British Film
Noir Guide

ALSO BY MICHAEL F. KEANEY

*Film Noir Guide: 745 Films of the Classic Era,
1940–1959* (McFarland, 2003; paperback 2011)

British Film Noir Guide

Michael F. Keaney

McFarland & Company, Inc., Publishers
Jefferson, North Carolina, and London

The present work is a reprint of the illustrated case bound edition of British Film Noir Guide, *first published in 2008 by McFarland.*

LIBRARY OF CONGRESS CATALOGUING-IN-PUBLICATION DATA

Keaney, Michael F., 1947–
British film noir guide / Michael F. Keaney.
p. cm.
Includes bibliographical references and index.

ISBN 978-0-7864-6427-2
softcover : 50# alkaline paper ∞

1. Film noir — Great Britain — Catalogs. I. Title.
PN1995.9.F54K427 2011   791.43'655 — dc22   2007052536

British Library cataloguing data are available

© 2008 Michael F. Keaney. All rights reserved

No part of this book may be reproduced or transmitted in any form or by any means, electronic or mechanical, including photocopying or recording, or by any information storage and retrieval system, without permission in writing from the publisher.

On the cover: Orson Welles in *The Third Man* (1949)
(Selznick Releasing Organization /Photofest)

Manufactured in the United States of America

*McFarland & Company, Inc., Publishers
Box 611, Jefferson, North Carolina 28640
www.mcfarlandpub.com*

Acknowledgments

Once again, my thanks to my wife, Doreen, for her kind indulgence of my strange fascination and its accompanying film collection expenses, for her patience while I spent so many hours holed up in the basement viewing and writing, and for taking the time to read the finished product and finding my many typos. My thanks to all of my fellow film noir fans for their emails of support and especially to my Canadian friends, Gordon Gates, Joe Santagata, and Gerry McCall, whose willingness to share their great enthusiasm for and knowledge of British films made the writing of this book an even more enjoyable experience.

Contents

Acknowledgments v

Preface 1

The Films 7

Appendix A. British Films Noirs Listed by Rating 227
Appendix B. British Films Noirs Listed by Year 230
Appendix C. British Films Noirs Listed by Director 233
Appendix D. British Films Noirs Listed by Cinematographer 238
Appendix E. Edgar Wallace Mystery Theatre 242
Bibliography 243
Index 245

Preface

For decades, film historians, authors and fans have differed on some aspects of film noir, including its definition (e.g., is it a style, a genre or a cycle?); the film that should be credited as the first genuine film noir (several candidates are usually offered, including 1940's *Stranger on the Third Floor* and 1941's *The Maltese Falcon*); the films that qualify for a place in the film noir "canon" and those that do not (e.g., are *Citizen Kane, Casablanca, Clash by Night*, and *Psycho* noirish enough for inclusion?); the acceptance into the canon of certain genre films such as Western, horror and science fiction films; and the questions of which film ended the classic noir era and whether or not films noirs continued to be made (as "neo-noirs") in yet another "noir cycle."

Because film noir itself is a such a subjective topic, I feel there is no definitive answer to any of the above questions. There are only opinions held by both the unbending and the flexible. Film noir, like beauty, is in the eye of the beholder, and as long as there are those who are interested in, even obsessed with, this fascinating subject there will be disagreements over such issues. I feel free to express my opinions on noir and encourage others to do the same. But in the end, I believe the argument is a futile one. I agree with author Spencer Selby, who I think puts many of these issues to rest in his book *Dark City: The Film Noir,** when he writes, "I believe that film noir must be and shall always remain something of an enigma." However, for the record I will state that I believe film noir is primarily a style, a dark visual style that accentuates certain "dark" plot elements and themes, such as crime, obsession, fatalism, cynicism, dread, loneliness and so on. Noir films have many recognizable characters (e.g., the femme fatale, bad cop or insurance investigator, hoodlum, fall guy, taxi dancer) and settings (e.g., the rain-drenched city, seedy hotels, nightclubs, dark alleyways and claustrophobic train compartments). The problem with this and other definitions is that there are exceptions to them. This explains the acceptance by fans and scholars alike of certain films whose noir styles are minimal but contain enough noir plot elements or characters to justify the film noir tag. *Cause for Alarm* and the Technicolor *Leave Her to Heaven* are good examples of this. Even crime, the most common noir element (and to some the most vital), may be missing, as it is in *Clash by Night*, which is considered a film noir by many. So the same question always remains. Just how noir is the film under consideration? Is it a full-blown noir like *Out of the Past*, considered by many to be the quintessential film noir? Or does it just squeak by with the bare minimum of noir essentials, such as many of the B crime films of the 1950s?

During the past decade, another debate began among the members of the ever-expanding noir community over the question of whether or not film noir is solely an American phenomenon. Since the 1979 publication of the book that has been referred to as "the film noir bible," Alain Silver's and Elizabeth Ward's *Film Noir: An Encyclopedic Reference to the American Style*, which

---

*For specifics about each book and article mentioned here, see the bibliography.

espouses the idea that film noir, like the Western, "is an indigenous American form" and that it is "the unique example of a wholly American film," a small number of articles, essays and books have been published that support the counter-theory that the American film industry has no claim to such exclusivity.

Contradicting Silver's and Ward's assertion, Andrew Spicer writes in his 2002 book *Film Noir*, "Film noir is not solely an indigenous American form.... British film noir was part of the same broad cultural interaction that gave rise to its American counterpart." Laurence Miller writes in his essay "Evidence for a British Film Noir Cycle," which appeared in Wheeler Winston Dixon's 1994 book *Re-Viewing British Cinema, 1900–1992*, that "film noir cannot be considered to be 'indigenous' only to America. "Rather," he writes, "it is likely that film noir developed in each country in response to a similar series of events that occurred at the same time." In his 1999 "British Film Noir" essay in Alain Silver's and James Ursini's *Film Noir Reader 2*, Tony Williams goes so far as to claim that "British film noir even begins a few years earlier than its American counterpart." As support for this, Williams cites several British films that predate the 1940–41 timeframe that usually marks the beginning of the American film noir classic period: *The Green Cockatoo* (1937), *They Drive by Night* (1938) (not to be confused with the American film noir of the same title), *I Met a Murderer* (1939) and *On the Night of the Fire* (1939). The multi-authored essays in Spicer's 2007 book *European Film Noir* suggest that film noir is a transnational phenomenon and not merely an American one.

Further complicating these issues is the premise put forth in some literature that much of British film noir differs substantially from its American counterparts in themes, characters and plot elements, as well as in its reliance on the influence of French cinema rather than on the German expressionistic movement. While some of these differences are apparent (e.g., the obsession with class is a distinctive British noir theme), many others are minor and, although a number of British noirs are not as stylistically dark as their American counterparts, American viewers should not assume that they will be shortchanged with the British film noir. In his essay, Miller seems to agree by placing fifty-one British titles side by side with American noirs according to their common themes, elements and characters (e.g., revenge, obsession, frame-ups, blackmail, amnesia, mental instability).

It has been noted by some writers that few British noirs revolve around the femme fatale, who supposedly has been supplanted by the homme fatale. However, I have found the opposite to be the case with at least thirty films noirs that present the femme fatale as a central or minor character (*Alias John Preston, The Bank Raiders, Black Widow, Blind Corner, Dear Murderer, The Depraved, Dual Alibi, The End of the Line, Face of a Stranger, The Flanagan Boy, Forbidden, The Frightened City, Great Expectations, The House Across the Lake, Information Received, The Long Memory, The Man Who Watched Trains Go By, Marilyn, Night Beat, Payroll, Playback, The Rough and the Smooth, The Set-Up, Soho Incident, Stage Fright, Take My Life, Tread Softly Stranger, Wicked as They Come*, and *Wings of Danger*.) The homme fatale can be found in fewer films, although he is usually featured prominently in them (e.g., *Blanche Fury, Cage of Gold, Daybreak, The Flesh Is Weak, The Last Page, Panic, The Secret Place, So Evil My Love, Street Corner, Turn the Key Softly*, and *Waterloo Road*).

Another supposedly rare character in British film noir is the private investigator. While private eyes are seldom the main protagonists (as they are in *Calling Bulldog Drummond, Girl Hunters*, and *Uneasy Terms*), they appear as supporting characters in a number of films, including *Hysteria, The Interrupted Journey, Locker Sixty-Nine, Never Mention Murder, The Share-Out, So Evil My Love*, and *The £20,000 Kiss*. Although she is British noir's lone female P.I., Marjorie Stedman (*The Man Who Was Nobody*) has more screen time than her American counterpart, Florence Cain, who is killed off early in 1945's *The Spider*. From the available literature, one might easily get the impression that the "dirty cop" is a nonexistent entity in British noir, but there are at least six films in which he makes an appearance as a major character (*Night Beat*, *Marriage of Convenience*, *Offbeat*, *One Way Out*, *Playback*, and *To Have and to Hold*). Unlike the ten American "boxing noirs"* that highlight the seedy world of prize fighting, the marginally noir *The Square Ring* is the only British film noir to do so, although boxers and ex-boxers are prominent characters in other films noirs, such as *Cloudburst*, *Daughter of Darkness*, *The Flanagan Boy*, *The Good Die Young*, *The Long Memory*, *No Way Back*, *Panic*, *Soho Incident*, *There Is Another Sun*, and *Three Crooked Men*.

In addition to femmes fatales, private eyes, and boxers, American visitors to the dark city on the other side of the Atlantic should expect to find a good representation of other noir characters: the stool pigeon (known in British crime films as a nose, snout or copper's nark), disillusioned war veteran, gambler, loan shark, blackmailer, shady lawyer, fall guy, wrongly accused man and his loyal wife or girlfriend, amnesia victim, and convict, along with a few uniquely British characters such as the spiv (the usually dapperly-dressed, small-time hoodlum who first came to notice in the post-war years) and the penniless and scheming aristocrat. American visitors will also spend more than a few nights in such recognizable haunts as the sleazy nightclub, fancy casino, fleabag hotel, overcrowded prison or warehouse hide-out.

In 1984, Selby wrote in *Dark City*, "If there is such a thing as a British noir cycle or a French noir cycle (and there very well may be), it is left to others to define and list such films." One of the first writers to attempt this was William K. Everson in a two-part magazine article entitled "British Film Noir," which appeared in the May and June 1987 issues of *Films in Review*. Here Everson offers a "rough" (and by his own admission a non definitive) "check list of British Noir: 1938–1963." Of the 135 films he lists, Everson categorizes thirty-six as "marginal" films noirs that contain "enough key elements to be considered."

In "Evidence for a British Film Noir Cycle," Miller states that his research resulted in the compilation of a list of 331 British noirs, of which he covers only fifty-one in the aforementioned category comparison with American noirs. Williams does not compile a list of British noirs in his 1999 essay, but includes many titles in his text. It is sometimes difficult, however, to distinguish between the films he considers to be noirs and the titles he mentions in passing but to which he does not assign the noir label. A best estimate is that he classifies ninety-four films as Brit noirs.

It is not until the 2002 publication of Spicer's *Film Noir* that a more complete British noir filmography can be found. Spicer presents three categories of British noir: "Antecedents/Experimental Period" (eighteen films beginning with 1926's *The Lodger* and ending with 1945's *Waterloo Road*); "Classical British Noir" (eighty films starting with 1946's *Carnival* and ending with 1964's *Face of a Stranger*); and "British Neo-Noir" (forty-two films beginning with 1965's *The Spy Who Came in from the Cold* and ending with 2000's *Sexy Beast*).

While working on my 2003 book *Film Noir Guide: 745 Films of the Classic Era, 1940–1959*, I viewed more than 700 American films and forty-two foreign films, including thirty-three British, and became convinced that there is indeed such a beast as the "foreign" film noir. (It is not my goal here to try to prove the existence of such a transnational style [genre or cycle], because I believe it cannot be proven. I refer readers who might enjoy the scholarly approach to this issue to the excellent books and essays mentioned in this introduction.)

In his essay in Spicer's *European Film Noir*, Robert Murphy lists 187 films, beginning with *The Lodger* (1926) and ending with *The Third Secret* (1964). Unlike Spicer, Murphy does not distinguish between "antecedents" and actual films noirs.

Like the debate over the origins of American film noir, there is disagreement among authors

---

*As described in *Film Noir Guide*: *The Big Punch*, *Body and Soul*, *Champion*, *City for Conquest*, *The Crooked Circle*, *Glory Alley*, *The Harder They Fall*, *Iron Man*, *The Set-Up*, and *Whiplash*.

over the same issue vis-à-vis British film noir. In *Film Noir*, Spicer goes with 1937's *The Green Cockatoo* as the first British noir (although he lists it as an antecedent in his filmography). In his essay, Williams states that *The Green Cockatoo* "is definitely the first British film noir in terms of visual style and content." In *European Film Noir*, Murphy does not commit himself but identifies *The Green Cockatoo* as "a film that has been identified as the first British film noir." In "Evidence for a British Film Noir Cycle," Miller, however, holds to the theory that film noir is a cycle and that British film noir and American film noir closely paralleled each other in terms of development. He lists several films from 1938 and 1939 as being noir "prototypes" and in a private correspondence identifies 1940 as the start of both the British and American cycles, with World War II serving as the catalyst for both. Everson disagrees with the other writers, as evidenced by his *Films in Review* article. In part one of the article, Everson states that he considers 1939's *On the Night of the Fire* to be "the first total, bona-fide British noir," but in part two he writes that *They Drive by Night* is "clearly the first authentic British noir" and includes it in the number one position of his filmography.

Based on this disagreement and on my personal opinion that film noir is primarily a style and not a cycle, I have decided to go with the earliest of the British noir contender films and begin my filmography with *The Green Cockatoo* (1937) and end it with the 1964 date propounded by Spicer and Murphy. (Everson's list covers the years 1938 to 1963.) Thus, I do not cover any of the earlier "antecedents" or "prototypes." Neither have I included any "neo-noirs," (i.e., post–1964 noirs), which are beyond the goals and scope of this book.

As a basis for my list, I first considered the writings of some of the authors listed in the bibliography. With a few exceptions, most of the "British Film Noir" descriptions on DVD packaging proved to be accurate. I also invited some fans of British noir to send me their suggestions and viewed each of their recommendations. As I did with the authors' filmographies, I eliminated the ones I believed had too few noir elements or lacked the noir style or were considered to be short features. From the filmographies, fan suggestions and my own hit-and-miss viewing, I compiled a list of British films I considered to be noir and, with a few exceptions (explained below), those that I believed could pass muster as "marginal" noirs or otherwise contained enough of "the noir style" to satisfy me personally. Of the 369 films covered in this book, 116 are titles not found in any other published filmography as of this writing. Many of these low-budget additions would compare in style and content to the American B noirs described in Arthur Lyons' innovative book *Death on the Cheap: The Lost B Movies of Film Noir!*

I recognize of course that compiling a list of noirs is a subjective process and that some noir fans and scholars will disagree with a number of my choices as they did with some of the films in *Film Noir Guide* (one reader charged that I seemed to have used the "kitchen sink method" of selection). As I did in my previous book, I readily admit that I have included some films from other authors' lists that I suspect do not qualify as even marginal noirs. I have done this because in these cases I found myself holding to the minority opinion and felt it best to give the majority the benefit of the doubt. Readers also can be assured that my judgments at least were come by honestly— with the exception of the twenty-eight films that were unavailable at the time of this writing, I viewed all of the films, the ones that eventually made it into the book *and* the ones that were rejected. It is my hope that a title omitted here will not someday be incorrectly attributed to me on a noir discussion web site, as was the case when a reader criticized me for including *Dr. No* in *Film Noir Guide*. I have yet to determine how he or she made this error when *Dr. No* is not even mentioned in passing.

Films that appeared on other authors' lists but were eliminated from mine include *Busman's Honeymoon, Death of an Angel, Dr. Strangelove or: How I Learned to Stop Worrying and Love the Bomb, The Entertainer, The Haunting, Holiday Camp, The Innocents, A Jolly Bad Fellow, Kind Hearts and Coronets, King & Country, The Ladykillers, The League of Gentlemen, Look Back in Anger, The Man Who Never Was, The Monkey's Paw, My Learned Friend, The Next of Kin, Night Comes Too Soon, Night of the Eagle, A Place of One's Own, The Servant, Taste of Fear, They Met in the Dark, This Man Is News, Three Cases of Murder, Thunder Rock, Time Bomb, Under Capricorn, Unpublished Story, Went the Day Well?*, and *The Wicked Lady*. In my opinion, these movies (comedies, costume films, horror films, spy films, melodramas and war films) lacked dark visual style or contained too few noir elements, settings or characters to be considered, or both.

In the filmography, each entry contains the title of the film, a subjective rating (based on the familiar five-star system), the film's release date, and a dialogue quote, along with the length, cast (not necessarily in the original credits order), production company, director, cinematographer (director of photography or where none mentioned, the lighting cameraman and/or camera operator), writer (usually listed in screen credits as "screenwriter" or "written by"), a synopsis that does not reveal the ending, and my personal opinions about the film's noir qualities or entertainment value. If a film was not available for viewing, I expressed no opinion about it and wrote only a one- or two-line plot description based on other synopses, the accuracy of which cannot be guaranteed.

As pointed out by some critics, I had been remiss in not including the names of cinematographers in my *Film Noir Guide*. Their inclusion here is an acknowledgment of the correctness of this critique. Others disapproved of the omission of musical composers. I tried to accommodate these critics but this proved a more difficult task. Many films listed only the musical directors, while others listed neither the composer nor the director. Therefore, I decided to exclude "Music by" as a category and, instead, mention composers in my write-ups only when I particularly enjoyed a film's score. Unlike those in many of the American films noirs listed in *Film Noir Guide*, the names of the actors and actresses presented in the synopses might be unfamiliar to most American viewers. Therefore, referring to them by their real names offers no clear recognition value and I refer to them instead by their characters' names.

When "Not credited" is used instead of a name it means that the name was not included in the screen credits and that I did not feel comfortable using the names provided by other sources.

The astute reader may notice that film lengths often differ among various movie databases. In the case of British films, it may be because the length was taken from the film's American release rather than the original British release, or because the only available copy of the film is an edited version shown on American television. Because some of the films I viewed were American releases that had been edited because of censorship issues or to make room for television commercials, I used British writer Denis Gifford's exceptionally useful book *The British Film Catalogue* as my guideline for original film lengths. When the names of production companies differed from database to database, I consulted Gifford and the British Film Institute's movie database (*http://www.bfi.org.uk*). Even release dates can differ and when this happened I again referred to Gifford. Gifford explains that his system does not follow the common industry practice of dating films by their release dates, but uses a film's actual first showing (e.g., a first review or the date the film was shown to the British Board of Film Censors), further explaining that the gap between the original showing and the film's actual release to theaters would sometimes amount to years.

I have spelled names as they appeared in the screen credits, making no attempt to identify cast or crew by their more familiar but differently spelled names. For example, cinematographer Hone Glendining is credited in some films as Hone Glendinning. However, when filmmakers used pseudonyms, as was often the case with blacklisted American filmmakers, working overseas I attempted to include their real names (e.g., "Mutz Greenbaum as Max Greene").

The five-star rating system is explained on the following page.

★ = Poor (for the hard core film noir fan only)
★★ = Fair
★★★ = Good
★★★★ = Very Good
★★★★★ = Excellent
NR = "Not Reviewed" (used for films that were not available at the time of writing)
Half-stars help to give some distinction to the definitions.

Appendix A breaks down each film by rating, Appendix B by year, and appendices C and D by director and cinematographer, respectively. Appendix E presents a list of crime and mystery films, some of which are included in The Films section of this book, that were based on the stories of British mystery writer Edgar Wallace and produced by Merton Park Productions for eventual showing on American and British television. The book ends with a bibliography listing the essays and books I found useful while writing *British Film Noir Guide*.

My goal in writing *British Film Noir Guide* was not to delve into the historical development of film noir in Great Britain nor to espouse any philosophical, sociological or psychological interpretations of individual films. I leave these things to the experts. Neither am I trying to persuade anyone that my opinions are inerrant or even correct. In addition to providing what I hope will be an entertaining read, my main purpose is to provide newcomers to film noir and the many (often self-described) rabid fans with a valuable reference that will serve as a starting point for, or a continuation of, their quest to seek out these dark and fascinating British films.

The Films

Across the Bridge
★★★★ (1957)

> I shall fix it so that he has nothing he wants. No shop will serve him. He'll have no food nor drink. There will be no bed in any hotel for him. As far as the people of this town are concerned he will cease to exist. [Catrina chief of police]

Length: 103 min. **Cast**: Rod Steiger, David Knight, Noel Willman, Bernard Lee, Bill Nagy. **Production Company**: The Rank Organisation. **Directed by**: Ken Annakin. **Photographed by**: Reginald Wyer. **Written by**: Guy Elmes, Denis Freeman.

Carl Schaffner (Steiger), a German-born financier with a British passport, is on business in New York when he learns that Scotland Yard has been investigating his company. Guilty of fraud and certain that the Yard will learn about his organization's $3 million deficit, Schaffner flees to Mexico. On the train, he meets Paul Scarff (Nagy), an American who holds a Mexican passport because of his marriage to a Mexican citizen. Schaffner notices that he and Scarff look somewhat alike and decides to steal his identity. He drugs the man, switches passports, and tosses him off the speeding train. Along with his new identity, however, comes something he had not anticipated — in order for his impersonation to be convincing he must take along Scarff's dog, Delores. The dog is miserable without her master yet refuses to leave Schaffner's side even after he kicks her and tries to abandon her in the desert. When Schaffner learns that Scarff was a political assassin wanted by the Mexican government, he doubles back to find the man's body and retrieve his own passport. Unfortunately for Schaffner, Scarff survived his ordeal and was rescued and taken to a motel in Flowerville, a small town on the American side of the border. After retrieving his passport from Scarff at gunpoint, Schaffner allows himself to be driven to Catrina, Mexico, by Flowerville resident Johnny (Knight), who thinks that turning in Schaffner will earn him the 100,000-peso reward placed on his head. Schaffner realizes he will be arrested when he arrives but is sure he can straighten out the case of "mistaken identity" and be released to retrieve the million dollars he has socked away in a Mexico City bank. Unfortunately, the corrupt Catrina police chief (Willman) refuses to return his passport unless Schaffner tells him where Scarff is hiding. Schaffner agrees, and as a result, Scarff is killed in a shootout with American police. The police chief then reneges on the deal, demanding ten percent of Schaffner's holdings in Mexico City. To complicate matters, Scotland Yard Inspector Hadden (Lee) arrives in town hoping to trick Schaffner into crossing the border so he can be arrested. Treated as a pariah by the townsfolk, Schaffner's only friend in the world is Delores, the mangy mutt he has been mistreating since the first day of his doomed impersonation. Based on a Graham Greene story, *Across the Bridge* is thematically noir but contains little of noir's dark visual style. It is a terrific film, expertly directed and enhanced by Steiger's performance as an on-the-run protagonist whose greed and treachery are responsible for his alienation from those whose help he so desperately needs and whose personal redemption comes from an unexpected source.

Act of Murder
★★★ (1964)

> For some reason people, like yourself, are inclined to hand over the entire contents of their houses to complete strangers on the strength of a piece of embossed note paper. Not much of an exchange, is it? [Police desk sergeant to scam victims]

Length: 62 min. **Cast**: John Carson, Anthony Bate, Justine Lord, Duncan Lewis, Richard Burrell, Dandy Nichols. **Production Company**: Merton Park Productions. **Directed by**: Alan Bridges. **Photographed by**: James Wilson. **Written by**: Lewis Davidson.

Ralph Longman (Bate) and his wife, Ann (Lord), are victimized by a trio of con artists (Lewis, Nichols and Burrell), who convince them to exchange their country home for a nonexistent flat in London for a couple of weeks. While the Longmans are speeding off to London to enjoy their vacation, the crooks prepare to steal their valuable collection of antiques. They are interrupted, however, by the Longmans' house guest, Tim Ford (Carson), who has returned to retrieve his suitcase. After chasing the crooks away, Ford puts the antiques back in place and returns to London. Meanwhile, Ralph and Ann, realizing they've been had, rush home expecting to find that the collection has been stolen. When they see that nothing is missing, they are at a loss to explain the reason for the con artists' charade. Ann's confusion turns to paranoia after she discovers that her budgie and hens have been poisoned. She begins throwing away food, even canned goods, suspecting that the crooks had something other in mind than merely robbing them. After stumbling upon her dog's body, she decides she needs to get away from the house and moves in with

Ralph Longman (Anthony Bate) does not want to lose his wife, Ann (Justine Lord), to her former lover in *Act of Murder* (Merton Park, 1964).

her mother in London. Ralph is not thrilled with her fear-motivated decision, but doggie killer Tim, who still loves former girlfriend Ann, is delighted to see that his plan is working. So he goes ahead with the next stage — seduction. In the meantime, Ralph has decided to track down the con artists to learn the reason for their mysterious scam. A highly original storyline, good acting and a grim ending help turn this little oddity into a pleasant surprise. (Part of the "Edgar Wallace Mystery Theater" series.)

The Adventuress see *I See a Dark Stranger*

Alias John Preston
★★ (1956)

I'm a little tired.... Fools always make me tired. [John Preston]

Length: 66 min. **Cast**: Christopher Lee, Betta St. John, Alexander Knox. **Production Company**: Danziger Photoplays. **Directed by**: David MacDonald. **Photographed by**: Jack Cox. **Written by**: Paul Tabori.

Aloof war veteran John Preston (Lee) arrives in the quaint town of Deanbridge and begins buying real estate and businesses, invigorating the town's stagnant economy. Before long, he becomes engaged to the banker's daughter, Sally Sandford (St. John), after stealing her away from her childhood sweetheart, who tries unsuccessfully to scare off his romantic rival with a gun. Happy that Preston has arrived to inject a little spark in their otherwise dreary town and that he has donated enough money to add a new wing onto the hospital, the city elders appoint him to the hospital's board of trustees. During his first meeting as a board member, Preston tells his colleagues, "I believe that pain exists in the world because people are too stupid or too lazy to do away with it." His first official act, however, is to oppose the hiring of psychiatrist Dr. Peter Walton (Knox) to oversee a new ward for mentally disturbed patients. It seems that Preston considers psychiatry to be nothing more than mumbo jumbo, but this doesn't prevent him from visiting the doctor several times under cover of darkness to tell him about a series of nightmares he has been having, in which a beautiful girl arrives in town, calls him by a different name and tries to blackmail him. In the first dream, Preston strangles the woman, but a man who identifies himself as her husband witnesses the murder and helps him bury the girl in the garden. Preston continues having nightmares and in his final one attacks both the stranger and Dr. Walton, who Preston seems to think has made a cameo appearance in his dream. Lee's performance as the schizophrenic veteran is enjoyable, which comes as no surprise to fans of the future British horror icon, but the rest of the cast is mostly forgettable. The film's editing process is particularly deficient, with numerous disjointed scene changes that disrupt the logical flow of the storyline. In addition, the camera catches too many clear facial shots of Lee's stunt double during the fistfight scene. The use of narrative and flashbacks in the three nightmare sequences, the presence of a disturbed war veteran as the main protagonist, a blackmailing femme fatale of sorts and low-key black and white photography qualify *Alias John Preston* as a film noir, albeit a lackluster one.

All Night Long
★★★ (1961)

I belong to that new minority: white American jazz musicians. They're going to hold a mass meeting in a phone booth. [Johnny Cousins]

Length: 95 min. **Cast**: Patrick McGoohan, Marti Stevens, Betsy Blair, Keith Michell, Paul Harris, Richard Attenborough. **Production Company**: Rank Organisation Film Productions. **Directed by**: Basil Dearden. **Photographed by**: Ted Scaife. **Written by**: Nel King, Peter Achilles.

In this modern-day reworking of Shakespeare's *Othello*, wealthy Londoner Rod Hamilton (Attenborough) throws a first wedding anniversary bash at a converted warehouse for his friends, jazz bandleader Aurelius Rex (Paul Harris) and Rex's wife, singer Delia Lane (Stevens). Among the guests are drummer Johnny Cousin (McGoohan) and his wife, Emily (Blair), pothead band manager Cass Michaels (Michell) and a number of musicians (Dave Brubeck,

John Dankworth, and Charlie Mingus, among others, who play themselves). Cousin is obsessed with starting his own band but must secure Lane as his top attraction before he can obtain any financial backing. The only problem is that Lane has retired at her husband's urging and has no intention of making a comeback. And so begins Cousin's plot to destroy the couple's year-old marriage, all in one night and in the middle of the coolest jam session in London. His cruel scheme involves convincing Rex that his wife has been having a torrid affair with their best friend, Michaels. His ability to do so strains viewer imagination somewhat but it's all part of the fun; that and the terrific jazz score directed by Phillip Green. McGoohan is excellent as the calculating drummer, but Attenborough has only a small, uninteresting role. For the era, the film daringly addresses a couple of controversial issues: two interracial relationships (the guests of honor and the band manager and his girlfriend) and the smoking of marijuana (although dutifully frowned upon by some of the musicians). Surprising also for the time, a waiter is shown raising his middle finger in response to some obnoxious band members.

Angel Street see Gaslight

Another Man's Poison
★★★½ (1951)

Will murder make your sales jump? [George Bates to author Janet Frobisher]

Length: 89 min. **Cast**: Bette Davis, Gary Merrill, Emlyn Williams, Anthony Steel, Barbara Murray. **Production Company**: Daniel Angel Films. **Directed by**: Irving Rapper. **Photographed by**: Robert Krasker. **Written by**: Val Guest.

Mystery writer Janet Frobisher (Davis) poisons her abusive estranged husband with a dose of horse medicine and is about to dispose of his body when George Bates (Merrill), the murdered man's accomplice in a recent bank robbery, shows up at her mansion in the English countryside. On the run, the former bank employee learns of his partner's murder and decides to blackmail Janet into pretending that he is her husband so he will have a safe haven while the cops are scouring the countryside for him. When Janet's house gets suddenly crowded, due to visits by her former lover (Steel), her secretary (Murray) and a noisy veterinarian (Williams), the already edgy Bates becomes highly agitated and dangerous, prompting Janet to start thinking about pulling out the old horse medicine once again. Based on the play "Deadlock," by Leslie Sands, *Another Man's Poison* is a showcase for Bette Davis, who always excelled as a haughty and dangerous female.

Appointment with Crime
★★½ (1946)

LEO MARTIN: What are you getting at?
CAROL DANE: I'm getting at the filthiest apology for a rat that ever crawled out of a sewer. The dirtiest little coward who ever hid behind a dog's frock, a hypocrite, a thief, a liar and a murderer.

Length: 97 min. **Cast**: William Hartnell, Robert Beatty, Joyce Howard, Herbert Lom, Alan Wheatley, Raymond Lovell, Victor Weske. **Production Company**: British National Films. **Directed by**: John Harlow. **Photographed by**: James Wilson. **Written by**: John Harlow.

Small-time crook Leo Martin (Hartnell) and his accomplices, Loman (Lovell) and Hatchett (Weske), attempt a "smash and grab" robbery of a jewelry store during broad daylight. Martin tosses a brick through the store window and tries to grab the jewels but is trapped when a metal blind slams down on his arms, breaking his wrists. His accomplices abandon him, leaving him to be captured by the police. After his release from prison, Martin seeks revenge, shooting Hatchett and demanding that Loman pay him £200 or else he will turn over the murder weapon, which has Loman's fingerprints on it, to Scotland Yard. Inspector Rogers (Beatty) begins his investigation at the Palais de Danse, where Martin's alibi is Carol Dane (Howard), a pretty, but none-too-bright taxi dancer who believes that the coppers are harassing Martin because of his criminal record. She pities the paranoid killer at first but eventually falls for his dubious charm and decides to run off with him. Meanwhile, Martin learns that the gun he used to kill Hatchett actually belongs to Loman's gangster boss, Gregory Lang (Lom), who is determined to get it back at any cost. *Appointment* is a gritty crime drama with a good cast, although Hartnell's attempts at hardboiled dialogue often come off as a poor imitation of Edward G. Robinson. See? Get me? The film's most interesting characters are Lang and his effete lieutenant, Noel Penn (Wheatley), whose relationship appears to be more than simply hoodlum boss and loyal goon. James Wilson's surreal nightmare sequence during Martin's wrist surgery, when the thief experiences a flashback to the time he was conned into participating in the robbery, is the highlight of the film and is reminiscent of similar sequences in the American films noirs *Stranger on the Third Floor* and *Blues in the Night*.

Assassin for Hire
★★★ (1951)

They don't play by the rules. Neither should we.
[Scotland Yard Inspector Carson about criminals]

Length: 67 min. **Cast:** Sydney Tafler, Ronald Howard, John Hewer, Katherine Blake. **Production Company:** Merton Park Productions. **Directed by:** Michael McCarthy. **Photographed by:** Robert LaPresle. **Written by:** Rex Rienits.

Assassin for Hire opens with a bang as killer Antonio Riccardi (Tafler) cold-bloodedly puts three slugs into the back of a mark in a darkened London alley. Investigating Riccardi's recent string of murders is Scotland Yard Inspector Carson (Howard), a no-nonsense detective with an unusual approach to solving cases (for a 1950s British movie cop, that is): "When it comes to catching criminals, it's always been my belief that the end justifies the means." Carson suspects Riccardi, who operates a rare-stamp business as a front, of being the killer, but Riccardi always has the same air-tight alibi—he was playing cards in the back room of Charlie's Pub at the time of the murders. Riccardi's loving wife, Maria (Blake), and kid brother, Giuseppe (Hewer), are unaware that the money Riccardi provides to help Giuseppe's career as a concert violinist comes not from selling stamps but from his one-man, murder-for-hire business. After Riccardi fulfills his latest contract outside a London nightspot, Inspector Carson concocts a plan to fool the killer into confessing to the crime. While *Assassin* relies heavily on an improbable coincidence to bring about the hit man's downfall, the screenplay is so competently written that the viewer should be able to forgive this minor defect. Tafler's portrayal of the killer as a sympathetic family man is believable (even though his Italian accent isn't), and Hewer does a good job as the resourceful but unethical detective.

Bad Blonde see *The Flanagan Boy*

Bang! You're Dead
(U.S. Title: *Game of Danger*)
★★½ (1954)

When a thing ain't wanted it's better off dead.
[Mr. Bonsell]

Length: 88 min. **Cast:** Jack Warner, Derek Farr, Veronica Hurst, Michael Medwin, Anthony Richmond, Sean Barrett, Philip Saville. **Production Company:** Wellington Films. **Directed by:** Lance Comfort. **Photographed by:** Brendan J. Stafford. **Written by:** Guy Elmes, Ernest Borneman.

Believing the gun he found at an abandoned American Army supply depot is a toy, Cliff Bonsell (Richmond), the 7-year-old son of a widowed farmer (Warner), shoots and kills neighbor Ben Jones (Saville) while "robbing" the man of his watch. Pleased with his new acquisition and unaware that Jones is not just playing dead, Cliff leaves behind the gun and goes on his merry way. Meanwhile, Bob Carter (Medwin), Jones' romantic rival for the affections of a pretty pub waitress (Hurst), discovers the body and the gun and is soon arrested and charged with murder. Detective Superintendent Grey (Farr) arrives in town and begins an investigation that leads him to the now-frightened Cliff, who tries to cover up the "theft" of the watch, and his older, slow-witted friend, Willy (Barrett), the only witness to the accident. Interesting but tortuously slow-moving at times, the storyline of this marginal noir revolves primarily around the two children and their unusual relationship (the younger boy being the leader) rather than the plight of the wrongly accused man.

The Bank Raiders
★★ (1958)

> Listen, Terry, either you're a big shot or you're not. I've no use for little men. If you want me to be with you then you've got to be big. [Della Byrne]

Length: 60 min. **Cast:** Peter Reynolds, Sandra Dorne, Sydney Tafler, Lloyd Lamble, Rose Hill, Arthur Mullard, Tim Ellison. **Production Company:** Film Workshop. **Directed by:** Maxwell Munden. **Photographed by:** Cyril Gray (camera operator), Henry Hall (lighting). **Written by:** Brandon Fleming.

Gigolo Terry Milligan (Reynolds), broke and between dames, pressures small-time hood Bernie Shelton (Tafler) into hiring him as a getaway driver for a planned heist on a North London bank. The robbers get away with a tidy sum but not before Terry is spotted by bank clerk Jack Connor (Ellison). Connor tells Scotland Yard Det. Inspector Mason (Lamble) that he is sure he can identify the driver if he sees him again. Meanwhile, the bank's cleaning woman dies after suffering a fractured skull administered by Shelton's overzealous goon, Linders (Mullard). This doesn't stop Terry, however, from flashing around his share of the take in an effort to impress barfly Delia Byrne (Dorne). After his spending spree attracts the attention of a civic-minded bartender who calls the cops, Terry is picked up by Inspector Mason for questioning and placed in an identification parade (the British version of a line-up). The bank clerk plays dumb, however, because Shelton has kidnapped his fiancé and has threatened to slash her face if he cooperates with the police. So the Yard is forced to release the cocky crook, whose good luck soon comes to an end. First, his landlady, Mrs. Marling (Hill), finds the money he has hidden under her bed and blackmails him for half. Then he accidentally kills Linders, who was sent by Shelton to silence him. Desperate and on the run, Terry shows up at Delia's flat. Delia, Shelton's former girlfriend, agrees to let him stay there for one night for £100 and encourages him to go after Shelton for the rest of the stolen dough. Lovesick Terry makes the mistake of following her advice. The film's nifty downbeat ending and its many noir elements (a heist gone bad, kidnapping, murder, blackmail, a protagonist who finds himself sinking quickly in the quagmire of crime while being victimized by a greedy femme fatale) do not compensate for the poor acting, especially that of the supporting cast. The dialogue is often laughable. "Why don't they let her go?" wails bank clerk Connor, distressed over his girlfriend's abduction. "I've done all they want. The thought of her in those devils' hands! And I'm helpless. I can't do anything." "Jack, you must try and steady yourself," says his mum. Quick to recover, Connor replies, "I know. I'm sorry. Let's have some tea."

Beat Girl
★★ (1960)

> STRIPPER: Who's the pal?
> GRETA: She's no pal. It's a bitch with a short memory.

Length: 85 min. **Cast:** David Farrar, Noëlle Adam, Christopher Lee, Gillian Hills, Delphi Lawrence. **Production Company:** Willoughby Film Productions. **Directed by:** Edmond T. Greville. **Photographed by:** Walter Lassally. **Written by:** Dail Ambler.

Architect Paul Linden (Farrar) returns from Paris with Nichole (Adam), his beautiful 24-year-old bride. Paul's equally gorgeous 16-year-old daughter, art student Jennifer (Hills), the product of a broken home, is not exactly thrilled with her new stepmother and proceeds to make Nichole's life a living hell. Jennifer spends most of her time with her pseudo-beatnik friends at The Offbeat, a Soho coffee bar, where one day she sees Nichole bump into Greta, a stripper who calls herself "The Duchess." Jennifer notices that Greta seems to know her stepmother, who gives the stripper the cold shoulder. When Jennifer comes to the conclusion that Nichole worked as a stripper before she met Paul, she decides to use this dark secret to break up the marriage. To get more dirt she starts hanging around the strip club, where she attracts the attention of Ken (Lee), the club's sleazy manager, who decides that girlfriend Greta is getting a bit long in the tooth and that a 16-year-old might be a good replacement. It may be a bit of a stretch to label *Beat Girl* a film noir, but Lassally's cinematography does contain some very darkly photographed scenes— a game of chicken on the railroad tracks comes to mind — and the teen characters, led by the nonviolent and surprisingly square Dave (future pop idol Adam Faith), are certainly cynical and alienated from mainstream society ("You've got to live for kicks," says one girl. "That's all you've got."). Gillian Hills, who appears to have been all of 13 or 14 years old when the film was made, is gorgeous and does a good job as the rebellious and spiteful sex kitten. Watch for Oliver Reed as the teenager in the plaid shirt who makes a play for Jennifer at The Offbeat. Christopher Lee, whose screen time is all too short, is terrific as the lecherous strip club manager. French actress Adam, however, doesn't fare as well, her accent being difficult to understand at times. And then there's that god-awful soundtrack. Keep your thumb poised over the mute switch, daddy-o.

Beautiful Stranger
(U.S. Title: *Twist of Fate*)
★½ (1954)

> Even when I was working in dirty little theaters and living in crummy hotels at least I had my pride. But now I have to be here in all this. To feel cheap for the first time in my life. [Joan Victor]

Length: 89 min. **Cast:** Ginger Rogers, Herbert Lom, Stanley Baker, Jacques Bergerac, Margaret Rawlings. **Production Company:** Marksman Films. **Directed by:** David Miller. **Photographed by:** Ted Scaife (lighting cameraman). **Written by:** Robert Westerby, Carl Nystrom.

Former chorus girl Joan "Johnny" Victor (American actress Rogers) lives in a beautiful French villa, compliments of her sugar daddy, Louis Galt (Baker), who swears that he will ask his wife (Rawlings) for a divorce any day now. When Johnny learns that Galt has been lying, she begins seeing Pierre Clemont (Bergerac, Rogers' real-life husband at the time), a local potter. Penniless gambler and two-bit crook Emil Landosh (Lom), an old friend, shows up in town and puts the bite on Johnny for some dough. Although Landosh works indirectly for industrialist Galt's gold coin counterfeiting ring (Galt finds "ordinary commerce dull"), Landosh is initially unaware of his boss' relationship with Johnny. But when he learns that Galt has hidden a half million dollars in cash in the wall safe at Johnny's villa, Landosh decides to help himself. Meanwhile, Galt wrongly believes that Landosh is Johnny's new lover and is determined to kill him. Johnny, however, thinks it is Pierre whom Galt is out to kill. Confusing? Yes, and dull too, but Lom is entertaining as the crook who thinks he has hit the jackpot for the first time in his weasely little life.

Bedelia
★★ (1946)

> I hate men. They're rotten beasts. I wish all the men in the world were dead. [Bedelia Carrington]

Length: 90 min. **Cast:** Margaret Lockwood, Ian Hunter, Barry K. Barnes, Anne Crawford, Jill Esmond, Julien Mitchell. **Production Company:** John Corfield Productions. **Directed by:** Lance Comfort. **Photographed by:** Frederick A. Young. **Written by:** Vera Caspary, Herbert Victor, M. Roy Fidley.

While vacationing in Monte Carlo, newlyweds Charlie and Bedelia Carrington (Hunter and Lockwood) meet artist Ben Chaney (Barnes), who convinces Charlie to allow him to paint a portrait of Bedelia despite her obvious reluctance. Bedelia doesn't even like to have her photograph taken. And for good reason. She has already poisoned three husbands to collect on their large insurance policies, and Charlie may be her fourth victim. When Charlie is called back to England on business, Bedelia thinks she is rid of the artist once and for all, but Ben follows them to Yorkshire and rents a nearby studio where he continues to work on her portrait while nosing around the Carrington household. When Charlie suddenly becomes ill, Ben convinces Dr. McAfee, Charlie's physician, to bring in a private nurse (Esmond) to care for Charlie and to keep Bedelia away from him until they can examine the mysterious medicinal

A wealthy businessman (Ian Hunter) is blissfully unaware that his bride (Margaret Lockwood) is a serial husband killer in *Bedelia* (John Corfield Productions, 1946).

powder she has been using to treat his condition. Meanwhile, Charlie's junior business partner and secret admirer, Ellen Walker (Crawford), suspects that something may be going on between Bedelia and Ben and is determined to find out what. *Bedelia* is a tedious and disappointing suspense thriller based on the novel by Vera Caspary, who also wrote *Laura*, the source for the classic 1944 American film noir of the same title. Despite a spirited effort by Lockwood, *Bedelia* has none of the elegance and style of *Laura*, but Lockwood fans, and there are many, should enjoy her portrayal of the psychotic villainess. Barnes, however, is stiff as a board and his character proves to be annoyingly aloof and not at all as mysterious as the filmmakers intended him to be.

Beyond This Place
(U.S. Title: *Web of Evidence*)
★★½ (1959)

Before they were murderers they were people.
[Paul Mathry to prison governor]

Length: 90 min. **Cast**: Van Johnson, Vera Miles, Emlyn Williams, Bernard Lee, Jean Kent, Moultrie Kelsall, Anthony Newlands, Jameson Clark, Ralph Truman. **Production Company**: Georgefield Productions. **Directed by**: Jack Cardiff. **Photographed by**: Wilkie Cooper. **Written by**: Ken Taylor.

In 1941, Patrick Mathry (Lee), a married man and the father of a young boy, is convicted of strangling his pregnant, 18-year-old lover during an air raid over Liverpool and is sentenced to hang. Eighteen years later Mathry's son, Paul (Johnson), arrives from the United States to learn about the father he believes died a hero during the war. When Paul discovers that the old man was convicted of murder and has been serving time in Wakefield Prison, thanks to a clemency petition initiated by shipping tycoon Enoch Oswald (Williams), he investigates with help from a rum-dum ex-cop (Clark), one of his father's arresting officers. Paul begins to suspect that the former prosecutor (Truman), now a prominent politician, and the other arresting officer (Kelsall), who is now a Chief Superintendent, have been covering up something for

The son (Van Johnson) of a convict falls for an emotionally unbalanced rape victim (Vera Miles) while trying to win a pardon for his father in *Beyond This Place* (a.k.a. *Web of Evidence*), (Georgefield Productions, 1959).

years. He also learns that the murdered girl's friend (Kent) may have blackmailed the real killer. Bob Dunn (Newlands), a reporter for the Liverpool Clarion, jumps on the story, and his newspaper articles pressure authorities into releasing the elder Mathry. Expecting fatherly gratitude for his productive efforts, Paul is shocked to learn that Mathry has become a hardened and bitter man who is concerned only with catching up on heavy drinking and womanizing. A pointless subplot has young Mathry falling for a librarian (Miles), who is frightened of men because years earlier she had been gang-raped — a crime the British filmmakers conveniently set in the United States. American stars Johnson and Miles give adequate but uninspired performances in this wrong man/whodunit noir that strays badly when it injects religious fanaticism into an otherwise plausible story.

The Big Chance
★★ (1957)

She never cleaned anything. It wasn't worth it she said. Any day now the Council would knock our street down and pack us into a pigeonhole in a nine-story heaven. That was the day Betty lived for. The day she'd become a model housewife. But for me it would be the end. Goodbye to the sea gulls, the river and all hope. [Narrator Bill Anderson]

Length: 61 min. **Cast:** William Russell, Adrienne Corri, Penelope Bartley, Ian Colin, Ferdy Mayne. **Production Company:** Major Productions. **Directed by:** Peter Graham Scott. **Photographed by:** Walter J. Harvey. **Written by:** Peter Graham Scott.

Disillusioned newlywed Bill Anderson (Russell) rues the day he married his drab, boring wife, Betty (Bartley). If only he had known before they married that she didn't like seagulls! Pining for the opportunity to run off to the Caribbean, where he can spend all of his time aboard a schooner, the travel agent gets his "big chance" when a businessman (Mayne) postpones his flight to Panama. Bill steals the man's ticket, switches passports and hurries off to the airport with a satchel filled with cash he stole from his agency's safe. At the airport, he manages to get by customs, but his flight is postponed until the next day because of heavy fog. And that's just the start of Bill's troubles. At the airport, he meets the beautiful Diana Maxwell (Corri), who is attempting to run off to Bermuda to get away from her middle-aged husband, Adam (Colin). Somehow Bill ends up as a passenger in her speeding car with Adam in hot pursuit. Before long, Bill and the socialite, who is so unlike his Betty, are making plans to go to Panama together. Fate, however, interrupts their pipe dream with a series of mishaps (including the tragedy of Diana's broken high heel), allowing Bill to get to know the real Diana Maxwell. And suddenly Betty no longer looks so awful. *The Big Chance* is filled with improbable coincidences, all designed to prevent the thief from making his getaway. Unlike another embezzler, banker Jim Osborne in the 1952 American film noir, *The Steel Trap*, Bill is unable to persuade the viewer to care much about whether or not he succeeds, is apprehended or is reconciled with his bride. Russell is a likeable enough actor with a cherub face and a charming manner, but he has little to work with here. Viewers might find their sympathies directed more toward his character's wife, who seems to have gotten the worst end of a bad deal when she married this dreamer. The film's biggest plus? Lots of atmospheric fog.

The Big Frame see *The Lost Hours*

Bitter Harvest
★★ (1963)

The world's full of old people fixing our lives for us. [Jennie Jones]

Length: 96 min. **Cast:** Janet Munro, John Stride, Anne Cunningham, Alan Badel. **Production Company:** Independent Artists. **Directed by:** Peter Graham Scott. **Photographed by:** Ernest Steward. **Written by:** Ted Willis.

Teenager Jennie Jones (Munro), a pretty grocery clerk in a small Welsh village, goes wild one night and allows herself to be picked up by an older man. After being plied with cheap champagne, she wakes up in the man's London apartment, deflowered, broke and too afraid to return home to her tyrannical father. She meets young Bob Williams (Stride), a waiter in a neighborhood pub, and takes advantage of his sympathetic nature by claiming to be pregnant. Bob moves her into his dingy one-room apartment overlooking the railroad tracks and begins to fall in love with her. Not satisfied to someday be the wife of a working class stiff and having to abandon the hope of getting that big break ("I want something good to happen to me before I die"), Jennie drops Bob and hooks up with the heartless Karl Denny (Badel), a hotshot producer of plays, thus ensuring her tragic plunge. Told in flashback following an introductory scene in which an obviously upscale Jennie, drunk and distraught, ransacks her fancy apartment, this color production of Patrick Hamilton's novel, "The Street Has a Thousand Skies," is a half-baked, sexualized retelling of the familiar tale of a dreamy-eyed innocent's downfall following a short but exciting stay in the big city. Munro seems miscast as the Lolita-type nymph that men, especially middle-aged ones, seem to find irresistible. Stride, however, is excellent as the obsessive youth who foolishly abandons the film's good girl, bartender Ella (Cunningham), for a selfish but needy stray.

The Black Glove see *Face the Music*

Black Limelight
(a.k.a. *Footsteps in the Sand*)
★★½ (1938)

All murderers are a source of amazement to their friends. [Lawrence Crawford]

Length: 70 min. **Cast:** Joan Marion, Raymond Massey, Walter Hudd, Henry Oscar, Elliott Mason, Coral Browne. **Production Company:** Associated British Picture Corporation. **Directed by:** Paul L. Stein. **Photographed by:** Claude Friese-Greene. **Written by:** Dudley Leslie, Walter Summers.

After a milkman discovers the body of Lily James (Browne), Scotland Yard sets up a dragnet for her married lover, Peter Charrington (Massey), who has gone on the run, leaving his wife, Mary (Marion), with a police cordon around their house and belligerent reporters seeking a scoop. Mary believes in her husband's innocence and is shocked to learn that Scotland Yard Inspector Tanner (Oscar) suspects that Peter is the "Dorset Killer," a "wholesale murderer" who has already knifed several young girls, including a 12-year-old. The Charrington family lawyer, Lawrence Crawford (Hudd), encourages Mary to persuade Peter to give himself up, but she adamantly refuses. When Peter sneaks back into the house to proclaim his innocence, he admits his love affair with the murdered woman. His story about the evening of the murder supplies Mary with the clue she needs to prove his innocence. She turns in her shocked husband, who accuses her of betraying him for the reward, and sets a trap for the killer. *Black Limelight* is not a particularly well-acted film. Canadian-born Hollywood star Raymond Massey, who doesn't have a word of dialogue until the movie is nearly half over, has a tendency to look wild-eyed in his scenes, while Australian actress Marion rattles off her lines like an auctioneer on speed. Elliott Mason, as the sharp-tongued housekeeper, provides some compensatory humor. What makes this dark and shadowy film unique is the portrayal of a 1930's housewife as bold, independent-minded, aggressive and courageous. Forgiving of her husband's unfaithfulness, perhaps implausibly so, she sets out to prove his innocence even at the risk of her own life. Interesting also is the filmmakers' depiction of Peter's affair with Lily, who is pregnant with his child. There is no attempt to whitewash the pregnancy or the fact that Lily has considered an abortion. "I've decided to go through with it," she tells her married lover, who is more than supportive of her decision. Definitely worth a viewing for fans of British film noir.

Black Memory
(NR) (1947)

Length: 73 min. **Cast**: Michael Atkinson, Myra O'Connell, Jane Arden, Michael Medwin, Sid James. **Production Companies**: Bushey Studios. **Directed by**: Oswald Mitchell. **Photographed by**: S.D. Onions. **Written by**: John Gilling.

Seeking to clear his father of a murder charge, a cockney youth goes undercover as a juvenile delinquent in the London underworld.

Black Narcissus
★★★★ ½ (1947)

You're objectionable when you're sober and abominable when you're drunk. [Sister Clodagh to Mr. Dean]

Length: 100 min. **Cast**: Deborah Kerr, Flora Robson, Jean Simmons, David Farrar, Sabu, Kathleen Byron, Jenny Laird, Judith Furse. **Production Companies**: Independent Producers, Archers Film Productions. **Directed by**: Michael Powell, Emeric Pressburger. **Photographed by**: Jack Cardiff. **Written by**: Michael Powell, Emeric Pressburger.

Five Anglican nuns (Kerr, Robson, Bryon, Laird and Furse) are transferred by their superiors in Calcutta to a former palace in the Himalayans to start a school and an infirmary for the locals. The "palace" was originally called The House of Women and was used to house the local ruler's harem. The palace decor reflects this, accentuating the contrast between the symbolically pure, white-clad nuns, whose objective is to serve God by serving others, and the palace's former occupants, concubines whose raison d'etre was to bring sexual pleasure to their master. Ambitious Irish nun Sister Clodagh (Kerr), her order's youngest ever Sister Superior, finds her new job more demanding than she had anticipated, having to deal with the constant wind, the bad drinking water, the superstitious people who are reluctant to come forward for medical treatment, a silent holy man who has not moved from his spot on the side of the mountain for years, and the local military leader's agent, Mr. Dean (Farrar), a sacrilegious Brit whose coarseness and lack of respect for her authority and her mission test her patience. Even worse, Sister Clodagh finds herself haunted by bitter memories of her secular life in Ireland when she was in love with a capricious young man who dropped her for the opportunity to emigrate to America. The dreary and lonely environment also seems to be affecting her staff, especially the increasingly psychotic and paranoid Sister Ruth (Byron), who has been betraying a sensual response to the handsome, often scantily clad, Mr. Dean. When the time comes for Sister Ruth to renew her vows, she refuses and, instead, paints her face, dons the sexy dress she ordered from a mail order catalog and heads off for Mr. Dean's cottage in the middle of the night. An early British Technicolor production, this tale of paranoia, sexual repression and conflicting loyalties is hauntingly beautiful (an Oscar for best color cinematography was awarded to Cardiff) and superbly acted, especially by the unforgettable Kerr and Byron, who turns in a bravura performance as the emotionally unstable nun whose shocking transformation slowly unfolds before the unwary viewer. Eighteen-year-old Simmons has a small but appealing role as a sultry dancing girl seeking to marry Mr. Dean but happily settling for a military bigwig (Sabu). The film's weakness lies in the character of the long-legged Mr. Dean, whom the viewer might have difficulty taking seriously with his silly outfits (short pants and a Sherwood Forest-type cap) and his laughable means of transportation — an obviously overburdened miniature pony.

Black Orchid
★★ (1953)

> I want my freedom and if in the course of getting it you suffer, I shan't give it a thought, I promise you. [Sophie Winnington to soon-to-be widower Dr. John Winnington]

Length: 60 min. **Cast:** Ronald Howard, Olga Edwardes, John Bentley, Mary Laura Wood, Sheila Burrell. **Production Companies:** Kenilworth Film Productions, Mid-Century Film Productions. **Directed by:** Charles Saunders. **Photographed by:** Eric Cross. **Written by:** Francis Edge, John Temple-Smith.

Trying to find a cure for meningitis while simultaneously maintaining a private medical practice makes it difficult for Dr. John Winnington (Howard) to give Sophie (Wood), his wife of ten years, the attention she constantly demands. Convinced that she is having an affair, John asks her for a divorce, but Sophie arrogantly replies that she is holding off until the right time. The right time coincides with the arrival of her younger sister, Christine (Edwardes), whom she hasn't seen in eight years. Sophie pushes John to hire Chris as his lab assistant and waits for nature to take its course. It doesn't take long before John and Chris fall innocently in love, prompting Sophie to hire a private detective to supply her with spurious evidence of an affair. Sophie happily files for divorce, is awarded a bundle in court and makes plans to leave the country by boat, but not before she breaks the bad news to John and Chris about a little known law. It seems that a man cannot legally marry his former wife's sister (while the wife is still alive, that is). Before Sophie can make it to the ship yard, she is hit by a lorry and killed. Not only does this save John a large cash settlement and a third of his earnings for life, it frees him to marry Christine. Sophie's devoted maid, Annette (Burrell), however, rushes off to Scotland Yard Inspector Markham (Napier) to inform him that she suspects John of poisoning her mistress. The subsequent autopsy finds that Sophie was suffering from nicotine poisoning when she was struck by the vehicle. John is soon convicted of murder and sentenced to hang, leaving Chris and John's friend, writer Eric Blair (Bentley), to search for the real killer. A lame script and run-of-the-mill performances contribute to the deserved obscurity of a film rarely seen on this side of the Atlantic. Stylistically, there is little to support a film noir designation for *Black Orchid*; however, the theme — that of a man wrongly convicted of murder who must depend on others to prove his innocence — is a prevalent one in American film noir. The script gives Dr. Winnington's noirish predicament, however, little emphasis, jumping hurriedly from the coroner's verdict of murder to Winnington's death row stay and offering the viewer only the vaguest notion that time is running out for him, thus the reason for the film's lack of suspense. The most interesting character turns out to be the maid, Annette, whose rabid devotion to her mistress seems to be sexually motivated.

Black 13
(NR) (1953)

Length: 77 min. **Cast**: Peter Reynolds, Rona Anderson, Patrick Barr, Lana Morris. **Production Company**: Vandyke Picture Corporation. **Directed by**: Ken Hughes. **Photographed by**: Gerald Gibbs. **Written by**: Pietro Germi.

A girl falls in love with the detective who wants to arrest her brother for murder.

Black Tide see Stormy Crossing

Black Widow
★★ (1951)

CHRISTINE: How soon will all this happen, Paul? Him finding out I mean.
PAUL: Well, tonight probably, tomorrow certainly, as soon as he sticks his nose outside the house.
CHRISTINE: But supposing he never leaves the house, Paul? Supposing he never leaves the house again, alive?

Length: 62 min. **Cast**: Christine Norden, Robert Ayres, Anthony Forwood, Jennifer Jayne, John Longden. **Production Company**: Hammer Film Productions. **Directed by**: Vernon Sewell. **Photographed by**: Walter J. Harvey. **Written by**: Alan MacKinnon.

A crook feigning injury causes Mark Sherwin (Ayres) to stop his car on an isolated country road to see if he can help. Mark's Good Samaritan deed earns him a good knock over the head, and the crook steals his wallet and drives away in Mark's car. After Mark regains consciousness, he manages to walk to a horse farm owned by Mr. Kemp (Longden) and his pretty daughter, Sheila (Jayne). The Kemps spend the next several days nursing Mark back to health, but there's nothing they can do for his retrograde amnesia, a consequence the local doctor says of his head injury and a pre-existing neurotic state. Meanwhile, the crook who stole Mark's car drives off a cliff while being chased by motorcycle cops for speeding and dies in a fiery explosion. Having recuperated from his injury, Mark finds a movie stub in his coat pocket, providing him with the only clue to his identity. With the name of the theater and the memory of a recurring dream, Mark finds his way to his estate. Once inside the house, he discovers a body in a coffin. Believing him to be dead, his shocked wife, Christine (Norden), faints when she sees him. Mark's memory returns immediately, and he realizes that the body thought to be his is the charred remains of the crook who stole his car and wallet. Mark is happy to be home, but Christine and her lover, Mark's best friend, Paul Kenton (Forwood), are devastated as they see their longed-for freedom and all of Mark's money slipping through their greedy fingers. However, since no one knows that Mark is alive, Christine goes ahead with the crook's burial in the family plot and concocts a murderous scheme to get rid of her husband. Unfortunately, her weak-kneed lover doesn't seem to have the stomach for it and needs a bit of a nudge. Unbeknownst to them, Mark has already figured out what they are up to and prepares to defend himself. The acting here leaves something to be desired, but the familiar noir plot and recognizable characters— an adulterous femme fatale wife and her lover plot to murder her husband, who happens to be a recently cured amnesiac (a nice little noir bonus from writer MacKinnon)— add to the enjoyment of this mildly entertaining, low-budget movie.

Blackmailed
(NR) (1951)

Length: 85 min. **Cast**: Mai Zetterling, Dirk Bogarde, Fay Compton, Robert Flemyng, Michael Gough. **Production Company**: H.H. Films. **Directed by**: Marc Allégret. **Photographed by**: George Stretton. **Written by**: Hugh Mills, Roger Vadim.

Whodunit about extortion victims attempting to cover up the murder of the man who was blackmailing them.

Blackout
★★ (1950)

SINCLAIR: Come on, start talking. Where do you come from?
PELLY: Mother said something about the stork but that was just to keep me quiet when the vicar came.

Length: 73 min. **Cast:** Maxwell Reed, Dinah Sheridan, Eric Pohlmann, Michael Evans, Michael Brennan, Patric Doonan, Annette Simmonds, Michael Balfour. **Production Company:** Tempean Films. **Directed by:** Robert S. Baker. **Photographed by:** Monty Berman. **Written by:** John Gilling.

Blind for the last eighteen months as a result of a car crash, Chris Pelly catches a ride with a hard-of-hearing driver (Balfour), who delivers him to No. 3 Lindale *Gardens* instead of a friend's house at No. 3 Lindale *Square*. When Chris enters the wrong building he stumbles over a dead body in the study. The killers, who are still in the house, nab Chris, but when they learn he is blind and will not be able to recognize them, they simply knock him unconscious and drop him off in the basement of the correct address. Later, when the police are unable to verify Chris' story, the assumption is that the knock on his head was accidental and that he imagined it all. Two months later, he regains his sight in a successful eye operation and goes looking for the house where he found the body. He hits pay dirt at the Dale residence, where he meets pretty Pat Dale (Sheridan) and convinces her that the body he found in her house that night must have belonged to her brother, Norman, a pilot who supposedly died in an airplane crash a year earlier. The two track down Chalky (Doonan), one of Norman's former crew members, who puts them onto the trail of the three killers, Otto Ford (Pohlmann), Guy Sinclair (Evans) and Mickey Garston (Brennan), smugglers involved in the currency exchange racket. Needless to say, the crooks are a bit dismayed when they discover that Reed can see and that he is excellent at recognizing voices. Because the protagonist does not become a "wrong man" who must prove he is not a killer, as the viewer expects will occur when he leaves his fingerprints on the knife protruding from the dead man's back, there is no satisfactory explanation for his obsession to hunt down the killers. Thus, *Blackout*, which begins so promisingly, evolves into an average, even hum-drum, mystery made even worse by the protagonist's many failed attempts at hardboiled sarcasm. Cinematographer Berman, however, has included plenty of tilted camera angles and dark menacing shadows, almost enough to compensate for the film's lackluster script and disappointing performances.

Blackout see *Contraband*; see *Murder by Proxy*

Blanche Fury
★★★½ (1948)

I know how cruelly unhappiness has twisted his nature. [Louisa about Philip Thorn]

Length: 95 min. **Cast:** Stewart Granger, Valerie Hobson, Michael Gough, Walter Fitzgerald, Susanne Gibbs. **Production Companies:** Independent Producers, Cineguild Productions. **Directed by:** Marc Allégret. **Photographed by:** Guy Green. **Written by:** Audrey Lindop, Cecil McGivern.

While Blanche Fury lies severely ill, perhaps dying, the viewer is presented with her sordid tale by way of a 90-minute flashback. Blanche Fuller (Hobson), a professional domestic and companion, takes a position as governess to her cousin's daughter at Clare Hall, an estate owned by Blanche's Uncle Simon (Fitzgerald). Simon changed the family name to Fury after coming into possession of the vast property formerly owned by Adam Fury. Fury's steward, Philip Thorn (Granger), swears that he is the true owner of the estate, being the illegitimate son of Adam and an Italian woman, but he has no way of proving his claim. After the ambitious Blanche marries her cousin, Laurence (Gough), father of her young charge, Lavinia (Gibbs), she immediately begins a torrid affair with the Philip, whose fanatical obsession with Clare Hall soon drives him to murder. After being fired by Laurence, Philip ambushes and kills both Laurence and Simon, framing a band of gypsies who earlier had threatened Simon for having two of their group arrested and prosecuted for arson. Complicit in the murder by her silence and inaction, Blanche is content to continue her secret affair with Philip, but after a coroner's jury determines that the murdered men had been victims of "gypsy vengeance," Philip becomes overly cocky, expecting to take immediate control of the Fury estate by marrying the widow. Blanche, however, has some bad news for him. It seems that the next in the line for inheritance is not her, but Lavinia, and Blanche has no intention of allowing Philip to murder an innocent child. Filmed in glorious Technicolor, this extravagant Period noir, which takes place in mid–19th century England, is beautifully produced and well acted, with Granger excellent as the servant with a real or imagined grievance that leads to his downfall. The film's beauty and many noirish elements (a convoluted plot, obsession, adultery, greed, ambition, betrayal, murder, a frame-up, a scheming homme fatale, a child in jeopardy and a downbeat ending) compensate for its weaknesses, such as poor character development and several plot holes. The most fascinating character is Blanche, ably portrayed by Irish-born actress Hobson as an independent-minded, even radical, Victorian female who has no qualms about putting her husband in his place. Soon after their wedding, Blanche informs her stunned groom that, "I have no intention, contrary to the fashion of our times, of being ordered about by my husband." Nor do Victorian mores prevent her from seeking out and giving herself to the ruggedly good looking stable master on her wedding night, while her effete groom is out chasing marauding gypsies with his wedding guests. Best scene in the film? When the viewer sees the invisible, ominous light bulbs going off over the heads of Blanche and Philip as he offhandedly remarks, "If only they would die." *Blanche Fury* is an admirable effort by Allégret, the Swiss-born French director, and a cinematographic coup for Brit noir veterans Green and Geoffrey Unsworth (credited with the film's exterior shots).

Blind Corner
(U.S. Title: *Man in the Dark*)
★★½ (1963)

ANNE GREGORY: The balcony has a very low parapet. It would be easy to push him over. Then I'd be free and we could be together.
RICKIE SELDON: Where? Swinging side by side on the scaffold?

Length: 80 min. **Cast**: William Sylvester, Barbara Shelley, Elizabeth Shepherd, Alexander Davion, Mark Eden. **Production Company**: Mancunian Film Corporation. **Directed by**: Lance Comfort. **Photographed by**: Basil Emmott. **Written by**: James Kelley, Peter Miller.

Blind songwriter Paul Gregory (Sylvester) manages to make a good living writing pop songs, although he would prefer to be composing classical music. His beautiful wife, Anne (Shelley), doesn't care much one way or the other as long as the money keeps rolling in. Anne is having an affair with penniless artist Rickie Seldon (Davion), whom she lures into a murder plot. Paul, it seems, has been warned by his friends not to go out on the balcony of his high-rise apartment when he has been drinking heavily, two things he does often these days. One day, Paul's best friend and manager, Mike Williams (Eden), who is known to despise Anne, tells him that he saw Anne cozying up with Rickie in a London restaurant. Paul confirms the story with the head waiter and sits back and waits for the inevitable confrontation. Meanwhile, Paul's secretary, Joan Marshall (Shepherd), who is in love with him, hopes the discovery of Anne's unfaithfulness will snap him out of his blind, pardon the pun, devotion to his wife. *Blind Corner* is fairly effective with a few nicely developed twists and solid performances by American actor Sylvester, a veteran of many British "B" films, and future Hammer horror icon Shelley. British crooner Ronnie Carroll makes a cameo appearance.

Blind Date
(U.S. Title: *Chance Meeting*)
★★½ (1959)

A city is like a mirror. When you look at it you see yourself. If you're happy, it's beautiful. If you're lonely, it's not so beautiful. [Van Rooyen's lover]

Length: 95 min. **Cast**: Hardy Krüger, Stanley Baker, Micheline Presle, Robert Flemyng. **Production Company**: Independent Artists. **Directed by**: Joseph Losey. **Photographed by**: Christopher Challis. **Written by**: Ben Barzman, Millard Lampell.

Jan Van Rooyen (Krüger), a Dutch artist barely eking out a living in London, has an affair with

Jacqueline Cousteau (Presle), "an expensive piece of French pastry" whose husband has an "appetite for cognac and slapping people around when he's drunk." Van Rooyen explains to Scotland Yard Inspector Morgan (Baker) (and to the viewer by way of several flashbacks) why police officers found him lounging around his lover's living room while her dead body was in the bedroom. Morgan, apprehensive of Rooyen's tale at first, begins to suspect that his Yard superior, Sir Brian Lewis (Flemyng), may be trying to cover up the involvement of one of his friends, an important diplomat. Richard Rodney Bennett's snappy jazz score helps to enliven this slow-moving film in which an obsession with class distinctions is an ever present plot element (Van Rooyen is the son of a Dutch coal miner, Inspector Morgan's father was a mere chauffeur, Cousteau is the wife of a government official, and Sir Brian has been hobnobbing with a highly placed public servant who may have been having an affair with Cousteau). The German-born Krüger is good as the eccentric, lovesick artist who eventually overcomes his initial discomfort with his British upper crust lover only to realize that he may be playing the patsy for someone much higher on the social ladder. Baker turns in his usual reliable performance, playing an unwavering detective under departmental pressure to close a murder case quickly and with as little media attention as possible, even if it means pinning the crime on an innocent man. Interesting for a British crime film at the time is the acknowledgment that such a creature as the corrupt police official actually may exist.

Blonde Bait see Women Without Men

Blonde for Danger see The Flamingo Affair

Blonde Sinner see Yield to the Night

The Blue Lamp
★★★½ (1950)

The case of Diana Lewis is typical of many—a young girl showing the effect of a childhood spent in a home broken and demoralized by war. These restless and ill-adjusted youngsters have produced a type of delinquent which is partly responsible for the post-war increase in crime. [Narrator]

Length: 84 min. **Cast:** Jack Warner, Jimmy Hanley, Dirk Bogarde, Peggy Evans, Patric Doonan. **Production Company:** Ealing Studios. **Directed by:** Basil Dearden. **Photographed by:** Gordon Dines. **Written by:** T.E.B. Clarke.

The Blue Lamp is a straightforward, semi-documentary police procedural with the good guys being, of course, the unarmed constables who patrol the streets of London, and the bad guys being the youthful lawbreakers who began roaming these same streets soon after the end of World War II. The film revolves around two pairs of characters— Police Constables (PCs) George Dixon, an experienced policeman approaching retirement, and Andy Mitchell, barely out of training, and hoodlums Tom Riley (Bogarde) and Spud (Doonan), two trouble-bound young men always on the lookout for an easy pound. The mood of the film changes from one of jolly good fun, with the good-natured bobbies at the Paddington Green police station playing darts and holding choir practice prior to starting their usually mundane duties, to a sense of impending disaster when Tom buys a gun to use in the heist he and Spud are planning at the Coliseum Cinema box office. The viewer senses from the disturbing scene in which Tom uses the gun to gleefully torment his 17-year-old girlfriend, Diana (Evans), that someone's days are numbered. Stumbling upon the stick-up at the Coliseum, a brave (some might say brash) constable steps forward just as the trembling, panicky gunman pulls the trigger. With the officer's shooting and subsequent death, the hunt begins for his murderer, with the police department combining technology, old-fashioned legwork and help from London's underworld figures, who are as much outraged over the constable's murder as are the coppers. The acting in *The Blue Lamp* (the title refers to the lamp hanging over the police station entrance) is good, with the one exception being the performance of Evans, who plays Tom's moll. Her hysteria method of acting must be seen to be believed. The film's best performance belongs to Bogarde as the cowardly psychotic gunman, whose look of astonishment when he pulls the trigger matches that of his victim's. Jack Warner went on to duplicate his role as PC George Dixon in the long-running (1955–1976) British television shown, "Dixon of Dock Green."

The Blue Parrot
★½ (1953)

CLUB HOSTESS 1: Does this happen often?
CLUB HOSTESS 2: What?
CLUB HOSTESS 1: Customers taking over the band.
CLUB HOSTESS 2: He's an American. They take over anything.

Length: 69 min. **Cast**: Dermot Walsh, Jacqueline Hill, Ballard Berkeley, June Ashley, Ferdy Mayne, Victor Lucas, Edwin Richfield, John Le Mesurier. **Production Company**: A.C.T. Films. **Directed by**: John Harlow. **Photographed by**: Bob Navarro. **Written by**: Allan MacKinnon.

Bob Herrick (Walsh), an American cop in London to study Scotland Yard's organizational expertise, pleads with Supt. Chester (Berkeley) to allow him to assist in the investigation of the murder of a blackmailing cab driver named Rocks Owen (Lucas). After taking away Bob's gun ("In this country we don't carry guns. They lead to shooting," Chester tells him), the superintendent permits the Yank to go undercover as an obnoxious American customer at a private Soho nightspot called The Blue Parrot. It is at The Blue Parrot where Rocks was last seen alive and where police officer Maureen Maguire (Hill) has been assigned to work undercover as a martini hostess alongside the club's veteran drink hustler, blonde bombshell Gloria (Ashley). While Scotland Yard investigates the club's owner (Le Mesurier), a waiter (Richfield) and a small-time gangster (Mayne), Bob finds himself falling for the policewoman, who he fears may have gotten in way over her pretty little head. Overlong even at 69 minutes, *The Blue Parrot* has little going for it except some unintentional humor.

Bombsight Stolen see ***Cottage to Let***

Both Sides of the Law see ***Street Corner***

Boys in Brown
★★½ (1949)

Everyone likes him ... even the screws. [Parolee Bill Foster to convict Jackie Knowles' mother.]

Length: 85 min. **Cast**: Jack Warner, Richard Attenborough, Dirk Bogarde, Jimmy Hanley, Barbara Murray. **Production Company**: Gainsborough Pictures. **Directed by**: Montgomery Tully. **Photographed by**: Gordon Lang, Cyril Bristow. **Written by**: Montgomery Tully.

Troubled youth Jackie Knowles (Attenborough) gets nabbed as the getaway driver in a botched jewelry store robbery. Already on probation for stealing a bicycle, Jackie is sent by a lenient judge to a borstal, a reformatory for delinquent boys between the ages of 16 and 21. The borstal is run by a reform-minded governor (Warner) and a staff of strict but well-intentioned masters, whose progressive system so far has been a failure, with a recidivism rate of approximately fifty percent. Once inside, Jackie is determined to serve his sentence and, hopefully with good behavior, get an early release. Unfortunately, he becomes involved with the wrong crowd, including Alfie Rawlins (Bogarde) and several others who are hell-bent on escaping. Desperate to see his girl, Kitty (Murray), who he thinks has dumped him for Bill Foster (Jimmy Hanley), a recently released inmate, Jackie decides to join the break-out attempt. During the escape, he clubs a master over the head with a lamp and thus faces a possible murder charge if he is caught. *Boys in Brown* is notable mainly for the presence of soon-to-be British superstars Attenborough and Bogarde and future British TV star Jimmy Hanley. All of the "boys" of Borstal Institution appear a bit long in the tooth. Attenborough was 26 at the time, Bogarde 28 and Hanley 31, and all look uncomfortable in their silly brown uniforms of short pants, knee socks and ties. Hurting the film's credibility is the portrayal of the three lads as hapless victims of society — Jackie has no father, Alfie's father beat him and Bill was an illegitimate child — rather than as the social misfits they seem to be. In addition, Alfie's offer to be the fall guy when the group is confronted with the attack on the master, is bewildering not only to the borstal governor but to viewer as well. With inmates named Plato, Sparrow, Barker, Spud and Dusty, the viewer may think that this is really an East Side Kids movie minus the comedy. Still, the film does have its enjoyable moments.

The Brain Machine
★★½ (1955)

> And get this. You bring the law with you, you'll have to fish your wife out of the river. Understand? [Frank Smith]

Length: 83 min. **Cast:** Elizabeth Allan, Maxwell Reed, Patrick Barr, Gibb McLaughlin, Edwin Richfield. **Production Company:** Merton Park Productions. **Directed by:** Ken Hughes. **Photographed by:** Josef Ambor. **Written by:** Ken Hughes.

Husband and wife psychiatrists Geoffrey Allen (Barr) and Philippa Roberts (Allan) have been studying their patients' electroencephalographs and have discovered a connection between the brain's electrical impulses and the psychopathic personality. When Frank Smith (Reed) is admitted to the North London Hospital suffering from partial amnesia, the supposed result of being hit by a bus, Philippa runs the standard tests. Smith admits under sodium pentothal that he had really been beaten by thugs working for Spencer Simon (McLaughlin), the elderly owner of a chemical company. An x-ray shows that Smith has a brain tumor, and an EEG indicates, according to Philippa's theory, that the patient has the potential to become violent. When Smith releases himself from the hospital without giving his home address, Philippa contacts the police, who are helpless to do anything until Smith commits a crime, which he does soon afterward when he returns to the hospital and kidnaps Philippa. Smith holes up with Philippa in a warehouse beneath the London Underground, where she finds a truck filled with stolen cortisone, a drug in short supply in England. Geoffrey, meanwhile, searches for his kidnapped spouse and indirectly causes the death of Smith's wife when Simon's thug, Ryan (Reed), who has been tailing Geoffrey, strangles her to prevent her from divulging Smith's whereabouts. Wounded during a shootout with Ryan, Smith moves Philippa to another hideout — Charlie's Gymnasium and Social Club — where they call Geoffrey and tell him to bring his surgical tools to remove the bullet. After performing the surgery, Geoffrey stupidly tells Smith, who according to Allen's own EEG hypothesis is exceptionally prone to violence, that Mrs. Smith has been murdered. Smith decides to pay Simon a visit at the chemical plant despite Allen's feeble pleas not to take the law into his own hands. At the plant, where workers are striking against their greedy boss, Smith will either prove or disprove the psychiatrists' theory. Decent performances and some nice noir-fortified photography overcome the film's weak premise. Unfortunately for Maxwell Reed, screenwriters overwrote his hardboiled dialogue, and his character comes off as a stereotyped Hollywood hoodlum.

The Breaking Point (U.S. Title: The Great Armored Car Swindle)
★★½ (1961)

> I've got myself in a hell of a jam, haven't I? [Eric Winlatter]

Length: 59 min. **Cast:** Peter Reynolds, Dermot Walsh, Joanna Dunham, Jack Allen, Brian Cobby. **Production Companies:** Falcon Pictures, Butcher's Film Service. **Directed by:** Lance Comfort. **Photographed by:** Basil Emmott. **Written by:** Peter Lambert.

Eric Winlatter (Reynolds) is broke. Even though he works for his uncle (Allen), Eric never seems to be able to get ahead, and his lack of financial success is affecting his marriage to Cherry (Dunham). Opportunity knocks, however, in the form of Lalvadore, an obscure Middle Eastern country "on the fringe of the Iron Curtain." The Lalvadorean government hires Winlatter's company to help it reorganize the country's currency. It seems that the Communists are planning to flood Lalvadore with counterfeit money to ruin its economy and force Lalvadore to turn to the Eastern bloc for aid. The Lalvadorean plan is to initiate a surprise call-in of their currency and replace it with new banknotes provided by Eric's company. When Eric is approached by a traitorous Lalvadorean embassy official (Cobby) and offered £1,000 to provide him with information about the switch, he happily accepts. But he soon finds himself involved in more than he bargained for when he is forced to take part in the actual heist. Meanwhile, Cherry has found solace in the arms of novelist Robert Wade (Walsh), whose writer's curiosity prompts him to wonder why Eric has been acting so suspiciously lately. *The Breaking Point* is a fairly suspenseful movie with a decent performance by Reynolds and a nicely done downbeat ending.

Brighton Rock
(U.S. Title: *Young Scarface*)
★★★★½ (1947)

Take my advice, Brown, and clear out of Brighton. You aren't big enough for the filthy racket you're in. [Police inspector to Pinkie Brown]

Length: 91 min. **Cast:** Richard Attenborough, Hermione Baddeley, William Hartnell, Carol Marsh, Nigel Stock, Wylie Watson, Alan Wheatley. **Production Company:** Associated British Picture Corporation. **Directed by:** John Boulting. **Photographed by:** Harry Waxman. **Written by:** Graham Greene, Terence Rattigan.

Spiv Pinkie Brown (Attenborough) and his thugs (Hartnell, Stock, and Watson) operate out of Brighton Beach, a seaside resort town in Sussex, about an hour's train ride from London. When reporter Fred Hale (Wheatley) arrives in town, Pinkie's boys recognize him as the journalist who coaxed their former gang leader into giving an interview during which the gangster disclosed too much about the slot machine racket in Brighton, resulting in his murder by rival mobsters. Pinkie takes revenge by pushing the reporter from a ride at the Palace Pier Amusement Park. When the coroner rules that Hale's fall from the ride was the result of a heart attack, Pinkie is certain he has gotten away with murder. His relief, however, is short-lived when he learns that Rose (Marsh), a waitress who never forgets a face, might be able to identify gang member Spicer (Watson) as the man who impersonated the reporter at Snow's Cafe in order to give Pinkie an alibi. Seeing both Rose and Spicer as threats, Pinkie decides to do something about them. Meanwhile, Ida Arnold (Baddeley), a middle-aged boardwalk performer who had befriended the murdered man, has been playing amateur detective, causing Pinkie even more anxiety. *Brighton Rock* is set against the backdrop of a now "jolly" seaside town, described by the filmmakers as having once been a place of dark alleys, festering slums, widespread crime, violence and gang warfare. Brown, a baby-faced 17-year-old criminal, is brilliantly portrayed by Attenborough as a cruel, razor-wielding sociopath who romances, marries and plots the death of a naive teen-aged girl in order to protect his alibi. An uncommonly violent film for the era, *Brighton Rock* is filled with religious allusions and symbolism. A racetrack evangelist carries a placard that reads, "The Wages of Sin Is Death" and during a fight breaks the sign over the head of one of the brawlers. At a night spot on the boardwalk, Rose's rosary beads fall from her purse and she and Pinkie discover that they are both Catholics. When asked by Rose if he thinks "it's true," Pinkie replies, "Of course it's true. These atheists don't know nothing. Of course they'll have flames, damnations, torments!" On their wedding day, Rose, who is guilt-ridden about helping Pinkie cover up the reporter's murder, tells him, "I wanted to be in a state of grace when I married you. But then I remembered, it wasn't any good confessing any more. Ever." The fate of Rose's immortal soul is further endangered when Pinkie tries to convince her to commit the unpardonable sin of suicide. Even the boozing Ida Arnold has a belief system, albeit a peculiar one that complements her eccentricity — she believes the dead can talk to her through the newspaper when she closes her eyes and points to letters. After six decades, *Brighton Rock* still holds up as a sensational crime film that compares favorably to many of its better known American gangster movies and film noir counterparts. Acting kudos go to Attenborough as the cowardly hoodlum, Marsh as the epitome of sweetness and naivety, Baddeley as the jovial barfly with a heart of gold and an unwavering sense of justice and Hartnell as Pinkie's loyal but prudent henchman.

The Brothers
★★★ (1947)

I tell you she is evil and evil breeds evil in those who meet it. [John Macrae]

Length: 98 min. **Cast:** Patricia Roc, Maxwell Reed, Finlay Currie, Duncan MacRae, Andrew Crawford. **Production Company:** Triton Films. **Directed by:** David MacDonald. **Photographed by:** Stephen Dade. **Written by:** Muriel and Sydney Box.

On the Scottish Island of Skye at the turn of the 20th century, an elderly, bootlegging widower and his two unmarried sons hire Mary Lawson (Roc), a pretty young girl fresh from the convent, as a live-in servant. After a stern warning from the village priest to safeguard the lass' chastity, the Macrae patriarch, Hector (Currie), swears that as long as he is alive the girl will be safe from harm. Hector's two sons, the elder John (MacRae) and the younger Fergus (Reed), despite their obvious yearning for Mary, are bound by the tradition of patriarchal obedience and keep their distance. Mary, however, has taken a particular liking to Fergus and a young man from the McFarish clan, with whom the MacRaes have had a longstanding feud. Willie McFarish (Crawford) takes advantage of Mary's interest by trying to force himself on her, but Fergus intervenes, thrashing the young man to protect the family honor, thus further exacerbating the Hatfield and McCoy–like feud. When Hector dies following a grueling rowing contest against the McFarishes (a traditional way of settling disputes on the island), all bets are off as far as Mary's chastity is concerned, and John, as the new head of household, sets his sight on marrying her, keeping secret his father's dying wish that she wed Fergus. Mary, however, wants nothing to do with her creepy, skeletal pursuer and turns once again to the libidinous Willie McFarish. When the priest orders John to find a wife for himself or he will remove Mary from her scandalous male-dominated surroundings, John marries a plain–Jane neighbor so that Mary won't be sent back to the convent. With his brother finally married, Fergus now feels free to pursue Mary, forgiving her for her dalliance with his mortal enemy, Willie, who has been boasting about his sexual conquest. This enrages and humiliates John and he begins thinking about revenge. Confusing? You bet. Enjoyable? You bet. The outdoor photography is spectacular with a beautiful coastal landscape as the film's unlikely noir setting. The characters are believable, with the elder, mad brother as the distinctive stand-out among an average, even boring, crowd of superstitious and tradition-bound islanders. The sexual allusions are obvious (one that can't be misread is a close-up of Mary's hand as it clenches tightly while Fergus accepts her submission). Not to be missed are Fergus' symbolic castration when he is forced to cut off his thumb to free himself from a fish's grip (or else drown in the oncoming tide) and an amazing execution-by-seagull scene. Not an outstanding film for sure but unique and worth searching out.

Cage of Gold
★★★ (1950)

BILL: *This doesn't smell so good.*
RAHMAN: *Money always smells good.*

Length: 83 min. **Cast:** Jean Simmons, David Farrar, James Donald, Herbert Lom, Madeleine LeBeau. **Production Company:** Ealing Studios. **Directed by:** Basil Dearden. **Photographed by:** Douglas Slocombe. **Written by:** Jack Whittingham.

War veteran Bill Glennon (Farrar) returns to London to find that Judith (Simmons), the teenaged girl who always had a crush on him, has grown up to be a beautiful woman. Bill romances her, steals her away from her boyfriend, Dr. Alan Kearn (Donald), makes her pregnant and marries her for her family's money. He learns after their quickie civil ceremony, however, that Judith's father lost all of his money during the war. So the caddish gold-digger, who has been earning his living smuggling gold, takes off the morning after the wedding and returns to Paris and Marie (LeBeau), a singer at the Cage of Gold nightclub, whose money and heart he recently stole. Always interested in making some easy dough, Bill sells his British passport to the nightclub's crooked owner, Rahman (Lom), who passes it on to one of his goons to use in a diamond smuggling operation. When the smuggler impersonating Bill dies in an airplane crash, the newspapers report that Bill was among the dead. The report of his death frees Judith and Alan to marry soon after the birth of Bill's son (the blessed event occurs only after Alan talks Judith out of an abortion). Meanwhile, Bill, on the run from the Paris police after trying to extort money from a banker whose daughter he had seduced, returns to London and sets his greedy sights on Alan and Judith, his unwittingly bigamist wife. Excellent low-key performances by Simmons, Donald and Farrar (who is especially good as the despicable homme fatale) and the dark and atmospheric cinematography spice up the familiar story, which in some ways resembles *No Man of Her Own*, an American film noir released the same year. Lom fans may be disappointed with his minor role, which has him doing little but coughing incessantly from too much smoking and ogling nightclub singer Marie, whose singing is almost as bad as that of Ida Lupino's in 1948's *Road House*.

Cairo
★★½ (1963)

PICKERING: After this it's South America for me.
NICODEMOS: Ah, gauchos, tangos and sunshine, eh?
PICKERING: No, simple lechery is more what I had in mind.

Length: 91 min. **Cast:** George Sanders, Richard Johnson, Faten Hamama, John Meillon, Ahmed Mazhar, Eric Pohlmann, Walter Rilla. **Production Company:** MGM. **Directed by:** Wolf Rilla. **Photographed by:** Desmond Dickinson. **Written by:** Joanne Court.

Major Pickering (Sanders), recently released from a German prison, arrives in Cairo with a plan to steal King Tut's jewels from the National Museum. With financial assistance from a small-time casino operator, Greek expatriate Nicodemos (Pohlmann), Pickering pulls together a professional team — gunman Ali Hassan (Johnson), safecracker Willy Roberts (Meillon), and getaway driver Kerim (Mazhar) — but makes the mistake of trusting bankrupt businessman Kamel Kuchuk (Rilla) to act as the fence for the stolen goods. An inferior but faithful remake of the American film noir classic *The Asphalt Jungle*, *Cairo* is interesting primarily for its use of an exotic Middle Eastern locale in lieu of the original's Midwestern American city. *Cairo*'s characters are almost identical to the original's (right down to the heist mastermind's fateful predilection for young girls, in this case a belly dancer). However, *Cairo* lacks the earlier filmmakers' meticulous and painstaking attention to detail in developing characters the viewer will care about. This is the major weakness of *Cairo*, an otherwise well-acted film that contains some clever dialogue ("I'm a policeman, not an Egyptologist," replies a police commandant to a persnickety museum official's questions concerning King Tut's stolen jewels). Egyptian actress Faten Hamama, who plays Amina (the counterpart of Jean Hagen's "Doll" in *The Asphalt Jungle*), was married at the time to future Hollywood superstar Omar Sharif.

Calculated Risk
★★ (1963)

I've got one last job lined up and it's easy street from then on. [Jailbird safecracker Kip]

Length: 72 min. **Cast:** William Lucas, John Rutland, Shay Gorman, Terence Cooper, David Brierly. **Production Company:** McLeod Productions. **Directed by:** Norman Harrison. **Photographed by:** William McLeod. **Written by:** Edwin Richfield.

On the day of his release from prison, recently widowed safecracker Kip (Rutland) tells his brother-in-law, Steve (Lucas), about an ingenious bank robbery plan that a dying convict shared with him. The scheme sounds good to Steve, who, fearing Kip's incompetence, decides to spearhead the robbery even though he has had no experience in planning a heist. After recruiting explosives expert Dodo (Gorman), getaway driver Ron (Brierly) and strong-arm goon

Calculated Risk   28

Heist mastermind Major Pickering (George Sanders, left) cases King Tut's jewels at the Egyptian National Museum in *Cairo* (MGM, 1963).

Nodge (Cooper), Steve plans to follow the dying prisoner's foolproof plan to the letter — digging through the walls of a bombed-out building next door to the bank and exiting into the vault, where they expect to find more than £200,000. When Kip suffers a mild heart attack just hours before the digging begins and is forced to remain at home, mastermind Steve reluctantly takes Kip's place at the dig. The rest of the crooks are relieved, however, because they figure that perhaps now the job won't be jinxed by Kip's notorious bad luck. Then, halfway through the excavating, they come across a 500-pound, unexploded German bomb buried in the debris. *Risk* is a tedious, low-budget suspense film that ultimately fails to satisfy as an interesting heist noir after a more than promising start.

Calling Bulldog Drummond
★★½ (1951)

ARTIE GUNNS: Scotland Yard ought to give you a medal for this....
BULLDOG DRUMMOND: Posthumously, of course.
GUNNS: Naturally. I'll be down for the final ceremonies.

Length: 80 min. **Cast:** Walter Pidgeon, Margaret Leighton, Robert Beatty, David Tomlinson, Peggy Evans, Charles Victor, Bernard Lee. **Production Company:** MGM British. **Directed by:** Victor Saville. **Photographed by:** F.A. Young. **Written by:** Howard Emmett Rogers, Gerard Fairlie, Arthur Wimperis.

After a series of daring heists committed by a gang of former soldiers, a desperate Scotland Yard Inspector McIver (Victor) visits war veteran and former amateur sleuth Capt. Hugh "Bulldog" Drummond (Pidgeon), now a professional pig breeder, and begs him to give the Yard a helping hand. Drummond, of course, agrees and is assigned to go undercover with Sgt. Helen Smith (Leighton), a beautiful but competent police officer. The two manage to infiltrate the gang, which operates out of The Last Word Club, a sleazy joint on the docks owned by Arthur Gunns (Beatty). Lee plays Col. Webson, a former Army officer who has turned to a life of crime out of boredom with civilian life. Evans is Gunns' appropriately named moll, Molly, and Tomlinson plays Drummond's fastidious sidekick, Algernon Longworth. An unexciting but nicely photographed heist film, with Canadian-born Hollywood star Pidgeon unimpressive in his only outing as the famous British sleuth. Leighton, however, does a good job as the street-smart female cop.

Candidate for Murder
★★½ (1962)

You engaged me to dispose of your wife, not to pander to your twisted, sadistic tastes. [Hit man Kersten to Donald Edwards]

Length: 60 min. **Cast:** Michael Gough, Erika Remberg, Hans Borsody, John Justin. **Production Company:** Merton Park Productions. **Directed by:** David Villiers. **Photographed by:** Bert Mason. **Written by:** Lukas Heller.

The delusional and paranoid Donald Edwards (Gough) wants his actress wife, Helene (Remberg), dead because he suspects, wrongly, that she is having an affair with barrister Robert Vaughan (Justin). Edwards hires Kersten (Borsody), a German hit man, to do the job, but Kersten suspects that his client is planning a double-cross. *Candidate* is fast-moving and suspenseful but the acting is a bit over the top. (Part of the "Edgar Wallace Mystery Theater" series.)

Carnival
★★ (1946)

MRS. TREWHELLA: What do you think of Cornwall?
JENNY PEARL: I think it's very dark.

Length: 93 min. **Cast:** Sally Gray, Michael Wilding, Stanley Holloway, Bernard Miles, Jean Kent, Catherine Lacey, Hazel Court, Michael Clarke. **Production Company:** Two Cities Films. **Directed by:** Stanley Haynes. **Photographed by:** Guy Green. **Written by:** Stanley Haynes, Guy Green.

Jenny Pearl (Gray), a strong-willed ballet dancer at the Orient Theater in Edwardian London, falls in love with sculptor Maurice Avery (Wilding), a free spirit who packs up one day and moves to Spain without even saying goodbye. When her mother (Lacey) dies, Jenny is left to care for her crippled sister, May (Court), because her happy-go-lucky father (Holloway) has always been too irresponsible to provide for his family. Having turned down a marriage proposal from Maurice's artist friend, Fuzz (Clarke), Jenny accepts an offer from her temporary lodger, Zachary Trewhella (Miles), a stern looking but seemingly compassionate farmer who promises to make a home for Jenny and May at his farm in Cornwall. It doesn't take long for Jenny to regret her decision after she meets her new mother-in-law, who like her son is a religious zealot with no tolerance for an independent-minded city woman. Marginally noir with a gratifyingly downbeat ending, *Carnival* is mostly dull and slow-moving. Gray, with her unusual raspy voice, is good as the fun-loving dancer but she is outshined by Kent, who plays her best friend and constant double-date companion. A young Peter Ustinov is credited with providing "additional dialogue" for the weak script, which was based on the 1912 novel by Compton MacKenzie. Ustinov's contribution didn't help much.

Case of the Frightened Lady
(U.S. Title: *The Frightened Lady*)
★★ (1940)

It's wonderful when people die quickly. [The killer]

Length: 81 min. **Cast**: Marius Goring, Helen Haye, Penelope Dudley-Ward, Patrick Barr, John Warwick, Felix Aylmer, George Merritt, Torin Thatcher, Elizabeth Scott, Roy Emerton, George Hayes. **Production Company**: Pennant Picture Productions. **Directed by**: George King. **Photographed by**: Hone Glendinning. **Written by**: Edward Dryhurst.

When Arthur Studd (Warwick), the Lebanon family chauffer, is strangled with a scarf made in India, suspicion immediately falls on groundskeeper Jim Tilling (Thatcher) because Tilling's wife (Scott) had been planning to run away with Studd. However, Scotland Yard Inspector Tanner (Merritt), who isn't convinced of Tilling's guilt, finds no shortage of suspects in the Lebanon household — Lady Lebanon (Haye), the family matriarch, and her confirmed bachelor son Lord William (Goring); William's cousin, Isla Crane, whom Lady Lebanon wants as a daughter-in-law; family doctor Lester Amersham (Aylmer), who feared that Studd was planning to blackmail him over an old forgery conviction; architect Richard Ferraby (Barr), hired to renovate the Lebanon mansion; and a pair of arrogant footmen (Emerton and Hayes), who have a strange habit of locking people in their rooms at night. *Frightened Lady* is a tedious whodunit revolving around a dysfunctional aristocratic family and their dark secret. Character actor Shiner provides the much needed comedy relief as Det. Sgt. Totty.

The Case of the Red Monkey
see *The Little Red Monkey*

Cast a Dark Shadow
★★★ (1955)

My Albert dropped dead in the saloon bar one night and I was drawing beer the next. Business has to go on, you know. [Widow Freda Jeffries]

Length: 82 min. **Cast**: Dirk Bogarde, Margaret Lockwood, Kay Walsh, Kathleen Harrison, Mona Washbourne, Robert Flemyng. **Directed by**: Lewis Gilbert. **Production Company**: Frobisher Productions. **Photographed by**: Jack Asher. **Written by**: John Cresswell.

Gold-digger Edward Bare (Bogarde) seems content to allow nature to take its course when it comes to his marriage to the much older Monica Bare (Washbourne) — that is, until he gets the wrong idea that Monica has written a will leaving everything to her sister. Unbeknownst to Edward, however, Monica has instructed her lawyer (Flemyng) to void her previous will and write one that would leave her entire estate to her "Teddy." Panicking, Edward murders her before she can sign the new will. After a coroner's verdict of accidental death, Edward learns the bad news — Monica's first will leaves him with only the house while her quirky maid, Emmie (Harrison), gets £200 and Monica's sister gets everything else. Determined that "somebody's got to pay my passage," Edward goes on holiday hoping to meet another rich widow. He is convinced that he has scored big when he encounters Freda Jeffries (Lockwood), a bawdy, middle-aged former bar maid, who tells him that when her husband died he left her his saloon business, which she promptly sold for a substantial amount of money. Only after he marries Freda does Edward learn that the joke is on both of them. She is equally broke and thought he was the wealthy one. The arrival in town of Charlotte Young (Walsh), a rich, attractive widow, prompts Edward to start making plans to get rid of Freda,

A wife killer (Dirk Bogarde) gives his latest spouse (Mona Washbourne) a nice neck rub before making a fatal adjustment to the gas fireplace in *Cast a Dark Shadow* (Frobisher Productions, 1955).

which proves a more difficult task than it did with the previous Mrs. Bare. Based on a play by Janet Green, this psychological thriller works nicely thanks to a believable job by Bogarde as a potential modern-day Bluebeard who seems to have a penchant for bodybuilding magazines. Supporting cast members, especially Lockwood, are equally good, and the surprise ending is, for a change, actually unexpected.

Cat Girl
★★½ (1957)

What is this place? A training school for ghouls? [Alan]

Length: 75 min. **Cast**: Barbara Shelley, Robert Ayres, Kay Callard, Ernest Milton, Jack May. **Production Company**: Insignia Films. **Directed by**: Alfred Shaughnessy. **Photographed by**: Peter Hennessy. **Written by**: Lou Rusoff.

Edmond Brandt (Milton) passes on a 700-year-old family curse to his niece, Leonora Johnson (Shelley), when he allows himself to be torn apart by the leopard that has been carrying his soul during its nightly hunts in the English countryside. Dubious at first of the lycanthropic-type curse pronounced upon her, newlywed Leonora soon becomes a believer when she catches her husband, Richard (May), in the arms of his lover, and telepathically orders the leopard to kill him. "The blood on my hands made me feel strange, excited," Leonora later tells her former boyfriend, psychiatrist Brian Marlowe (Ayres), who understandably has her committed to an institution. Not one to hold a grudge, Leonora has decided that she is still in love with Marlowe and jumps at his suggestion that she spend a therapeutic day with his wife, Dorothy (Callard), who foolishly agrees to play nursemaid to an insanely

A psychiatrist's wife (Kay Callard) is pursued by her husband's murderous patient, a woman victimized by an ancient family curse in *Cat Girl* (Insignia Films, 1957).

jealous woman who believes she can take over the body of a leopard. Atmospherically reminiscent of the superior 1942 American horror noir *Cat People*, this early vehicle for Barbara Shelley, Britain's future Queen of Horror, is marred not only by the wooden performance of American actor Robert Ayres but by the corny dialogue, such as when creepy Uncle Edmund points to his collection of stuffed wild cats and their prey and explains the family curse to his niece, adding, "To be condemned to live a life of horror and anguish; to have the form and intellect of a man yet the cunning and savagery and bloodlust of these creatures." Despite the film's weaknesses, *Cat Girl* is a fairly suspenseful movie with a nicely orchestrated climax in a dark alleyway near the London docks.

The Challenge
(U.S. Title: *It Takes a Thief*)
★½ (1960)

> JIM: You get to hear a lot of things even in stir. Such as you and Kristy. I've been thinking a lot about you and Kristy.
> BILLIE: What'dya expect me to be? A nun?

Length: 89 min. **Cast:** Jayne Mansfield, Anthony Quayle, Carl Möhner, Peter Reynolds, Edward Judd, John Bennett, John Stratton. **Production Company:** Alexandra Film Studios. **Directed by:** John Gilling. **Photographed by:** Gordon Dines. **Written by:** John Gilling.

Widower Jim Maxton (Quayle) is persuaded by his girlfriend, Billie (Mansfield), to participate in an armored car heist with her gang. Billie is the brains of the outfit as well as the getaway driver, while Jim's job is to transport the stolen loot in his truck. After the heist, Jim buries the money in a secret hiding place, looking forward to the day when he and Billie will be able to raise his infant son on a farm bought with their share of the dough. He soon learns, however, that Billie and gang members Kristy (Möhner), Buddy (Reynolds), Spider (Bennett), and Rick (Stratton) have planned from the beginning to double-cross him. Wrongly thinking that Billie knows where the stolen money is, Kristy calls in an anonymous tip to the cops and Jim receives an eight-year sentence. Five years later, he is released from prison and returns home with the intention of retrieving the stolen money. While Jim was in prison, Billie and her gang were committing a rash of robberies, with Billie pocketing enough dough to buy herself a nightclub. Billie, who is now Kristy's girl, tries unsuccessfully to get Jim to divulge the location of the hidden money. Too impatient to wait for Billie to seduce Jim into talking, Kristy kidnaps Jim's 6-year-old son and threatens to kill him unless Jim comes up with the money in six days. Meanwhile, Det. Sgt. Gittens (Judd), who is seeking vengeance for the injury he suffered during the earlier armored car heist, suspects that the recent epidemic of robberies have been committed by the same gang and believes that the recently freed jailbird will lead him to them. The hot jazz sound and the dimly lit, smoked-filled rooms of the film's first few minutes promise much, but the shoddy script and some horrid acting ruin what could have been an interesting crime drama. Quayle, who would go on to bigger and better things, beginning with 1961's *The Guns of Navarone*, turns in a decent performance, but American actress and sex kitten Mansfield and Austrian actor Möhner fail miserably. Mansfield's wardrobe is nothing short of laughable, with one outrageously puffy outfit looking like something straight out of *What Ever Happened to Baby Jane?* Even worse, there are numerous holes in the plot. For instance, why would the gang report Jim to the police even if they knew where he had hidden the money? Mightn't he just spill his guts about the identity of his accomplices? The determined viewer might resolve some of the many questions by sitting through the film a second or third time. But that would be cruel and unusual punishment. This one is for Mansfield fans only.

Chamber of Horrors see *The Door with Seven Locks*

Chance Meeting see *Blind Date*

Chase a Crooked Shadow
★★★★ (1958)

We would appreciate it very much if you joined with us in not telling *anybody* how Chase a Crooked Shadow Ends." [Producer Douglas Fairbanks, Jr. to movie audience]

Length: 87 min. **Cast:** Anne Baxter, Richard Todd, Herbert Lom, Faith Brook, Alexander Knox. **Production Company:** Associated Dragon Films. **Directed by:** Michael Anderson. **Photographed by:** Erwin Hillier. **Written by:** David Osborn, Charles Sinclair.

A stranger (Todd) claiming to be the dead brother of Kimberley Prescott (Baxter), a South African diamond company heiress, shows up at her villa off the coast of Spain with austere lady friend Mrs. Whitman (Brook). Despite Kimberley's protestations, the man proves to the satisfaction of local police comisario Vargas (Lom) that he is who he says he is. The viewer knows better, of course, but hasn't a clue as to the reason for the charade. Kimberley has a history of emotional problems, having been hospitalized for "acute anxiety" after her father's suicide. The stranger, who seems to know everything there is to know about Kimberley, including her favorite "swimming drink," carries on his impersonation even when he is alone with her. Is he trying to drive her mad? If so, for what reason? Or could he and Mrs. Whitman be after the fortune in diamonds that Kimberley is thought to have stolen from the vault of her father's mining company? Confusing Kimberley (and the viewer) even more is the fact that her beloved Uncle Chan (Knox) seems to be involved in the sham. A tense thriller directed by Michael Anderson of *Around the World in 80 Days* fame, *Chase a Crooked Shadow* works as well as it does thanks to American film noir veteran Anne Baxter (*The Blue Gardenia*, *The Come-On*, *Guest in*

A police detective (Herbert Lom) is skeptical about the report by a seemingly paranoid woman (Ann Baxter) that her home has been invaded by a stranger claiming to be her brother in *Chase a Crooked Shadow* (Associated Dragon Films, 1958).

the House, I Confess). She is in top form as the heiress whose already unstable mental health has worsened as a result of a home invasion by a man everyone thinks is her brother. Todd nicely underplays his role as the somber and mysterious stranger, and Brook is appropriately menacing as the woman assigned to keep a close eye on their victim. Lom works his usual magic in a rare good-guy role.

Christ in Concrete see Give Us This Day

Circle of Danger
★★ (1951)

He's what the book means when it says an officer and a gentleman. You and I, we take the oath of service and we forget it before the words are half out of our mouths. [Sholto Lewis to Clay Douglas]

Length: 86 min. **Cast**: Ray Milland, Patricia Roc, Marius Goring, Hugh Sinclair, Naunton Wayne. **Production Company**: Coronado Productions. **Directed by**: Jacques Tourneur. **Photographed by**: Oswald Morris. **Written by**: Philip MacDonald.

American Clay Douglas (Milland) is obsessed with discovering the truth behind the combat death of his kid brother, Hank, a commando in the British army during World War II. It seems that Hank was the only casualty during a minor raid behind enemy lines, and Clay finds this disturbing. Of the thirteen men involved in the raid only a few are still alive, and Douglas travels to England, Scotland and Wales to question the unit's survivors. The information he receives seems to confirm his suspicion that his brother was murdered by a fellow commando, perhaps the outwardly effete choreographer, Sholto Lewis (Goring); the shady car salesman, Reggie Sinclair (Wayne); or Scottish landowner Hamish McArran (Sinclair). During his search for his brother's killer, Douglas falls in love with McArran's girlfriend, Elspeth Graham (Roc), who doesn't much appreciate playing second fiddle to Douglas' single-minded mission. Although Milland, the Welsh-born Hollywood star who won an Oscar for 1945's *The Lost Weekend*, does a decent job as the obsessed protagonist, the tedious plot might tempt some viewers to indulge in an 80-minute snooze. The distinctly recognizable speaking voice of veteran British character actress Dora Bryan, who plays a nightclub singer named Bubbles, is guaranteed, however, to awaken nap-inclined viewers, ensuring that they will not miss the strange climax and Douglas' peculiar reaction to the truth about his brother's death.

Circle of Deception
★★½ (1960)

LUCY: He said it was my job and I did it.
PAUL: Your job? You're a woman, aren't you? That's your job.

Length: 100 min. **Cast:** Bradford Dillman, Suzy Parker, Harry Andrews, Robert Stephens. **Production Company:** Twentieth Century–Fox Film Corporation. **Directed by:** Jack Lee. **Photographed by:** Gordon Dines. **Written by:** Nigel Balchin, Robert Musel.

Based on a hastily conducted psychological profile, British army officer Lt. Paul Raine (Dillman), a French-Canadian, is under consideration by Navy intelligence officer Capt. Tom Rawson (Andrews) for a dangerous mission behind enemy lines. Raine is gung-ho about the opportunity to be of service even though he is aware that he may be captured and tortured by the Nazis, who have secretly been tipped off about the mission, the purpose of which Raines believes is to prepare an area inside occupied France for the forthcoming Allied invasion. What he doesn't know is that Rawson has deliberately given him the wrong information, expecting him to crack under torture (but not after putting up a valiant effort), thus convincing the Germans that the phony invasion details are genuine. Also unbeknownst to Raine, the girl he has been romancing, Lucy Bowen (Parker), Rawson's assistant, has been a reluctant spy for her boss and has provided Rawson with her own assessment of how Raine might behave in the Nazi torture chambers. She believes that he would die before talking. After proving more resourceful and elusive than his superiors gave him credit for, Raines is finally caught by Capt. Stein (Stephens) of the German Army and turned over to two particularly nasty Gestapo torturers, who don't know about the hidden cyanide pill under Raine's false tooth. This suspenseful morality play is told via a post-war flashback from Raine's room at the seedy Bar Aldo in Tangier, where the remorseful Lucy arrives to find that the once eager wannabe spy who "had to fight both sides alone" is now a pathetic, guilt-ridden drunkard, who doesn't yet realize he had been played for a patsy by his superiors. The film takes a tough look at the ethics of sacrificing one unwitting man's life in order to save thousands of others. The strong performances of Americans Dillman and Parker and of veteran English character actor Andrews help to enliven the often lethargic script.

The Circle see *The Vicious Circle*

Cloudburst
★★★ (1951)

You've made me a perfect murderer, Mick. You've taken away everything I want to live for.
[John Graham to Mick Fraser]

Length: 92 min. **Cast:** Robert Preston, Elizabeth Sellars, Colin Tapley, Sheila Burrell, Harold Lang. **Production Company:** Hammer Film Productions. **Directed by:** Francis Searle. **Photographed by:** Jimmy Harvey. **Written by:** Francis Searle, Leo Marks.

Government cryptologist John Graham (Preston), a commando during the war, seeks revenge against the fleeing killers who ran down his pregnant wife after murdering a night watchman in a botched warehouse robbery attempt. Boxer-turned-crook Mick Fraser (Lang), a.k.a. Kid Python, and his accomplice, Lorna Dawson (Burrell), not only refused to stop their car after striking Carol Graham (Sellars) but backed over her in their panic to get away. Withholding information from the police about the fatal hit-and-run, Graham plans to hunt down the couple with the unwitting aid of some former commando buddies. Wily Scotland Yard Inspector Davis (Tapley), however, may have stumbled upon Graham's plot and a battle of wits begins. In its early moments *Cloudburst* revolves around the guilt and torment suffered by the former commando over his war-time experiences. Graham's life, the viewer learns, had been saved during the war by his then wife-to-be, who became permanently disabled as a result of refusing to disclose Graham's whereabouts to her Gestapo torturers. Later, as the plot shifts to Graham's planned revenge, it becomes apparent that he views his actions as having the tacit approval of his late wife, who moments before the her death had expressed outrage about the night watchman's murder and had indicated that vengeance should be sought by the victim's family. American actor Preston, a veteran of several other films noirs (*Blood on the Moon*, *The Lady Gambles*, *The Macomber Affair* and *This Gun for Hire*) and British noir veteran Sellars turn in nicely understated performances, but their short time together on the screen is almost too depressing to watch. Look for Stanley Baker in a minor role as a milkman.

The Clouded Yellow
★★½ (1950)

It's very bad for her to be reminded of the past. We have to watch her. She gets things twisted and wrong. It can be dangerous. [Jess Fenton]

Length: 96 min. **Cast:** Jean Simmons, Trevor Howard, Kenneth More, Barry Jones, Sonia Dresdel, André Morell, Maxwell Reed. **Production Company:** Carillon Films. **Directed by:** Ralph Thomas. **Photographed by:** Geoffrey Unsworth. **Written by:** Janet Green.

British secret service agent David Somers (Howard) is fired after fouling up an assignment and is forced to seek nongovernmental employment. With jobs for men with his particular skills difficult to find in civilian life, he accepts a temporary position in the English countryside, cataloguing butterflies for amiable lepidopterist Nicholas Fenton (Jones), who lives with his unfaithful wife, Jess (Dresdel), and her emotionally unstable niece, Sophie Malraux (Simmons). Somers befriends the mysterious but beautiful Sophie, whose psychological problems stem from her childhood when she stumbled upon the bloodied bodies of her mother and father, victims of an apparent murder-suicide. Gameskeeper Hick (Reed), who once had an affair with Mrs. Fenton, begins to aggressively pursue her uninterested niece. When he is found with a letter opener in his back, Sophie becomes Scotland Yard's prime suspect. Believing she has been framed, Somers goes on the run with her, using his Secret Service skills to help them avoid capture. Meanwhile, Chubb (Morell), Somers' former superior, assigns Willy Shepley (More) to find Somers before the newspapers, which have already made the "Butterfly Girl" front page news, learn about the fugitive's government connection. While on the run, Somers and Sophie fall in love and decide to flee the country, but Scotland Yard, the Secret Service and the real killer have other plans for them. The first half of *The Clouded Yellow* (a species of butterfly), promises more than the film can deliver. What starts out as a suspenseful psychological thriller ends up as an outdoorsy chase flick with side trips to nicely photographed city locales such as London, Newcastle and Liverpool. However, it is still an enjoyable film thanks mainly to good performances by Howard and Simmons, whose unlikely romantic pairing is surprisingly credible.

The Clue of the New Pin
★★½ (1961)

What do you think of that? Serving chop suey to the scum of the earth and he should be a millionaire. [Ramsey Brown about John Trasmere's long-lost Chinese son]

Length: 58 min. **Cast:** Paul Daneman, James Villiers, Bernard Archard, Clive Morton, David Horne. **Production Company:** Merton Park Productions. **Directed by:** Allan Davis. **Photographed by:** Bert Mason. **Written by:** Philip Mackie.

Rex Lander (Daneman), the ill-treated nephew of cruel millionaire John Trasmere (Horne), murders his uncle when he learns that the old man is planning to leave him out of his will. Lander frames Trasmere's old enemy, Ramsey Brown (Morton), for the crime. TV interviewer Tab Holland (Villiers) and Scotland Yard Superintendent Carver (Archard) try to figure out how Trasmere was killed inside his locked vault with the only key found on a table within the vault. In the meantime, Brown makes the mistake of trying to blackmail the cocky Lander, who thinks a similarly planned second murder might be in order. *Clue*'s storyline is quite innovative because, for a change, the answer to an ingenious locked-room puzzle is revealed to the viewer before it is solved by the investigating detective. (Part of the "Edgar Wallace Mystery Theater" series.)

The Code of Scotland Yard
see *The Shop at Sly Corner*

The Concrete Jungle
see *The Criminal*

Confession
(U.S. Title: *The Deadliest Sin*)
★★½ (1955)

> I know your type. All tough on the outside but all soft on the inside. You know what happens to guys like you? They wind up all alone and nobody cares. [Barfly to Mike Nelson]

Length: 90 min. **Cast:** Sydney Chaplin, Audrey Dalton, John Bentley, Peter Hammond, John Welsh, Patrick Allen. **Production Company:** Anglo-Guild Productions. **Directed by:** Ken Hughes. **Photographed by:** Philip Grindrod. **Written by:** Ken Hughes.

Having committed a robbery in New York, Mike Nelson (American actor Chaplin) returns to Tenbridge, his peaceful and relatively crime-free hometown in England. (Mike's obvious American accent is explained away as a consequence of his two-year stay in the States.) Mike's former accomplice, Corey (Allen), whom he double-crossed, has followed him across the Atlantic hoping to retrieve his share of the loot. When Corey catches up with Mike he tries to strangle him but is shot and killed by Mike's childhood friend, Alan (Hammond). A deeply religious Catholic, the guilt-ridden Alan heads straight for church and confesses to Father Neil (Welsh), implicating Mike by name. Mike, who has followed Alan there, shoots him dead in the confessional booth and begins making plans to get rid of Father Neil, even though the priest is bound by the seal of the confessional and unable to divulge Mike's role in Corey's death, However, Father Neil agrees to cooperate with Scotland Yard Inspector Kessler (Bentley) by acting as a decoy. Meanwhile, Mike's sister, Louise, Alan's girlfriend, suspects that her brother may be a murderer, and she is torn between her loyalty to her sibling and her sense of justice. Vaguely reminiscent of Alfred Hitchcock's American film noir *I Confess* (1953), director Hughes' *Confession* starts out promisingly enough with Alan's nocturnal visit to the confessional and the subsequent flashback explaining his admission of murder. Minimizing the benefit of its dark and ominous cinematography, the film suffers from a weak script. Chaplin, the son of actor-director Charles Chaplin and actress Lita Grey, hands in a decent performance, but his character has to be one of the dumbest and most impulsive of screen criminals, straining viewer credibility to the limits.

Contraband
(U.S. Title: *Blackout*)
★★★ (1940)

> Marriage ends adventure. [Capt. Anderson to Mrs. Sorensen]

Length: 92 min. **Cast:** Conrad Veidt, Valerie Hobson, Raymond Lovell, Esmond Knight, Phoebe Kershaw, Leo Genn, Stuart Latham, Peter Bull. **Production Company:** British National Films. **Directed by:** Michael Powell. **Photographed by:** F.A. Young. **Written by:** Brock Williams, Michael Powell.

In November 1939, the Danish freighter *Helvig*, captained by Hans Anderson (Veidt), is stopped by British naval authorities, who are searching for contraband that could end up in Nazi hands. The Brits force the ship into anchorage at the holiday town of Eastgateon-Sea. The *Helvig* is carrying desperately needed medical supplies to Denmark, and although the Brits have orders to rush the ship through clearance if all is in order, it will still take at least twenty-four hours before the freighter will be permitted to continue on its way. Being congenial hosts, the English officers invite Capt. Anderson to dinner and leave him two shore passes, which are promptly stolen by English passengers Mr. Pidgeon (Knight) and Mrs. Sorensen (Hobson). Irate, the captain sneaks ashore by rowboat and catches up with the two as they board a train for London. He eventually loses track of Pidgeon but sticks close to Sorensen, determined to return her to the ship. While on their trek through the streets of London during a blackout period, the two are kidnapped by German spies (Lovell, Kershaw, Genn, Latham and Bull). It is then that Anderson learns a secret about his wayward passenger, with whom he has already fallen in love. The convoluted espionage plot is not what makes *Contraband* so enjoyable. Neither is it the unsuccessful effort at establishing romantic chemistry between the cynical, middle-aged captain and his young, cheeky passenger. The film succeeds because of the dark, at times expressionistic, cinematography of Freddie Young, future Oscar winner for *Lawrence of Arabia, Doctor Zhivago,* and *Ryan's Daughter,* and his fascinating depiction of the London blackout milieu — street vendors hawking gas masks and flashlights, nervous air raid wardens distressed over a pedestrian lighting his pipe, darkened buildings — which testifies to Londoners' sense of paranoia justified later in the war by the savage German blitzkriegs. The filmmakers make ingenious use of the blackout as a plot device in a scene in which Capt. Anderson turns on all the lights in the building where he and Mrs. Sorensen are being held captive in order to attract the attention of air raid wardens and constables, who break into the building intent on giving bloody hell to the blackout scofflaws. Noir fans may have difficulty with the light comedy overkill, especially coming from German-born actor Conrad Veidt, who was noted for his portrayals of disturbed villains, but all in all the film is an hour and a half well spent.

Corridor of Mirrors
★★½ (1948)

I could always tell the moment he came into the club. Even your voice would take on a hungry note. Like a yowling cat on the tiles. [Nightclub singer's jealous boyfriend]

Length: 105 min. **Cast:** Eric Portman, Edana Romney, Barbara Mullen, Joan Maude. **Production Company:** Apollo Films. **Directed by:** Terence Young. **Photographed by:** André Thomas. **Written by:** Rudolph Cartier, Edana Romney.

By way of flashback and voice-over narration, the viewer becomes acquainted with the wealthy Paul Mangin (Portman), a London painter and art critic who no longer works at either profession because of a mysterious obsession. Mangin falls for Mifanwy Conway (Romney), a chic young lady who bears a perfect resemblance to the beautiful woman whose 400-year-old portrait hangs in his home. It seems that Mangin has been haunted since his time in an Italian castle-turned-makeshift hospital, where he became fixated with the painting, which he swears stared enticingly down at him while he recuperated from his war wounds. After returning to England and achieving extraordinary financial success in the London art world, Mangin went back to Italy and purchased the portrait, making it the center not only of his exquisite mansion but of his life. His obsession leads him to imagine that Mifanwy is the reincarnation of Venetia, the woman in the painting, and that he is her one-time lover, born again in modern-day England and destined to be reunited with her. With this fantasy in mind, Mangin attempts to transform Mifanwy into his dream woman (much like *Vertigo*'s John Ferguson does with *his* obsession, Judy Barton, a decade later). Mifanwy, unfortunately, has different ideas, as do the two jealous women who desire to have Mangin for themselves — his fiftyish housekeeper (Mullen), "a poor creature with the mind of a child," and a cynical nightclub singer (Maude), who is angry at being discarded by the upscale gentleman who once found her so attractive and desirable. The noirish result is murder. Interesting, yet often tedious for viewers with little patience for Gothic mysteries, *Corridor of Mirrors* is a visually beautiful film, oozing with atmosphere, compliments of French cinematographer Thomas. Director Young (best known for his later James Bond films, *Dr. No*, *From Russia with Love*, and *Thunderball*) makes his directorial debut. Look for future British horror film icon Christopher Lee as a nightclub patron.

Cosh Boy
(U.S. Title: *The Slasher*)
★★½ (1952)

If she's done herself in, she's done herself in and that's the end of that. [Walshy about his suicidal girlfriend]

Length: 75 min. **Cast:** James Kenney, Joan Collins, Betty Ann Davies, Robert Ayres, Hermione Baddeley, Hermione Gingold, Ian Whittaker. **Production Company:** Riverside Studio. **Directed by:** Lewis Gilbert. **Photographed by:** Jack Asher. **Written by:** Vernon Harris, Lewis Gilbert.

Psychotic teenager Roy Walsh (Kenney) leads a gang of four other youths in "coshing" elderly women (that is, hitting them over the head with a cosh, a blackjack-type weapon, and stealing their purses). The cowardly "Walshy," as he is known to the gang, hasn't the courage to participate in the crimes so he has his underlings, especially his main patsy, the slow-witted Alfie Collins (Whittaker), do all of the dirty work. Afterward, Walshy takes the lion's share of the paltry spoils and divides the remainder among his crew. (After one job that nets Walshy and Alfie twenty-five bob, the two boys split the money "fifty-fifty," with fifteen going to Walshy and ten to his oblivious but grateful accomplice.) Completely amoral, Walshy even steals his elderly grandmother's life savings. When confronted by his war-widowed mother (Davies) and her Canadian boyfriend (American actor Ayres) about the missing money, Walshy replies, in front of his gran, "Under the mattress I suppose. That's where the old fool usually keeps it." After deflowering Alfie's 16-year-old sister, Rene (Collins), our hero dumps her when she informs him that she is pregnant. If she thought she could get sympathy from him by throwing herself in the river, she is proven to be mistaken when Walshy, believing she has killed herself, goes about the business of robbing the Palidrome box office of its evening receipts from a wrestling match. The heist, of course, goes awry and Walshy finds himself abandoned by his buddies to face the music in his usual cowardly fashion. Why the film was released in the United States under such an inappropriate title as *The Slasher* is anyone's guess, but it was likely done because American audiences would have had no idea what a "cosh boy" was. "Slasher" is likely a reference to the scene in which Walshy waves a straight razor in his stepfather's face. As the statement prior to the opening credits informs us, *Cosh Boy* deals with the "post-war tragedy" of juvenile delinquency and lays the blame for this social evil squarely on the shoulders of parents who have failed to administer early discipline. The filmmakers demonstrate what they mean by "discipline" in a brutal scene in which two policemen give Walshy's new stepfather ten minutes alone with the terrified boy to beat the devil out of him with a belt, while Walshy's neighbors gather outside to enjoy his anguished screams of pain. The acting is fair with Kenney giving a convincing if oftentimes frenzied performance as the incorrigible delinquent, and a young Joan Collins doing well in an early role.

Cottage to Let
(a.k.a. *Bombsight Stolen*)
★★½ (1941)

BARRINGTON: *Don't tell me you're a German spy?*
GERMAN SPY: *Agent. Spies work for the other side.*
BARRINGTON: *Nice point.*

Length: 90 min. **Cast:** Leslie Banks, Alastair Sim, John Mills, Michael Wilding, Carla Lehman, George Cole, Wally Patch. **Production Company:** Gainsborough Pictures. **Directed by:** Anthony Asquith. **Photographed by:** Jack Cox. **Written by:** A. de Grunwald, J.O.C. Orton.

During World War II, German spies using an employment agency in Scotland as their front seek to prevent inventor John Barrington (Banks) from completing a new airplane bombsight device for the British war effort. Occupying a cottage on the Barrington estate are Flight Lieutenant George Perry (Mills), a wounded British flyer who has parachuted into the area, and Charles Dimble (Sim), an eccentric tenant, both of whom could be either Nazi spies or British intelligence agents. Authorities also suspect that Barrington's assistant, Alan Trently (Wilding), is working for the enemy, prompting Scotland Yard to send in one of its detectives (Patch) to work undercover as a butler in order to keep an eye on him. A subplot has both Perry and Trently vying for the affections of Barrington's pretty daughter (Lehman) while Ronald (Cole), a precocious teenaged evacuee, noses around and becomes a thorn in the side of the Third Reich. About an hour into the film everyone's identity becomes apparent and the film finally becomes interesting. Except for the convoluted storyline and the nicely shot climax in a mirrored maze at a charity bazaar, there are few noirish traits that can be attributed to *Cottage*, a film that is marred by too many failed attempts at humor.

Counterblast
(U.S. Title: *The Devil's Plot*)
★★★ (1948)

> Start killing the rodents. I don't want anything left alive. [Dr. Brucker to Martha]

Length: 99 min. **Cast:** Robert Beatty, Mervyn Johns, Nova Pilbeam, Sybilla Binder. **Production Company:** British National Films. **Directed by:** Paul L. Stein. **Photographed by:** James Wilson. **Written by:** Jack Whittingham.

Soon after World War II, German prisoners of war, including the infamous "beast of Ravensbruk," bacteriologist Dr. Brucker (Johns), escape from a British POW camp outside London. Brucker earned his reputation by conducting experiments on concentration camp inmates during the war in an effort to develop a vaccine against the plague that the Nazis planned to unleash against the Allies. While understandably anxious to escape England and avoid his upcoming trial at Nuremberg, Brucker, still the loyal Nazi, reluctantly obeys orders from his Fourth Reich superiors to continue his experiments. Coincidentally, Dr. Forrester, a relatively unknown British bacteriologist, who has been away in Australia for years, has returned to England, and Brucker, who speaks perfect English, seizes the opportunity by murdering him and stealing his identity and new job. Dr. Rankin (Beatty), Brucker's inherited assistant, suspects there is something not quite right with his new boss, but he can't put his finger on it. When pretty Tracy Hart (Pilbeam) shows up unexpectedly, claiming she had received a job offer from Dr. Forrester by mail, Brucker considers killing her, but when he realizes that she has not seen Forrester since she was a child and therefore poses no threat to him, he takes her on. (After all, he has to infect somebody with the plague in order to test his vaccine.) Meanwhile, Rankin and Tracy fall in love, complicating Brucker's plans, and Martha (Binder), the Nazi housekeeper from hell, arrives on the scene to keep Brucker in line. This is a violent but effective film with Johns convincing as a maniac who, after murdering one of his own soldiers because the man dared to disparage the Nazi dream of world domination, is able to persuade his loyal assistant to volunteer as a human guinea pig by appealing to her British patriotism. *Counterblast* is marginally noir, but the acting is solid and the ironic ending is satisfying.

Crimes at the Dark House
★★★ (1940)

> LADY GLYDE: Surely I ought to know what I'm signing before I write my name.
> LORD GLYDE: Nonsense, my dear. What do women know about business? If I explained it, you wouldn't understand it.

Length: 69 min. **Cast:** Tod Slaughter, Sylvia Marriott, Hilary Eaves, Geoffrey Wardwell, Hay Petrie, Rita Grant, Elsie Wagstaff, David Horne. **Production Company:** Pennant Picture Productions. **Directed by:** George King. **Photographed by:** Hone Glendining. **Written by:** Frederick Hayward, Edward Dryhurst, H.F. Maltby.

In Australia, a maniac kills a fellow gold prospector in a hideous manner (by hammering a stake into his brain) and steals his paltry gold find. Luckily for the killer (Slaughter), he finds a letter on his victim's body indicating that the man's father recently died and has left him his estate in London. The murderer also learns that the family servants and business associates haven't seen the boy since he was 12 years old, so he travels to England as Percival Glyde to claim the dead man's inheritance. When he arrives, he learns the bad news: Glyde's father died owing a tidy sum of money, and the younger Glyde is expected to make good on the debt. There is some good news, however: Jessica (Grant), a pretty servant girl, seems more than willing to accept his lecherous advances, and the beautiful and wealthy Laura Fairlie (Marriott) is honor-bound to follow her late father's wishes that she marry Glyde after his return from Australia. Laura's boyfriend (Wardwell) and sister (Eaves) cannot persuade the Fairlie family patriarch, hypochondriac Uncle Frederick (Horne), to release Laura from her obligation. But back to the bad news. Mrs. Catherick (Wagstaff) shows up claiming that Glyde had made her pregnant two decades earlier and that their insane daughter, Anne, is confined to a mental institution. Of course, Mrs. Catherick immediately recognizes the killer as an imposter, and she and her daughter's doctor, "mental specialist" Isidor Fosco (Petrie), see an opportunity to make a few pounds for themselves. Complicating things, Jessica becomes pregnant and starts to pester her master to make an honest woman out of her, while Anne Catherick, who holds a grudge against the father who abandoned her as a child, escapes from the lunatic asylum. The imposter isn't at all concerned about all of the potential obstacles to his plan to steal Laura's fortune, however; he simply invites the troublemakers to meet him at night at the old boat house by the lake. Based on a Wilkie Collins novel "The Woman in White," *Crimes* is not a film for everyone. Some will certainly hate it, while others will consider it a fun experience, primarily because of Tod Slaughter's entertaining histrionics. Once again he proves that his mustache-twirling villains are among the screen's most enjoyable. Despite the brutality here of his character's murders and the repulsiveness of his lechery, his stereotypical villainous laughter should bring a smile to the appreciative viewer's face. Many of the film's theatrically delivered lines are often side-splitting, and the blackmailing Dr. Fosco's has one of the best: "Her insane hatred of you is bound to bring her here with the intention of venting her spleen upon you."

The Criminal
(U.S. Title: *The Concrete Jungle*)
★★★★ (1960)

QUANTOCK: You were big inside.
JOHNNY: Oh, yeah. Big enough to be three in a cell all through last year's stinking summer.

Length: 97 min. **Cast:** Stanley Baker, Sam Wanamaker, Grégoire Aslan, Margit Saad, Jill Bennett, Patrick Magee, John Molloy, Brian Phelan, Kenneth Warren. **Production Company:** Merton Park Productions. **Directed by:** Joseph Losey. **Photographed by:** Robert Krasker. **Written by:** Alun Owen.

Released on remission (i.e., parole), convict Johnny Bannion (Baker) dumps his former moll, Maggie (Bennett), hooks up with the beautiful Suzanne (Saad) and plans a racetrack heist he has been thinking about for the past three years. After the robbery, he and his accomplices, including friend Mike Carter (American actor Wanamaker), get away with £40,000, which Johnny secretly buries in the middle of a country field until things cool down. But before covering the dough with dirt, he helps himself to a small handful of bills, which he later launders to buy a piece of jewelry for Suzanne. Unfortunately for him, Maggie witnesses the purchase and squeals to the coppers. Six weeks after his release, Johnny finds himself back in prison, this time facing a fifteen-year sentence. Meanwhile, Carter, who has no desire to wait fifteen years to get his hands on the dough, has made secret arrangements with his connection on the inside, prison baron Frank Saffron (Aslan), for Johnny's escape. Johnny, however, seems to have no motivation to break out now that he's back to being a respected prison king-pin. He also considers the buried £40,000 as his future retirement fund. So Carter kidnaps Suzanne and lets it be known that he is holding her until Johnny reveals the location of the dough, prompting Johnny to escape in order to save Suzanne. In the concrete jungle, the convicts run the show while the bureaucratic and weak-kneed prison governor ignores their illegal activities, as well as the complaints of the humane but ineffective prison doctor (a tip of the hat to the American film noir, *Brute Force* and its equally ineffective medico, Dr. Walters).

On the outside, Johnny's ex-moll hate him, and his pals began to treat him with disdain. Although he still seemed to be in charge of the gang, it was only at the indulgence of his underling, Carter, who informed him that "your sort doesn't fit into an organization." In other words, Johnny is a dinosaur, out of date and useful to syndicate bosses only for the heist money he has promised to share with them. The robbery is a success but it occurs so quickly on screen, unlike the meticulously planned racetrack heist in the American film noir *The Killing*, that it could be mistaken by the viewer for a practice run. Afterward, Johnny's downfall, like that of so many other noir protagonists, is caused by a woman. Back in stir, Johnny finds he still has the respect of his fellow cons and is allowed by the cruel chief warder, Barrows (Magee), to once again run Cellblock B as his personal fiefdom as long as Barrows knows what's going on at all times. Losey does his usual expert job of directing, focusing on an obsolete and doomed criminal (perfectly played by the Welsh-born Baker). Daring for the era, the film contains a scene in which the viewer is treated to a peek at the nude backside of German actress Margit Saad. Homosexuality is strongly implied in the character of neurotic convict Pauly Larkin (Phelan), who is portrayed as having a strong attachment to his cellmate, the jovial but dangerous Clobber (Warren). Robert Krasker's cinematography, while beautifully stark, is not typically noir (i.e., there are no odd camera angles and virtually no shadows), although the plot is convoluted enough that even the most astute viewer might need a second viewing to recuperate from the initial confusion.

Crossroads to Crime
★★ (1960)

> This is a transport cafe. We don't cater to the upper classes here. [Connie Williams to Constable Ross]

Length: 57 min. **Cast:** Anthony Oliver, Patricia Heneghan, Miriam Karlin, George Murcell, Ferdy Mayne, David Graham. **Production Company:** A.P. Films. **Directed by:** Gerry Anderson. **Photographed by:** John Read. **Written by:** Alun Falconer.

Disregarding his superior's orders and the sage advice of his wife, Joan (Heneghan), village constable Don Ross (Oliver) single-handedly tries to nab a gang of truck hijackers led by Miles (Mayne) and Diamond (Murcell), who have forcibly enlisted roadside cafe owner Connie Williams (Karlin) as their accomplice. Ross pretends to be a dirty cop, accepting bribes from Diamond and actually participating in the theft of a shipment of nickel, during which a guard is murdered. Despite Barry Gray's enjoyable musical score, this rarely seen, low-budget crime drama is unconvincing and dull but redeems itself with an exciting and surprising climax.

Cross-Up see *Tiger by the Tail*

Crow Hollow
★★½ (1952)

> AUNT JUDITH: She's a very sensuous creature.
> AUNT POLLY: Don't use those queer adjectives, Judith.

Length: 69 min. **Cast:** Donald Houston, Natasha Parry, Pat Owens, Esma Cannon, Nora Nicholson, Susan Richmond. **Production Companies:** Merton Park Productions, Bruton Film Productions. **Directed by:** Michael McCarthy. **Photographed by:** Robert LaPresle. **Written by:** Vivian Milroy.

Ann Amour (Parry), newlywed wife of Dr. Robert Amour (Houston), whom she has known for only a week, moves into her husband's house at Crow Hollow, where his three eccentric maiden aunts, Judith (Cannon), Opal (Nicholson) and Hester (Richmond) also live, along with their beautiful maid, Willow (Owens), whom the women refer to as Aunt Opal's companion. Strange events begin to take place that convince Ann that someone is trying to kill her: a poisonous spider from Aunt Judith's collection finds its way into Ann's gardenia corsage, and a bowl of Aunt Hester's soup makes Ann deathly ill. Ann attempts to convey her fears to Robert, who is too busy with his medical duties to take her seriously. But then she finds a body in her bedroom, that of a woman dressed in Ann's evening gown with a knife buried in her back. It is obvious now, even to Robert, that the killer mistook the woman for Ann. Similar in plot to a number of American films noirs (*Christmas Holiday, Cry Wolf, Rebecca, Secret Beyond the Door, Shadow of a Woman* and *Undercurrent*), in which newlywed brides learn too late that they have married into dysfunctional, if not dangerous, families, *Crow Hollow* is a bland thriller that nevertheless does a good job in its depiction of the bride's mounting paranoia and alienation.

Curse of the Demon
see *Night of the Demon*

The Damned (U.S. Title: *These Are the Damned*)
★★★½ (1962)

> I like to listen to people who know what they are talking about. The only trouble is I never believe anything they say. [Simon Wells]

Length: 96 min. **Cast:** Macdonald Carey, Shirley Anne Field, Oliver Reed, Alexander Knox, Viveca Lindfors, Walter Gotell, James Villiers. **Production Companies:** Hammer Film Productions, Swallow Productions. **Directed by:** Joseph Losey. **Photographed by:** Arthur Grant. **Written by:** Evan Jones.

Simon Wells (Carey), a middle-aged American vacationing in the seacoast resort town of Weymouth, tries to pick up a 20-year-old sexpot named Joan (Field), who promptly lures him into a trap set by her brother, King (Reed), the leader of a gang of leather-jacketed motorcycle-riding hoodlums. The lads pounce on Simon, giving him a good thrashing and stealing his money. Later, Joan visits Simon and, despite her brother's orders to stay put, goes off with the bruised, forgiving victim for a short boat ride. King witnesses Simon trying to seduce Joan and swears that he will kill this rival for his sister's affections. After the surprisingly virginal Joan rejects Simon's advances, he rows her back to shore, where King and his gang are waiting for them. The couple flee, seeking shelter at a barbed-wired government facility, where an operative named Bernard (Knox) and his military staff are secretly raising a brood of nine radioactive children whose mothers had accidentally been exposed to lethal doses of radiation during their pregnancies. Bernard expects the inevitable someday — a nuclear holocaust — and believes that the hope of the human race lies with these children, who are naturally immune to the fatal effects of radiation. Unfortunately for the children, however, they must be isolated from the rest of the world because death is the inevitable consequence for all who come in direct physical contact with them. All of this, of course, is unknown to Simon, Joan and King, who, while trying to escape the facility's armed guards, are taken in by the curious children. The kids are fascinated with their first nontelevised adult contact, and wonder if any of these grownups could be their parents. Meanwhile, the high levels of radioactivity are beginning to have an effect on the three unwitting trespassers. The transformation from banal juvenile delinquent story to powerful message movie is abrupt but not terribly surprising because we get an inkling early on that, although the violence at times is brutal, the film is going to be more than just another crime movie about a victim standing up to vicious street thugs. This happens when we are introduced to Bernard and his girlfriend, Freya (Lindfors), and learn that Freya has complaints about her lover's secretiveness. Bernard looks her straight in the eye and says, "If I were to tell you even a little bit about what you call my secrets, I might be condemning you to death." And we believe him. Knox and Lindfors give flawless performances as lovers trapped in, forgive the pun, a toxic relationship, and Reed is convincing as the gang leader with a questionable concern for his younger sister's sexual purity. *The Damned* is a fascinating movie, although the May-December romance between Field and Carey lacks credibility. Even more unbelievable is the protagonist's bombshell marriage proposal to the biker girl who had lured him into a mugging only hours earlier.

Dancing with Crime
★★½ (1947)

> Don't come so close to me. I'm a little fastidious. [crime boss E.J. Gregory]

Length: 83 min. **Cast:** Richard Attenborough, Barry K. Barnes, Sheila Sim, Garry Marsh, Barry

Jones, John Warwick, Bill Rowbatham. **Production Companies:** Coronet Films, Alliance Film Studios. **Directed by:** John Paddy Carstairs. **Photographed by:** Reginald Wyer. **Written by:** Brock Williams.

To the vexation of Scotland Yard Inspector Carter (Warwick) and Det. Sgt. Murray (Marsh), London taxi driver Ted Peters (Attenborough) and his girl, Judy Goodall (Sim), decide to investigate the murder of childhood friend Dave Robinson (Rowbatham). Robinson, a spiv who thought he had become so big that he could get away with double-crossing black marketeer E.J. Gregory (Jones), was shot by Gregory's vicious henchman, Paul Baker (Barnes), the emcee the Palais de Danse, Gregory's dancehall front. Fatally wounded, Robinson had escaped Baker but died in the back seat of Ted's taxi. Judy goes undercover as a dance hostess at the club to keep Peter up to date on the gangsters' operation. Meanwhile, Gregory and Baker, fearful that the nosy taxi driver may know too much, decide to kill him. The viewer shouldn't expect any big surprises or innovations. The film's noir style is evident and the themes and plot elements are familiar: life-long buddies take separate paths, one choosing the straight and narrow while the other is lured by the criminal lifestyle; a veteran turns to crime as a cure for his post-war economic problems; a beautiful woman goes undercover in a dangerous environment to ferret out a killer; criminals attempt to frame the protagonist for murder; and an amateur detective outperforms the city's mostly bungling police force. What is really enjoyable about *Dancing* is watching the baby-faced Sir Richard Attenborough (the elderly dinosaur entrepreneur in *Jurassic Park*) grinning jovially and fist fighting his way through this early role. The gorgeous Diana Dors has a small part as a dance hostess, and Dirk Bogarde, in an uncredited role, appears momentarily as a police officer.

The Dark Eyes of London
(U.S. Title: *The Human Monster*)
★★½ (1939)

The Yard is a dour, soulless type of business where hijinks and horseplay of the more imaginative kind are severely discouraged. [Yard commissioner to American cop]

Length: 75 min. **Cast:** Bela Lugosi, Hugh Williams, Greta Gynt, Edmon Ryan, Wilfred Walter, Alexander Field. **Production Company:** John Argyle Productions. **Directed by:** Walter Summers. **Photographed by:** Bryan Langley. **Written by:** Patrick Kirwan, Walter Summers, J.F. Argyle.

Insurance broker Feodor Orloff (Lugosi) has been lending money to desperate clients and for collateral having them make him the beneficiary of their life insurance policies. He then orders his patsies to be drowned by a deformed blind man (Walter), who lives at Orloff's supposedly favorite charity, Dearborn's Home for the Destitute Blind. Under pressure from his boss to find the common denominator in the past five drownings, Scotland Yard Det. Inspector Larry Holt (Williams) and his new friend, visiting Chicago cop Lt. O'Reilly (American actor Ryan), step up the investigation. When police scientists determine that the latest victim, the father of pretty Diana Stuart (Gynt), was drowned in tap water and his body dumped in the Thames, suspicion falls on Orloff, the beneficiary of the man's new life insurance policy. When Holt learns that there is a connection between Orloff and a well-known forger (Field), he becomes convinced of Orloff's guilt and begins to worry about Diana's safety, especially since she has taken a secretarial position at the home for the blind. This is a dark film, both thematically and stylistically, with Lugosi turning in a nicely restrained performance (for him, that is) as the villainous murderer. Williams and love interest Gynt are enjoyable, but Ryan's stereotypical American is an embarrassment to all decent gun-toting U.S. coppers. Two particularly gruesome scenes stand out—the eerily filmed murder of a small-time criminal in his bathtub by the hideous blind giant, Jake, and Orloff's gleeful drowning of a defenseless blind and mute accomplice whose conscience had gotten the best of him.

The Dark Man
★★ (1951)

INSP. VINER: You had a black market deal with Mostyn.

STOOL PIGEON: I wouldn't say black exactly, more what they call sepia.

INSP. VINER: Never mind the shade, what did he supply?

Length: 91 min. **Cast:** Edward Underdown, Maxwell Reed, Natasha Parry, William Hartnell. **Production Company:** Independent Artists. **Directed by:** Jeffrey Dell. **Photographed by:** Eric Cross. **Written by:** Jeffrey Dell.

Fearing she may be able to identify him, a killer (Reed) goes after Molly Lester (Parry), who has described him to police as a "dark man." Inspector Jack Viner (Underdown) is assigned the task of protecting the pretty stage actress and soon finds himself falling in love with her. A police superintendent (Hartnell) tries to keeps the riled Viner in line after the murderer attacks Molly (a nicely shot strangulation scene reflected in the mirror in Molly's dim, candle-lit flat). The film's final fifteen minutes are devoted to a boring chase, during which the killer is pursued by soldiers and police officers. Cross' cinematography is appropriately dark and the film is quite atmospheric, but these do not compensate for the lackluster direction and boring script. Film veteran Hartnell, later the first "Dr. Who" in the long-running British TV series, is enjoyable as Inspector Viner's crusty superior, and Reed does a good job as the murderous "dark man." Underdown, reportedly author Ian Fleming's first choice to play British secret agent James Bond, is a bit stiff and not credible as a Scotland Yard inspector who, according to the woman he is assigned to protect, is too young looking to be a policeman. He was in his early forties at the time and looked it.

Dark Secret
(NR) (1949)

Length: 85 min. **Cast:** Dinah Sheridan, Emrys Jones, Irene Handl, Hugh Pryse. **Production Company:** Nettlefold Productions. **Directed by:** Maclean Rogers. **Photographed by:** Walter J. Harvey. **Written by:** A.R. Rawlinson, Moie Charles.

A pilot's wife becomes obsessed with the murder of the previous occupant of their cottage.

The Dark Tower
★★ (1943)

Fate has kicked me around. [Stephen Torg]

Length: 93 min. **Cast:** Ben Lyon, Anne Crawford, David Farrar, Herbert Lom, William Hartnell. **Production Companies:** Warner Brothers First National Productions. **Directed by:** John Harlow. **Photographed by:** Otto Heller. **Written by:** Brock Williams.

Stephen Torg (Lom), a down-and-out drifter, seeks a job with a near-bankrupt traveling circus owned by Phil Danton (Lyon). As it turns out, the drifter is an accomplished hypnotist and Phil decides to use him as part of a trapeze act that stars Phil's brother, Tom (Farrar), and Tom's girlfriend, Mary (Crawford). Torg's role is to hypnotize "Miss Mary" so that she will be able to perform a high-wire stunt without a balancing parasol. For some reason, this rather unspectacular feat seems to delight and amaze audiences and manages to set the circus back on its feet once again. Sensing the power he now has to determine the pecuniary success or failure of the circus, the former tramp begins making demands and soon ends up owning a third interest in the business. Not satisfied with this, he sets his evil eyes on the lovely Mary, but she won't give him the time of day because she is loyal to Tom, who is seething with jealousy. But this doesn't stop Torg, who merely uses his hypnotic powers to give her a suggestion that when it comes time to catch her partner during their trapeze act she will begin to feel weak, very weak. The normally dependable Farrar and Lom are big disappointments thanks to this marginal noir's absurd premise and its even more ridiculous climax. Veteran character actor Hartnell is enjoyable as the circus' publicity man.

Daughter of Darkness
★★★ (1948)

No one likes to find a young gypsy dead in his barn. [Mr. Tallent]

Length: 91 min. **Cast:** Anne Crawford, Siobhan McKenna, Maxwell Reed, Liam Redmond, Honor Blackman, George Thorpe, Barry Morse. **Production Companies:** Kenilworth Film Productions, Alliance

Film Studios. **Directed by:** Lance Comfort. **Photographed by:** Stanley Pavey. **Written by:** Max Catto.

Father Cocoran (Redmond), under pressure from angry women in his congregation, gives the boot to Emmy Beaudine (McKenna), a comely lass who has been working as a servant in the Irish priest's rectory and who spends her free time playing mournful dirges on the church organ. The village women see Emmy as a "brazen slut" out to seduce their men. They make it very clear to the reluctant cleric that they intend to drive her out of town. Before she goes, however, Emmy has a run-in with "Battling" Dan (Reed), a carnival boxer with a roving eye that nearly gets scratched out by the seductive but plain-Jane young girl, who seems strangely unaware of the power she has over men. Father Cocoran (possibly a victim himself of Emmy's charms) gets her a job on an English horse farm run by Bob Stanforth (Morse) and his wife, Bess (Crawford), who surprises herself by taking an immediate dislike to the new servant girl. Soon after Emmy's arrival, a traveling carnival shows up in town to entertain the locals. One of its sideshow attractions, the now facially scarred boxer "Battling" Dan, is found murdered on opening night, and his German Shepherd dog, howling and barking menacingly, can be seen lurking around the horse farm, where the bodies of two other men are soon discovered. Meanwhile, the young men of the church choir intend to find out who has been playing the organ late at night, suspecting that it may be the killer. Belfast-born McKenna gives a hauntingly weird but effective performance as a female serial killer, a veritable cinematic rarity at the time. Supporting cast members are excellent, including veteran Crawford, screen newcomer Honor Blackman (Pussy Galore in *Goldfinger*), and Reed, who was often typecast as an obnoxious ladies' man. *Daughter of Darkness* may be an acquired taste for some viewers, who may hate or love the film. Most, however, will agree after their first viewing that it is unusual.

Daybreak
★★½ (1946)

The hangman's job is not an enviable one, is it?
[Prison governor]

Length: 81 min. **Cast:** Ann Todd, Eric Portman, Maxwell Reed, Bill Owen. **Production Company:** Triton Films. **Directed by:** Compton Bennett. **Photographed by:** Reginald H. Wyer. **Written by:** Sydney and Muriel Box.

Eddie Tribe (Portman), a barber moonlighting as a prison hangman, refuses to execute a prisoner and must inform authorities as to the reason why. Explained in a flashback, Eddie's motives slowly unfold. After inheriting his father's barge business, he gives up his half of his interests in the barber shop to his partner, Ron (Owen), falls in love with and marries the much younger Frankie (Todd), a dance hall hostess he has only recently met, and sets up house with her on one of his barges. Determined to quit his job as executioner, which he has been performing under an assumed name, Eddie gives the government six months notice (they do need to train a new hangman, after all), while struggling to keep the reasons for his frequent out-of-town visits a secret from his increasingly lonely bride. When Eddie hires Olaf (Reed), to help with the barge business, Frankie finds herself both repulsed by and attracted to the young Dane's cockiness and rugged good looks. After a night of dancing, while Eddie is on one of his frequent "business trips," Olaf and Frankie return to the barge, where the Dane forces himself on his boss' not-so-reluctant wife, beginning an affair that prompts the guilt-ridden Frankie to beg her husband, without disclosing her reasons, to fire Olaf. Eddie refuses, however, and goes on his merry way to hang the next condemned man. When the prisoner receives a last-minute pardon, Eddie hurries home only to find Olaf and Frankie together. To say any more would be to divulge too much, even though the unnecessary opening scene is pretty much the film's own spoiler. Portman and Todd give touching performances as the doomed lovers. Reed, however, overacts as the homme fatale who thinks he is God's gift to women. *Daybreak* is an extremely dark and depressing tale that unfolds too slowly yet somehow manages to remain interesting.

Dead Men Are Dangerous
(NR) (1939)

Length: 69 min. **Cast:** Robert Newton, Betty

Lynne, John Warwick, Peter Gawthorne. **Production Company**: Welwyn Studios. **Directed by**: Harold French. **Photographed by**: Unknown. **Written by**: Victor Kendall, Harry Hughes, Vernon Clancey.

A penniless writer discovers a body, switches clothes with the dead man and soon finds himself accused of murder.

Dead of Night
★★★★ (1945)

I tell you, doctor, there's something horrible waiting for me here. Perhaps even death itself. [Walter Craig]

Length: 104 min. **Cast**: Mervyn Johns, Michael Redgrave, Roland Culver, Mary Merrall, Googie Withers, Frederick Valk, Ralph Michael, Anthony Baird, Judy Kelly, Sally Ann Howes, Barbara Leake. **Production Company**: Ealing Studios. **Directed by**: (Alberto) Cavalcanti, Charles Crichton, Basil Dearden, Robert Hamer. **Photographed by**: Stan Pavey (lighting), Douglas Slocombe (lighting). **Written by**: John Baines, Angus MacPhail.

London architect Walter Craig (Johns) is invited by Eliot Foley (Culver) to spend the weekend at the Foley estate in the English countryside to discuss a possible job. When Craig arrives, he experiences a strange sense of déjà vu and comes to the conclusion that he knows the estate and the people inside the mansion from a recurring nightmare he has been having for years. Craig, whose dream slowly unfolds, seems to have foreknowledge of things that are about to happen inside the house. The host and some of the houseguests enjoy the spooky conversation even though Craig seems particularly distraught over his predicament, and they begin to share bizarre tales about supernatural events that have occurred in their own lives (presented in flashback). Racecar driver Hugh Grainger (Baird) relates how he met his wife, Joyce (Kelly), who was working as a nurse at the time of his near fatal car crash, and how a late-night vision of a waiting hearse driver would later save his life. Teenager Sally O'Hara (Howes) tells of her experience at a Christmas party with the ghostly apparition of a crying child, and Joan Cortland (Withers) describes how an antique mirror with a sordid history drove her fiancé, Peter (Michael), to the brink of insanity. Host Foley attempts to lighten things by telling a humorous story about a pair of middle-aged golfers who fall in love with the same girl and determine their romantic fate over a game of golf, with the loser having to commit suicide. Unfortunately for the winner, the loser returns to haunt his rival. Finally, psychiatrist Dr. van Straaten (Valk) tells the group about a former patient, ventriloquist Maxwell Frere (Redgrave), whose obsession with his life-like dummy, Hugo, leads him to shoot another ventriloquist, who he believes is trying to recruit Hugo as part of his own act. While justly considered an important pre–Hammer horror film, *Dead of Night* has always been somewhat overrated, being especially marred by the ridiculous and unfunny golfing story. The hearse driver and Christmas party segments are well-done, while the haunted mirror story is much more polished, but even these fail to produce the chills or goose bumps one would expect from a film of its reputation. What makes this a true horror classic, however, are Redgrave's *tour de force* performance in the film's noirish ventriloquist sequence and the final scenes in the linking narrative, during which the dreamer, Craig, revisits the segments in a wild, nightmarish collage of superbly photographed and, at last, genuinely frightening images.

Dead on Course see *Wings of Danger*

The Deadliest Sin see *Confession*

The Deadly Game see *Third Party Risk*

Deadly Nightshade
★½ (1953)

The atom bomb is the scientist's national weapon against the dark force of stupidity. [Dr. Ferrari, defecting atomic scientist]

Length: 61 min. **Cast**: Emrys Jones, Zena Marshall, John Horsley. **Production Company**: Kenilworth Film Productions. **Directed by**: John Gilling. **Pho-

tographed by: Monty Berman. **Written by:** Laurence Huntington.

Escaped convict John Barlow and artist Robert Matthews (both played by Jones) have something in common — they could be identical twins (and for purposes of this implausible story their voices happen to be identical also). Barlow reads in the newspaper that the artist, who had been mistaken for him by a local barkeep, was arrested but released after police discovered the error. Figuring that Matthews' cottage in the English countryside will now be the last place the coppers will look, Barlow shows up there with the intention of tying up Matthews and getting a good night's sleep before slipping away in the morning. Unfortunately, Matthews puts up a fight and Barlow accidentally kills him. (That's two accidental killings by Barlow in the past two years, the first being a fatal drunk driving accident, for which he was sentenced to serve seven years in prison). After hiding Matthews' body in a shed, Barlow gets the surprise of his life when police inspector Clements (Horsley) shows up in the middle of the night with some shipwreck survivors, including Barlow's former girlfriend, Ann Farrington (Marshall). Ann, guilt-ridden over Barlow's drunk-driving accident because she believes he began drinking heavily as a result of their break-up, recognizes him immediately. The nervous convict soon learns that Matthews had been on the payroll of Communist spies and had been responsible for the recent sinking of Ann's ship. Both the police and Matthews' Communist accomplices suspect something is amiss (Matthews was left-handed and didn't smoke, while Barlow ... well, you get the picture). So the desperate impersonator is forced to make a choice: escape with Matthews' blood money or prevent an atomic scientist's defection, which would give the other side the upper hand in the post-war struggle for nuclear superiority. The weak script relies entirely on far-fetched coincidences and brazenly plays on the post-war fears of Communist world domination. The acting, however, is adequate and the film's short length makes watching it a bit more tolerable. The title refers to the password used by the defecting scientist to identify himself to the spies.

Dear Murderer
★★★★ (1947)

RICHARD FENTON: I suppose Vivian told you that we've been out together.
LEE WARREN: I didn't mind your going out. It was the staying in that I objected to.

Length: 90 min. **Cast:** Eric Portman, Greta Gynt, Dennis Price, Jack Warner, Maxwell Reed, Hazel Court. **Production Company:** Gainsborough Pictures. **Directed by:** Arthur Crabtree. **Photographed by:** Stephen Dade. **Written by:** Muriel and Sydney Box, Peter Rogers.

While on business in the States for eight months, Lee Warren (Portman) frets over his beautiful wife Vivien's (Gynt) lack of correspondence and decides to return home early to surprise her. Unfortunately, it's Lee who gets the surprise when he discovers that she has been having an affair with barrister Richard Fenton. Jealousy drives Lee to kill Richard in a unique fashion, making it look like a suicide. Like so many other film noir killers, Lee believes he has committed the perfect murder, but it isn't long before his scheme backfires on him. Problem number one shows up in the person of handsome Jimmy Martin (Reed), whom Vivien has stolen from Avis Fenton, who also happens to be Richard's sister. Ignoring his wife's advice that "you can't kill them all, you fool," Lee decides to get rid of Jimmy, also, so he frames him for Richard's murder. Problems two and three are Inspector Penbury, a shrewd cop from the New Scotland Yard branch in the City of Westminster, and Vivien, who, it turns out, really loves Jimmy and has a devious scheme of her own. *Dear Murderer*, the title of which comes from the salutation of a goodbye note written by Vivien to Lee, is an enjoyable low-budget noir with top-notch performances from Portman as the sympathetic killer and Greta Gynt as his unfaithful femme fatale wife, who, when she wrongly believes her former lover has committed suicide, can't hide a self-satisfied little smirk. "He killed himself for me," she boasts. The film is rife with noirish elements—a strong sense of fatalism, the use of flashbacks and voice-over narration, a convoluted storyline, a fall guy, a femme fatale and an obsessive and desperate protagonist.

Delayed Action
(NR) (1954)

Length: 60 min. **Cast:** Robert Ayres, Alan Wheatley, June Thorburn, Michael Kelly. **Production Company:** Kenilworth Film Productions. **Directed by:** John Harlow. **Photographed by:** Gerald Gibbs. **Written by:** Geoffrey Orme.

A suicidal writer accepts an offer from robbers to confess to their crime and, if the scheme begins to go wrong, to kill himself.

The Depraved
★★½ (1957)

I believe that when a man learns to kill he becomes an animal. After that, he's never completely human, completely civilized. [Tom Wilton]

Length: 70 min. **Cast:** Anne Heywood, Robert Arden, Carroll Levis, Basil Dignam, Denis Shaw, Robert Ayres. **Production Company:** Danziger Productions. **Directed by:** Paul Dickson. **Photographed by:** Jimmy Wilson. **Written by:** Brian Clemens, Edith Dell.

When his jeep runs out of gas on the isolated road to Camp Deningley, Capt. Dave Dillon (Arden), an American Army officer, stops at the Wiltons' house to use the telephone. Thus begins a torrid love affair between Dillon and Laura Wilton (Heywood), a victim of her abusive alcoholic husband, Tom (Dignam). When Laura suggests that Dave help her murder Tom for the insurance money, the war veteran balks, but after mulling it over he comes up with what he thinks is a foolproof plan involving a treacherous curve on the road between the Wiltons' home and the Army camp. Forging an invitation to a party thrown by his commander (Ayres) for the locals, Dave lures Tom to the camp, knowing that when the arrogant, in-your-face pacifist leaves he will drive home drunk on that lonely stretch of road, ensuring that Scotland Yard will assume that he had an accident. After their ambush of the unwary drunk, the lovers think they have gotten away with murder. Dave prepares for his future with Laura, but his plans are rudely interrupted by a pair of determined investigators in his long-time Army buddy, Major Roy Kellaway (Levis), and the wily Scotland Yard Inspector O'Flynn (Shaw). Not a bad clone of the classic American film noir *Double Jeopardy*, with the elegant Heywood standing out as the femme fatale. After his lackluster performance in Orson Welles' 1955 multinational production of *Mr. Arkadin*, Arden is convincing here as the clueless noir patsy.

Design for Murder see Trunk Crime

Desperate Moment
★★½ (1953)

There comes a point when all that matters is to be free. [Simon Van Halder]

Length: 88 min. **Cast:** Dirk Bogarde, Mai Zetterling, Philip Friend, Albert Lieven, Theodore Bikel. **Production Company:** British Film Makers. **Directed by:** Compton Bennett. **Photographed by:** C.M. Pennington-Richards. **Written by:** Patrick Kirwan, George H. Brown.

Bogarde plays Simon van Halder, a former Dutch resistance fighter sentenced to life in a German prison for killing a British soldier during the theft of a truckload of penicillin in postwar Germany. After serving five years, he learns that his lover, Anna DeBurg (Zetterling), who he thought had been killed during the war, is alive and well. Anna's sudden return from the grave gives Simon a new lease on life, and he confesses for the first time that it was not he who killed the British soldier but Paul Ravitch (Lieven), another member of the resistance. Simon also maintains that he was not even mixed up in the drug heist, which he thought had involved only a small amount of stolen penicillin to treat his wounds. In fact, Simon now claims that he had voluntarily taken the rap to protect his friends since he had no reason to live after Anna's supposed death. The authorities, however, are not buying his story. Realizing that Paul framed him, Simon escapes and, with help from Anna, traces his former friends to Hamburg and Berlin, hoping that they will be willing to testify on his behalf. Unfortunately, one by one the men become victims of suspicious "accidents." Meanwhile, Capt. Bob Sawyer

The Devil Inside

An escaped convict (Dirk Bogarde) and his lover (Mai Zetterling) meet clandestinely in a theater in ***Desperate Moment*** (British Film Makers, 1953).

(Friend), an American military intelligence officer who is hopelessly in love with Anna, vows to track down his romantic rival. Bikel, in an early role, plays one of the men being sought by Simon. There is a lot of activity in this Wrong-Man/On-the-Run noir — Simon attempting but failing to escape from a prison train, eventually breaking out of jail, being chased by cops in two cities, passionately hugging and kissing Anna in bombed-out buildings and cheap hotel rooms and disguising himself as a prison guard, seaman and chimney sweep — most of it not contributing to the strained plot. Bogarde, however, salvages the film merely by showing up on screen.

The Devil Inside see *Offbeat*

The Devil's Plot see *Counterblast*

Dial 999 (U.S. Title: *The Way Out*)
★½ (1955)

> TERRY: The police at the ports will be on the lookout for you.
> GREG: Not if we use the way out.
> TERRY: The way out?
> GREG: It's an undercover way of getting in and out of the country for criminals and smugglers. I've heard about it.
> TERRY: Darling, we don't know any criminals or smugglers.

Length: 86 min. **Cast:** Mona Freeman, Gene Nelson, John Bentley, Michael Goodliffe, Paula Byrne, Sydney Tafler, Charles Victor. **Production Company:** Merton Park Productions. **Directed by:** Montgomery Tully. **Photographed by:** Philip Grindrod. **Written by:** Montgomery Tully.

Womanizing salesman Greg Carradine (Nelson), an American in London on an expired passport, kills his bookmaker at the Zanzibar Club and runs home crying about it to his loving British wife, Terry (Freeman). Risking arrest for aiding and abetting, both Terry and her brother, John (Goodliffe), manage to prevent Sgt. Seagrave (Bentley) from finding Greg as Terry scurries about trying to make arrangements with some local hoods (Tafler and Victor) to sneak her husband out of the country via "the way out," a secret escape route used by on-the-lam criminals. Even Terry's best friend, Vera (Byrne), puts her pretty neck on the line when she hides Greg in her apartment, and he rewards her kindness with a sexual assault. When Sgt. Seagrave starts closing in on Greg, Terry convinces her criminal contacts to push up the schedule, even though it means that she and John will have to do their own driving — she in the truck with Greg and John in a decoy vehicle. After making multiple vehicle switches, the fugitives find themselves at England's southeast coast ready to put Greg on a boat to France. By now Terry is fed up with her whiny, paranoid husband and breaks the bad news to him that she does not plan to accompany him. Agonizingly slow and boring, *The Way Out* suffers from a dreary script and lackluster performances by American co-stars Freeman and Nelson and British actor Bentley as the inept policeman. This is one of the few crime films in which the revised American title makes more sense than the original British one.

Do You Know This Voice?
★★★ (1964)

That little kid's better off than most of us. He's dead. He died while he was clean and innocent.
[John Hopta]

Length: 75 min. **Cast**: Dan Duryea, Isa Miranda, Gwen Waterford, Peter Madden, Barry Warren. **Production Companies**: Parroch-McCallum Productions. **Directed by**: Frank Nesbitt. **Photographed by**: Arthur Lavis. **Written by**: Neil McCallum.

Hospital orderly John Hopta (Duryea) kidnaps and murders a 6-year-old Bristol boy and convinces his wife, Jackie (Waterford), who is unaware of the murder, to make a telephone call to the boy's working class parents demanding a ransom they cannot afford to pay. Jackie disguises her voice to sound like a man but makes the mistake of using a neighborhood telephone booth, where she is almost recognized by a neighbor, Rosa Marotta (Italian actress Miranda), with whom John has a cordial relationship. Police trace the call but by the time they arrive at the call box only Rosa is there. When she learns that a boy has been killed, Rosa offers herself as bait to catch the killer, but police superintendent Hume (Madden) nixes the idea. So she contacts the local newspaper, which runs a front-page story claiming that she can identify the murderer. When John asks her if the story is true, Rosa tells him that while she didn't see the caller's face she is sure there is something that she is forgetting and that it is certain to return to her. This bit of shocking news convinces John that he must get rid of his likable neighbor and, despite his wife's objections and the presence of Det. Sgt. Connor (Madden) in Rosa's home for protection, John makes plans to kill her with a vial of poison stolen from the hospital where he works. This obscure crime film is notable mostly for American film noir icon Duryea's performance as Hopta, the enigmatic child killer who adores his wife (although obviously not enough to stop him from slapping her around occasionally) and is kind to his neighbors. When asked by his wife why he killed the little boy, Hopta replies calmly, "Sure I killed the kid ... but I didn't mean to kill him. I just tied him up a little too tight." The film's title refers to a television newscast that plays the tape of Jackie's conversation with the boy's father and asks for help from the public in identifying the voice.

Don't Talk to Strange Men
★★★ (1962)

I don't know where you are or who you are. But I know something else. I wish I *did* know you.
[Adult voice on telephone to teenaged girl]

Length: 65 min. **Cast**: Christina Gregg, Cyril Raymond, Gillian Lind, Janina Faye. **Production Company**: Derrick Williams Productions. **Directed by**: Pat Jackson. **Photographed by**: Stephen Dade. **Written by**: Gwen Cherrell.

Just before dark, teenager Jean Painter (Gregg), on her way home from babysitting, answers the telephone in a call box at a rural bus stop in the English countryside and quickly becomes enchanted by the voice on the other end, an obviously older man who, it seems, dialed the number by accident. The man cleverly pumps her for information—is she alone? are there any houses around? does she wait for the bus every night at the same time?—before asking for permission to call her again the next evening, thus beginning a nightly routine. Finally, Jean, who has promised the caller that she wouldn't tell anyone about their conversations (although she cheats and tells her younger sister), makes a date to meet him at the isolated bus stop after dark. Jean, a typical teenager, offhandedly dismisses newspaper stories about a killer of young girls being on the loose, as well as her mystery man's ominous requests for secrecy, and sneaks out of the house for an exciting rendezvous, using a movie date with her accomplice sister Ann (Faye) as an alibi. Before long, both girls, especially the more level-headed Ann, begin to have second thoughts about the wisdom of their rebellious behavior. But is it too late? Although this film is only marginally noir, this should not affect the viewer's ability to both enjoy it and to suffer distress over the timeliness of the decades-old film, which immediately brings to mind the danger to gullible children in today's Internet chat rooms. The somewhat implausible storyline is sadly familiar by now—a naive teenage girl foolishly disregards her parents' sage advice and warnings and, as a result, places her life in danger. The jovial middle-aged parents (Raymond and Lind), unaware that their daughter's sudden romantic feelings are for a complete stranger, and a grown man at that ("at this age, they'll fall in love with anyone," says mom), regularly express fear and concern each time her bus is only a few minutes late. Jean's safety, however, seems not enough of an incentive for them to leave the comfort of their cozy home to pick her up each night from her babysitting job. (Mr. Painter, after all, hates taking the car out after dark.) To provide their audience with a suspense-filled viewing experience, director Jackson and cinematographer Dade resort to their bag of cinematic magic tricks, like the opening long shot, which contains no dialogue and captures a young girl walking along a dimly lit highway as an ominous car slowly follows and eventually offers her a ride. The camera catches the expression of shock on her face when once inside his car, she learns his true intention. In another scene, the filmmakers make use of thunder and wind in lieu of a musical score to build suspense and, later, show only the hulking back of the sex killer while the camera focuses on Jean's look of horror when she sees his face for the first time. An interesting cultural sighting: among the celebrity photographs hanging on the English teens' bedroom wall are one of Frank Sinatra and, surprisingly, one of American actor Dale Robertson wearing the cowboy outfit from his then hit TV show, *Tales of Wells Fargo*.

The Door with Seven Locks (U.S. Title: *Chamber of Horrors*)
★½ (1940)

> Women are like tiger cats. They ought to be caged at sixteen and shot at twenty. [Inspector Andy Sneed]

Length: 89 min. **Cast:** Leslie Banks, Lilli Palmer, Romilly Lunge, Gina Malo, David Horne, Richard Bird. **Production Company:** Rialto Productions. **Directed by:** Norman Lee. **Photographed by:** Alex Bryce, Ernest Palmer. **Written by:** Norman Lee, Gilbert Gunn.

On his deathbed, Lord Selford (Mallalieu) confirms his will, leaving his entire estate to his young son, John, a sickly child with a paralyzed hand. He also stipulates that if John dies June Lansdowne (Palmer), John's cousin, is to inherit everything. Selford entrusts his solicitor, Edward Havlock (Horne), with seven keys that will open the tomb in which Selford is to be interred along with the family jewels for John's retrieval when he comes of age. Ten years later, cousin June arrives in England from Canada with her Aunt Glenda (Malo). After witnessing the murder of John Selford's guardian (Roberts), who was about to inform her of the carefully guarded secret of the missing keys, June soon finds herself seeking help from Dick Martin (Lunge), a romantically inclined ex-cop, and his former boss, Inspector Andy Sneed (Bird).

Conspiracy, embezzlement, betrayal, an Inquisition torture chamber, criminal impersonation, a mop-headed butler with a gun and silencer — it all sounds much more exciting than it really is. Based on a novel by Edgar Wallace, this overlong film should have contained a snooze warning in its credits. German-born actress Palmer, however, is beautiful and oh so perky. Malo's annoying, man-hungry character, however, should have been killed-off early in the film.

Double Confession
★★ (1950)

I didn't have a drink myself in three months. Aren't you proud of me. All right, I had one, but I didn't even get into a fight. [Dipsey Paynter]

Length: 85 min. **Cast:** Derek Farr, Joan Hopkins, Peter Lorre, William Hartnell, Nautnon Wayne. **Production Company:** Harry Reynolds Productions. **Directed by:** Ken Annakin. **Photographed by:** Geoffrey Unsworth. **Written by:** William Templeton.

Jim Medway (Derek Farr) shows up at the resort city of Seagate to check up on his adulterous wife and becomes a suspect in her death and the apparent accidental death of a man who had been visiting her. On the beach, Jim meets a quiet and obviously depressed young woman named Ann Corday (Hopkins). They quickly fall in love while Inspector Tenby (Wayne) investigates the dual murder. Meanwhile, the late Mrs. Medway's former lover, Charlie Durham (Hartnell), the owner of the Primrose Bar, and his associate, misogynist "Dipsey" Paynter (Lorre), "a little drunk he fished out of the river some years ago," scheme to kill Jim and make it look like an accident. Slow moving, the film comes alive only during Lorre's and Hartnell's scenes. Based on several subtly affectionate touches between the men and the mournful reaction of one when the other dies, Durham and his close friend appear to be involved in more than just a business relationship. The romance between Jim and Ann touches on the subject of illegitimacy with admirable dignity, but a subplot involving a middle-aged woman's fruitless romantic pursuit of an unreceptive man is silly and pointless.

Downfall
★★½ (1964)

He's a menace. He attracts women, plays the ladies' man right up to the hilt. But all the time, deep down, he really hates them. When the point's reached where they want something more than just his advances, that's where he snaps. [Psychiatrist about Martin Somers]

Length: 59 min. **Cast:** Maurice Denham, Nadja Regin, T.P. McKenna, Ellen McIntosh. **Production Company:** Merton Park Productions. **Directed by:** John Moxey. **Photographed by:** James Wilson. **Written by:** Robert Stewart.

Barrister Sir Harold Crossley (Denham) successfully defends his client, driving school instructor Martin Somers (McKenna), against the charge of murdering another man's wife. While even Sir Harold's associate, attorney Jane Meldrum (McIntosh), has misgivings about the evidently psychotic Somers, Sir Harold makes a point of expressing complete confidence in his client's innocence. When Sir Harold learns that his wife, Suzanne (Regin), has been having an affair, he hires the acquitted man as his chauffeur and, hoping for the best, or rather the worst, arranges for Somers and Suzanne to spend a lot of time together ... alone. This interesting suspense drama is highlighted by a good performance by Denham as the middle-aged cuckold with lofty career ambitions. (Part of the "Edgar Wallace Mystery Theater" series.)

Dual Alibi
★★★ (1947)

You string along with me, baby, and you'll be dripping in diamonds. We're going places. [Mike Bergen to Penny]

Length: 81 min. **Cast:** Herbert Lom, Terence de Marney, Phyllis Dixey, Ronald Frankau. **Production Company:** British National Films. **Directed by:** Alfred Travers. **Photographed by:** James Watson. **Written by:** Alfred Travers, Stephen Clarkson, Vivian Adés.

Twins Georges and Jules de Lisle (Lom in a dual role), a famous French trapeze act, sign on with London circus owner Vincent Barney (Frankau). When Barney's publicity agent, Mike Bergen (de Marney), intercepts a letter addressed to Jules from French lottery officials advising him that he has won a million francs, the schemer decides to claim the prize money for himself. As part of his plan to get his hands on the winning ticket, Bergen convinces his girlfriend, Penny (Dixey), to seduce Jules, who falls hard for the pretty wannabe singer, much to the consternation of his more staid brother, Georges. When the brothers learn about their winning lottery ticket, the fast thinking Bergen manages to pull a nifty switcheroo, replacing the ticket with a mere twenty-franc winner, and Bergen and Penny rush off to Paris to claim the grand prize. By the time the brothers arrive at the lottery office in Paris, the thieves have already been paid off. With no proof, they have little recourse but to hunt Bergen down and demand their money. When they finally find the thief living high on the hog in Paris, all they receive for their trouble is a nice working over by his sycophantic associates (i.e., goons). Out for vengeance now, the de Lisles concoct a foolproof murder plan that involves one of the twins shooting the thief in a public place while the other performs a solo trapeze act, leaving the mystified authorities to sort out which one is the killer. The interesting if far-fetched storyline of this obviously low-budget film is told by way of one long flashback. The film's fine cast and its exceptionally dark and shadowy cinematography are impressive. Brit noir veteran Lom does well in the dual role, and the twin special effects are surprisingly good, except for the trapeze scenes when it's obvious that it is not Lom who is swinging forty feet above the ground. De Marney is appropriately repugnant as the con artist and Frankau gives a good performance as the circus owner whose easygoing and trusting nature would probably make P.T. Barnum turn over in his grave.

Dulcimer Street
see *London Belongs to Me*

East of Piccadilly
(U.S. Title: *The Strangler*)
★½ (1941)

Look at that fog out there. It comes down over London as though the Almighty is sick and tired of its noise and din. The people creep about the street. Everything's quiet and sly 'cause nothing's real until the fog goes again. [Cafe waiter Joe]

Length: 79 min. **Cast:** Judy Campbell, Sebastian Shaw, Henry Edwards, Naill MacGinnis, George Pughe, Edana Romney, George Hayes, Martita Hunt. **Production Company:** Associated British Picture Corporation. **Directed by:** Harold Huth. **Photographed by:** Claude Friese-Greene. **Written by:** J. Lee Thompson, Lesley Storm.

Crime reporter Penny Sutton (Campbell), mystery novelist Tamsie Green (Shaw) and Scotland Yard Inspector MacKenzie (Edwards) investigate the murder of a prostitute, who was strangled in her tenement flat by a serial killer known as "The Soho Strangler." Their suspects include the building's other tenants, an apparent Jekyll and Hyde American businessman (Pughe) and an obviously crazed wannabe Shakespearean actor (Hayes). Tamsie and Penny spend much of their time discussing the case at a nearby cafe managed by a doting mother (Hunt) and her weird son (MacGinnis). Stylistically dark, *East of Piccadilly* opens with a nicely staged strangulation scene but soon deteriorates into a zany comedy-mystery revolving around a missing corpse and the conviction of a man wrongly accused of the murders. While torturously slow at times, the film compensates with some humorous dialogue, like this exchange between Inspector MacKenzie and his subordinate in the flat where the murder occurred: "George, get down to the yard and have a look around," MacKenzie orders. "The Yard, sir?" asks his bewildered underling. "Not Scotland Yard, you idiot," replies the inspector, pointing out the window. "*This* yard."

Eight O'clock Walk
★★★ (1954)

I should not like it to be thought that the giving of sweets to children was evidence of homicidal intent. [Queen's Justice Harrington]

Length: 87 min. **Cast:** Richard Attenborough, Cathy O'Donnell, Derek Farr, Ian Hunter, Maurice Denham, Harry Welchman. **Production Company:** British Aviation Pictures. **Directed by:** Lance Comfort. **Photographed by:** Brendan Stafford. **Written by:** Katherine Strueby, Guy Morgan.

Jovial London taxi driver and war veteran Tom Manning (Attenborough), the victim of an 8-year-old girl's April Fool's prank, is wrongly charged with the child's murder when her strangled body is found near the river. A victim of fate and circumstantial evidence, the hapless Manning swears he is innocent, but only his Canadian wife, Jill (O'Donnell), and his junior QC (Queen's Counsel), Peter Tanner (Farr), believe him. Tanner, who takes on Manning's defense when the senior solicitor of his law firm becomes too ill to do so, must go up against his own father, Geoffrey (Hunter), who is prosecuting the case. Not as suspenseful as one might hope, the film nevertheless takes an interesting look at the particulars of a British murder trial that hopefully are not commonplace (e.g., the defendant's original attorney doesn't even bother to visit his client until just before the trial and then only at the desperate urging of the accused's wife). Attenborough is superb as the "wrong man," but American film noir veteran O'Donnell's loyal and sweet wife routine wears thin very quickly. Noted British character actor Denham gives a stand-out performance as one of the prosecution's more damning witnesses. A superfluous subplot about the emotional distress suffered by the trial judge (Welchman) while his critically ill wife undergoes surgery detracts from the otherwise effective script.

The Embezzler
★★½ (1954)

> The rotten thing about prison life is that they don't pay you any salary there. Oh, they give you a few bob when you leave, but that's all. Rotten system, isn't it? It means that a man's got to rely on the generosity of a few old friends until he gets on his feet. I could do with £50 right now. [Blackmailer Alec Johnson to victim]

Length: 61 min. **Cast:** Charles Victor, Zena Marshall, Cyril Chamberlain, Michael Gregson. **Production Companies:** Kenilworth Film Productions, Mid-Century Film Productions. **Directed by:** John Gilling. **Photographed by:** Jonah Jones. **Written by:** John Gilling.

After learning he has only about two years to live, elderly London bank cashier Henry Paulson (Victor), tired of his boring existence and nagging wife, turns down a promotion and decides to rob the bank's vault and flee to Rio de Janeiro over the weekend. Unfortunately for Henry, his manager returns to the bank unexpectedly and catches him in the act. Henry manages to get away with the money but is forced to abandon his escape plans. So he hops aboard a train to the coastal resort city of Eastbourne, where he takes a room at the Eastcott Hotel, a local boarding house. When ex-con Alec Johnson (Chamberlain) shows up and blackmails one of the guests, Claire Forrest (Marshall), a former girlfriend now married to a doctor (Gregson), Henry risks exposure by trying to help her. Before long, Johnson discovers Henry's true identity and sets his sights on the embezzled dough. *The Embezzler*'s strong point is the solid character development of the lead protagonist, capably portrayed by Victor as a sympathetic, law-abiding milquetoast who sees a golden, albeit illegal, opportunity and audaciously grabs it despite the risk involved. His ultimate downfall and redemption come as a result of fulfilling his life-long desire to "make somebody very happy." A pleasant but unexciting viewing experience.

The End of the Line
★½ (1957)

> Look, honey, let's talk straight. What have you got in mind? A little accident? A little slip on the bathtub soap? [Mike Selby to married lover]

Length: 64 min. **Cast:** Alan Baxter, Barbara Shelley, Jennifer Jayne, Arthur Gomez, Geoffrey Hibbert. **Production Company:** Fortress Productions. **Directed by:** Charles Saunders. **Photographed by:** Walter J. Harvey. **Written by:** Paul Erickson.

American writer Mike Selby (Baxter), hired to edit the script for an English play, runs into an old girlfriend, Liliane (Shelley), now married to middle-aged nightclub owner and fence John Crawford (Gomez). Liliane convinces Mike to help her steal her husband's latest hot jewelry acquisition so they can run off together. Lovesick Mike reluctantly agrees and the planned heist turns into a nightmare of murder, blackmail and double-cross. American actor Baxter is not believable as the noir patsy, but Britain's future horror icon, Barbara Shelley, does a good job as the treacherous femme fatale. Unfortunately, even she can't save this time-waster.

Epitaph for a Spy see *Hotel Reserve*

Escape
(NR) (1948)

Length: 79 min. **Cast:** Rex Harrison, Peggy Cummins, William Hartnell, Norman Wooland, Jill Esmond. **Production Company:** Twentieth Century Productions. **Directed by:** Joseph L. Mankiewicz. **Photographed by:** Frederick A. Young. **Written by:** Philip Dunne.

A man who accidentally killed a constable escapes from Dartmoor Prison and is aided by a sympathetic girl.

Escape by Night
★★ (1954)

> You guys *look* for the news. But in this paper jungle, I *make* it. [Reporter Tom Buchan to colleagues]

Length: 79 min. **Cast:** Bonar Colleano, Sid James, Andrew Ray, Ted Ray, Simone Silva, Patrick Barr, Martin Benson, Eric Berry, Ronan O'Casey. **Production Company:** Tempean Films. **Directed by:** John Gilling. **Photographed by:** Monty Berman. **Written by:** John Gilling.

Alcoholic reporter Tom Buchan (Colleano) gets fired from his job at *The Comet* because while other London newspapers were running front-page stories about the recent conviction of some big-time racketeers he was busy getting drunk. Determined to prove that he is a better reporter than his colleagues and competitors, Buchan warns gangster Gino Rossini (James) about an imminent police raid and allows Rossini to take him hostage in exchange for an exclusive story. The pair hole up in an abandoned theater and wait for the arrival of Rossini's brother Guillio (Benson), goon Pietro (O'Casey), mouthpiece Con Blair (Berry), who are to bring with them the cash from the sale of stolen diamonds. Unbeknownst to Rossini, his gang has abandoned him and run off with the dough. While they wait, Rossini tells Buchan his life story, and the reporter uses a neighborhood kid, Joey (Andrew Ray), to deliver his stories to the newspaper. Meanwhile, Joey's dad (radio personality Ted Ray, Andrew's real-life father) reads about a £500 reward being offered by *The Comet* for Rossini's capture, and, having figured out what his son has been up to, makes a call to the police. Joey manages to warn his new friends just before the cops arrive, and Rossini and Buchan go on the run once again. Wrongly believing that his moll, singer Rosetta Mantania (Silva), has betrayed him, Rossini shows up at The Painted Smile Club seeking revenge. American-born actor Colleano, who was noted for his supporting roles in British films as a wise-cracking American, plays (what else?) a wise-cracking American, but this time it is in a starring role. Unfortunately, he doesn't have much to work with here. His character is a one-dimensional egotist able only to elicit viewer antipathy. In an obvious attempt to make him more likeable, the writers turn him into a widower whose wife was the victim of a violent death (it is never explained but an automobile accident is assumed). It doesn't work. The usually dependable Sid James doesn't fare much better with his stereotypical Italian gangster impersonation. *Escape*, however, does have its noirishly atmospheric moments, especially the claustrophobic hideout setting and the exciting climax in a darkened London alleyway.

Escape Route
(U.S. Title: *I'll Get You*)
★★ (1952)

> What are they running down there? Immigration control or a game of find the missing alien? [Inspector Reid]

Length: 79 min. **Cast:** George Raft, Sally Gray, Reginald Tate, Clifford Evans. **Production Company:** Banner Pictures. **Directed by:** Seymour Friedman. **Photographed by:** Eric Cross. **Written by:** John Baines, Nicholas Phipps.

Undercover F.B.I. agent Steve Rossi (Raft) sneaks into England to pursue Michael Grand

(Evans), the head of a ring of kidnappers who have been boldly snatching scientists off the streets of major Western cities and transporting them to countries behind the Iron Curtain. While Scotland Yard detectives scour London trying to find Steve, whose cover is that of a jet production expert seeking to defect, Col. Wilkes of British Intelligence assigns the beautiful Joan Miller (Gray) to work with the supposedly "illegal alien" in finding the bad guys. Of course, Steve and Joan fall for each other during their efforts to save Western civilization. However, the romance between Raft, who was pushing 60 at the time, and the 30-year-old Gray is not very credible. *Escape Route*, strangely entitled "*I'll Get You*" for its U.S. release, is interesting primarily for the presence of one-time Hollywood great Raft, whose film noir repertoire includes *A Bullet for Joey*, *A Dangerous Profession*, *Johnny Angel*, *Loan Shark*, *Nocturne*, *Race Street*, *Red Light*, *Rogue Cop*, *They Drive by Night* (1940) and *Whistle Stop*. The silliness of the plot is underscored by Scotland Yard's treatment of the protagonist's illegal entry into the country as if it were the crime of the century, having his photograph published on the front page of every daily in London and assigning scores of detectives to track him down. Fans of George Raft and those holding to a liberal definition of film noir might enjoy this lackluster B movie, especially the scene in which one of screendom's toughest gangsters struts around the kitchen wearing a dainty apron while preparing dinner.

Escape to Danger
(NR) (1943)

Length: 84 min. **Cast:** Eric Portman, Ann Dvorak, Karel Stepanek, Ronald Ward. **Production Company:** RKO Radio Pictures. **Directed by:** Lance Comfort, Mutz Greenbaum (as Max Greene). **Photographed by:** Unknown (Guy Green credited as camera operator). **Written by:** Wolfgang Wilhelm, Jack Whittingham.

The Nazis unwittingly send a British double agent to England to steal top-secret invasion plans.

The Face at the Window
★★½ (1939)

I shall apply my discovery to the next victim of "The Wolf" and from his dead brain extract the identity of his murderer. [Prof. LeBlanc]

Length: 65 min. **Cast:** Tod Slaughter, John Warwick, Aubrey Mallalieu, Marjorie Taylor, Wallace Everrett, Robert Adair. **Production Company:** Pennant Picture Productions. **Directed by:** George King. **Photographed by:** Hone Glendining. **Written by:** A.R. Rawlinson, Ronald Fayre.

Paris, 1880 — Chevalier Lucio de Gardo (Slaughter) lusts after Cecile de Brisson (Mallalieu), the daughter of a financially strapped banker (Mallalieu). M. de Brisson is strapped because the Chevalier has recently robbed his bank. The robber now offers him financial aid in exchange for permission to court Cecile. (The middle-aged Chevalier's idea of courting is to grab and violently smooch the shocked girl, who understandably recoils in disgust at his lecherous advances.) When the Chevalier learns that Cecile has given her heart to penniless bank clerk Lucien Cortier (Warwick), he frames the young man for the bank robbery and then for the murder of Cecile's father by a serial killer known as The Wolf, whose victims are known to have witnessed a grotesque face staring at them through a window only moments before their brutal murders. Lucien goes on the run and is hunted by Inspector Gouffert (Adair). However, an eccentric scientist (Everrett), who has been conducting experiments with electricity, may have figured a way to trap the real killer. This is strictly a low-budget, high-camp melodrama made palatable by stage actor Slaughter's over-the-top performance. For a while viewers may believe that the only villainous gesture Slaughter does not make use of is the gleeful rubbing together of his hands. That moment finally arrives during the film's hoot of a climax when the identity of the killer is revealed. By the way, the rest of the cast are no slouches either when it comes to histrionics.

Face of a Stranger
★★½ (1964)

I've served over three years for that money. I figure I'm entitled to it by now. [Convict Johnny Bell]

Length: 56 min. **Cast:** Jeremy Kemp, Bernard Archard, Rosemary Leach, Philip Locke, Jean Marsh. **Production Company:** Merton Park Productions. **Directed by:** John Moxey. **Photographed by:** James Wilson. **Written by:** Jimmy Sangster (as John Sansom).

Johnny Bell (Locke), expecting to be released after serving three years of a five-year sentence for robbery, loses ninety days of his remission time for hiding another convict's shiv and refusing to divulge the identity of the weapon's owner. The dejected con asks his soon to-be-released cellmate, Vince Howard (Kemp), to visit Mary Bell (Leach), Johnny's blind wife, to break the bad news about the delay of his release. When Howard gets out he learns that own wife, Grace (Marsh), has been living with another man and is not interested in a reconciliation. So the ex-convict makes the trip to Bell's country cottage to make good on his promise. When he arrives, Howard is shocked to discover that the blind woman believes that he is her husband. So he decides to string her along since she is pretty easy on the eyes. Now if he can only figure a way to get his hands on the robbery money Bell has hidden away before Mary gets wise to his impersonation. Meanwhile, Michael Forrest (Archard), a local gamekeeper who has been helping the blind woman write letters to her incarcerated husband, has been skulking around the cottage and spying on the seemingly happy couple. This fast-moving film is based on a rather flimsy premise — that a woman who went blind after her husband was imprisoned might not recognize the man she had lived with for almost a year before their separation. Nevertheless, director Moxey does an excellent job in keeping the viewer interested right up to the satisfying, if predictable, climax. Kemp is enjoyable as the alienated jailbird who jumps at the opportunity for a bit of happiness. (Part of the "Edgar Wallace Mystery Theater" series.)

Face the Music
(U.S. Title: *The Black Glove*)
★★ (1954)

You know whose guy he is? Nobody's. You know who he's in love with? A diminished seventh chord. [Singer Barbara Quigley about her piano player]

Length: 84 min. **Cast:** Alex Nicol, Eleanor Summerfield, Paul Carpenter, John Salew, Geoffrey Keen, Ann Hanslip, Arthur Lane, Paula Byrne, Martin Boddey, Fred Johnson. **Production Company:** Hammer Film Productions. **Directed by:** Terence Fisher. **Photographed by:** Jimmy Harvey. **Written by:** Ernest Borneman.

Brad Bradley (American actor Nicol), a jazz trumpeter playing at the London Palladium, meets singer Maxine Halbert (Hanslip), has dinner at her flat and becomes a murder suspect when her body is discovered the next morning. Playing detective, Brad investigates on his own, to the consternation of his manager (Salew) and the Scotland Yard cops (Johnson and Boddey) investigating the murder. Suspects include singer Barbara Quigley (Summerfield) and her piano player, Johnny Sutherland (Carpenter), record producer Maxie Margulies (Salew) and jazz pianist Jeff Colt (Lane) and his wife, Gloria (Byrne). The clue to the killer's identity, Brad learns, lies in a demonstration record found at the murder scene. Although unable to compensate for the film's sluggish storyline, a good number of noir elements and characters are present (seedy jazz joints, a wrongly suspected protagonist, voiceover narration, a flashback, a nightclub singer), as well as some entertaining hardboiled dialogue (such as, "I felt like yesterday's corpse when I finally got away that night.").

Faces in the Dark
★★½ (1960)

My world has changed. It's black. It's a world of voices and smells. [Richard Hammond]

Length: 85 min. **Cast:** John Gregson, Mai Zetterling, John Ireland, Michael Denison, Tony Wright, Nanette Newman. **Production Company:** Penington-Eady Productions. **Directed by:** David Eady. **Photographed by:** Ken Hodges. **Written by:** Ephraim Kogan, John Tully.

During the testing of an experimental light bulb, an explosion occurs that permanently scars and blinds ruthless businessman Richard Hammond (Gregson), who will require constant care from his beautiful wife, Christiane (Zetterling). Christiane, who had been planning to divorce Richard before the accident, brings him to their country home to recuperate after his six-month stay in the hospital. In Hammond's absence, his partner, David Merton (Denison), an opponent of the light bulb venture, takes over the business operations. After arriving at the country estate, Richard begins to notice things are not as he remembered — the existence of a unfamiliar peach tree his wife insists he planted himself, the smell of pine in an area where pine trees have never grown, church bells that no one hears but Richard, the wrong kinds of flowers. Believing he may be cracking up, as his doctor had suggested could happen, Richard is relieved and delighted when his wild younger brother, nightclub pianist Max (American actor Ireland), shows up to borrow money. He is mystified, however, when Max leaves without a word after getting into an argument with the chauffeur, Clem (Wright), over Janet (Newman), the Hammonds' maid. Richard then overhears a conversation between his wife and Janet that causes him to believe that Christiane has been lying to him about Max's disappearance. Next, he begins to suspect that somebody is planning to kill him. Are his suspicions a result of his increasing paranoia? Or are they based on reality? Suspenseful and at times riveting, despite some mediocre performances and an overly familiar storyline, *Faces in the Dark* contains a dandy of a climax.

The Fallen Idol
(a.k.a. *The Lost Illusion*)
★★★★ (1948)

These foreigners like a bit of dirt. [British scrub woman at French embassy]

Length: 95 min. **Cast:** Ralph Richardson, Michèle Morgan, Bobby Henrey, Sonia Dresdel, Denis O'Dea, Jack Hawkins. **Production Companies:** London Film Productions. **Directed by:** Carol Reed. **Photographed by:** Georges Périnal. **Written by:** Graham Greene.

The French ambassador departs London, leaving his precocious young son, Phillipe (Henrey), in the hands of his two trusted servants, Baines (Richardson) and Baines' shrewish wife (Dresdel). Phillipe loves Baines and the feeling is obviously mutual. Unnecessarily spiteful and cruel (she burns Philippe's pet snake alive), Mrs. Baines, however, is not highly thought of by either her mellow husband or her imaginative young charge. For the past seven months, Baines has been involved with Julie (Morgan), a member of the embassy typing pool. He is devastated when she tells him she is leaving him because she can no longer love in the shadows. So Baines promises her that he will ask his wife for a divorce and confess to the affair. He bravely fulfills the first half of his promise but can't quite bring himself to mention Julie to Mrs. Baines. Young Phillipe has been taking all of this in, yet is unable to understand what has been going on in the strange adult world (Baines has told him that Julie is his niece). The boy accidentally spills the beans to Mrs. Baines, who schemes to catch her husband and his lover together. She tells Baines that she is off to visit a sick relative and later sends him a telegram saying she will be gone for several days. But she secretly returns to skulk around the darkened embassy hoping to surprise the couple. But it is she who gets the surprise when she takes a fatal fall down a stairwell after a violent argument with Baines. Phillipe sees just enough of the accident to get it into his head that the man he idolizes has just murdered his wife. When Scotland Yard Inspector Crowe (O'Dea) and his men arrive to question Baines, Phillipe tries to protect his friend by telling them childish and irrational lies ("We've got to think of lies and tell them all the time," he screams in desperation, "and then they won't find out the truth."). The boy's lies, of course, serve only to bolster the cops' suspicions that Mrs. Baines' death was no accident. Based on Graham Greene's story, "The Basement Room," *The Fallen Idol* is an absolute pleasure to view. Richardson is perfect as the dignified adulterer wrongly suspected of murder, and Dresdel couldn't be any better as the witch (spelled with a capital B) to whom he is married. Young Henrey is surprisingly capable and does a good job suppressing the cuteness factor. Reed's direction, while not matching the brilliance of his best-known noir masterpieces, *The Third Man* and *Odd Man Out*, is nevertheless commendable. Perhaps the most heart-stopping scene is the one in which Mrs. Baines' telegram, which Baines does not want the police to discover, goes sailing around the embassy hallway in the form of a paper airplane, landing squarely at the feet of Detective Ames (Hawkins in a minor role). While the film fails to live up to its full noir potential with a more satisfying, darker ending, Périnal's cinematography is first-rate, especially the scene in which the panicky child flees through darkened London alleyways after witnessing what he believes is a murder.

Fanny by Gaslight
(U.S. Title: *Man of Evil*)
★★★ (1944)

It's time people are judged on what they are, not on their parentage. [Harry Somerford]

Length: 108 min. **Cast**: Phyllis Calvert, James Mason, Stewart Granger, Jean Kent, Wilfrid Lawson, John Laurie, Stuart Lindsell, Margaretta Scott, Nora Swinburn. **Production Company**: Gainsborough Pictures. **Directed by**: Anthony Asquith. **Photographed by**: Arthur Crabtree. **Written by**: Doreen Montgomery.

In Victorian London, on the day of her return from a long absence abroad, 19-year-old Fanny (Calvert) witnesses Lord Manderstroke (Mason) push her father, William Hopwood (Laurie), in front of a horse-drawn cab during a brawl outside of Hopwood's pub, The Happy Warrior. Manderstroke is found not guilty of murder and goes free, while Fanny learns that her father and mother (Swinburn) had been operating a bordello, called The Shades, out of the pub's basement. Before the critically ill Mrs. Hopwood dies, she makes arrangements for Fanny to live in the household of cabinet minister Clive Seymour, who shocks the young girl by confessing that he is her real father. When Seymour's wife, Alicia (Scott), accuses him of having an affair with their new maid, Fanny, he reluctantly admits his paternity, prompting Alicia to blackmail him into giving her a divorce. Alicia, who been having an affair with none other than the penniless Manderstroke, plans to take her husband for all he's got so she can support her penniless lover. Unwilling to give in to her demands, Seymour commits suicide, leaving Fanny an orphan once again. But not to worry, Seymour's loyal private secretary, the handsome Harry Somerford (Granger), falls in love with the long-suffering lass, who by now has taken a job as a barmaid at a pub owned by Chunks (Lawson), her adoptive father's chum and her childhood protector. Harry's obsession with Fanny does not go over well with his class conscious mother and sister, who insist that he drop the bar maid and find a more suitable girl. Harry, of course, refuses, and proposes to Fanny, who, fearing their marriage would destroy his career, runs off and goes to live with her childhood friend, chorus girl Lucy (Kent). In the meantime, Manderstroke, who has tired of Alicia, keeps showing up to make life even more miserable for the stepdaughter of the man he murdered. Lucy, however, thinks he's kind of cute. And so it goes on and on, this flamboyant tale of murder, suicide, adultery, prostitution and class distinction, until its gripping climax. Not a great film but certainly an entertaining one, with Mason at his evil best and Granger showing the stuff that would propel him to stardom as a romantic lead. Calvert, too, does a good job as the unfortunate bastard child of a spineless, but repentant, government official. Calvert and Granger co-starred with Mason in the 1943 British noir *The Man in Grey* and the two would team up again for the 1945 noir *Madonna of the Seven Moons*. (As an example of the maturity of British filmmakers of the era as compared to their American counterparts, the viewer should note the scene in which the unmarried Fanny and Harry are portrayed as having shared a bed in a Paris hotel room. In American movies of the 1940s and 1950s even husbands and wives almost always were depicted as sleeping in separate beds.)

The Fatal Night
(NR) (1948)

Length: 50 min. **Cast**: Lester Ferguson, Jean Short, Leslie Armstrong, Brenda Hogan, Patrick Macnee. **Production Company**: Anglofilm. **Directed by**: Mario Zampi. **Photographed by**: Cedric Williams. **Written by**: Gerald Butler.

Two Englishmen dare an American to spend a night in a supposedly haunted house. (Early film role for Macnee, future star of the TV series, *The Avengers* and *The New Avengers*.)

Finger of Guilt
see *The Intimate Stranger*

Five Angles on Murder
see *The Woman in Question*

Five Days (U.S. Title: *Paid to Kill*)
✯✯ (1954)

> For the sake of the past, I've taken your sponging, your chiseling and your cheap little tricks. Now you're going to pay me back for some of that. [James Nevill to Paul Kirby]

Length: 72 min. **Cast:** Dane Clark, Paul Carpenter, Thea Gregory, Cecile Chevreau, Anthony Forwood, Arthur Young, Avis Scott. **Production Company:** Hammer Film Productions. **Directed by:** Montgomery Tully. **Photographed by:** Walter Harvey. **Written by:** Paul Tabori.

Jim Nevill (Clark), the American president of British-owned Amalgamated Industries, receives some devastating news — the important business deal he had gambled on has fallen through and, as a result, his company will be ruined. With things looking "black and hopeless," Neville concocts a bizarre plan that involves his own murder so that his beautiful wife, Andrea (Gregory), can collect on his substantial life insurance policy. He blackmails his former best friend, Paul Kirby (Carpenter), who had committed a murder years earlier, into killing him sometime in the next five days. A reluctant assassin, boozer Kirby takes his down payment of £500 and skips town, leaving behind his unhappy girlfriend, Eileen (Scott), a Soho barmaid. In the meantime, Nevill asks a handsome young member of Amalgamated's board, Peter Glanville (Forwood), to see to it that Andrea is entertained while he is busy attending to the details of his own murder. When the failed business transaction is suddenly resurrected, Nevill assigns his loyal secretary, Joan (Chevreau), who is secretly in love with him, to track down Kirby and tell him that their deal is off. Someone else, however, has decided to take over Kirby's assignment, making several attempts on Nevill's life, leaving him frightened and paranoid but

A London businessman (Dane Clark) tries desperately to cancel the hit he has taken out on his own life in *Five Days* (a.k.a. *Paid to Kill*) (Hammer, 1954).

determined to find the wannabe killer. His main suspect is irate board member Hyson (Young), who doesn't much care for Nevill's business tactics. "The methods you introduced may be all right among cutthroats and adventurers," Hyson had told him, "but not here in the city of London." Similar in plot to Director Robert Siodmak's 1931 German film, *Der Mann, der seinen Mörder sucht* (a.k.a. *Looking for his Murderer* or *The Man Who Seeks His Murderer*), and two American films noirs, 1944's *The Whistler* and 1947's *The Pretender* (1947), *Five Days* takes the potentially exciting idea of a desperate man seeking to call off a contract on his life and somehow manages to accomplish very little with it. One skillfully photographed noir scene saves the movie from being a total bust: when the panicky victim flees through London's dark alleyways trying to avoid a driver who is intent on running him down.

Five to One
★★½ (1963)

> BURGLAR JOHNNY: With a plan it ought to be flexible. You want to be able to improvise on it.
> BURGLAR ALAN: Improvise? What do you think this is? A jazz band?

Length: 56 min. **Cast**: Lee Montague, Ingrid Hafner, John Thaw, Brian McDermott, Ewan Roberts. **Production Company**: Merton Park Productions. **Directed by**: Gordon Flemyng. **Photographed by**: James Wilson. **Written by**: Roger Marshall.

Alan Roper (Thaw), a small-time but ingenious crook, convinces London bookmaker and illegal money changer Larry Hart (Montague) that Roper and his two accomplices, Pat Dunn (Hafner) and Johnny Lea (McDermott), are planning a heist that will net them £60,000. The greedy Hart agrees to pay Roper £12,000 for the traceable currency. Unbeknownst to Hart, there is no heist except the one the three crooks are planning against him once he transfers the twelve grand from the bank to his office safe. Step number one of their convoluted plan is to photograph a married, middle-aged insurance company executive (Roberts) in a compromising position with Pat, and then blackmail him into turning over the combination to Hart's office safe. Unfortunately, the only combination their victim is able to retrieve is the one to Hart's home safe, so the determined Roper figures a way to trick the fence into moving the money from his office to his home. The film's distinctive storyline is quite enjoyable up until the disappointing climax, the outcome of which is overly dependent upon coincidence. (Part of the "Edgar Wallace Mystery Theater" series.)

The Flamingo Affair
(U.S. Title: *Blonde for Danger*)
(NR) (1948)

Length: 58 min. **Cast**: Denis Webb, Colette Melville, Arthur Chesney, Eddie Matthews. **Production Company**: Inspiration Pictures. **Directed by**: Horace Shepherd. **Photographed by**: Frederick Ford. **Written by**: Maurice Moisiewitsch.

A war veteran falls in love with a femme fatale involved in black market activities, who convinces him to rob the safe at the garage where he works.

The Flanagan Boy
(U.S. Title: *Bad Blonde*)
★★ (1953)

> I've seen better bodies hanging in a butcher shop. [Lorna Vecchi]

Length: 81 min. **Cast**: Barbara Payton, Frederick Valk, John Slater, Sid James, Tony Wright. **Production Company**: Hammer Film Productions. **Directed by**: Reginald Le Borg. **Photographed by**: Walter Harvey. **Written by**: Guy Elmes, Richard Landau.

After learning that he has innate boxing ability, merchant seaman Johnny Flanagan (Wright) hooks up with a pair of seasoned trainers (James and Slater) and signs on with big-time fight promoter Giuseppe Vecchi (Valk). Standing between Johnny and his shot at a lightweight championship title, however, is the elderly Vecchi's voluptuous young wife, Lorna (Payton), a former taxi dancer who can barely hide her disgust for her older husband and who has her own big plans. Mistaking the sexual tension between the handsome young boxer and his sexy wife as merely mutual dislike, Vecchi foolishly pushes the two together so that the group will become "one big happy family." Soon, Lorna and Johnny become involved in a torrid affair, causing a super-sized guilt complex in Johnny ("I feel dirty," he laments). After lying to Johnny about being pregnant with his child, Lorna begins pressuring him to murder Vecchi, something the weak-kneed boxer finds distasteful. *The Flanagan Boy* is a pale imitation of the classic film noir *The Postman Always Rings Twice*, although Le Borg's ending is more satisfying than the original. While no Lana Turner, American actress Payton is believable enough as the scheming femme fatale. Wright, in his movie debut, is uninteresting as the patsy, and Valk, a German-born Czechoslovakian actor, overdoes the Italian accent and buffoonery routine. Sid James, however, is quite good as the fight manager-turned-sideshow barker who sees in the Flanagan boy a golden opportunity to return to the legitimate business of prizefighting.

The Flesh Is Weak
★★½ (1957)

You cross me again and, brother or no brother, I'll cut your throat. [Angelo Giani to Tony Giani]

Length: 88 min. **Cast:** John Derek, Milly Vitale, William Franklyn, Martin Benson, Freda Jackson, Harold Lang, Patricia Jessel, Patricia Plunkett, Shirley Anne Field, Joe Robinson. **Production Company:** Raymond Stross Productions. **Directed by:** Don Chaffey. **Photographed by:** Stephen Dade. **Written by:** Leigh Vance.

Newly arrived in London and seeking employment, 21-year-old eye candy Marissa Cooper (Vitale) is unfortunate enough to be spotted by Henry (Lang), a goon who works for

A small town girl (Milly Vitale) falls for a sleazy London pimp (John Derek), who cons her into turning tricks in *The Flesh Is Weak* (Raymond Stross Productions, 1957).

vice racketeers Angelo and Tony Giani. Henry gets Marissa a job as a "hostess" at The Golden Bucket, the Giani brothers' Piccadilly Circus nightspot, which serves as a front for their prostitution racket. Recognizing a hard sell when he sees one, Angelo (Benson) assigns his handsome younger brother, Tony (Derek), to work his magic on the naive young girl (i.e., to romance her into pulling tricks for the gang). Before long, the contemptible heel has his victim going out on "dates," supposedly to help him pay off his debts, and, like Susan (Field) before her, she soon becomes a "Giani girl." Tony is quick to relegate her to walking the sidewalks beside old pros like Millie (Jessel) and Doris (Plunkett). (On her first night out the petrified girl is advised by one of her more experienced colleagues, "Don't stand there as if you're in the Army. Pretend you're enjoying yourself.") When Marissa walks off with her first customer, Tony and his goon, Lofty (Robinson) can barely contain their glee as they peer from the shadows. Later, when Marissa finally wises up, she decides to leave Tony, telling Trixie (Jackson), an aging ex-prostitute charged with looking after the new girls, that she feels she can make it on her own. This prompts the vengeful Giani brothers to frame Marissa in a staged knife attack on another of their prostitutes. Marissa is sentenced to six months at HM Prison Holloway for armed assault, a fairly lenient punishment that causes Angelo to remark, "What's this country coming to?" Meanwhile, Lloyd Buxton (Franklyn), a writer who is working on an exposé of the prostitution racket in London, tries to convince Marissa to testify against her former lover, a risky ploy indeed. Viewers have a pretty good idea of what kind of movie they are in for when the opening screen credits are flashed atop a sewer grating. The story is a familiar one — a naive country girl is victimized by a smooth city slicker — and it has certainly been done better. The main attraction in this darkly claustrophobic film is American actor Derek, who turns in a fine performance as the handsome homme fatale who has caused the downfall of an unknown number of gullible young girls before finally meeting his match in Marissa Cooper.

Floods of Fear
★★½ (1958)

PRISON GUARD SHARKEY: That little rat was mauling the girl.
ESCAPED CONVICT DONOVAN: Well, she's on your side of society. Why don't you look after her?

Length: 84 min. **Cast:** Howard Keel, Anne Heywood, Cyril Cusack, Harry H. Corbett, John Crawford. **Production Company:** Rank Film Productions. **Directed by:** Charles Crichton. **Photographed by:** Christopher Challis. **Written by:** Charles Crichton.

When a severe rainstorm threatens to flood an area in the American northwest, convicts from the nearby state prison are sent out to buoy the dikes and levies holding back the Humboldt River. When a dike falls apart due to the incessant pounding of the raging river, most of the cons drown, but wrongly imprisoned Donovan (Keel) survives and manages to save the lives of fellow convict Peebles (Cusack), the marooned Elizabeth Matthews (Heywood), and injured prison guard Sharkey (Corbett). After taking shelter in Elizabeth's half-submerged and rapidly deteriorating house, Donovan and Peebles lock up Sharkey and Elizabeth to prevent them from trying to attract rescuers. Donovan, determined to make his way to the town of West Mills to kill former business partner Jack Murphy (Crawford), the man who framed him for murder, finds himself having to protect his two hostages from the psychopathic Peebles, who wants to kill the guard and rape Elizabeth. When Donovan finally leaves for West Mills to fulfill his six-year-old dream of revenge, Elizabeth, who now believes in his innocence, tries desperately to prevent him from committing murder. Marginally noir but for the most part exciting and well-made, this adventure film was American actor Howard Keel's second nonmusical role since his movie debut in the 1948 British film *The Small Voice*, the first being *Three Guys Named Mike*, a 1951 romantic comedy. He does well here as the escaped convict torn between his obsessive desire for revenge and his basic sense of decency. Heywood is convincing as the hostage who falls for her handsome captor, but Cusack is not a homicidal maniac.

An escaped convict (Howard Keel) and his hostage (Anne Heywood) in *Floods of Fear* (Rank, 1958).

The Flying Scot
(U.S. Title: *Mailbag Robbery*)
★★★ (1957)

JACKIE: You'll get the best treatment South America can offer.
PHIL: That's the idea exactly. One last big job. A decent payoff. Get myself better. Take it easy the rest of my life.

Length: 69 min. **Cast:** Lee Patterson, Kay Callard, Alan Gifford, Mark Baker. **Production Company:** Insignia Films. **Directed by:** Compton Bennett. **Photographed by:** Peter Hennessy. **Written by:** Norman Hudis.

Crooks Patterson, Callard, Gifford and Baker think their plan to rob the mail compartment of the Flying Scot, a passenger train bound for London, can't fail. Ingenious as the scheme is, like most noir heists, if something *can* go wrong it *will* go wrong. This time it's the robbers' miscalculation about the ease of breaking into the locked compartment that contains a half million pounds, the ill-timed perforation of the older thief's ulcer and the unwitting interference of two passengers: an alcoholic on his way to the hospital to submit to "the cure," and a pesky little boy with a big imagination. This low-budget crime drama offers a unique "surprise beginning" with 12 minutes of no dialogue. American actor Lee Patterson does a good job as the heist mastermind who has taken to carrying a gun despite the misgivings of his partners.

Footsteps in the Fog
★★★★ (1955)

Look out for that one. She's got something up her sleeve besides her arm. [Mrs. Pack about Lily Watkins]

Length: 90 min. **Cast:** Stewart Granger, Jean Sim-

Footsteps in the Fog

Inspector Peters (Finlay Currie, seated) and his staff interview a murderer's girlfriend (Belinda Lee) and a blackmailer (William Hartnell) about the death of a constable's wife in *Footsteps in the Fog* (Film Locations, 1955).

mons, Bill Travers, Belinda Lee, Finlay Currie, William Hartnell. **Production Company:** Film Locations. **Directed by:** Arthur Lubin. **Photographed by:** Christopher Challis. **Written by:** Dorothy Reid, Lenore Coffee.

In turn-of-the-twentieth century London, Stephen Lowry (Granger), fed up after ten years of marriage to a wealthy older woman, poisons his wife. He seems to have gotten away with the murder when her doctor declares that death was caused by gastroenteritis. Unfortunately for Lowry, one of his servants, Lily Watkins (Simmons), has proof that he killed his wife and is not afraid to rub that proof right in his aristocratic face. With misguided love as her motivation, Lily blackmails him into promoting her to housekeeper, enabling her to get even with her former superiors, who had been mistreating her. Of course, the other servants resent having to take orders from a lowly chambermaid and eventually quit. Lily sees to it that Lowry hires no one to replace them so she alone can care for him. Needless to say, Lowry isn't happy with the recent turn of events and decides that Lily must go. So he follows her one night out onto the dark and foggy London streets, his heavy walking stick in hand. When he catches up with her, he bludgeons her with the cane and flees in a panic, losing the weapon after colliding with a pedestrian. Back at home, he gets the surprise of his devious life when Lily walks through the doorway. Lowry has killed the wrong woman. His victim? None other than the wife of the friendly neighborhood constable. When police find Lowry's walking stick with his initials emblazoned on the handle, he has no choice but to admit it is his. Stolen, says Lowry, but when witnesses identify him as the killer, he is arrested by Inspector Peters (Currie) and brought before a grand jury to determine if he should stand trial. Lowry's lawyer, David MacDonald (Travers), isn't thrilled with the task of defending him because the woman MacDonald loves, Elizabeth Travers (Lee), has fallen for the killer. With Elizabeth insisting that he take on the case, what can a love smitten barrister do but ignore the obvious conflict of interest and offer his services? As it turns out, MacDonald doesn't have a lot of defending to do because Lily, who knows that Lowry intended to kill her, comes forward and testifies that he never left the house on the night of the murder. Case dismissed. Lowry two, Crown zero. Feeling his oats, especially now that he knows Elizabeth is in love with him, Lowry plans to marry her for her money. But again he is faced with having to do something about Lily, who has written her sister an incriminating letter to be opened only in the event of her death. After sweet talking her with promises of marriage, which the gullible servant is astounded to hear, Lowry convinces her to retrieve the letter. While the direction is superb, the Technicolor cinematography gorgeous and Benjamin Frankel's musical score forcefully beautiful, it is the solid cast that ensures *Footstep*'s success. Real-life husband and wife Granger and Simmons turn in excellent performances as the upper-class murderer and lower-class blackmailer whose twisted obsession brings about not only *his* downfall but her own. Character actor Hartnell also stands out as Lily's despicable brother-in-law, who tries to do a little blackmailing of his own. For those who like their films noirs with a Victorian flavor, *Footsteps in the Fog* should do the trick.

Footsteps in the Sand
see *Black Limelight*

For Them That Trespass
★★★ (1949)

It's filth that fertilizers and rejuvenates the earth. [Christopher Drew]

Length: 95 min. **Cast:** Stephen Murray, Richard Todd, Patricia Plunkett, Rosalyn Boulter, Michael Laurence. **Production Company:** Associated British Picture Corporation. **Directed by:** (Alberto) Cavalcanti. **Photographed by:** Derick Williams. **Written by:** J. Lee Thompson.

The place is London. The year is 1936. After having his first poem published in the Daily Telegraph, struggling writer Christopher Drew (Murray) decides that in order to be successful he must get down in the dirt with the commoners and start writing from experience. Thus he finds himself drawn to the Wild Swan Pub in Lenten Town, a particularly seedy section of London, where he befriends a tart named Frankie (Boulter), who has no trouble squeezing him into her busy schedule between her other lovers, the amiable Herbie Logan (Todd) and the man she lives with, the violently jealous Jim Heal (Laurence). Jim returns home one night and catches a glimpse of the startled writer jumping out of Frankie's back window. Jim, thinking Christopher was his romantic rival, Herbie, murders Frankie, and Herbie, who had been involved in a boisterous row with her that evening at the Wild Swan, becomes Scotland Yard's prime suspect. While on the run, Herbie meets and falls in love with Rosie (Plunkett), who, out of fear of being arrested for abetting a criminal, reluctantly turns him in to the police. Herbie's protestations of innocence and his insistence that he knows the identity of the real killer — a poet named "Kit Marlowe" (Christopher's condescending attempt at anonymity with Frankie, who would never know one of England's most famous literary figures) — fall on amused ears. Found guilty, Herbie is sentenced to hang, while Christopher, who knows who the real killer is, remains silent to protect his reputation and budding career. Herbie's death sentence is ultimately commuted to life, and he spends the next fifteen years in prison swearing that if he ever gets out he will clear his name. When he is finally released, he marries the guilt-stricken Rosie, who has been waiting for him all this time. Socially ostracized and unable to find work to support his wife and new-born child, the ex-con spends his time searching for "Kit Marlowe." A visit to Frankie's old flat results in the discovery of Christopher's first published poem, which Frankie had cut out of the Daily Telegraph and hid in a heating vent. It isn't long before Herbie figures out that "Kit Marlowe" is the now famous novelist and playwright Christopher Drew. Cavalcanti's Lenten Town, the epitome of film noir's "dark city" with its smoky and boisterous bars, dark perilous alleyways and seedy characters, is the centerpiece of the film, an early starring vehicle for Richard Todd, who does a fine job as the innocent man wrongly convicted of murder.

Forbidden
★★★ (1949)

You never really understood what was behind it all — the sordid little hell I was trying to hide when I first came to the fair grounds here. [Jim Harding]

Length: 87 min. **Cast:** Douglass Montgomery, Hazel Court, Patricia Burke, Garry Marsh, Kenneth Griffiths. **Production Company:** Pennant Picture Productions. **Directed by:** George King. **Photographed by:** Hone Glendinning. **Written by:** Katherine Strueby.

Jim Harding (Montgomery), a chemist-turned-carnival huckster, opens shop at a Blackpool amusement park, selling a product his hawker claims is a combination corn remover, hair restorer and stomach elixir. What Jim really wants to do, however, is serious chemical research, but he needs to earn enough money to support the extravagant lifestyle of his wannabe actress wife, Diana (Burke). Diana has been having an affair with the owner of a local theater, Jerry Burns (Marsh), who has been leading her on with empty promises about helping her acting career. Lonely and depressed, Jim begins seeing Jeannie Thompson (Court), a nice girl who sells cotton candy and taffy apples at the amusement park. Even after spending several nights with Jeannie while Diana is away, Jim has yet to tell her that he is married. Diana, having been informed of the affair by Jeannie's spiv suitor, Johnny (Griffith), shows up at Jeannie's door and arrogantly hands her a wad of bills as a bribe to stop seeing her husband. After promising Jeannie that he will find a way out of his predicament, Jim confronts his wife and demands a divorce, but she plans to cling as long as possible to her money earner. Furious, Jim decides to double Diana's thyroid medication, which has a tendency to speed up the heart rate, hoping that it will induce a heart attack. His anger is short-lived, however, and he has a change of heart. But despite his frantic attempts to locate Diana, he is too late. He finds her body and, in a panic, buries her beneath his carnival tent only to learn afterward that she never took the pills. So he spreads the word around that his wife has left to take an acting job and immediately goes on the run. *Forbidden* is dark and entertaining despite the irritating class references often found in British films of this era ("I tried looking up the fence once," Jeannie says, adding, "now I'm back in me own yard and it suits me fine."). Told almost entirely in flashback and bolstered by Glendinning's skilled cinematography, *Forbidden* successfully utilizes several common noir plot elements (a morally ambivalent protagonist is wrongly suspected of murdering his cheating wife and goes on the run) but ultimately is weakened by its Hollywood-like ending. The film is still enjoyable, thanks to the fast-moving script and the capable acting of American actor Montgomery (in his last film role before moving on to guest spots on American television in the 1950s). Burke, by the way, could portray a femme fatale along with the best of them.

Fortune Is a Woman
(U.S. Title: *She Played with Fire*)
★★½ (1957)

If you'll take my advice, you won't make the mistake of trying to defend me. You'll just bury me as decently and as quietly as possible. [Oliver Branwell to his employers]

Length: 95 min. **Cast:** Jack Hawkins, Arlene Dahl, Dennis Price, Greta Gynt. **Production Company:** John Harvel Productions. **Directed by:** Sidney Gilliat. **Photographed by:** Gerald Gibbs. **Written by:** Sidney Gilliat, Frank Launder.

While investigating a claim for valuable paintings supposedly destroyed in a minor fire at Lowis Manor, London insurance adjuster Oliver Branwell (Hawkins), is shocked to learn that the owner of the house, asthmatic war veteran Tracey Moreton (Price), is married to Branwell's former lover, Sarah (Dahl). Branwell approves the claim while trying to rekindle his romance with the reluctant Mrs. Moreton. He soon begins to suspect that her husband has scammed the insurance company by selling the original art and purposefully destroying replacement forgeries in the fire. While following up on his hunch, Branwell chances upon Moreton's body at Lowis Manor while the house is ablaze from a deliberately set fire. Branwell suspects Sarah of starting the fire but keeps quiet about his suspicions, allowing her to collect £30,000 from his insurance company. Later, he becomes convinced of her innocence and marries her with the intention of returning the insurance money. But a mousy little blackmailer, who claims he is representing a "client," shows up and interferes with Branwell's plans. A couple of flashbacks and a few interestingly photographed scenes, as well as decent performances by Hawkins, American actress Dahl and Greta Gynt as a flirtatious suspect, help make this mildly entertaining film noir more interesting.

Four Dark Hours see *The Green Cockatoo*

Frenzy see *Latin Quarter*

Frieda
★★★★ (1947)

JUDY MANSFELD: Hitler is dead.
RICHARD MANSFELD: Christ also died.

Length: 98 min. **Cast:** David Farrar, Glynis Johns, Mai Zetterling, Flora Robson, Albert Lieven, Barbara Everest, Ray Jackson, Gladys Henson. **Production Company:** Ealing Studios. **Directed by:** Basil Dearden. **Photographed by:** Gordon Dines. **Written by:** Angus MacPhail, Ronald Millar.

During fierce fighting in the spring of 1945, RAF flyer Robert Dawson (Farrar) marries German nurse Frieda Mansfeld (Zetterling) in a Krakow church. Frieda had helped Robert escape from a German POW camp and marrying her and bringing her home to England is his way of ensuring that she doesn't fall victim to Nazi retaliation. In Robert's hometown of Denfeld, the local newspaper runs a story about the marriage, and the majority of townsfolk seem prepared to despise Frieda because she is "the enemy." Robert's household—his mother (Everest), kid brother (Jackson), war-widowed sister-in-law (Johns), and even the maid (Henson)—give Frieda a cool reception but eventually come to accept her as part of the family. (In a particularly poignant scene, Robert's mother and her new daughter-in-law talk about losing loved ones in a British air attack on Cologne—Frieda's parents and Mrs. Dawson's son, Alan, a pilot whose bombs could have been the ones that killed the Mansfelds.) Only Aunt Nell (Robson), a candidate for Parliament, continues to reject the German girl, whom she regards as an obstacle to her election. After the war ends, Denfeld's bitterness and resentment toward Frieda all but disappear, and she is accepted by everyone but Nell, who manages to maintain an air of civility about having a German in the family. Just as things are looking up for the newlyweds, Frieda's brother, Richard (Lieven), arrives in town wearing a Polish uniform but secretly harboring Nazi sentiments. When Richard is recognized as a sadistic concentration camp guard by a former inmate, the consequences for Frieda are potentially tragic. Nell finds herself in a position to save her favorite nephew's wife. But will she? A thought provoking and provocative film, especially since it was made so soon after the war, *Frieda* tackles the understandable anti–German attitude of the English people. (At a government office, Frieda applies for a ration card while a roomful of civilians give her the evil eye. When one woman complains about "giving our rations to a German girl," the clerk responds, "We'll be feeding a whole nation before long.") Remarkably understated performances by Farrar and Zetterling, whose characters are a joy to watch as they slowly fall in love, are the highlight of the film. German actor Lieven is convincing as the rabid Nazi, and his character more than likely reaffirmed the conviction of many post-war viewers that not all of their former enemies would be as repentant as the sweet Frieda and that some might jump at the opportunity for yet another shot at world domination.

The Frightened City
★★★½ (1961)

The criminal mind. It's the dark side of the moon. [Inspector Sayers]

Length: 96 min. **Cast:** Herbert Lom, John Gregson, Sean Connery, Alfred Marks, Yvonne Romain, Olive McFarland, Kenneth Griffith, David Davies. **Production Company:** Zodiac Productions. **Directed by:** John Lemont. **Photographed by:** Desmond Dickinson. **Written by:** Leigh Vance.

Scheming accountant Waldo Zhernikov (Lom) teams up with mobster Harry Foulcher (Marks) to organize London's protection racket, much to the exasperation of Scotland Yard's Inspector Sayers (Gregson), who, as a milder British precursor to San Francisco's Inspector (Dirty) Harry Callahan, is always in trouble with his superiors for nabbing bad guys without obtaining the proper warrants. Foulcher easily convinces Paddy Damion (Connery), a nonviolent cat burglar, to be his new chief enforcer because Paddy is guilt-ridden over the accidental crippling of his former accomplice, Wally (Griffiths), and feels his new position in Foulcher's organization will help Wally with his financial problems. Zhernikov, meanwhile, assigns his lover, femme fatale Anya (Romain), to keep an eye on his handsome new employee. After getting her first eyeful, Anya takes on the job in earnest. Paddy's girlfriend, nightclub chanteuse Sadie (McFarland), watches in frustration as Anya, a wannabe singer, not only moves in on her man but also begins horning in on her act at the Taboo Club, a front for Foulcher's illegal activities. With the exception of cantankerous gang leader Alf Peters (Davies), a good friend of Paddy, all of the formerly splintered gangs are happy with the new syndicate. When Peters tries to break away, Zhernikov and Foulcher decide that Peters must go, and they use the unwitting Paddy to set him up for a hit. Big mistake. *The Frightened City*, released just a year before Sean Connery's first James Bond blockbuster, *Dr. No*, is a gratifying crime drama with many noir elements—a morally ambiguous protagonist, a femme fatale, a nightclub setting, acts of betrayal, low-key black and white cinematography, a downbeat ending, and a convoluted storyline. Lom is in his usual top form as the villain, and Connery is enjoyable as the soft-hearted, two-fisted patsy who's lucky enough to have a forgiving girlfriend.

The Frightened Lady see The Case of the Frightened Lady

The Fugitive see On the Night of the Fire

The Gambler and the Lady
★½ (1952)

That's where you belong, Jim Forster, in the gutter with all the other trash. [nightclub singer Pat]

Length: 74 min. **Cast:** Dane Clark, Kathleen Byron, Noami Chance, Eric Pohlmann. **Production Company:** Hammer Film Productions. **Directed by:** Patrick Jenkins, Sam Newfield. **Photographed by:** Walter Harvey. **Written by:** Sam Newfield.

Nightclub owner and illegal casino operator Jim Forster (American actor Clark), a reformed alcoholic who once killed a man while drunk, wants so desperately to fit in with London society that he takes etiquette lessons in his spare time. After the American-born street thug falls in love with Lady Susan Willens (Chance), he drops his obsessively jealous girlfriend, nightclub dancer Pat (Byron), and becomes involved in a shady gold mining deal with Susan's aristocratic but penniless father and brother. Meanwhile, gangster Arturo Colonna (Pohlmann) and his ruthless brother arrive in London to take over Forster's gambling operation, the easy way or the hard way. Inane dialogue ("I was so broke I had wrinkles on my stomach") and weak editing hurt this fairly well-acted film.

Game of Danger see Bang! You're Dead

Gaslight (U.S. Title: *Angel Street*)
★★★★★ (1940)

>There are a lot of dirty things in London. [former policeman Sgt. Rough]

Length: 88 min. **Cast**: Anton Walbrook, Diana Wynyard, Frank Pettingell, Cathleen Cordell, Robert Newton. **Production Company**: British National Films. **Directed by**: Thorold Dickinson. **Photographed by**: Bernard Knowles. **Written by**: A.R. Rawlinson, Bridget Boland.

Several years after murdering his elderly aunt in her Victorian London home and failing to find her collection of valuable rubies, Louis Barlow (Walbrook) returns as newlywed Paul Mallen. Accompanying him is his emotionally unstable bride, Bella (Wynyard), a wealthy socialite who purchased the residence at his request. Upon their arrival at the long-vacant house, Bella chances upon an envelope addressed to "Louis Barlow" and thus becomes a threat to her husband and his plan to find the rubies, which he believes were hidden by his aunt somewhere in the house. Paul schemes to nullify his wife's effectiveness as a potential witness against him by slowly driving her mad. Moving objects around the house, he accuses Bella of hiding them. She denies his accusations at first, but before long he has her convinced that she has been stealing these things and simply doesn't remember doing so. While Bella is fretting over the apparent loss of her sanity, Paul takes up with Nancy, the brazen parlor maid who is only too happy to find herself on an almost equal footing with her mistress. Unbeknownst to Paul, an alert former policeman named Rough (Pettingell) has recognized him as Louis Barlow and begins following him around town. Rough only suspects what the killer has been up to but is forced to act quickly and without evidence when he learns that Paul is going to have Bella committed. Most American viewers are probably more familiar with the 1944 U.S. version of *Gaslight*, and with good reason. MGM purchased the rights to the British film and then, it has been alleged, attempted to destroy all copies before releasing its own version. Fortunately, the studio's reported efforts to squelch the competition were unsuccessful and the British film is now seen occasionally on American television. Although the 1944 film was more lavishly produced and boasted of big-name stars such as Ingrid Bergman, Charles Boyer and Joseph Cotten, the original still compares favorably and, for some, is actually superior to the remake, thanks in large part to the talented cast. Austrian actor Walbrook's portrayal of the murderer obsessed with finding the missing gems is entertaining despite being a bit over the top; Wynyard is in top form as his unsuspecting victim; and Newton does well in a small role as Bella's concerned cousin. The plot of both versions are similarly presented except for American filmmakers' predilection for spicing up a thriller by dangling in front of viewers the possibility of a superfluous screen romance. Such was the case in the casting of the young and handsome Joseph Cotten in the role of the original version's middle-aged, portly detective, played here with exuberance and humor by veteran character actor Pettingell. *Gaslight* is a must see for all fans of period films noirs.

The Gentle Gunman
★★★★ (1952)

>MAUREEN FAGAN: He died for Ireland.
>MOLLY FAGAN: Better had he lived for her.

Length: 86 min. **Cast**: John Mills, Dirk Bogarde, Robert Beatty, Elizabeth Sellars, Barbara Mullen, James Kenney. **Production Company**: Ealing Studios. **Directed by**: Basil Dearden. **Photographed by**: Gordon Dines. **Written by**: Roger MacDougall.

Sibling IRA gunmen Terry and Matt Sullivan have a falling out over the organization, with Terry (Mills) having become disillusioned with the violence and Matt (Bogarde) believing that his big brother and mentor has turned traitor or coward, or both. Their IRA comrades, led by the fanatically anti–British Shinto (Beatty), also have their doubts about where Terry's loyalties lie and plan to conduct a tribunal to determine his fate. Shinto, whom Molly Fagan (Mullen) holds responsible for the death of her IRA husband, has recruited Molly's young son, Johnny (Kenney), and has a special mission for him in Belfast. Molly's daughter, Maureen (Sellars), a

His former comrades and girlfriend (Elizabeth Sellars) are not happy about an IRA soldier (John Mills, right) leaving the organization in *Gentle Gunman* (Ealing, 1952).

girl who seems strangely turned on by violence and death, transfers her affections from pacifist Terry to the idealistic Matt, a relative newcomer to the organization, and encourages him to participate in Shinto's foolhardy operation to rescue two IRA soldiers from their British captors. Determined to save his brother's neck, Terry hurries to spring the prisoners before Shinto can implement his own foolhardy plan. Based on screenwriter MacDougall's play, *The Gentle Gunman* takes a hard look at the violence of the era between the Irish Republican Army and the English. The character of Terry Sullivan is a representation of the British pipe dream that all IRA gunmen should awaken to the senseless violence and be born again to a healthy sense of humanism (and, of course, acceptance of British rule over Northern Ireland). Unfortunately, many of the rebel organization's members probably have been closer philosophically to Shinto and his henchmen when it comes to the violent tactics they consider necessary to achieve their goal of a free Ireland. The somewhat self-serving portrayal of Terry Sullivan's conversion in no way diminishes the ultimate truth of the film's message — that violence is horrific. Well-acted, especially by Mills, Bogarde and Sellars, with a riveting storyline (even though the protagonist's struggle with his seared conscience is neglected and therefore a bit unconvincing), *The Gentle Gunman* succeeds as entertainment, which in the movie business is a film's most important achievement.

The Girl Hunters
★★ (1963)

Hell, I never belt dames. I always kick them.
[Mike Hammer]

Length: 103 min. **Cast**: Mickey Spillane, Shirley Eaton, Lloyd Nolan, Scott Peters, Murray Kash, Hy Gardner. **Production Companies**: Present Day Productions, Fellane Productions. **Directed by**: Roy Rowland. **Photographed by**: Ken Talbot. **Written by**: Mickey Spillane, Roy Rowland, Robert Fellows.

Private eye Mike Hammer (Spillane), now a "filthy drunken bum" according to his former best friend, New York City police Captain Pat Chambers (Peters), gives up his love affair with the sauce to search for his former secretary and girlfriend, Velda, who he had believed was murdered years earlier. Mike gets information about Velda from dying FBI agent Richie Cole (Kash) and soon learns that she is on the run from a Red assassin called "The Dragon" and that she has been trying to reach her former boss with information about a commie spy ring. Aiding Mike in his investigation are FBI Agent Art Rickerby (American film noir veteran Nolan), who is out to avenge the murder of his friend, Cole; *Herald Tribune* columnist Hy Gardner (playing himself); and Laura Knapp (Eaton), the widow of a murdered U.S. senator. Watching closely is Capt. Chambers, whose anger stems from his belief that Mike was to blame for Velda's supposed murder. Overly convoluted and horribly acted (especially bad is Peters who seems to be stuck on angry overkill for the entire film), *The Girl Hunters* is entertaining in a bizarre, campy sort of way but is certainly no *Kiss Me Deadly* (the 1955 classic noir with Ralph Meeker in the Mike Hammer role). Hardboiled writer Spillane does a better job playing his P.I. creation than did Biff Elliot and Robert Bray in the other two Mike Hammer noirs, *I, the Jury* (1953) and *My Gun Is Quick* (1957), but not much better. He tries hard to emulate his hard-drinking, two-fisted, misogynistic protagonist but fails miserably with his lame attempts at hardboiled dialogue, boring fisticuffs, and laughable romantic encounter with Eaton, who has problems maintaining an American accent. During one hysterical scene, Hammer decides to break into the apartment of a suspect. He removes his trench coat and hat, props up his suit collar (who knows why?), and gingerly approaches the already half-opened door. He then charges into the room, stumbles over his own feet and falls onto a coffee table. The casting of Spillane's columnist friend Hy Gardner was a big mistake mainly because the alumnus of the American TV classic game show "To Tell the Truth" just couldn't act. Nevertheless, Gardner manages to deliver one memorable line of dialogue in his scene with Hammer: "He (the late senator) hated the commie punks just like we do." The highlight of the film is its climax, when Mike sets an ingenious, but risky, death trap for his betrayer.

The Girl in the Painting
see *Portrait from Life*

Give Us This Day (U.S. Title: *Christ in Concrete, Salt to the Devil*)
★★★★ (1949)

> GEREMIO: You're beautiful. Annunziata's hands are rough. She's worked. She's had children. She's old. But no older than you. What right have you to be beautiful?
> KATHLEEN: I took care of myself. Men want their women beautiful.

Length: 120 min. **Cast**: Sam Wanamaker, Lea Padovani, Kathleen Ryan, Charles Goldner, Bonear Colleano, William Sylvester, Sidney James. **Production Company**: Plantaganet Films. **Directed by**: Edward Dmytryk. **Photographed by**: C. Pennington-Richards. **Written by**: Ben Barzman.

In 1921, Italian immigrant Geremio (Wanamaker), who barely ekes out a living as a bricklayer building skyscrapers in New York City, proposes to his Irish-American girlfriend, Kathleen (Ryan). The practical lass turns him down, citing his poor economic prospects. So Geremio begins writing to Annunziata (Padovani), a young girl in Italy whom he knows only from a photograph carried by his best friend Luigi (Goldner). Annunziata accepts his proposal of marriage on one condition — that he provide them with a house she can call her own. Unfortunately, Geremio doesn't own such a house but writes back saying that he does, and Annunziata makes the trek across the Atlantic to marry her fibbing pen pal. Too afraid to admit his lie, Geremio marries the girl and takes her to a house in Brooklyn that he has rented for a three-day honeymoon and tells her that this is their new home. He promises himself that he will break the bad news to her at the right moment, something he forgets to do while enjoying his newlywed reverie. When she learns of his deceitfulness from their landlord and is forced to move to his tenement apartment in Manhattan, Annunziata proves to be both forgiving and patient. The owner of the house will permit them to move back in when they can raise at least $500 toward the $1,000 asking price. Earning $1.50 an hour at his bricklaying jobs and working, even during the best of times, only one week a month, Geremio sees no hope, but his frugal and optimistic bride declares that they will move into the house within a year. She even has Geremio starting to believe it. Then the babies start arriving. Four of them over the next seven years. Then the Great Depression hits, and the family begins dipping into their savings just to survive. "Eating our dream" is the way Geremio describes his predicament to friends and coworkers, Luigi, Julio (Colleano), and Giovanni (Sylvester), who are not much better off than he. The dream, however, promises to revive when contractor Murdin (James) offers Geremio a position as foreman on a construction job he has won with an exceptionally low bid, a job that Geremio knows will be unsafe. Reluctantly and guiltily, he accepts the job despite the possibility of tragedy. When he begins cracking the whip at the construction site and downplaying the safety issues, his friends turn against him, prompting him to seek solace in the bottle and in the arms of former girlfriend Kathleen. Blacklisted from Hollywood during the Red Scare in the States, Director Dmytryk, whose American films noirs included *Cornered*, *Crossfire*, *The Sniper* and *Murder, My Sweet*), turns in one of his better British efforts with *Give Us This Day*. Fellow blacklist victim, American Sam Wanamaker, in only his second film, does a fine job as the hardworking but unmotivated laborer who finds himself married to a wonderful woman with one major fault: an all-consuming obsession to own her own home. (During her difficult at-home delivery of their first child, Annunziata refuses to allow her husband to get a doctor because it would mean reducing their house fund by $25.) *Give Us This Day* is a gloomy and depressing film (with no religious overtones despite the American titles) about how one man attempts to deal with the pressure of extreme poverty. The film boasts of a fine international supporting cast in Padovani (Italian), Ryan (Irish), Goldner (Austrian), James (British), and Colleano and Sylvester (Americans). At the time of the film's release, Colleano was already becoming a familiar face to fans of low-budget British films, and Sylvester, who made his debut here, would soon be following in his footsteps.

Golden Salamander
★★★ (1950)

Can't dance the English. Too stiff. Can't let themselves go. [Rankl]

Length: 87 min. **Cast**: Trevor Howard, Anouk (Aimée), Herbert Lom, Walter Rilla, Miles Malleson, Jacques Sernas, Wilfrid Hyde-White. **Production Company**: Pinewood Films. **Directed by**: Ronald Neame. **Photographed by**: Oswald Morris (lighting). **Written by**: Leslie Storm, Victor Canning, Ronald Neame.

David Redfern (Howard), an archaeologist for a London museum, drives to Kabarta from Tunis to oversee the retrieval of Etruscan antiques stored since the war in the cellar of local businessman Paul Serafis (Rilla). On his way there, David is forced to abandon his vehicle because of a mud slide. He witnesses two gunrunners, Rankl (Lom) and Max (Sernas), retrieving their contraband from a stalled truck. Once in Kabarta, David keeps his mouth shut about what he has seen, but his guilty conscience eventually gets the best of him. Before reporting the incident to the chief of police, Douvet (Malleson), David gives Max the opportunity to flee the country for the sake of the gunrunner's sister, Anna (Anouk), with whom David has fallen in love. Rankl meanwhile learns of Max's plans to escape to Paris and kills him. David now must face the ire of the gunrunners' boss, none other than Serafis, whose control of the police chief, the telephone switchboard and the mail isolates Max from the rest of the world until a convenient time can be found to kill him. *Golden Salamander* is a stylishly filmed but slow-moving adventure yarn with Howard handing in a good performance, and French actress Anouk Aimée (billed simply as Anouk) lighting up the screen with her beauty and low-key acting. Lom once again appears as a villain, and Hyde-White plays a Hoagy Carmichael-like nightclub pianist whose relationship with the gunrunners becomes strained after they murder his friend. The title refers to an artifact containing a Greek inscription ("not by ignoring evil does one overcome it but by going to meet it"), an adage that gnaws at the archaeologist's conscience, prompting him to report the crime he witnessed.

The Good Die Young
★★★ (1954)

No money is safe where a woman can get her hands on it. [Eddie Blaine]

Length: 98 min. **Cast**: Laurence Harvey, Gloria Grahame, Richard Basehart, Joan Collins, John Ireland, René Ray, Stanley Baker, Margaret Leighton. **Production Company**: Remus Films. **Directed by**: Lewis Gilbert. **Photographed by**: Jack Asher. **Written by**: Vernon Harris, Lewis Gilbert.

Four men with three things in a common — they are veterans, they have no criminal records and they desperately need money — attempt to pull off an armored car heist. A series of flashbacks shows how the men met and how they came to be involved in a crime that the savvy viewer instinctively knows from the start is doomed. American Joe Halsey learns that his British wife, Mary (Collins), is pregnant and emotionally distraught because of her clinging, selfish mother, who wants her to stay in England so badly that she fakes a suicide attempt. When a doctor tells Joe that he should get Mary away from her mother as soon as possible because of the obvious risk to her mental and physical health, Joe must come up with a way to pay for air fare back to the States. Another American, Eddie Blaine (Ireland), an Air Force Tech Sergeant who has deserted to keep an eye on his cheating actress wife (American film noir icon Grahame), needs dough to hold onto her. British boxer Mike Morgan goes into the final fight of his career with a broken hand and ends up having to have it amputated. With no hope of getting a job ("There are plenty of jobs you can do with one hand," he says, "but they want two-handed men to do them."), Mike decides to use the thousand quid he won in his last fight to buy a tobacconist shop. Unfortunately, his wife, Angela (Ray), has already used the money to bail her ex-convict brother out of jail. Mike's money and his dreams of owning his own business go down the drain when his good-for-nothing brother-in-law skips town. Finally, there is Miles Ravenscourt (Harvey), a roguish "gentleman of leisure," a decorated war hero whose own father hates him so much that he suggests that the six Germans Miles killed during the war must have "lost their way, were out of ammunition, and were unconscious" when Miles came upon them. Miles is an inveterate gambler who has been relying on the generosity of his wife, Eve (Leighton), to pay off his bookies. When Eve learns he has been cheating on her, she cuts off his allowance and gives him an ultimatum — get a job or she will leave him. Given that choice, Miles concludes it is much simpler to hold up the post office's armored car and walk away with £90,000. The men first meet and get to know each other at the Four In Hand Saloon, where Joe, Mike and Eddie spend hours griping about their marital situations and the raw deals they have received as deserving war veterans. Miles, who has been taking it all in, finally discloses his daring plan. Despite some initial protests (Eddie's being the strongest with, "There are some things I am and some things I'm not. One of the things I'm not is a thief."), the men ultimately go for it, their confidence growing the closer their car gets to the post office ... until Miles pulls out a case filled with guns. There can be no complaints about the cast of fine actors assembled here, although Harvey comes off a bit stiff as the stereotypical upper-class English scoundrel with no ambitions other than to chase women and gamble. American noir veterans Basehart, Ireland and Graham turn in capable performances, as do British actresses Ray, Leighton (later Mrs. Laurence Harvey for several years), and Collins. The acting kudos, however, go to Baker as the

Good-Time Girl

broken-down boxer, whom film noir fans might favorably compare with the Stoker Thompson character in *The Set-Up*. (Interestingly, Baker, like *The Set-Up*'s Robert Ryan, was once an amateur boxer in real life.) Robert Morley appears in a noteworthy cameo as Miles' not-very-fatherly old man. All in all, this tale of disillusioned veterans, who see no solution to their problems but the commission of a major crime, is enjoyable. Especially memorable is the film's downbeat ending.

Good-Time Girl
★★★½ (1948)

JIMMY: Got you a nice job, didn't I?
GWEN: So what?
JIMMY: Well, do I get nothing in return?
GWEN: I said "thank you." What more do you want?
JIMMY: Plenty.

Length: 93 min. **Cast**: Jean Kent, Dennis Price, Herbert Lom, Peter Glenville, Bonar Colleano, Hugh McDermott, Jill Balcon, Griffith Jones, Flora Robson, Diana Dors. **Production Company**: Triton Films. **Directed by**: David MacDonald. **Photographed by**: Stephen Dade. **Written by**: Muriel Box, Sydney Box, Ted Willis.

In post-war London, understaffed borstals, or reformatories, are overcrowded with teenagers "whose natural growth has been marred by bad upbringing, bad companions or plain bad luck." The unfortunate story of one of these youngsters, 16-year-old Gwen Rawlings (Kent), is told by a Juvenile Court worker (Robson) to rebellious teen Lyla Lawrence (Dors). Via flashbacks, Lyla and the viewer first meet Gwen when she is caught trying to return a valuable brooch that she borrowed from the pawn shop where she works. After turning down her opportunistic boss' sexual advances, she returns home to find out that he has

A troubled teen (Jean Kent) hits rock bottom and ends up in a borstal (reformatory) in *Good-Time Girl* (Triton Films, 1948).

reported the "theft" to her father, who, as is his custom when she steps out of line, takes a belt to her. Determined that she will no longer accept such abuse (and probably tired of sleeping in the same bed with her two sisters), Gwen leaves home. Fortune seems to smile on her when she finds a small flat, and her next-door neighbor, spiv Jimmy "The Waiter" Rosso (Glenville, in a wonderfully slimy performance) gets her a coat check job at the Swan's Down Club, which is managed by underworld figure Max Vine (Lom). When Jimmy sees that Gwen is never going to be "grateful" for his assistance and that she has taken a shine to Red Farrell (Price), one of the club's musicians, he socks her. When Max notices her shiner, he fires Jimmy, who takes revenge by slashing Max's face and framing Gwen for a jewelry theft, for which she is arrested and sentenced to three years in the borstal. (Interestingly, after Gwen's hearing, Red, who is an otherwise decent sort of chap, feels comfortable enough to passionately kiss this 16-year-old in front of a court official after he has already been chastised for putting her up in his apartment without his wife being present). At the reformatory, Gwen is befriended by tough inmate Roberta King (Balcon). Together the two girls run their dormitory with an iron fist, shaking down the other girls for cigarettes and roughing them up when they complain about it. After escaping during a dining hall brawl, Gwen returns to London and hooks up with lecherous black marketeer Danny Martin (Jones) and later with two U.S. Army deserters (McDermott and Colleano), who lead her further down the path of self-destruction with drunken carousing and petty robbery, culminating in the death of two innocent men. Kent, in her late twenties at the time, gives a very convincing performance as the unfortunate teen who is sexually harassed, physically abused, and wrongly imprisoned in a borstal where, it is subtly hinted, she forms a lesbian bond with a savvy "good conduct girl." Overall, *Good-Time Girl* is a believable tale, with a few unfortunate exceptions, including the brazen pedophilic kiss and Gwen's implausibly rapid metamorphosis from sweet, victimized girl to rebellious and vicious reformatory inmate. (See The American film noir *Caged* for a similar but more believable transformation). In addition, the subplot involving Diana Dors' character contributes nothing to the otherwise riveting storyline and detracts from the film's textbook noir climax.

The Great Armored Car Swindle see *The Breaking Point*

Great Day
★★★ (1945)

Sometimes it's braver to live than to die. [Margaret Ellis]

Length: 79 min. **Cast**: Eric Portman, Flora Robson, Sheila Sim, Walter Fitzgerald, Philip Friend. **Production Company**: RKO Radio Pictures. **Directed by**: Lance Comfort. **Photographed by**: Erwin Hillier. **Written by**: John Davenport, Lesley Storm, Wolfgang Wilhelm.

In the village of Denley, the members of the Women's Institutes excitedly prepare for a visit by America's first lady, Eleanor Roosevelt, who wants to learn what British women "in the towns, in the factories, in the services and in the villages" are doing for the war effort. Denley has been chosen as the representative British village. The patriotic women of Denley have been keeping themselves busy while their men are off fighting the Germans and Japanese — making such item as fur gloves for British convoy men, wool sweaters for bomber crews, rabbit skin coats for Russian troops, and even 7,000 pounds of home-made jam. In addition, the young women do the work that the Denley men used to do — heavy farm chores, like driving tractors and planting crops — as well as finding time to serve hot tea to troops preparing to ship out. The women of Denley are indeed untiring and seemingly unified in their efforts to support the troops, but the unity is mostly a facade that is clearly demonstrated by their constant gossiping and backbiting. The films revolves primarily around the Ellis family. John Ellis (Portman) is a World War I hero with low self-esteem, an alcohol problem and an outstanding bar bill so large that the local pub will no longer serve him on credit. John is bossed around somewhat by his wife, Women's Institutes member Liz Ellis (Robson), who is so sick of his squandering their hard-earned money on booze that she has emasculated him by taking control of the household purse and doling out a few bob here and there when he resorts to begging for it. The Ellises' pretty daughter, Margaret (Sim), is so neurotic as a result of having grown up in this environment that she has decided to drop her carefree fiancé, Lt. Geoffrey Winthrop (Friend), and enter into a loveless marriage with Bob Tyndale (Fitzgerald), a middle-aged farmer who can offer her the security she craves. At some point between the preparation for Mrs. Roosevelt's visit and all the infighting among the women, John Ellis loses it. While playing the big spender for a group of Allied soldiers at the pub, John realizes that he has spent all of the money he managed to borrow from Geoffrey and worm out of Liz. He drunkenly attempts to steal a carelessly placed ten shilling note from a woman's open purse and is caught by bar patrons and turned over to the police. If there is anything noir about this little-known film, whose strength is the interesting look it offers into the war role of British rural women, it begins at this point. Suddenly the film becomes very dark, with the viewer sensing that a terrible tragedy is about to occur. Noir fans, however, shouldn't get their hopes up. Well acted, with Portman giving a good performance but speaking his lines so quickly that he is barely understandable at times.

Great Expectations
★★★★★ (1946)

> Estella, you must leave this house. It's a dead house. Nothing can live here. [Pip]

Length: 118 min. **Cast:** John Mills, Anthony Wager, Valerie Hobson, Jean Simmons, Bernard Miles, Francis L. Sullivan, Finlay Currie, Martita Hunt, Freda Jackson, Torin Thatcher. **Production Company:** Cineguild Productions. **Directed by:** David Lean. **Photographed by:** Guy Green. **Written by:** David Lean, Ronald Neame, Anthony Havelock-Allan, Kay Walsh, Cecil McGivern.

In early 19th century England, young orphaned Pip (Anthony Wager) lives with his cruel sister (Jackson) and her browbeaten but kindly husband, blacksmith Joe Gargery (Miles). Pip's childhood is rather ordinary except for two life-changing events. The first is his chance encounter in a cemetery with escaped convict Abel Magwitch (Currie), who threatens to cut out his liver and eat it if the boy doesn't get him some food and a file for his leg irons. The second is being sent by his sister to the murky and run-down mansion of a crazed hermit, Miss Havisham (Hunt), a bitterly resentful woman who was jilted at the altar in her youth and who now says she would like to have a young boy playing around the house on occasion. At Miss Havisham's he meets Estella (Simmons), the unkind but flirtatious girl he will come to love. Prior to his twenty-first birthday, Pip (Mills), now an apprentice blacksmith, learns from lawyer Jaggers (Sullivan) that an anonymous benefactor has decided to support the young man financially and to see to it that he becomes a "young gentleman of great expectations." Pip moves to London where he learns manners from his roommate, Herbert Pocket (Guinness), turns into a grand snob and falls in love all over again with the girl of his childhood dreams, Estella (Hobson), now a beautiful and much admired woman with no romantic interest in him at all. In fact, she is boldly encouraging the courtship of Bentley Drummie (Thatcher), an even bigger snob than Pip. Then one day Pip receives a visit from the convict he helped as a young boy and his world is turned upside down. David Lean's film has been called a masterpiece, and rightfully so. It is about as close to perfection as a screen version of a Dickens classic can get. Lean's direction is flawless and the acting is superb even though Mills, in his late thirties, is a bit long in the tooth to be playing a twenty year-old; however, he is such a good actor that the viewer manages to forget this very quickly. Sixteen-year-old Simmons is stunningly beautiful as the femme fatale, and Hobson does a fine job as her adult counterpart. While noir fans, especially the hardboiled variety, may scratch their heads over the attempted insertion of a screen version of a Charles Dickens novel into the ever-changing film noir "canon," the noirish elements of *Great Expectations* cannot be denied: a wrongly convicted escaped convict, a beautiful femme fatale, a morally ambiguous attorney operating on the outside fringes of the law, a frustrated and vengeance-minded old woman living in self-imposed decay and squalor, social injustice in the form of capital punishment imposed haphazardly on the lower classes, voiceover narration and occasional dark and shadowy cinematography (Green won the Academy Award for Best Black and White Photography). As the cliché goes, they just don't make them like this any more.

The Green Cockatoo (a.k.a. *Four Dark Hours; Race Gang*)
★★½ (1937)

> Every time a copper comes in here I want to open all the windows. [Jim Connor]

Length: 63 min. **Cast**: John Mills, Rene Ray, Robert Newton, Charles Oliver, Bruce Seton, Julien Vedey. **Production Company**: New World Pictures. **Directed by**: William Cameron Menzies. **Photographed by**: Mutz Greenbaum. **Written by**: Edward O. Berkman.

This unintentionally funny take-off on American gangster movies of the thirties has John Mills in the role of Jim Connor, the owner of a Soho night spot called The Green Cockatoo. Jim, who also doubles as the joint's song-and-dance man (Mills' training as a dancer shows here), is a bit ambiguous as to which side of the law he prefers. He hates coppers but at the same time refuses to accept dirty money from his gambler brother, Dave (Newton), whom he jokingly describes as a "cheap, petit larceny crook." Jim learns that gangster Terrell (Oliver) and his goons, Madison (Seton) and Steve (Vedey), are after Dave because Dave double-crossed them by accepting their money to fix a dog race and then betting it on the mutt he was supposed to have put out of commission. The hoods go looking for the double-crosser and find him at the train station, where they knife him. Badly wounded, Dave runs into Eileen (Ray), a small-town girl who has just arrived in London hoping to find a job and a place to stay. He takes her to a seedy hotel, where he dies of his wounds but not before telling her to get a message to his brother at The Green Cockatoo. The hotel owner and the chambermaid think Eileen killed Dave for his money and call the police after she runs away without sharing the spoils with them. Now Eileen has become a murder suspect with only one place to go—The Green Cockatoo. There she meets Jim but because of a mix-up when the police arrive, she is unaware that he is the dead man's brother. Likewise, Jim doesn't know that she is involved in his brother's death or even that his brother has been killed. But because, he's not terribly fond of coppers, he decides to help her get away. On the run, the two must avoid not only the police but Terrell and his boys. Mills is miscast in the role of the suave nightclub owner who, judging by his hardboiled slang ("cut yourself a slice of sleep," "the joint is knee-deep in coppers") and his two-fisted antics, has seen too many American gangster movies. Newton, the inveterate ham actor, is around only long enough for the viewer to wish he had more screen time. Ray is believable as the naive country bumpkin whose bad luck is prophesized by the oddball who shares her compartment aboard the train: "You must be careful in London because London is full of iniquity," he warns her. The stock footage of London during the day, the tourist's London, is in stark contrast to the other London portrayed here—the dark, violent city so aptly described by the train passenger as being populated by "lecherous men, strange women, robbers, thieves, gamblers," all of whom, even the nightclub owners, seem to carry shivs. *The Green Cockatoo* has been cited by several film scholars as the first British film noir.

Green for Danger
★★★★ (1946)

> He's sick of me and I'm sick of myself. [Marion Bates]

Length: 91 min. **Cast**: Sally Gray, Alastair Sim, Trevor Howard, Rosamund John, Leo Genn, Judy Campbell, Megs Jenkins. **Production Companies**: Independent Producers, Individual Pictures. **Directed by**: Sidney Gilliat. **Photographed by**: Wilkie Cooper. **Written by**: Sidney Gilliat, Claud Gurney.

In this intriguing murder mystery set against the backdrop of World War II and the vicious

German bombing raids over England, the sardonic Inspector Cockrill (Sim) investigates two deaths at a small emergency hospital. The first victim was a postman who died on the operating table under mysterious circumstances, while the second was Marion Bates (Campbell), a nurse who had assisted during the lethal surgery. Crazed with jealousy after spotting her surgeon boyfriend, Mr. Eden (Genn), kissing pretty nurse "Freddie" Linley (Gray), both of whom were present at the time of the mailman's death, Marion had announced at a hospital dance that she knew the identity of the killer. Shortly after this unwise public declaration, she was stabbed to death in the dark operating theater and her body found by Freddie. Inspector Cockrill naturally considers Eden and Freddie to be suspects, as well as the other medical staff present during the postman's surgery — anesthetist Dr. Barney Barnes (Howard), Nurse Linley's jealous boyfriend; Esther Sanson (John), an emotionally unstable and guilt-stricken woman who blames herself for her mother's death in a bombing raid; and Nurse Woods (Jenkins), whose voice seemed shockingly familiar to the mailman just prior to his being put under by Dr. Barnes. Of course, Inspector Cockrill eventually gets his man. Or is it his woman? Highly satirical (as one would expect from producers Sidney Gilliat and Frank Launder, whose forte was comedy), *Green for Danger* is also a very dark film, both stylistically and thematically, at least early and late in the story. However, the comedic appearance of Sim as the eccentric cop may dash the noirish expectations of hard-core noir fans as the plot evolves into a standard, although decidedly enjoyable, whodunit culminating in a disappointing and head-scratching climax vis-à-vis the fate of the killer.

The Green Scarf
(NR) (1954)

Length: 96 min. **Cast:** Michael Redgrave, Leo Genn, Ann Todd, Kieron Moore, Michael Medwin.

A deaf, dumb and blind writer (Kieron Moore) who has confessed to murder seems disturbed by the scarf worn by his wife (Ann Todd) in *The Green Scarf* (B & A Productions, 1954).

Production Company: B & A Productions. **Directed by**: George More O'Ferrall. **Photographed by**: Jack Hildyard. **Written by**: Gordon Wellesley.

A prominent lawyer defends a deaf, dumb and blind novelist, who has confessed to a murder.

Guilt Is My Shadow
★★ (1950)

I feel no guilt. [Kit Ferguson]

Length: 86 min. **Cast**: Patrick Holt, Elizabeth Sellars, Peter Reynolds, Avice Landone, Lana Morris. **Production Company**: Associated British Picture Corporation. **Directed by**: Roy Kellino. **Photographed by**: William McLeod. **Written by**: Roy Kellino, Ivan Foxwell.

Jaime Lovell (Reynolds), the getaway driver in a botched bank heist in London, goes on the run, taking refuge in his uncle's farmhouse outside the village of Welford. Kit Ferguson (Holt) is a hermit and not happy about his nephew barging in like this, but he kindly consents to give him a roof over his head. A top-notch mechanic, Jaime lands a job at the local gas station and immediately begins ripping off the customers and stealing from his boss. When Jaime's estranged wife, Linda (Sellars), arrives unexpectedly, Kit takes her in as well and suffers the loss of his privacy in silence. Linda slowly develops a rapport with her husband's handsome uncle, who admires her willingness to help with the chores and her obvious love of animals. Meanwhile, Jaime has been running around with a high-maintenance local girl (Morris). When Linda catches him with his hand in Kit's cash box she threatens to squeal unless he returns the money. Jaime roughs her up and, in self-defense, she strikes him over the head with a heavy candle holder, killing him. After Kit buries his nephew's body in an abandoned tin mine on his property, he and Linda settle down and begin to fall in love, causing village tongues to wag. Unfortunately, Linda, whose guilty conscience is beginning to get the best of her, appears headed for a breakdown, experiencing terrible nightmares and imagining that she has been seeing Jaime walking around Welford. When Jaime's mother (Landone) arrives unannounced, Linda cracks. *Guilt* is a fair rural noir revolving around a cover-up by two otherwise decent law-abiding people and the relentless guilt one of them experiences. The film's best part is its cleverly photographed nightmare sequence, in which Linda finds herself climbing up a steep cliff and arriving at a creepy, fog-laden cemetery, where she encounters her dead husband. Reynolds is enjoyable as the unlucky ne'er-do-well, and Sellars, who does a good job as his longsuffering wife, is very easy on the eyes. The script, however, is tedious and somewhat pretentious.

A Gunman Has Escaped
(NR) (1948)

Length: 58 min. **Cast**: John Harvey, John Fitzgerald, Robert Cartland, Frank Hawkins, Jane Arden. **Production Company**: Condor Film Productions. **Directed by**: Richard Grey. **Photographed by**: Cedric Williams. **Written by**: John Gilling.

Three jewel thieves fall out after going on the run.

Hatter's Castle
★★★★ (1941)

Why do you think I stuck with you? Because you're young or so handsome? No. No money, no music. [Nancy to James Brodie]

Length: 102 min. **Cast**: Robert Newton, Deborah Kerr, Beatrice Varley, James Mason, Emlyn Williams, Enid Stamp-Taylor, Andrew Bateman. **Production Company**: Paramount British Productions. **Directed by**: Lance Comfort. **Photographed by**: Mutz Greenbaum (as Max Greene). **Written by**: Paul Merzbach, R. Bernaur, Rodney Ackland.

In the late 19th century, in the Scottish town of Levenford, James Brodie (Newton) runs his hat business and his family with an iron fist. Cruel, arrogant and obnoxious, Brodie shows a modicum of decency only to his lover, Nancy, a young waitress at the Winton Arms Pub, saving his impatience and wrath for his wife (Varley), daughter, Mary (Kerr), and teenaged son, Angus (Bateman), who live with him in the opulent mansion he had built as a monument to himself. The house is "a realization of a dream" to him, but the townspeople derogatorily call it

"Hatter's Castle." When love-smitten Mary calls in the town's handsome young physician, Dr. Renwick (Mason), to tend to the rapidly deteriorating health of her long-abused mother, James explodes with fury and orders his daughter never to see Renwick again. She obeys but soon finds herself being seduced by Brodie's new store clerk, Dennis (Williams), who Brodie believes is Nancy's step-brother but is really her former lover. Naive and innocent, Mary allows the caddish Dennis to worm his way into her bedroom, where he rapes her, using only, he claims later, "a bit of coaxing." After learning she is pregnant, Mary confronts Dennis, who is more than happy to propose marriage, believing that he will be marrying into a wealthy family. When Dennis learns that Brodie is bankrupt, he leaves town quickly, but not before rubbing his former boss' nose in the news about his daughter's pregnancy. Irate, Brodie literally throws Mary out of his home on a stormy night, leaving her no alternative but to join Dennis on his outbound train. When Dennis makes it clear that he has no intention of marrying her, she gets off at the next stop and disappears into the night. (We later learn that her baby dies, which, since this is Victorian times, allows for a future romance between her and Dr. Renwick.) The train crashes because of a washed-out bridge, killing Dennis and the other passengers, and everyone believes that Mary died also. Brodie's life soon begins to unravel — his wife is diagnosed with cancer, he loses his store, his lover leaves him, and Angus, for whom he had great social aspirations, is caught cheating on a scholarship test. Events that may have simply depressed a normal man now drive Brodie to the brink of insanity, personifying the expression "mad as a hatter," and causing him to suffer "a fate no tyrant can escape." Based on the novel by A.J. Cronin, *Hatter's Castle* is a genuine noir for those viewers who accept the premise that such dark period films can rightfully be referred to as films noirs. Expressionistic, low-key, black and white cinematography; a downbeat ending; a strong sense of fatalism; plot elements such as family dysfunction, adultery, rape, attempted murder, betrayal, double suicide. It's all here, topped off by a sensational performance by Robert Newton, whose wild-eyed style some might associate with the Vincent Price school of ham acting. Most of the supporting cast members are excellent, but these performers go almost unnoticed in the scenes they share with Newton, one of Britain's great film icons.

The Heart of the Matter
★★★½ (1953)

> The dying. That's what I'm here for. They send for me when they're dying. I've never been much use to the living. [Father Rank]

Length: 105 min. **Cast:** Trevor Howard, Elizabeth Allan, Maria Shell, Denholm Elliott, Gérard Oury, Peter Finch. **Production Company:** London Film Productions. **Directed by:** George More O'Ferrall. **Photographed by:** Jack Hildyard. **Written by:** Ian Dalrymple.

During World War II, middle-aged Harry Scobie (Howard) serves as the assistant police commissioner of Freetown, the capital of the British colony of Sierra Leone. Having been passed over for promotion in favor of a younger man, Harry also must deal with the constant grumbling of his shrewish wife, Louise (Allan), who wants to get away from the sweltering city for a while and begs him to book her a passage to South Africa. To pay for the ticket, Harry accepts a loan from Yusef (Oury), a suspected diamond smuggler who claims he wants to be Harry's "friend." Harry's relationship with Yusef triggers an investigation by his superiors, who have heard rumors that Yusef is a protected man. Wilson, a police department clerk who has been romancing Mrs. Scobie and is angry about her sudden departure, begins looking for ways to destroy Harry's career and break up his marriage. His big chance comes when Harry becomes romantically involved with 19-year-old widow Helen Rolt (Schell), a survivor of a German U-boat attack. Hoping Louise will catch Harry in the other woman's arms, Wilson deliberately withholds a letter that says she is returning to Freetown. Meanwhile, Yusef blackmails the policeman by threatening to expose his affair unless he delivers a package of diamonds to a ship about to leave port. Guilt-ridden about his affair and not wanting to hurt either his wife or his mistress, Harry, a strict Roman Catholic whose only real friend seems to be Father Rank (Finch), begins thinking about suicide, something he believes to be an unforgivable sin. Howard turns in an outstanding performance as the cop with a big heart, a seared conscience and a rapidly deteriorating reputation. What little violence the film contains is explicit, and the downbeat ending, while a bit forced, should be satisfying to noir fans willing to overlook the film's exotic locale and lack of other "typical" noir characteristics.

Heat Wave see *The House Across the Lake*

Hell Drivers
★★★½ (1957)

Nothing you ever touched was clean. [Tom Yately's mother to Tom]

Length: 108 min. **Cast**: Stanley Baker, Herbert Lom, Peggy Cummins, Patrick McGoohan, William Hartnell. **Production Companies**: Aqua Film Productions, Rank Organisation Film Productions. **Directed by**: C. Raker Endfield. **Photographed by**: Geoffrey Unsworth. **Written by**: John Kruse, C. Raker Endfield.

Ex-convict Tom Yately (Baker), broke and desperate for work, takes a job hauling gravel for contractor Cartley (Hartnell). What Tom doesn't know is that the corrupt Cartley and his bullying foreman, Red (McGoohan), are operating with five fewer truck drivers than they claim to have on their payroll. They are doing

Hell-raising truckers (left to right, Patrick McGoohan, Sid James and George Murcell) torment a jailbird (Stanley Baker), who is determined to keep a low profile in *Hell Drivers* (Aqua Films, Rank, 1957).

this so they can take a huge cut of the pay that would normally go to the drivers, who are reimbursed, instead, according to the number of gravel pick-ups and deliveries they make. With thrill-seeker Red as the company pacesetter, Cartley encourages speeding and reckless driving despite the recent near fatal accidents that have sidelined some drivers. Tom sets his eye on the prize for making the most runs each day — a solid gold cigarette case currently in Red's possession. But Red is not about to let him or any other driver take it away from him. Front office secretary Lucy (Cummins) is immediately attracted to the ruggedly handsome Tom, who wants nothing to do with her because his new friend, trucker Gino Rossi (Lom), is in love with her. At first, Tom is well-liked by his fellow truckers. However, when he refuses to get involved in a fight with locals at a town dance because of his convict past (a secret only Gino knows about), the men do a one-eighty and begin taunting him as a "yellow-belly," victimizing him with practical jokes designed to slow him down on the road. This, along with his mother's resentment over having a jailbird for a son, makes for a lonely and unhappy trucker who clearly wants to reform his life and make proper amends for his past. The scenes in which the truckers speed recklessly on precarious dirt rows, narrowly missing unsuspecting motorists, are exciting and suspenseful, and the script, while not brilliant, is intelligent and well-executed. What makes the film such a delight to watch are the outstanding performances of Baker and McGoohan as the truckers at loggerheads with each other from day one. While Baker gives his usual solid performance, McGoohan outshines him as crazy Red, who's so tough that he fights with a cigarette butt hanging from his lips. (Marring the exciting fight between Tom and Red is a glitch where the cigarette falls from Red's mouth but magically reappears by the time he swings his next punch.) According to Baker in a later interview, the fight scene resulted in bruises and loose teeth for both men. In addition to Lom, American actor McGoohan and British film noir icon Baker, other faces likely familiar to American viewers include Cummins (best known to noir fans for *Gun Crazy*), David McCallum (who later co-starred in the American TV series *The Man from U.N.C.L.E.*), Jill Ireland (*The Valachi Papers*, *The Mechanic*, *Death Wish 2*), and Sean Connery, the screen's future James Bond.

Hell Is a City
★★★½ (1960)

When the hell did a copper worry about what was good for anyone but himself? [Doug Savage]

Length: 98 min. **Cast:** Stanley Baker, John Crawford, Donald Pleasence, Maxine Audley, Vanda Godsell, Charles Houston, Joby Blanshard, Charles Morgan. **Production Company:** Hammer Film Productions. **Directed by:** Val Guest. **Photographed by:** Arthur Grant. **Written by:** Val Guest.

While searching for the robbers who stole £4,000 from local bookmaker Gus Hawkins (Pleasence) and killed his young secretary in the process, Manchester Police Inspector Harry Martineau (Baker) must deal with a constant barrage of criticism from his bored wife Julia (Audley), who seems intent on keeping their unhappy marriage childless. Harry also must fend off the romantic advances of a flirtatious barmaid named "Lucky" (Godsell), while remaining on the lookout for her former boyfriend, Don Starling (Crawford), an escaped convict who has returned to the city to retrieve the hidden jewels from his last heist and to take revenge on Harry, the cop who helped put him away. Although Harry is unaware that Starling was the brains behind the recent Hawkins robbery, the malachite green-treated bills that stain the hands of anyone who touches the money lead him to Starling's accomplices, Clogger Roach (Houston), Tawny Jakes (Blanshard) and Laurie Lovett (Morgan). Meanwhile, Starling finds tenuous refuge in the home of his lover, Chloe Hawkins (Whitelaw), Gus Hawkins' beautiful but unfaithful wife. While co-stars Baker and American actor Crawford provide enjoyably gritty performances, the centerpiece of this often underrated crime thriller is the city of Manchester. Although not quite as seedy looking as many of its dark city counter-

An escaped convict (John Crawford) kidnaps a bookmaker's secretary for her bank deposits in *Hell Is a City* (Hammer, 1960).

parts across the Atlantic, Manchester, as presented in the black-and-white splendor of "Hammerscope" (a CinemaScope clone), is a worthy noir battleground for any tough city cop who is forced to take on an irredeemably corrupt killer.

Her Panelled Door see *The Woman with No Name*

Here's the Knife, Dear: Now Use It see *Nightmare*

The Hidden Room see *Obsession*

The Hideout see *The Small Voice*

Home at Seven (U.S. Title: *Murder on Monday*)
★★★ (1952)

> Everybody trying to prove a false alibi says they were at "the pictures." There was one the other day. They're hanging him on Friday. [Dr. Sparling]

Length: 85 min. **Cast:** Ralph Richardson, Margaret Leighton, Jack Hawkins, Campbell Singer. **Production Companies:** London Film Productions, British Lion Production Assets. **Directed by:** Ralph Richardson. **Photographed by:** Jack Hildyard, Edward Scaife. **Written by:** Anatole de Grunwald.

Bank clerk and former air-raid warden David Preston (Richardson), a stickler for schedule, arrives home at his usual time, 7 P.M., only to learn from his wife, Janet (Leighton), that he has been missing for twenty-four hours. Disbelief turns to shock when she proves her assertion by showing him the dates on two newspapers. The family doctor (Hawkins) is called in and the couple's anxiety is somewhat assuaged by his lack of concern and dismissive bedside manner. However, when they're told by a neighbor that a large sum of money has been stolen from their social club's safe and that the club steward claims he saw David take the money, their apprehension is replaced by fear and desperation. To make matters worse, they learn that the club steward has been found murdered. David, who admits to having hated the man, begins to suspect that he may have killed him and blocked it out of his memory. While trying to prevent his wife from learning an embarrassing secret he has kept from her over the years, David begins a cover-up that Scotland Yard Inspector Hemingway (Singer) easily sees through. Sir Ralph Richardson's first and last directing effort is an enjoyable film with a plot that revolves around the common noir theme of an amnesia victim who learns he may have committed a horrible crime during his temporary lapse of memory. Richardson is perfect as the good-natured bank clerk whose structured existence becomes noirishly chaotic during a frightening forty-eight-hour period. Unfortunately, the cinematography does not emphasize the otherwise dark nature of the film, which was based on a play and has the look of one.

Hotel Reserve
(a.k.a. *Epitaph for a Spy*)
★★★ (1944)

> Don't try any tricks. Don't write any letters. If you do, imprisonment, deportation, the Gestapo. [Michel Beghin to Peter Vadassy]

Length: 89 min. **Cast:** James Mason, Herbert Lom, Lucie Mannheim, Raymond Lovell, Julien Mitchell, Patricia Medina. **Production Company**: RKO Radio Pictures. **Directed by**: Victor Hanbury, Lance Comfort and Mutz Greenbaum (as Max Greene). **Photographed by**: Not credited. **Written by**: John Davenport.

At the Hotel Reserve on the French Riviera, sometime in 1938, hotel guest Peter Vadassy (Mason), an Austrian medical student and part-time language instructor seeking to become a French citizen, is picked up by the French police on charges of espionage after having a roll of film developed at a local shop. It seems that one of the other hotel guests accidentally used Peter's identical camera to take photographs of top-secret military operations. French Intelligence officer Michel Beghin (Mitchell) takes advantage of Peter's unlucky predicament by forcing him to flush out the Nazi spy from among the ten hotel guests. Solid performances by Mason and Lom highlight this interesting espionage thriller, which climaxes in an exciting rooftop chase.

Hour of Glory see *The Small Black Room*

The House Across the Lake
(U.S. Title: *Heat Wave*)
★★★ (1954)

> With some people, it's liquor. With me, it's always been women. [Mark Kendrick]

Length: 68 min. **Cast:** Alex Nicol, Hillary Brooke, Sid James, Alan Wheatley. **Production Company**: Hammer Film Productions. **Directed by**: Ken Hughes. **Photographed by**: Walter J. Harvey. **Written by**: Ken Hughes.

American novelist Mark Kendrick (Nicol) is befriended by Bev Forrest (James), a wealthy neighbor. Although, harshly critical at first of Forrest's adulterous wife, former model Carol (Brooke), Mark soon finds that he has fallen under her spell. When he informs her that Bev, who is ill and not expected to live much longer, plans to write her out of his will, Carol suggests that it might not be such a bad thing if her husband were to die before his lawyer could return from the States. Disgusted with Carol's suggestion and guilt ridden for betraying his friend, the writer attempts to leave town, but fate intervenes, causing him to miss his train. He allows Bev to talk him into just one more fishing outing aboard Bev's boat. Carol tags along, and it turns out to be Bev's last fishing trip. Told in flashback by Mark to police Inspector MacLennan (Wheatley) over drinks in a bar, the story, as seen from the perspective of the morally ambiguous protagonist, has many noir elements—a femme fatale and her patsy, voice-over narration, betrayal, and low-key black and white cinematography. *The House Across the Lake* seems to improve with each viewing. American actor Nicol does a fine job as the patsy, Brooke is terrific as the greedy femme ("Carol goes where the money is; she has an instinct for it," Bev tells Mark) and the South African-born James does a fine job as the cuckolded husband.

The House in the Woods
★★½ (1957)

There's a dark side to every man's character. [Writer Geoffrey Carter]

Length: 60 min. **Cast:** Ronald Howard, Patricia Roc, Michael Gough. **Production Company:** Film Workshop. **Directed by:** Maxwell Munden. **Photographed by:** Edwin Catford (lighting), Cyril Gray (camera operator). **Written by:** Maxwell Munden.

Agitated lately due to writer's block and being surrounded by noisy and annoying neighbors, London writer Geoffrey Carter (Gough) talks his wife, Carol (Roc), into renting a country house for the summer. Located in the middle of nowhere, hours from London, the house is owned by eccentric artist Spencer Rowland (Howard), who claims to be going on a trip shortly. He convinces his prospective tenants to spend a few days with him while his solicitors draw up the rental paperwork. As Carol poses for a portrait at Spencer's request, Geoffrey begins writing a murder mystery. He is sidetracked, however, by the artist's strange behavior (specifically, his habit of staring at a portrait of his late wife while playing over and over a recording of "Fantasy of Lost Love"). Geoffrey also suspects that his host has been lying about a number of things, including the date of his wife's death, and that something other than a beloved family cat is buried under a large rock in the woods. Geoffrey eventually comes to the conclusion that Spencer has murderous intentions and discloses his worries to Carol, who she thinks they are merely the result of a writer's vivid imagination. Nicely acted psychological melodrama with Howard giving a spooky performance.

House of Darkness
★★½ (1948)

It's a wonderful feeling to be puffed up with delusions of grandeur. It makes everybody else appear so damned insignificant. [Francis Merivale]

Length: 77 min. **Cast:** Lawrence (Laurence) Harvey, Lesley Brook, Alexander Archdale, Lesley Osmond, John Teed, Grace Arnold. **Production Company:** International Motion Pictures. **Directed by:** Oswald Mitchell. **Photographed by:** Cyril Bristow. **Written by:** John Gilling.

Often described as a horror film, *House of Darkness* is more a psychological period noir about an obsessed ne'er-do-well slowly losing his mind after deliberately causing his stepbrother to suffer a fatal heart attack. In Victorian England, pianist Francis Merivale (Harvey), believing he was cheated out of his rightful inheritance by his two stepbrothers, causes the death of one of them, violinist John (Archdale), and drives away the other, the superstitious and easily manipulated Noel (Teed), by pretending that their house is haunted by John's ghost. The new master of the house, with only his longsuffering wife (Osmond) and their gruff housekeeper (Arnold) for company, starts drinking heavily and begins to fear that the haunted house rumors he himself started may be true. Guilt-induced madness envelops Francis as he begins seeing strange things and hearing a violin accompany his piano playing. Is it only he who hears the violin? Did that portrait of John, which he had destroyed, supernaturally reassemble and hang itself over the mantle? Although it's really up to the viewer to decide whether or not the Merivale mansion is haunted, the filmmakers try to influence that decision by introducing a flashback narrated by the film's musical composer, George Melachrino (in a cameo as himself), who explains how he came to write a rhapsody for a new movie. He claims to have visited the long-abandoned house and to have actually heard music playing. This leads into another flashback that tells the story. Melachrino's stirring music is the highlight of the film. Loyal Harvey fans should enjoy his film debut, but others may find his performance a bit over the top.

Mad pianist Francis Merrivale (Laurence Harvey) and nervous housekeeper Tessa (Grace Arnold) in *House of Darkness* (International Motion Pictures, 1948).

The Human Monster
see *The Dark Eyes of London*

Hunted (U.S. Title: The Stranger in Between)
★★★ (1952)

> I went to see the man and he laughed. Laughed straight in my face. Then he said, "What do you think girls marry sailors for?" [Sailor Chris Lloyd about his wife's lover]

Length: 84 min. **Cast:** Dirk Bogarde, Jon Whiteley, Elizabeth Sellars, Geoffrey Keen. **Production Companies:** British Film Makers, Independent Artists. **Directed by:** Charles Crichton. **Photographed by:** Eric Cross. **Written by:** Jack Whittingham.

Robbie Campbell (Whiteley), a 6-year-old boy who has been physically abused by his adoptive father, runs away from his London home after setting fire to the kitchen curtains. He hides in the cellar of a bombed-out building, where he stumbles upon Chris Lloyd (Bogarde), a seaman who has just murdered the man who had been having an affair with his wife (Sellars). Unsure of what to do with the young witness, Chris takes him along on a cross-country trek, during which the killer and the boy develop an inseparable bond. After a pair of privacy-seeking lovers find the murdered man's body in the ruins, and the boy's teddy bear next to it, Scotland Yard Inspector Deaken (Keen), unsure of why the fleeing killer is taking the child along but fearing the worst, issues a call for a manhunt that covers England and Scotland. A sensitively told story that despite some slow moments manages to stay interesting, this on-the-run noir was released the same year as American director Joseph Losey's similarly plotted Italian film, *Imbarco a mezzanotte* (*Stranger on the Prowl*).

Crichton's film is much better thanks to sensitive performances by Bogarde as the desperate killer-turned-surrogate-father and Whiteley, who is convincing as the young lad sadly victimized by his adoptive parents. Sellars' screen time is much too short, but her provocative portrayal of Mrs. Lloyd is remarkable and shocking for the era. "You were away," she tells her husband after being caught cheating. "I couldn't help it." Even while the killer is desperately trying to sneak out of their flat because he fears being caught there by the cops watching the building, the sex-crazed dame tries to tempt him into spending the night.

The Hypnotist (U.S. Title: *Scotland Yard Dragnet*)
★ (1957)

INSPECTOR ROSS: Have you any addresses of any of her relatives?
WITNESS: No sir.
INSPECTOR ROSS: Where'd she bank?
WITNESS: Sorry, sir, I don't know.
INSPECTOR ROSS: You're not very helpful, are you?

Length: 88 min. **Cast**: Roland Culver, Patricia Roc, Paul Carpenter, William Hartnell, Ellen Pollock. **Production Company**: Merton Park Productions. **Directed by**: Montgomery Tully. **Photographed by**: Phil Grindrod. **Written by**: Montgomery Tully.

Test pilot Val Neal (Carpenter) is hospitalized after being injured during his ejection from a malfunctioning jet. While in the hospital, he begins experiencing attacks of severe pain accompanied by blackouts and temporary amnesia. His fiancée, Mary Foster (Roc), entrusts him to the care of family friend, Dr. Francis Pelham (Culver), a retired psychiatrist, who subjects Val to hypnotic therapy. While he has his new patient under hypnosis, Pelham tries to compel him to murder novelist Barbara Barton (Pollock), the doctor's estranged wife. Not surprisingly, the hypnotized Val can't go through with the crime, as Pelham, a supposed authority on hypnosis, suspected might happen. So the good doctor decides to go with Plan B — murdering her himself and framing his trusting patient. The sardonic Inspector Ross (Hartnell) investigates Barbara's murder, and Mary plays psychiatrist/detective by visiting Val's childhood home, where she learns the dark secret that her fiancé has blocked out of his memory for decades. Against all medical advice, she decides to divulge the secret to Val, hoping the knowledge will snap him out of his condition. Why the amnesia victim had to be a test pilot or the psychiatrist's wife a famous novelist is a matter of conjecture. Ditto regarding a strange scene involving the London jazz club Val wanders into while under hypnosis. Perhaps the filmmakers thought these superfluous details would inject some life into the deadly boring script. If so, their ploy failed. Carpenter seems very comfortable playing the whiny protagonist, a role he was not unfamiliar with, while the rest of the talented cast, including the usually reliable Hartnell, give it the old college try.

Hysteria
★★★½ (1964)

I was born four months ago by the side of a road. Anything that went before happened to somebody else. [Amnesia victim Chris Smith]

Length: 85 min. **Cast**: Robert Webber, Anthony Newlands, Jennifer Jayne, Maurice Denham, Lelia Goldoni, Peter Woodthorpe. **Production Company**: Hammer Film Productions. **Directed by**: Freddie Francis. **Photographed by**: John Wilcox. **Written by**: Jimmy Sangster.

A victim of amnesia as a result of a car crash in which he suffered a fractured skull, American hitchhiker Chris Smith (Webber) has spent months recuperating in a London hospital, where he has been treated by psychiatrist Dr. Keller (Newlands) and loved by Nurse Gina McConnell (Jayne). When he is finally released, Chris receives pills for his violent headaches, as well as the key to a luxurious penthouse in an empty apartment building that is currently under renovation. Keller tells him that the same anonymous benefactor who has been paying his medical bills is also covering the rent. With the only clue to his identity being a magazine photograph, Chris hires Hemmings (Denham), a middle-aged private detective, to find the girl in the photo. On his own, Chris tracks down

Overly medicated amnesia victim Chris Smith (Robert Webber, left) has been seeing things lately and wonders if this body-in-the-shower scene is real in **Hysteria** *(Hammer, 1964).*

photographer Marcus Allan (Woodthorpe), who tells him that the girl in the photo was stabbed to death six months earlier. So Chris is understandably puzzled when Denise James (Goldoni), the supposedly dead model, shows up claiming not only to be the wealthy widow of the driver who died in the accident but also Chris' anonymous benefactor and the owner of his apartment building. Juggling two women now (Gina and Denise) and faithfully popping his headache pills, Chris battles relentless hallucinations in which he hears a couple quarrelling in the supposedly empty next-door apartment. The arguments always end with the woman being stabbed to death in the shower. Unfortunately, no one believes Chris because each time he tries to tell someone about it, the blood, weapon and body mysteriously disappear. Not the usual Hammer fare of vampires and ghouls, *Hysteria* is a thinking man's suspense thriller that is presented almost flawlessly. (The film's major weakness is a confusing and badly introduced flashback intended to explain how Chris ended up in the car accident.) Nevertheless, writer-producer Sangster and director Francis, who worked together in Hammer's earlier films *Paranoiac* and *Nightmare*, present a very enjoyable thriller. Veteran American television actor Robert Webber, whose only prior noir had been the ultra-violent 1950 American film, *Highway 301*, gives an able performance as the amiable drifter caught up in a dizzying psychological quagmire as a result of a series of unrelated mishaps. Especially notable is the campy performance of well-known British character actor Denham as the unlikely P.I.

I Became a Criminal
see *They Made Me a Fugitive*

I Believe in You
★★★½ (1952)

> You've made a mug of me. I've gone straight and you've made a mug of me. [Charlie Hooker to his parole officer]

Length: 95 min. **Cast:** Cecil Parker, Celia Johnson, Harry Fowler, Joan Collins, George Relph, Laurence Harvey. **Production Company:** Ealing Studios. **Directed by:** Michael Relph, Basil Dearden. **Photographed by:** Gordon Dines. **Written by:** Jack Whittingham, Michael Relph, Basil Dearden.

A former colonial service officer and now a retired "gentleman of leisure," stuffy Henry Phipps (Parker) discovers his second calling after helping car theft accomplice Norma (Collins) elude the police. After turning her over to her probation officer, Matty (Johnson), Henry takes a position as an assistant parole officer. On his first day on the job, he witnesses Norma's car-thief boyfriend, spiv Jordie Bennett (Harvey), being sentenced to six months in prison while Norma, although a repeat offender, receives leniency as a result of Matty's recommendation. Henry's new boss, Mr. Dove (Relph), assigns him to first-time offender Charlie Hooker (Fowler), whose crime has earned him a year's probation in a hostel. Antagonistic toward his new probation officer at first, Charlie eventually warms up, takes a day job as a lorry driver and meets Norma. The two fall in love and plan to marry, if Henry can make good on a well-meaning but rash promise to get Charlie permission to rent a flat away from the hostel. Things start going badly for the two lovers when a judge turns down Henry's petition and gun-toting ex-con Jordie shows up seeking to renew his romance with Norma while involving Charlie in the heist of a truckload of whisky. *I Believe in You* is a nicely done semi-documentary that traces the day-to-day, often routine, tasks of two dedicated parole officers—an awkward newcomer and his veteran female counterpart. Seasoned with humor and a few noirish moments during the second half when ne'er-do-well Jordie is released from prison, this unpretentious film takes a look at a pretentious upper class Brit's change of heart regarding the working class poor. Parker gives an exceptionally low-key and likeable performance as the tyro probation officer, while Fowler, Harvey and the mesmerizing 19-year-old Collins are enjoyable as the criminally inclined youths.

I Met a Murderer
★★★½ (1939)

> Here is a dual personality. A Jekyll and Hyde. And who can say when that phlegmatic and gentle exterior will be torn aside and the mad fires that smolder beneath revealed? [excerpt from Jo Trent's unfinished manuscript of "Dear Murderer"]

Length: 78 min. **Cast:** James Mason, Pamela Kellino, Sylvia Coleridge, William Devlin. **Production Company:** Gamma Films. **Directed by:** Roy Kellino. **Photographed by:** Roy Kellino. **Written by:** Pamela Kellino, Roy Kellino, James Mason.

Hard-working farmer Mark Warrow (Mason) murders his cruel and shrewish wife, Martha (Coleridge), after she shoots his favorite dog. He buries her behind the house, but the grave is immediately discovered by Martha's lazy brother, Jay (Devlin), prompting Mark to go on the run. While eluding police, he meets Jo Trent (Kellino), a mystery writer driving across country with a mini-caravan in tow. She seems to take a liking to the handsome stranger and invites him to tag along. Mark, feeling safe now, soon finds himself falling in love with Jo only to discover that the motivation behind her surprising interest in him is a new manuscript she has begun, entitled, "I Met a Murderer," in which she details her meeting and subsequent relationship with the wanted wife killer. Meanwhile, Mark has been spotted, and the manhunt takes on a revived fury, as locals arms themselves to the teeth. (A brilliantly inspired chase scene that simultaneously revolves around a fox hunt and the man hunt has Mason fleeing vigilantes and police while a fox tries desperately to escape its pursuers and their bloodthirsty dogs. At one point, the fox and Mason find themselves hiding in the same dark corner, two terrified creatures experiencing a sense of empathy and kinship. Made by Gamma Films (a production company founded by Mason and Roy and Pamela Kellino), *I Met a Murderer* is an amazingly simple, almost amateurish, movie in all respects. Filmed entirely in a nontypical noir setting (the great outdoors), the film's dark storyline revolves around a familiar noir character (a sympathetic, reluctant killer), who, while on the lam, meets and falls in love with a beautiful woman who learns to love him. The dialogue is relatively sparse (Devlin's character never utters a word), but the acting is first-rate, with Mason and his future wife, Kellino, perfectly paired as lovers drawn together by fate. Coleridge is appropriately detestable as the farmer's wife who is so frustrated that she knows exactly where to strike to hurt the man she believes is responsible for her misery. This film should not be missed, especially by Mason fans.

I Promised to Pay see *Payroll*

I See a Dark Stranger (U.S. Title: *The Adventuress*)
★★★★ (1946)

BRIDEY: The upper classes are cringing and always moaning about their troubles and the lower classes are arrogant and think they own the earth.
MILLER: I thought it was the other way around.

Length: 111 min. **Cast:** Deborah Kerr, Trevor Howard, Raymond Huntley, Liam Redmond. **Production Companies:** Independent Producers, Individual Pictures. **Directed by:** Frank Launder. **Photographed by:** Wilkie Cooper. **Written by:** Frank Launder, Sidney Gilliat.

On her twenty-first birthday, Irish lass Bridie Quilty (Kerr), having been reared on her uncle's tall tales about his younger days during the fight for Irish independence, heads off to Dublin to join the IRA. Rebuffed in Dublin, she is recruited there by German spy J. Miller (Huntley), who brings her to the English village of Wynbridge, where he capitalizes on her beauty by having her seduce an Army sergeant into disclosing the day and time an imprisoned spy will be transferred there. When Lt. David Baynes (Howard) shows up in town, Miller suspects he is an intelligence officer whose job it will be to oversee the prisoner transfer. Miller has Bridie keep David busy while the escape is being engineered. As it turns out, David is not an intelligence officer at all but just a soldier on sick leave who has now become infatuated with Bridie. After the escape plan goes sour and both German spies are shot while fleeing, the dying Miller assigns Bridie to help retrieve a code book hidden on the Isle of Man. She hops a train, only to be followed by the pining officer, who is determined not to let her out of his sight, and a mysterious man in a straw hat. Humor plays a large part in this film, as it does in so many of the Launder-Gilliat efforts, but it detracts little from the film's dark and gloomy ambiance and the protagonist's noirish predicament. (The Three Stooges-style fight in a bathroom in a Northern Ireland inn is a bit much, however.) Kerr is terrific as the Irish girl with a large British chip on her shoulder, and Howard gives a good account of himself as the lovesick English soldier who is faced with a tough dilemma when he learns that the lives of thousands of British soldiers are in his hands.

I'll Get You see *Escape Route*

I'll Get You for This (U.S. Title: *Lucky Nick Cain*)
★★½ (1951)

NICK CAIN: Don't you scream until I get out.
CLAUDETTE AMBLING: I never scream. I swoon.

Length: 83 min. **Cast:** George Raft, Coleen Gray, Charles Goldner, Walter Rilla, Martin Benson, Peter Illing, Greta Gynt, Enzo Staiola. **Production Companies:** Kaydor Productions, Romulus Films. **Directed by:** Joseph M. Newman. **Photographed by:** Otto Heller. **Written by:** George Callahan, William Rose.

When he arrives in Sao Paolo, Italy, for a vacation, American gambler Nick Cain (Raft) gets the royal treatment from casino operator Francisco "Frankie" Sperazza (Benson), who claims that the presence of a famous gambler will be a big draw for his club. Sperazza hires penniless American tourist Kay Wonderly (Gray) to cozy up to her countryman and encourage him to stay in Sao Paolo. After returning to Nick's hotel room for a drink after their first night out, Nick and Kay quickly learn that somebody has doped their whiskey. When they awaken, they find a dead body and a roomful of policemen ready to arrest them. Knowing a frame-up when he sees one, Nick gets the drop on the cops, forces them to drink the spiked booze and takes off into the night with Kay. Aided by an orphaned waif (Staiola) and a florist (Goldner), Nick searches for the real killer and learns that the dead man was a U.S. Treasury agent intent on busting a gang of counterfeiters who are using the infamous "Hitler plates," designed by Germany during the war to destroy the American economy. Before the night is over, Nick has a few more surprises in store for him. The action in this darkly photographed movie takes place mostly at night in the narrow, shadowy alleyways of the small Italian town. A few tilted angle shots and a hallucinatory sequence contribute to its noir ambiance. Noir icon and former hoofer Raft plays, no big surprise here, a charming ladies' man, and he even manages to squeeze in a tango with Gray, responding to her question "Do you tango?" with a sly reference to his former dancing days. "I used to," he says as he begins to glide gracefully across the floor. Very smooth, George.

Immoral Charge
see *Serious Charge*

Impact
★★ (1963)

THE DUKE: Melanie, you're a bitch, aren't you?
MELANIE: All women are, but then you've told me that I'm all woman.

Length: 61 min. **Cast:** Conrad Phillips, George Pastell, Ballard Berkeley, Linda Marlowe, Richard Klee, Anita West, John Rees. **Production Company:** Butcher's Film Service. **Directed by:** Peter Maxwell. **Photographed by:** Gerald Moss. **Written by:** Conrad Phillips, Peter Maxwell.

Crusading crime reporter Jack Moir (Phillips) is framed by Sebastian Dukelow (Pastell), a.k.a. "The Duke," the racketeer owner of a private London nightspot where customers twist the nights away to a swinging jazz band and are entertained by The Duke's moll, singer Melanie Calf (West). The Duke has one of his trusted goons, Wally Wheeler (Klee), frame Jack for mail robbery and assault on a police officer, for which the reporter is sentenced to two years at HM Prison Wormwood Scrubs. During his imprisonment, Jack's obsession with vengeance grows. He convinces his soon-to-be released cellmate, Charlie Wright (Rees), to help him concoct a plan. Once on the outside, Jack is ready to put the plan into action, but it appears that Charlie may be more interested in selling him out to The Duke for a tidy sum. *Impact* is a tame crime drama in which the protagonist attempts to use duress to extract a confession, which would hardly be enforceable in court of law.

Impulse
★★ (1955)

You're a smart aleck. You wouldn't listen. Now you've got yourself a murder rap. How does it feel to be one of the criminal element? [Jack Forrester to Alan Curtis]

Length: 80 min. **Cast:** Arthur Kennedy, Constance Smith, Joy Shelton, James Carney, Bruce Beeby. **Production Company:** Tempean Films. **Directed by:** Cy Endfield (as Charles De Lautour). **Photographed by:** Jonah Jones. **Written by:** Jonathan Roche, Lawrence Huntington.

While his wife (Shelton) is visiting her mother, Alan Curtis (American actor Kennedy), an American real estate agent in the village of Ashmore in Suffolk, meets Lila Ray (Smith), a London nightclub singer. His one-night stand turns into something more than he bargained for when he agrees to help Lila's "brother," Harry Winters (Beeby), a jewel thief on the run from shady nightclub owner Jack Forrester (Carney) and his goons. When Harry is found dead in his flat, Curtis, who believes he accidentally killed him during a fight, goes on the run. Despite the old college-try by the usually reliable Kennedy, a veteran of more than a dozen films noirs, the storyline never manages to grab the viewer's complete attention as it drags on and on toward its predictable climax.

In the Wake of a Stranger
(NR) (1959)

Length: 64 min. **Cast:** Tony Wright, Shirley Eaton, Danny Green. **Production Company:** Crest. **Directed by:** David Eady. **Photographed by:** Eric Cross. **Written by:** John Tully.

A Liverpool schoolmistress helps a sailor prove that he is not a murderer.

Incident at Midnight
★★ (1963)

> BOY BRENNAN: You're not knickin' old ladies' hang bags now, Foster. This is the big time, son.
> FOSTER: If murder's big time, I don't wanna know. What's the use of fifty thou' if we take the nine o'clock walk?

Length: 56 min. **Cast:** Anton Diffring, William Sylvester, Justine Lord, Martin Miller, Tony Garnett, Philip Locke, Sylvia Langova, Jacqueline Jones. **Production Company:** Merton Park Productions. **Directed by:** Norman Harrison. **Photographed by:** James Wilson. **Written by:** Arthur la Bern.

An all-night chemist's shop is the scheduled post-heist meeting place for three narcotics thieves, one of whom has been critically wounded, and their customer, a former Nazi who has assumed the medical identity of a concentration camp inmate he murdered during the war. Unbeknownst to the phony doctor and his accomplice wife (Langova), a stool pigeon has spilled the beans to the cops about the narcotics deal. Scotland Yard has assigned an undercover cop to the case but hadn't counted on a warehouse security guard being shot and killed during the heist. Meanwhile, the thieves' psychotic ringleader forces an unlicensed surgeon, no longer allowed to practice medicine because of his addiction to drugs, to operate on his wounded comrade. There are just too many characters and too much happening for a crime drama this short to be effective, and it leaves viewers scratching their heads when an important plot element is not explained sufficiently. (Part of the "Edgar Wallace Mystery Theater" series.)

Information Received
★★½ (1961)

> No wonder crime's on the up and up with every blessed copper chasing all the skirts in London. [Maudie]

Length: 77 min. **Cast:** William Sylvester, Sabina Sessleman, Edward Underdown, Robert Raglan, Walter Brown, Bill Dancy. **Production Company:** United Co-Productions. **Directed by:** Robert Lynn. **Photographed by:** Nicolas Roeg. **Written by:** Paul Ryder.

Word in the London underworld is that American safecracker Johnny Stevens (Dancy) has been hired for a big job. Stevens is arrested when his ship docks and is tried and convicted on outstanding burglary and safecracking charges. After being sentenced to seven years in prison, Stevens is placed in solitary confinement by order of Superintendent Jeffcote (Raglan), who replaces him in the prison population with an undercover impersonator, former safecracker Rick Hogan (Sylvester). The hope is that someone will break Hogan out of jail, allowing Jeffcote to kill two birds with one stone — learning who is behind a recent spate of jail breaks and who brought Stevens to London and why. It doesn't take long before Hogan escapes with the aid of safecracker Vic Farlow (Brown), who was hired by a local criminal named Drake (Underdown) to steal secret NATO documents. Farlow hides Hogan at his home while he waits for Drake to pay him off. Big mistake. Hogan finds himself alone with Farlow's beautiful German wife, Sabina (Sesselman), and begins to fall in love with her. And it looks like the feeling is mutual. *Information Received* is a fast-moving, well-written Undercover noir. American actor Sylvester, a familiar face in British crime movies and films noirs, gives a solid performance as the unpredictable impersonator, who has been known to work both sides of the law. German siren Sesselman is good as the scheming femme fatale. Comedic actress Hermione Baddeley has a small role as an over-the-hill tart who takes a liking to Hogan.

The Informers (U.S. Title: *Underworld Informers*)
★★★ (1963)

> I used to think a snout was the lowest kind of vermin, but now I know there's one thing lower. That's the copper that keeps him at it. [Charlie Ruskin to Inspector Johnnroe]

Length: 105 min. **Cast**: Nigel Patrick, Margaret Whiting, Catherine Woodville, Colin Blakely, Derren Nesbitt, Harry Andrews, John Cowley, Allan Cuthbertson, Frank Finlay, Roy Kinnear. **Production Company**: Rank Organisation Film Productions. **Directed by**: Ken Annakin. **Photographed by**: Reginald Wyer. **Written by**: Alun Falconer.

Against the orders of his boss (Andrews), Inspector Johnnroe (Patrick) continues to rely on his favorite "snout" (i.e., informant), Jim Ruskin (Cowley), to help him snag the safecrackers who have pulled off a string of recent bank jobs. When the booze loving Ruskin gets careless while spying on Bertie Hoyle (Nesbitt) and Leon Sale (Finlay) and their gang, he is murdered, and both Johnnroe and Ruskin's brother, ex-convict Jim Ruskin (Cowley), vow to take their own form of revenge on the killer. Bertie, meanwhile, uses his prostitute girlfriend, Maisie (Whiting), to frame Johnnroe for bribery and attempts to make one of his own men, Shorty Sparks (Kinnear), the patsy for the snout's murder. *The Informers* is a tightly scripted and ultraviolent crime drama with Nesbitt delightfully psychotic as the gang's ringleader, and Patrick convincing as an honest cop faced with being labeled "dirty." Woodville plays the Inspector's loyal wife, and Australian-born actor Cuthbertson is an apple polishing detective who couldn't be happier about his colleague's predicament.

The Inheritance see *Uncle Silas*

An Inspector Calls
★★★ (1954)

> INSPECTOR POOLE: The Palace Bar has, I understand, an unsavory reputation.
> GERALD CROFT: Yes, it's the favorite haunt of women of a certain sort.
> MRS. BIRLING: Women of a certain sort? Here in Brumley?

Length: 79 min. **Cast**: Alastair Sim, Jane Wenham, Brian Worth, Eileen Moore, Olga Lindo, Arthur Young, Bryan Forbes. **Production Company**: Watergate Productions. **Directed by**: Guy Hamilton. **Photographed by**: Edward Scaife. **Written by**: Desmond Davis.

At the conclusion of a Birling family dinner celebrating the engagement of daughter Sheila (Moore) to Gerald Croft (Worth), an uninvited guest arrives, disrupting not only the happy occasion but also the lives of those present. Identifying himself as Inspector Poole (Sim), the enigmatic visitor tells the upper-crust Gerald and the aspiring upper-crust Birling family that he has come to question them about a girl named Eva Smith (Wenham), who apparently has just committed suicide in a most horrible way — by drinking disinfectant. One by one, each family member learns that he or she has unwittingly contributed in some way to the girl's death — factory owner Arthur Birling (Young) by firing Eva for asking for a raise; spoiled Sheila for having the girl dismissed from her new job at a clothing store for alleged disrespect; Mrs. Birling (Lindo), a member of a charitable organization, for denying financial aid to the girl, who claimed to be pregnant by a "silly and wild" boyfriend; and Eric (Forbes), the Birlings' alcoholic son, the silly and wild boyfriend who got Eva pregnant. Even good old reliable Gerald had a link to the dead girl, admitting to an affair with her at the same time he was seeing Sheila. While the family members are busy rationalizing away or guiltily accepting their responsibility for Eva's suicide, Gerald learns that Inspector Poole may be an imposter and that, perhaps, Eva isn't dead after all. Based on a 1947 play by J.B. Priestly, *An Inspector Calls* takes some interesting potshots at Edwardian (and contemporary) social mores during "a time of steadily increasing prosperity and progress" and advocates the premise that people, no matter their class, are all somehow connected. The film does not work well as a social commentary but fares better (albeit with a modicum of film noir style and elements) as a compelling drama, thanks to its fine supporting cast. Unfortunately, the viewer is shortchanged by the relatively brief screen time of veteran Alastair Sim as the eerily perceptive visitor.

The Interrupted Journey
★★ (1949)

> If whoever pulled that (emergency) cord for any flippant reason, I'll see that his name stinks from one end of the country to the other. [Mr. Clayton, railway investigator]

Length: 80 min. **Cast:** Richard Todd, Valerie Hobson, Christine Norden, Tom Walls, Alexander Gauge. **Production Company:** Valiant Films. **Directed by:** Daniel Birt. **Photographed by:** Erwin Hillier. **Written by:** Michael Pertwee.

Aspiring writer John North (Todd) leaves Carol (Hobson), his slightly nagging wife (the nerve of her expecting him to actually work for a living until he becomes successful as a writer!) and runs off with, of all people, the wife of a London publisher, thus ensuring the continuing flow of rejection slips. Once on board the love train with Susan Wilding (Norden), John begins to have second thoughts. So when he sees the cuckolded husband (Gauge) and a private eye tailing them, he pulls the emergency cord and jumps from the train only a short distance from his house. Minutes later, with John back in the arms of his unwitting wife, the unimaginable happens— the stopped train is rear-ended by another and the resulting collision kills twenty people, injuring scores more. Among the reported dead are Susan, her husband and the private dick. John's guilty conscience causes him to suffer nightmares about the wreck, but he really begins to sweat when a suspicious railway investigator (Walls) shows up at his house asking embarrassing questions in front of Carol. Eventually, Scotland Yard discovers that Susan did not die as a result of the crash but was shot in the back. After somebody plants the murder weapon in John's back yard pond, the writer does what any framed noir protagonist would do— he goes on the run. A promising idea, which could have been taken straight out of Alfred Hitchcock's dream diary, plus a top-notch cast and a dark, moody atmosphere do not necessarily equal a well-made film, as *The Interrupted Journey* proves with its muddled script, slack direction and unoriginal, cop-out ending.

The Intimate Stranger
(U.S. Title: *Finger of Guilt*)
★★½ (1956)

> I feel as though I'm out in the open with somebody ready to take a pot shot at me and I don't know who or where or how. [Reggie Wilson]

Length: 95 min. **Cast:** Richard Basehart, Mary Murphy, Constance Cummings, Roger Livesey, Faith Brook, Mervyn Johns. **Production Companies:** Anglo-Guild Productions, Merton Park Productions. **Directed by:** Joseph Losey (as Joseph Walton). **Photographed by:** Gerald Gibbs. **Written by:** Howard Koch (as Peter Howard).

In London after being driven out of Hollywood because of an affair with his boss' wife, American filmmaker Reggie Wilson (Basehart) is now the executive producer at Commonwealth Pictures, which is owned by his new father-in-law, Ben Case (Livesey). Reggie begins receiving letters from Evelyn Stewart (Murphy), an American actress in Newcastle, who has been expressing her desperate desire for a reconciliation. According to Reggie, however, he doesn't know the letter writer. Suspecting blackmail, he divulges all to Ben, as well as to American actress Kay Wallace (Cummings), his former lover and the star of his new production. At Ben's urging, Reggie fearfully confides in his wife, Lesley (Brook), who doesn't at all doubt his fidelity. He then takes Lesley along on a trip to Newcastle to confront Evelyn, who makes a believer out of Lesley causing her to return to daddy. Desperate now, Reggie pays a visit to a Newcastle police station and has the local constables bring Lesley in for questioning. But even they seem to believe the girl's story. Unsure of himself now, Reggie begins to suspect that he be suffering from multiple personality disorder. He returns to the studio and receives more bad news— Ben has canceled the new film, Reggie's pet project, and has ordered him to take a long vacation. It seems that Reggie's worst nightmare is coming to pass—another sex scandal that threatens to end his promising film career. Told mostly in flashback, *Intimate Stranger* is a slow-moving thriller that relies heavily on the abilities of its outstanding cast to keep viewers interested. American film noir veteran Basehart is good as the baffled movie executive, as is noted British character actor Mervyn Johns, who plays the studio chief's loyal assistant. Mary Murphy, best known for her role as an innocent small-town girl who falls for a motorcycle gang leader in 1953's *The Wild One*, turns in fine performance as the mysterious actress.

The Intruder
★★½ (1953)

There's only one rule in this world and I've learned it at last: it's each man out for himself. [Ginger Edwards]

Length: 84 min. **Cast**: Jack Hawkins, Hugh Williams, Michael Medwin, George Cole, Dennis Price, Duncan Lamont, Arthur Howard. **Production Company**: Ivan Foxwell Productions. **Directed by**: Guy Hamilton. **Photographed by**: Ted Scaife. **Written by**: Robin Maugham, John Hunter, Anthony Squire.

Wolf Merton (Hawkins), a tank commander during the war, returns from a round of golf to find his home is being robbed. He is shocked to discover that the burglar is Ginger Edwards (Michael Medwin), a former enlisted man who once served under him. Ginger flees when he wrongly concludes that Wolf has called the police, and Wolf, wanting to help his former comrade, tracks down the other men (Cole, Price, Lamont and Howard) from his old regiment in the hopes that one of them will know where Ginger is hiding. During the film's multiple flashbacks, Wolf pieces together the events leading to the tragic downfall of a war hero: immediately after his return from the front, Ginger learns that his girlfriend has been cheating on

A troubled war hero (Michael Medwin) flees after attempting to rob the home of his former commanding officer in *The Intruder* (Ivan Foxwell Productions, 1953).

him; his little brother dies in a car accident; in a rage, he accidentally kills the abusive uncle who raised him and his kid brother; and after serving seven years of a ten-year prison term for manslaughter, he escapes and unwittingly burglarizes his former commanding officer's home. Hawkins does well in a mostly unexciting role, and Price is enjoyable as a gutless officer, now an arrogant businessman who enjoys flaunting his former military rank and wartime exploits. However, it is veteran character actor Medwin, with an amazing Jekyll-and-Hyde transformation from exemplary soldier to hardened criminal, who takes top acting honors in this marginal film noir that looks into the tribulations of a returning combat soldier.

It Always Rains on Sunday
★★★ (1947)

> BESSIE HYAMS: What's wrong with the East End, anyway?
> LOU HYAMS: It smells.

Length: 92 min. **Cast**: Googie Withers, Jack Warner, Edward Chapman, Susan Shaw, Patricia Plunkett, David Lines, Sydney Tafler, Betty Ann Davies, John Slater, John McCallum. **Production Company**: Ealing Studios. **Directed by**: Robert Hamer. **Photographed by**: Douglas Slocombe. **Written by**: Angus MacPhail, Robert Hamer, Henry Cornelius.

On a rainy and dreary Sunday in Bethnal Green, a neighborhood in London's working class East End, escaped convict Tommy Swann (McCallum) seeks shelter at the home of his former girlfriend, Rose (Withers), an ex-barmaid who is now unhappily married to George Sandigate (Chapman), a decent but boring man fifteen years her senior. (The highlight of George's week is a dart tournament at the local pub.) Brushing aside the legal and domestic consequences of her actions, Rose feeds Tommy and hides him in her bedroom, while George and the stepchildren, grownups Vi (Shaw) and Doris (Plunkett) and teenager Alfie (Lines), wander in and out of the house. Having served time at Dartmoor Prison for a botched "smash and grab raid," Tommy prefers death to recapture. So when reporter Slopey Collins (Michael Howard) comes nosing around the Sandigate home, the ungrateful jailbird, who has already rekindled his romance with Rose, shows his true colors by saving his own skin and leaving Rose to take the rap. Before the film's exciting climax—a chase scene through a dangerous railway yard—the viewer must first sit through several subplots: a love affair between Vi and Morry Hyams (Tafler), a music shop owner and part-time band leader; young Alfie's quest for a harmonica, which he finally obtains by blackmailing Vi and Morry, whose wife, Sadie (Davies), is fed up with his philandering; Doris' shaky romance with her boyfriend (Nigel Stock), who is jealous of the attention she has been receiving from shady arcade owner Lou Hyams (Tafler), Morry's brother; and the determined efforts of a wily police detective (Warner) to nab a trio of incompetent thieves (Jimmy Hanley, John Carol and Alfie Bass), who are trying to unload a truckload of stolen roller skates. A depressing film heightened by the seemingly constant downpour of rain and Slocombe's dark cinematography, the film ends on a low but hopeful note. The acting is excellent with Withers turning in a stand-out performance as the shrewish stepmother who melts like butter at the sight of her former lover and is willing to risk prison to help him escape. *It Always Rains* has been described by one prominent film historian as the "definitive" British film noir.

It Takes a Thief
see *The Challenge*

Jassy
★★ (1947)

> There's no need to be mealy-mouthed about it. That's your mother all over again. Sweet. Sweet and rotten. Sweet as honey and full of poison.
> [Nick Helmar to Dilys]

Length: 102 min. **Cast**: Margaret Lockwood, Patricia Roc, Dennis Price, Basil Sydney, Dermot Walsh, Esma Cannon. **Production Company**: Gainsborough Pictures. **Directed by**: Bernard Knowles. **Photographed by**: Geoffrey Unsworth. **Written by**: Dorothy Christie, Campbell Christie, Geoffrey Kerr.

After marrying the father of her former friend (Patricia Roc, right), a scheming former house servant (Margaret Lockwood) is confronted by the former friend and her husband (Grey Blake) after the older man's suspicious death in *Jassy* (Gainsborough, 1947).

Jassy is a confusing costume drama about a half-breed gypsy girl gifted with the "second sight," who manages to work her way up from kitchen maid in a small cottage to mistress of a mansion by wedding the middle-aged lord of the estate, the same man who drunkenly shot and killed her godly father during a minor tenant uprising. The girl, Jassy (Lockwood), starts out working for the Hatton family, whose gambling addicted patriarch, Christopher (Price), has just lost his entire fortune to crass drunkard Nick Helmar (Sydney). When Jassy becomes infatuated with young Barney Hatton (Walsh), Barney's mother fires her but gives her a letter of recommendation that lands her a menial job at a private girl's school attended by Nick's spoiled daughter, Dilys (Roc). Dilys befriends Jassy but only to exploit her as a gypsy fortune teller to entertain her snobbish classmates. After being expelled for trying to run off with a soldier, Dilys goes home and takes along Jassy, who was fired for covering up for her. After meeting his daughter's pretty young friend, Dily's divorced father, Nick, quickly ends his affair with a bawdy kitchen maid, hires Jassy as his housekeeper to straighten out the incompetent staff and ultimately proposes to her, after apologizing for killing her father, of course. Jassy agrees to marry the old sod if he will sign over the estate to her. He foolishly does so and then learns that she has no intention of consummating the marriage. Next, Jassy hires mute peasant girl Lindy Wicks (Cannon), referred to by the other servants as "the loony," whose inability to speak was brought about by her brutish father's use of a horse whip to punish her. The simple-minded but grateful Lindy, it turns out, will do just about anything for her new mistress. On and on it goes until somebody is murdered and Jassy is charged with the crime and placed on trial. Without divulging too much, it can be said charitably that the courtroom climax is laughable and the ending forced and unbelievable. Who would have thought that a movie filmed in glorious Technicolor and starring such capable actresses as Lockwood and Roc could be this dull, despite a plethora of noirish plot elements, such as murder, suicide, gambling, alcoholism, adultery, guilt, promiscuity and physical abuse?

Jigsaw
★★★½ (1962)

If she hasn't learned how to wait, she's the wrong girl for a copper. [Det. Inspector Fellows]

Length: 108 min. **Cast:** Jack Warner, Ronald Lewis, Yolande Donlan, Michael Goodliffe, Moira Redmond. **Production Company:** Figaro Films. **Directed by:** Val Guest. **Photographed by:** Arthur Grant. **Written by:** Val Guest.

Jigsaw opens in a bedroom of a house located five miles outside the English city of Brighton. A pretty woman (Redmond) discusses relationship problems with a man whose face the camera does not show. She tells him that she's three months pregnant and that it's time to inform his wife of their affair. This turns out to be a deadly mistake. The man strangles her and begins to chop up her body into small pieces for the furnace (all of this occurs off-screen, of course). Unable to finish the job, he stuffs the remaining body parts in a trunk, which is discovered by Brighton police detectives Inspector Fellows (Warner) and Sgt. Wilks (Lewis), who are investigating a burglary at the real estate office that managed the house. Among the items stolen from the office, the detectives later learn, is the lease with the killer's signature. Fellows and Wilks begin a long and arduous murder investigation as they attempt to put together the many clues they hope will lead to the killer. Pieces of the jigsaw puzzle include a lonely spinster (Donlan) who once was seduced by the killer and a convicted sex criminal (Goodliffe) who uses his job as a vacuum cleaner salesman to meet lonely and willing housewives. Based on the play "Sleep Long My Lovely" by Hilary Waugh, this police procedural is reminiscent of the American classic film noir *Naked City*, revolving around a grueling murder investigation by a crusty middle-aged detective and his younger assistant. Like their counterparts in *Naked City*, the two cops do a lot of pavement pounding that often promises more than it delivers; yet they persist. The film's fast-pace storyline, which includes several flashbacks, never seems to let up and eventually delivers the goods with a stunning climax at the Brighton police station. Veteran British character actor Warner is perfectly cast as the determined cop, and Donlan (director Guest's wife) gives a gripping performance as the forlorn woman taken in by the charming killer.

Joe MacBeth
★★½ (1955)

You can't stop what's coming, Joe. You can only get in the way. [Lily MacBeth]

Length: 90 min. **Cast:** Paul Douglas, Ruth Roman, Bonar Colleano, Grégoire Aslan, Sid James, Minerva Pious. **Production Company:** Film Locations. **Directed by:** Ken Hughes. **Photographed by:** Basil Emmott. **Written by:** Philip Yordan.

Newlywed gangster Joe MacBeth (Douglas) heeds the advice of his ruthlessly ambitious bride, Lily (Roman), and murders his boss, Duca (Aslan), putting the finger on Banky (James), Joe's loyal ally and friend. Afterward, Joe becomes the self-proclaimed underworld "kingpin" of an American city that, judging from the elevated train tracks, appears to be Chicago. Despite the seemingly blind obedience and acceptance by Duca's hoods, the new boss begins to experience bouts of paranoia, triggering in him yet another wave of violence, and he hires two out-of-town hit men to kill Banky. The goons go too far, however, and also murder Banky's daughter-in-law and infant grandchild, prompting Banky's son, mob soldier Lennie (Colleano), to seek revenge. The filmmakers updated Shakespeare's *Macbeth* to modern times and gave it a 1930s American-style gangster setting. What works well are the clever sequences in which the name of a local nightclub changes with the murder of each owner—

Mobster Joe MacBeth's loyal underling (Sid James, seated) tries to dissuade his hot-headed son (Bonear Colleano, right) from stirring up rebellion among his fellow mob soldiers in *Joe MacBeth* (Film Locations, 1955).

"Tommy's" becomes "Duca's" after Duca has Joe poison his rival and then changes to "Mac's" after Joe knifes Duca during an early morning swim. What also works well is the acting. Americans Douglas, Roman, and Colleano, and British actor James are the glue that keeps the film together, giving it its fascinating, if oddball, quality. Something that doesn't work well, however, is the character of Rosie (Pious), the Tarot card reader and street vendor, whose inane character is supposed to correspond to the three hags of Shakespeare's play.

Johnny Nobody
✯✯ (1961)

The only people qualified to talk about sin are sinners like myself. [James Mulcahy]

Length: 88 min. **Cast**: Nigel Patrick, Yvonne Mitchell, William Bendix, Aldo Ray. **Production Company**: Viceroy Films. **Directed by**: Nigel Patrick. **Photographed by**: Ted Moore. **Written by**: Patrick Kirwan.

James Mulcahy (Bendix), a hard-drinking writer living as an outsider in a small Irish village, takes sadistic pleasure in provoking the locals with his blasphemous proclamations. He goes too far one day and, in front of a crowd of angry onlookers and the village priest, Fr. Edward Carey (Patrick), he drunkenly dares God to prove His existence by striking him dead, whereupon a stranger (Ray) appears out of nowhere and puts a bullet in the defiant atheist's back. When asked by the priest who he is and why he has murdered the man, the stranger replies that he is "nobody" and that a voice told him to "destroy that man." Claiming to be suffering from amnesia about events prior to the shooting, "Johnny Nobody," as the press has dubbed him, stands trial in Dublin. His shaky defense (that the mysterious voice telling him to kill Mulcahy must have belonged to God) seems to be reasonable enough to the many Irish citizens who see him as a hero and are clamoring for a not guilty verdict. When Fr. Carey is grilled on the stand by Johnny's counsel and asked if he thinks a miracle has occurred, the presiding judge at first refuses to allow the question but delays his final decision until after the weekend recess. Carey, whose village has become a popular tourist attraction since the killing, is forced to examine his conscience during the next forty-eight hours. With journalist Mary Floyd (Mitchell) following him around, the priest tries to learn something about the amnesiac killer. What Carey discovers proves hazardous to his health, and he becomes a fugitive on the run from the police, a frame-up victim trying desperately to get back to Dublin before the jury reaches a verdict. The best thing about *Johnny Nobody* is the excellent cast the film's director and star, Patrick, has brought together. The plot is absolute nonsense and at times insulting to the Irish, who are portrayed as a bunch of superstitious vigilantes quick to attack anyone who mocks their religious beliefs. The Irish criminal justice system doesn't fare much better and is shown to be easily misled by the religious ramifications of an open-and-shut murder case. The film premiered in the United States in 1965, nearly a year after the death of 58-year-old American actor Bendix, a noir veteran who had seen much better roles during his illustrious career.

Jungle Street
(U.S. Title: *Jungle Street Girls*)
★★ (1961)

Things're getting warmer and me tongue is getting loose. [blackmailer Joe Lucas]

Length: 82 min. **Cast:** David McCallum, Kenneth Cope, Jill Ireland, Brian Weske, John Chandos, Martin Sterndale, Howard Pays. **Production Company:** Theatrecraft. **Directed by:** Charles Saunders. **Photographed by:** Jimmy W. Harvey. **Written by:** Alexander Doré.

London loser Terry Collins (McCallum) gun butts an elderly mugging victim, accidentally killing the man. Investigating the crime are Inspector Bowen (Sterndale) and Sgt. Pelling (Pays), who plan to take the fingerprints of all the locals living in Terry's district. The edgy killer, meanwhile, takes up with a former pal, recently released convict Johnnie Calvert (Cope), who took a jail term for robbery without squealing about Terry's participation in the crime. The jailbird is not happy to learn that while he was in prison Terry lost the stolen loot on the horses. Terry, however, convinces Johnnie to help him break into the safe at The Adam & Eve Club, a strip joint on Jungle Street where Johnnie's girl, Sue (Ireland), performs and fends off advances by the club's middle-aged owner, Jacko Fielding (Chandos). In the meantime, club employee Joe Lucas (Weske) has figured out that Terry is the killer sought by police and decides to blackmail him. McCallum gives an outrageously high-strung performance as the cowardly thug who doesn't like people laughing at him, especially women. Cope is more low-key in his role of the patsy jailbird who manages to last about 24 hours on the outside without committing a major crime. This is a fair-to-middling B-crime movie that offers viewers a sneak peak at a young David McCallum in his pre–*Man from U.N.C.L.E.* days.

Jungle Street Girls
see *Jungle Street*

The Key (U.S. Title: *Stella*)
★★★½ (1958)

War has nothing noble or sensible about it. It's simply an epidemic of madness and anyone who takes part in it is a lunatic and a murderer. [Capt. Van Dam]

Length: 134 min. **Cast:** William Holden, Sophia Loren, Trevor Howard, Oskar Homolka, Kieron Moore, Bernard Lee. **Production Company:** Open Road Films. **Directed by:** Carol Reed. **Photographed by:** Oswald Morris. **Written by:** Carl Foreman.

Just prior to America's entry into the war, American David Ross (Holden), a former tugboat captain and a now a sergeant in the Canadian Army, is sent to Westport, England, to command a rescue tugboat operated by the Salvage Service, popularly known as the "Red Cross of the Ocean." The job of the salvage crews is to tow back to port the "lame duck" ships that have been badly damaged by German aircraft or U-boats. Unfortunately, the poorly armed tugboats often become sitting ducks for the Germans, who lay in wait for the rescuers' inevitable arrival. Coincidentally, Ross' old friend, Chris Ford (Howard), is also a captain in the Service and the two have a grand reunion. Ford invites Ross to his two-room flat, a prize in a town where tugboat crews must share six to a room at the local fleabag, and introduces him to his girlfriend, Stella (Loren), who, Ross later learns, apparently comes with the lease. Due to the tugboat crews' high mortality rate, it has become a tradition for Stella's current boyfriend, always a tugboat captain (and Ford is number three), to pass the apartment key on to a comrade, just in case. Although he has fallen in love with Stella and plans to marry her, Ford seems relieved to be able to turn over his duplicate key to his best friend and makes Ross promise that, should the worst happen, he will do the same someday to ensure that Stella is taken care of. Meanwhile, the beautiful Swiss-Italian girl, who has never gotten over the death of her first Salvage Service fiancé, seems to have stoically accepted her role as a romantic perquisite of the rent payer. She has come to believe, however, that the men who fall in love with her are destined to die at sea. *The Key* is not your average war movie (although there is plenty of action for those so inclined) and, with its bleak ambience and cynical and paranoid characters, is considered by at least one respected film historian to be a film noir. Its storyline, at times, is Twilight Zone-like spooky, but preventing the plot from becoming too implausible are the terrific performances of British film veteran Howard (who won a Best Actor BAFTA award for his role), American actor Holden and latest Hollywood sensation, Italian actress Loren in an early English-speaking role. Lee plays the officer-in-charge of the rescue operations, and Homolka is the religious tugboat captain who warns Ross that a "bad kind of woman" will bring him bad luck.

Kill Her Gently
★★ (1957)

> We broke away without killing anybody and we're not going to start now. We're not clean, but we don't have to get messy. [Escaped convict Connors]

Length: 63 min. **Cast:** Griffith Jones, Maureen Connell, Marc Lawrence, George Mikell, Shay Gorman, Marianne Brauns. **Production Company:** Fortress Productions. **Directed by:** Charles Saunders. **Photographed by:** Walter J. Harvey. **Written by:** Paul Erickson.

Fate arranges a meeting on a dark country road between musician Jeff Martin (Jones) and two escaped convicts, American William Connors (Lawrence), serving twelve years for armed robbery, and Swede Lars Svenson (Mikell), doing eight years for his role in a bank heist that resulted in a customer's death. Martin helps the desperate men get through a police barricade because he has a proposition for them —£1,000, a getaway vehicle and help in obtaining phony passports if they will murder his wife, Kay (Connell). Martin, a former mental patient, wrongly believes his wife had him committed because she was having an affair with the family doctor, Jimmy Landers (Gorman). Pretending to be their hostage, Martin brings the men home, where they wait for the bank to open the next morning so he can withdraw the blood money. The plan begins to go bad when Martin learns that his pretty young maid, Raina (Brauns), whom he had recently fired, is still in her apartment over the garage, and Connors, who hasn't seen a woman in years, seems more than a little interested in making her acquaintance. Meanwhile, Kay, who is determined to escape, senses that the young Swede may have a conscience and pleads with him to help her. The promising script suffers from weak performances, especially by Connell, who overdoes the hostage act with persistent screaming and ridiculously futile escape attempts. (Why no one ever bothers to disconnect the telephone outside her bedroom is anyone's guess). Even character actor Lawrence, a veteran baddie of numerous American crime movies and films noirs, seems lethargic as the desperate convict.

Kill Me Tomorrow
★★½ (1957)

You're scared, aren't you? Been squealing again, huh? Brother, if the price is right you sing like a bird, dontcha? [Bart Crosbie to stool pigeon Nikko]

Length: 80 min. **Cast:** Pat O'Brien, Lois Maxwell, George Coulouris, Freddie Mills, Ronald Adam, Wensley Pithey, Claude Kingston. **Production Company:** Delta Films. **Directed by:** Terence Fisher. **Photographed by:** Geoffrey Faithfull. **Written by:** Robert Falconer, Manning O'Brine.

American Bart Crosbie, a middle-aged, rum-dum reporter, is fired from the London Clarion. Soon afterward, he witnesses the murder of his former editor (Adam) by jewel thieves Heinz Webber (Coulouris) and Waxy Lister (Mills). Rather than go to the police, Crosbie blackmails the killers, offering to take the murder rap for enough money to pay for an eye operation for his young son, who is going blind. Webber and Lister agree but when Scotland Yard Inspector Lane (Pithey) refuses to accept Crosbie's confession, the crooks kidnap young Jimmy Crosbie (Kingston) as insurance. With a little help from reporter Jill Brook (Maxwell), Bart forgets about booze for awhile and goes after his son's kidnappers. *Kill Me* is a fast-paced crime drama with middle-aged American actor O'Brien trying his best to be convincing as the two-fisted romantic interest for Maxwell, who later won fame as British intelligence's dowdy secretary, Miss Moneypenny, in the James Bond films.

Lady in Distress
see *A Window in London*

Lady of Vengeance
★★ (1957)

He's blood-walked his way across two continents. [William Marshall about Larry Shaw]

Length: 74 min. **Cast:** Dennis O'Keefe, Ann Sears, Anton Diffring, Patrick Barr, Vernon Greeves, Eileen Elton. **Production Company:** Rich and Rich. **Directed by:** Burt Balaban. **Photographed by:** Ian Struthers. **Written by:** Irve Tunick.

The American publisher of The London Clarion, William T. Marshall (American actor O'Keefe), learns that his ward, Melissa Collins (Elton), has leaped to her death in front of a train, just two years after he kicked her out of his home for having an affair with playboy musician and blackmailer Larry Shaw (Greeves). After Inspector Madden (Barr) brings him to the morgue to identify the body, Marshall receives a letter written by Melissa just prior to her death asking that he take revenge against the man who destroyed her life. In response, Marshall convinces criminal mastermind and avid philatelist Karnak (Diffring) to come up with a foolproof and sadistic plan that will cause the intended victim to suffer a series of increasingly severe "emotional impacts" before the *coup de grace* is administered by Marshall himself. Reluctant at first, even when threatened with blackmail, Karnak eagerly accepts the job when Marshall offers him as payment an extremely rare stamp that would be the centerpiece of his already priceless stamp collection. While Marshall is carrying out the last phase of his scheme, his loyal and loving secretary, Katie (Sears), and Inspector Madden rush to stop him. After a dramatic beginning (Melissa's suicide), the potentially interesting film falls apart as a result of lackluster direction and acting and a disappointing surprise ending.

The Large Rope
(U.S. Title: *The Long Rope*)
★★ (1953)

INSPECTOR: Did he look like a murderer?
VILLAGE CONSTABLE: I don't know what a murderer looks like, sir. I've only ever seen photographs.

Length: 72 min. **Cast:** Donald Houston, Susan Shaw, Robert Brown, Vanda Godsell, Peter Byrne. **Production Company:** Insignia Films. **Directed by:** Wolf Rilla. **Photographed by:** Geoffrey Faithfull. **Written by:** Ted Willis.

Released from prison after serving three years for a crime he did not commit, Tom Penney (Houston) returns to his village a pariah. His best friend, Jeff Stribling (Byrne) and the village hussy, Amy Jordan (Godsell), both of whom who had framed Tom for Jeff's assault on Amy, fear he has returned for revenge. Adding insult to Tom's injury, Jeff is scheduled to marry Tom's former girlfriend, Susan Hamble (Shaw), on the day the jailbird arrives in town. When somebody strangles Amy, angry villagers, led by Amy's husband, Mick (Brown) and the local coppers, seek out Tom, who takes it on the lam, but not before paying a visit to his former best friend and ex-girlfriend. Entertaining at times, this low-budget Jailbird/Whodunit noir contains no big surprises.

The Last Page (U.S. Title: *Man Bait*)
★★½ (1952)

You've got to give me a hundred [pounds]. If you don't I shall tell about what you did to me last night. [Ruby Brice to her boss]

Length: 84 min. **Cast**: George Brent, Marguerite Chapman, Peter Reynolds, Diana Dors. **Production Company**: Hammer Film Productions. **Directed by**: Terence Fisher. **Photographed by**: Walter Harvey. **Written by**: Frederick Knott.

Working late one evening, London bookstore manager John Harman (American actor Brent) responds to some aggressive flirting by one of his clerks, Ruby Brice (Dors), and lives to regret it. Ruby's new boyfriend, ex-convict Jeffrey Hart (Reynolds), sees the harmless kiss as an

Homme fatale ex-convict (Peter Reynolds) pressures his new girlfriend (Diana Dors) into blackmailing her boss in *The Last Page* (a.k.a. *Man Bait*) (Hammer, 1952).

opportunity to blackmail Harman for £100 of his recent insurance policy cash-in and convinces Ruby to confront her employer with the demand. Harman, who is preoccupied with an upcoming operation for his invalid wife, shrugs off the extortion attempt as the folly of youth and refuses to pay. Hart, seeing that more drastic measures are necessary, tells Ruby to warn Harman that she will report his behavior to the bookstore's owner and makes her write a letter to Mrs. Harman to prove that she means business. When Mrs. Harman reads the letter, the shock kills her, and the inconsolable widower, not caring any longer, turns over his entire cash-in of £300 to the initially reluctant but now unrelenting little blackmailer, who foolishly attempts to cheat her boyfriend out of his share of the unexpected bounty. American actress Chapman plays Harman's loyal secretary, who has worshiped him from afar for years and now must help him out of the jam of his life. This is an average but entertaining blackmail noir but its big weakness is the blackmail victim's nonchalant response to numerous extortion attempts by his employee. Reynolds' sociopathic homme fatale is the film's biggest attraction.

The Late Edwina Black
(U.S. Title: *Obsessed*)
★★ (1951)

Sick people sometimes find funny things to worry about. They get notions, you know. [Dr. Prendergast]

Length: 78 min. **Cast:** David Farrar, Geraldine Fitzgerald, Roland Culver, Jean Cadell, Harcourt Williams. **Production Company:** Elvey Gartside Production. **Directed by:** Maurice Elvey. **Photographed by:** Stephen Dade. **Written by:** Charles Frank, David Evans.

Schoolteacher Gregory Black (Farrar) has been having an affair with his invalid wife Edwina's hired companion, Elizabeth Grahame (Fitzgerald). After Edwina's death, snoopy Scotland Yard Inspector Martin (Culver) shows up to inform the couple that Edwina's body will be exhumed and a post-mortem performed because the attending physician (Prendergast) has had second thoughts about his diagnosis of a heart attack. Edwina's devoted nurse, Ellen (Cadell), seems particularly pleased at this turn of events and even more so when it is discovered that her mistress died of arsenic poisoning. Inspector Martin knows that at least one of the three, all of whom stand to benefit by Edwina's death, must be the killer and sets out to trap him or her. Meanwhile, the stress of the investigation causes the lovers to turn on each other. *The Late Edwina Black*, based on a play by William Dinnie and William Murum, is a mostly tedious Victorian whodunit with a well-done surprise ending. The most interesting character in the film is the victim, who never makes an appearance on screen. Even the usually reliable David Farrar and Hollywood film noir veteran Geraldine Fitzgerald (*Nobody Lives Forever, So Evil My Love, The Strange Affair of Uncle Harry, Three Strangers*) come off as boring as a result of the mind-numbing dialogue. There is one unintentionally funny scene that relieves a bit of the tedium: after an argument about their reciprocal murder accusations, Gregory swears to Elizabeth on his dead wife's bible that he is innocent. This leads them to engage in what moderns now refer to as make-up sex (off screen, of course), but Elizabeth becomes furious when she learns the next morning that the "bible" was actually a dictionary. "Was that why you made love to me last night," she asks. "To stop me from saying what I think? Was that the idea? To make me shut up?" "No, it wasn't," he replies, "but shut up, you hear, shut up."

Latin Quarter (a.k.a. *Frenzy*)
★½ (1945)

I always put the pretty ones by the window. [Morgue attendant]

Length: 80 min. **Cast:** Derrick de Marney, Frederick Valk, Joan Greenwood, Joan Seton, Beresford Egan. **Production Company:** British National Films. **Directed by:** Vernon Sewell. **Photographed by:** Günther Krampf. **Written by:** Vernon Sewell.

In 1893, Dr. Ivan Krasner (Valk), "France's most famous criminologist," aids Parisian police in a murder and missing persons investigation that leads him to Paris' well-known Latin

Quarter, "the Mecca of artists of all nationalities." Artist Charles Garrie (de Marney) tells him the story of Anton Minetti, a mad sculptor and murderer whose missing wife had been having an affair with Garrie. The missing person mystery is solved during a séance conducted by Garrie's new girlfriend, Lucille (Seton), at Minetti's haunted studio. Atmospheric but tedious. Those who might prefer their Parisian mad artist noirs with more pizzazz are referred to the far superior American film *Bluebeard* (1944).

The Life and Adventures of Nicholas Nickleby
see *Nicholas Nickleby*

The Limping Man
★★ (1953)

He was a bad boy and somebody was out to get him. I got the benefit. He got the bullet. [Kendall Brown]

Length: 74 min. **Cast:** Lloyd Bridges, Moira Lister, Alan Wheatley, Leslie Phillips, Héléne Cordet. **Production Company:** Banner Films. **Directed by:** Cy Endfield (as Charles De Latour). **Photographed by:** Jonah Jones. **Written by:** Ian Stuart Black, Reginald Long.

Frank Prior (American actor Bridges) returns to London to visit actress Pauline French (Lister), a woman he had fallen in love with while he was stationed there as a U.S. serviceman six years earlier. Shortly after his plane lands, a limping sniper shoots one of the passengers just as Frank is asking the victim for a light. After being questioned at the airport by Scotland Yard Inspector Braddock (Wheatley) and Detective Cameron (Phillips), Frank catches up with Pauline and learns that she had been romantically involved with the murdered man and that she is high on the cops' list of suspects. While trying to prove Pauline's innocence, he uncovers a few dirty secrets about her, including her connection to a contraband smuggling operation for which she apparently is being blackmailed by the dead man's ex-wife (Cordet). After a promising beginning (the murder is photographed through the telescopic lens of the killer's rifle), the filmmakers resort to numerous red herrings right up until the movie's deceitful ending. The dialogue is hysterical at times. For example, when the theater manager asks the whereabouts of the stage door man, an employee replies, "He took his crutch and went downstairs," which prompts the ever alert Scotland Yard inspector to shout, "Did you say crutch?"

The Little Red Monkey (U.S. Title: The Case of the Red Monkey)
★★ (1955)

SPY #1: Sometimes I think monkeys have more manners than people.
SPY #2: People don't smell.
SPY #1: And that too is a matter of opinion.

Length: 74 min. **Cast:** Richard Conte, Rona Anderson, Russell Napier, Sylva Langova, Colin Gordon, Arnold Marlé. **Production Company:** Merton Park Productions. **Directed by:** Ken Hughes. **Photographed by:** Josef Ambor. **Written by:** James Eastwood, Ken Hughes.

A ring of commie assassins led by blonde bombshell Hilde Heller (Langova) is responsible for the recent murders of several nuclear scientists in London. Greatly embarrassed by newspaper reports about an accomplice monkey (!) seen at the crime scenes, Scotland Yard wants to ensure that the defecting Prof. Leon Dushenko (Marlé) arrives safely in the States with his briefcase of nuclear secrets. Superintendent John Harrington (Napier) is assigned to protect the elderly scientist at a small hotel while awaiting the arrival of the frightened man's American escort, G-man Bill Locklin (American noir veteran Conte). After a failed attempt on Dushenko's life results in the shooting death of a police detective, the cops move the scientist to a sanatorium and wait for a thick fog to lift at the airport. While Locklin is busy romancing the hotel receptionist (Jackson), the spies are desperately trying to discover their target's hiding place. They find an unwitting ally in nosy reporter Harry Martin (Gordon). This wouldn't be a bad little spy thriller if it weren't for the dumb monkey angle and the ridiculous

Locker Sixty-Nine

An American G-man (Richard Conte) in London is tortured by Red spies seeking a defecting scientist in *The Little Red Monkey* (a.k.a. *The Case of the Little Red Monkey*) (Merton Park, 1955).

surprise ending that relies entirely on coincidence.

Locker Sixty-Nine
★★½ (1962)

> P.I. CRAIG: Hey, if you print this it's going to make me look pretty stupid.
>
> REPORTER YORK: Oh, in the newspaper game the truth can sometimes be twisted.

Length: 56 min. **Cast:** Eddie Byrne, Paul Daneman, Walter Brown, Penelope Horner, Edward Underdown, Edwin Richfield, Clarissa Stolz, John Glyn-Jones. **Production Company:** Merton Park Productions. **Directed by:** Norman Harrison. **Photographed by:** Bert Mason. **Written by:** Richard Harris.

Craig (Brown), a cop-turned-private investigator, follows an intruder into the house of his client, wealthy London exporter Bennett Sanders (Underdown), and is thumped over the head after finding Sanders' bloodied body. By the time Craig regains consciousness, the body has disappeared. Craig calls his former colleague, Scotland Yard Inspector Broom (Glyn-Jones), who refuses to treat the crime as a murder until the body is found. Meanwhile, an anonymous tipster informs *Daily Sketch* reporter Simon York (Byrne) of the mysterious goings-on at the Sanders' mansion, and Simon convinces his editor to allow him to investigate the case of the missing body. York's investigation leads him to a number of suspects—Sanders' business partner (Daneman); a singer (Horner) at the Blue Parakeet Club; a food distributor (Richfield); and a brother and sister from Uruguay who have been seeking revenge against Sanders and the food distributor for shipping deadly tainted food to their village during an emergency.

Locker offers a convoluted plot with enough twists and familiar noir characters (nightclub singer, nosy reporter, femme fatale and a P.I.) to keep viewers interested until the big let-down of a climax. (Part of the "Edgar Wallace Mystery Theater" series.)

London Belongs to Me
(U.S. Title: *Dulcimer Street*)
★★½ (1948)

> MRS. JOSSER: I don't know what the young ones are coming to. I really don't.
> UNCLE HENRY: What can you expect? They're a doomed generation. Born doomed.

Length: 112 min. **Cast**: Richard Attenborough, Alastair Sim, Fay Compton, Wylie Watson, Stephen Murray, Susan Shaw, Andrew Crawford, Eleanor Summerfield. **Production Company**: Individual Pictures. **Directed by**: Sidney Gilliat. **Photographed by**: Wilkie Cooper. **Written by**: Sidney Gilliat, J.B. Williams.

An odd assortment of characters make their home at a Dulcimer Street rooming house operated by a widow who regularly attends séances at the South London Psychical Society in the hopes of contacting her dead husband. When one of the lodgers, a young mechanic who lives there with his mother, is convicted of murdering a female arcade cashier and is sentenced to hang, the tenants organize to collect thousands of signatures demanding clemency. The soon-to-be famous Attenborough stars as the naive lad who, while in the process of stealing an automobile, accidentally pushes a girl out of the speeding car, killing her. Sim and Watson steal the show as a phony spiritualist and a middle-class retiree, respectively. Thirty-six-year-old Murray, who seems to have made a career out of playing old men, overdoes it as a raving socialist, and Andrew Crawford silly-grins his way through the film as a police detective in love with Shaw. The film's numerous attempts at humor mar its otherwise noirish ambiance.

The Long Dark Hall
★★½ (1951)

> What good is the truth when it doesn't sound true? [defendant Arthur Groome]

Length: 86 min. **Cast**: Rex Harrison, Lilli Palmer, Raymond Huntley, Patricia Wayne, Anthony Dawson, Eric Pohlmann. **Production Companies**: Five Ocean, Cusick International Films. **Directed by**: Anthony Bushell, Reginald Beck. **Photographed by**: Wilkie Cooper. **Written by**: Nunnally Johnson.

Middle-class businessman Arthur Groome (Harrison), a married father of two, stumbles upon the body of his showgirl lover, Rose Mallory (Wayne), and soon finds himself accused of stabbing her to death. The prosecutor's case is composed entirely of circumstantial but damaging evidence that could be offset if only an unidentified witness (Pohlman) would come forward. Unfortunately, the man is a smuggler who fears the police will ask too many questions. Meanwhile, the real murderer (Dawson), a misogynistic psychopath who has struck at least once before in a dark London alley, begins stalking Groome's wife, Mary (Palmer, Harrison's real-life wife at the time), whose surprising marital loyalty the killer deeply admires. The title refers to the passageway leading to the murder scene, traversed first by the victim, then by the killer, and ultimately by the unfortunate adulterer moments before discovering the body of the beautiful woman with whom he was admittedly obsessed. As in similar American noirs, such as *Phantom Lady*, a protagonist accused of a murder he did not commit must rely on the woman who loves him and the detection skills of the arresting police detective (Huntley). Bushell, the film's co-director, plays a well-meaning but mostly inept lawyer. This Wrong-Man noir is nicely photographed and well-acted, with Harrison giving a strong performance. It suffers, however, from a script that contains little suspense and no surprises.

The Long Haul
★★★ (1957)

> Listen, you were serving in a pig house like this when I picked you up, baby. Watch out I don't drop you right back among the pigs. [Joe Easy to Lynn]

Length: 100 min. **Cast**: Victor Mature, Diana Dors, Gene Anderson, Patrick Allen, Michael Wade. **Production Company**: Marksman Films. **Directed by**: Ken Hughes. **Photographed by**: Basil Emmott. **Written by**: Ken Hughes.

The Long Haul 110

With the exception of a temporarily happily married trucker (Victor Mature, drinking coffee at right), appreciative diners eyeball a hoodlum's girlfriend (Diana Dors) in *The Long Haul* (Marksman Films, 1957).

American Army Corporal Harry Miller's discharge comes through while he is stationed in post-war Germany. Harry (Mature) wants to return to America but his English wife, Connie (Anderson), pressures him to make a stopover in her hometown, Liverpool, where she hopes that a job as a driver with her Uncle George's trucking firm will persuade Harry to give up his plans to return to America. Assigned the route between Liverpool and Glasgow, Harry soon becomes a victim in an insurance scam when crooked haulage contractor Joe Easy (Allen) and his boys hijack Harry's truckload of whiskey while he is busy romancing Easy's moll, Lynn (Dors), at a cheap roadside motel. Blackballed by the insurance company as a result of the theft and unable to find work to support his wife and little boy, Butch (Wade), Harry hires on with Easy. Before long, he finds himself estranged from his wife, who has learned about his affair with Lynn, and on the run from the police, who suspect he had something to do with the death of a trucker in a staged hijacking incident. Meanwhile, Lynn, who has dumped Easy and now works as a bar girl at The Congo Club in Liverpool, tries to convince Harry to leave his wife. Reluctant at first, Harry agrees after the angry Connie lets a dark secret slip. Before he and Lynn board a ship bound for America, Harry agrees to help Easy pull one more illegal job, a big one involving the theft of a shipment of furs. Two often underrated actors, British actress Dors and American import Mature, are surprisingly good in this highly melodramatic but fast-moving noir. The script leaves a lot to be desired with its hackneyed dialogue, but compensates for its weaknesses with its dark noir style, themes and elements.

The Long Memory
★★★ (1953)

> When I first saw you there in that place of bad people I knew that you were not bad. [Elsa]

Length: 96 min. **Cast:** John Mills, John McCallum, Elizabeth Sellars, Eva Bergh, John Chandos, John Slater, Harold Lang. **Production Company:** Europa British. **Directed by:** Robert Hamer. **Photographed by:** Harry Waxman. **Written by:** Robert Hamer, Frank Harvey.

After spending twelve years in prison for a murder he did not commit, Philip Davidson (Mills) seeks revenge against those who framed him — his former girlfriend, Fay (Sellars), who betrayed him to protect her drunkard father, and Tim Pewsey (Slater), a punchy ex-boxer who was involved with Fay's father in a fugitive smuggling ring. Fay is now married to the man who arrested Davidson, Scotland Yard Inspector Lowther (McCallum). The bitter jailbird takes refuge aboard a decrepit, abandoned barge and stews about the injustice of it all. Elsa (Norwegian actress Bergh), a pretty war refugee, enters his life and causes him to rethink his desire for revenge ... until he learns that Boyd (Chandos), the small-time crook he supposedly killed, is alive and operating a scrap metal business as a front for his criminal activities. Despite a plethora of familiar noir plot elements (a wrongly convicted protagonist is betrayed by a reluctant yet destructive femme fatale and finds the support of a good woman whose love causes him to seek redemption instead of vengeance), *The Long Memory* seems overly lengthy, the consequence of a weak script that portrays the resentful convict as a wishy-washy dreamer who has a tendency to falter when faced with the opportunity to achieve his dream of vengeance. In addition, the surprise ending is predictable and disappointing. Waxman's cinematography, however, is terrific, centering on dreary but spectacular onsite locations along the marshy banks of the Thames Estuary. Hamer's taut direction and the fine cast are big pluses. There are vague but fascinating hints of a homosexual relationship between gangster Boyd and his effeminate but menacing chauffeur/receptionist (Lang), whom the alert viewer will catch thumbing through a men's bodybuilding magazine. Also interesting is the film's similarity to the American noir *Moontide* (1942), in which the two alienated protagonists, Bobo (Jean Gabin) and Anna (Ida Lupino), find each other, set up house aboard a barge and provide each other with the incentive to seek some degree of normalcy in their seemingly ill-fated lives.

The Long Rope
see *The Large Rope*

The Lost Hours
(U.S. Title: *The Big Frame*)
★★ (1952)

> He was born in an icebox. [Dianne Wrigley about Paul Smith]

Length: 72 min. **Cast:** Mark Stevens, Jean Kent, John Bentley, Dianne Foster, Garry Marsh, Cyril Smith, John Harvey. **Production Company:** Tempean Films. **Directed by:** David MacDonald. **Photographed by:** Monty Berman. **Written by:** John Gilling, Steve Fisher.

Test pilot Paul Smith (Stevens), a former Yank in an RAF squadron during the war, reunites with his pilot buddies at the Golden Lion pub, gets into a fight with one (Harvey), is accidentally served a Mickey Finn by a clumsy waiter and wakes up in a cheap hotel the next morning with a hangover and a bad case of alcoholic blackout. When he reads in the newspaper that the man he fought with has been found dead, Paul smells a frame-up. He goes on the lam to find the real killer with help from his girlfriend, Louise Parker (Kent), and his best friend, Clark Sutton (Bentley). Paul's investigation threatens to uncover a smuggling ring whose members will stop at nothing, including murder, to prevent him from proving his innocence and exposing their activities. Foster plays one of the war veterans' temptress wife, whose charms are wasted on the uninterested murder suspect. *The Lost Hours* is standard whodunit noir enhanced by the hardboiled performance of American actor Stevens, whose impressive U.S. film noir pedigree includes *Between Midnight and Dawn, Cry Vengeance, The Dark Corner, The Snake Pit, The Street With No Name* and *Timetable* (which he also directed). Marsh and Smith, who play the investigating policemen strictly for laughs, have the film's best dialogue exchange: "We've been on the case thirty hours nonstop," Smith remarks, adding that "dawn is now breaking." "Well, don't get lyrical about it," Marsh responds.

The Lost Illusion
see *The Fallen Idol*

Love on the Dole
★★★★ (1941)

> You need money to get away. Not many get out of Hanky Park except through cemetery gates and even that costs you money. [Sally Hardcastle]

Length: 100 min. **Cast:** Deborah Kerr, Clifford Evans, Frank Cellier, Mary Merrall, George Carney, Geoffrey Hibbert. **Production Company:** British National Films. **Directed by:** John Baxter. **Photographed by:** Jimmie Wilson. **Written by:** Walter Greenwood, Barbara K. Emary, Rollo Gamble.

Along with their law-abiding neighbors, coal miner Mr. Hardcastle (Carney), his wife (Merrall) and their grown children, factory workers Sally (Kerr) and Harry (Hibbert), struggle in poverty during the Depression in the early 1930s while petty crooks and bookmakers thrive. Despite government promises of an imminent economic boom, conditions only worsen, but life goes on for the working class residents of Hanky Park, a district in Salford, Lancashire. In the Hardcastle household, Sally falls in love with Larry Meath (Evans), a young Labour Party dreamer, and 18-year-old Harry plans to marry his factory worker girlfriend. With lay-offs on the rise and jobs becoming almost impossible to find ("God, give me some work," cries the desperate Hardcastle family patriarch), the government takes the extreme measure of cutting the dole (i.e., the unemployment benefits), causing angry workers to attempt an ill-advised protest march. After Larry, the calming influence in the mob, is accidentally killed by police, Sally faces a difficult choice — allowing her loved ones to starve or, equally repellant to both her and her proud family, becoming the mistress of Sam Grundy (Cellier), a libidinous old bookie who can provide her father and brother (now married with a baby) with the jobs they need to survive. Adapted from the novel by Walter Greenwood, *Love on the Dole,* an off-genre, social-problem noir, is a depressing, realistic, and blatantly politicized look at the plight of the poor working class in Great Britain in the early 1930s. After a successful run as a play in 1934, a movie version of the novel was planned, but filmmakers were stymied by the British Board of Film Censors. The film, now considered a classic, was eventually released in 1941 but not in the United States until 1945. Scottish-born actress Deborah Kerr, in her first starring role, is sensational, exhibiting early on the talent and beauty that would propel her to international stardom in the 1950s and 1960s.

Lucky Nick Cain
see *I'll Get You for This*

Madeleine
★★★½ (1950)

> There seems to be something about your character that prevents you from acting naturally. [Mr. Smith to daughter Madeleine]

Length: 114 min. **Cast:** Ann Todd, Norman Wooland, Ivan Desny, Leslie Banks, André Morell. **Production Companies:** Pinewood Films, Cineguild Productions. **Directed by:** David Lean. **Photographed by:** Guy Green. **Written by:** Stanley Haynes, Nicholas Phipps.

In 1857 Glasgow, Madeleine Smith (Todd) has been meeting her working class French lover, Emile L'Anglier (Desny), behind her wealthy father's back. James Smith (Banks), however, has already decided that he wants his daughter to wed the very eligible William Minnoch (Wooland). Madeleine thinks William is kind, but the stuffy gentleman is certainly no Frenchman. Emile, a highly sexual and ambitious man, insists that he be formally introduced to the Smith family and not be forced to sneak around like a servant. When Madeleine offers to run away with him rather than confront her dictatorial father, Emile refuses. This slight prompts her to break off their affair and to accept William's marriage proposal. In response, Emile resorts to blackmailing her, using as ammunition the love letters she had written him during happier times. Not long after the extortion encounter, Emile becomes ill and dies, and the police determine that he has been poisoned. Madeleine, who claims that the arsenic she recently purchased was for cosmetic use, is charged with the crime. (Some Victorian women had the habit of using powder laced with arsenic to lighten their skin.) The Glasgow citizenry, outraged over the alleged murder, take to the streets, with the religious element especially hostile, referring to Madeleine as the "daughter of Satan." Madeleine's lawyer (Morell) has his work cut out for him in trying to convince the jury that Emile more than likely was despondent over the breakup and committed suicide. *Madeleine* is based on the true story of accused Glasgow poisoner Madeleine Smith, so the disappointing real-life ending cannot be blamed on the filmmakers. Todd gives an outstanding performance as the romance-minded Victorian lady with a genteel facade, who learns that she has been risking her reputation for a man who is more interested in climbing the social ladder than in returning the love she has to offer. Initially a very shadowy film, both in style and theme, it soon develops into a tepid courtroom drama during the second half. British noir veteran Elizabeth Sellars, in her second film, plays Madeleine's maid, Christina.

Madonna of the Seven Moons
★★★½ (1944)

Only fools pray. [Maddalena Labardi, a.k.a. Rosanna]

Length: 110 min. **Cast:** Phyllis Calvert, Stewart Granger, Patricia Roc, Peter Glenville, John Stuart, Jean Kent. **Production Company:** Gainsborough Pictures. **Directed by:** Arthur Crabtree. **Photographed by:** Jack Cox. **Written by:** Roland Pertwee.

Maddalena (Calvert), a teenaged student at a Catholic boarding school in Italy, is raped by a gypsy, and, after keeping her ordeal a secret, is sent home by the nuns at the request of her father, who has made arrangements for her to marry an older man, kindly wine merchant Giuseppe Labardi (Stuart). The story picks up years later when the couple's grown-up daughter, Angela (Roc), returns home to Rome after being away at an English boarding school. Upon her return, she learns that her mother is seriously ill and that she has run away several times over the years only to return with no memory of where she had been. Soon after Angela's return, Maddalena suffers another of her attacks. This time, the viewer is permitted to witness the transformation of prim and proper Maddalena into the fiery Rosanna, the peasant lover of Nino Barucci (Granger), a Florentine thief who is so happy to see her and the jewels she has stolen from her own household that he dumps his current girlfriend, Vittoria (Kent), whom he demotes to household scullery maid. The scorned Vittoria soon goes to work on Rosanna, planting the image in her mind of Nino and other women. Meanwhile, Nino wonders where and with whom Rosanna has spent the past four years, and is egged on by his gigolo brother, Sandro (Glenville), who suggests that she did not steal those jewels after all but that someone, a lover perhaps, may have given them to her. Angela soon arrives in Florence to search for her mother, her only clue being a drawing on Maddalena's bedroom mirror of seven moons and the name "Rosanna" uttered during one of her blackout spells. The vile Sandro, who knows nothing of Rosanna's other life, is only too happy to be of assistance to this wealthy and beautiful girl. Slow to get moving, *Madonna* eventually picks up speed around the time Maddalena suffers her transforming blackout, steals her own jewelry and takes off to Florence, leaving behind a confused husband and a traumatized daughter. The film is filled with darkly photographed religious symbolism and iconography, which Maddalena embraces but which her alter ego, Rosanna, seems to dread. Cast members, especially Calvert and Granger, do an outstanding job of making the far-fetched dual personality premise a good deal more convincing. Four decades later, Granger would call *Madonna* "fairly terrible" and "dreadful" but said that this and other films served wartime audiences well as entertainment and escapism.

Mailbag Robbery
see *The Flying Scot*

The Malpas Mystery
★★ (1960)

> Marshalt's ready for another double-cross. Only this time *you've* been elected the fall guy. Or should I say dame? [Gordon Seager to Dora Elton]

Length: 69 min. **Cast:** Maureen Swanson, Allan Cuthbertson, Geoffrey Keen, Ronald Howard, Sandra Dorne. **Production Company:** Independent Artists-Langton Productions. **Directed by:** Sidney Hayers. **Photographed by:** Michael Reed. **Written by:** Paul Tabori, Gordon Wellesley.

Released from prison after a wrongful conviction as an accomplice to a jewel robbery, Audrey Bedford (Swanson) finds life on the outside a bit more complicated than when she left: she takes a secretarial job with Mr. Malpas, a murderous hermit who wears a mask to conceal his identity; she finds herself being courted by Inspector Dick Shannon (Howard), the cop who arrested her; she meets her wealthy, long-lost father (Keen), himself a wrongly convicted ex-convict; and she is used as a patsy once again by her step-sister, Dora Elton (Dorne), and Dora's jewel thief boyfriend, Lacey Marshalt (Cuthbertson). And if that weren't enough excitement for an innocent jailbird, a private detective agency offers her an undercover assignment to spy on Malpas, who has just murdered one of his informants and dumped the man's body into the Thames. The only film in the "Edgar Wallace Mystery Theatre" series not produced by Jack Greenwood, at 69 minutes it is also the longest. After being cut to approximately 55 minutes to make room for American television commercials, the plot is almost unintelligible.

Man Bait see *The Last Page*

The Man Between
★★★ (1953)

> I was born to hang. [Ivo Kern]

Length: 101 min. **Cast:** James Mason, Claire Bloom, Hidegarde Neff, Geoffrey Toone, Aribert Waescher, Ernst Schroeder. **Production Companies:** London Film Productions, British Lion Production Assets. **Directed by:** Carol Reed. **Photographed by:** Desmond Dickinson. **Written by:** Harry Kurnitz.

Londoner Susanne Mallison (Bloom) visits her brother, Martin (Toone), a British officer serving in post-war Berlin. Martin is married to German national Bettina (Neff), a worried looking woman who has been meeting clandestinely with troubled war veteran Ivo Kern (Mason). Susanne is attracted to Ivo, a former attorney who abandoned his profession when the Nazis gained power. She soon learns that his romantic interest in her has been a ruse to obtain her unwitting help in kidnapping Martin's friend, Olaf Kastner (Schroeder), who is wanted by the East Germans. Susanne also finds out that Ivo is actually Bettina's first husband, who was believed to have been killed during the war, and that he has been threatening to expose his wife's unintentional bigamy unless she lures Kastner into the eastern sector. West German authorities convince Susanne to help them capture Ivo as he tries to kidnap Kastner, but their plan fails when Ivo discovers that he has been set up. So Ivo's boss, Halendar (Waescher), a gangster on the East Germans' payroll, decides to kidnap Bettina in the hopes that Kastner will enter the Russian sector to try to save her. Unfortunately, Halendar's goons grab Susanne by mistake, leaving Ivo with the task of getting her back safely to West Berlin, where he hopes the police will go easy on him for his past criminal "difficulties." The film's overly convoluted storyline and the questions it leaves unanswered are its weakest features. (For example, the viewer is never quite sure why the communists want Kastner so badly or what crimes Ivo has committed that have forced him to become a flunky for a small-time criminal.) Making up for this shortcoming,

A troubled German war veteran (James Mason) tries to help a kidnap victim (Claire Bloom) escape from East Berlin in *The Man Between* (London Films, British Lion, 1960).

however, are a classic Reed climax and the film's overall bleak and claustrophobic atmosphere, which is heightened by Dickinson's noirish cinematography in and around Berlin's bombed-out ruins. Not surprisingly, Mason turns in a strong performance as the morally ambiguous protagonist who surprises himself by finding redemption in the love of a former wartime enemy.

Man Detained
★★½ (1961)

HELDER: We must do something before he phones again.
BRAND: *If* he phones again. Suppose he goes straight to the law?
HELDER: He wants money, not a clear conscience.

Length: 59 min. **Cast:** Bernard Archard, Elvi Hale, Paul Stassino, Michael Coles, Ann Sears, Victor Platt, Clifford Earl. **Production Company:** Merton Park Productions. **Directed by:** Robert Tronson. **Photographed by:** Bert Mason. **Written by:** Richard Harris.

Small-time thief Frank Murray (Coles) assumes he has hit the jackpot when he breaks into the office safe of photographer Thomas Maple (Platt) and walks away with £10,000. Maple's secretary, Kay Simpson (Hale) calls the police when she discovers the theft and is shocked when her boss doesn't tell them about the money he had in the safe. It turns out that the dough is counterfeit and that Maple is in cahoots with hoodlum James Helder (Stassino). After Helder kills Maple to prevent the police from learning about the phony dough, Inspector Verity (Archard) and Det. Sgt. Wentworth (Earl) get a lead on Murray. They arrest him and charge him with breaking and entering, expecting they will soon be able to prove that he killed

Maple. Meanwhile, Maple's wife (Sears), who has been having an affair with Helder, learns that the murderer plans to shut her mouth as well. *Man Detained*, from the "Edgar Wallace Mystery Theater" series, moves at a brisk pace and is fairly entertaining. The climax, during which the gun-wielding Helder proves he is the worst shot in London's underworld, is especially enjoyable.

Man in Black
★½ (1950)

Danger stalked her in this house of terror. [The man in black]

Length: 75 min. **Cast:** Sidney James, Betty Ann Davies, Sheila Burrell, Hazel Penwarden, Valentine Dyall. **Production Company:** Hammer Film Productions. **Directed by:** Francis Searle. **Photographed by:** Cedric Williams. **Written by:** John Gilling.

This is a boring and inane tale about Henry Clavering (James), a critically ill yoga expert who is "obsessed with the fear of impending death," and his dysfunctional family. Clavering's sudden demise during an exhibition in his home of "physical catalepsy," is deliberately caused by his "merciless, vindictive, scheming" second wife (Davies), who, along with her daughter (Burrell), then tries to drive her stepdaughter (Penwarden) insane in order to steal her inheritance. Introduced by a mysterious *Whistler*-like character called "the Man in Black" (Dyall), this "story of intrigue and jealousy and murder" falls flat despite the presence of noted character actor James. B noir fans will see a similarity between this bomb and an equally bad American B noir, 1945's *The Strange Mr. Gregory*, which revolves around a stage magician's use of the infamous "Kalamudra Death Trance."

The Man in Grey
★★★½ (1943)

No matter how I have to do it, or who has to suffer, one day I'll get the things I want. [Hesther Barbary]

Length: 116 min. **Cast:** Margaret Lockwood, Phyllis Calvert, James Mason, Stewart Granger. **Production Company:** Gainsborough Pictures. **Directed by:** Leslie Arliss. **Photographed by:** Arthur Crabtree. **Written by:** Margaret Kennedy, Leslie Arliss.

During England's Regency period, young beauty Clarissa Richmond (Calvert) is pressured by her family into entering a loveless marriage with the very eligible Lord Rohan (Mason), an arrogant aristocrat whose only interest in the girl is her ability to bear him an heir. Once a son is born, Rohan takes the child away from Clarissa and hires servants to raise the boy at another of his castles. He permits Clarissa to do pretty much as she pleases at his other estate as long as she doesn't intrude on his privacy. When Clarissa runs across Hesther (Calvert), a former classmate now working as a strolling player, she invites the girl to be a nursemaid for her young son in the hopes that Rohan will allow the boy to come back home. Rohan refuses but once he gets a look at the gorgeous Hesther he permits Clarissa to take her on as a companion. Before long, Rohan and his wife's best friend are involved in an affair, while the unwitting Clarissa finds herself falling in love with Rokeby (Granger), Hesther's charismatic friend, a former plantation owner in the West Indies who is now a jack of many trades. The scheming Hesther, determined to become the lady of the manor, encourages the two to run off together. When that plan fails and Rohan decides to kick Hesther out ("Society has been pleased to resent your presence here," he coldly tells her), Hesther realizes that only one option remains. Regarded by fans and film scholars as the movie that made James Mason a star, albeit typecasting him for awhile as a villain, *The Man in Grey* is a well-scripted Period noir revolving around the familiar storyline of a sociopathic interloper (superbly played by Lockwood) who tries to destroy her friend's marriage for her own selfish gain. Calvert is believable as the "good girl" of the film and is perfectly complemented by Granger as the charming, slightly rascally "other man." Granger and Calvert have dual roles, also playing descendants of Clarissa and Rokeby whose meeting during World War II at an auction at the Rohan family mansion results in the lengthy flashback to Regency times. Mason, Granger and Calvert would team up again in 1944's *Fanny by Gaslight*.

Man in Hiding see *Mantrap*

The Man in the Back Seat
★★★½ (1961)

> When the law gets a dead body they never let it alone. Like maggots. Only maggots don't want to know where it comes from. The law does. [Tony]

Length: 57 min. **Cast**: Derren Nesbitt, Keith Faulkner, Carol White, Harry Locke. **Production Company**: Independent Artists. **Directed by**: Vernon Sewell. **Photographed by**: Reginald Wyer. **Written by**: Malcolm Hulke, Eric Paice.

Two young connivers, Tony and Frank (Nesbitt and Faulkner), mug a bookie (Locke) outside the Brookvale Greyhound Stadium. Tony, the supposed brains behind the plan, knocks the bookie over the head with a cosh (a blackjack-type weapon) before noticing that the money bag is chained to the man's wrist. They dump their unconscious victim into the back seat of his own car and take off into the dark London night, unaware that the bookie has left the keys to the money bag and chain back at the racetrack office. When they discover this inconvenient fact, they stop by Frank's home to get a hammer and chisel. Frank's concerned wife, Jean (White), insists that they take the man to the hospital. Realizing that Jean is right in her assessment that their victim looks like he is dying, the two spend the rest of the evening trying to get him to the hospital without getting caught. Like so many noir crooks before them, Tony and Frank begin to bicker, with Frank constantly reminding Tony that if the man should die it would be Tony, the more coldhearted of the two, who actually killed him. Tony, always thinking, has a remedy for that possibility. *The Man in the Back Seat* is a short but highly entertaining adaptation of an Edgar Wallace novel. The criminals' luck is almost too bad to believe, but director Sewell, scriptwriters Hulke and Pace and the two leads, Nesbitt and Faulkner, manage to pull off everything so smoothly that you might not realize the implausibility of the plot until the film is over. By that time, it's too late to wipe the smile from your face.

Man in the Dark see *Blind Corner*

Man of Evil see Fanny by Gaslight

Man on the Run
★★ (1949)

> I'm not having any stiffs in the house. [Charlie, a fence]

Length: 82 min. **Cast**: Derek Farr, Joan Hopkins, Edward Chapman, Laurence Harvey, John Bailey, Edward Underdown, Kenneth More. **Production Company**: Associated British Picture Corporation. **Directed by**: Lawrence Huntington. **Photographed by**: Wilkie Cooper. **Written by**: Lawrence Huntington.

After a former service buddy (More) shows up by pure chance at the London pub where Peter Burden (Farr) works as a barman and attempts to blackmail him, Army deserter Burden heads off to a jeweler's shop with his military revolver. Planning to pawn the gun to pay off the extortionist, as well as his landlord for past-due rent, Burden arrives at the shop and pulls out his gun at the same time that two robbers (Bailey and Underdown) pop in for a quick heist. The crooks knock the jeweler unconscious and one of them shoots and kills a cop outside the store. In the confusion, Burden slips away unnoticed but later learns that the store owner claims there were three gunmen, not two as the police initially determined. Stopping for a sandwich at a pub (a wrongly suspected cop killer on the run has to eat, you know), Burden is accused by a drunken soldier of stealing his money and flees in a panic when a constable arrives. He runs into an alley across the street, where he bumps into war widow Jean Adams (Hopkins) who, for reasons that are not clear even to herself, agrees to help him find the real criminals. (Her first act of helpfulness is to toss Burden's gun off a bridge only to have it land on a passing tugboat whose captain promptly turns it over to Scotland Yard.) The only clue the amateur detectives have to go on is that one of the robbers is missing half of his two middle fingers and speaks with an Australian accent. Later, when Jean stops into the same pub to make a telephone call, she luckily notices an Australian sounding customer with two missing finger digits. After following the crook to his hideout, she is arrested by Scotland Yard Inspector Mitchell (Chapman) but not before giving Burden, with whom she has now fallen desperately in love, the cop killers' address. The filmmakers rely completely on absurd coincidences in a desperate effort to make this movie work. However, other than the presence of 20-year-old Laurence Harvey in one of his earliest roles (that of Det. Sgt. Lawson), and some interesting social commentary on the post-war plight of British Army deserters, *Man on the Run* has little to offer. Farr turns in a good performance, but Hopkins expresses the same limited emotive range—surprise to wild-eyed surprise—throughout the entire movie.

The Man Upstairs
★★ (1958)

People are getting used to seeing the police pushed around. And everybody weeps buckets over these rotten little thugs whose fathers were boozers and mothers didn't love them. [Inspector Thompson]

Length: 88 min. **Cast**: Richard Attenborough, Bernard Lee, Donald Houston, Dorothy Alison, Patricia Jessel, Virginia Maskell, Kenneth Griffith, Charles Houston, Maureen Connell, Amy Dalby. **Production Company**: A.C.T. Films. **Directed by**: Don Chaffey. **Photographed by**: Gerald Gibbs (lighting), Gerald Massie-Collier (camera operator). **Written by**: Alun Falconer.

Around two A.M. on a cold winter morning, John Wilson (Attenborough), an emotionally disturbed scientist who lives in a flat on the

London police take drastic measures to apprehend a disturbed armed man who has locked himself in his room in *The Man Upstairs* (A.C.T. Films, 1958).

third floor of a London boarding house, reaches his breaking point while trying to get his broken gas fireplace to work. In his neurotic frenzy, he wakes up the other boarders, attacking one of them, the gossipy Mr. Pollen (Griffith), who tried to help him. The slightly injured Pollen overreacts and calls in the police. When two bobbies show up to investigate, Wilson shoves one of them, causing the cop to fall over the third-floor railing, critically injuring him. Wilson then locks himself in his room, where he waits nervously with a gun. Before long, Sanderson (D. Houston), a mental welfare officer, and a no-nonsense police inspector named Thompson (Lee) show up, along with reporters, the fire brigade, numerous constables for crowd control, and a worried Army officer with a canister of tear gas that can be used legally only during wartime and on foreign soil. Meanwhile, Thompson has rounded up all of the tenants and placed them in Mr. and Mrs. Barnes flat. Of the group, only Mrs. Barnes (Alison) has expressed concern for the welfare of her upstairs neighbor, the kindly gentleman who has been tutoring her children for free. The others, Pollen, artist Mr. Nicholas (C. Houston) and his overnight female guest (Connell), the elderly Miss Acres (Dalby), and Mrs. Lawrence (Jessel), the hard-drinking landlady, spend their time bickering among themselves. Sanderson's pleas to be allowed to continue his conversation with the armed man are ignored by Inspector Thompson, who seems determined to storm Wilson's room and the consequences be damned. Mrs. Barnes telephones Wilson's fiancée, Helen Grey (Maskell), who arrives at the boarding house to disclose that the scientist's mental problems were caused by a head injury he suffered in an experiment gone bad. Although Thompson allows Helen to talk to Wilson through the locked door, her efforts fail to convince her fiancé to surrender. The inspector, who has taken the drastic measure (for English cops, that is) of having a gun delivered from headquarters, prepares to send in his men, while Mrs. Barnes attempts to organize her neighbors to stand up to the cop in an effort to save Wilson's life. As can be seen from the preceding plot summary, a lot happens during the film's 88 minutes. Some of what happens is fairly suspenseful; the rest is merely a lot of chatter that tries to pass itself off as serious character development. The only character the viewer probably will care about is the mentally ill scientist, and, unfortunately, he is the one the filmmakers have neglected the most. Attenborough is wasted in the role. With very little dialogue, he is relegated to tugging wildly at the fireplace's gas receptacle and alternately looking worried and puzzled. Lee's police inspector is annoyingly wishy-washy, constantly postponing his decision to end the standoff with a possible cop killer as a result of being pushed around by a meddling superior and a couple of outspoken civilians. The ending, unfortunately, is as predictable as it is lame.

The Man Who Was Nobody
★★ (1960)

SOUTH AFRICA SMITH: Miss Stedman, I'm neither an escaped lunatic nor a sex maniac.
MARJORIE STEDMAN: Which just shows how deceptive appearances can be.

Length: 58 min. **Cast**: Hazel Court, John Crawford, Lisa Daniely, Paul Eddington, Robert Dorning, Kevin Stoney, William Abney. **Production Company**: Merton Park Productions. **Directed by**: Montgomery Tully. **Photographed by**: Brian Rhodes. **Written by**: James Eastwood.

A lawyer (Dorning) hires reporter-turned-private investigator Marjorie Stedman (Court) to find his client, James Tynewood (Abney), who disappeared after writing a rubber check at a jewelry store for an £8,500 diamond ring. When Tynewood's strangled body is found, Marjorie joins forces with a mysterious stranger who calls himself South Africa Smith (Crawford) to find the killer. Their search leads them to a floating roulette game run by a couple of diamond thieves (Dorning and Stoney) and to Tynewood's former girlfriend (Daniely), a rum-dum model with a guilty conscience. This entry in the "Edgar Wallace Mystery Theatre" series is mildly entertaining, but its main noir significance is the presence of a female P.I., albeit a rather soft-boiled one, who goes undercover as a beatnik and a gambler's girlfriend in order to find the missing diamond thief.

The Man Who Watched the Trains Go By (U.S. Title: The Paris Express)
★★ (1952)

Tell them not to waste any money dragging the canal for my body. [embezzler Julius de Koster, Jr.]

Length: 80 min. **Cast:** Claude Rains, Marius Goring, Märta Torén, Ferdy Mayne, Herbert Lom. **Production Company:** Raymond Stross Productions. **Directed by:** Harold French. **Photographed by:** Otto Heller. **Written by:** Harold French.

Kees Popinga (Rains), a mild-mannered, middle-aged Dutch bookkeeper, accidentally kills his boss, Julius de Koster, Jr. (Lom), when he catches the man in the act of destroying financial records and trying to run off with an attaché case filled with company funds. Without a word to his wife and two children, Kees takes the dough and catches the next Paris-bound train, realizing a life-long dream of visiting the French capital. Once in Paris, he contacts de Koster's lover, Michele Rozier (Torén), who pretends to be interested in helping him escape but is really panting over the money she had expected to con out of de Koster, who was on his way to join her before his untimely demise. Kees, proving the old adage that there's no fool like an old fool, falls for Michele but remains justifiably suspicious that she and her French boyfriend, Louis (Mayne), plan to steal the money he has stolen. Meanwhile, Paris police inspector Lucas (Goring), who knows that de Koster's death was accidental, is scouring the city for Kees hoping to capture him before he really does kill somebody, like Michele for instance, if he learns that she has betrayed him. Filmed in Technicolor, the film's bland script and direction ruin what could have been an interesting viewing experience. The transformation of the bookkeeper from easygoing daydreamer to wild-eyed psycho is just not believable. The acting is not up to par, either. Rains is a big disappointment, overplaying the small-town hayseed, and Swedish actress Torén's femme fatale seems to be an unintentionally perplexing character. Lom is enjoyable but his screen time is much too short. The banter between Goring and both Lom and Rains is filled with what the screenwriters must have imagined were brilliant chess metaphors but, like almost everything else here, the routine is overdone. On a positive note, cinematographer Keller provides a nicely done, expressionistic dream sequence. Look for French actress Anouk Aimée, future star of *A Man and a Woman* (1966), as a French prostitute.

The Man Who Wouldn't Talk
★★½ (1958)

MARY RANDALL: I've known other men who wouldn't talk, who died because they wouldn't. For good reason. They were good men.

MR. BELLAMY: There's great deal of difference, Miss Randall, between your husband, a prisoner of war who refused to tell how his comrades escaped, and a man charged with murder.

Length: 97 min. **Cast:** Anna Neagle, Zsa Zsa Gabor, Anthony Quayle, Katherine Kath, Leonard Sachs. **Production Company:** Everest Pictures Limited. **Directed by:** Herbert Wilcox. **Photographed by:** Gordon Dines. **Written by:** Edgar Lustgarten.

American Frank Smith (Quayle) is recruited by his government to travel undercover to London as a honeymooner, supposedly married to Eve Trent (Gabor), a secret agent. Smith is told he is to meet secretly with Professor Hovard (Sachs), a Hungarian biologist who claims he has vital information to share but only with an American virologist, which is what Frank just happens to be. It turns out that the guilt-stricken Hovard has helped the Russians develop a deadly virus they may eventually use against the West. Fearing for his life and that of his family in Hungary, Hovard makes Frank promise not to divulge the scientific information he has just given him to anyone but Dr. Blaylock, a prominent virologist back in the States. Frank agrees, giving him his solemn word. By now the two honeymoon impersonators have fallen in love, but Frank's resolve not to divulge the scientific information to Eve's superiors does not go down well with her. That night a shot rings out, and Frank is seen fleeing his hotel room. He is captured in Dublin and soon charged with a murder. With Frank facing trial, his solicitor convinces Mary Randall, QC (Neagle), to take his case, but Frank, remembering his promise to Prof. Hovard, refuses to testify on his own behalf. Things quickly go downhill for the defense when Yvonne Delbeau (Kath), who claims to have witnessed the murder, shows up in court to testify against Frank. An interesting but not very suspenseful courtroom drama with good performances by Quayle as the scientist who takes his word very seriously and Neagle as his frustrated attorney. Zsa Zsa does a good job of playing, well, Zsa Zsa.

The Man Within
(U.S. Title: *The Smugglers*)
(NR) (1947)

Length: 90 min. **Cast**: Michael Redgrave, Jean Kent, Joan Greenwood, Richard Attenborough, Francis L. Sullivan. **Production Company**: Production Film Service. **Directed by**: Bernard Knowles. **Photographed by**: Geoffrey Unsworth. **Written by**: Muriel and Sydney Box.

In the early 19th century, a smuggler takes in an orphan who grows up to hate him and later informs on him to the authorities.

Mantrap
(U.S. Title: *Man in Hiding*)
★★ (1953)

I'm not going to be on the run for the rest of my life. I'll be out of this mantrap for good. [Mervyn Speight]

Length: 78 min. **Cast**: Paul Henreid, Lois Maxwell, Kieron Moore, Hugh Sinclair, Anthony Forwood, Bill Travers, Lloyd Lamble, Kay Kendall. **Production Company**: Hammer Film Productions. **Directed by**: Terence Fisher. **Photographed by**: Reginald Wyer. **Written by**: Paul Tabori, Terence Fisher.

Suave London lawyer Hugo Bishop (Henreid), a former intelligence officer during the war, plays private detective at the request of a friend who wants him to find and help escaped convict Mervyn Speight (Moore), who was convicted of murdering a girl at a bombed-out lot two years earlier. At the time of his conviction, Speight claimed temporary amnesia but now says he is positive that he can identify the real killer; thus, the reason for his escape. Speight's ex-wife Thelma (Maxwell), a beauty editor at Venus Magazine, is fearful, however, that he plans to take revenge on her for divorcing him and remarrying. While trying to ferret out the real killer, attorney Bishop manages to stay two steps ahead of his old friend, Scotland Yard Inspector Frisnay (Lamble). There is no shortage of suspects— Thelma's new husband (Travers), her boss (Sinclair), and a romance-minded reporter (Forwood). *Mantrap* is a slow-moving whodunit with a modicum of noir elements. Henreid, a veteran of several films noirs, such as *Hollow Triumph* (a.k.a. *The Scar*), *Stolen Face*, and *Deception* and, depending on your definition of noir, *Rope of Sand*, *A Woman's Devotion*, and *Casablanca*, gives a disappointing performance as a lawyer who enjoys his work, especially the part where he gets to play kissy-huggy with his pretty secretary (Kendall), something he does every chance he gets.

Marilyn
(U.S. Title: *Roadhouse Girl*)
★★ (1953)

You've changed, Marilyn. You're hard. [Tom Price]

Length: 70 min. **Cast**: Maxwell Reed, Sandra Dorne, Leslie Dwyer, Vida Hope, Ferdy Mayne. **Production Company**: Nettlefold Productions. **Directed by**: Wolf Rilla. **Photographed by**: Geoffrey Faithfull. **Written by**: Wolf Rilla.

Vagrant auto mechanic Tom Price (Reed) gets a job at a roadhouse (a combination cafe, garage and gas station) owned by the mean-spirited George Saunders (Dwyer). Saunders also happens to have a beautiful but bored wife, Marilyn (Dorne), of whom he is extremely possessive. Like drifter Frank Chambers in the classic American noir *The Postman Always Rings Twice*, Tom becomes romantically involved with his boss' wife. When Saunders catches Marilyn in Tom's bedroom, he attacks her, and Tom is forced to come to her aid. His punch sends the smaller man to the floor, where Saunders bangs his head and dies. The lovers cover up the killing to make it look like the drunken

A drifter (Maxwell Reed) falls for the fickle wife (Sandra Dorne) of an abusive cafe owner in *Marilyn* (a.k.a. *Roadhouse Girl*) (Nettlefold Productions, 1953).

husband fell down a flight of stairs. What they don't know is that Marilyn's fiercely loyal maid, Rosie (Hope), witnessed the staged accident. A coroner's jury believes their story, and Marilyn inherits the roadhouse, which she turns into a hot nightspot with the help of Nicky Everton (Mayne), a wealthy playboy with an active libido, much to the chagrin of Tom and Rosie, who are watching the developing romance with more than a casual interest. Because of the low production values and mediocre acting, the similarity to *Postman* is merely superficial. A more accurate comparison might be made to some of director Hugo Haas' low-budget Hollywood B films, such as *Bait* and *Pickup*. Hope is almost robotic as Marilyn's possibly lesbian maid, and the awkwardly tall Reed, whose character seems a bit slow-witted, is not convincing as a loverboy. Dorne, who isn't bad on the eyes, does okay as the femme fatale, albeit a reluctant one whose primary failing after the deliberate cover-up of her husband's death, is her childlike tendency to manipulate friends and lovers to get what she wants. The final scene, although predictable, is nicely staged and photographed.

The Mark of Cain
★★ (1948)

> Sarah's going to die. They're going to put the noose around her neck. She's going to hang until she's dead. You can't run away from that, Richard. [Jeremy Thorn]

Length: 88 min. **Cast**: Sally Gray, Eric Portman, Patrick Holt, Dermot Walsh. **Production Company**: Two Cities Films. **Directed by**: Brian Desmond Hurst. **Photographed by**: Erwin Hillier. **Written by**: Francis Crowdy, Christianna Brand.

In turn-of-the-century France, two feuding brothers, Richard (Portman) and John Howard

(Holt), fall for the beautiful Sarah Bonheur (Gray). (The antagonism between the boys began as youngsters when Richard tied John to the bedpost and beat him, something John has never forgotten.) Successful businessman John wins Sarah's hand and brings her back to Manchester, England, as his wife, further alienating his jealous brother. The marriage, however, is not a success, with John embarrassed by his wife's lack of social skills and jealous of the attention paid to her by the young and dashing Jerome Thorn (Walsh). Richard whispers rumors in Sarah's ear about John's unfaithfulness, encouraging her to file for divorce. When husband and wife reconcile, however, Richard takes matters into his own hands, poisoning John and framing Sarah for the murder, all the while convinced that he will be able to get her off the hook. When his plan fails and Sarah is sentenced to hang for her husband's murder, John suddenly develops an "oh well, that's the breaks" attitude and concentrates on the prosperous business he has inherited as a result of his brother's death. But young Thorn takes to stalking the killer in the hopes that the constant harassment will pressure him into confessing. *The Mark of Cain* is a disappointing Period noir that promises much but delivers little. Portman, however, is dandy as the killer.

Marriage of Convenience
★★½ (1960)

FORMER INSPECTOR JOHN MANDLE: Interesting change. The criminal who tracks down the detective.

ESCAPED CONVICT LARRY WILSON: Don't you think the crook that catches the crook might be better?

Length: 58 min. **Cast**: John Cairney, Harry H. Corbett, John Van Eyssen, Jennifer Daniel, Moira Redmond, Russell Waters. **Production Company**: Merton Park Productions. **Directed by**: Clive Donner. **Photographed by**: Brian Rhodes. **Written by**: Robert Stewart.

Granted permission to marry Barbara Blair (Daniel), his supposedly pregnant girlfriend, convict Larry Wilson escapes from custody at the courthouse where the ceremony was to have taken place. It turns out that Barbara is really the stepdaughter of Larry's former cellmate, Sam Spencer (Waters), whom Larry has promised to pay £8,000 for Barbara's part in the charade. On the outside, Larry expects to hook up with his accomplice and girlfriend, Tina (Redmond), who has the £20,000 from Larry's stickup of the bank where she used to work. Unfortunately, Tina has married John Mandle (Van Eyssen), the Scotland Yard inspector who arrested Larry for the bank robbery! Bent on revenge and determined to retrieve the dough, Larry seeks out former Inspector Mandle, who now writes a newspaper column about his Yard exploits and operates a boat business. On the case is Mandle's successor at the Yard, Inspector Jock Bruce (Corbett), who is nursing a king-size inferiority complex as a consequence of Mandle's low opinion of his provincial background. This typically convoluted entry in the "Edgar Wallace Mystery Theatre" series is especially interesting for its look at a Scotland Yard inspector who has turned bad over stolen dough and a beautiful dame. South African born actor Van Eyssen does a good job as the dirty cop, as does Corbett as his paranoid foil.

Midnight Episode
(NR) (1950)

Length: 78 min. **Cast**: Stanley Holloway, Leslie Dwyer, Reginald Tate, Meredith Edwards, Wilfrid Hyde-White. **Production Company**: Triangle Films. **Directed by**: Gordon Parry. **Photographed by**: Hone Glendining. **Written by**: Paul Vincent Carroll, David Evans, William Templeton.

A has-been actor discovers a body and steals the dead man's wallet, which turns out to be a valuable clue to the killer's identity.

Mine Own Executioner
★★★★ (1947)

The world is full of neurotics. Absolutely full. [Dr. Norris Pile]

Length: 108 min. **Cast**: Burgess Meredith, Dulcie Gray, Christine Norden, Michael Shepley, Kieron Moore, Barbara White. **Production Companies**: London Film Productions, Harefield Productions. **Directed by**: Anthony Kimmins. **Photographed by**: Wilkie Cooper. **Written by**: Nigel Balchin.

A London psychoanalyst (Burgess Meredith) has an affair with his wife's best friend (Christine Norden) in *Mine Own Executioner* (London Films, Harefield Productions, 1947).

London psychoanalyst Felix Milne (Meredith) takes on a new patient, Adam Lucien (Moore), at the request of Lucien's wife, Molly (White), who tells him that Adam has "had a go at murdering me." Using a powerful hypnotic drug on Adam, Felix learns that as a P.O.W. in a Japanese camp the young man had been tortured mercilessly by his captors before killing a Japanese sentry and escaping. Now back home, Adam limps badly and suffers guilt as a result of his inability to hold out to the death rather than divulge information to his captors. Felix has diagnosed Adam as "markedly schizophrenic" and, although happy with the man's noticeable improvement, he is concerned for Molly's safety, advising her to avoid being in the dark with her husband unless she is close beside him. "Don't let him see you as a vague or shadowy figure," he warns her. Felix, meanwhile, has psychological problems of his own — he has feelings of inferiority about his lack of formal psychiatric credentials, which could lead to his termination at the free clinic where he volunteers his service, and has a tendency to bully his loving but clumsy wife, Pat (Gray). He also has been guiltily pursuing a sexual tryst with Pat's best friend, Barbara (Norden), who is married to the good-natured Peter Edge (Shepley). Both stylistically and thematically noir, *Mine Own Executioner*, which is based on screenwriter Balchin's novel, is fascinating stuff. Meredith turns in a bravura performance as the flawed but sympathetic protagonist, Gray is wonderfully low-key as his longsuffering but forgiving wife, and Moore is appropriately creepy as his anguished patient.

Mr. Denning Drives North
★★★½ (1951)

You could go a long way before you'd find a better mortuary than mine. [caretaker Wright]

Length: 93 min. **Cast**: John Mills, Phyllis Calvert, Sam Wanamaker, Herbert Lom, Eileen Moore. **Production Companies**: London Film Productions, British Lion Production Assets. **Directed by**: Anthony Kimmins. **Photographed by**: John Wilcox. **Written by**: Alec Coppel.

Soon after a vivid nightmare (an expressionistic sequence reminiscent of those in several American films noirs) about his own murder trial, aircraft designer Tom Denning (Mills) tells his wife, Kay (Calvert), about his recent visit to the flat of his daughter's boyfriend, Vic Mados (Lom), a ne'er-do-well immigrant with a criminal background. As told in flashback, Denning offers Mados £500 to leave the country, an offer that Mados accepts. But after taking the dough, he tells Denning that he will bring Denning's daughter, Liz (Moore), with him to the Continent. When Denning suggests that his daughter will never agree to accompany him, Mados responds with an evil grin and replies, "Suppose I told you she has already been with me?" Not a bright thing to say to an irate father, and Mados receives a well-deserved uppercut to the jaw for the flippant remark. Unfortunately for Denning, his knockout punch does more damage than he intended, as Mados' head hits the fireplace, killing him instantly. Denning disposes of Mados' body in the countryside, beginning a cover-up that will torment the unintentional killer to the point of contemplating suicide. Denning's anguish is not due to guilt, however, but is a result of his anxious concern that there has been no indication that Mados' body has been found. After Denning confides in Kay, the two visit the ditch on the side of the road where Denning tossed the body to make it appear that Mados had been a victim of a hit-and-run driver. When they find no corpse, Kay is relieved, but Denning realizes that he can never have peace until he solves the puzzle. While his business is going to the dogs, he takes off on a cross-country jaunt in an attempt to track down a band of gypsies he believes was in the area where he dumped Mados' body. Meanwhile, Liz has found herself a new boyfriend, Chick Eddowes (American actor Wanamaker), a patent attorney from Chicago, who becomes unwittingly involved in the case and is determined to solve it to make an impression on the Denning family. The reason Denning gives Kay for not going to the police after killing Mados is that they would have wanted to know what the creep had said to cause Denning to hit him. The newspapers would have had a field day reporting his daughter's scandalous behavior. (Why he couldn't have simply told the police that Mados had made a nasty comment about, say, his mother's combat boots, is anybody's guess.) But then there wouldn't be much of a story, and this film relies heavily on plot, with so many twists and turns that it's difficult at times to keep track of them. Highly entertaining (with Mills giving an excellent performance), and very well-crafted, *Mr. Denning*'s running time could be thirty minutes longer and probably still be suspenseful. Although Denning is not a sympathetic protagonist (as shown by his lack of real guilt over the accidental killing), viewers will find themselves rooting for him simply because his victim was such a louse. Lom, who always played scoundrels with remarkable flair, is excellent as the naive girl's lover.

Mr. Perrin and Mr. Traill
★★★½ (1948)

> I loathe the whole place and everyone in it... This place will sap your ambition. It will put out every spark of decency you've got. It will destroy you just like it's destroyed every one of us. [Schoolmaster Berkland to new teacher]

Length: 92 min. **Cast**: David Farrar, Marius Goring, Greta Gynt, Raymond Huntley, Mary Jerrold. **Production Company**: Two Cities Films. **Directed by**: Lawrence Huntington. **Photographed by**: Erwin Hillier. **Written by**: L.A.G. Strong, T.J. Morrison.

The pathetic world of Vincent Perrin (Goring), a stuffy, tradition-bound mathematics master at Banfield's College, a school for young boys, begins to collapse when war hero David Traill (Farrar) arrives for his first semester as an assistant in Perrin's math department and as the new sports master. Because of Traill's popularity with the students, Perrin fears that he is losing the loyalty of one of his favorite pupils and, worse, the affections, imaginary though they are, of Isobel Lester (Gynt), the school's widowed nurse. Egged on by his doting mother (Jerrold), the middle-aged Perrin can never work up enough courage to make his feelings known to the pretty Miss Lester, who views him sympathetically but remains romantically uninterested in him. Miss Lester does, however, take quickly to the handsome Traill. And the attraction is mutual. Contributing to Perrin's impending emotional breakdown is the tyrannical rule of the sadistic headmaster (Huntley), who seems to take great pleasure in bullying him in public. Then one day Traill and Miss Lester announce their engagement, and Perrin begins to gaze strangely at a hunting knife he impounded from one of his students. *Mr. Perrin and Mr. Traill* is considered by at least one film scholar to be a marginal noir containing "enough key elements to be considered." While these elements are scarce, the film manages to succeed as a noteworthy social commentary on the hallowed halls of the stereotypical private English school, portraying them as breeding grounds for rumor mongering, envy, discontent, mean-spirited pettiness and obnoxious authoritarianism. Farrar gives a nicely restrained performance as the embodiment of an apparently new breed of schoolmaster, while Goring overdoes it a bit as his threatened colleague. Huntley, a veteran of similar roles, is appropriately hateful as the malicious headmaster.

Murder at 3 A.M.
★★ (1953)

> I wish I had the brains to hold down a job like yours. [Mystery writer to Scotland Yard inspector]

Length: 60 min. **Cast**: Dennis Price, Peggy Evans, Philip Saville, Rex Garner. **Production Company**: David Henley Productions. **Directed by**: Francis Searle. **Photographed by**: S.D. Onions. **Written by**: John Ainsworth.

Scotland Yard Inspector Peter Lawton (Price) and his underling, Sgt. Bill Todd (Garner), seek a serial robber who always strikes at 3 A.M. and whose victims are always society dames on their way home from fancy London nightclubs. After the criminal kills his last two victims using a military style "commando blow," Lawton and his superiors come under intense media pressure to find the killer before he strikes again. Their prime suspect is Teddy King (Saville), a mystery writer who also happens to be a war hero and the fiancé of Lawton's kid sister (Evans), who volunteers as a decoy to prove their suspicions wrong. *Murder* is a predictable, low-budget police procedural with some noir ambience.

Murder by Proxy
(U.S. Title: *Blackout*)
★½ (1955)

> It's a big jump from garbage cans to mink. [Casey Morrow]

Length: 87 min. **Cast**: Dane Clark, Belinda Lee, Betty Ann Davies, Andrew Osborn, Eleanor Summerfield, Harold Lang. **Production Company**: Hammer Film Productions. **Directed by**: Terence Fisher. **Photographed by**: Jimmy Harvey. **Written by**: Richard H. Landau.

American war veteran Casey Morrow (Clark), broke and stewed to the gills, meets London socialite Phyllis Brunner (Lee), who offers him £500 to marry her. Casey wakes up in an alcoholic fog in the Chelsea apartment of artist Maggie Doone (Summerfield), where he finds a portrait of Phyllis and discovers that he is £500 richer. He reads in the newspaper that Phyllis' wealthy father has been murdered and that the woman he may or may not have married has mysteriously disappeared and is feared dead. Presuming he is now a murder suspect, Casey goes on the run and begins searching for the real killer. Among his suspects are Phyllis' con artist fiancé, Lance Gordon (Osborn); Gordon's goon, Travis (the perennially shifty Lang); Phyllis' widowed mother (Davies); and Phyllis herself, who eventually shows up to assure Casey that she is indeed his wife. Even American noir veteran Clark, whose charisma and acting skills have been known to salvage more than a few boring films, can do little to improve this overly complicated story. The screenwriters fail in their attempts to inject humor into the sluggish plot, while Clark's overuse of hardboiled dialogue causes some unintended laughs

("When he turns up, if he ever turns up, he's going to be the deadest man ever killed."). *Murder by Proxy* is a must-have for the Brit noir completist but it is a film that the average viewer might wish to avoid.

Murder Can Be Deadly
see *The Painted Smile*

Murder in Reverse (U.S. Title: *Query*)
(NR) (1945)

Length: 88 min. **Cast**: William Hartnell, Jimmy Hanley, Chili Bouchier, John Slater. **Production Company**: British National Films. **Directed by**: Montgomery Tully. **Photographed by**: Ernest Palmer. **Written by**: Montgomery Tully.

Having been wrongly convicted and imprisoned for a murder that never occurred, an ex-convict kills the supposed murder victim that framed him.

Murder in Soho (U.S. Title: *Murder in the Night*)
✯ (1939)

> So you double-crossed me. I fell for you and you made a sucker out of me. I thought you had class. I thought you were better than me and all the time you were just a stool pigeon for the police. [Steve Marco to Ruby Lane]

Length: 70 min. **Cast**: Jack La Rue, Sandra Storme, Bernard Lee, Martin Walker, Arthur O'Connell, Edmon Ryan, Googie Withers, James Hayter, Francis Lister. **Production Company**: Associated British Picture Corporation. **Directed by**: Norman Lee. **Photographed by**: Claude Friese-Greene. **Written by**: F. McGrew Willis.

Class-conscious Steve Marco (American actor La Rue), the gangster owner of the Cotton Club, a Soho night spot, falls for his new dance hostess, Ruby Lane (Storme), unaware that she is married to Joe (Lister), one of his more untrustworthy thugs. Marco murders Joe for double-crossing him and threatening to turn stoolie. Inspector Hammond of the Vine Street police station convinces the widow to stay on at the club and romance the love-smitten Marco and pump him for information that could prove he is the murderer. Meanwhile, reporter Roy Barnes (Lee) has also fallen for Ruby and can't understand why a nice girl like her would be interested in a slimy hood like Marco. This is simple-minded fare with too many failed attempts at comedy by Withers and Hayter as a nightclub act and by American actors O'Connell and Ryan as Marco's goofy but vicious thugs, Lefty and Spike, respectively. The acting is terrible, even by future Academy Award nominee O'Connell who goes way overboard with the Brooklyn accent. The 1930s' ambiance is heavy, weakening any claims of a film noir style, although noirish characters and themes are found in abundance.

Murder in the Night
see *Murder in Soho*

Murder on Monday
see *Home at Seven*

Murder Without Crime
✯✯½ (1950)

> I'm no good, Steve, no good at all. [Grena]
>
> Well, why try to be something you're not. [Steve]

Length: 76 min. **Cast**: Dennis Price, Derek Farr, Patricia Plunkett, Joan Dowling. **Production Company**: Associated British Picture Corporation. **Directed by**: J. Lee Thompson. **Photographed by**: Bill McLeod. **Written by**: J. Lee Thompson.

Stephen (Farr), a has-been novelist whose wife, Jan (Plunkett), has just walked out on him for cheating on her, visits The Teneriffe Club in Piccadilly Circus with his landlord, Matthew (Price), who introduces him to barfly Grena (Dowling). Stephen and Grena make a perfect couple—she's drunk and suicidal and he's drunk and depressed over losing his wife. When they arrive at Grena's apartment, Stephen has second thoughts about taking up with another woman on the very evening his wife has left him, so he brushes off Grena's advances and goes home. Grena, not one to take no for an answer, follows him to his apartment. Stephen seems to play much better on his home field and responds eagerly, but their lovemaking is interrupted by a telephone call from Jan, who wants to come home and make up. Concerned that Jan may walk in on him and Grena, Stephen tries to convince the clinging woman to leave quietly. She kicks up a fuss and a struggle ensues. She falls and hits her head on a piece of furniture. Meanwhile, Matthew, who lives downstairs, hears the commotion and heads upstairs to see what is going on. Hearing Matthew's persistent knock on the door, the panicky writer hides Grena's limp body inside an ottoman, but his shrewd landlord figures out what has happened and soon concocts a strange blackmail plan that has Stephen contemplating the merits of suicide. The acting in this thriller is certainly up to par, with Price entertaining as the pretentious and sadistic landlord and Dowling appealingly cheap as the bar girl. Farr gives an intense performance as the straying husband whose sexual conquests could result, in a worst case scenario, in an undeserved date with the hangman or, at the very least, the break-up of his marriage. Unfortunately, however, this otherwise dark and entertaining adaptation of a play written by director Thompson, is gimmicky to the point of implausibility. The film uses the common noir technique of voiceover narration to tell the story, but there seems to be no connection between the storyteller (evidently a visiting American with a Walter Winchell narration style) and the characters.

My Brother's Keeper
★★★½ (1948)

The biggest mistake of all is to get caught. [George Martin]

Length: 91 min. **Cast:** Jack Warner, Jane Hylton, David Tomlinson, George Cole, Yvonne Owen, Beatrice Varley. **Production Company:** Gainsborough Pictures. **Directed by:** Alfred Roome. **Photographed by:** Gordon Lang. **Written by:** Frank Harvey, Jr.

Facing a robbery-with-violence conviction, George Martin (Warner), a war hero gone bad, jumps from a police car, dragging with him the reluctant prisoner to whom he is handcuffed, Willie Stannard (Cole), an innocent young man wrongly facing trial for attempted rape (subtly described as his having "tried to interfere" with a girl). Willie has no choice but to play follow the leader as the escaping prisoners try to stay one step ahead of the manhunt that is slowly enveloping them. Martin receives help from the two women in his life, his longsuffering wife (Varley) and his mistress (Hylton), but their unenthusiastic assistance is of little use after he kills a hunter that stumbled upon him in the woods, causing police to double their efforts to capture the men. After Martin manages to hacksaw through the handcuffs, he quickly abandons his hapless and obtuse companion. On his own, Willie immediately gives himself up only to find himself charged with the hunter's murder. Only Martin and his mistress know that the lad is innocent and Martin has no intention of stopping to explain. The exciting long-shot climax, during which Martin madly flees dozens of fast approaching bobbies, is strangely surreal and only one example of the film's enjoyable cinematography. Jack Warner, who specialized in playing mostly sympathetic roles, is excellent as the Jekyll-and-Hyde jailbird who one moment is seen mercilessly ridiculing his tearful partner for acting like a crybaby and the next expressing sorrow for his callousness. A subplot intended to inject humor into the film's glum storyline involves a London reporter and his wife (Waring and Owen), whose honeymoon is interrupted when his editor forces him to cover the manhunt. A precursor to the American film *Defiant Ones* (1958), but minus the race issue, this fast-moving noir was the first of two directorial efforts by Roome before his return to his usual film editing chores, which included work on the popular *Carry On* comedy film series.

Mystery at Tiger Bay
see *Tiger Bay*

Naked Fury
(U.S. Title: *The Pleasure Lovers*)
★★½ (1959)

I always knew you were bent. I never thought you were *that* crooked. [Heist mastermind Eddie to ship's captain]

Length: 60 min. **Cast:** Reed De Rouen, Kenneth Cope, Leigh Madison, Arthur Lovegrove, Alexander Field, Tommy Eytle, Ann Lynne, Arthur Gross. **Production Company:** Coenda Films. **Directed by:** Charles Saunders. **Photographed by:** Jimmy W. Harvey. **Written by:** Guido Coen.

Robbers break into a warehouse safe and get away with £50,000 but not without difficulty. After knocking out the elderly night watchman and kidnapping his daughter, Carol (Madison), who witnessed the robbery, they hole up in their hideout on the top floor of a dilapidated building. Heist mastermind Eddy (American De Rouen) nixes the idea of killing Carol and promises to release her as soon as they are safely aboard their getaway ship. However, Johnny (Cope), who has a weakness for pretty girls, has other, less noble, plans for her. Meanwhile, troubles continue to plague the men while they wait for their chance to get out of town: Syd (Lovegrove) is blackmailed by his scheming wife, Stella (Lynn), for half of his share of the loot; Steve (Guyana-born Eytle) needs his money quickly for medical expenses for his son; Johnny is being forced by a former robbery accomplice, ex-con Tom Parker (Gross), to betray his friends and steal the dough; Carol's father dies in the hospital, prompting the ship's captain to raise his price for the robbers' safe passage out of England; and the precarious hideout, where the crooks' elderly accomplice (Field) works as the caretaker, seems ready to crumble to the ground. The acting is nothing to write home about but the brisk storyline is interesting enough to hold viewer interest until the nicely done special-effects climax.

The Narrowing Circle
★★½ (1956)

> NELSON: From what I hear, Miss Speed is everything I hate most in women. She's a careerist. She's hard and she's unfeminine.
> PACEY: You *are* mad.
> NELSON: Well, if it's insane to like your women soft and sweet and kind of dependent, okay, I'm mad.

Length: 66 min. **Cast:** Paul Carpenter, Hazel Court, Russell Napier, Trevor Reid, Paula Byrne, June Ashley, Ferdy Mayne. **Production Company:** Fortress Productions. **Directed by:** Charles Saunders. **Photographed by:** Jonah Jones. **Written by:** Doreen Montgomery.

Dave Nelson (Carpenter), a writer for a crime magazine, loses his promotion and his girl (Martin) to coworker Bill Strayte (Mayne). While out on a bender, Dave picks up a floozy named Christy (Ashley) at the Rubicon Bar and takes her to the Norfolk Hotel, where she leaves him to sleep it off. When he returns to his apartment the next morning, Dave discovers Strayte's body and calls Scotland Yard. Inspector Crambo (Reid) is assigned to investigate and makes no bones about considering Dave his prime suspect. When Dave takes the inspector to the seedy London hotel to verify his alibi, the desk clerk claims he does not recognize Dave and has never heard of a girl named Christy. A lie on both accounts. Before long the clerk and the floozy are murdered and Dave is the one who discovers their bodies. Crime writer Dave smells a frame-up and goes on the run in the hopes of finding the real killer, whom he suspects was being blackmailed by Strayte over a 15-year-old murder. Dave turns to Rosemary Speed (Court), a writer at the magazine and the only person who believes he is innocent. Although she risks being arrested as an accessory, she decides to help him clear his name, falling in love with him in the process. The storyline is familiar to noir fans — an innocent man is framed for murder and, with the aid of a beautiful woman, sets out to prove his innocence. Canadian-born actor Paul Carpenter appeared in a number of low-budget British films in the 1950s. Fast-paced and moderately suspenseful, *The Narrowing Circle* is one of his better ones, although like a number of his films it is plagued with insipid dialogue.

Never Let Go
★★★½ (1960)

> LIONEL: What's wrong with the club?
> JACKIE: Those tarts are too fat to turn around with nothing on.

Length: 91 min. **Cast:** Richard Todd, Peter Sellers, Elizabeth Sellars, Adam Faith, Carol White, Mervyn Johns, David Lodge, Noel Willman. **Production Company: Independent Artists. Directed by: John Guillermin. Photographed by: Christopher Challis. Written by: Alun Falconer.

With his monthly sales figures plummeting due to his late arrivals for sales appointments, London cosmetic salesman John Cummings (Todd) buys a Ford Anglia to avoid having to rely on public transportation. Just two weeks later the car is stolen outside his office by motorcycle gang leader Tommy Towers (Faith), who works for Lionel Meadows (Sellers), the owner of a garage business that fronts for his stolen car racket. When reporting the crime to the police, John learns that there's a good chance he will never see his car again. Because he had been unable to afford insurance, there is now no way he can buy another car. So, with his livelihood at stake, the mousy salesman begins his own investigation. Alfie Barnes (Johns), the slow-witted newspaper vendor who witnessed the theft, reluctantly directs him to the Victory Tavern where Tommy and his gang hang out. From here John is able to make the connection to Meadows, a violent psychotic who doesn't want this "lipstick peddler" nosing around and jeopardizing his operation. After Meadows' goon, Cliff (played by Sellers' long-time friend and supporting actor Lodge), beats up John, Mrs. Cummings (Sellers) tries to persuade her husband to abandon his obsessive quest to find his car. She's not very convincing, however, indelicately informing him that he has always been pretty much a loser who never finished a thing he started. "You're not tough enough, Johnny," she tells him. This, coupled with the seeming indifference of Inspector Thomas (Willman), increases John's resolve, and he goes after the car thieves with a vengeance, leading to a violent showdown at Meadows' garage. While not a sensational film (after its U.S. premiere in 1963, a critic referred to it as "nonsense" and its plot as "drearily routine"), *Never Let Go* is highly enjoyable for two reasons— Peter Sellers and Richard Todd, both of whom were cast way out of type. Comedian Sellers is surprisingly convincing as the violent gangster who terrorizes everyone, including his abused girlfriend, Jackie (White), and his cry-baby underling, Tommy, played by pop singer Adam Faith. Sellers has a tendency to overdo the psycho act at times, but his scene with the goldfish and the turtle should remain in viewers' minds for a long time. Todd makes the transition from romantic leading man to drab Caspar Milquetoast seem effortless. The only disappointment here is the usually reliable Sellars, who really didn't have much to work with in her role as the loving but tactless wife.

Never Mention Murder
★★ (1964)

All you husbands are the same. They call on blokes like me to do the dirty, you might say, but the minute they get what they're paying for they start taking it out on the bloke that got it. [P.I. Felx Carstairs]

Length: 56 min. **Cast**: Maxine Audley, Dudley Foster, Michael Coles, Pauline Yates, Brian Haines. **Production Company**: Merton Park Productions. **Directed by**: John Nelson Burton. **Photographed by**: James Wilson. **Written by**: Robert Banks Stewart.

Philip Teasdale (Foster), the resident heart surgeon at the hospital on Honeymoon Island, a resort for newlyweds, hires private investigator Felix Carstairs (Haines) to follow his wife, Liz (Audley). Carstairs presents his client with evidence that Liz has been having a fling with Tony Sorbo (Coles), who performs a mind-reading act with his wife, Zita (Yates), at the island hotel. Seeking vengeance, Teasdale replaces Tony's smoking-deterrent pills with pills that are known to cause a simulated stroke. After Tony is admitted to the hospital, Teasdale schedules him for an unneeded heart operation, which he himself will perform. Tony, who doesn't even know Liz's real name, suspects nothing, but Liz panics when she learns the identity of her husband's latest patient. Meanwhile, Carstairs, who has already tried to sell information about Tony and Liz's affair to Zita, becomes wise to Teasdale's plan and makes the mistake of attempting to blackmail him. *Never Mention Murder* is an interesting revenge film with Foster turning in a good performance as the remarkably blasé cuckold. (Part of the "Edgar Wallace Mystery Theater" series.)

Nicholas Nickleby (a.k.a. *The Life and Adventures of Nicholas Nickleby*)
★★ (1947)

This isn't a school. It's a hell on earth. [Nicholas Nickleby to Wackford Squeers]

Length: 105 min. **Cast:** Cedric Hardwicke, Derek Bond, Stanley Holloway, Alfred Drayton, Bernard Miles, Sally Ann Howes, Mary Merrall, Aubrey Woods, Jill Balcon. **Production Company:** Ealing Studios. **Directed by:** (Alberto) Cavalcanti. **Photographed by:** Gordon Dines. **Written by:** John Dighton.

When her husband dies, Mrs. Nickleby (Merrall) is forced to accept the unenthusiastic and paltry charity of her brother-in-law, Ralph (Hardwicke), a mean-spirited miser who promptly ships off his nephew, Nicholas (Bond), to work as teacher at a orphaned boys' school and gets his niece, Kate (Howes), a job in a sweat shop. It isn't long before Nicholas flees the school and its cruel overseer, Wackford Squeers (Drayton), taking with him Squeers' badly mistreated servant, Smike (Woods). The two wander the countryside seeking work and eventually take positions as actors with a traveling Shakespearean troupe led by the kindly Vincent Crummles (Holloway). When he learns that his Uncle Ralph has been taking advantage of Kate's beauty to stimulate business, Nicholas rushes home to his sister's side. There he meets Madeline Bray (Balcon), a pretty girl whose father has just been sent to prison for being unable to pay off a large debt owed to Ralph. Ralph, however, is quite willing to forgive the old man's debt if Madeline can be persuaded to take a trip to the altar with him. Meanwhile, Ralph's servant, Newman Noggs (Miles), gleefully tells Nicholas a secret about his employer that could send Ralph to prison for a long time. Cinematically pretentious and overacted by almost every player, this screen version of the Dickens novel has been described as a film noir by several prominent film scholars, who likely see the film's dark visual style and grotesque characters as menacing and evoking a sense of dread, adding more ammunition to the premise that film noir is indeed in the eye of the beholder.

Night and the City
★★★★½ (1950)

BOUNCER: Out.
HARRY FABIAN: What do you mean? This is a public place.
BOUNCER: So's the morgue. Move.

Length: 101 min. **Cast:** Richard Widmark, Gene Tierney, Googie Withers, Francis L. Sullivan, Herbert Lom, Stanislaus Zbyszko, Mike Mazurki. **Production Company:** 20th Century–Fox Productions. **Directed by:** Jules Dassin. **Photographed by:** Mutz Greenbaum (as Max Greene). **Written by:** Jo Eisinger.

London spiv Harry Fabian (American noir icon Widmark), small-time hustler, dreamer, thief, and loser, longs to *be* somebody, to give up his job as a club touter (i.e., a conniver who steers unsuspecting tourists to the Silver Fox, a clip joint owned by Phil Nosseross [Sullivan]) and finally make it big. Harry's latest scheme involves gaining control over the "sport" of wrestling in London, something shady wrestling promoter Kristo (Lom) does not consider to be a wise move. Harry, however, has conned Kristo's dear old dad, legitimate wrestling's legendary Gregorius the Great (Zbyszko), into backing his plan, thus ensuring his own safety when Kristo learns about his wannabe rival's plans. Harry's scheme must wait, however, until he can come up with the initial investment, and, as usual, he's not having much luck getting the money together ... until Helen Nosseross (Withers), Phil's wife and Harry's former lover, foolishly hands over £200 to Harry to bribe a government bureaucrat for a liquor license for a club she is opening in an effort to get away from her fat, groping husband. Harry double-crosses Helen by supplying her with a forged license, using the money to set up Fabian Enterprises. Noir fate steps in and interferes with Harry's plans once again, this time with the death inside the ring of the elderly Gregorius during an impromptu grudge match against Kristo's star wrestler, The Strangler (American noir veteran Mazurki). With his ace in the hole gone, Harry goes on the run, seeking refuge with his underworld cronies, whose loyalty and friendship fail him with the temptation of the large reward Kristo has placed on his head. Fearing Harry has gone too far this time, his devoted but longsuffering girl, Mary Bristol (Tierney), a singer at the Silver Fox, sets out to find him before Kristo and his thugs do. American film noir icon Richard Widmark is sensational as noir's most inept and pathetic hustler. Although the supporting cast is terrific (especially Sullivan and Withers) and Dassin's direction flawless, the film belongs primarily to Widmark in perhaps his best role and to cinematographer Greene (Mutz Greenbaum), whose skills are in evidence from the film's spectacular opening of Harry racing through the dark streets in a frantic effort to escape a shadowy pursuer. London has never looked seedier. Blacklisted director Dassin admitted decades later that, fearing he would be pulled from the film before having a chance to finish it, he did not find the time to read Gerald Kersh's novel, on which the film was based, until well after the film's release. As a consequence, the film was vastly different than the novel, and Kersh reportedly was displeased with the end result. In addition, an American and a British version of the film were released, the slightly longer British version containing several additional scenes and a radically different musical score. In 1992, a less satisfying American remake was released, starring Robert De Niro as the hapless hustler and the corrupt boxing setting replacing the wrestling backdrop.

Night Beat
★★½ (1948)

> You came from the gutter. Now here's your fare back. To me, you're dirt. Dirt! [Felix Fenton to Jackie]

Length: 91 min. **Cast:** Anne Crawford, Maxwell Reed, Ronald Howard, Christine Norden, Hector Ross, Sid James. **Production Company:** British Lion Production Assets. **Directed by:** Harold Huth. **Photographed by:** Vacklav (Václav) Vích. **Written by:** Guy Morgan, T.J. Morrison, Robert Westerby.

War veterans Andy Kendall (Howard) and Don Brady (Ross), who served together as commandos in the British Army, return from the front and, like thousands of other vets, wonder where they will be able to find jobs. Both end up joining the police department as constables, but Andy's dishonest nature soon gets him into trouble, and he is forced to resign after only a little more than a year on the force. Andy's sister, Julie (Crawford), angrily breaks her engagement to Don (now a detective) because she blames him for reporting Andy's infraction. On the rebound, she marries a crooked Piccadilly club owner, ex-con Felix Fenton (Reed), and gets her brother a job with him. Meanwhile, Andy's girl, nightclub singer Jackie (Norden), has taken up with Felix and continues their relationship after Felix's marriage to Julie. When Andy is caught smuggling illegal whiskey for Felix, he is sentenced to three months in prison, where he learns from a fellow con that there is a "nose" (a stool pigeon) at Felix's nightclub—"Nightlife" Nixon (James), the crippled piano player, who reported the whiskey heist to the police. Andy wrongly assumes that Felix betrayed him and plans to take revenge after his release. When somebody gets murdered, Andy becomes convinced that his sister is the killer and, deliberately directing suspicion on himself, goes on the run. His former buddy, Don, decides to bring him to justice. The storyline—buddies going their separate ways, one on the straight and narrow as a cop and the other toward a life of crime—is a familiar one, and there is nothing exceptional about this version except for its well-constructed character development. Norden's femme fatale is the film's most interesting character. It is said of her that "money is the one sacred thing in her life," but when she is spurned by her married lover she is surprisingly convincing in her claim that she would stand by him even if he were a beggar. *Night Beat* also offers a look at a British "bad cop," in the person Constable Kendall, who loses his job for knowingly purchasing hot jewelry to impress a girl.

Night Boat to Dublin
★★ (1946)

> TONY: She was talking in her sleep last night and she kept on saying, "No, Frank. No, Frank." Not once, old boy, but over and over again.
> DAVID: Well what are *you* worrying about. She was saying "no," wasn't she?
> TONY: Yes, yes, I think you've got something there.

Length: 99 min. **Cast:** Robert Newton, Raymond Lovell, Muriel Pavlow, Guy Middleton, Herbert Lom, John Ruddock, Martin Miller, Leslie Dwyer, Brenda Bruce. **Production Company:** Associated British Picture Corporation. **Directed by:** Lawrence Huntington. **Photographed by:** Otto Heller. **Written by:** Lawrence Huntington, Robert Hall.

British military intelligence agents Captains David Grant (Newton) and Tony Hunter (Middleton) seek a Swedish atomic scientist (Miller) who has either defected or been kidnapped. To infiltrate a spy ring led by Paul Faber (Lovell) and his goon, Bowman (Ruddock), Grant goes undercover as an on-the-run Army deserter charged with espionage. To test his reliability, Faber has Grant marry the sweet Marion Decker (Pavlow), the niece of an infamous Gestapo chief, so she can obtain British citizenship (thus the justification for the romantic subplot). The usually flamboyant Newton turns in one of his more subdued performances but, miscast in a rare romantic role, looks a bit out of place in his scenes with Pavlow. Lom makes a brief appearance as a Nazi spy at a Dublin hotel.

The Night Has Eyes
(U.S. Title: *Terror House*)
★★★ (1942)

> The moors are like quicksand. They never give up their dead. [Stephen Deremid]

Length: 79 min. **Cast:** James Mason, Wilfrid Lawson, Mary Clare, Joyce Howard, Tucker McGuire, John Fernald. **Production Company:** Associated British Picture Corporation. **Directed by:** Leslie Arliss. **Photographed by:** Günther Krampf. **Written by:** Leslie Arliss.

Composer Stephen Deremid (Mason) holes up in his mansion in the middle of Yorkshire Moors. He is a troubled and possibly demented victim of his years in an internment camp in Spain, where he fought on the side of the republicans during the Spanish Civil War. No longer able to compose ("I gave up music for war," he says), Deremid spends his time playing his old compositions and being cared for by his two servants, Mrs. Ranger (Clare) and Jim Sturrock (Lawson). After a young teacher from the Carne House Secondary School for Girls disappears during a trip to the moors, her colleagues Marian Ives (Howard) and wisecracking American Doris (McGuire), visit the area in the hopes of discovering what happened to her. What they find is the paranoid composer, who may or may not have murdered their friend, and a number of dead household pets that the man willingly admits to having strangled. *Night* is a bit slow-moving, but Mason is excellent as the troubled, morally ambiguous war veteran, as is Clare as the overly cheerful housekeeper.

Night of the Demon
(U.S. Title: *Curse of the Demon*)
★★★★½ (1957)

> I know the value of the cold light of reason, but I also know the deep shadows that light can cast, the shadows that can blind man to truth. [Prof. Mark O'Brien]

Length: 95 min. **Cast:** Dana Andrews, Peggy Cummins, Niall MacGinnis, Maurice Denham, Athene Seyler. **Production Company:** Sabre Film Production. **Directed by:** Jacques Tourneur. **Photographed by:** Ted Scaife. **Written by:** Charles Bennett, Hal E. Chester.

American psychologist John Holden (Andrews) travels to England to collaborate with Prof. Henry Harrington (Denham) on an exposé of the Order of the True Believer, a "devil cult" led by black arts magician Julian Karswell (MacGinnis). When Holden arrives, he learns that Harrington is dead, the apparent victim of his car's collision with a power line. In reality, as the viewer witnesses during the film's first five minutes, Harrington was killed by a fire demon conjured up from the depths of hell by Karswell, who used his magical powers to put a stop to Harrington's investigation. Holden believes that Karswell is a fraud despite some rather impressive evidence to the contrary and picks up the investigation where Prof. Harrington left off. When Karswell is unable to convince the determined psychologist to stop interfering with his religious sect, he secretly passes him an ominous parchment containing runic symbols and later informs him that he will die in three days. Although remaining as skeptical as ever, Holden allows himself to be persuaded by Harrington's pretty niece, Joanna (Cummins), to start taking things more seriously. After dragging Holden to a séance conducted by a friend of Karswell's mother (Seyler), Joanna drives him to the Karswell estate in the middle of the night. He breaks into the mansion in an attempt to learn whether or not Karswell has discovered the key to an ancient coded book on black magic. Indeed, Karswell has, and when Holden leaves by way of the woods, he experiences a supernatural run-in with the fire demon, which leaves him scratching his disbelieving head. What finally convinces him of the reality of Karswell's curse is a session with one of the conjurer's insane former followers, who, while under hypnosis, informs him that the only way he can remove the curse is to pass the parchment back to the person who gave it to him. With less than 15 minutes to live, the psychologist boards a train and confronts the obviously terrified magician who, for fear of being slipped the parchment, adamantly refuses to accept anything from the man he has doomed to a horrible death. *Night of the Demon* (released in the U.S. as the severely truncated *Curse of the Demon*) is top-notch fare from director Tourneur, whose American film noir pedigree includes *Berlin Express*, *Experiment Perilous*, *Nightfall*, and the quintessential film noir *Out of the Past*, as well as his three Horror noir collaborations with legendary producer Val Newton, *Cat People*, *I Walked with a Zombie*, and *The Leopard Man*. *Night* was intended by Tourneur to be much more subtle in its presentation, but executive producer Hal E. Chester reportedly insisted that the fire demon be shown on screen. The result was an almost comical looking Godzilla-type monster, which, fortunately, detracted only slightly from the film's otherwise scary atmosphere. Peggy Cummins, best known to American viewers for her starring role in the classic 1950 noir *Gun Crazy*, and American film noir icon Dana Andrews (*Beyond a Reasonable Doubt*, *Boomerang*, *Daisy Kenyon*, *Edge of Doom*, *Fallen Angel*, *Iron Curtain*, *Laura*, *Ox-Bow Incident*, *Where the Sidewalk Ends* and *While the City Sleeps*) turn in good, low-key performances. But it is Scaife's dark, shadowy cinematography that is primarily responsible for the film's reputation as a masterpiece of cinematic horror.

Night Was Our Friend
★★ (1951)

I'm not really mad. Just twisted somewhere, I suppose. [Martin Raynor]

Length: 61 min. **Cast:** Elizabeth Sellars, Michael Gough, Ronald Howard. **Production Company:** A.C.T. Films. **Directed by:** Michael Anderson. **Photographed by:** Gerald Gibbs. **Written by:** Michael Pertwee.

Sally Raynor (Sellars) is found not guilty of poisoning her husband, Martin (Gough), and returns home a free woman only to confess to her lover, Dr. John Harper (Howard), that she did indeed kill Martin. When John leaves in disgust, Sally remembers the events that changed her life forever. Via flashback, the viewer learns that Martin's private plane crashed in Brazil two years earlier and that he was presumed killed. Sally went on with her life, falling in love with the handsome doctor, only to be told just prior to their wedding that Martin had been found wandering the jungle, having escaped from an Indian tribe that held him captive all this time. Determined to be the good wife, Sally dumps John to care for her obviously disturbed husband, who has arrived home with some heavy emotional baggage. It seems he has taken to wandering the woods at night ("I love the night," he tells Sally.) Then one day a local lad is attacked by a mad man who attempts to strangle him. Good performances by Gough, Sellars and Howard (son of actor Leslie Howard) cannot save this unexciting film, which, after a promising start, quickly deteriorates into a substandard psychological melodrama. Some filmographies credit Moray Grant with the film's lackluster cinematography but the credits list Gibbs as the director of photography and Grant as the camera operator. Director Anderson went on to make the more memorable *Around the World in 80 Days*, *The Quiller Memorandum*, and *The Shoes of the Fisherman*.

Night Without Stars
★★★ (1951)

Louis Malinay: Like you, I thought the world was a fine, healthy place to live in. But it's not. No, it's rotten, poisoned and sick.
Giles Gordon: It's you that's sick.

Length: 86 min. **Cast:** David Farrar, Nadia Gray, Maurice Teynac, Gilles Quéant, Gérard Landry. **Production Company:** Europa Films. **Directed by:** Anthony Pélissier. **Photographed by:** Guy Green. **Written by:** Winston Graham.

As a result of a shell blast during the war, British lawyer Giles Gordon (Farrar) is now legally blind, and surgery has left him with minimal sight in only one eye. Fearing complete blindness, he refuses experimental eye surgery and goes on holiday to the south of France. There he meets pretty shoe-store clerk Alix Delaisse (Gray), who at first befriends him out of sympathy but soon becomes quite fond of him. Giles quickly falls in love with the war widow but learns that she is engaged to Pierre Chaval (Landry), a shady character rumored to have been a Nazi informant during the war. Chaval warns Giles to stay away from his "property," but the blind war hero doesn't scare off that easily. Then one night Giles receives a frantic telephone call from Alix and rushes off to Chaval's apartment, where he stumbles upon a dead body, which he assumes is Chaval's. Believing he is protecting Alix, who has disappeared, Giles does not report the body to the police. Days later, after having heard no news about the dead man, he confides in lawyer Louis Malinay (Teynac), who tells him that the victim could not have been Chaval because he had just seen Chaval preparing for his wedding to Alix. After weeks of not hearing from Alix, Giles returns to London, undergoes that risky eye operation, and, with his sight fully restored, flies back to France to learn the truth about what happened. What he finds is a gang of dangerous black marketeers, a nosy French detective (Quéant), a newspaper story about Chaval's death in a car accident and a strangely distant Alix, who seems to have become quite cozy with Malinay. Cynicism, self-pity, obsession, and revenge are the noir themes that are portrayed, fairly successfully, in *Night Without Stars*. Unfortunately, the scenes relating to the precarious eye surgery seem to have been thoughtlessly added and thus seem more of an intrusion than a vital plot ingredient. On the bright side, however, David Farrar is excellent, turning in a relaxed but dignified performance as the troubled war veteran who seeks redemption in the love of an equally troubled woman.

Nightmare (a.k.a. *Here's the Knife, Dear: Now Use It*)
★★★½ (1963)

> Don't talk to me like that. You're not talking to some idiot neurotic teenager now. [Mrs. Baxter to Mr. Baxter]

Length: 82 min. **Cast:** David Knight, Moira Redmond, Jennie Linden, Brenda Bruce, George A. Cooper, Irene Richmond. **Production Company:** Hammer Film Productions. **Directed by:** Freddie Francis. **Photographed by:** John Wilcox. **Written by:** Jimmy Sangster.

Teenager Janet Freeman (Linden) is sent home from boarding school because of her deteriorating mental health and her disruptive recurring nightmares about her insane mother, who was incarcerated in a mental institution after stabbing Janet's father to death, a murder Janet witnessed when she was only eleven. Janet fears that she has inherited her mother's insanity and may one day be placed in an asylum. She becomes convinced of the reality of these fears when she begins seeing a ghostly lady in white walking around the house. The mystery woman always ends up as did Janet's father — with a bloodied knife sticking out of her chest. Expressing concern for Janet's rapidly deteriorating mental health are Janet's guardian, lawyer Henry Baxter (American actor Knight); Grace Maddox (Redmond), her companion and nurse; Mary Lewis (Bruce), her former teacher; and household servants Mrs. Gibbs (Richmond) and John (Cooper). Their worst fears are realized when Janet attempts suicide and later stabs and kills a woman she believes is the ghostly figure who has been tormenting her. Consequently, Janet's greatest fear is realized and she is placed in the asylum that held her mother. But this is not the end of the story, which now begins to revolve around the other characters. However, to divulge any more of the plot would be giving away too much. Director Francis, cinematographer Wilcox and screenwriter Sangster, who would work together again the following year on the similarly themed *Hysteria*, do an excellent job of turning the now overly familiar storyline into an unexpectedly suspenseful film, despite a bit of cheating with a few dishonest red herrings. Redmond's over-the-top performance is delightful.

1984
★★★½ (1956)

WINSTON: You're late. What happened to you?
JULIA: The anti-sex meeting went on forever.

Length: 90 min. **Cast**: Edmond O'Brien, Jan Sterling, Michael Redgrave, Donald Pleasence, David Kossoff. **Production Company**: Holiday Film Productions. **Directed by**: Michael Anderson. **Photographed by**: C.M. Pennington-Richards. **Written by**: William P. Templeton, Ralph Bettison.

Winston Smith, Number 6748, a history reviser for the Records Department of Oceania's Ministry of Truth, purchases an old diary at a London antiques shop, sneaks it past the ever-present, all-seeing eye of the video camera posted inside the doorway to his flat and begins to record his thoughts. Although his written rants against the malevolent state, especially his brazen declaration "Down with Big Brother," could mean death for him if the Thought Police were to find the diary, Winston writes, "I don't care any more." He also has noticed that he is being followed by a woman who works in his office's Fiction Department and believes she may being planning to report him. He contemplates killing her. But one day she slips him a piece of paper containing the words, "I must talk with you. I love you." Thus, the two begin a love affair forbidden by a Party that sponsors two-minute "hate breaks" at government offices and "Hate Week," a nation-wide celebration in which mind-numbed citizens hurl Party-approved slogans at traitors and other perceived enemies of Big Brother. In addition, the Party alone claims the right to arrange marriages for the so-called "privileged" class of the Outer Party, of which Winston and Julia are members. Content at first to sneak around the countryside where no cameras can capture their perilous trysts, Winston and Julia, a member of the Women's Anti-Sex League, daringly rent a room above the antiques shop where Winston purchased the diary. The shop is owned by a seemingly understanding and compassionate middle-aged widower (Kossoff), who still remembers the old days before the 1965 atomic war that devastated the world and resulted in the creation of three present-day superpowers, Oceania, East Asia and Eurasia, the latter currently fighting a conventional war against Oceania. Yet the lovers quickly become dissatisfied with their few stolen moments together, and Winston, seething against Big Brother and the Inner Party members who rule Oceania, ultimately decides to make his traitorous feelings known to his superior, O'Connor (Redgrave), who he has come to believe is involved with the anti–Big Brother underground — a decision that is the beginning of the end for the lovers and will result in visits for both of them to the ominous Room 101 at the Ministry of Love. "Freely adapted" from the satirical, dystopic novel by George Orwell, this second version of *1984* (the first being a 1954 British television play starring Peter Cushing as Smith) has its share of admirers, especially those who can appreciate the pairing of noir veterans Edmond O'Brien, an unlikely choice for a romantic lead, and Jan Sterling as the ill-fated lovers. Many critics, however, feel that in addition to being too dull, the film does little justice to Mr. Orwell's famous literary creation. Some see the novel as being more faithfully represented by a later version, *Nineteen Eighty Four*, a 1984 film starring John Hurt as Smith and Richard Burton as O'Brien (the character called O'Connor in the earlier film). Both films are darkly atmospheric and entertaining and both ably portray the doomed protagonist's alienation, cynicism and paranoia, as well as the gloominess of the society in which he finds himself trapped. It is understandable, however, if fans of classic films noirs are partial to the 1956 film, especially the American release, which ends on a more noirishly downbeat note than does the British version.

No Orchids for Miss Blandish
★★ (1948)

EDDIE SHULTZ: She's got class.
BAILEY: Sure, they've all got it now. It's the movies.

Length: 104 min. **Cast**: Jack La Rue, Hugh McDermott, Linden Travers, Lily Molnar, Walter Crisham, Macdonald Parke. **Production Companies**: Tudor Films, Alliance Film Studios. **Directed by**: St. John L. Clowes. **Photographed by**: Gerald Gibbs. **Written by**: St. John L. Clowes.

The Grisson mob, headed by the brutal Slim Grisson (LaRue) and his cruel and obnoxious mother, affectionately known in local gangster circles as Ma Grisson (Molnar), murder a couple of maverick kidnappers and walk off with their prize, the wealthy Miss Blandish (Travers) and her $100,000 necklace. It turns out that Slim has been wooing Miss Blandish with bouquets of orchids, which she had always haughtily refused to accept. Now, with the beautiful socialite a hostage at his Black Dice nightclub and casino, Slim faces a difficult decision—demand a million-dollar ransom from Miss Blandish's father and then kill her after payment is received, be satisfied with the necklace and kill her immediately, or let her go. Love wins out. To his shock, she refuses his offer of freedom, having fallen in love with the man she knows is a vicious murderer. This, of course, makes Ma Grisson and Slim's goons, Eddie (Crisham) and Doc (Parke), very nervous, and a coup seems imminent. Meanwhile, obnoxious newspaper reporter Fenner seeks the story of a lifetime and goes searching for the missing woman with gun in hand. Despite its directorial crudity, mediocre acting and a screenplay overburdened with clichés and exaggerated hardboiled dialogue ("It's just a flesh wound" and "You crazy rat, you croaked him"), *No Orchids* is a must-see film simply because of its infamous reputation. Although the violence is tame by today's standards, it was distressful for the somber British critics of the late 1940s who vehemently condemned the film. The Monthly Film Bulletin described it as "the most sickening exhibition of brutality, perversion, sex and sadism ever to be shown on a cinema screen." Americans seemed less upset. When the film opened in New York several years later, The New York Times commented that "when sex rears up ... it is so studiously contrived that it is laughable." Director Clowes took the lion's share of the blame for the notoriety of his final film, but it should be noted that he became sick during filming and producer Oswald Mitchell assumed directorial duties. The film was remade in 1971 as *The Grissom Gang*, with Robert Aldrich directing.

No Road Back
★★ (1957)

Don't worry about looking dumb. They're dumb themselves. They'll never notice. [bartender about Scotland Yard detectives]

Length: 83 min. **Cast**: Skip Homeier, Paul Carpenter, Patricia Dainton, Norman Wooland, Margaret Rawlings, Alfie Bass, Sean Connery. **Production Company**: Gibraltar Film Productions. **Directed by**: Montgomery Tully. **Photographed by**: Lionel Banes. **Written by**: Charles Leeds, Montgomery Tully.

A perfectly planned £250,000 jewel heist goes bad when the gang's mastermind, the vicious Clem Hayes (Carpenter), kills a night watchman and the frightened getaway driver, Rudge Harvey (Bass), who wanted to turn himself him to the police to avoid the gallows. The gang's fence, nightclub owner Mrs. Railton (Rawlings), a deaf and blind sculptress who chose a life of crime so she could afford to send her son, John (American actor Homeier), to medical school in the States, turns against Clem when he tries to frame John for Rudge's murder. German-born actor Wooland co-stars as the Scotland Yard inspector taken in by Mrs. Railton's decent citizen act, and Dainton plays Mrs. Railton's finger-spelling interpreter. Two scenes stand out in this otherwise slow-moving film: when Clem shoots Rudge in front of the deaf and blind Mrs. Railton, who mundanely goes about her chores unaware of the victim crawling toward her and pleading for help, and when Mrs. Railton tries to shoot Clem with a little help from her seeing-eye dog. *No Road Back* is a minor heist noir of some interest thanks to the presence of Sean Connery, in his second film role, as a stuttering jewel thief named Spike.

No Room at the Inn
★★★ (1948)

Mary O'Rane was a sweet and gentle girl. Now she's coarse and savage and sly. [Miss Drave]

Length: 82 min. **Cast**: Freda Jackson, Joy Shelton, Hermione Baddeley, Ann Stephens, Robin Netscher, Harcourt Williams, Sydney Tafler. **Production Company**: British National Films. **Directed by**: Daniel

Birt. **Photographed by**: James Wilson. **Written by**: Dylan Thomas, Ivan Foxwell.

On Christmas Eve, Mary O'Rane, a Buntings department store sales clerk, witnesses the arrest of a childhood friend, Norma Bates (Dowling), for shoplifting, prompting Mary to recall the events that put Norma on the path to crime. The story picks up, by way of flashback and voiceover narration, with a social worker turning Mary over to Aggie Voray (Jackson), a local widow who has custody of four other war-time evacuees, including Norma. With her merchant marine father away at sea and her mother having been killed in a German bombing raid, Mary has no better place to go, despite the tireless efforts of her kindly teacher, Judith Drave (Shelton), to have her removed from Mrs. Voray's house, a place Miss Drave considers a den of "swinish filth and spiritual corruption." Mrs. Voray is accustomed to spending the government money she receives for the children on booze, men and fancy clothes, while her charges live in squalor and degradation. The only boy in the house, the mischievous Ronnie (Netscher), seems to be Mrs. Voray's favorite target for abuse, prompting Mary to befriend him and step forward as his protector. Miss Drave's vociferous complaints, meanwhile, go unheeded by the local vicar (Williams) and the city council, which has as members several of Mrs. Voray's ardent, middle-aged admirers. *No Room* is a horribly depressing film, appropriately complemented by James Wilson's gloomy photography. Tame compared to movies today about child abuse, the film must have stirred up some strong social feelings among English viewers after its release. Hermione Baddeley has a small part as Mrs. Voray's housekeeper, and character actor Sydney Tafler plays a barroom Casanova who dumps Mrs. Voray for a younger tart, causing the disappointed drunkard to take her frustrations out on the children, especially poor Ronnie, who she feels is long overdue for an overnight stay in the coal bin.

No Trace
★★★ (1950)

> MAISIE: When I got back to my room I thought I'd drop a few lines to me old man. It gets very lonely, you know.

> INSPECTOR MACDOUGALL: Yeah, right. Husband?
>
> MAISIE: Me father. He's got another eighteen months to go.

Length: 76 min. **Cast**: Hugh Sinclair, Dinah Sheridan, John Laurie, Barry Morse, Dora Bryan, Michael Brennan, Beatrice Varley. **Production Company**: Tempean Films. **Directed by**: John Gilling. **Photographed by**: Monty Berman. **Written by**: John Gilling.

Popular crime novelist and London radio personality Robert Southley (Sinclair) runs into a bit of difficulty in the person of an uncouth American hoodlum, Mike Fenton (Brennan), his one-time criminal accomplice in the days before the successful author changed his name and went straight. Fenton demands £500 for a letter Southley wrote to him years earlier implicating himself in a Philadelphia jewel robbery. Southley pays but learns that he purchased a copy and that the blackmailer is holding on to the original letter with the intention of bleeding him forever. So the author dons a phony beard and seaman's clothes and rents a room at Fenton's boarding house, where he murders his tormentor and retrieves the letter and the money. Southley's friend, Scotland Yard Inspector MacDougall (Laurie), challenges the writer to a friendly competition of solve-the-latest-murder and takes him along to interview the two witnesses, Fenton's landlady (Varley) and streetwise neighbor Maisie (Bryan), who do not recognize the killer without his beard. While Southley successfully misleads the police, his secretary, Linda (Sheridan), decides to help her boss win the crime-solving contest and begins to investigate on her own. What she discovers threatens to expose Southley as the killer, prompting him to decide that she, too, must be eliminated. A suspenseful script and a good directing job by Gilling make this crime melodrama seem a lot shorter than its 76 minutes. The highlight of the film is Berman's photographic interpretation of the murder, where the camera makes good use of tilted angles and close-ups of killer and victim. The blaring jazz music emanating from the radio is also a nice touch. The acting is credible, with Bryan's comedy relief role being especially entertaining. Thirteen years later Barry Morse, who plays

Inspector MacDougall's assistant and Linda's boyfriend, would land the role he is most famous for — that of Detective Philip Gerard in the hit American TV series, *The Fugitive*.

No Trees in the Street
★★½ (1959)

> It's the street. The smell gets worse. It doesn't get any better. It gets worse. [Wilkie]

Length: 96 min. **Cast:** Sylvia Sims, Herbert Lom, Melvyn Hayes, Ronald Howard, Joan Miller, Carole Lesley. **Production Company:** Allegro Films. **Directed by:** J. Lee Thompson. **Photographed by:** Gilbert Taylor. **Written by:** Ted Willis.

Jess Martin (Miller) and her children, teenager Tommy (Hayes) and grown-up Hetty (Syms), live in a pre–World War II London slum. Tommy can't hold a legitimate job and is not really interested in doing so. When neighborhood crime boss Wilkie (Lom) offers him a job as a getaway driver, Tommy jumps at the opportunity, with the blessing of his mum, who knows that Wilkie is attracted to Hetty and hopes that Hetty will play up to the rich criminal. Hetty, however, has never been interested in Wilkie, and now that he has involved her brother in his criminal activities she has come to despise him. When Tommy double-crosses Wilkie and runs off with £20 and a gun he scored from a recent heist, and Hetty threatens to leave their crummy neighborhood for good, Jess realizes that her dream of financial security is slipping away. So she invites Wilkie into their flat to seduce her daughter, whom she has plied with whiskey. Incredibly, Hetty falls in love with Wilkie after the incident. Happy at last, the jealous gangster doesn't care much for the attention his new girl has been receiving from the neighborhood copper, Det. Sgt. Frank Collins (Howard), who is mainly interested in finding Hetty's brother before he uses the stolen gun on someone. *No Trees* is told via flashback two decades later by Sgt. Collins who hopes the story will scare a tough, leather-jacketed, knife-carrying teen into going straight. The script is too ridden with clichés to be interesting — the concerned cop, the crook who falls for a good girl, the juvenile delinquent with a chip on his shoulder, and the premise that society is entirely to blame for good people going bad. Hayes' performance as the unsympathetic and annoyingly whiny punk is way over the top, but Lom and Syms are good as the gangster and the girl with whom he has become obsessed to the detriment of his loyal moll, Lova (Lesley). Gilbert Taylor's cinematography is appealing and is especially noirish during the climactic scene involving the standoff between the police and young Tommy.

No Way Back
(NR) (1949)

Length: 72 min. **Cast:** Terence de Marney, Eleanor Summerfield, Jack Raine, John Salew. **Production Company:** Concanen Recordings. **Directed by:** Stefan Osiecki. **Photographed by:** Robert Navarro. **Written by:** Stefan Osiecki, Derrick de Marney.

A depressed former boxer finds himself framed for a robbery.

The Noose
(U.S. Title: *The Silk Noose*)
★★ (1948)

> I can be nice. But I can be not nice. [Sugiani]

Length: 95 min. **Cast:** Carole Landis, Joseph Calleia, Derek Farr, Stanley Holloway, Nigel Patrick, Hay Petrie. **Production Company:** Associated British Picture Corporation. **Directed by:** Edmond T. Greville. **Photographed by:** Hone Glendining. **Written by:** Richard Llewellyn.

London underworld figure Eduardo Sugiani (Calleia) and his spiv henchman, Bar Gorman (Patrick), manage their black market operation out of The Blue Moon Club, Sugiani's Soho nightspot. When the body of a woman connected to the mob is discovered, Linda Medbury (Landis), an American fashion reporter for the London Evening Echo, begins snooping around, much to the irritation of the violence-prone Sugiani (nicknamed "Knucksie" because of his fondness for brass knuckles). At first, Sugiani tries using charm to dissuade the spunky reporter from her mission, but when that fails, he sends his troll-like hit man, "the Barber" (Petrie), to pay her a visit. In the meantime,

Linda's war-hero fiancé, sportswriter Jumbo Hoyle (Farr), and his vigilante buddies organize at a local gymnasium and come up with a plan that includes wearing football jerseys as a means of identifying each other during their upcoming raid on Sugiani's illegal operations. Keeping a close eye on their activities is the incorruptible Inspector Rendall (Holloway) of Scotland Yard, who is seeking evidence to put Sugiani and Gorman away for good. Despite Hone Glendining's stylish noir photography, a good performance from Calleia (a character actor familiar to American film noir fans) and an incredibly hyperactive but enjoyable acting job from Patrick, *The Noose* is a muddled attempt to mix gangsterism with British zaniness, and the result is disappointing. To help follow the plot, American viewers should keep a British slang dictionary close at hand, although a few expressions are explained for the benefit of Landis' American character. Best known perhaps for her role as the ill-fated waitress-turned-celebrity in *I Wake Up Screaming*, American actress Landis committed suicide with an overdose of seconal in 1948, the year *The Noose* was released.

Now Barabbas (a.k.a. *Now Barabbas Was a Robber*)
(NR) (1949)

Length: 87 min. **Cast:** Richard Greene, Cedric Hardwicke, Kathleen Harrison, Ronald Howard, Stephen Murray, William Hartnell, Richard Burton. **Production Company:** Anatole de Grunwald Productions. **Directed by:** Gordon Parry. **Photographed by:** Otto Heller. **Written by:** Gordon Parry.

Episodic film revolving around the lives of prisoners.

Now Barabbas Was a Robber
see *Now Barabbas*

Nowhere to Go
★★½ (1958)

The porter found him last night. Him and a girl tied up in a bedroom. His false teeth rammed halfway down his throat. [George]

Length: 97 min. **Cast:** George Nader, Maggie Smith, Bernard Lee, Geoffrey Keen, Bessie Love. **Production Company:** Ealing Studios. **Directed by:** Seth Holt. **Photographed by:** Paul Beeson. **Written by:** Seth Holt, Kenneth Tynan.

Canadian con artist and thief Paul Gregory (Nader) breaks out of an English prison with help from an accomplice, Victor Sloane (Lee), and attempts to retrieve stolen money from his safety deposit box at a local bank. Via flashback, the viewer watches Gregory worm his way into the confidence of wealthy widow Harriet Jefferson (Love) and abscond with her collection of rare coins, selling it for £55,000. Realizing he will be captured quickly, Gregory stores the dough in the safety deposit box and waits for Inspector Scott (Keen) to show up to arrest him. A first time offender in England, Gregory expects to be sentenced to five years for his crime, reckoning that the dough waiting for him will be well worth the time served, especially with time off for good behavior. He is shocked, however, when the no-nonsense judge sentences him to ten years, thus prompting his daring breakout. The unexpectedly harsh sentence is only the beginning of Gregory's troubles as he soon learns when Sloane double-crosses him by stealing the key to the box and then dying when Gregory roughs him up in an effort to retrieve it. On-the-run now for murder, Gregory seeks help from socialite Bridget Howard (Smith), who is able to get him as far as Wales before Inspector Scott shows up at her family estate. An early co-starring vehicle for future Oscar winner Smith, and the beginning of a downward career spiral for American actor Nader, *Nowhere to Run*, with its noirishly convoluted storyline, is a fast-moving treat right up to its downbeat ending.

Obsessed see *The Late Edwin Black*

Obsession
(U.S. Title: *The Hidden Room*)
★★★ (1949)

You've heard of the last straw, haven't you, Bill? We'll, you're it. [Dr. Clive Riordan]

A psychiatrist (Robert Newton) surprises his adulterous wife (Sally Gray) and her American lover (Phil Brown) in *Obsession* (a.k.a. *The Hidden Room*) (Independent Sovereign Films, 1949).

Length: 98 min. **Cast**: Robert Newton, Phil Brown, Sally Gray, Naunton Wayne. **Production Company**: Independent Sovereign Films. **Directed by**: Edward Dmytryk. **Photographed by**: C.M. Pennington-Richards. **Written by**: Alec Coppel.

Psychiatrist Clive Riordan (Newton) learns that his faithless wife, Storm (Gray), has been at it again, this time gallivanting around London with a young American, Bill Kronin (Brown). Having decided that enough is enough, the cuckolded doctor kidnaps Bill and keeps him chained for months to a bed in the cellar of a bombed-out ruin. Clive visits Bill regularly, feeding him and tending to his other needs. On each visit, however, he brings bottles of acid, which he empties into a bathtub, as part of his plan to eventually dispose of his victim's body. Storm suspects that Clive has already murdered Bill but, aware of the inevitable scandal if it becomes known, keeps quiet about her suspicions. Meanwhile, Storm's intelligent little dog, Monty, has the opportunity to spend some time with the appreciative prisoner, and a relentless Scotland Yard detective, Superintendent Finsby (Wayne), is assigned to investigate the case of the missing American. Hollywood film noir veteran Dmytryk (*Murder, My Sweet; Cornered; Crossfire; The Sniper*) brings to the screen a suspenseful and tightly woven thriller based on a novel by screenwriter Coppel called appropriately, "A Man About a Dog." Sally Gray and American actor Phil Brown do a fine job as the flabbergasted lovers not at all ready to pay the price for their dalliance. Newton, as always, is a pleasure to watch.

The October Man
★★★½ (1947)

I'd paste the living daylights out of you only it would be like kicking a dead man. [Mr. Wilcox to Jim Ackland]

Length: 110 min. **Cast:** John Mills, Joan Greenwood, Edward Chapman, Kay Walsh, Frederick Piper, Jack Melford. **Production Company:** Two Cities Films. **Directed by:** Roy Baker. **Photographed by:** Erwin Hillier. **Written by:** Eric Ambler.

The film's opening scene focuses on two bus passengers seated directly behind the driver—industrial chemist Jim Ackland (Mills) and a little girl, entrusted to Jim's care by his friends. Throughout the trip on this dark, rain-swept evening, the bus driver has been troubled by poor visibility. Thanks to several close-ups of the bus's failing brake system, the viewer is privy to the accident that is about to occur. As a train rolls by in the distance, the bus begins to skid and, as Jim's wraps his protective arms around the girl, slams into a brick wall. It is an accident that will kill the little girl and leave Jim with a skull fracture and a tormented conscience. His subsequent depression provokes him to attempt suicide twice during his convalescence period, and when he is eventually released from the hospital he is warned by his doctor that people may begin to get on his nerves. Jim starts a new job and takes a flat at the Brockhurst Commons Hotel, a small rooming house with an odd assortment of guests, one of whom, clothing model Molly Newman (Walsh), will soon become a murder victim. Molly is being stalked by another hotel guest, Mr. Peachy (Chapman), who doesn't mind that Molly, an inveterate moocher, never pays her debts so long as she continues to be "nice" to him. Molly, who is having an affair with Mr. Wilcox, a married gent from Birmingham, tires of Peachy's advances and tries to discourage them by pretending that she and the new guest, Jim, have become cozy. This only succeeds in making Peachy jealous, and when Molly's body is found on the Commons one Sunday evening (with a rolled-up check for £30 bearing Jim's signature lying nearby), Peachy begins spreading rumors that Jim had been visiting Molly in her room every night. Jim, of course, had no interest in the woman because by now he has fallen in love with his employer's sister, Jenny Carden (Greenwood), whom he is afraid to marry because of his suicidal tendencies. (Lately, Jim has developed the habit of standing on a railroad trestle, remembering the train from his ill-fated bus ride, and thinking about jumping—not exactly a mental state, he admits, that is conducive to a long-term relationship). Meanwhile, Detective Inspector Godby (Piper) of the Criminal Investigation Department (CID), who believes the killer is a man "with mental trouble in the background, a paranoiac," is certain that Jim is his man. The only thing that remains, Godby believes, is to extract a confession from Jim after assuring him that a jury would deliver a verdict of guilty but insane, thus sparing him from the hangman. Roy Ward Baker made his debut here as a director, and producer-screenwriter Ambler also wrote the novel on which the film was based. (The title refers to the month of the protagonist's birth, as noted by amateur astrologist Molly Newman just prior to her murder.) British film icon Mills gives an impressive performance as the vulnerable, tormented chemist seeking redemption in suicide but finding it in the love of a beautiful woman. The little girl on the bus is played by Mills' daughter, Juliet, older sister of Hayley, and future star of the American TV series *Nanny and the Professor*.

Odd Man Out
★★★★½ (1947)

> KATHLEEN: Sooner or later the police will get him. Let me have him until then.
> DENNIS: As long as he lives, he'll belong to the organization.

Length: 116 min. **Cast:** James Mason, Robert Newton, Cyril Cusack, Kathleen Ryan, F.J. McCormick, W.G. Fay. **Production Company:** Two Cities Films. **Directed by:** Carol Reed. **Photographed by:** Robert Krasker. **Written by:** F.L. Green, R.C. Sherriff.

Belfast IRA chief Johnny McQueen (Mason), having escaped from prison six months earlier, pulls a payroll heist with several of his men, is shot while escaping and kills a civilian during a struggle on the front steps of the targeted mill. While two of his accomplices attempt to pull Johnny into the back seat of the getaway car, the panicky driver speeds off, causing Johnny to lose his grip and fall to the street. Afraid to go back to pick him up, the driver takes off, hoping that his wounded chief will make it back to head-

A Belfast parish priest (W.G. Fay) and a local girl (Kathleen Ryan) meet to discuss her wounded and missing IRA boyfriend in *Odd Man Out* (Two Cities Films, 1947).

quarters on foot. Johnny makes it as far as an old air raid shelter, where he collapses and the blood drains slowly from his body. Weak and beginning to hallucinate, Johnny waits until dark to try to make it back to his men. The word is out on the street, however, and those he seeks help from are too fearful of both the police and the IRA to become involved. Eventually Johnny is found by a tramp named Shell (McCormick), who hides him in a junkyard and offers to disclose his location to Johnny's priest, Fr. Tom (Fay), for a reward. (What Shell gets instead of money is a mini-sermon on faith). While, Fr. Tom and Johnny's girl, Kathleen (Ryan), set out to find the wanted man before the police do, Shell's psychotic artist friend, Lukey (Newton), forces Shell to bring Johnny to his studio so he can capture the eyes of a dying man on canvas. James Mason turns in a *tour de force* perform-ance that alone is responsible for any compassionate viewer response to a rebel (some would say terrorist) who has just killed an innocent man. Carol Reed's direction is perfect, almost hypnotizing the viewer into staying glued to the screen and the troubling but beautifully photographed scenes, including one in which the dying gunman experiences a religious vision and recites in the manner of a Shakespearean actor a well-known biblical call to charity (i.e., love). Laden with religious symbolism and dialogue, this violent and thought provoking film is hardly religious fare and tends to provoke more political discussion than spiritual. Although the word Belfast is never mentioned, the viewer knows exactly where this film takes place thanks to the opening aerial shot of the city. Just as easily figured out is the name of the "organization" to which these robbers owe their allegiance. Mason is terrific and Newton, as usual, indulges in the type of enjoyable histrionics that only he could get away with.

Offbeat
(U.S. Title: *The Devil Inside*)
★★★ (1961)

> STEVE: What's all this about guilt? Everyone I meet nowadays feels it about something. Lets be realistic. This is an age of betrayal.
> RUTH: If you loved a woman, would you betray her?
> STEVE: I suppose so. I'm a man.

Length: 72 min. **Cast**: William Sylvester, Mai Zetterling, John Meillon, Anthony Dawson, Victor Brooks. **Production Company**: British Lion Production Assets. **Directed by**: Cliff Owen. **Photographed by**: Geoffrey Faithfull. **Written by**: Peter Barnes.

To nab the thugs who have been robbing London banks and jewelry stores, MI5 intelligence officer Layton (Sylvester), on loan to Scotland Yard, goes undercover as "Steve Ross," a recently deceased international criminal with a reputation for professionalism among London underworld figures. With the cooperation of the South London Bank, Layton commits a robbery using the "Willie Sutton technique" (surprising bank employees as they arrive for work). After the bogus robbery, he seeks out a fence for the hot money, and his contacts point him in the direction of an unlikely gang of thieves, a corporate-like syndicate of happily married family men operating under the guise of a legitimate business. The gang leaders, James (Dawson) and Johnny (Meillon), even have plans to develop a retirement fund for their "employees," something they refer to as "welfare for the wayward." They investigate Layton, whose cover holds up, and put him on the payroll as a salaried employee with a cut in the action. A cynical and hardened cop who trusts no one, not even his law enforcement colleagues, Layton is surprised to find that the gang members are a civilized and good-natured lot, just everyday people "trying to make a living dishonestly." He befriends the crooks, one of whom saves his life, and falls in love with Ruth Lombard (Zetterling), the sexy widow of a gang member who died in prison. When the crooks decide to rob a cache of diamonds from the vault of a London jewelry store, Layton comes up with a daring plan to drill deep into the sidewalk outside the store, in broad daylight, and then dig a tunnel into the strongroom. Into the heist with a passion now, Layton decides to betray his real employer, Her Majesty's Government, and to flee to South America with Ruth and their share of the money after the diamonds have been fenced. Meanwhile, Scotland Yard Inspector Adams (Brooks), who dislikes Layton and doesn't have much use for outside agencies interfering in the Yard's jurisdictional cases, begins tailing the undercover cop. Ken Jones' upbeat jazz score highlights this fast-moving crime film, the primary theme of which is betrayal. It also contains some common noir plot elements (an undercover police operation, a convoluted heist scenario and a bad cop). American actor Sylvester does a good job as the bitter MI5 officer, and Swedish-born actress Zetterling is effective as the widowed moll who falls for him.

Oliver Twist
★★★★½ (1948)

> MRS. SOWERBERRY: The boy must be mad.
> MR. BRUMBLE: It's not madness, ma'am. It's meat.... If you'd kept the boy on gruel this never would have happened.

Length: 116 min. **Cast**: Robert Newton, Alec Guinness, Kay Walsh, John Howard Davies, Henry Stephenson, Anthony Newley, Francis L. Sullivan, Ralph Truman. **Production Companies**: Independent Producers, Cineguild Productions. **Directed by**: David Lean. **Photographed by**: Guy Green. **Written by**: David Lean, Stanley Haynes.

Novelist Charles Dickens' waif, Oliver Twist (Davies), so named by the obese Mr. Brumble (Sullivan), the beadle at the parish workplace where the orphaned lad's mother died giving birth, suffers abuse at the hands of exploitative adults before finding his rightful place in Victorian London society. After having the audacity to ask for a second helping of broth, 9-year-old Oliver is handed over by the workplace board to a local funeral parlor to serve as an apprentice. Cruelly treated once again, Oliver runs away to London, where he is recruited by the ragamuffin Artful Dodger (played by 16-year-old Anthony Newley) as a pickpocket for the villainous Fagin (Guinness) and his gang of young thieves. Fagin learns that he has not lucked upon just another boy who will steal for him but a lad whose identity a mysterious stranger named Monks (Truman) will pay handsomely to keep secret. After Oliver is rescued from the gang by the grandfatherly Robert Brownlow (Stephenson), the murderous criminal Bill Sikes (Newton) and his lover, Nancy (Walsh), kidnap the boy and return him to Fagin's hideout, where he remains a prisoner while Brownlow tries desperately to find him. Of the numerous film versions of the Dickens classic tale, David Lean's is perhaps the best and certainly the darkest, thanks to Green's magnificent black and white cinematography, which, paradoxically, manages to depress as well as invigorate the viewer with some dark and disturbing images. Contributing to the rewarding viewing experience are Lean's vibrant direction and intense performances by Newton and Guinness, whose controversial portrayal of Fagin as a hook-nosed, money-grubbing Jew led to accusations of anti–Semitism and resulted in the expurgation of ten minutes of his screen time, as well as the delay of the film's American premiere for three years. Look for a young Diana Dors as a funeral parlor owner's kitchen maid.

On the Night of the Fire
(U.S. Title: *The Fugitive*)
★★★ (1939)

Let's be a bit balmy. Being sane don't get us nowhere. [Will Kobling]

Length: 94 min. **Cast**: Ralph Richardson, Diana Wynyard, Romney Brent, Mary Clare, Henry Oscar. **Production Company**: G&S Films. **Directed by**: Brian Desmond Hurst. **Photographed by**: Vacklav (Václav) Vích. **Written by**: Brian Desmond Hurst, Patrick Kirwan, Terence Young.

While out for a stroll, barber Will Kobling (Richardson) peers through a window left open by a careless cashier and notices a table filled with bills and coins. He climbs through the window and walks off with £100. The only clue the police have to the identity of the thief is the distinctive jacket button he lost. When Will asks his wife, Kit (Wynyard), to sew on a new one she becomes suspicious and confronts him about the theft. Rather than trying to convince him to return the money, even anonymously, Kit convinces Will to allow her to pay off a substantial debt she owes to Pilegar, the hated neighborhood loan shark who also owns a tailor shop across the street from the Kobling Shaving Saloon. After Pilegar deposits the money, he is paid a visit by the cops, who have identified the bills as being part of the stolen money. Pilegar refuses to cooperate, saying the money had been given to him by a number of different customers. He then proceeds to blackmail Will. When a huge fire breaks out in the city and the police and neighbors rush off to it, Will uses the opportunity to strangle Pilegar. The only person who knows that Will was at Pilegar's shop on the night of the fire is Lizzie Crane (Clare), a crazy old drunk who spreads the word about Will around the neighborhood. Before long the barber finds himself being tailed twenty-four hours a day by the police, ostracized by angry neighbors and victimized by vigilantes who try to destroy his shop. This prompts him to send his wife and baby daughter out of town, and when things get too hot he goes on the run. His only apparent friend is Jimsey Jones (Brent), a merchant seaman, and even Jimsey is beginning to be tempted by the £200 reward offered for Will's capture. Well acted, especially by Richardson, and sensationally photographed, *On the Night of the Fire* attempts to portray the protagonist in a sympathetic light. At first, the viewer is empathetic about Will's sudden larcenous behavior. After all, who has never given in to the temptation to do something wrong? However, he loses all claim to understanding when he cold-bloodedly murders his blackmailer and threatens to kill the man who has been trying to help him. Even the behavior of his loving and devoted wife, who probably never committed an unlawful deed in her entire life, is not very admirable. Not to fear, though. Noir fate steps in, as it always does, and resolves all issues.

On the Run
★★½ (1963)

PRISON GOVERNOR: I just can't understand it. Only a month to serve and he does something as stupid as this. Completely out of character. Model prisoner. First known offense. Already under a year's remission. And he spoils it all like this.
WARDER: He's no fool. He must know what it will mean.
PRISON GOVERNOR: There must be some reason. But he's an idiot.

Length: 59 min. **Cast:** Emrys Jones, Sarah Lawson, Patrick Barr, Delphi Lawrence, Kevin Stoney, Philip Locke. **Production Company:** Merton Park Productions. **Directed by:** Robert Tronson. **Photographed by:** James Wilson. **Written by:** Richard Harris.

Deeply in debt to crooked London bookie Wally Lucas (Stoney), Frank Stewart (Jones) embezzles funds from his employer and finds himself being blackmailed by Lucas into helping rob £30,000 worth of gold-bearer bonds. The heist goes awry, but before being nabbed by the police Stewart and his accomplice, David Hughes (Locke), manage to stash the bonds in a sewer. Both men are sent to prison, and three years later Lucas convinces Stewart that Hughes will be getting an early release. Fearing he will be cheated out of his share of the take, Stewart, scheduled for early release himself, breaks out and heads for London. The wily bookie then double-crosses Stewart by reporting his whereabouts to the cops, knowing that when he is captured more time will be added to his sentence, allowing Hughes to be released before him. While on the run, Stewart hooks up with his daughter's employer, Helen Carr (Lawson), and romantic sparks fly. But when Helen tries to convince him to surrender to the police, Stewart refuses, telling her that he's earned the dough and nothing will stop him from retrieving it. Lucas and his lover, Stewart's greedy wife Yvonne (Lawrence), have other plans, however, and a couple of Lucas' flunkies pay Helen a visit. *On the Run* is a slow-moving film that contains some interesting noir characterizations—a paranoid escaped convict, his femme fatale wife, a small-time but dangerous bookie, two sadistic goons, a seemingly psychotic safe cracker— and a noirish confrontation in a London sewer. There are worse ways to spend an hour. (Part of the "Edgar Wallace Mystery Theater" series.)

Once a Sinner
★★½ (1950)

I need Irene more than I need respectability. [John Ross]

Length: 80 min. **Cast:** Pat Kirkwood, Jack Watling, Joy Shelton, Sydney Tafler, Thora Hird, Stuart Latham. **Production Company:** John Argyle Productions. **Directed by:** Lewis Gilbert. **Photographed by:** Frank North. **Written by:** David Evans.

Flashy Irene James (Kirkwood) quits her barmaid job, leaves her despicable counterfeiter boyfriend, Jimmy Smart (Tafler), and weds John Ross (Watling), a young bank clerk who has recently become obsessed with her. Taken aback by John's risky proposal (his boss has hinted that he could lose his job at the bank for even being seen with the likes of such a woman) but willing to try anything at least once, Irene trades in her spiked heels and tight skirt for an ill-fitting kitchen apron. Needless to say, John's stuffy parents are more than just a little confounded by his choice of a wife. They had in mind a more sensible girl like pretty socialite Vera Lamb (Shelton), whom John callously dropped after meeting Irene. Six months into their marriage, John learns from his vicious mother-in-law (Hird) that Irene has been hiding a dark secret. It turns out that his bride is a mother, having given birth to Jimmy Smart's baby. Unable to accept the bad news, John forces Irene back into the arms of her baby's father, who has been brazenly passing counterfeit bills around town. Complicating things for her unhappy son, John's mother has been hiding Irene's desperate sounding letters. *Once a Sinner* is a slow-moving tale that is held together primarily by Kirkwood's effortless performance. She is reminiscent of another provocative new girl in town, Billie Nash in the 1954 American noir *Wicked Woman*. While neither girl might be considered beautiful, both Irene and Billie can stop a conversation simply by sashaying into a room. John Ross, like many of Billie Nash's victims, is hooked the moment he lays eyes on

Irene. *Sinner* might have been better if the filmmakers had had the foresight to give renowned British character actress Thora Hird a bit more screen time. The last fifteen minutes of the film are the most noirish, with some really top-notch nighttime scenes (including a darkened alley confrontation à la *Killer's Kiss*) and an ending that should satisfy even the most finicky film noir fan.

One Way Out
★★★ (1955)

LESLIE: We're just friends, that's all.
DANVERS: You *were* friends. Right now she's lying on a slab in the mortuary.
LESLIE: She's dead?
DANVERS: She's not playing hunt the slipper.

Length: 61 min. **Cast:** Eddie Byrne, Jill Adams, Lyndon Brook, John Chandos. **Production Company:** Major Productions. **Directed by:** Francis Searle. **Photographed by:** Walter Harvey. **Written by:** Jonathan Roche.

With only two weeks to go before his retirement, police detective John Patrick Hartcourt (Byrne) has only one regret: he has not been able to nab his long-time nemesis, Jim Danvers (Chandos), a vicious London fence. After the body of Danvers' distraught lover is found floating face down in the canal, an apparent suicide, Hartcourt connects her emerald necklace to a recent jewelry store robbery. Fearing that an investigation will expose his role in the heist, Danvers has his flunky, Leslie Parrish (Brook), frame Hartcourt's widowed daughter, Shirley (Adams), as an accomplice in a gas station robbery. He then blackmails the cop, forcing him to convince his superiors that his lead connecting the fence to the jewelry robbery did not pan out. Sealing the arrangement, Danvers also forces Hartcourt to accept a £1,000 bribe. When the cop retires, Danvers breathes a sigh of relief that quickly turns to panic when an attendant he assaulted in the gas station robbery dies of his injuries. With his former colleagues closing in on his daughter as the killer, Hartcourt concocts an alibi for her and Parrish, but the police aren't buying it, leaving the former cop only one way out. A veteran police officer with an unblemished record, Hartcourt doesn't turn bad because of greed or a dame as do many of his American noir counterparts (for instance, the dirty cops of *Night Editor*, *Murder Is My Beat*, *Private Hell 36*, *The Prowler*, *Pushover*, *Rogue Cop*, or *Shield for Murder*), but he does so to protect his daughter, the widow of a slain police officer. But no matter the motive, the label "dirty cop" is the ultimate consequence of his decision. He is so guilt-ridden, however, and so desperate to protect his daughter that he comes up with a daring scheme to take down Danvers. Solid, low-key performances, especially by the distinguished looking Byrne, and a sensational ending make for an interesting and enjoyable film.

Operation Diplomat
★★½ (1953)

SISTER ROGERS: Is everything all right?
FENTON: Yes, everything's fine. Mrs. Terry's in there dead.

Length: 70 min. **Cast:** Guy Rolfe, Lisa Daniely, Patricia Dainton, Sydney Tafler, Ballard Berkeley, Anton Diffring. **Production Company:** Nettlefold Productions. **Directed by:** John Guillermin. **Photographed by:** Gerald Gibbs. **Written by:** A.R. Rawlinson, John Guillermin.

Mr. Fenton (Rolfe), a London surgeon (yes, Mr. is the correct title for British surgeons), is whisked away in a phony ambulance to a house where a man lay dying. There he performs surgery with the aid of Mr. Shroder (Diffring), a surgeon whose license has been revoked for undisclosed reasons, and Lisa Durand (Daniely), a nurse who has been blackmailed into assisting. After the successful operation, Fenton is paid 350 guineas by a man named Wade (Tafler), who refuses to identify the patient. Wade drugs the unsuspecting doctor and has him dropped off unceremoniously on a park bench in the middle of the night. The next evening Fenton is visited by a man who claims he is a Foreign Service officer and says that Shroder has something to do with the disappearance of the chairman of Western Defence, Sir Oliver Peters. A photograph convinces Fenton that Peters is the man whose life he saved the previous evening. When Shroder is murdered in Fenton's flat, the doctor assumes he was killed by the government agent, but Inspector Austin (Berkeley) informs him that no such person exists and that Scotland Yard considers Fenton the prime suspect. When Fenton's head nurse and assistant mystery solver, Sister Rogers (Dainton), is kidnapped, the doctor races against time to find her before Wade and his boss, an enigmatic figure known only as "the chief," can smuggle Peters out of the country. Bodies and red herrings litter this convoluted, but action-packed, film, which was based on a British TV series of the same name. It's a fast seventy minutes with the long and lanky Rolfe enjoyable as the prominent surgeon wrongly suspected of multiple murders.

Outcast of the Islands
★★★★ (1951)

> CAPT. LINGARD: You have been possessed of a devil.
> WILLEMS: Yes. Isn't she pretty?

Length: 102 min. **Cast:** Ralph Richardson, Trevor Howard, Robert Morley, Wendy Hiller, George Coulouris, Kerima, Peter Illing, Betty Ann Davies, A.V. Bramble. **Production Companies:** London Film Productions, British Lion Production Assets. **Directed by:** Carol Reed. **Photographed by:** John Wilcox, Edward Scaife. **Written by:** William Fairchild.

Embezzler Peter Willems (Howard), fired from his managerial position at a colonial trading post in Singapore and kicked out of his house by his wife (Davies), hops a ride on a schooner captained by his good friend, Tom Lingard (Richardson), a prosperous trader. Lingard's secret route to and from Sambir is the envy of all businessmen in the area, especially the Arab Alagappan (Illing), who has convinced tribal elder Babalatchi (Coulouris) and the aged blind chief, Badavi (Bramble), to help him gain river access to Sambir so he can drive Lingard out of business. Lingard's manager, Almayer (Morley), fears that the newly arrived Willems, who has been assigned to assist him, is planning to take over his job. Almayer refuses to let Willems do any work, hoping that when Lingard returns from his next trading excursion he will have a change of heart and send the upstart back to Singapore. Meanwhile, Willems, with plenty of free time on his hands, becomes obsessed with Badavi's beautiful daughter, Aissa (Algerian-born Kerima), following her around like a lovesick teenager and sharing his secret desires with Almayer's kindly wife (Hiller), who is also Lingard's adopted daughter. Babalatchi encourages Aissa to play up to the ruttish white man, who has become an entertaining spectacle to the perceptive natives, in order to persuade him to reveal the way through the rocky waterways that lead to Sambir. Instead, Willems, hoping to worm his way into Lingard's established trading business, makes Almayer a business proposition. The insecure manager turns him down. This prompts Willem to accept the Arab's offer, thus betraying his only friend in the world and ultimately paying a high personal price for his treachery. *Outcast* is a spectacular adaptation of Joseph Conrad's novel by one of Britain's most important directors, Carol Reed (*Odd Man Out, The Third Man, The Fallen Idol*). A steamy tale of lust, betrayal and moral degeneration expertly photographed against an atmospheric jungle village backdrop, the film relies heavily on the superb acting skills of its three co-stars: Howard as the pathetic scoundrel, whose lustful obsession for a sultry native girl is the beginning of his downfall; Morley, the fat, pompous trading post manager, who was "trapped" into marrying the boss' daughter and worries obsessively about the intrusion of a potential business rival; and Richardson, in a smaller role, as Willem's loyal friend who lives to regret his decision to once again take the troubled man under his wing. The film's final scenes are unforgettable if a bit mystifying in deciphering Aissa's motive for encouraging Willems to murder his former friend. Perhaps the explanation lies in the nine minutes that were cut from the film's American release in 1952.

Paid to Kill see Five Days

The Painted Smile (U.S. Title: Murder Can Be Deadly)
★★ (1962)

> KLEINIE: It's a matter of principle. You trespassed.... You're going to do something for me.

The Painted Smile

A nightclub hostess (Liz Fraser) lures an intoxicated college student (Tony Wickert) to her apartment, where she thinks her extortionist boyfriend is waiting in *The Painted Smile* (a.k.a. *Murder Can Be Deadly*) (Blakeley's Films, 1962).

> Something very useful for once in your life. Just for once.
> MARK: Useful?
> KLEINIE: Yes, Mark. You're going to be a good example to other trespassers.

Length: 60 min. **Cast:** Liz Fraser, Kenneth Griffith, Peter Reynolds, Tony Wickert, Nanette Newman, David Hemmings. **Production Company:** Blakeley's Films. **Directed by:** Lance Comfort. **Photographed by:** Basil Emmott. **Written by:** Pip Baker, Jane Baker.

Three college students out on the town end up in a London clip joint where Jo Lake (Fraser) works as a hostess. Jo and her boyfriend, Mark (Reynolds), have a nice little racket going for themselves. She picks up drunks and brings them home, where Mark, playing the irate husband, takes them for all the dough they have on them. Of the three celebrating students, Jo chooses Tom (Wickert) because he has £50 and is drunk as a skunk. When they arrive at her flat, Jo discovers that Mark has been murdered by her former lover, Kleinie (Griffith), and she is quick to blackmail Tom into disposing of her unlucky accomplice. While driving to the countryside to bury the body, Tom is chased by a police car and abandons his vehicle. The next day he wakes up in a warehouse suffering from alcoholic blackout about the events of the previous evening. A quick look at the morning newspaper, however, serves as a depressing reminder, and Tom goes on the run with his girlfriend, Mary (Newman), hoping to find Jo, who also is trying to leave town. This is a somewhat entertaining piece of fluff with several darkly photographed scenes, such as the crippled Kleinie climbing the dark stairwell that leads to his victim's flat. Its main interest, however, lies in the presence of former child actor and future jack of all movie trades, producer, director and actor David Hemmings.

Panic
★★½ (1963)

> JOHNNIE: I'd poison her mother and she'd still protect me.
> TOM: She must have a beautiful maternal instinct. Towards you, I mean, not her mother.

Length: 69 min. **Cast:** Janine Gray, Glyn Houston, Dyson Lovell, Duncan Lamont, Stanley Meadows, Brian Weske, Philip Ray, Charles Houston. **Production Company:** Ingram. **Directed by:** John Gilling. **Photographed by:** Geoffrey Faithfull. **Written by:** John Gilling.

Jazz trumpeter Johnnie Cobb (Lovell) plays his Swiss girlfriend, Janine Heining (Gray), for a patsy when two of his cohorts, Tom (Meadows) and Ben (Weske), rob and kill her diamond merchant boss. The robbers knock Janine unconscious, and when she awakens she finds she has lost her memory. Suspecting that Janine was involved in the heist and murder, Scotland Yard Inspector Saunders (Lamont) searches for the secretary while she deliriously wanders in and out of several London dives, including a cafe patronized by violent beatniks and a sleazy hotel, where she is sexually attacked by a brazen desk clerk. After being befriended by kindly ex-boxer Mike Connor (Houston), Janine finds herself in even deeper trouble when Johnnie kills his accomplice brother, Louis (Houston), and tries to frame her for the crime. Meanwhile, Mike, badly out of condition, returns to the boxing ring to earn enough money to help Janine get out of the country. *Panic* is similar in theme to a number of American films noirs (*Clay Pigeon, Somewhere in the Night, Two O'Clock Courage*), in which an amnesia victim is wrongfully suspected of a crime and goes on the run to learn his real identity with the help of a beautiful woman. An otherwise mundane crime film, *Panic* offers several unique twists to the amnesia theme. Here the memory loss victim is a beautiful woman and her newly found friend and ally is a trustworthy man. The presence of an homme fatale, a few tilted camera angle shots, and an exciting climax in a darkened alleyway outside the boxing arena are nice noir touches. Ultimately, however, *Panic* suffers from a lack of character development and a tortuously slow pace. "A" for effort, though.

Paranoiac
★★★½ (1963)

I'm mad. I'm insane. I'm dirty! [Eleanor Ashby]

Length: 80 min. **Cast:** Janette Scott, Oliver Reed, Sheila Burrell, Alexander Davion. **Production Company:** Hammer Film Productions. **Directed by:** Freddie Francis. **Photographed by:** Arthur Grant. **Written by:** Jimmy Sangster.

Several years after his parents were killed in an airplane accident, 15-year-old Tony Ashby committed suicide by jumping off a cliff into the ocean. His body was never found, having been washed out to sea. At least that's what his loving but emotionally unbalanced sister, Eleanor (Scott), believed until a young look-alike imposter shows up at her mansion seven years later just in time to save her from a suicide attempt. The sudden appearance of her supposedly dead brother gives Eleanor a new lease on life but depresses the hell out of her other brother, alcoholic playboy Simon (Reed), who suddenly realizes he can kiss his £600,000 inheritance goodbye ... unless he can come up with a way to get rid of both the imposter and Eleanor, whose descent into insanity he had counted on and encouraged. Meanwhile, the head of the dysfunctional Ashby clan, spinster Aunt Harriet (Burrell), is having a difficult time keeping secret her favorite nephew's worsening mental condition and controlling his heavy drinking (the inconsiderate lout has been going well over the family's weekly £20 wine allowance). As if things couldn't get any worse at the Ashby mansion, a psychopath in a clown mask has been slithering around brandishing a meat hook. Hammer Films, riding Hitchcock's *Psycho* band wagon, produced in *Paranoiac* a high-quality psychological thriller. The cast is excellent, especially Reed, although his borderline histrionics approaches that of a Robert Newton or Vincent Price performance. Director Francis throws in enough twists and turns to muddle the plot for a while but eventually clears up everything satisfactorily. Screenwriter Sangster offers a provocative script that touches fleetingly on the possibility of incest between Eleanor and her imposter brother and suggests that all may not be perfectly normal in the nephew-aunt relationship either. Cinematographer Grant's atmospheric black and white photography gives ammunition to those film noir fans who consider *Paranoiac* to be a late entry in the "noir cycle." The title is terrific but puzzling since the film's dangerous characters probably would not be diagnosed as merely "paranoid" by mental health professionals.

The Paris Express see *The Man Who Watched the Trains Go By*

The Passing Stranger
(NR) (1954)

Length: 84 min. **Cast**: Lee Patterson, Diane Cilento, Duncan Lamont, Olive Gregg. **Production Company**: Harlequin Productions. **Directed by**: John Arnold. **Photographed by**: Walter Lassally. **Written by**: Anthony Simmons, John Arnold.

In need of dough to run off with his girl, an American Army deserter becomes involved with a gang of gunrunners.

Passport to Shame
(U.S. Title: *Room 43*)
★★½ (1959)

A woman is like a guitar. It depends on the player. [Nick Biaggi]

Two reluctant prostitutes (Odile Versois, left, and Diana Dors, right) peddle their wares on a London street corner for their vicious pimp in *Passport to Shame* (a.k.a. *Room 43*) (United Co-Productions, 1959).

Length: 91 min. **Cast**: Eddie Constantine, Odile Versois, Diana Dors, Herbert Lom, Brenda de Banzie. **Production Company**: United Co-Productions. **Directed by**: Alvin Rakoff. **Photographed by**: Jack Asher. **Written by**: Patrick Alexander.

London pimp Nick Biaggi (Lom) and his madam, Aggie (de Banzie), frame an innocent French waitress, Marie Louise Beaucaire (Versois), for theft at the Paris restaurant where she works and trick her into emigrating to London, where they plan to make her part of their stable of prostitutes—not a common streetwalker like the rest of their girls, but a high-priced call girl "reserved for special customers" and, of course, for Nick. In order for them to keep her in England permanently, however, they first have to find a patsy who will marry her and then file for an annulment. They decide on taxi driver Johnny McVey (Constantine), an ambitious Canadian who has borrowed money from Nick's front, the United Loan Company, to buy a cab, the beginning, Johnny hopes, of his own fleet. After having Johnny's new vehicle destroyed in a planned "accident," Nick claims to be a war veteran whose life was saved during the war by a member of Johnny's outfit. He offers to pay off Johnny's debt to United Loan, and from here it is a simple task to convince the broke taxi driver to marry a foreigner for money. What Nick doesn't count on is Johnny falling in love with the beautiful French girl and, with a bit of help from scores of tough taxi driver buddies, attempting to rescue her from a fate worse than death. A subplot has one of Nick's prostitutes, Vicki (Dors), walking the streets in order to pay for plastic surgery for a victim of Nick's psychotic cruelty, her acid-scarred younger sister, "a girl who wouldn't look at a man; now no man will look at her." The U.S. release, entitled *Room 41* (the room in which Nick imprisons Marie Louise after she refuses to prostitute for him), runs five minutes shorter than the original British production. Missing is a narrative introduction by real-life Inspector Robert Fabian, whose career the 1954 British TV series "Fabian of Scotland Yard" was based upon. Here Fabian condemns the social evils of prostitution (the filmmakers' bow to the British Board of Film Censors, which at the time permitted the topic of prostitution to be portrayed only if preceded by such an abjuration). With the exception of a bit part in a 1936 Hollywood musical (*Born to Dance*), this is the first English-language film for American-born actor Eddie Constantine, who eventually made such a name for himself in French movies that he became a citizen of France. He does well here as the sympathetic but tough taxi driver. Lom is appropriately revolting, and French actress Versois is convincingly sweet and innocent. Cinematographer Jack Asher treats the viewer to a vivid expressionistic nightmare, in which Marie Louise, after two drags on a cigarette laced with some pretty strong stuff, hallucinates about running through a street lined with prostitutes, tossing herself into a pit filled with naked men, breaking a wooden stool over a john's head, being trapped by prison bars that are closing in on her, and seeing herself in a mirror as a hardened prostitute. Look for Michael Caine in an early bit role as a bridegroom.

Payroll
(U.S. Title: *I Promised to Pay*)
★★★ (1961)

> There isn't a thief alive who can crack our system. [overconfident security man Harry Parker]

Length: 105 min. **Cast**: Michael Craig, Françoise Prévost, Billie Whitelaw, William Lucas, Kenneth Griffith, Tom Bell, Barry Keegan, William Peacock. **Production Companies**: Lynx Films, Independent Artists. **Directed by**: Sidney Hayers. **Photographed by**: Ernest Steward. **Written by**: George Baxt.

A motor works factory hires Harry Parker (Peacock), a security expert who promises executives that their payroll will be as safe as if it were in the bank when they use his new "tank on wheels," an armored van that is supposedly impregnable to robbery attempts. Harry, it is proven later by Johnny Mellors (Craig) and his gang (Griffith, Bell and Keegan), was mistaken. Harry dies during the brazen robbery and the gang gets away with £100,000, the factory's entire payroll. Harry's widow, Jackie (Whitelaw), impatient with the slow police investigation, seeks revenge and starts sending anonymous notes to the factory's accountant, Dennis Pearson (Lucas), whom she correctly suspects was the inside man on the heist. Pearson's shrewish wife, Katie (Prévost), meanwhile, has been throwing herself at the lecherous Johnny and has some heist ideas of her own. The first half-hour of this heist noir is devoted to the tedious planning stage, but the action soon picks up, revolving around the infighting among the thieves, Katie's seduction of Johnny, and Jackie's stalking of the guilt-ridden accountant. Comparisons to *The Killing* are inevitable but it should be noted that any resemblance between *Payroll* and the classic American film noir is mostly superficial (although the beautiful Prévost as the femme fatale housewife with adultery and dough on her mind certainly gives a high-quality, Marie Windsor-like performance). Craig and Lucas ham it up at times to the point of silliness, but the rest of the supporting cast, especially Bell, give good performances. The irony-drenched climax is particularly enjoyable. *Payroll* was filmed on location in Newcastle Upon Tyne, and the street scenes are attention grabbing, especially those leading up to the robbery. The armored van, however, is almost laughable, falling apart easily when sandwiched between two ramming trucks while a tape recorder in the back broadcasts an SOS over a loud speaker mounted on the roof: "Help. Bandits. Help." Surprisingly, a good number of workers from the motor works factory respond to the appeal and make a valiant effort to nab the robbers. Good citizens or did they realize that they might not be getting paid that week?

Peeping Tom
★★★★½ (1960)

> You're safe as long as I can't see you frightened, so stand in the shadows, please. Please. [Mark Lewis to Helen Stephens]

Length: 109 min. **Cast**: Carl Boehm, Moira Shearer, Anna Massey, Maxine Audley, Jack Watson. **Production Company**: Michael Powell Theatre. **Directed by**: Michael Powell. **Photographed by**: Otto Heller. **Written by**: Leo Marks.

Photographer Mark Lewis (Boehm), a focus-puller at a London motion picture studio, moonlights by taking pictures of naked women for a shopkeeper, who sells them under the counter to his male customers. Mark also happens to be a psychotic killer suffering from scoptophilia, or voyeurism, evidently caused by his late psychiatrist father's experiments in which he filmed his young son in terrifying situations. Turned on by the fear in his victims' faces, Mark photographs the women as he is about to plunge into their necks a blade he has hidden in a leg of his tripod. Mark's first on-screen victim is an aging Soho prostitute, whom the viewer sees through the lens of Mark's movie camera. His next victim is a movie extra (Shearer), who stays at the studio late one evening to allow Mark to film her. Mark tells her to try to act terrified for the camera, but after listening to some up-tempo music and dancing around the vacant set, she has difficulty doing so. But not for long. While Scotland Yard Chief Inspector Gregg (Watson) investigates the murders, Mark is fast becoming friends with one of his tenants, Helen Stephens (Massey), a plain-Jane librarian who cares for her blind mother (Audley) in a room they rent in Mark's house. Helen, an aspiring writer, has written a children's book called "The Magic Camera" and seeks technical advice from her upstairs neighbor, who seems flattered by her request. Although her daughter seems to be falling for the handsome photographer, Mrs. Stephens senses that there is something very wrong about him and takes to sneaking into his darkroom, where he regularly views his snuff films and listens to his father's taped experiments. Highly controversial at the time of its release, *Peeping Tom* badly damaged the career of director Powell, although the film is now considered by many a work of genius thanks to American director Martin Scorcese's efforts to have the film, which had been badly chopped up for its American release, restored to its original form. Mild in comparison the splatter films that would hit the theaters not long afterward, this fascinating psychological thriller nevertheless was anathematized by irate English critics. German actor Boehm is aptly spooky as the perverted killer, whose shyness hides a deadly persona. The color cinematography is spectacular and one would imagine that noir veteran Heller must have had a grand time photographing this peek at life behind a madman's camera.

Personal Affair
★★★ (1953)

> I can't think any more. My mind is full of horrors. Whichever way it turns it runs into horror. [Henry Vining]

Length: 83 min. **Cast:** Gene Tierney, Leo Genn, Glynis Johns, Walter Fitzgerald, Megs Jenkins, Pamela Brown. **Production Company:** Two Cities Films. **Directed by:** Anthony Pélissier. **Photographed by:** Reginald Wyer. **Written by:** Lesley Storm.

Seventeen-year-old student Barbara Vining (Johns) has fallen in love with her Latin teacher Stephen Barlow (Genn), and a tactless comment by Stephen's jealous and insecure wife, Kay (American actress Tierney), drives the humiliated girl from her private tutoring session at the Barlow house. Angered at his wife's insensitivity, Stephen leaves the house and telephones Barbara to ask to her to meet him ... near the river. When Barbara's mother (Jenkins) and father (Fitzgerald) return home later that evening they become worried that their daughter hasn't returned. The next day, a search party finds the girl's beret in the river and the Vinings begin to fear the worst. In the days that follow, Stephen tells the police that he accidentally ran into Barbara during an evening walk before putting her on a bus for home. Three days into Barbara's disappearance, Stephen officially becomes a murder suspect and loses his job at school, Kay begins receiving obscene telephone calls and the townsfolk begin to gossip about a torrid love affair between the teacher and his teen-aged student. Meanwhile, Barbara's spinster aunt (Brown), a bitter and cynical woman who hasn't forgotten the lover who spurned her twenty years earlier, pays a malicious visit to Kay to confirm the gossip. The splendid cast overcomes the somewhat talky script with sensitive performances, while Wyer's shadowy cinematography adds to the suspense and overall depressing atmosphere. Genn is particularly good as the man suspected of seducing and possibly murdering his trusting student, and Fitzgerald is convincing as the heartbroken and bewildered father torn between wanting to believe the teacher's protestations of innocence and suspecting that the man is a dangerous psychopath who may have sexually violated and killed his daughter.

Piccadilly Third Stop
★★★ (1960)

> I know that look. Somebody's going to get double-crossed. [Christine Preedy]

Length: 90 min. **Cast:** Terence Morgan, Mai Zetterling, Yoko Tani, John Crawford, William Hartnell, Charles Kay. **Production Company:** Ethiro Productions. **Directed by:** Wolf Rilla. **Photographed by:** Ernest Steward. **Written by:** Leigh Vance.

Small-time London crook and all-around cad Dominic Colpoys-Owen (Morgan) meets Phina (Tani), the daughter of the ambassador of a small country in the East Indies and, having nothing better to do that week, seduces her. When Phina lets it slip that her father has more than £100,000 stashed in the embassy safe and that he will be out of town on business, Dominic hurriedly recruits a heist team. He even convinces the naive Phina, who thinks he wants to run away with her after the robbery, to unlock the door to the basement room where the safe is located. The wannabe robbers, Dominic, veteran safe blower Colonel Whitfield (Hartnell), money man Joe Preedy (American actor Crawford) and Dominic's friend and former accomplice, Toddy (Kay), plan to break into the embassy by digging through a tunnel wall in the Underground subway system. Preedy, however, who is deeply in debt to a dangerous gambler, decides he doesn't want to split the take four ways and, violating the team's agreement, packs a gun on the night of the heist. Dominic learns about Preddy's planned double-cross from Preedy's adulterous wife, Christine (Zetterling), and brings his own revolver. Meanwhile, the men learn that Toddy has been picked up by cops for trying to sell hot jewelry and that the ambassador is returning a day earlier than expected. Agreeing that they have no alternative, the men reluctantly go ahead with their plans, confident that Toddy would never squeal. As a heist noir, *Piccadilly* falls short when compared to some of its classic American counterparts, such as *The Asphalt Jungle* or *The Killing*, but it is surprisingly effective in its gradual plot and character development, picking up momentum with the formation of the heist team around midpoint in the film, and capping off everything with a suspenseful, if predictable, climax. The acting is decent, with veteran character actor Hartnell taking top honors as the persnickety safecracker. Phillip Green's jazz score is the icing on this noir cake.

Pink String and Sealing Wax
★★½ (1945)

> If I swing, he swings as well. I'll take him with me if it's the last thing I do. [Pearl Bond]

Length: 89 min. **Cast:** Mervyn Johns, Googie Withers, Gordon Jackson, Garry Marsh, John Carol. **Production Company:** Ealing Studios. **Directed by:** Robert Hamer. **Photographed by:** Richard S. Pavey. **Written by:** Diana Morgan, Robert Hamer.

Chemist Edward Sutton (Johns) rules his Victorian household with an iron fist, dominating his longsuffering wife and terrorizing his five children, one of whom, David (Jackson), begins drinking heavily and pursing the unresponsive Pearl Bond (Withers), the faithless and battered wife of the owner of a Brighton pub called The Dolphin. While in the chemist's shop being treated by David for a cut hand, Pearl snatches some strychnine and later puts it in her husband's whiskey. When the police become suspicious, Pearl's lover, Dan Powell (Carol), advises her to blackmail store owner Sutton, who also has the job of analyzing contaminated substances for the court, into standing by the physician's verdict of death by tetanus. When she tells Sutton that his son had given her the strychnine and told her it was merely a medicine designed to put her alcoholic husband, Joe (Marsh), "off the drink," Sutton doesn't buy her story. So she tries a different approach, telling him that David had told her it was poison all right and that they plotted the murder together. So Sutton decides it's time for a heart-to-heart with his naive boy, and Pearl nervously awaits his decision. Other than Googie Withers' stand-out performance as the victimized wife driven to murder, *Pink String and Sealing Wax* (referring to the chemist's method of wrapping his products) is predictable and often slow moving. Interesting though is the film's portrayal of two very different types of abusers—one a member of the privileged upper middle class, a self-righteous despot who bullies his entire family, and the other a lower class barkeep with a loose wife and a serious drinking problem that triggers outbursts of physical violence.

Pit of Darkness
★★½ (1961)

> AMNESIAC RICHARD LOGAN: You've got to believe me. There is no other woman.
> JULIE LOGAN: How do you know if you've lost your memory?

Length: 76 min. **Cast:** William Franklyn, Moira Redmond, Leonard Sachs, Bruno Barnabe, Anthony Booth, Nanette Newman, Humphrey Lestocq, Michael Balfour. **Production Company:** Butcher's Film Service. **Directed by:** Lance Comfort. **Photographed by:** Basil Emmott. **Written by:** Lance Comfort.

Safe designer Richard Logan (Franklyn) awakens in the rubble of an old bomb site in London after being dumped there by two men who, had they not been frightened away by a group of children, would have murdered him. Having suffered a bad knock on the head, Richard doesn't recall what happened to him and returns home thinking he has been away for three hours. Instead, he learns from his wife, Julie (Redmond), that he has been missing for three weeks. She thinks he has been cheating on her, but Richard fears, as have many noir amnesia victims before him, that he has done something horrible and is tormented by his inability to remember what it is. Julie also tells him that the private investigator she hired to find him has been murdered. Richard tries to retrace his steps and, little by little, after numerous mental flashbacks, he discovers that Clifton Conrad (Sachs), the shady owner of a Soho night spot called The Blue Baboon, and his goons, Bruno (Barnabe) and Fisher (Balfour), are involved somehow in his predicament. He also learns that some important office files are missing, files reporting that one of his company's safes has been broken into and that the famous Ethiope's Ear Diamond has been stolen. He begins to suspect that this is the horrible thing he feared and that either his business partner, Bill (Lestocq), or his secretary, Mary (Newman) and her seedy boyfriend, Ted (Booth), are in cahoots with Conrad. After several attempts on his life, Richard finally remembers everything only to learn that now it is his wife who is missing. *Pit* is an average amnesia noir that contains some highly implausible moments, such as the safe-cracking scene in which the six people crammed into a room in the middle of the night make enough noise to awaken the dead but go unnoticed by the people living there. Saving the film, however, are the nicely photographed mini-flashbacks and a enjoyable musical score by Martin Slavin.

A Place to Go
★★½ (1963)

> It's just one night's work. That's all I'm in it for. Just enough money to get me independence. [Ricky Flint]

Length: 86 min. **Cast:** Bernard Lee, Rita Tushingham, Mike Sarne, Doris Hare, David Andrews, John Slater. **Production Company:** Excalibur Films. **Directed by:** Basil Dearden. **Photographed by:** Reginald H. Wyer. **Written by:** Michael Relph.

Bethnal Green neighborhood lad Ricky Flint (Sarne) seeks to escape his dead-end existence by hijacking cigarettes from the factory where he is employed. In league with local gangster Jack Ellerman (Slater), Ricky convinces his brother-in-law, Jim (Andrews), to be the getaway driver while he himself works on dismantling the factory's burglar alarm system. Ricky also manages to find time to become involved with Catherine (Tushingham), the sardonic girlfriend of one of his accomplices. Meanwhile, Ricky's father, Matt (Lee), quits his job and suffers the indignation of being forced by his wife, Lil (Hare), to give up his seat at the head of the dinner table to Ricky, who has now become the family bread winner. Humiliated and desperate, Matt takes to performing a foolish escape artist act outside London movie theaters in order to earn a few bob. This potentially solid heist yarn is marred by too many attempts at light comedy. Pop singer Sarne, best known for directing and writing the disastrous 1970 film *Myra Breckenridge*, is enjoyable as the novice crook, and Tushingham, a unique actress in every respect, does a good job as his romantic interest.

Playback
★★★ (1962)

> When I said I'd do anything for you it didn't include *that*! [Constable Dave Hollis to Lisa Shillack's murder plan]

Length: 62 min. **Cast:** Margit Saad, Barry Foster, George Pravda, Nigel Green. **Production Company:** Merton Park Productions. **Directed by:** Quentin Lawrence. **Photographed by:** Bert Mason. **Written by:** Robert Stewart.

Constable Dave Hollis (Foster) has big hopes for his career, with a promotion to detective in the Criminal Investigation Division (CID) expected shortly. On his regular beat one night, he meets Lisa (Saad), the wife of international jeweler Simon Shillack (Pravda). Lisa has locked herself out of her flat and Dave dutifully assists her. He hangs around for a couple of drinks, just long enough to miss a robbery being committed in the neighborhood, prompting him to file false report about where he was at the time of the crime. Dave soon becomes romantically involved with Lisa, who takes him to her favorite casino, where he loses a bundle. Casino manager Ralph Monk (Green) isn't the type of guy who likes waiting for his dough so he has a couple of his goons work Dave over and gives him two weeks to come up with the dough or else. Sensing his desperation, Lisa drops the bomb — she suggests that they kill her husband, who is worth £250,000. Shocked and indignant at her suggestion, Dave storms off but, like his American film noir cousin, *Double Indemnity*'s Walter Neff, he soon warms to the idea. Before he realizes what's happening, he's standing in front of Simon Shillack and pointing a gun at him. *Playback* is about as noir as a Brit noir gets. It falls a bit short with its unimpressive cinematography but is packed with noir themes, elements and characters. The film begins with former cop Dave Hollis on trial for murder and continues with a lengthy flashback with voiceover narration during which he informs the viewer about how he had the misfortune to hook up with a dangerous femme fatale. In addition to being a war veteran, Constable Dave is an inveterate gambler who transforms into a bad cop just a short time into his adulterous affair with Lisa. Because of the flashback scenario, the viewer knows he will eventually succumb to her evil charms, but what the killer faces afterwards is nothing short of film noir hell. (Part of the "Edgar Wallace Mystery Theater" series.)

The Pleasure Lovers
see *Naked Fury*

Poison Pen
★★★★ (1939)

> There is someone amongst us with the cunning of a fiend. [Rev. Rider]

Length: 79 min. **Cast:** Ann Todd, Flora Robson, Geoffrey Toone, Robert Newton, Reginald Tate, Belle Chrystall, Edward Chapman, Catherine Lacey. **Production Company:** Associated British Picture Corporation. **Directed by:** Paul L. Stein. **Photographed by:** Philip Tannura. **Written by:** William Freshman, Doreen Montgomery.

The villagers of Hilldale, a small town in the English countryside, are being tormented by the mean-spirited author of anonymous letters that accuse some of the citizens of various sexual escapades. Even the town's most prestigious families, including the Riders— Rev. Rider (Tate); his spinster sister, Mary (Robson); and his

While the citizens of Hilldale are being inundated with anonymous hate mail, the town's most eligible bachelor (Cyril Chamberlain), the vicar's spinster sister (Flora Robson) and her niece (Ann Todd, rear right) enjoy a church social in *Poison Pen* (Associated British Pictures, 1939).

daughter, Ann (Todd) — as well as Ann's fiancée, David (Toone), are not immune to the vicious slander that eventually results in the suicide of Connie Fateley (Lacey). The emotionally fragile Connie, a "foreigner" (i.e., a village newcomer), had been wrongly targeted by angry townsfolk as the culprit. Shortly after the Rev. Rider calls in Scotland Yard to investigate the letters, Sam Hurrin (Newton), a depressed and out-of-work local, guns down a shopkeeper (Chapman) whom the letter writer accused of having an affair with Hurrin's pregnant wife (Chrystall). Working with a renowned handwriting expert, the Yard watches every mailbox in Hilldale and begins interviewing everyone who mails a letter. Based on a play by Richard Llewellyn, *Poison Pen* is a dark and depressing look at the turmoil faced by an already gossip-ridden village when one of its own resorts to slander of the most vicious kind in order to compensate for the lack of normalcy in his or her own life. Reginald Tate is excellent as the righteously indignant vicar, and Flora Robson does an exceptional job as his well-respected and much-loved sister. The film's climax, beginning with the revelation of the letter writer and ending with the slanderer's well-deserved punishment, is so expertly done that it can easily be watched over and over. *Poison Pen* compares favorably to the similarly themed but more famous *Le Corbeau* (1943) and its American film noir remake *The 13th Letter* (1951).

Pool of London
★★★ (1951)

You wonder perhaps why I never set foot in this accursed city. Well, I'll tell you. Behold from afar it gleams like a jewel. But walk within the shadow of its walls and what do you find? Filth. Squalor. Misery. [Ship's engineer Trotter]

Length: 85 min. **Cast:** Bonar Colleano, Susan Shaw, Earl Cameron, Moira Lister, Max Adrian. **Production Company:** Ealing Studios. **Directed by:** Basil Dearden. **Photographed by:** Gordon Dines. **Written by:** Jack Whittingham, John Eldridge.

Two merchant seamen, Dan (Colleano) and his buddy, Johnny (Cameron), hit the streets of London during a weekend stopover. Wheeler and dealer Dan smuggles small contraband items, such as cigarettes, which he sells to a steady customer, and nylons, which he gives to his girlfriend, Maisie (Lister). ("Wonderful what a woman will do for a pair of these," he tells a shipmate.) His Jamaican friend, Johnny, although pretty much a straight-shooter and determined to stay out of trouble, is not above helping his friend sneak an occasional item ashore. When Dan is offered a hundred quid to deliver a small box to Rotterdam, he jumps at the opportunity but, fearing that the customs official has it in for him and is sure to search him, he asks Johnny to bring the box aboard the ship. To impress Maisie, Johnny violates the terms of his agreement with the robbers by opening the sealed box. He discovers that it contains stolen diamonds from a recent heist in which an elderly watchman was murdered. Although reluctant now to involve his best friend, Dan is convinced by the greedy Maisie to go ahead with the arrangement in order to "put ourselves on velvet." Meanwhile, Maisie's sister, who has overheard their conversation, accidentally spills the beans in front of a constable and is hauled off to Scotland Yard for a little talk with the officers investigating the robbery and murder. *Pool of London* is a fascinating and tightly woven thriller containing interesting on-location photography in and around post-war London and a nicely done heist scene involving some daring acrobatics by the heist mastermind (Adrian). Colleano and Cameron convincingly portray interracial buddies whose friendship will soon be put to the test. A subplot involves the possibility of a romance between Johnny and a friendly white theater cashier (Shaw, later the real-life wife of Colleano) and his encounters with racial prejudice.

Port of Escape
★½ (1956)

Dames! They've got tongues as long as your arm. She'll tie you in knots. [Dinty Missouri]

Length: 76 min. **Cast:** Googie Withers, John McCallum, Bill Kerr, Joan Hickson, Wendy Danielli, Alexander Gauge. **Production Company:** Wellington Films. **Directed by:** Tony Young. **Photographed**

by: Philip Grindrod. **Written by:** Barbara S. Harper, Tony Young.

Two recently dismissed seamen, Australian Mitchell Gillis (McCallum) and American "Dinty Missouri" (Kerr), take it on the lam around the London docks after Mitch accidentally kills a sailor while protecting Dinty in an alley brawl. The former war heroes take refuge aboard a barge used as a residence by three women, gossip columnist Anne Stirling (Withers), who witnessed the fight and believes that Mitch murdered the man; her 17-year-old sister, Daphne (Danielli) and their maid, Rosalie (Hickson). While holding the women against their will, Mitch tries to explain that the sailor's death was accidental, but they're having none of that ... until Anne begins to fall for the ruggedly handsome fugitive. The potentially violent Dinty, suffering from amnesia as a result of a head injury sustained in an airplane crash, teeters on the verge of a psychotic breakdown. Fearing that his best friend will dump him for their pretty hostage and forget his promise to get him safely back to his hometown in Missouri for a brain operation, Dinty inserts a clip into the unloaded gun Mitch allows him to carry. Meanwhile, Scotland Yard Inspector Levins (Gauge) scours the waterfront in an effort to find the fugitives before they make their escape upriver. The god-awful silliness is compensated for by the noir atmosphere of the seedy pub, shadowy waterfront alleyways and claustrophobic barge scenes, along with several interesting hints that the two desperate seaman are more than just friends.

Portrait from Life (U.S. Title: *The Girl in the Painting*)
★★½ (1948)

Who knows what horrors she has forgotten? [Hendlemann]

Length: 90 min. **Cast:** Mai Zetterling, Guy Rolfe, Robert Beatty, Herbert Lom, Arnold Marlé, Philo Hauser. **Production Company:** Gainsborough Pictures. **Directed by:** Terence Fisher. **Photographed by:** Jack Asher. **Written by:** Frank Harvey, Jr., Muriel and Sydney Box.

After the war, Maj. Lawrence (Rolfe) returns to England and learns that his girlfriend has just gotten married. A bit down in the dumps, he wanders around London and eventually finds himself at a Piccadilly Circus art exhibition, where he is attracted to "Portrait of Hildegarde," a painting of a beautiful young girl standing beneath a sign that reads, "Displaced Persons Camp." Also mesmerized by the painting is Prof. Menzel (Marlé), an Austrian emigrant who is struck by the uncanny resemblance Hildegarde bears to his wife when she was younger, causing him to conclude that the girl must be his missing daughter, Lydia, whom he last saw ten years earlier when she was only seven or eight. Lawrence and the professor track down the artist, Campbell Reid (Beatty), a dying alcoholic whose cryptic last words are, "Hendlemann knows what Hildegarde has forgotten." Obsessed now with solving the mystery behind the painting, Lawrence spends the remainder of his military leave scouring German refugee camps for Hildegarde/Lydia (Zetterling). He finally finds her, suffering it seems from amnesia about her childhood and living with her "parents," Hendlemann (Lom) and his wife. Having had no success in his attempts to spark Hildegarde's memory, Lawrence finally begins to unravel the mystery with the help of Hans (Hauser), the camp gossip, who is happy to sell information for a few British cigarettes. Meanwhile, the Hendlemanns, who seem nervous about the British officer's probing questions, try to discourage him by hiding the girl. The story of the search for Lydia Menzel is told via flashback and voiceover narration, techniques found in two similarly plotted American films noirs that revolved around a protagonist's obsession with a beautiful woman's portrait—*Laura* and *Portrait of Jennie*. Qualitywise however, the similarities end there. Although the story of Lawrence's hunt for the missing girl had the potential to be fascinating, the filmmakers fail to convince the viewer that there is a logical reason for his obsession, a problem that a bit more character development might have solved. Sometimes Lawrence's interest in the missing girl seems a result of his sympathy for her elderly father, and at other times it's because he thinks she's quite the looker. And she is. The beautiful Swedish-born Mai Zetterling does an excellent job as the victimized young girl who, deliberately or subconsciously, has blocked out a decade of her young life. Beatty, as the hard-drinking soldier-artist who spurns Hildegarde's romantic overtures because of his deteriorating health, also gives a good performance. There are several gaping holes in the script, including the problem of how two British Army officers could question the camp squealer in a small recreation room without noticing that Hendlemann, the only other occupant, is lurking nearby and listening to their conversation. In addition, the viewer twice assumes that the squealer has been killed yet is still left in doubt about his ultimate fate. Despite its weaknesses, this hard-to-find film is worth tracking down.

Portrait in Smoke
see *Wicked as They Come*

Portrait of a Sinner
see *The Rough and the Smooth*

A Prize of Arms
★★★½ (1962)

> You're on your own. You get no help from anyone. You're a mug if you expect it. If you want anything in this world you've just got to go out and take it. [Turpin]

Length: 105 min. **Cast:** Stanley Baker, Helmut Schmid, Tom Bell, Patrick Magee. **Production Company:** Inter-State Films. **Directed by:** Cliff Owen. **Photographed by:** Gilbert Taylor, Gerald Gibbs. **Written by:** Paul Ryder.

Three men attempt to heist £100,000 from the paymaster's office of a British Army camp on the day troops are being shipped to the Middle East to deal with the Suez Canal Crisis—Turpin (Baker), a former Army captain who was dishonorably discharged because of his black market activities in Germany after the war; Swavek (Schmid), a former explosives expert for the Polish army; and Fenner (Bell), an automobile mechanic with a drinking problem. The heist has been meticulously planned, but with everything that goes wrong for the three hapless crooks the film could have been subtitled, "The Three Stooges Pull a Heist." Fenner gets caught drinking by the Regiment Sergeant Major (Magee) and is assigned to KP duty scrubbing pots and pans. English soldier impersonator Swavek has to answer questions with a piece of paper in his mouth to disguise his noticeable Polish accent. At one point, Turpin and Swavek take refuge in the bunkers on the artillery target range and must flee in the middle of an unscheduled practice session. Then the two men are forced to receive a series of inoculations, which causes Swavek to become incapacitated during their getaway in a thirty-truck convoy. No, this isn't a comedy. Interestingly, other than a couple of female cafeteria workers on the Army post, the characters are all male, and after twenty minutes of developing the characters of the three crooks, the remainder of the script focuses on the mechanics of the actual heist. Despite the expected crime-doesn't-pay ending, the film succeeds as pure entertainment thanks primarily to the first-rate acting, especially by Baker, who is perfectly cast as the hardboiled heist leader.

Psyche 59
★★ (1963)

> Beat her. Use your hand. Use your belt. When she's had enough, make love to her. [Eric Crawford]

Length: 94 min. **Cast:** Curt Jürgens, Patricia Neal, Samantha Eggar, Ian Bannen, Beatrix Lehmann. **Production Company:** Troy-Schenck Productions. **Directed by:** Alexander Singer. **Photographed by:** Walter Lassally. **Written by:** Julian Halevy.

A housewife and mother of two, Alison (Neal) desperately tries to remember what happened immediately prior to her fall down a flight of stairs, which left her blinded. Doctors have informed her that the blindness is not physical but was caused by psychological trauma and assure her that her sight will return once she faces the truth about whatever happened. Unaware that her husband, Eric (Jur-

Up until now, the husband of a blind woman (Curt Jürgens) seems to have been restraining himself while being romantically pursued by wife's sister (Samantha Eggar) in *Psyche 59* (Troy-Schenck Productions, 1963).

gens), and her newly divorced younger sister, Robin (Eggar), once had an affair, Alison invites Robin to stay with her family. Robin deliberately begins flirting with Eric, who seems to be making a valiant effort to remain faithful to his wife. As Eric's willpower slowly deteriorates, family friend Paul (Bannen), Robin's former lover, finds himself falling once again for the woman who once cruelly dumped him. On vacation at the countryside home of the sisters' astrology crazed grandmother (Lehmann), the sexual tension reaches a boiling point. Beautifully photographed and well-acted, *Psyche 59*, unfortunately, reaches a dead-end at about the half-way point when the viewer suddenly realizes that not much is going to happen to enliven the excruciatingly slow-moving storyline.

American actress Neal, fresh from her Oscar winning performance in *Hud*, is believable enough as the blind and tormented housewife, and Eggar oozes with sexuality, but that's about as good as this psychological drama gets.

PT Raiders see *The Ship That Died of Shame*

Queen of Spades
★★½ (1949)

I cannot afford to risk the necessary in the hopes of winning the superfluous. [Capt. Herman Suvorin]

Length: 95 min. **Cast:** Anton Walbrook, Edith Evans, Yvonne Mitchell, Ronald Howard. **Production **Company**: Associated British Picture Corporation. **Directed by**: Thorold Dickinson. **Photographed by**: Otto Heller. **Written by**: Rodney Ackland, Arthur Boys.

Capt. Herman Suvorin (Walbrook), an engineering officer in the Russian Army in 1806, is looked down upon by some of his more aristocratic colleagues. His only friend, an officer named Andrei (Howard), has been bringing him to the local drinking establishment, where the young officers enjoy the company of beautiful gypsy dancers and gamble away their pay in Faro games. Herman, however, refuses to spend his hard-earned money on such pursuits, even though he desperately wishes he could. In fact, as much as he despises his fellow officers he longs for nothing more than to be on an equal if not a higher social stratum than they, but without money, and plenty of it, his situation is hopeless. Then one day he wanders into a bookstore and walks out with an occult tome entitled, "The Strange Secrets of the Count de Saint Germain." In it he finds the story of "Countess R," who, sixty years earlier, according to the book, sold her soul to the devil in return for the "secret of the cards," a system for winning at Faro. Realizing that "Countess R" is none other than the elderly Countess Renevskaya (Evans) of St. Petersburg, Herman becomes determined to have the secret for himself. Pretending to be in love with the countess' ward, the badly treated and lonely Lizaveta Ivanova (Mitchell), Herman worms his way into the house with the intention of convincing Countess Renevskaya, one way or the other, to turn over the secret to him. Meanwhile, Andrei, who has fallen in love with Lizaveta, learns that Herman is up to no good and risks his friendship with the naive girl by telling her of his suspicions. Nominated for a BAFTA award for Best British film of 1949 but losing to *The Third Man*, this film version of an Alexander Pushkin short story offers some outstanding performances, with Dame Edith Evans terrific in her role as the persnickety 80-year-old countess, and Anton Walbrook giving an entertaining, albeit over-the-top, performance. A beautifully photographed ghost story but lacking the requisite chills, *The Queen of Spades* stumbles all over itself due to an inane and poorly developed storyline. Too many plot questions go unanswered, and the climactic Faro game is just plain silly.

Query see *Murder in Reverse*

The Quiet Woman
★★½ (1951)

I knew the moment I set eyes on her she was nothing more than a cheap slut. [Helen]

Length: 71 min. **Cast**: Derek Bond, Jane Hylton, Dora Bryan, Michael Balfour, John Horsley, Harry Towb, Dianne Foster. **Production Company**: Tempean Films. **Directed by**: John Gilling. **Photographed by**: Monty Berman. **Written by**: John Gilling.

Jane Foster (Hylton), a mystery woman concealing a dark secret, moves to a small coastal village, where she buys a local pub called The Quiet Woman. Duncan McLeod (Bond), an artist and part-time smuggler of contraband liquor, falls in love with Jane despite her seeming aloofness and her disapproval of his criminal activities. Things become complicated when escaped convict Jim Cranshaw (Towb) shows up on Jane's doorstep carrying a gun and demanding that she help him cross the Channel to France. Meanwhile, Duncan's former girlfriend, artist's model Helen (Foster), jealously threatens to squeal to the police about Jane harboring a criminal, while customs officer, Inspector Bromley (Horsley), Duncan's wartime buddy, struggles between his duty and his loyalty to the man who saved his life during the war. Some very nice outdoor photography compensates for the bland script. Balfour and Bryan play it strictly for laughs as sidekicks for the hero and heroine, respectively. Foster, whose American noirs include *The Brothers Rico* and *Drive a Crooked Road*, shines as Duncan's vindictive former lover.

Race Gang see *The Green Cockatoo*

Radio Cab Murder
★★ (1954)

SAFECRACKER: You can't burn them. They're made of a special alloy. Dissipates the heat. You have to blow them. Will that fit in with your set-up
SPENCE: I should think so.
SAFECRACKER: Would you like to tell me the set-up?
SPENCE: Possibly.
HENRY: Look, why don't you two stop scratching around and get down to laying?

Length: 70 min. **Cast:** Jimmy Hanley, Lana Morris, Sonia Holm, Pat McGrath, Bruce Beeby. **Production Company:** Insignia Films. **Directed by:** Vernon Sewell. **Photographed by:** Geoffrey Faithfull. **Written by:** Vernon Sewell.

Inspector Rawlings (Beeby) convinces London cab driver Fred Martin (Hanley), an ex-convict who once served hard time for safecracking, to go undercover to help pinch a gang of robbers. As part of the ruse, Fred's boss pretends to fire him because he's a jailbird, prompting Fred's unwitting driver buddies to threaten a retaliatory walk-out. Meanwhile, Henry (McGrath), Fred's former criminal accomplice, makes contact with him on behalf of gang members, who want to enlist him for a big bank job. Fred reports back to his girlfriend, cab dispatcher Myra (Morris), who passes the specifics on to Inspector Rawlings. Unfortunately for Fred, the untrusting crooks have given him the name of a bank on the other side of town. There are some enjoyable moments in this low-budget crime drama, and veteran Hanley turns in a good performance as the likeable ex-con.

Rag Doll (U.S. Title: Young, Willing and Eager)
★★ (1961)

STEPDAD: I'm still your dad, legally anyway.
CAROL: Then call the police. Tell them about it. They'll give you about five years.

Length: 67 min. **Cast:** Jess Conrad, Hermione Baddeley, Kenneth Griffith, Christina Gregg. **Production Company:** Blakeley's Films. **Directed by:** Lance Comfort. **Photographed by:** Basil Emmott. **Written by:** Brock Williams, Derry Quinn.

Carol (Gregg), a pretty 17-year-old waitress who works at her stepfather's roadside cafe, hitches a ride to London after fending off one too many pawings by male customers who, in exchange for cheap bottles of booze, have the tacit approval of her seedy stepfather. In London, she chances upon a kind-hearted arcade fortune teller, known to her marks as Princess Saphita (Baddeley) but to her friends as "Auntie," who invites her to move in with her. Auntie introduces her to middle-aged Mort Wilson (Griffith), who, despite Carol's rejection of his advances, gives her a job working at the Spanish Dive, one of several London coffee bars he owns. Carol soon hooks up with Joe Shane (Conrad), a pop singer who "got his name from a movie." A former Soho gang member, Joe hasn't had a decent gig in months but manages to survive by burglarizing homes. After Carol gets pregnant, Joe does the decent thing and marries her, thus dooming his chances forever, he claims, of making it big as a pop singer. So with a baby coming, Joe decides to pull just one more burglary and then move to Canada with Carol. His target? Mort Wilson, who keeps a pistol in his home to ensure that nobody messes with his weekly receipts. This is a odd movie with an overacted, out-of-place ending. There is barely a hint of Joe's illegal activities before we are witnessing the dramatic downfall of a hardened criminal. It's almost humorous. Another thing that is strange is that "chick" lover Wilson, who doesn't hesitate to put the quick make on under-aged girls, is presented in such a favorable light instead of being portrayed as a lecherous molester. Despite its provocative American release title of *Young, Willing and Eager*, *Rag Doll* is a dud. Its biggest plus is the sensational nighttime shots of London's busy streets, including a theater marquee advertising its current movie, *The Alamo*, with huge head shots of John Wayne, Richard Widmark, Richard Boone and British actor Laurence Harvey.

Recoil
★★ (1953)

I learned a lot when I was working with you, Farnborough. I found out what made you tick. You've got a nice line-up and I'm cutting myself in. The easy way or the hard way. [Nick Conway to his gangster boss]

Length: 79 min. **Cast**: Kieron Moore, Elizabeth Sellars, Edward Underdown, John Horsley, Martin Benson. **Production Company**: Tempean Films. **Directed by**: John Gilling. **Photographed by**: Monty Berman. **Written by**: John Gilling.

Jean Talbot (Sellars) tracks down Nick Conway (Moore) after he robs and kills her jeweler father, but Scotland Yard Inspector Tunbridge (Horsley) needs more evidence before he can make an arrest. Meanwhile, Nick's boss (Benson) learns that Nick has held back the proceeds from the robbery and sends a couple of his goons to work him over, prompting Nick to start his own gang. The frustrated Jean decides to go undercover as a lodger at the home of Nick's brother, Dr. Michael Conway (Underdown), who has reluctantly given his evil sibling an iron-clad alibi for the night of the murder. Michael falls for his pretty tenant, but it seems that she has eyes only for Nick, whom she seduces in order to report his movements to the Yard. Although *Recoil* contains an exciting fiery car crash and is well acted by Sellars as the justice-seeking civilian, the implausible plot becomes especially hard to swallow when late in the story Jean convinces her father's killer she just happens to be a petty jewel thief, which is very convenient for his next heist. Surprisingly, the undercover meddler receives not one word of censure from the cops for interfering in an official investigation. In fact, they actually encourage her in this dangerous charade.

Return to Sender
★½ (1963)

I want him lame. Very lame. [Dino Steffano about prosecutor Robert Lindley]

Length: 61 min. **Cast**: Nigel Davenport, Yvonne Romain, Geoffrey Keen, William Russell, Jennifer Daniel. **Production Company**: Merton Park Productions. **Directed by**: Gordon Hales. **Photographed by**: James Wilson. **Written by**: John Roddick.

Big-time swindler Dino Steffano (Davenport) hires Mike Cochrane (Russell) to discredit honest prosecutor Robert Lindley (Keen), who is about try Steffano on a charge that will put the crook away for at least seven years. Cochrane, who has a personal grudge against Lindley because of an 18-month prison term he once received at the prosecutor's hands, quickly agrees. Cochrane comes up with an elaborate scheme to make it appear that Lindley has been having an affair with Steffano's wife, Lisa (Romain). Meanwhile, Steffano is plotting to double-cross both Cochrane and his own lover, Beth Lindley (Daniel), the prosecutor's daughter, who was an accomplice in Steffano's latest swindle. The cast is good, but the plot is a highly convoluted mess that offers little compensation when the climax finally arrives. (Part of the "Edgar Wallace Mystery Theater" series.)

Ricochet
★★½ (1963)

JOHN BRODIE: I've never touched blackmail.
ALAN PHIPPS: Well, you've got to start sometime. You can't afford scruples.

Length: 64 min. **Cast**: Maxine Audley, Richard Leech, Alex Scott, Dudley Foster, Patrick Magee. **Production Company**: Merton Park Productions. **Directed by**: John Moxey. **Photographed by**: James Wilson. **Written by**: Roger Marshall.

Divorce attorney Alan Phipps (Leech) concocts a convoluted plan to get his wife's money. He approaches her former lover, gigolo John Brodie (Scott), and pays him to contact her about some old love letters she had written to Brodie. As part of the scheme, Phipps expects Yvonne (Audley), who is unaware that her gun is loaded with blank cartridges, to shoot Brodie. Then Phipps will blackmail her. At least that's the way Brodie understands the plan. Unfortunately for him, though, Phipps loads the gun with real bullets and sends Yvonne on her way to meet with her supposed blackmailer. After she shoots and kills Brodie during a struggle for the gun, Scotland Yard Inspector Cummins (Magee) shows up at the Phipps' home to arrest her. Believing he has gotten away with murder, Phipps relaxes, but his relief is short-lived when he is surprised by the sudden appearance of Brodie's partner, Peter Dexter (Foster), who has blackmail plans of his own. Competently acted and augmented by Wilson's dark photography, *Ricochet* is marred by several holes in its otherwise distinctive plot. (Part of the "Edgar Wallace Mystery Theater" series.)

The Rivals
★★½ (1963)

KIDNAPPER: Where's the money?
CAR THIEF #1: What are you talking about?
KIDNAPPER: ... There was a package in the glove compartment. It's missing.
CAR THIEF #2: Try the lost property office.

Length: 56 min. **Cast:** Jack Gwillim, Erica Rogers, Brian Smith, Howard Greene, Barry Linehan, Tony Garnett, Murray Hayne, Maria Lennard, Donna Pearson. **Production Company:** Merton Park Productions. **Directed by:** Max Varnel. **Photographed by:** James Wilson. **Written by:** John Roddick.

A pair of small-time car thieves, Steve Houston (Smith) and Eddy McGuire (Greene), stumble onto a kidnapping when they find a ransom note in the glove compartment of a car they have just pinched. Despite the misgivings of his girlfriend (Rogers), who wants to call the cops, Steve comes up with a daring plan to deliver the note and collect the £75,000 ransom. The owner of the car, kidnapping accomplice Phillipa Martin (Lennard), is the secretary of a Swedish millionaire (Gwillim), whose daughter (Pearson) has been nabbed by Paul Kenyon (Linehan) and his two goons (Garnett and Hayne). In a panic, the kidnappers move their victim from Phillipa's house to a docked boat and set out to find the car thieves who are trying to cut in on their action. *The Rivals* is fast-moving and fairly enjoyable despite a few silly scenes, such as the climactic meeting of the kidnappers and car thieves when a gun changes hands four times. Or the scene in which the car thieves are staking out the millionaire's hotel while parked in a no-parking zone, and Eddy, the dumber of the two, nearly ruins the plan by antagonizing the constable who has pointed out their infraction. (Part of the "Edgar Wallace Mystery Theater" series.)

Roadhouse Girl see Marilyn

The Rocking Horse Winner
★★★★½ (1949)

Good money? It's evil money. Dreadful, evil money. How could anybody ever touch money like that? [Hester Grahame]

Length: 90 min. **Cast:** Valerie Hobson, John Howard Davies, Ronald Squire, John Mills, Hugh Sinclair. **Production Company:** Two Cities Films. **Directed by:** Anthony Pélissier. **Photographed by:** Desmond Dickinson. **Written by:** Anthony Pélissier.

Hester Grahame (Hobson) is a middle-class spendthrift living above her family's means. When her husband, Richard (Sinclair), goes into debt over a poker loss and then loses his job, things around the Grahame household become intolerable for their sensitive young son, Paul (Davies), who desperately wants to help satisfy his mother's craving for money. Paul's opportunity arrives on Christmas in the form of a rocking horse, which handyman Bassett (Mills), a former jockey and now a handicapped war veteran, shows him how to ride. And ride the boy does. Frantically. Feverishly. Obsessively. And after he gets where he is going in his child mind, he somehow manages to come up with the name of the winner in the next real-life horse race. Secretly, Paul and Bassett go into partnership, placing small wages on each race. Their horses always win and the money begins to pile up, quieting the whispers the boy has been hearing from the house itself about his mother's financial needs ("There must be more money, there must be more money"). It isn't long before Hester's brother, Oscar (Squire), catches wind of his nephew's unusual ability and joins in the partnership. The two adults agree that the winnings are primarily Paul's and that the money should be put aside for his mother according to the boy's wishes. Obligingly, Oscar makes secret arrangements for Hester to receive an annual disbursement of £1,000 to be made on her birthday over the next five years. Hester sees the windfall, an inheritance from a relative she is told, as her chance to start living high on the hog once again. But then Paul's powers begins to fail him and the three partners start to lose money, placing unbearable pressure on the boy to ensure that his mother remains happy. With the English Derby approaching, it is a sickly and frail Paul who hops back on the rocking horse in a brave effort to come up with just one more winner. And the horse he names, if it wins, should net the worried gamblers £70,000. But at what cost? Based on a story by D.H. Lawrence, *The Rocking Horse Winner* is an absorbing but morbid fantasy and a stunning achievement for writer-director Pélissier and cinematographer Desmond Dickinson, whose expressionistic shots of the boy's frenzied rocking horse rides are terrifying yet strangely beautiful. Child actor Davies (*Oliver Twist*) turns in an amazing performance as the innocent little boy who is obsessed with his mother's happiness, and Hobson is excellent as his loving but money-hungry mother, who soon learns a hard lesson about life's priorities.

Room 43 see *Passport to Shame*

Room at the Top
★★★★½ (1959)

Too many pansies about these days. I knew a lot of real men once. They're all dead now. [Elspeth]

Length: 117 min. **Cast:** Simone Signoret, Laurence Harvey, Heather Sears, Donald Wolfit, Hermione Baddeley, John Westbrook, Allan Cuthbertson. **Production Company:** Remus Films. **Directed by:** Jack Clayton. **Photographed by:** Freddie Francis. **Written by:** Neil Paterson.

Joe Lampton (Harvey), raised in a working class family in the factory town of Dufton, arrives in the more upscale Warnley Town ostensibly to begin a new job in the Treasury Department at the Town Hall but in reality to find acceptance and social advancement. Joe quickly sets his sights on pretty Susan Brown (Sears), the daughter of the wealthiest man in town (Wolfit) and the fiancée of Jack Wales (Westbrook), who, like Joe, had been interred in a P.O.W. camp during the war. Wales, a former officer, takes great delight in taunting Joe, a former sergeant, about Joe's lack of social standing and the futility of trying to ingratiate himself with the snobbish Brown clan. Susan, however, sees the handsome young man in a different light and ultimately succumbs to his charms. When he fails in his attempt to buy Joe off with a good job back in Dufton, Mr. Brown sends his daughter on a trip abroad in the hopes that she will forget the brash young social climber. While Susan is away, Joe begins an affair with stage actress Alice Aisgill (Signoret), an older woman who is unhappily married to a callous and unfaithful husband (Cuthbertson). The two fall in love and make plans for a happy, if penniless, future. Unfortunately, George Aisgill refuses to give his wife a divorce and threatens to ruin both of their lives if they continue their affair. In a seeming death blow to the couple's romance, Susan returns from Europe declaring her love for Joe and proving it by giving him her virginity and becoming pregnant with his child. Joe is pleasantly surprised when Mr. Brown, who has resignedly accepted his family's embarrassing predicament, offers him a high-paying position in his company and the hand of his daughter in marriage. Joe now faces a choice — true love with Alice or the attainment of his dream of social improvement. His decision comes hard and results in tragedy. While the film contains many familiar noir themes, such as betrayal, adultery, rabid ambition and the distinctive British theme of class obsession, the film succeeds stylistically as a noir only as it approaches its conclusion. Here, in a scene reminiscent of Stoker Thompson's beating in *The Set-Up*, Joe is viciously attacked in a darkened alley by a pub floozy's jealous boyfriend and his pals, who leave him for dead, face down in a muddied pool of water. Noir or not, *Room at the Top* is a great film, worthy of multiple viewings if only because of Signoret's dazzling performance and the opportunity to witness Baddeley's superb acting skills. Although tame by today's standards, its overt sexual themes earned the film an "X" (adult) rating from the British Board of Film Censors. Considered one of the first of the British New Wave films (prominent others include *Look Back in Anger, Saturday Night and Sunday Morning, The Loneliness of the Long Distance Runner, Billy Liar*), *Room at the Top* is a tough, unyielding denunciation of the British class system. The film, which would win BAFTA awards for Best

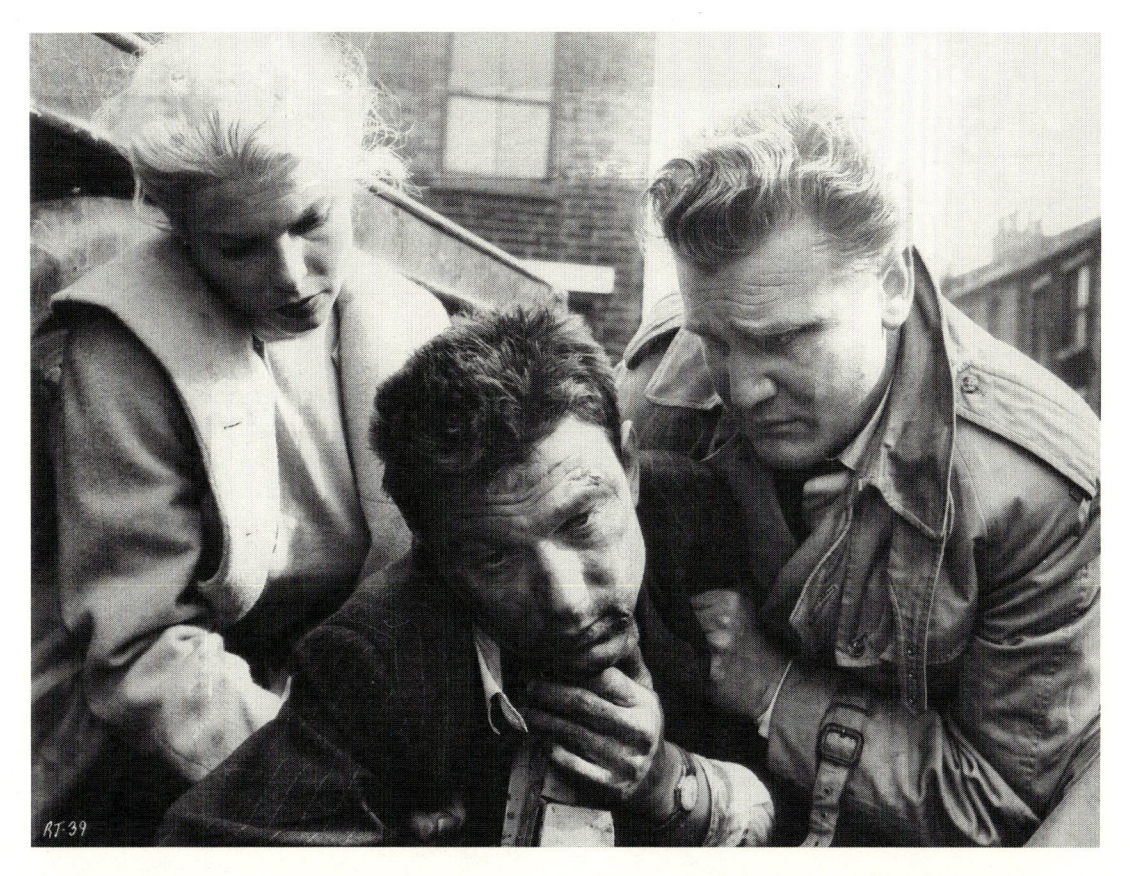

Social climber Joe Lampton (Laurence Harvey) is helped by friends (Mary Peach and Donald Houston) after being beaten up by a jealous boyfriend and his pals in *Room at the Top* (Remus Films, 1959).

British Picture and Best Film from Any Source and receive an Oscar nomination for Best Picture, is a showcase for French movie star Simone Signoret. Signoret won both a Best Actress Oscar and a BAFTA award for her portrayal of the abused and longsuffering wife whose surrender to adultery offers only fleeting happiness and inevitable devastation. Well-known British character actress Hermione Baddeley, nominated for both an Oscar (Best Actress in a Supporting Role) and a BAFTA award (Best British Actress), turns in a sensational performance as Alice's concerned best friend. Laurence Harvey lost the Oscar race for Best Actor to Charlton Heston (*Ben Hur*) and both Harvey and Wolfit lost the BAFTA award for Best British Actor to Trevor Howard (*The Key*). Neil Paterson won the Academy Award for his screenplay, but Jack Clayton lost the Best Director Oscar to William Wyler (*Ben Hur*).

Room to Let
★½ (1950)

> I like maps, don't you? They're such useful things when one wants to move about in a hurry. [Dr. Fell]

Length: 68 min. **Cast:** Jimmy Hanley, Valentine Dyall, Christine Silver, Merle Tottenham, Constance Smith, Charles Hawtrey. **Production Company:** Hammer Film Productions. **Directed by:** Godfrey Grayson. **Photographed by:** Cedric Williams. **Written by:** John Gilling, Godfrey Grayson.

In 1904, following a deadly fire at a London mental hospital, a mysterious stranger calling himself Dr. Fell (Dyall) seeks lodging at the home of wheelchair-bound Mrs. Musgrave (Silver) and her daughter, Molly (Smith). Financially strapped, the two take him in despite the social embarrassment it would bring if their peers learn of their desperation. One of Molly's suitors, newspaper reporter Curly

Minter (Hanley), has been investigating the fire and a rumor that a mental patient escaped during the blaze, something the hospital superintendent flatly denies. Could Dr. Fell be the missing patient? He certainly acts the part, skulking about, shutting all of the drapes, locking the doors and forbidding Molly to leave the house or to have visitors. The frightened Musgraves and their equally spooked housekeeper, Alice (Tottenham), soon find themselves regretting the decision to accept Fell's three-month advance on the rent. Meanwhile, the reporter's investigation leads him to the conclusion that Dr. Fell may be none other than the notorious serial killer Jack the Ripper, who has been missing since 1888. Somewhat similar to the American films noirs *The Lodger* (1944) and *Man in the Attic* (1953), *Room to Let*, which is presented in flashback with voiceover narration by the now elderly Curly, adds its own unique twists—the missing mental patient scenario and a silly locked-room murder puzzle that has supposedly kept British true-crime enthusiasts stumped for decades, which says very little for British true-crime enthusiasts. The acting leaves a lot to be desired with Hawtrey, a string-bean actor famous for his comedic roles in the *Carry On* film series, giving a weird performance as Hanley's unlikely romantic rival for the affections of the beautiful Molly Musgrave, and Dyall, well-known for his velvety radio announcer voice, almost laughable in his attempts to appear menacing. Hanley, whose character is aptly nicknamed "Curly," turns in the film's best performance.

The Rough and the Smooth
(U.S. Title: *Portrait of a Sinner*)
★★½ (1959)

> Sometimes men try things with foreign girls they wouldn't dare with their own. [Ila Hansen]

Length: 99 min. **Cast:** Tony Britton, Nadja Tiller, William Bendix, Natasha Parry, Tony Wright. **Production Company:** George Minter Productions. **Directed by:** Robert Siodmak. **Photographed by:** Otto Heller. **Written by:** Audrey Erskine-Lindop, Dudley Leslie.

Archaeologist Mike Thompson (Britton) is seeking Noah's Ark but instead finds Ila Hansen (Tiller). Ila is a sultry German girl with a history of psychological problems attributable to her sexual molestation as a child and her love for her no-good sailor boyfriend (Wright), a vicious drug dealer who needs money fast. Mike's fixation with Ila threatens to destroy his relationship with his fiancée, Margaret Goreham (Parry), as well as his career. Complicating things is Ila's middle-aged boss, American Reg Barker (Bendix), who seems to be more than just her employer. A sordid little tale, *The Rough and the Smooth* benefits from noir icon Siodmak's expert direction and Heller's dark cinematography, but otherwise it's an unremarkable film. Austrian actress Tiller's portrayal of a femme fatale is lacking, but American actor Bendix, a veteran of a dozen films noirs, turns in a gritty performance as the obsessed businessman.

Rough Shoot
(U.S. Title: *Shoot First*)
★★★ (1953)

> You'll tell your wife what any good husband should tell his wife in matters of importance— absolutely nothing. [Col. Sandorski]

Length: 88 min. **Cast:** Joel McCrea, Evelyn Keyes, Herbert Lom, Marius Goring, David Hurst. **Production Company:** Raymond Stross Productions. **Directed by:** Robert Parrish. **Photographed by:** Stanley Pavey. **Written by:** Eric Ambler.

Robert Tanie (American actor McCrea), a Yank Army officer renting a cottage and a hunting "shoot" in the Dorset countryside, stumbles across an intruder he believes is either a poacher or a black marketeer. After he shoots the stranger with a load of buckshot, he is shocked to discover that the man is dead. What Tanie doesn't know is that a foreigner named Hiart (Goring) shot the intruder with a high-powered rifle at the instant Tanie pulled the trigger. Tanie, who thinks the stranger must have died of a heart attack caused by the blast of buckshot, panics and hides the body, thus beginning a reluctant association with an eccentric former Polish Army colonel, Peter Sandorski (Lom), who claims he is working

A former American Army officer (Joel McCrea) hides the body of the man he thinks he accidentally killed in *Rough Shoot* (a.k.a. *Shoot First*) (Raymond Stross Productions, 1953).

for British intelligence to bust up a Communist spy ring headed by Hiart. American film noir veteran Evelyn Keyes plays Tanie's wife, Cecily, and German-born actor Hurst is an affable scientist trying to pass atomic secrets to his Communist contact in London. Marginally noir, this Hitchcockesque thriller offers a familiar noir character (the wrong man) involved in a familiar noir activity (covering up a crime). Lom, whose forte was villainous roles, is miscast as the quirky spy chaser who lives in a county mental hospital as part of his cover. The explosive climax at London's Madame Tussaud's Wax Museum is the highlight of the film.

Salt to the Devil
see *Give Us This Day*

Sapphire
★★★★ (1959)

> Our father was a doctor. White. Our mother, a singer. Black as I am. You never know which way it's going to be. [Dr. Robbins]

Length: 92 min. **Cast:** Nigel Patrick, Michael Craig, Yvonne Mitchell, Paul Massie, Bernard Miles, Earl Cameron, Olga Lindo, Gordon Heath, Harry Baird. **Production Company:** Artna Films. **Directed by:** Basil Dearden. **Photographed by:** Harry Waxman. **Written by:** Janet Green.

A mother and her two children find the body of a murdered girl in a London park. The police identify the knifing victim as Sapphire Robbins, a 21-year-old Royal Academy of Music student. An autopsy determines that she was pregnant. When Superintendent Robert Hazard (Patrick) meets the girl's brother (Cameron), a black Birmingham doctor, he is surprised to learn that Sapphire, who he had assumed was white, was actually a "colored" girl, or a "lily-skin," as her black friends refer to those who pass for white. Sapphire had been dating white architectural student David Harris (Massie), who decided to marry her when he learned she was pregnant. Neither David nor his bigoted parents (Miles and Lindo) and sister, Millie (Mitchell), had been aware that Sapphire was black until shortly before her death, and Hazard suspects that one of the Harris family could be the killer. The motive? David's marriage would mean the loss of an important scholarship and the end of his dream of becoming an architect. But when Hazard finds one half of a photograph showing Sapphire at a local dance, he begins looking for the dance partner cut from the photo. His search leads him to two black men, attorney Paul Slade (Heath) and a switchblade carrying spiv called Johnnie Fiddle (Baird), both of whom dated Sapphire before she "went white." A super-efficient cop, Hazard eventually finds the murderer thanks to a clue carelessly left behind when the killer disposed of the Sapphire's body in the park. Filmed in Eastman color, *Sapphire* is an intelligently made police procedural that takes a look at miscegenation and racism in England in the 1950s. There is no preaching, but no punches are pulled either. Racism seems shockingly rampant but even more surprising is the casualness of the manner in which it is portrayed. The usual racial slurs are tossed around a bit but not excessively except during the film's weakest scene, apparently intended by filmmakers to depict a microcosm of the racism experienced at the time by blacks in England. This occurs when murder suspect Johnnie Fiddle flees from cops through darkened London neighborhoods and runs into more nasty or dangerous bigots than one might expect to encounter in such a short period of time. In an attempt at fairness, the filmmakers portray the other side of the coin by depicting the black attorney as having his own racial prejudices, while other black characters freely express their disdain for Sapphire's attempts to pass as white. Even Scotland Yard detectives are portrayed as being not immune from prejudice, as evidenced by the character of Inspector Phil Learoyd (Craig), an otherwise decent cop with an obvious inclination toward bigotry, who at one point refers to his black suspects as "spades." His superior, Superintendent Hazard, evidently doesn't feel the same way but makes no effort to scold his colleague or attack his remarks as being especially inappropriate during an official police investigation. Good acting, solid directing, and a pulsating jazz score from Philip Green highlight this unusually sophisticated film. In 1960, *Sapphire* won a BAFTA award for Best British Film of 1959, beating out *Look Back in Anger*, *Tiger Bay*, *Northwest Frontier* and *Yesterday's Enemy*.

Saraband see *Saraband for Dead Lovers*

Saraband for Dead Lovers (U.S. Title: *Saraband*)
★★½ (1948)

I prefer dirt of my own choosing. I don't like being pushed into it. [Count Konigsmark]

Length: 96 min. **Cast:** Stewart Granger, Joan Greenwood, Flora Robson, Peter Bull, Françoise Rosay, Frederick Valk, Michael Gough. **Production Company:** Ealing Studios. **Directed by:** Basil Dearden. **Photographed by:** Douglas Slocombe. **Written by:** John Dighton, Alexander Mackendrick.

To pay off a gambling debt, Swedish Count Philip Konigsmark (Granger) becomes a soldier for Germany's Hanoverians, Electress Sophia (Rosay) and Elector Ernest August (Valk) and their two sons, Prince George Louis (Bull) and Prince Charles (Gough). The royal family wants to seat a Hanoverian on the throne of England, and Countess Clara Platen (Robson), Ernest's lover, is determined to see to it that they get their wish. Things become complicated when Clara begins an affair with the handsome Swedish officer, who has fallen desperately in love with George Louis' young wife, Sophie Dorothea (Greenwood). Although miserable in her loveless, politically arranged marriage, Sophie struggles with the temptation to stray from her repugnant and adulterous husband, the future George I of England. And Countess Platen, who is losing her battle against the aging process, has no intention of giving up Philip without a fight. Ealing's first color film and first big-budget costume melodrama, *Saraband* was not well received despite the presence of box office draw Stewart Granger, on loan to Ealing from Gainsborough Pictures. Primarily a tale of political machinations and an ill-fated romance told from Sophie's deathbed via one long flashback, this slow-moving film is interesting primarily for the superb performance of Flora Robson as the scheming Countess. Some scholars and fans see this costume film as noir or "marginally noir," but the noir designation may be problematic for hard-core aficionados and even the more liberal-minded who otherwise accept the existence of "Period noirs." Director of photography Slocombe provides a few outstanding scenes, such as the dream-like sequence, in which Sophie stumbles her way through a crowd of masked revelers in a street festival, and the dueling sequence, which takes place in the darkened corners of a castle hall. Anthony Quayle has a small role as the Countess' spy, Durer.

Scotland Yard Dragnet
see *The Hypnotist*

Seance on a Wet Afternoon
★★★★★ (1964)

I committed a criminal act. I kidnapped her. I didn't "borrow" her, and they're onto us. [Bill Stanley]

Length: 116 min. **Cast:** Kim Stanley, Richard Attenborough, Judith Donner, Mark Eden, Nanette Newman. **Production Companies:** Allied Film Makers, Beaver Films. **Directed by:** Bryan Forbes. **Photographed by:** Gerry Turpin. **Written by:** Bryan Forbes.

Seeking public recognition for her supposed psychic abilities, suburban housewife and medium Myra Savage (Stanley) pushes her milquetoast husband, Bill (Attenborough), into kidnapping the young daughter of a wealthy businessman (Eden) and his wife (Newman). The idea behind Myra's mad scheme is to demand a ransom, collect the money and then come forward with supposedly supernaturally obtained clues that will reunite the frantic parents with their daughter and their money, thus satisfying Myra's neurotic craving for attention and approval. Bill grabs the little girl, Amanda Clayton (Donner), in front of her school, drugs her and locks her in the bedroom that used to belong to the couple's late son, Arthur, convincing the girl that she has been hospitalized for "double German measles." Disguised as a doctor and a nurse and wearing surgical masks to prevent Amanda from identifying them later, Bill and Myra keep the child drugged most of the time while they continue to follow Myra's detailed plan. The pseudo-psychic promptly makes contact with the Claytons, but while she receives an especially warm welcome from Amanda's desperate mother, she also attracts the attention of the Scotland Yard detectives investigating the kidnapping. Meanwhile, Bill, who is extraordinarily loyal and patient with his wife's obviously deteriorating mental state, is becoming more and more concerned for the little girl's well-being, and justifiably so because Myra has been insisting that dead Arthur asked during a recent séance that Myra send Amanda to him. Nearly fifty years after its release, *Seance* remains, unfairly, a much neglected classic. With the passage of time, some previously renowned films lose that special something that once marked them as cinematic masterpieces. Sir Richard Attenborough's production is not one of these films, thanks in particular to his own performance, which resulted in his winning a BAFTA award for Best British Actor, and that of American actress Kim Stanley, who received a BAFTA nomination for Best Foreign Actress and an Academy Award nomination for Best Actress in a Leading Role. While the suspenseful child-in-jeopardy theme makes this is a disturbing film to watch, what should trouble viewers even more is the sympathy they may find themselves feeling for the kidnappers, especially the character of the beaten-down husband. This can be attributed, once again, to the superb performances by the two stars, but director/screenwriter Byran Forbes (BAFTA nominee for Best British Screenplay) and cinematographer Gerry Turpin (another BAFTA nominee) cannot be overlooked when considering the overall brilliance of the film.

Secret People
★★★ (1952)

> MARIA: What about the others?
> LOUIS: My orders are to save myself and I obey orders.

Length: 96 min. **Cast:** Valentina Cortese, Serge Reggiani, Charles Goldner, Audrey Hepburn, Irene Worth, Reginald Tate. **Production Company:** Ealing Studios. **Directed by:** Thorold Dickinson. **Photographed by:** Gordon Dines. **Written by:** Thorold Dickinson, Wolfgang Wilhelm.

In 1930, Maria Brentano (Cortese) and her pre-teen sister, Nora, flee to England after their activist father is murdered by General Galbern, the tyrannical dictator of their European homeland, presumably Fascist Italy. After living for the next seven years with their father's best friend, Anselmo (Goldner), the owner of a small London cafe, the girls take the oath of allegiance to their adoptive country. On a celebratory holiday in Paris, Anselmo and the girls run into Maria's former boyfriend, Louis (Reggiani), who they thought had been killed along with Maria's father. Louis is now a member of an organized group of assassins who plan to kill Galbern at the first opportunity. Louis romances Maria, swears his love for her and follows her to London, where he pressures her into to delivering a bomb disguised as a cigarette case to a garden party to be attended by the visiting dictator and where the now grown-up Nora (Hepburn), an accomplished ballerina, will be performing. Things go badly, however, when a member of the organization places the bomb under the General's chair only seconds before the intended victim gets up and walks away. The bomb explodes, killing a waitress and seriously injuring a Scotland Yard detective, whose life Maria saves by applying first aid. Louis and his group of assassins, worried now about Maria's loyalties, warn her to remain silent if she wants her sister to stay healthy. Plagued by guilt, however, Maria spills all to Scotland Yard Inspector Eliot (Tate) and policewoman Miss Jackson (Worth), who use her as bait in an effort to nab the killers before they make another assassination attempt. Meanwhile, Louis, realizing that Maria is no longer useful, turns his attention to Nora. *The Secret People* is an interesting commentary on the use of violence to achieve political ends and an even more interesting study of a love damned by conflicting political and moral convictions. The opportunity to view the Belgian-born Hepburn, soon to be a major Hollywood star, in one of her earliest film roles, and the stand-out performances of Cortese and Reggiani as the ill-fated lovers compensate for the film's slow moments, which culminate in a shockingly downbeat climax.

The Secret Place
★★★½ (1957)

> I've wanted to live in a place that's elegant, where all the people are nice and beautifully dressed and no one comes home at night drunk, singing and shouting like they do on Gentry Street. Oh, I hate the sound of their voices. [Molly Wilson]

Length: 98 min. **Cast:** Belinda Lee, Ronald Lewis, Michael Brooke, Michael Gwynn, Geoffrey Keen, David McCallum, George Selway, George A. Cooper. **Production Company:** Rank Organisation Film Productions. **Directed by:** Clive Donner. **Photographed by:** Ernest Steward. **Written by:** Linette Perry.

Molly Wilson (Lee), a kiosk sales clerk, has fallen in love with small-time crook Gerry Carter (Lewis), who along with his hastily assembled gang, Steve (Gwynn), Harry (Cooper), and Paddy (Selway), is planning to rob a diamond merchant. Before he can go ahead with the robbery, Gerry needs a police officer's uniform. It so happens that the father of Molly's 14-year-old friend, Freddie (Brooke), is a constable, and Freddie, who has a huge crush on the pretty older girl, agrees to let her borrow the uniform, thinking she wants to play a joke on a friend. Molly feels guilty about lying to Freddie, but her love for Gerry and his promise to marry her and take her out of the slums win out over a guilty conscience. After Steve and his gang pull off the heist of £60,000 worth of diamonds, Molly returns the uniform to the relieved boy, who sneaks it back into his father's closet. While waiting for his fence to locate a cutter for the bigger stones, Steve hides the diamonds inside Molly's phonograph. Unfortunately for the crooks, Molly unwittingly gives the record player to Freddie, and now Steve must figure a way to retrieve his stash from the flat of a London constable (Keen). Meanwhile, after reading about the heist in the newspaper, Freddie figures out the real reason why Molly wanted the uniform and in a rage smashes the phonograph, finding the diamonds. Feeling betrayed and worried about getting his father into trouble, Freddie tries to decide what to do with the stolen jewels. One thing he does know, however, and that is he is not going to turn them over to Molly or to her impatient hoodlum boyfriend, who by now is contemplating violence. *The Secret Place* is a low-budget noir that successfully combines the heist and child-in-jeopardy plot elements to produce a highly suspenseful and enjoyable story, the exciting climax of which is somewhat reminiscent of the American film noir *The Window*. Steward's capable cinematography and good performances, especially by Michael Brooke as the young patsy, Belinda Lee as the love-smitten girl who becomes involved with a charming but dangerous homme fatale and David McCallum as her none-too-bright and cowardly brother, make this a must-view British noir.

Serious Charge (a.k.a. *Immoral Charge*)
★★★½ (1959)

Let someone else take on this flock. Only he'd better watch out or his sheep will tear him to pieces. [Rev. Howard Phillips]

Length: 99 min. **Cast:** Anthony Quayle, Sarah Churchill, Andrew Ray, Irene Browne, Cliff Richard, Liliane Brousse, Leigh Madison. **Production Company:** Alva Films. **Directed by:** Terence Young. **Photographed by:** Georges Périnal. **Written by:** Guy Elmes, Mickey Delamar.

The Reverend Howard Phillips (Quayle) operates a youth center in Bellington and assists the local social worker in helping juvenile delinquents, or "juves," such as the repentant Curley Thompson (Richard), who have had brushes with the law. Curley's brother, gang leader Larry (Ray), however, has no use for the minister and his goody-two-shoes attempts to straighten out wayward youths. After getting Mary Williams (Madison) pregnant, Larry sets his sights on Rev. Phillips' young, and somewhat wild, French housekeeper, Michelle (Brousse). During a visit to Rev. Phillips vicarage, the now suicidal Mary tells all, and on her way home witnesses Larry and Michelle smooching at a bus stop. Distraught, she runs blindly into traffic and is struck by a vehicle and killed. After the coroner's report reveals that the girl was pregnant, Rev. Phillips has a heart-to-heart with Larry, who scoffs at the minister's charge that he was somehow responsible for Mary's death. When Phillips threatens to tell Larry's abusive old man about the boy's near brush with fatherhood, Larry begins tearing at his clothes and screaming. At this point, spinster Hester Peters (Churchill), whose advances the vicar has shyly refused, walks into the house and witnesses Larry's act. Before long, word of a sexual assault spreads around town, resulting in torrents of anonymous hate mail to the minister, icy stares from the citizenry, slashed tires and empty church pews. The only person who believes the vicar's story is his sagacious and strong-willed mother (Browne). Based on a play by Philip King, *Serious Charge* is very mature stuff, indeed, for 1959. Anthony Quayle turns in a sensitive yet powerful performance as the soccer star minister who is wrongly accused of attempting to commit a horrible sexual crime and, as a result, begins to question his calling. British rock'n'roller Cliff Richard makes his film debut.

The Set-Up
★★★ (1963)

I never thought of murdering my wife until I met her. [Theo Gaunt about Nicole Romain]

Length: 58 min. **Cast:** Maurice Denham, John Carson, Maria Corvin, Brian Peck, Anthony Bate. **Production Company:** Merton Park Productions. **Directed by:** Gerard Glaister. **Photographed by:** Bert Mason. **Written by:** Roger Marshall.

While traveling by train, prominent businessman Theo Gaunt (Denham) meets penniless jailbird Arthur Payne (Peck) and decides that Payne is the patsy he needs to help him pull off his wife's murder. Gaunt's accomplice, Ray Underwood (Bate), contacts Payne and offers him £200 to break into a safe in Gaunt's home to steal jewelry, supposedly as part of an insurance fraud plan. Payne, believing that the house belongs to the man who hired him, agrees. Instead of finding jewelry in the safe, however, he finds a gun, leaving his fingerprints all over the weapon later identified as the one used to kill Mrs. Gaunt. Payne goes on the run but gives himself up to Inspector David Jackson (Carson), who thinks that the ex-convict's story about being hired to break into Gaunt's house has a ring of truth to it. Meanwhile, the middle-aged Gaunt plans to live happily ever after with his younger lover, Nicole Romain (Corvin), but soon learns that instead of just one patsy in the frame-up there are actually two. A convoluted but clever storyline, decent acting, and some familiar noir elements and characters (wife killer, ex-convict, patsy, blackmailers, femme fatale) make this an enjoyable entry in the "Edgar Wallace Mystery Theater" series.

Seven Days to Noon
★★★★ (1950)

The dream has become a nightmare. [Professor Willingdon, renegade atomic scientist]

Length: 94 min. **Cast:** Barry Jones, André Morell, Hugh Cross, Sheila Manahan, Olive Sloane, Joan Hickson, Ronald Adam. **Production Companies:** London Film Productions, British Lion Production Assets. **Directed by:** Roy Boulting, Frank Harvey. **Photographed by:** Gilbert Taylor. **Written by:** Roy Boulting, John Boulting.

After sending a letter to the Prime Minister (Adam) threatening to blow up London if Britain does not cease its nuclear weapons production, Professor Willingdon (Jones), a prominent atomic scientist, disappears with a "UR12" bomb the size of a portable typewriter. Scotland Yard Superintendent Folland (Morell) is the first to investigate, and he determines that the letter is no hoax. Meanwhile, the on-the-run scientist seeks refuge at a rooming house run by a paranoid cat lover (Hickson), who thinks he may be the murderer the newspapers have labeled the "landlady killer." Later, he is taken in by an aging former showgirl (Sloane), who has romance on her mind. With help from Willingdon's daughter (Manahan) and personal assistant (Cross), Supt. Folland initiates a manhunt that is soon taken over by the Army following the complete and rapid evacuation of London. With a theme that is way ahead of its time, *Seven Days* is suspenseful, well-acted, skillfully directed and superbly photographed with many touches of the noir style, especially in its London-at-night sequences in which the authorities hunt for the elderly fugitive in dark alleyways, seedy bars, junk yards and sewers. Veteran character actor Jones, in his only starring role, is convincing as the deluded protagonist whose guilt over his role in the development of the atomic bomb drives him mad. The realism of the film's portrayal of London's evacuation — down to the shooting of a looter by soldiers enforcing martial law — is a remarkable cinematic accomplishment. *Seven Days to Noon* is one of those rare gems that, when you luck upon it, makes you wonder why you've never heard of it before.

The Seventh Veil
★★½ (1945)

His name is Peter Gay. He's the apostle of a new religion called Swing. [Nicholas]

Length: 94 min. **Cast:** James Mason, Ann Todd, Herbert Lom, Hugh McDermott, Albert Lieven. **Production Companies:** Theatrecraft, Ortus Films. **Directed by:** Compton Bennett. **Photographed by:** Reginald H. Wyer. **Written by:** Muriel and Sydney Box.

After an automobile accident injures her hands, concert pianist Francesca Cunningham (Todd) sneaks out of her hospital room and jumps from a bridge into the river. Rescued by a constable, she is returned to the hospital, where, like Louise Howell Graham in the American film noir *Possessed*, she undergoes drug-induced hypnosis to break through her wall of silence and depression. Psychiatrist Dr. Larson (Lom) hopes to remove his patient's final mental barrier, something he calls the seventh veil. He attempts to learn the cause of her mental illness, which is preventing her from even attempting to play the piano. By way of voiceover narration and multiple flashbacks, the viewer follows Francesca from her early teenaged years in a boarding school, where a minor infraction of the rules leads to a severe caning of her hands, through her later teens and early adult years as the orphaned ward of a misogynistic distant cousin, crippled "Uncle" Nicholas (Mason). Under Nicholas' authoritarian tutelage Francesca becomes a famed international pianist. We also witness her two brief affairs with marriage-minded suitors—an American saxophone player (McDermott) and a German artist (Lieven). Will Dr. Larson cure his new patient? Will Francesca ever play the piano again? Which of the men in her life will she choose? These questions will be answered for the determined viewer who manages to stay awake until the slow-moving film's contrived ending. While Muriel and Sydney Box won an Academy Award for their screenplay, the film's strongest attribute is Wyer's dark and shadowy cinematography. Those responsible for teaming James Mason with Ann Todd should receive an award of their own. They are terrific together.

Shadow Man
see *Street of Shadows*

Shake Hands with the Devil
★★★★ (1959)

> We're underground. We have to take death as it comes. Ugly and friendless. [Sean Lenihan]

Length: 111 min. **Cast:** James Cagney, Don Murray, Dana Wynter, Glynis Johns, Michael Redgrave, Sybil Thorndyke, Cyril Cusack. **Production Companies:** Troy Films, Pennebaker Inc.. **Directed by:** Michael Anderson. **Photographed by:** Erwin Hillier. **Written by:** Ivan Goff, Ben Roberts.

In 1921, Irish-American Kerry O'Shea (Murray), a World War I veteran and Dublin medical student, becomes a member of the Irish Republican Army after his best friend is killed by a group of British soldiers who thought the boy was part of an IRA ambush. Kerry is surprised to learn that his professor, Dr. Sean Lenihan (Cagney), is a secret commandant in the rebel group and that he had been a friend of Sean's father, an IRA soldier who years earlier died fighting the British. Soon after taking his oath of allegiance to the organization ("once in, never out"), Kerry begins an affair with Kitty Brady (Johns), a local prostitute with ties to the underground. He falls in love however, with Lenihan's beautiful English hostage, Jennifer Curtis (Wynter), whom the commandant has taken captive as part of a plan to negotiate the release from prison of IRA accomplice Lady Fitzhugh (Thorndike). Meanwhile, the IRA leader known as "The General" (Redgrave thinly disguised as Irish rebel leader Michael Collins) announces that he is prepared to sign a peace treaty with the English. Lenihan, obsessed with a no-compromise military victory over the British, turns renegade and swears to continue the battle on his own. His fanatical militarism turns personal when he wrongly suspects that Kitty Brady, in his eyes a moral stain on Irish purity, has betrayed the cause. And when Lady Fitzhugh dies in prison after a lengthy hunger strike, he turns his attention to his innocent hostage, whom he has sworn to execute once she proves no longer useful. The Irish Republican Army is never mentioned by name, the filmmakers taking its cue from similar movies (such as *Odd Man Out*) that have addressed the sensitive political issue of the Irish independence from British rule. It is not uncommon for viewers to walk away from these IRA-related movies believing that filmmakers have favored one side in the conflict over the other. In the case of *Shake Hands with the Devil*, which was based on the novel by Irish author Rearden Conner, the film seems pro-Irish to those who see the filmmakers as bending over backwards to portray the English-Irish hostilities, known historically as The Troubles, in a manner that makes the British appear vicious, cruel and largely at fault for the appalling conditions under which the Irish were forced to live. At the same time, those who make this accusation note, the Irish rebels are portrayed as amazingly patient and courageous. Still others see as evidence of the filmmakers' intent to disparage the Irish cause the portrayal of IRA commandant, Sean Lenihan, as a fanatical militant, a sociopath and a sexually repressed and violent misogynist who wants the war and the violence to continue unabated. From the nonpolitical movie fan's viewpoint, however, this is top-notch entertainment highlighted by Michael Anderson's superb direction and Erwin Hillier's noirish cinematography. Irish-American actor James Cagney gives his most intense performance since *White Heat*, and viewers are treated to an early peek at a young actor named Richard Harris, who plays IRA fighter and loverboy Terence O'Brien.

The Shakedown
★★★ (1960)

> AUGIE CORTONA: Look me up when you get out. I'll have a job for you.
> CELLMATE: What cemetery will you be in?

Length: 92 min. **Cast:** Terence Morgan, Hazel Court, Donald Pleasence, Bill Owen, Robert Beatty, Harry H. Corbett, Gene Anderson. **Production Company:** Ethiro Productions. **Directed by:** John Lemont. **Photographed by:** Brendan J. Stafford. **Written by:** Leigh Vance, John Lemont.

London gangster Augie Cortona (Morgan) is released after three years in prison and returns home to find that his prostitution ring has been taken over by rival Gollar (Corbett), who also has laid claim to Augie's prostitute girlfriend, Zena (Anderson). Not inclined to return to the street racket because he feels that new laws have made prostitution an unprofitable and risky business, Augie steals money from Gollar and opens a modeling school with alcoholic photographer Jessel Brown (Pleasence). Augie begins using the school as a front for pornography and blackmail, extorting dough from pathetic middle-aged men who like to take pictures of naked women. Scotland Yard Inspector Bob Jarvis (Beatty) and beautiful police officer Mildred Eyde (Court), who unenthusiastically romances Augie after going undercover as a modeling student, hope to find out what the jailbird has been up to since his release from prison. Meanwhile, Augie's old cellmate, Spettigue (Owen), shows up looking for a job, and Gollar foolishly attempts to run Augie out of town. Despite its noticeable low budget, this somewhat racy gangster movie hits the spot with good acting, some invigorating jazz from composer Philip Green, including a silly but sexy rendition of the title song by singer Sheila Buxton, and lots of enjoyable hardboiled dialogue.

The Share-Out
★★★ (1962)

> I shan't keep you long. Not until I've got something to keep you with. [Superintendent Meredith to murder suspect]

Length: 61 min. **Cast:** Bernard Lee, Alexander Knox, Moira Redmond, William Russell, Richard Vernon, John Gabriel, Jack Rodney, Richard Warner. **Production Company:** Merton Park Productions. **Directed by:** Gerard Glaister. **Photographed by:** Bert Mason. **Written by:** Philip Mackie.

The board members of Calderwood Properties, Ltd. are a group of blackmailers who dig up dirt on prominent citizens, like Member of Parliament Mark Speller (Warner), and then blackmail them into selling their real estate holdings at half the market value. Superintendent. Meredith (Lee), determined to get the goods on Col. Calderwood (Knox), Diana Marsh (Redmond), John Crewe (Vernon) and Mr. Monet (Gabriel), recruits shady P.I. Mike Stafford (Russell) to infiltrate the company after Calderwood's own P.I. (Rodney), a spy for Scotland Yard, is found murdered. From this point on, viewers of this enjoyably convoluted film, part of producer Jack Greenwood's "Edgar Wallace Mystery Theatre" series, will need a score sheet to keep track of the multiple double-crosses. This is entertaining stuff with Lee and the Canadian born Knox handling their adversarial roles with skill. The title refers to the blackmailers' "sinking fund," a half-million pounds worth of diamonds locked safely away in Calderwood's safe until the day the police get too close. Two keys are required to open the safe — Calderwood has one and the other three board members each has a second key. Greed, of course, threatens to be the crooks' ultimate undoing.

She Played with Fire
see ***Fortune Is a Woman***

The Ship That Died of Shame
(U.S. Title: *PT Raiders*)
★★★★ (1955)

> She said, "Don't do anything silly with that ship of yours, will you?" Well, Birdie, we did do something silly, useless, futile and pathetic. [Bill Randall]

Length: 95 min. **Cast**: Richard Attenborough, George Baker, Bill Owen, Virginia McKenna, Roland Culver, Bernard Lee. **Production Company**: Ealing Studios. **Directed by**: Basil Dearden. **Photographed by**: Gordon Dines. **Written by**: John Whiting, Michael Relph, Basil Dearden.

During the war, motor gun boat (MGB) number 1087, skippered by newlywed Bill Randall (Baker) and manned by a group of British sailors known as "the beat-up boys," was a thorn in the flesh of German forces on the other side of the English channel. The boat's main mission was to blow up mines, but the crew also managed to sink a few German torpedo boats and trawlers and downed several enemy aircraft. With the death of Bill's bride, Helen (McKenna), in a bombing raid, Bill tries to pick up the pieces of his broken life at the end of the war. After his venture into the boat building business fails, he learns that his old job is no longer available. So when shipmate George Hoskins (Attenborough) shows up one day with a proposition — buying the mothballed MGB 1087 from the government and using it to smuggle contraband luxury items into the country — Bill, broke, depressed and longing to return to the sea, jumps at the opportunity. They are soon joined by their former coxswain, Birdie (Owen), and the three men begin to smuggle into the country harmless consumer items, enjoying their small slice of the post-war black market pie. Then George gets greedy, joining forces with Army officer-turned-gangster Maj. Fordyce

War veterans turned smugglers (Richard Attenborough, left, and George Baker, right) help a child killer (John Chandos) escape the police in *The Ship that Died of Shame* (a.k.a. *PT Raiders*) (Ealing Studios, 1955).

(Culver), who soon puts the men among the ranks of big-time smugglers with items such as counterfeit money and automatic weapons. It is at this time that MGB 1087 begins to exhibit mechanical difficulties that mysteriously disappear when illegal cargo is lost overboard or abandoned to the sea. When Bill and Birdie, who are basically decent chaps, learn that the boat has been used to transport a fleeing child murderer, they decide they want out. George, however, has already taken precautions against such rebellion. As Fordyce and George prepare to flee, having forcing Bill to agree to transport them out of the country aboard 1087, a nosy customs officer (Lee) investigating the disappearance of the child killer shows up at their hideout. Attenborough can portray a rotter with the best of them, and the hateful character he portrays here contributes greatly to the entertainment. The familiar film noir theme of troubled war veterans turning to crime is given a unique twist with the sometimes overdone fantasy theme (the suggestion that some ships can have a conscience). In addition, the cinematography and special effects are excellent, while the suspense and excitement rarely let up.

Shoot First see Rough Shoot

The Shop at Sly Corner (U.S. Title: The Code of Scotland Yard)
★★★½ (1947)

I'm like a stick of dynamite, aren't I? Simply no discretion. [Archie Fellows]

Length: 92 min. **Cast:** Oskar Homolka, Derek Farr, Muriel Pavlow, Manning Whiley, Garry Marsh, Kenneth Griffith. **Production Company:** Pennant Picture Productions. **Directed by:** George King. **Photographed by:** Hone Glendining. **Written by:** Katherine Strueby.

Widower Desius Heiss (Homolka), a middle-aged French émigré who runs a London antiques shop, dotes on his beautiful daughter, Margaret (Pavlow), a talented violinist who is engaged to Navy doctor Robert Graham (Farr). Heiss is a scrupulously fair businessman, at times paying his customers more for their items than they are actually worth. The same cannot be said about Heiss' shop assistant, Archie Fellows (Griffith), a dishonest and weak-willed scoundrel, who cheats customers at every opportunity and pockets the profits. Slithering around in the after-hours darkness of the shop, Archie overhears a conversation between Heiss and cat burglar Corder Morris (Whiley). The two friends have had an illegal arrangement for years, with Heiss acting as a fence for Corder's stolen goods. During their conversation, Heiss reveals his desire to end their criminal partnership and shows him the flogging scars he received while serving time on the French penal colony at Devil's Island, where he had been wrongly imprisoned as a young man for a murder he did not commit. He eventually escaped and, thus, can never return to his native land. Taking all of this in, Archie later confronts Heiss and demands money in return for keeping his mouth shut about his boss' criminal past. Like most blackmailers, Archie keeps returning for more, bleeding the antiques dealer dry until Heiss makes him a final offer—£15,000 and a ticket to Canada, where Archie is to remain for five years. The slimy extortionist, however, has come up with a plan of his own. He has decided to become a partner in the business and to marry Corer's daughter. In a fit of rage, Heiss strangles Archie and recruits his friend, Morris, to help him dispose of the body. With his old friend, antiques aficionado Major Elliot (Marsh) of Scotland Yard, on the case, Heiss relaxes and begins to enjoy his daughter's musical triumphs ... until he learns that a woman witnessed two men dumping a body in the woods. Highly atmospheric and quite suspenseful, *The Shop at Sly Corner* is top-notch entertainment, thanks mostly to Griffiths' portrayal of the despicable Archie Fellows. Archie serves as the glue that holds this little movie together. Once he passes from the scene, however, things slow down and it's just a matter of waiting until the inevitable happens. Homolka is good as the charming antiques dealer driven to murder in order to protect his daughter from the clutches of one of the most distasteful rouges in British film noir. The title change to *The Code of Scotland Yard* for the film's American release is puzzling.

Silent Dust
★★★★ (1949)

Since you died I've had time to recover from your rotten, sadistic, little mind. [Angela Rawley]

Length: 82 min. **Cast**: Stephen Murray, Nigel Patrick, Derek Farr, Sally Gray, Beatrice Campbell, Seymour Hicks. **Production Company**: Independent Sovereign Films. **Directed by**: Lance Comfort. **Photographed by**: Wilkie Cooper. **Written by**: Michael Pertwee.

Days before the scheduled unveiling of an ostentatious memorial to his son, Simon (Patrick), who is believed to have been killed in combat three years earlier, Robert Rawley, a wealthy, blind businessman, is asked by Lord Clandon (Hicks) to dedicate the memorial instead to the town's fifty young men of all economic classes who lost their lives in combat. Rawley, obsessed with paying homage to his beloved son, steadfastly refuses. Meanwhile, Robert's daughter-in-law, Angela (Gray), pays him a visit with new husband Max (Oliver) in tow and nervously waits for the best time to tell Robert about her recent marriage. Before she can do so, however, she discovers that Simon, an Army deserter and on the run for killing a motorist whose car he stole, is very much alive and has sneaked into the house. (Simon flippantly tells her that "I was too young to die, so I didn't.") As it turns out, Simon has always been quite the heel, and Angela was never happy about being married to him. In desperate need of money, Simon sees Angela's bigamy predicament as an opportunity to blackmail her. Robert's new wife, Joan (Campbell), and the rest of the guests are determined to keep Simon's presence a secret from Robert. Disturbed by their weird behavior, Robert is left to rely on his reasoning and deductive powers to figure out what is going on around him. When he does, the inevitable confrontation occurs. Suspenseful, intelligently scripted and well-acted (Patrick especially stands out), *Silent Dust* deftly presents an imaginative twist on the war veteran-turned-criminal theme. The unique, even comical, presentation of the film's narrative flashbacks, in which the cowardly Simon's version of his desertion story is entirely different from the way the viewer sees it unfolding on screen, is only one of the highlights of this moving tale of a father's journey through sorrow, pride and eventual disillusionment over his good-for-nothing son.

The Silk Noose see The Noose

The Six Men
★½ (1951)

The only singing you'll do now is at the end of a harp. [Bill "Alibi" Lewis]

Length: 65 min. **Cast**: Harold Warrender, Olga Edwardes, Peter Bull, Desmond Jeans, Michael Evans, Ivan Craig, Reed De Rouen, Christopher Page, Edward Malin. **Production Company**: Vandyke Picture Corporation. **Directed by**: Michael Law. **Photographed by**: S.D. Onions. **Written by**: Reed De Rouen, Richard Eastham, Michael Law.

The members of a six-man robbery ring (Bull, Jeans, Craig, De Rouen, Page, and Malin) are individually framed by a showgirl (Edwardes) and a mysterious "blind" character calling himself "The Mole." Meanwhile, the investigating police detective, Superintendent Holyroyd (Warrender), seeks to nail the crooks. Filled with cliché-ridden hardboiled dialogue ("Here's where you get yours, copper!") and cutely nicknamed villains (Alibi Lewis, Johnny the Kid, Keyhole Russell, and Jimmy the Fence), this intolerably slow-moving, but aesthetically noir, tale of revenge fails at almost every level. The film opens promisingly enough with Alibi Lewis (American actor De Rouen, who collaborated on the script) cold-bloodedly shooting his boss (Bull), but it soon deteriorates into a predictable and boring mystery embellished by the slapstick antics of a bumbling Scotland Yard inspector (Evans) seeking to advance his career. The opening murder scene serves as the introduction to the flashback narrative but it merely accentuate the weaknesses of the film's editing and screenwriting processes. After the flashback, when the scene is revisited, the dialogue is slightly different and instead of firing only five rounds Lewis shoots six times, which proves to be an important detail when "The Mole" walks in and advises Lewis that his gun is now empty. For hard-core British crime fans only.

The Slasher see *Cosh Boy*

The Sleeping Tiger
★★½ (1954)

He's tough enough, but he's immature and unhappy and I think frightened under that hard shell of his. [Dr. Esmond about sociopath Frank Clemmons]

Length: 89 min. **Cast:** Dirk Bogarde, Alexis Smith, Alexander Knox, Hugh Griffith. **Production Company:** Insignia Films. **Directed by:** Joseph Losey (as Victor Hanbury). **Photographed by:** Harry Waxman. **Written by:** Harold Buchman (as Derek Frye), Carl Foreman (as Derek Frye).

Rather than being tossed in jail for a botched mugging, petty thief Frank Clemmons (Bogarde), accepts an invitation from his intended victim, psychiatrist Dr. Clive Esmond (Knox), to participate in a unique social experiment whereby Clemmons will live in Esmond's home for six months while the doctor studies him. One of crook's unexpected perquisites as a houseguest turns out to be the doctor's beautiful American wife, Glenda (Smith), who at first is repulsed by the criminal but soon finds herself attracted to him. Before long the two are involved in a torrid affair that evidently does little to lessen Clemmons' criminal aspirations since he and an accomplice have been committing burglaries all over London, attracting the attention of a Scotland Yard detective (Griffith), who has little patience for psychiatric mumbo jumbo and criminal coddling. The cast turns in fine performances, especially Bogarde and American actress Smith, but the story crawls at a snail's pace before culminating in a shocking and noirish ending. American exiles Losey, Buchman and Foreman had to use pseudonyms because of the blacklisting of suspected Communist Party members and sympathizers in the entertainment industry back in the States, prompted by the House Un-American Activities Committee's infamous investigation.

The Small Back Room
(U.S. Title: *Hour of Glory*)
★★★½ (1949)

This dope the doctor gives me doesn't do my foot any good. It makes me feel bad. That noble remedy (whiskey) on the other hand doesn't do me any good either. But at least it leaves me not caring whether it hurts or not. [Sammy Rice]

Length: 108 min. **Cast:** David Farrar, Kathleen Byron, Jack Hawkins, Michael Gough, Robert Morley. **Production Companies:** London Film Productions, British Lion Production Assets, Archers Film Productions. **Directed by:** Michael Powell, Emeric Pressburger. **Photographed by:** Christopher Challis. **Written by:** Michael Powell, Emeric Pressburger.

The "back room" in the title of this war melodrama refers to the research department of a British corporation seeking to win Army contracts in support of the war effort. One of the company's scientists, Sammy Rice (Farrar), is secretly living with secretary Susan (Byron), although Susan claims to be living in the flat next door. It is not an easy relationship for Susan, however, who must comfort the pain-ridden Sammy almost daily because of the loss of his foot and his paranoia about refusing to remove his tin replacement in front of her, despite the immense relief it would bring. Instead, he swallows his pain killers, which he refers to as his dope, and when they stop working he hits the bottle heavily. In fact, the only alcohol that is safe from Sammy, temporarily at least, appears to be the bottle of Highland Clan whiskey the couple are saving for a future V-Day celebration. When Sammy is visited by Captain Stewart (Gough) and informed that German aircraft have been dropping booby-trapped devices that are exploding all over England and killing children, former demolitions expert Sammy promises to help the next time the Army comes across one. That time arrives quickly and Sammy has the opportunity to bolster his self-worth or die trying, if he can sober up that is. Farrar, Byron and Hawkins turn in excellent performances as the troubled lovers and their unprincipled boss, respectively. Challis' clever photography includes an expressionistic hallucinatory sequence in which Sammy imagines he is being terrorized by giant alarm clocks and chased by a giant-sized bottle of whiskey. Morley's cameo as a quirky cabinet minister (his screen credit reads "Guest") was an attempt to infuse a bit of gratuitous humor into an otherwise dark and depressing film.

The Small Voice
(U.S. Title: *The Hideout*)
★★ (1948)

You're surprised I have feelings? What do you think I am? A block of wood or a garbage can? That's how you look at me. But it doesn't matter that much to you if I rot my heart and mind away in a small stone cell. [Boke]

Length: 85 min. **Cast:** Howard Keel, Valerie Hobson, James Donald, David Greene, Michael Balfour. **Production Company:** Constellation Films. **Directed by:** Fergus McDonell. **Photographed by:** Stan Pavey. **Written by:** Julian Orde, Derek Neame.

A car containing three escaped prisoners (Keel, Green and Balfour) collides with a limousine. The accident kills the limousine chauffeur but not his passengers, two children whom the convicts kidnap and bring to the home of the hapless couple who stopped to help them. The estranged couple, Murray and Eleanor Byrne (Donald and Hobson), learn soon enough that the men they helped are on the run from the police and that the little boy, who is suffering from meningitis, will die unless he gets prompt medical attention. The convict ringleader, a particularly nasty cop killer named Boke (Keel), refuses to leave or to allow the couple to bring the boy to the hospital. Until now it has been the spunky Mrs. Byrne who has stood up to the killer, while her playwright husband, a former P.O.W. with a lame leg, has been playing mind games with Boke, hoping to convince him to leave. But when the boy's agonizing screams become too much for even the convicts to bear, prompting Boke to consider shooting the child, the Byrnes finally realize that their pleas for compassion have fallen on deaf ears and that drastic action must be taken. This was American actor Howard Keel's movie debut (being credited as Harold Keel in the British production). Although he gave a capable performance as the conscienceless killer, Keel went on to become famous for his musical leading roles soon afterward. The British title refers to the "small, clear voice of conscience," something the Liverpool-born, Chicago-raised Boke seems intent on proving he does not have. The American release of the film is shorter than the original British production by eighteen minutes (which may account for the script's seemingly poor character development and the resultant apathetic feeling viewers may come away with at the end). Strangely, the credits in the American release (*The Hideout*) list the names of the director, cinematographer and screenwriter, as "Burgess McDonnell," "Stan Davey," and "Julian Oroe," respectively.

The Small World of Sammy Lee
★★★½ (1963)

SAMMY: Want to buy a watch?
BIG ALF: Now what makes you think I want to buy a watch?
SAMMY: Well, you asked me the time, didn't you?
BIG ALF: If I asked you the way to Buckingham Palace it doesn't mean I want to buy the bloody place, does it?

Length: 107 min. **Cast:** Anthony Newley, Robert Stephens, Wilfrid Brambell, Julia Foster, Warren Mitchell, Miriam Karlin, Toni Palmer. **Production Company:** Elgin Films. **Directed by:** Ken Hughes. **Photographed by:** Wolfgang Suschitzky. **Written by:** Ken Hughes.

Sammy Lee (Newley) is a loser. Even worse, he is an inveterate gambler. In the hole to his bookie for 300 quid, if Sammy doesn't come up with the dough in six hours a couple of bad-intentioned goons are going to show up at the Peepshow Club, the seedy Soho strip joint where he works as house emcee and comic. As the deadline approaches, Sammy rushes off to brother Lou's grocery store to beg for money. Lou (Mitchell) reluctantly agrees to bail him out, but Lou's shrewish wife, Milly (Karlin), quickly nixes that idea. Sammy is too proud to accept money from the friendly hooker who lives next door or to allow his country bumpkin girlfriend, Patsy (Foster), to start stripping to help him out of his jam. So between afternoon sets, he rushes madly around Soho trying to raise the dough, using every trick in his hustler's manual. At the end of the day, he comes up short and the bookie's two goons arrive as promised. Although seemingly resigned to an imminent beating, or worse, Sammy is always open to suggestions. So when the club gofer (Brambell) wonders aloud why Sammy is still hanging around, the comic decides that now would be a good time to beat a path to the bus terminal and catch up with Patsy, whom he had sent packing earlier in the day. Sammy Lee's sordid world of gamblers, prostitutes, strippers and lecherous middle-aged men whose idea of a good time is spending an afternoon ogling the "slags" who play sultan's harem for their viewing pleasure, is much like the world of fellow Londoner, hustler Harry Fabian (*Night and the City*). Sammy and Harry, in fact, are birds of a feather — two losers on the run after messing with the wrong guy. Newley gives a solid performance as the desperate gambler.

The Smugglers
see *The Man Within*

The Snorkel
★★★½ (1958)

You've been a naughty girl. I don't like naughty girls. [Paul Decker to Candy Brown]

Length: 90 min. **Cast:** Peter van Eyck, Betta St. John, Mandy Miller. **Production Companies:** Hammer Film Productions, Clarion Film Productions. **Directed by:** Guy Green. **Photographed by:** Jack Asher. **Written by:** Peter Myers, Jimmy Sangster.

In northern Italy near the French border, Paul Decker (van Eyck) murders his wife for her money and makes it look like she committed suicide by gas inhalation. His plan is complicated but ingenious. He drugs her, locks the room from the inside, duct tapes the windows and doors, attaches a pair of hoses to a diving snorkel, goes down a secret trap door hidden under an area rug and runs the hoses out a small opening in a tight crawlspace. He then returns to the room, puts on the snorkel and makes himself comfortable while he waits for his wife to die. In the morning, when the maid finds the room locked but reeking of gas, Decker hides in the crawlspace and stays hidden there while police swarm over the apparent suicide scene. Later that day, Decker "returns" from France, his passport stamped appropriately since he swam the short distance on the night of the murder and then back again the next morning.

He begins to play the shocked and grief-stricken husband and easily fools family friend Jean Edwards (St. John), who sees it as her duty to comfort the grieving widower. Unfortunately for Decker, Candy Brown (Miller), his wife's teenaged daughter from a previous marriage, is not duped by his act. When Candy was eight, she witnessed Decker deliberately drown her father, but nobody believed her. Surely someone will believe her now, she thinks. No such luck. The police and Jean shrug off her accusations as the delusions of a troubled child. Despite her detractors, Candy audaciously tells Decker she is determined to figure out how he committed the murder. Decker, who has already poisoned Candy's dog because of its habit of retrieving his snorkel, believes her. So he decides to push his luck a bit by getting out the old breathing apparatus just one more time. Depending on the toleration level of the viewer for implausible premises, *The Snorkel*, with its noirish child-in-jeopardy scenario, will be viewed as either a very good suspense thriller or a rather silly time-waster. German-born actor van Eyck does a terrific job of being menacing (oh, that attempted murder scene in the ocean!). The ending, however, is a let-down.

Snowbound
★★ (1948)

Make no mistake, my British friends. There will be another Reich. Only this time it will spread all over the world. [Keramikos, alias Von Kellerman]

Length: 85 min. **Cast:** Dennis Price, Robert Newton, Mila Parély, Herbert Lom, Stanley Holloway. **Production Company:** Gainsborough Pictures. **Directed by:** David MacDonald. **Photographed by:** Stephen Dade. **Written by:** David Evans, Keith Campbell.

Former Army intelligence officer Derek Engles (Newton), now a movie director, hires war buddy Neil Blair (Price) to go undercover for him at a ski lodge in the Italian Alps, where Blair is to pretend to be writing a screenplay for Engles' next movie. His real task, however, is to report to Engles about the goings-on there. What Blair doesn't know is that the other guests at the lodge — Carla Rometta, a beautiful con artist pretending to be a countess; Keramikos (Lom), a Gestapo agent pretending to be a Greek citizen; and an assortment of other unsavory characters who are also not what they seem — are there to find the buried Italian gold that a Nazi officer rerouted at the close of the war. Double-crosses and betrayals abound (both in the present and the past as shown in flashbacks) as the group gets snowed in by a raging blizzard. Those who categorize *Snowbound* as a film noir should expect arguments. The nighttime photography both in and outside the lodge is quite atmospheric, however, and may trigger a feeling of fatalism and impending doom in some viewers. (The film's most impressive scene is when scores of torch-carrying skiers head out into the dark night, single file, to search for a missing person.) The characters, unfortunately, are one-dimensional, with Lom's stereotypical Nazi fanatic being the most interesting. While some performers get too much screen time, Newton's role is insignificant, thus shortchanging his many fans. Stanley Holloway, beloved British actor and comedian, provides the comedy relief.

So Evil My Love
★★★★ (1948)

A missionary's widow, a painter before his time. We belong among the rejected. [Mark Bellis to Olivia Harwood]

Length: 109 min. **Cast**: Ray Milland, Ann Todd, Geraldine Fitzgerald, Raymond Huntley, Leo G. Carroll. **Production Company**: Paramount British Productions. **Directed by**: Lewis Allen. **Photographed by**: Mutz Greenbaum (as Max Greene). **Written by**: Leonard Spigelgass, Ronald Millar.

While onboard a schooner from Jamaica to Victorian England, Olivia Harwood (Todd), the recently widowed wife of a British missionary, nurses malaria-stricken passengers, including artist Mark Bellis (Milland), whose life she saves. The grateful artist, an international criminal wanted for murder, burglary and art theft, shows up later at Olivia's London home seeking to rent a room. Despite the threat to her reputation, she allows him to move in, thus beginning a love affair that involves her in a downward spiral toward moral degeneracy and murder. Mark learns that Olivia's beautiful best friend, Susan (Fitzgerald), a pathetic alcoholic who is married to the cold-as-ice Edgar Bellamy (Lovell), has been unfaithful and that Olivia has letters from her to prove it. Mark convinces Olivia to use the letters to blackmail Bellamy for £5,000. Reluctant at first, the missionary quickly adapts to her new criminal persona, going so far as to encourage her friend to write new letters to her former lover just in case Bellamy already knows about his wife's earlier affair and believes it is over. The cuckolded Bellamy, a mean-spirited and despotic man, is not one to sit still for such criminal audacity and hires Jarvis (Carroll), a private investigator, to dig up dirt on Olivia. The dirt Jarvis digs up turns out to be Mark's criminal activities, allowing Bellamy to turn the tables on his blackmailer. Although Olivia hands over Susan's letters in exchange for the incriminating evidence against her lover, Bellamy informs her that he has held back copies of Jarvis' report and that he intends to use them. During their confrontation, the sickly lawyer suffers a heart attack, and Olivia replaces his medicine with poison and watches Susan unwittingly administer the fatal dose. With the failure of the blackmail plan and Susan being charged with murder, Mark leaves town but convinces Olivia that she must stay behind to throw suspicion off herself. But while in Paris, Mark realizes that he truly loves Olivia and rushes back to London to whisk her off to America, where they can be married. Unfortunately for Mark, being alone has given Olivia plenty of time to be tormented by guilt over her betrayal of her best friend, whose fragile mental and emotional state has been worsening each day. Things really begin to turn nasty, however, when Mark's secret girlfriend, Kitty (Lister), shows up to gloat. *So Evil My Love*, from a novel by Joseph Shearing and supposedly based on a true story, is a dark tale of guilt, adultery, betrayal, blackmail, and murder, which propounds the familiar 1940's moral lesson that no crime can go unpunished. Hollywood star Ray Milland, a native of Wales, is perfect as the homme fatale con man who realizes too late that money isn't everything, a questionable conversion that viewers suspect would never last anyway. Todd, in a very stoic performance, is the epitome of voluntary victimhood as the religious widow who allows herself to be manipulated into committing the most heinous of crimes by her love and sexual desire for the most dishonorable of men. Fitzgerald, too, does a good job as the emotionally abused Victorian wife whose finds solace only in the bottle. Perhaps too melodramatic and slow moving for nonfans of, or those who doubt the existence of, the Period noir, *So Evil* has an ending that is well worth the wait.

So Long at the Fair
★★★½ (1950)

> BRITISH AMBASSADOR: Well, now that you are here what is it you've lost? Your purse or your pet dog?
> VICKY BARTON: My brother.

Length: 86 min. **Cast:** Jean Simmons, Dirk Bogarde, David Tomlinson, Marcel Poncin, Cathleen Nesbitt, Honor Blackman. **Production Company:** Gainsborough Pictures. **Directed by:** Terence Fisher, Antony Darnborough. **Photographed by:** Reginald Wyer. **Written by:** Hugh Mills, Anthony Thorne.

English citizens Vicky Barton (Simmons) and her brother Johnny (Tomlinson) arrive in Paris amidst confusion and chaos as a multitude of visitors pour into the city to visit the 1889 Great Exposition. With all of the hotels booked solid, they consider themselves fortunate that Johnny had the foresight to write the Hotel de la Licorne for reservations. Unfortunately, however, Johnny disappears on their first night in Paris and the hotel owners (Poncin and Nesbitt) and staff claim that no such person ever registered (Johnny, it seems, forgot to sign the register). No one, from the British Ambassador to the Paris Police Commissioner, believes Vicky's story and who could blame them since Vicky is also claiming that the room Johnny was staying in also has disappeared? To the quiet dismay of marriage-minded Rhoda O'Donovan (Blackman), Vicky finds an ally in fellow countryman, George Hathaway (Bogarde), Rhoda's fiancé, who is barely eking out a living as an artist. This is a highly enjoyable film, but its intriguing Hitchcockesque plot, supported by superb acting, direction and photography, is ruined by an ending that stretches the imagination and prompts more questions about the disappearance puzzle than it actually answers.

So Well Remembered
★★★ (1947)

> I'm not responsible for their stupidity or their filth. [Olivia Channing about the diphtheria-infected children of Browdley]

Length: 114 min. **Cast:** John Mills, Martha Scott, Trevor Howard, Patricia Roc, Richard Carlson, Frederick Leister. **Production Company:** Alliance Film Studios. **Directed by:** Edward Dmytryk. **Photographed by:** Frederick A. Young. **Written by:** John Paxton.

George Boswell (Mills), a councilman and the muckraking editor of Browdley's only newspaper, falls in love with Olivia Channing (Scott), the daughter of the town pariah, John Channing (Leister). Mr. Channing is the shady owner of the now defunct mills and the townsfolk hold him responsible for the bleak ghetto conditions being experienced by most of the working class populace. When Channing dies in an automobile accident, the ambitious Olivia accepts George's marriage proposal and proceeds to scheme her way into London society by pushing George to run for Parliament. When George learns, however, that he is being used by his party backers to enrich themselves at the expense of his neighbors, he ruffles more than a few feathers by terminating his candidacy and devoting his attention to a diphtheria epidemic that has begun to ravage Browdley. Believing George's humanitarian philosophy to be at odds with the well-being of his family, Olivia leaves him and eventually marries a wealthy London big-wig, returning twenty years later as a widow to reopen the unsafe and unsanitary mills. Meanwhile, wounded war veteran Charles (Carlson), Olivia's son from her second marriage, falls in love with Julie (Roc), a local girl who had been adopted by the town's alcoholic doctor (Howard) after her parents died during the diphtheria epidemic. Obsessed with controlling her weak-kneed son, Olivia does all she can to prevent Charles' marriage to Julie, prompting Dr. Whiteside to divulge to George his ex-wife's dreadful secret. Well-acted and expertly directed, *So Well Remembered* takes a look at the pitiable pre- and post-war social conditions experienced by the lower class poor throughout England and lays the blame on corrupt capitalists and politicians. Told via flashback at the end of World War II and narrated by novelist James Hilton, whose book was the basis for the movie, it is also a noirish story of a humanitarian politician (Mills in an enjoyably low-key performance) who has the misfortune of falling in love with a greedy and ambitious femme fatale of sorts.

Soho Incident (U.S. Title: *Spin a Dark Web*)
★½ (1956)

You do what you're told. I like that. [Bella Francesi complimenting Jim Bankley]

Length: 77 min. **Cast:** Faith Domergue, Lee Patterson, Rona Anderson, Martin Benson, Robert Arden, Peter Burton, Bernard Fox. **Production Company:** Film Locations. **Directed by:** Vernon Sewell. **Photographed by:** Basil Emmott. **Written by:** Ian Stuart Black.

Down and out in London, Canadian Jim Bankley (Patterson) pressures his former Army pal (Arden) into getting him a job with local crime lord Rico Francesi (Benson). Rico's sister Bella (American actress Domergue), the real brains behind the Francesi gang, is quick to seduce the handsome newcomer. With dough in his pocket and a swell-looking dame at his side, Jim thinks his successful foray into the world of crime will be limited to Rico's gambling scams, but he soon learns that a boxer friend, the brother of his former girlfriend, Betty Walker (Anderson), has been killed for refusing to throw a fight and that Scotland Yard Inspector Collis (Burton) is seeking one of Rico's boys, MacLeod (Fox), for the murder. When Jim sees Rico kill MacLeod at Bella's cold-blooded insistence, he decides it's time to drop both Bella and the rackets. The spurned femme fatale, however, has other plans for him. A dreadful film, *Soho Incident* contains some terrific nighttime shots of London.

Solo for Sparrow
★★ (1962)

INSP. SPARROW: You did a wire tapping job for Scotty Gordon six years ago, you and your little gray van.
LARKIN: Who told you?
SPARROW: He told me. You surprised? He sang like the Newton Girl's Choir.

Length: 56 min. **Cast:** Glyn Houston, Anthony Newlands, Nadja Regin, Michael Coles, Allan Cuthbertson. **Production Company:** Merton Park Productions. **Directed by:** Gordon Flemyng. **Photographed by:** Bert Mason. **Written by:** Roger Marshall.

A gang of thieves kidnap an elderly jewelry shop employee who has the key to the store and its safe. The woman accidentally dies during her short confinement, and police Inspector Sparrow suspects that Reynolds (Newlands), the shop owner, was the inside man in the robbery. However, Sparrow is removed from the investigation when his nervous boss (Cuthbertson) turns over the high-profile case to Scotland Yard. So Sparrow, who has no qualms about "bending the law" in his pursuit of criminals, takes two weeks of vacation and spends them trying to trap Reynolds and Reynolds' accomplice wife (Regin), as well as heist mastermind Pin Norman (Coles) and his goons. Notable only for an early film appearance by future Hollywood superstar Michael Caine, who has a small role as one of Pin Norman's thugs. (Part of the "Edgar Wallace Mystery Theater" series.)

The Spell of Amy Nugent see *Spellbound*

Spellbound (U.S. Title: *The Spell of Amy Nugent*)
★★ (1941)

Out of the infinitely mysterious void, beyond our knowing, has come a personality, strong, malignant, depraved and whose purpose it is *to* deprave. [Mr. Cathcart]

Length: 82 min. **Cast:** Derek Farr, Vera Lindsay, Frederick Leister, Hay Petrie, Diana King, Winifred Davis, Felix Aylmer. **Production Company:** Pyramid Amalgamated Productions. **Directed by:** John Harlow. **Photographed by:** Walter J. Harvey. **Written by:** Miles Malleson.

College student Laurie Baxter (Farr) falls in love with Amy Nugent (King) and plans to marry her despite his mother's blatantly expressed distaste at the thought of having a shopkeeper's daughter in her upper class family. Mrs. Baxter (Davis) would much rather her son marry socialite Diana Hilton (Lindsay), but Laurie considers Diana to be merely a friend. Unfortunately, Amy, a nervous and sickly girl her whole life, dies soon after Laurie proposes. Depressed over her sudden demise, Laurie becomes fascinated by spiritualism and begins attending séances conducted by well-known medium Mr. Vincent (Leister), who discovers in the young man a psychic ability stronger than he has ever known. Vincent convinces Laurie to attend a potentially dangerous session in which he will attempt to materialize Amy. Obsessed now with seeing his fiancée again, Laurie ignores the concerns of Diana; his college professor, Mr. Morton (Aylmer); and Mr. Cathcart (Petrie), a former spiritualist who now actively opposes all such meddling in the supernatural. The ceremony succeeds in its intended purpose but at a heavy cost to Laurie's mental state. Mr. Cathcart comes to believe that the now potentially violent young man was possessed during the séance and leaves it to Diana to try a bit of exorcising. Will her love save Laurie from being taken over permanently by a malignant spirit? What do you think? Also known as *The Spell of Amy Nugent*, *Passing Clouds* and *Ghost Story*, *Spellbound* (not to be confused with Alfred Hitchcock's 1945 film noir) takes a look at the world of spiritualism during a time in England when it enjoyed intense popularity. The filmmakers treat the spooky stuff as if it were an accepted reality, unlike later American noirs such as *Fallen Angel* and *The Amazing Mr. X*, which depict the spirit world as a realm ruled not by ghosts but by con artists out to scam rich elderly widows. While the atmosphere and photography are noirishly dark, something that should satisfy noir fans, the outdated musical score gives it a 1930s feel. Farr's histrionics make Lindsay's stilted acting style all the more noticeable. Irish actor W.G. Fay (Father Tom in *Odd Man Out*) has a minor role as the Baxters' wizened groundskeeper.

The Spider and the Fly
★★★½ (1949)

Don't cry, Mademoiselle. I've seen too many people cry. Tears don't move me any more. [Police Chief Maubert]

Length: 95 min. **Cast:** Eric Portman, Guy Rolfe, Nadia Gray, John Carol, Harold Lang. **Production Companies:** Pinewood Films, Mayflower Pictures. **Directed by:** Robert Hamer. **Photographed by:** Geoffrey Unsworth. **Written by:** Robert Westerby.

Just prior to the outbreak of World War I, cat burglar and expert safecracker Philippe Lodocq (Rolfe) and Paris Chief of Police Fernand Maubert (Portman), continue their long-running battle of wits. Maubert knows that it is Lodocq, an adversary he has arrested and helped convict several times in the past, who has recently robbed a bank in the countryside, but he can't prove it because the thief has an ironclad alibi — he was in a church at the time visiting with the parish priest. So Maubert arrests Lodocq's girlfriend and accomplice, Madeleine Saincaize (Gray), hoping she will crack and betray her lover. She does neither and Maubert is forced to release her, becoming in the process an ardent admirer of the loyal moll, whom he advises to steer clear of Lodocq to avoid certain heartbreak. The cop's prediction proves true and Lodocq dumps Madeleine, albeit in a gentlemanly fashion, hoping she won't retaliate by betraying him to his nemesis. She doesn't, much to Maubert's chagrin. Opportunity soon presents itself to Maubert in the person of a small-time crook Belfort (Lang), who turns stool pigeon after being arrested as a pickpocket. Maubert gives Belfort his freedom after he fingers Lodocq for an imminent bank heist. The police chief sets a trap that goes horribly awry when Lodocq's accomplice, Jean Louis (Carol), accidentally kills himself and a policeman. Lodocq escapes but, realizing he can now be charged with murder and desperate for an alibi, he turns once again to Madeleine. Still in love with him, she accommodates, telling Maubert that Lodocq was with her at the time of the fatal burglary. Defeated once again, Maubert manages to come up with yet another plan to capture Lodocq. This one works. By the time World War I has broken out, Lodocq has served two years of a five-year sentence, while Maubert has been working for the French counterespionage service. Representing the French government, Maubert makes Lodocq a tempting offer — if he will break into a safe at the German legation in Berne, Switzerland, and steal some secret documents, he will be pardoned. Staying true to form, Lodocq holds out for 50,000 francs, the expunging of his criminal record, a medal and a five-minute visit with Madeleine, whom Maubert has grown to love, albeit from a distance. And so the two former adversaries become fellow conspirators, one for love of France and the other for love of money and personal freedom. Be prepared for a nifty surprise ending. While dark, shadowy, and convoluted, *The Spider and the Fly* is also slow-moving, not a big enticement for the impatient viewer. The film has, however, a surprising air of sophistication about it, thanks in large part to likeable performances by costars Portman and Rolfe, both of whom portray staid, almost emotionless characters, belying their obvious affection and respect for one another. Rolfe, a tall and gaunt actor, has a very unusual, not unpleasant, walking style. At times, he seems almost to glide to his destination. American viewers may recognize the actor from his appearances more than forty years later as Andre Toulon in *Puppet Master* sequels.

Spin a Dark Web see Soho Incident

The Spy in Black
(U.S. Title: *U-Boat 29*)
★★★★ (1939)

> BOAT PASSENGER: We're all in the hands of Providence.
> JILL BLACKLOCK: No you're not. You're in the hands of a man who cares nothing for his life or yours.

Length: 82 min. **Cast:** Conrad Veidt, Sebastian Shaw, Valerie Hobson, June Duprez. **Production Companies:** London Film Productions, Harefield Productions. **Directed by:** Michael Powell. **Photographed by:** Bernard Browne. **Written by:** Emeric Pressburger.

During World War I, German U-boat commander, Capt. Hardt (Veidt), is ordered to go behind enemy lines as a spy and to coordinate with Frau Tiel (Hobson), who has taken on the identity of a schoolteacher in a small village off the coast of Scotland. Frau Tiel is impersonating newly hired Anne Burnett (Duprez), whom German spies have put out of commission by chloroforming her and then tossing her from a cliff into the ocean. After making contact with Frau Tiel, Hardt learns that British traitor Lt. Ashington (Shaw) has gotten hold of top secret plans concerning the transit schedule of fifteen English destroyers, information that Hardt relays to his U-boat comrades, setting in motion a deadly trap that will mean the end of the line for all the ships and a milestone in the German war effort. Unique, exciting and suspenseful, *The Spy in Black* was produced on the eve of World War II, and is exceptionally interesting because of its sympathetic portrayal of the U-boat commander, played brilliantly by German-born actor Veidt, and a darkly inspired plot twist, as well as a thrilling at-sea climax.

Squadron Leader X
(NR) (1942)

Length: 100 min. **Cast:** Eric Portman, Ann Dvorak, Walter Fitzgerald, Barry Jones. **Production Company:** RKO Radio Pictures. **Directed by:** Lance Comfort. **Photographed by:** Mutz Greenbaum. **Written by:** Wolfgang Wilhelm, Miles Malleson.

A German agent disguised as a British pilot parachutes into Belgium as part of a Nazi plot to convince the pro–English Belgians that British pilots plan to bomb their civilians.

The Square Ring
★★★ (1953)

The blokes that don't go into the ring, they're the ones that get rich out of boxing [heavyweight Rick Martell]

Length: 83 min. **Cast:** Jack Warner, Robert Beatty, Bill Owen, Maxwell Reed, George Rose, Bill Travers, Ronald Lewis, Alfie Bass, Sidney James, Bernadette O'Farrell, Joan Collins. **Production Company:** Ealing Studios. **Directed by:** Basil Dearden. **Photographed by:** Otto Heller. **Written by:** Robert Westerby.

At a small boxing arena managed by a cigar-chomping fight promoter (James), six English fighters anxiously await their bouts in a dressing room manned by attendants Danny Felton (Warner) and Frank Forbes (Bass) — the aging Kid Curtis (Beatty), a former light heavyweight champion who dreams of making a comeback and reuniting with his estranged wife, Peg (O'Farrell), who would rather seem him lose than take any more beatings; Happy Burns (Owen), an up-and-coming lightweight with a string of female admirers and an as-yet unbroken nose; Rick Martell (Reed), a heavyweight who has taken "more dives than Esther Williams" but plans to double-cross the razor-toting hoods who are betting against him because his new girlfriend (Collins, Reed's real-life wife) is in the audience, a decision that could result in her disfigurement; Rowdie Rawlings (Travers), a slow-witted heavyweight who relaxes by reading science fiction pulp magazines before his fights; Whitey Johnson (Rose), a punch-drunk boxer has-been who has taken one too many hard lefts to the head; and Eddie Lloyd (Lewis), a talented young amateur making his professional boxing debut against one of the sport's dirtiest fighters. Reminiscent of *The Set-Up*, one of the great American boxing noirs, *The Square Ring* takes a fast-moving and entertaining look at the seedy side of the sport and the oftentimes pathetic combatants who have chosen it as their path to a richer life. Although the film is marginally noir, the intelligent script and solid acting (except for George Rose's overdone punchy routine) contribute to an enjoyable viewing experience.

Stage Fright
★★★★ (1950)

The only murderer here is the orchestra leader.
[singer Charlotte Inwood]

Length: 111 min. **Cast:** Jane Wyman, Marlene Dietrich, Michael Wilding, Richard Todd, Alastair Sim, Kay Walsh. **Production Company:** Warner Brothers First National Productions. **Directed by:** Alfred Hitchcock. **Photographed by:** Wilkie Cooper. **Written by:** Whitfield Cook.

Fleeing the police, Jonathan Cooper (Todd) turns to Eve Gill (Wyman) for help, explaining to her (and the viewer by way of flashback) his role in the attempted cover-up of the murder of his lover's husband. The lover, stage and singing star Charlotte Inwood (Dietrich), shows up at Jonathan's flat, her dress stained with blood, to tell him how she has accidentally killed her husband. Jonathan volunteers to return to her apartment to retrieve a dress so she can go on with her scheduled performance that evening. While at the apartment, he tries to make it look like the murder was committed during a burglary gone wrong, but he is interrupted by Charlotte's maid, Nellie Goode (Walsh), who recognizes him. When the police arrive at his flat to question him, he escapes and heads directly for The Royal Academy of Dramatic Art (RADA), where Eve, a budding actress who is secretly in love with him, is auditioning for a role. She drives him to her father's cottage in the countryside where he hides out as she plays amateur detective in the hopes of clearing him. While pretending to be a newspaper reporter, the actress bribes Nellie to take sick leave and to recommend Eve, supposedly a yokel cousin, for the temporary maid position. During her amateur sleuthing, she is romanced by the handsome policeman investigating the murder, Det. Inspector Wilfred Smith (Wilding), who goes along with a plan concocted by Eve's father (Sim) to trick Charlotte into confessing to the murder. Wyman is marvelous as the wannabe actress who gets a chance to practice her craft in real life, but Dietrich, the German-born Hollywood icon, steals the show as the scheming femme fatale. Hitchcock's daughter, Patricia, who was attending RADA at the time, has a small role as a student actress and even filled in as a stunt driver for Wyman, explaining later that her famous father was concerned about his star's safety. Upon the film's release, a controversy erupted (which cannot be explained here without revealing the film's ending) with critics claiming that Hitchcock did not play fair with his audience. Nevertheless, *Stage Fright*, while not one of the director's best efforts, is highly entertaining, often humorous and offers viewers a very dark and frightening climax.

Stella see The Key

Stolen Face
★★★ (1952)

> We can blame the war for her condition. She got badly smashed up in the blitz, and it so embittered her that she turned criminal. [HM Prison Holloway physician]

Length: 72 min. **Cast:** Paul Henreid, Lizabeth Scott, André Morell, Mary Mackenzie. **Production Company:** Hammer Film Productions. **Directed by:** Terence Fisher. **Photographed by:** Walter Harvey. **Written by:** Martin Berkeley, Richard H. Landau.

While on holiday, Philip Ritter (Henreid), a successful London plastic surgeon, falls in love with American concert pianist Alice Brent (Scott), who turns down his offer of marriage because she feels obligated to her manager and fiancé (Morell). Dejected, Ritter returns to London, where he continues his prison charity work by operating on a horribly scarred convict, Lily Conover (Mackenzie), turning her into the spit and image of Alice. Hoping that Lily will go straight, as his other convict patients have done, Ritter marries her on the rebound. Unfortunately, the old lifestyle beckons to Lily, whose promise to "be everything you want me to be" lasts about as long as her ability to stay away from old boyfriends, shoplifting, heavy drinking and wild parties. Meanwhile, Alice's manager frees her from her commitment to marry him, so she rushes off to London to break the good news to Ritter, who by now doesn't need much incentive to ask his wife for a divorce. Alice, of course, refuses and plans to take Ritter for every penny he's got. After a tedious first half, the film picks up considerably once Dr. Ritter turns Lily Conover into a pale imitation of his true love and foolishly marries her. There is no medical reason why Lily's voice changes after the operation to sound like Alice Brent with a Cockney accent, but this minor problem should not affect the viewer's fun while watching noir icon Scott overdo it just a bit as the wife from hell.

Stormy Crossing
(U.S. Title: *Black Tide*)
★★½ (1958)

> INSPECTOR PARRY: We went through all this at the inquest. The jury was not impressed.
> DANNY PARKER: They're a bunch of creeps.

Length: 69 min. **Cast:** John Ireland, Derek Bond, Leslie Dwyer, Maureen Connell, Sheldon Lawrence, Joy Webster, John Horsley. **Production Company:** Tempean Films. **Directed by:** C. Pennington-Richards. **Photographed by:** Geoffrey Faithfull. **Written by:** Brock Williams.

Former model Kitty Tyndall (Webster), now a long-distance swimmer, makes the mistake of telling her lover, Paul Seymour (Bond), that if *he* doesn't inform his wife about their affair *she* will. During her attempt to swim the English Channel alongside American swimmer Danny Parker (Lawrence), who has fallen in love with her after knowing her for only a few days, Kitty is drowned by Seymour under cover of a dense fog. After the coroner rules her death an accident, Danny tells the cynical Dover police inspector Parry (Horsley) that he knows she was murdered and vows to find the killer. Fearing Danny will make good on his vow, Seymour hops into his motor boat and follows the swimmer into yet another thick fog. When Danny doesn't return from his swim, his brother and trainer, Griff Parker (Ireland), begins to think that maybe Danny was right about Kitty being murdered and that, as a result, has become victim number two. Griff and hotel desk clerk Shelley Baxter (Connell) team up to hunt down the, by now, nervous killer. American film noir veteran Ireland makes a good effort despite the silliness of the plot. Screenwriters had to come up with a way to murder Kitty while she was swimming across the English channel and being followed by her trainer, a boatload of official observers and a helicopter. They decided on fog. They forgot, however, to explain how the killer knew there was going to be such a severe fog on the day of the swim when no one involved with the event knew about it. The obvious nonactor playing the swim organizer is Sam Rockett, who swam the Channel in a 1950 race sponsored by the *Daily Mail* and eventually wrote a book about his exploits entitled "It's Cold in the Channel."

The Stranger Came Home
(U.S. Title: *The Unholy Four*)
★½ (1954)

> I don't know what hit me or how long it was before I came to, but when I did I was aboard a Mexican tramp with nothing in my pockets to tell me who I was. Nothing in my head either, except a big hole. [Philip Vickers]

Length: 80 min. **Cast:** Paulette Goddard, William Sylvester, Patrick Holt, Paul Carpenter, Alvys Maben, Russell Napier. **Production Company:** Hammer Film Productions. **Directed by:** Terence Fisher. **Photographed by:** James Harvey. **Written by:** Michael Carreras.

Missing amnesia victim Philip Vickers (Sylvester) returns home after four years to settle scores. He believes that one of his three friends, all of whom are in love with his wife, Angie (American actress Goddard), knocked him over the head and left him for dead during a fishing trip off the Portuguese coast. After Philip arrives home, one of the three men is murdered and Scotland Yard Inspector Treherne (Napier) compiles a long list of suspects—Philip; Angie; Angie's social secretary, Joan Merrill (Maben); and Mrs. Vickers' two remaining admirers, Job Crandall (Holt) and Bill Saul (Carpenter). Three bodies, two phony confessions, one blackmail and two frame-ups later, Treherne solves the case. By this time, however, the viewer more than likely has lost interest. The film, based on the novel "Stranger at Home" by actor George Sanders (actually ghost-written for him by writer Leigh Brackett), contains enough noir plot and character elements to satisfy those hardcore fans who may not be bothered by the weak performances of a jaded-looking cast and the overall dreariness of the film.

The Stranger in Between
see *Hunted*

The Stranger's Hand
★★½ (1954)

> Your world, my world is sinking. There's nothing we can do about it. [Dr. Vivaldi to Major Court]

Length: 85 min. **Cast:** Trevor Howard, Alida Valli, Richard Basehart, Eduardo Ciannelli, Richard O'Sullivan, Stephen Murray. **Production Company:** Independent Film Producers. **Directed by:** Mario Soldati. **Photographed by:** Enzo Serafin. **Written by:** Guy Elmes, Giorgio Bassani.

Major Court (Howard) arrives in Venice to be reunited with his 8-year-old son, Roger (O'Sullivan), whom he hasn't seen in three years. After boarding a water bus to the hotel where Roger is staying, Court notices a dazed acquaintance being propped up by two men. He makes the mistake of questioning the men about his friend's condition, letting on that he recognizes him, and, as a result, finds himself kidnapped and drugged in order to be secreted out of the country by Dr. Vivaldi (Ciannelli), who apparently works for a communist government somewhere in Europe. Much baffling conversation goes on between Major Court and his surprisingly kind captor, who cautiously refers to the country that employs him as "over there." When Court doesn't show up at the hotel, his worried son alerts the staff, and the police are called in to investigate, but they don't take the boy seriously. Roberta Glabri (Valli), a hotel employee, befriends the child and, along with her unenthusiastic American boyfriend, Joe Hamstringer (Basehart), tries to help him locate his father, who by now has been smuggled aboard a ship of Eastern European registry that is scheduled to leave Venice in a few hours. Child actor O'Sullivan has the major portion of screen time and manages to hold his own. The filmmakers skimp on character development when it comes to Howard and American noir veteran Basehart, who are relegated to small supporting roles. Howard's character, a war hero judging by his cane and pronounced limp, is drugged much of the time, and Basehart doesn't even appear on screen until almost an hour into the film. The refugee character portrayed by Italian actress Valli quickly links the boy's missing father to the recent disappearance of a prominent fellow countryman, whom she correctly suspects has been kidnapped by her former government. However, she seems strangely annoyed at times because of the child's single-minded determination to convince the adults around him to help him find his father. The beautiful on-location photography is the biggest plus in this joint British and Italian film, which was based on a Graham Greene story. The title refers to a spontaneous bonding ceremony, which involves the kidnapper tying a piece of string around his finger as a reminder of his new friendship with his victim's son.

The Strangler see East of Piccadilly

Street Corner
(U.S. Title: *Both Sides of the Law*)
★★ (1953)

> I've always told Stan that you're a slut and now I can prove it. [Mrs. Foster to daughter-in-law, Bridget]

Length: 94 min. **Cast:** Anne Crawford, Peggy Cummins, Terence Morgan, Rosamund John, Barbara Murray, Eleanor Summerfield, Ronald Howard, Michael Medwin, Charles Victor. **Production Company:** London Independent Producers. **Directed by:** Muriel Box. **Photographed by:** Reginald H. Wyer. **Written by:** Muriel and Sydney Box.

Sgt. Pauline Ramsey (John) of the London Metropolitan Police and her "coppers in skirts" (Crawford, Murray et al.) tackle crime and social problems in London. Their cases include abusive parents who went to work and left their baby at home alone to climb out on a window ledge, and Edna (Summerfield), a homeless Army deserter who also happens to be a bigamist happily married to husband number two, David Evans (Howard), a sickly one-armed man. (Evans' one arm is never explained but the viewer can only assume that the writers made him a cripple so there would be a reasonable excuse for Edna to be the one to jump into the river to save a drowning child.) Several subplots, including one about a misogynist constable, revolve around the noirish story of 18-year-old shoplifter Bridget Foster (Cummins). Bridget becomes involved with homme fatale Ray (Morgan), a small-time criminal who lures her away from her decent lorry driver husband and infant son with an expensive brooch that he and his goon, Chick (Medwin), stole during a recent jewelry heist. After Chick manages to get only a measly £85 for the stones from fence Muller (Victor), Ray pretends to be a cop on the take and blackmails the elderly German emigrant into handing over the jewels and paying him £500 to keep his mouth shut. Things begin to go wrong for Ray when Muller's angry wife pays a visit to the local police station. This tepid police procedural should have concentrated on the more interesting wayward housewife plot instead of jumping around to insignificant subplots intended to pay homage to London's female police officers. Cummins' spunky performance, several years after her starring role in the spectacular 1949 American film noir *Gun Crazy*, is the film's highlight. Also enjoyable are two humorous scenes with well-known British character actresses Dora Bryan as a prostitute fed up with being arrested by women cops and Thora Bird as the mother of a boy who goes missing just so he can get candy at the police station.

Street of Shadows
(U.S. Title: *Shadow Man*)
★★½ (1953)

> When you're a cripple you have to drag yourself about for years by your arms. It makes you strong. ["Limpy" Thomas]

Length: 84 min. **Cast:** Cesar Romero, Kay Kendall, Edward Underdown, Victor Maddern, Simone Silva. **Production Companies:** Merton Park Productions, William Nassour Productions. **Directed by:** Richard Vernon. **Photographed by:** Phil Grindrod. **Written by:** Richard Vernon.

Luigi (Romero), the owner of a Soho pin table saloon, a combination pub and penny arcade, finds the body of former girlfriend Angele Abbe (Silva) in his flat. Believing he is protecting his new lover, married society dame Barbara Gale (Kendall), whom he saw leaving the scene of the murder, Luigi goes into hiding, hoping to prevent Scotland Yard Inspector

Johnstone (Underdown) from closing in on Barbara. Unaware that his crippled employee, "Limpy" Thomas (Maddern), had been romantically obsessed with the murdered woman, Luigi mistakenly relies on him to convince the police that they should be looking for the merchant seaman who had been manhandling her the evening before. Not much effort seems to have been put into constructing a plausible, fast-moving plot, but the film's intense noir atmosphere more than makes up for its baffling storyline, which doesn't really start making any sense until the half-way point. There are some interesting but unexplained characterizations in the film, such as Barbara's apparently open marriage to her upper-class husband who, along with some pompous middle-aged friends, runs a crooked poker game and is somehow involved with "pick-up girls." American actor Romero is unexciting as the morally ambiguous protagonist who finds himself the victim of a frame-up, but Maddern is more than persuasive as his club-footed employee, a pathetic creature with an urgent but unrequited longing for female companionship.

Strongroom
★★★½ (1962)

> Perfect crime, you know. Practically not a crime at all really. The bank's been robbing the poor for years. We're practically Robin Hoods. [Griff to heist accomplice Len]

Length: 80 min. **Cast:** Derren Nesbitt, Colin Gordon, Ann Lynn, Keith Faulkner, Morgan Sheppard, Jack Stewart. **Production Company:** Theatrecraft. **Directed by:** Vernon Sewell. **Photographed by:** Basil Emmott. **Written by:** Max Marquis, Richard Harris.

Three struggling auto scrap dealers, Griff (Nesbitt), Len (Faulkner) and Len's brother,

A conscience stricken bank robber (Derren Nesbitt, left) tries to convince his worried accomplice (Keith Faulkner) to help him free the bank employees from a locked vault before the air runs out in *Strongroom* (Theatrecraft, 1962).

Alec (Sheppard), turn to bank robbery, pulling off their first (and, they swear, their last) heist. It's Easter weekend and the whip-cracking bank manager, Mr. Spencer (Gordon), has unexpectedly asked his secretary, Rose (Lynn), to work late, leaving the daring trio with two employees to worry about instead of the one they expected. The amateur crooks manage to overcome Rose and Spencer, find the keys to the vault and start helping themselves. Just when it seems that all they have left to do is to tie up their hostages and make their getaway, two charladies arrive for an unscheduled office cleaning. In a panic, the robbers lock their two victims in the air-tight vault and sneak past the cleaning women. Generally good-natured guys, the three decide that Alec should drop off the keys at a call box a good distance away and telephone the police to let them know about the employees locked in the safe. Plenty of time, plenty of air, they figure. Unfortunately, Alec is killed in a car accident before he has the chance to accomplish his assignment, and the keys wind up in the personal property bin at the morgue. After being notified of Alec's death, Griff pressures Len, who wants to skip town, to go with him to the morgue, where they end up having to deal with a by-the-rules bureaucrat who won't release the keys without police approval. While the ever weakening Rose and Mr. Spencer are bonding in the vault, an inquisitive police detective (Stewart) wonders why a now-deceased automobile scrap dealer had been carrying two sets of keys that look like they could open, say, a vault. Thematically dark, visually claustrophobic, well-acted and, for a low-budget B film, surprisingly thought provoking, *Strongroom* is another of those gems that make hunting down rare films a worthwhile effort. The working stiffs-turned-bank robbers are sympathetically portrayed and one can't help but hope they come out on top. The unexpected ending is one that noir fans are sure to appreciate.

Take My Life
★★★ (1947)

She was going to divorce me for cruelty. Not because I'd been cruel but because she hated me. [Sidney Fleming on why he killed his wife]

Length: 79 min. **Cast**: Hugh Williams, Greta Gynt, Marius Goring, Francis L. Sullivan, Rosalie Crutchley. **Production Company**: Cineguild Productions. **Directed by**: Ronald Neame. **Photographed by**: Guy Green. **Written by**: Winston Graham, Valerie Taylor, Margaret Kennedy.

Londoner Nicholas Talbot (Williams), husband of opera singer Phillipa Shelley (Gynt), stands trial for the murder of his former girlfriend, Elizabeth Rusman (Crutchley). During the first ten minutes or so, viewers may think they are about to see a British take-off on *The Thin Man*— suave husband, beautiful wife, sophisticated repartee, a murder. It soon becomes apparent, however, that the movie bears a stronger resemblance to the American film noir *Phantom Lady* (1944), with Phillipa desperately seeking to prove that her husband, a victim of fate, is innocent of murder, while the real killer, Sidney Fleming (Goring), remains free to continue his headmaster duties at an exclusive boys' school in Edinburgh. Many familiar noir elements are presented, including the fall guy (Nicholas) and the femme fatale (Elizabeth), flashbacks and voice-over narration, a claustrophobic compartment on a speeding train and plenty of mirrors for cinematographer Green to utilize. Much of the film is slow moving, with the suspense hitting its peak during the last ten minutes. Goring is especially good as the killer who loves his job enough to kill to keep it. Sullivan (familiar to noir fans as the portly owner of the Silver Fox Club in *Night and the City*) plays the prosecutor and serves as the film's narrator.

Temptation Harbor
see *Temptation Harbour*

Temptation Harbour
(U.S. Title: *Temptation Harbor*)
(NR) (1947)

Length: 104 min. **Cast**: Robert Newton, Simone Simon, William Hartnell, Margaret Barton. **Production Company**: Associated British Picture Corporation. **Directed by**: Lance Comfort. **Photographed by**: Otto Heller. **Written by**: Victor Skutezky, Frederic Gotfurt, Rodney Ackland.

William Hartnell and Dave Crowley fight over a valise filled with dough in *Temptation Harbour* (a.k.a. *Temptation Harbor*) (Associated British Pictures, 1947).

After witnessing a murder, a harbor signalman finds a suitcase filled with stolen dough, leaves England for France with his daughter and femme fatale girlfriend, and is stalked by a greedy burglar who is after the money. *Temptation Harbour* is another of the coveted "lost films" of British noir that, hopefully, will surface someday in the near future.

Terror House see The Night Has Eyes

Terror Street see Thirty-Six Hours

There Is Another Sun
(U.S. Title: *The Wall of Death*)
★★½ (1951)

They bury the dead at the pit end. [Motorcycle racer Eddie Peskett]

Length: 95 min. **Cast:** Susan Shaw, Maxwell Reed, Laurence Harvey, Leslie Dwyer, Meredith Edwards, Robert Adair, Hermione Baddeley. **Production Company:** Nettlefold Productions. **Directed by:** Lewis Gilbert. **Photographed by:** Wilkie Cooper. **Written by:** Guy Morgan.

Carnival "Wall of Death" performer "Racer" Peskett (Reed), who accidentally but recklessly killed a man during a motorcycle race three years earlier, is obsessed with entering an upcoming event that offers a £100 first prize. The money is important to Racer but more important is the adulation of the crowd, which he has sorely missed since the fatal accident. His devoted pal, carnival boxer Mag Maguire (Harvey), is determined to help Racer come up with the £50 fee he needs to rent a motorcycle from the racetrack manager and resorts to stealing from his friend, boxing booth proprietor Mick Foley (Dwyer). Despite the possibility of losing his shot at a genuine boxing career and the desperate appeals of his new girlfriend, Lillian

(Shaw), to disassociate himself from Racer, Mag's misguided sense of loyalty soon attracts the attention of Det. Sgt. Bratcher (Edwards), who has been seeking Racer for an undisclosed previous crime and now wants him for his recent assault on the carnival's Wall of Death owner, Sarno (Adair). In 1952, a reviewer described this film as being "listless and dismal." Noirishly dismal, yes; listless, hardly. The plot moves briskly toward its not unexpected climax, and the performances, especially Harvey's, are more than satisfactory. A couple of well-orchestrated boxing scenes might lead the viewer to wonder if Harvey had had some amateur ring experience before turning to acting; he looks that good.

These Are the Damned
see *The Damned*

They Can't Hang Me
★★½ (1955)

> What is the life of one insignificant street walker when the biggest secret you ever had may be behind the Iron Curtain in twenty-four hours? [condemned killer Robert Pitt]

Length: 75 min. **Cast:** Terence Morgan, Yolande Donlan, Anthony Oliver, André Morell. **Production Company:** Vandyke Picture Corporation. **Directed by:** Val Guest. **Photographed by:** Stanley Pavey. **Written by:** Val Guest, Val Valentine.

Five days before his execution for the murder of a prostitute, Robert Pitt (Morell), a senior civil servant, reveals that he is also a traitor and offers the British government a deal—release him and he will disclose the name of a Communist spy known as "Leonidas," who is expected to smuggle atomic secrets out of the country in the next few days. Inspector Ralph Brown (Morgan) of Scotland Yard's Special Branch and his associate, Inspector Newcombe (Oliver) of the Murder Squad, try to learn the identity of the spy while the prime minister mulls over Pitt's deal. This is a low-budget but fast-paced thriller that opens with a silhouetted murder committed behind the window of dingy London tenement. American actress Donlan, director Guest's wife at the time, plays Brown's perky but neglected fiancée, and veteran British character actor Beckwith is his jailbird manservant.

They Drive by Night
★★★★½ (1938)

> I thought perhaps some of me pals might help me but I was lucky the swines didn't turn me in. [Shorty Matthews]

Length: 84 min. **Cast:** Emlyn Williams, Ernest Thesiger, Anna Konstam. **Production Company:** Warner Brothers First National Productions. **Directed by:** Arthur Woods. **Photographed by:** Basil Emmott. **Written by:** Paul Gangelin, James Curtis, Derek Twist.

Released from Pentonville Prison only moments before a man is hanged there, small-time crook Shorty Matthews (Williams) looks forward to visiting his dancehall girlfriend, Alice. When he arrives at her lodging house, roses in hand, he is shocked to discover that she has been strangled. Fearing he will be blamed for the murder (and hanged like the bloke at Pentonville), he flees the scene and hitchhikes north with a couple of truckers. He eventually crosses paths with Molly O'Neill (Konstam), Alice's dancehall friend, who has caught a ride back to London with a particularly nasty trucker who, mistaking her for a "lorry girl" (a prostitute who services truck drivers), attempts to rape her on an isolated road. After saving her from her attacker, Shorty finds himself back in London with Scotland Yard hot on his trail and Molly his only ally. Convinced of Shorty's innocence, Molly volunteers to play detective at the high-class Palais de Danse, where she works as a taxi dancer (a "professional dancing partner"), thinking that perhaps one of Alice's former customers could be the murderer. At the club, she encounters several of Alice's regulars (most of whom are "dumb but harmless"), but one really sparks her interest—the creepy Walter Hoover (Thesiger), a middle-aged student of criminal psychology, who expresses more than a passing interest in the, by now, well-publicized murder case. Hoover follows Alice to Shorty's hide-out in an abandoned house and

They Made Me a Fugitive

offers Shorty sanctuary in his home until the real killer is found. Hoover's proposal causes Molly and Shorty to believe that Alice's killer has finally surfaced. Taut direction by Arthur Woods (whose promising career was cut short with his combat-related death in World War II), moody and ominous cinematography, and terrific acting all contribute to making this rarely seen gem a classic film fan's delight. Standing out among the cast is Ernest Thesiger (best known to American movie fans as Dr. Pretorius in 1935's *Bride of Frankenstein*) as the gaunt amateur psychologist with a taste for girlie magazines and who has a library filled with provocative reading material ("Sex in Relation to Society," "Sex in Prison," "The Thrill of Evil"). His character, an enigmatic, cat-loving oddball, is frightening and yet strangely sympathetic, and Thesiger is just perfect for the role. Regrettably, *They Drive by Night* was not distributed in the U.S. because Warner Brothers, whose British sub-division, First National, produced the film, decided to use the snappy title for Raoul Walsh's 1940 movie starring George Raft and Humphrey Bogart. The title, as it turned out, proved more appropriate for the American film, the plot of which revolves around the arduous and dangerous profession of long-distance truck drivers. In terms of "noirness," however, the American film, excellent though it is, can't hold a candle to this gem.

They Made Me a Fugitive (U.S. Title: *I Became a Criminal*)
★★★★½ (1947)

CONVICT VOICE 1: There's the new one.
CONVICT VOICE 2: What's he in for?
CONVICT VOICE 1: Manslaughter. Killed a cop.
CONVICT VOICE 3: That's not manslaughter. It's fumigation.

Length: 103 min. **Cast:** Sally Gray, Trevor Howard, Griffith Jones, Rene Ray, Jack McNaughton, Eve Ashley. **Production Companies:** Gloria Films, Alliance Film Studios. **Directed by:** (Alberto) Cavalcanti. **Photographed by:** Otto Heller. **Written by:** Noel Langley.

The gang leader's former moll (Sally Gray, right) tries in vain to convince another gang member's girlfriend (Rene Ray) to help a convict framed for killing a cop in *They Made Me a Fugitive* (a.k.a. *I Became a Criminal*) (Gloria Films, Alliance Film Studios, 1947).

Clem Morgan (Howard), a former RAF pilot and P.O.W., takes a job with Narcy (Jones), a London gangster who specializes in the black marketeering of rationed items such as whiskey, nylons and cigarettes. When Clem learns that Narcy is also dealing in dope, he threatens to quit the gang. Not one to accept rebellion in the ranks, the brutal gang leader frames Clem for the murder of a bobby, and the decorated war veteran receives a fifteen-year prison sentence for manslaughter. In prison, Clem is visited by Narcy's vindictive former moll, chorus girl Sally (Gray), who tells him that Narcy has stolen Clem's girlfriend, Ellen (Ashley), and that there's a possibility that Soapy (McNaughton), one of Narcy's thugs, may be persuaded to turn King's evidence in the cop killing case. Hoping to clear himself, Clem breaks out of prison and heads for London to seek out the frightened Soapy, who has been in hiding because Narcy plans to shut him up for good. *They Made Me a Fugitive* is one of the more well-known British films noirs among American noir fans, and deservedly so. The film's overall style and cinematography are inarguably noirish. The familiar noir characters include a disillusioned and cynical war veteran whose decision to involve himself in criminal activities after the war leads to a wrongful cop killing conviction; a showgirl who tries to help him clear his name and falls hard for him in the process; a misogynist crime lord and his gang of weasely thugs; a moll who makes a patsy out of the protagonist; and a potential squealer who flees in panic from a knife-wielding hood. The noirish locales include a warehouse hideout, a sleazy night spot called Tiny's Place run by an obese underworld figure, and a dimly lit alleyway where a girl (Ray) is dragged off by a pair of thugs to be tortured for information). Cavalcanti's splendid direction and Heller's dark cinematography, as well as the top-notch acting, especially by Howard, Gray and Jones, help make this a memorable viewing experience. The film climaxes with a nail-biter of a confrontation at the gang's hideout and front, the coffin-strewn Valhalla Undertaking Company, an eerie place where the walls are decorated with appropriately ominous slogans, such as "It Is Later Than You Think," "R.I.P." and "Death Is Always Around The Corner — Insure Against Accidents."

The Third Man
★★★★★ (1949)

I don't want another murder in this case and you were born to be murdered. [Maj. Calloway to Holly Martins]

Believed dead, drug thief Harry Lyme (Orson Welles) shows up in Vienna's bombed-out ruins in *The Third Man* (London Film Productions, 1949).

Length: 104 min. **Cast**: Joseph Cotten, Alida Valli, Orson Welles, Trevor Howard, Bernard Lee, Ernst Deutsch, Erich Ponto. **Production Company**: London Film Productions. **Directed by**: Carol Reed. **Photographed by**: Robert Krasker. **Written by**: Graham Greene.

Penniless Holly Martins (Cotten), an American author of Western adventure novels, arrives in post-war Vienna at the invitation of his best friend, Harry Lyme (Welles). Not long after his arrival, Martins is told that Lyme had been struck recently by a car and killed. In disbelief, Martins attends the funeral service, where he meets British military cop Maj. Holloway (Howard), who seems overly eager for the writer to leave Vienna. After looking up Lyme's Czech girlfriend, Anna Schmidt (Valli), and several of the dead man's acquaintances, including his physician, Dr. Winkel (Ponto), and business associate, Baron Kurtz (Deutsch), Martins begins to think that his friend may have been murdered and decides to remain in Vienna to find "the third man," an unsubstantiated witness to the car accident. Martin soon learns that Lyme, considered by Maj. Calloway and his subordinate, Sgt. Paine (Lee), to be "the worst racketeer that ever made a dirty living in this city," had been involved in a shameful racket — the black marketing of watered-down penicillin, a drug desperately needed by Vienna's war-ravaged hospitals. Of all the British films noirs, *The Third Man* is perhaps the most familiar to American viewers. A well-deserved Oscar went to cinematographer Krasker, Reed was nominated for Best Director and the film received a BAFTA award for Best British Picture. In addition to its astute direction, moody photography, and Anton Karas' unforgettable musical score, *The Third Man* offers compelling performances by its three talented co-stars, Welles, Cotten and Valli and is a film that should be seen by all movie lovers and not just noir aficionados.

Third Party Risk
(U.S. Title: *The Deadly Game*)
★½ (1955)

Policemen frighten me. [war veteran Philip Graham]

Length: 70 min. **Cast**: Lloyd Bridges, Maureen Swanson, Finlay Currie, Simone Silva, Ferdy Mayne, Peter Dyneley, George Woodbridge, Russell Waters. **Production Company**: Hammer Film Productions. **Directed by**: Daniel Birt. **Photographed by**: Walter Harvey. **Written by**: Robert Dunbar, Daniel Birt.

While visiting Spain, Phil Graham (Bridges), an American veteran of the RAF, runs into Tony Roscoe (Dyneley), an old war buddy who asks him to deliver a car and an envelope to London. When Phil arrives at Tony's London flat, he discovers his friend's body and hightails it out of there before the police show up. With rumpled Scotland Yard Inspector Goldfinch (Woodbridge) breathing down his neck, Phil does some sleuthing and learns that Tony had been a blackmailer and that the envelope contains the microfilm of a new, top-secret antibiotic formula. There are a number of suspects who seemingly had good reason to kill Tony — the mysterious Mr. Darius (Currie), chemical scientist Dr. Gray (Waters), theatrical entrepreneur Maxwell Carey (Mayne) and Carey's singer girlfriend, Mitzi Molnaur (Silva). Along the way, Phil manages to avoid Mitzi's self-serving romantic overtures while falling in love with Darius' niece, Spanish folk dancer Marina (Swanson). American film noir veteran Bridges gives it his best effort, but the lifeless plot and insipid cast of characters are too heavy a load for him to bear on his own.

The Third Secret
★★★½ (1964)

He limited his patients to good, healthy neurotics. [Dr. Milton Gillen about Dr. Leo Whitset]

Length: 103 min. **Cast**: Stephen Boyd, Richard Attenborough, Jack Hawkins, Diane Cilento, Pamela Franklin. **Production Company**: Hubris Productions. **Directed by**: Charles Crichton. **Photographed by**: Douglas Slocombe. **Written by**: Robert L. Joseph.

After his analyst's death is ruled a suicide, neurotic TV news commentator Alex Stedman (Boyd) feels betrayed that the doctor who had convinced him that life was worth living would put a bullet in his own head. When the analyst's 14-year-old daughter, Catherine Whitset (Franklin), approaches the cynical newsman and tells him she suspects that one of her father's patients murdered him, Alex investigates because he wants to believe that his trusted analyst would never kill himself. He soon learns that there is a world of difference between a neurotic and a psychotic and that one of Dr. Whitset's active patients may have been a paranoid schizoprehenic with violent tendencies. Catherine supplies Alec with the names of her father's active patients, and he interviews each one: Sir Frederick Belline (Hawkins), a judge with a career-busting secret only his late analyst knew; Alfred Price-Gorham (Attenborough), an art gallery manager and wannabe artist who desperately seeks recognition; and Anne Tanner (Cilento), a self-conscious, sexually frustrated secretary for whom Alex has his own special method of treatment. Meanwhile, the teen-aged Catherine is beginning to get very close to the handsome American TV star, and her uncle suspects that the older man's intentions may not be honorable. Beautifully filmed in black and white and containing a visually striking nightmare sequence, *The Third Secret* (two are mentioned early on and the third is revealed at the end) is mostly a talk fest, albeit a captivating one that manages to hold the viewer's attention until the shocking and disturbing climax. Youngster Pamela Franklin, who made her debut in 1961's *The Innocents*, is quite good as the troubled teen determined to learn the truth about her father's death. The Irish-born Boyd, a big Hollywood star at the time, easily manages to gain viewer sympathy despite his character's arrogance. The alert viewer will notice that certain words were edited in at least two scenes involving Catherine and Alex. The reason for the editing is most likely that, as has been reported, a sequence with Patricia Neal was deleted from the film's final cut and making sound edits was more economical than re-filming.

13 East Street
★★½ (1952)

Dames only spell trouble. Joey "the Dameless" they call me. [Joey Long]

Length: 71 min. **Cast:** Patrick Holt, Sandra Dorne, Sonia Holm, Robert Ayres, Michael Balfour, Michael Brennan, Michael Ward. **Production Company:** Tempean Films. **Directed by:** Robert S. Baker. **Photographed by:** Monty Berman. **Written by:** John Gilling.

Scotland Yard Inspector Gerald Frazier (Holt) goes undercover as a small-time crook named Gerald Blake to infiltrate a ring of black marketeers headed by Larry Conn (Ayres), an American Army deserter. As Blake, Frazier is sentenced to four years in prison after pretending to rob a London jewelry store but escapes with Joey Long (Balfour), a member of Conn's gang. On Long's recommendation, Conn gives the undercover cop a job, but another of Conn's gang, George Mack (Brennan), believes he has seen the new man someplace before and is determined to remember where. Conn's moll, Judy (Dorne), a floozy with a reputation for eating men alive ("she opens her mouth and swallows them whole"), likes what she sees in Blake and makes plans to betray her lover to run off with the undercover cop after the next big fur heist. Meanwhile, Frazier's wife (Holm) worries about the safety of her husband and must deal with the suspicions of a nosy neighbor who thinks she's having an affair with her husband's Yard contact, Sgt. Follett (Ward). An entertaining crime drama told entirely in flashback but with little noir style, *13 East Street* (the address of the gang's haulage front) seems at times a pale imitation of the American film noir *The Street with No Name*. The warehouse climax is exciting, however, and includes a nice touch of irony involving a vicuna coat ("It looks like camel hair, but it ain't camel hair. It's vicuna.").

Thirty-Six Hours
(U.S. Title: Terror Street)
★★ (1954)

BILL ROGERS: Your uncle. What's he done so bad that Orville can shake him down?
HENRY: He's a terrible man. My life has been corrupted and dirtied by him. He deals in every shady business in the gutter of mankind.
BILL: Will you cut out the dramatics?
HENRY: He's a diamond smuggler.

Length: 80 min. **Cast:** Dan Duryea, Elsy Albiin, Ann Gudrun, John Chandos, Kenneth Griffith, Eric Pohlmann, Harold Lang. **Production Company:** Hammer Film Productions. **Directed by:** Montgomery Tully. **Photographed by**: Walter Harvey. **Written by**: Steve Fisher.

American Army-Air Force Major Bill Rogers (Duryea) hitches an unauthorized flight to England to try to find out why his wife has stopped writing. (Via flashback and Bill's voiceover narration, the viewer learns how Bill met and fell in love with the Norwegian-born Katie soon after the war's end.) When he arrives in London, Bill discovers that their flat is empty and that Katie (Albiin) has moved to the West End, where she lives in an expensive apartment that seems to be paid for by a customs intelligence officer named Orville Hart (Chandos). While confronting his wife, Bill is knocked over the head by Orville, who then shoots and kills Katie with Bill's gun, placing the weapon in the unconscious man's hand. Realizing he has been framed, Bill escapes before the cops arrive and hides out in the apartment of Sister Jenny Miller (Gudrun), who works at a local soup kitchen. Jenny believes his story and together they try to learn who killed Katie and why. In the meantime, Orville convinces the psychologically disturbed Henry Slosson (Griffith), who worshipped Katie from afar, that Bill murdered her in cold blood. When Henry shows up at Bill's flat to take revenge, knife at the ready, Bill disarms him and pumps him for information. Bill learns that Orville has been blackmailing Henry's uncle (Pohlmann), an antiques dealer with a diamond smuggling sideline, and that Katie's relationship with Orville was not what it seemed. American noir icon Duryea looks like he regrets ever getting involved in this slow-moving suspense tale with its poorly staged fisticuffs and hackneyed hardboiled dialogue. The title refers to the amount of time Bill has to find his wife's killer before his flight leaves for the States and he is charged with being AWOL, which, as a very recent widower and murder suspect, should be the least of his worries. Lang brightens things up with a humorous performance as a grubby desk clerk who listens in on his tenants telephone conversations.

This Was a Woman
(NR) (1948)

Length: 104 min. **Cast**: Sonia Dresdel, Barbara White, Walter Fitzgerald, Cyril Raymond. **Produc-**

A son (Emrys Jones) suspects his mother (Sonia Dresdel) of being a dangerous psychotic who poisoned his father in *This Was a Woman* (Excelsior Films, 1948).

tion Company: Excelsior Films. Directed by: Tim Whelan. Photographed by: Hal Britten, Günther Krampf. Written by: Val Valentine.

A mentally disturbed, power-hungry woman ruins her daughter's marriage, kills the family dog and slowly poisons her husband.

Three Crooked Men
★★ (1958)

> You know how I feel about carrying rods on a job. Something goes wrong, a gun goes off and you've got a short walk and a long drop ahead of you. [Vince]

Length: 71 min. **Cast:** Gordon Jackson, Sarah Lawson, Eric Pohlmann, Philip Saville, Michael Mellinger, Warren Mitchell. **Production Company:** Danziger Photoplays. **Directed by:** Ernest Morris. **Photographed by:** Jimmy Wilson. **Written by:** Brian Clemens, Eldon Howard.

Three crooks (Pohlmann, Saville and Mellinger) arrive in the village of Riverford to rob the local bank of a big payroll deposit. They break into the vault after hours by digging through the brick wall the bank shares with a small grocery store owned by handicapped former boxer Don Wescott (Jackson) and his wife, May (Lawson). The robbers kidnap Don and Mr. Prinn (Mitchell), a bank teller who stumbles onto the heist, and release them just outside London after reading that Scotland Yard considers the two victims to be suspects in the bank robbery. To clear their names, Don and Prinn try to track down the robbers. Making good use of character development, the filmmakers try gamely to make something interesting out of a silly premise. Former boxing champ Don is depressed and filled with self-pity over the loss of his leg in an automobile accident ("I was going to get somewhere, be somebody, and now look at me") and takes his frustrations out on his customers and his longsuffering wife. Meek Mr. Prinn leads a secret life as a soon-to-be-exposed kleptomaniac. The three bank robbers argue about the use of guns on the job and discuss how they plan to spend their loot. (One of them is going to save his share so he can hire a good lawyer the next time he gets caught committing a crime.) Veteran character actors Pohlmann and Jackson provide good performances, but Mitchell, who went on to star as bigot Alf Garnett in the hit British TV series "Till Death Do Us Part," the inspiration for the American comedy series "All in the Family," overdoes the timid routine.

Three Silent Men
(NR) (1940)

Length: 72 min. **Cast:** Sebastian Shaw, Derrick de Marney, Patricia Roc, Arthur Hambling. **Production Company:** Butcher's Film Service. **Directed by:** Thomas Bentley. **Photographed by:** Geoffrey Faithfull. **Written by:** Dudley Leslie, John Byrd.

An anti-war surgeon operates to save the life of the inventor of a new weapon but the man dies of an overdose of ether. The surgeon is charged with murder and his daughter seeks to prove his innocence.

3 Steps to the Gallows
(U.S. Title: *White Fire*)
★★ (1953)

> Don't worry, nobody's going to kill you. If they do, I'll speak sharply to them. [Gregor Stevens to Sartago's worried goon]

Length: 81 min. **Cast:** Scott Brady, Mary Castle, Ferdy Mayne. **Production Company:** Tempean Films. **Directed by:** John Gilling. **Photographed by:** Monty Berman. **Written by:** Paul Erickson, John Gilling.

While his ship is docked in London for four days, American merchant seaman Gregor Stevens (Brady) decides to visit his kid brother, Larry, whom he hasn't seen in years. He's shocked to find Larry sitting in a British prison awaiting execution in three days for a murder he swears he didn't commit. Gregor believes him and goes looking for bad guys. And he finds plenty of them, beginning with Mario Sartago (Mayne), the manager of the Gay Mask Club, a front for diamond smugglers, and his crew of incompetent henchmen. He also meets Yvonne Durante (Castle), the club's sexy singer, who appears to know something about his brother's frame-up but isn't talking. Will the two-fisted American find the killer before his brother is hanged? Who cares? Even with its terrific noir title (the British one, that is) and its familiar wrong-man-condemned-to-die theme, this mildly entertaining, occasionally dark, action romp, might be a disappointment to some noir fans. The viewer is advised, however, to sit back and enjoy the on-location photography and the always reliable performance of noir icon Lawrence Tierney's kid brother, Scott Brady, whose own film noir pedigree (*Canon City, He Walked by Night, Port of New York, Undertow, Johnny Guitar,* and *Terror at Midnight*) is nothing to sneeze at. A word of caution: don't spend too much time being amazed at American actress Mary Castle's uncanny resemblance to Rita Hayworth. You may lose track of the convoluted storyline and have to watch the movie again.

Three Sundays to Live
★½ (1957)

> You wake up at night, find yourself in a cell and you think that you're dreaming. But as the days go by, you begin to realize that it's true, that those cell doors are real, that those barred windows are real, that the guards are real, that the two warders who stay with you day and night are real. And that in a few days they'll come in, take you out, put a rope around your neck and hang you for something you haven't done. [Frank Martin]

Length: 71 min. **Cast:** Kieron Moore, Jane Griffiths, Basil Dignam, Sandra Dorne, John Stone. **Production Company:** Danziger Photoplays. **Directed by:** Ernest Morris. **Photographed by:** Jimmy Wilson. **Written by:** Brian Clemens.

London bandleader Frank Martin (Moore) is framed for the murder of his boss, the owner of the Flamingo Club. Frank is arrested, found guilty and sentenced to be hanged. Days before his scheduled execution, he escapes and with the help of his girl, Judy Allen (Griffiths), and his attorney, Howard Davitt (Dignam), tries to find the only witness who can prove his innocence, Ruth Chapman (Dorne), a singer who has gone missing since the night of the murder. Inspector Morgan (Stone) is determined to find the escaped con and send him back to death row where he is convinced he belongs. *Three Sundays* is a bland wrong man noir that is marred by choppy editing and an implausible storyline, in particular the condemned man's overly easy escape and his ability to track down the missing witness so quickly. The title refers to the British practice of not executing a condemned man until three Sundays have elapsed following sentencing.

Three Weird Sisters
★★★ (1948)

> I wish you'd never come here. Oh, don't misunderstand me. I know you're charming, cool, clever, efficient, cultivated, but you're, you're stupid, Miss Prentiss. [Dr. Davies]

Length: 82 min. **Cast:** Nancy Price, Mary Clare, Mary Merrall, Nova Pilbeam, Anthony Hulme, Raymond Levell, Elwyn Brook-Jones, Marie Ault. **Production Company:** British National Films. **Directed by:** Dan Birt. **Photographed by:** Ernest Palmer. **Written by:** Louise Birt, Dylan Thomas.

In Wales, the three spinster Morgan-Vaughan sisters, blind Gertrude (Price), deaf Maude (Clare) and arthritic Isobel (Merrall), try to convince their tightwad half-brother, Owen (Lovell), to fork over some money to help rebuild a string of cottages destroyed by a recent cave-in of the coal mine once owned by their late father. Businessman Owen, whose mother was the household cook, adamantly refuses and pays a visit to his sisters' mansion, itself structurally unsound as a result of the recent cave-in, to let them know in no uncertain terms that he is through supporting them and their ridiculous causes. Owen brings his secretary, Claire Prentiss (Pilbeam), along for moral support. The sisters, however, are not easily put off and decide that if Owen won't help the villagers rebuild they'll just have to kill him and collect his money as his heirs. After the old girls make several attempts on Owen's life with a little help from Thomas (Brook-Jones), the slow-witted son of the cook (Ault), Owen decides to change his will, making Claire his beneficiary, supposing that the murderous attempts will stop if his sisters have nothing to gain by his death. Not to be outwitted, the three weird sisters turn their attention to Claire, who has been having no success in her attempts to convince the handsome Dr. Davies (Hulme), about the old hags' treachery. This aptly titled film is dark and atmospheric and, although it may be embarrassing to admit this, quite spellbinding. Try taking your eyes off the screen whenever Price, Clare or Merrall are in a scene and you may find it impossible to do, because of their eerily campy performances. Equally campy is Hans May's score, which accentuates the hilarity of the script. *Three Weird Sisters* is great fun and would really pack them in at a midnight cult film festival in the States.

Tiger Bay (U.S. Title: *Mystery at Tiger Bay*)
★★★★ (1959)

I'm not an animal for a little boy to keep in a cage. I'm a woman. A woman with a heart and a body which is my own to give how I like, when I like. [Anya]

Length: 105 min. **Cast**: John Mills, Horst Buchholz, Hayley Mills, Yvonne Mitchell, Anthony Dawson. **Production Company**: Independent Artists. **Directed by**: J. Lee Thompson. **Photographed by**: Eric Cross. **Written by**: John Hawkesworth, Shelley Smith.

Gillie (Hayley Mills), a tomboy being raised by her seamstress aunt in a poor neighborhood in Cardiff, Wales, witnesses Polish sailor Korchinsky (Buchholz) shoot and kill former concentration camp inmate Anya (Mitchell) because of her unfaithfulness. Gillie, who has been unable to play "cowboys and Indians" with the other neighborhood children because she has no toy gun, steals the murder weapon from the killer's hiding place and proudly shows it off to a fellow choir member during a wedding ceremony at the church. After the wedding,

A sailor (Horst Buchholz) returns from a sea voyage to find that his girlfriend (Yvonne Mitchell) has been cheating on him in *Tiger Bay* (Independent Artists, 1959).

Korchinsky traps Gillie in the belfry. It is here in a darkened church that the bond of a fiercely loyal friendship between a murderer and a child who is noted for telling tall tales has its beginning. "You should have killed *him* instead," Gillie tells Korchinsky, referring to Anya's other lover, Barclay (Dawson), whom Gillie later will try to frame in an effort to protect her new friend. Much like the characters in 1952's *Hunted*, the killer and child go on the run while the police search frantically for clues and motives. Superintendent Graham (John Mills, Hayley's real-life father), who is in charge of the murder investigation, finally locates the missing girl but is led astray by her lies, which are intended to give Korchinsky time to make his getaway aboard a Venezuelan steamer. This superb but marginally noir film, which won BAFTA awards for Best Film from Any Source and Best British Screenplay, belongs entirely to 12-year-old Hayley Mills, whose unaffected performance won her a BAFTA award for Most Promising Newcomer and helped pave the way for her starring roles in a successful string of Walt Disney movies. (Hayley actually made her film debut as an infant in *So Well Remembered*, which starred her father.) Buchholz does a good job as the sympathetic killer, and John Mills is fun to watch as the frustrated detective getting nowhere with the stubbornly loyal tomboy, who refuses to be a witness against the killer she has come to love.

Tiger by the Tail
(U.S. Title: *Cross-Up*)
★★ (1955)

So this is London. Rain, a hotel in Kensington and a feeling of depression. [John Desmond]

Length: 85 min. **Cast:** Larry Parks, Constance Smith, Lisa Daniely, Cyril Chamberlain, Ronan O'Casey, Russell Westwood. **Production Company:** Tempean Films. **Directed by:** John Gilling. **Photographed by:** Eric Cross. **Written by:** John Gilling, Willis Goldbeck.

John Desmond (Parks), an American reporter working for a London newspaper, becomes obsessed with the mysterious and beautiful Anna Ray (Daniely). "There was no escaping her," he says. "She was like a drug. Beautiful. Sometimes hateful." His infatuation with her causes him to miss an important story deadline, much to the exasperation of his pretty secretary, Jane Claymore (Smith). After Anna decides to dump him, Desmond grabs her diary from her in a fit of jealousy and finds that she has pulled a gun on him. During the ensuing struggle, the gun goes off, and Anna slumps to the floor, dead. Desmond seeks help from Jane, who does as any loyal noir secretary would do and helps him cover up the death. The diary, it turns out, is a coded book of contacts belonging to a counterfeiting gang known as "The Committee." C.A. Foster (Chamberlain), the head of the ring's bumbling London branch, desperately wants to retrieve the diary before Desmond figures out how to decode it. So he has his sadistic goons, Nick (O'Casey) and Sam (Westwood), torture Desmond. (Well, perhaps torture is too harsh of a word. They do slap him a few times, twist his arm real hard and shine a desk lamp in his face.) Desmond manages to escape and it is at this point that the film's storyline begins its downward trek, deteriorating into a sort of madcap comedy with the fleeing reporter finding refuge at a farm run by two flighty women (Thora Hird and Joan Heal), and Jane concocting a ridiculous amnesia story to protect Desmond's job at the newspaper. The film, composed of one long flashback accompanied by voiceover narration, begins promisingly (and very noirishly) as the reporter, evidently dying, collapses on a dark London street corner and is found by police. "You're a little late, pal," he tells one of the officers. "I guess I had a tiger by the tail and I couldn't let go." While Daniely does a good job as the dangerous female, blacklisted American actor Parks can't quite pull off his role as the two-fisted reporter victimized by fate.

Tiger in the Smoke
★★½ (1956)

What is a soul? When I was a small boy, I used to think of it as a little, ghostly, kidney-shaped bean. Now I think of it as the man I am with when I am alone. Neither definition would satisfy a theologian. [Canon Avril]

Length: 94 min. **Cast**: Donald Sinden, Muriel Pavlow, Tony Wright, Laurence Naismith, Christopher Rhodes. **Production Company**: Rank Film Productions. **Directed by**: Roy (Ward) Baker. **Photographed by**: Geoffrey Unsworth. **Written by**: Anthony Pélissier.

While trying to find out why someone has been impersonating the late husband of his fiancée, Meg Elgin (Pavlow), Geoffrey Levett (Sinden) is kidnapped by a gang of veterans working as street musicians. Meanwhile, psychotic killer and escaped convict Jack Havoc (Wright), former leader of the gang, seeks a treasure in Meg's home but learns that it is actually hidden in a mansion off the French coast. Chief Inspector Luke (Rhodes) investigates the untidiness, and Canon Avril (Naismith) fritters around being kind and, well, canonly. The plot of *Tiger* is torturously slow in divulging its secrets, and the goings-on during the film's first hour are nearly incomprehensible. Pavlow is annoying as the weepy widow who is itching to remarry but can't seem to find her fiancé and is not even sure if her husband is dead or alive. Wright, better known to American noir fans as Barbara Payton's patsy in *The Flanagan Boy* (a.k.a. *Bad Blonde*), gives the film's best performance as the treasure obsessed killer with a fervent belief in what he calls "the science of luck," otherwise known as "the pursuit of death," according to Canon Avril. What *is* impressive about this otherwise dreary film is Geoffrey Unsworth's extraordinary cinematography, which is so dark that the characters are barely recognizable at times, especially in smoggy London Town. In one remarkable scene, Havoc is shown climbing out of a window in Meg's home and leaping onto the fog-smothered streets below. It appears that instead of jumping he simply evaporates into the night.

Time to Remember
★★ (1962)

> FRENCH VICTOR: The worst fall-out in the world is when thieves fall out.
> JUMBO JOHNSON: Yeah, well, all I want to see fall out is the door to that safe.

Length: 58 min. **Cast**: Harry H. Corbett, Yvonne Monlaur, Robert Rietty, David Lodge, Genine Graham, Ray Barrett. **Production Company**: Merton Park Productions. **Directed by**: Charles Jarrott. **Photographed by**: Bert Mason. **Written by**: Arthur la Bern.

During a heist-gone-bad at the London home of a recently deceased millionaire, thief Jumbo Johnson (Lodge) drops £100,000 worth of stolen gems down the chimney of a boarded up fireplace before falling from the rooftop during a struggle with a police officer. In the hospital, he betrays his accomplice, safecracker "French" Victor (Rietty), by informing the police that Victor has fled to Paris with the jewels and a valuable stamp collection stolen from the house. Before dying, Jumbo lets his wife, Kitty (Graham), in on the location of the hidden jewels. Under an assumed name, Kitty contacts real estate agent Jack Burgess about purchasing the home, but her real intention is to get inside the house so she can retrieve the jewels. Jack, an inveterate loser, figures out her plan and decides to look for the jewels himself. In Paris, Victor learns he is being sought by French police and, after selling the stolen stamp collection, returns to London to retrieve the jewels, leaving behind his girlfriend, Suzanne (Monlaur), to deal with the cops and the heist's angry getaway driver, Sammy (Barrett), who shows up demanding his share of the loot. The convoluted plot eventually succeeds in explaining itself, but until then it's a tedious experience. (Part of the "Edgar Wallace Mystery Theater" series.)

Time Without Pity
★★★★½ (1957)

> Everyone has a secret. It's not always written in the face. [David Graham]

Length: 88 min. **Cast**: Michael Redgrave, Leo McKern, Ann Todd, Peter Cushing, Alec McCowen, Paul Daneman. **Production Company**: Harlequin Productions. **Directed by**: Joseph Losey. **Photographed by**: Frederick Francis. **Written by**: Ben Barzman.

Recently released from a sanatorium, where he underwent the "cure," alcoholic writer David Graham (Redgrave) rushes off to London to see if he can prevent the government from hanging his son, Alec (McGowan), in the next 24 hours for the murder of a chorus girl. Convinced of Alec's innocence, David frantically tries to prove it while the real killer, automobile manufacturer Robert Stanford (McKern), nervously anticipates the execution. David is surprised to learn that Stanford's wife, Honor (Todd), has been trying to convince the government to issue a reprieve and that she may have been having an affair with Alec. With time running out, David begins losing his battle to stay sober, much to the delight of Stanford, whose arrogance and confidence grows with each passing hour. Redgrave, who was nominated for a BAFTA award as Best British Actor for his performance, is sensational as the desperate rum-dum who cannot resist a visit to a local pub even though his son's life depends on his sobriety. McKern's performance, however, is so over the top that his character comes off more like a campy James Bond villain than an adulterous husband with a really bad temper tantrum problem. The film, directed by blacklisted American director Losey, tiptoes gracefully around its anti-capital punishment message while providing excellent character development and a bittersweet surprise ending. Future British horror icon Peter Cushing plays Alec Graham's attorney, and Daneman is Stanford's weak-kneed adopted son.

To Have and to Hold
★★★ (1963)

> INSPECTOR ROBERTS: Since when has police procedure stated that if you can't find the number one suspect you forget him and pick on the number two?
> SGT. FRASER: So you admit he's number two?
> INSPECTOR ROBERTS: Yes I do but that doesn't mean anything. You're the number three.

Length: 71 min. **Cast**: Ray Barrett, Katharine Blake, Nigel Stock, William Hartnell. **Production Company**: Merton Park Productions. **Directed by**: Herbert Wise. **Photographed by**: James Wilson. **Written by**: Jimmy Sangster (as John Sansom).

After responding to a report of a hysterical woman who suspects that her former boyfriend is planning to kill her, a London police detective, Sgt. Henry Fraser (Barrett), finds himself falling for the woman, Claudia Matthews (Blake), whose husband, George (Stock), is out of town on business. Before long, police find a dead woman whose badly disfigured body is identified as Claudia's, indicating that her fears were well-founded. Despite orders from his supervisor, Inspector Roberts (Hartnell), to drop the case, Fraser sets out to prove that Matthews murdered his wife. His investigation leads him to a seaside cottage where a woman named Pauline Carstairs, who claims to be Claudia's identical twin, is living with Matthews. At first, Fraser and Pauline join forces in an attempt to prove that Matthews killed Claudia, but before long they are plotting his demise. An entirely predictable but nonetheless enjoyable variation of the *Double Indemnity* storyline, replete with flashbacks, voiceover narration, bad cop, patsy, and femme fatale. (Part of the "Edgar Wallace Mystery Theater" series.)

The Torso Murder Mystery
see *Traitor Spy*

Tower of Terror
★★ (1941)

> When you've been locked up for months like I've been, when you've got nothing else to do but think — of home, of your family — then there's room for only one thought in your brain: how to break out and escape all that filth and misery.
> [Concentration camp escapee Marie Durand]

Length: 78 min. **Cast**: Wilfrid Lawson, Michael Rennie, Movita, Charles Rolfe. **Production Company**: Associated British Picture Corporation. **Directed by**: Lawrence Huntington. **Photographed by**: Walter Harvey. **Written by**: John Reinhardt.

The complicated lives of three people converge at the Westerrode lighthouse, a little piece of Nazi real estate in the North Sea — sullen Wolfe Kristan (Lawson), the lighthouse keeper; English spy Anthony Hale (Rennie); and Marie Durand (Movita), an escapee from a Nazi concentration camp who had been imprisoned for innocently taking photographs in a forbidden zone. Kristan is obsessed with the memory of his late wife, who is said to have drowned fifteen years earlier, and when he fishes Marie from the sea after her escape he is convinced that Mrs.

Kirstan has returned to him. Hale, meanwhile, has gotten hold of top-secret photographs of a German installation, stolen the identity of Kirstan's new lighthouse assistant and arrived at the island to work while he waits for the arrival of a Dutch freighter to return him to England. Kristan, whose severed hand was replaced years earlier with a hook that he finds useful in barroom brawls, is not pleased with the arrival of his handsome new assistant, and an age-old jealousy begins to raise its ugly head. Rennie appears ill at ease as an on-the-run, undercover spy, and beautiful Mexican-American actress Movita, future second wife of Marlon Brando, is miscast as a former concentration camp prisoner. If you're looking primarily for dark and gloomy atmosphere and care little about intelligent plotting, this is your film. Others may find enjoyment in Lawson's campy, over-the-top performance, which at times is reminiscent of Dwight Frye's outrageous portrayal of the mad Renfield in 1931's *Dracula*. But for the most part, *Tower of Terror* is a time waster.

Traitor Spy (U.S. Title: *The Torso Murder Mystery*)
(NR) (1939)

Length: 75 min. **Cast:** Bruce Cabot, Marta Labarr, Tamara Desni, Romilly Lunge. **Production Company:** Rialto Productions. **Directed by:** Walter Summers. **Photographed by:** Robert LaPresle. **Written by:** Walter Summers, John Argyle, Jan Van Lusil, Ralph Gilbert Betterson.

A British agent steals his country's top secret plans for a new patrol boat and tries to sell them to the Germans.

Tread Softly Stranger
★★★ (1958)

He didn't do it *for* me. He did it to get me. [Calico, in response to Johnny's accusation that his lovesick brother is robbing the foundry for her]

Length: 90 min. **Cast:** Diana Dors, George Baker, Terence Morgan, Patrick Allen. **Production Company:** Alderdale Films Limited. **Directed by:** Gordon Parry. **Photographed by:** Douglas Slocombe. **Written by:** George Minter, Denis O'Dell.

London gambler Johnny Mansell (Baker) flees from an angry bookmaker who has promised that if he doesn't get his dough immediately Johnny will end up needing plastic surgery. Johnny returns to his hometown, Rawborough, and joins his brother, Dave (Morgan), at a seedy rooming house, only to find even more trouble. It seems that bookkeeper Dave has fallen for the beautiful Calico (Dors), a hardened club girl, and has embezzled £300 from the foundry where he works, spending it all on her. After Dave tells his brother that the foundry is about to perform an audit, the results of which are certain to send him to prison, Johnny wins enough money at the track to replace the stolen funds. By the time he returns with the good news, however, Calico has already convinced his weak-kneed brother to break into the foundry to steal more money and, of course, share the proceeds with her. Johnny races off to stop Dave before it is too late, but the two are surprised by the foundry's night watchman, who is a family friend. The skittish bookkeeper accidentally shoots the old man, killing him. After the murder, the brothers fret that an eyewitness who has mysteriously disappeared will return to identify them and that the night watchman's son, Paddy Ryan (Allen), is trying to trap them into confessing. Meanwhile, Johnny and Calico fall for each other, leaving the already neurotic Dave in a state of anxiety that threatens to expose them all. Director Parry sees to it that it is always night time in the bleak industrial city of Rawborough, adding to the film's strong sense of fatalism and impending disaster. Twenty-seven year-old Dors is perfect as the insatiably greedy femme fatale. Enjoyable too are Morgan and the Bulgarian-born Baker as normally devoted brothers who are at each throats because of a beautiful woman and a foolish crime. The unexpected twist ending is very satisfying.

Trunk Crime (U.S. Title: *Design for Murder*)
(NR) (1939)

Length: 51 min. **Cast:** Manning Whiley, Barbara Everest, Michael Drake, Hay Petrie. **Production Company:** Charter Film Productions. **Directed by:** Roy Boulting. **Photographed by:** Wilkie Cooper. **Written by:** Francis Miller.

A bullied student plans revenge against one of his tormentors by drugging him and burying him alive in a trunk.

Turn the Key Softly
★★★ (1953)

> There you are, ladies, London. The biggest city in the world and it's all yours. [Prison guard to released prisoners]

Length: 81 min. **Cast:** Yvonne Mitchell, Terence Morgan, Joan Collins, Kathleen Harrison, Glyn Houston. **Production Company:** Chiltern Film Productions. **Directed by:** Jack Lee. **Photographed by:** Geoffrey Unsworth. **Written by:** Jack Lee, Maurine Cowan.

Three women prisoners are released from London's HM Prison Holloway: Monica Marsden (Mitchell), who served a year as an accomplice for burglary after being abandoned at the crime scene by her good-for-nothing lover, David (Morgan); Stella Jarvis (Collins), a prostitute who looks forward to marrying her forgiving and loving boyfriend, bus conductor Bob (Houston); and the elderly Mrs. Quilliam (Harrison), a compulsive shoplifter whose only friend is her faithful mutt, Johnny. While Stella and Mrs. Quilliam are tempted to return to their old criminal ways, Monica's only desire is to find an office job and forget about David. The charming but cunning cat burglar, however, has other plans and Monica soon finds herself a reluctant participant in yet another robbery and forced to make a choice between her freedom and the homme fatale who once betrayed her. This is a well-crafted but ultimately maudlin film, the star of which is really the teeming city of London as seen through the lens of skilled cinematographer Unsworth (an Oscar winner for 1972's *Cabaret* and, posthumously, for 1979's *Tess*). Mitchell nicely underplays her role, and the 20-year-old Collins, in an early starring vehicle, is believable as the money-loving prostitute with a good chance for a normal if unexciting life as a housewife. Character actress Harrison, who lived to be 105 years old, gives a tug at viewer heartstrings as the booster of only petty items (taking more expensive goods, after all, would be stealing).

21 Days
(U.S. Title: *21 Days Together*)
★★★½ (1937)

> I want to suffer. God may forgive me if I suffer. [John Evan, wrongly accused of murder]

Length: 75 min. **Cast:** Leslie Banks, Vivien Leigh, Laurence Olivier, Hay Petrie, Esme Percy. **Production Companies:** London Film Productions, Denham Productions. **Directed by:** Basil Dean. **Photographed by:** Jan Stallick. **Written by:** Basil Dean, Graham Greene.

During a struggle with his girlfriend's estranged blackmailing husband (Percy), who also is a secret bigamist, Larry Durrant (Olivier) strangles the man and dumps his body in an archway near her flat. Guilt-stricken, Larry pays a visit to his barrister brother, Keith (Banks), who encourages him to cover up the crime for his own selfish reason — he expects to be appointed to a judgeship and the scandal would ruin him. Meanwhile, John Evan (Petrie), a vagrant ex-clergyman, has found the body and robbed the dead man of his money. Evan is later arrested for the murder and placed on trial. When Larry learns of the man's arrest, he refuses to leave the country despite Keith's desperate insistence, and swears to his girl, Wanda (Leigh), that he will not let the wrongly accused man hang. During the next several weeks while the trial is in progress, Larry and Wanda get married and live it up, hoping that Evan will be found not guilty but prepared to save him if he is. (Strangely, the accused believes he deserves to die because of his robbery of the dead man and seems ready and willing to be hanged.) The moment of truth arrives, and Keith makes one last desperate attempt to persuade his brother to give up this foolish idea of confessing. The film was not greeted with enthusiasm when it was first released several years after it was made. Considered by some to be rather slow-moving, the film moved quickly enough for this viewer, who found it to be suspenseful and highly enjoyable. Olivier and Leigh more than pass muster with their low-key performances as star-crossed and guilt-ridden lovers whose expectation of thirty years of happiness together may soon drop to a mere three weeks. Character actor Petrie gives an interesting performance as the oddball vagrant with a death wish, while Banks is suitably hateful as Olivier's callously ambitious brother.

The £20,000 Kiss
★½ (1963)

You've joined a goodly company, Sir Harold: the wealthy men of this country who are being milked morning and night because they haven't the guts to face a public scandal. [P.I. John Durran]

Length: 57 min. **Cast**: Dawn Addams, Michael Goodliffe, Richard Thorp, Anthony Newlands, Alfred Burke, Mia Karam. **Production Company**: Merton Park Productions. **Directed by:** John Moxey. **Photographed by:** James Wilson. **Written by:** Philip Mackie.

Barrister Sir Harold Trevitt (Goodliffe), a Queen's Counsel and member of Parliament is about to marry into a prestigious family. Unfortunately, he finds himself the victim of blackmailing maid Paula Blair (Karam), who has snapped a photo of him kissing her employer, his next-door neighbor, Mrs. Maxine Hagen (Addams). Before handing over the £5,000 Blair is demanding, Trevitt hires private detective John Durran (Thorp) to look into the matter. Meanwhile, Maxine's husband, Leo (Newlands), returns from a business trip and offers to lend fellow gun aficionado Trevitt one of his antique dueling pistols, conveniently fitted with a silencer. Before long, the price of that "innocent kiss" reaches £20,000 and Durran's friend, Scotland Yard Inspector Waveney (Burke), finds himself investigating two murders. Part of the "Edgar Wallace Mystery Theater," series, the marginally noir *Kiss* is a confusing and unsatisfying whodunit.

Twilight Women see Women of Twilight

Twist of Fate see Beautiful Stranger

U-Boat 29 see The Spy in Black

Uncensored
(a.k.a. *We Shall Rise Again*)
(NR) (1942)

Length: 108 min. **Cast**: Eric Portman, Phyllis Calvert, Griffith Jones, Raymond Lovell. **Production Company**: Gainsborough Pictures. **Directed by:** Anthony Asquith. **Photographed by:** Arthur Crabtree. **Written by:** Terrence Rattigan, Rodney Ackland.

A Belgian nightclub owner publishes an anti–Nazi underground newspaper.

Uncle Silas
(U.S. Title: *The Inheritance*)
★★★ (1947)

So much for your prayers of atonement, you sinful little wanton. [Uncle Silas to Caroline]

Length: 103 min. **Cast**: Jean Simmons, Katina Paxinou, Derrick de Marney, Derek Bond, Manning Whiley. **Production Company**: Two Cities Films. **Directed by:** Charles Frank. **Photographed by:** Robert Krasker. **Written by:** Ben Travers.

When Austin Ruthyn dies, his 16-year-old daughter, Caroline (Simmons), the heiress to his fortune, goes to live with her Uncle Silas (De Marney). Silas, wrongly found innocent years earlier of murdering a man, greets his niece with a great display of affection, but Caroline soon learns that there is more to her seemingly eccentric uncle than meets the eye. Silas is intent on stealing Caroline's inheritance, and if killing her is the only way to accomplish that, then so be it. A skilled forger, Silas writes letters to her friends in her name telling them of an intended trip abroad, but in reality he and his two accomplices, his libidinous son, Dudley (Whiley), and Caroline's dipsomaniac governess, Madame de la Rougierra (Paxinou), both of whom seem to take great pleasure in tormenting the young girl, are keeping her captive in Silas' decrepit mansion until a convenient time for her murder. Caroline's only hope of escape lies with the gamekeeper's little boy and her handsome suitor, Lord Richard Ilbury (Bond). Darkly atmospheric, this gothic melodrama (some call it a horror film) is tortuously slow at times, but that is compensated for by Krasker's expressionistic cinematography, which includes lots of grotesque close-ups, especially of the evil governess. Paxinou and De Marney play their parts with wonderful Vincent Price-like hamminess, and Simmons (27 years old at the time) gives a believable performance as the imperiled teenager.

Underworld Informers
see *The Informers*

Uneasy Terms
★★ (1948)

If you knew how much I hated him. How I've always hated him. Yet when I'm with him, I love him. He's got something. It's like a snake wrapped itself around you. You can't get away. When I'm with him, I'm fascinated. When I'm away from him, God knows how I hate him. [Viola Alardyse]

Length: 91 min. **Cast**: Michael Rennie, Moira Lister, Faith Brook, Joy Shelton, Patricia Goddard, Barry Jones, Paul Carpenter. **Production Company**: British National Films. **Directed by**: Vernon Sewell. **Photographed by**: Ernest Palmer. **Written by**: Not credited (based on a Peter Cheyney novel).

Private investigator Slim Callaghan (Rennie) takes on a case involving the three Alardyse sisters (Lister, Brook and Goddard), their murdered stepfather and a shady nightclub owner (Patrick). The motive for the stepfather's murder is the retrieval of an anonymous letter informing him that one of the sisters is in violation of their mother's will, which stipulates that if the girls ever marry they will forfeit their share of the inheritance. This is a boring and downright silly whodunit (the killer actually promises to confess if Callaghan will beat somebody up) containing a plethora of familiar noir elements (an extremely convoluted storyline, a private eye, a war veteran, a flashback, murder and suicide, an attempted frame-up, blackmail, betrayal, bigamy, family dysfunction, a nightclub setting, and even impersonation by plastic surgery). It falls short, though, with its weak character development and silly dialogue. Suave and gentlemanly private investigator Slim Callaghan, however, does have several things in common with his crude Yank counterpart, hardboiled P.I. Sam Spade in *The Maltese Falcon*—a secretary named Effie (Shelton); a bout with a Mickey Finn that knocks him unconscious; a policeman buddy (Jones) whose investigation is always one step behind his own; and a heart of stone when it comes to the criminal female.

The Unholy Four
see *The Stranger Came Home*

The Upturned Glass
★★★ (1947)

DR. JOYCE: I never like losing a patient.
DR. FARRELL: Well, that's the sort of sentimentality you get over when you've killed as many patients as I have.

Length: 86 min. **Cast**: James Mason, Rosamund John, Pamela Kellino, Ann Stephens. **Production Company**: Triton Films. **Directed by**: Lawrence Huntington. **Photographed by**: Reginald H. Wyer. **Written by**: Pamela Kellino, Jno (John) P. Monaghan.

In his spare time, brain surgeon Michael Joyce (Mason) teaches a university class on the psychology of crime, and his latest lecture is, unbeknownst to his students, about himself and his plan to murder the woman he believes is responsible for the death of his former lover, Emma Wright (John). Via flashbacks and the protagonist's voice-over narration, the viewer witnesses the genesis of a romantic relationship between the married woman and the surgeon whose skills saved the sight of her young daughter (Stephens). After the couple realize the futility of their affair and end it, Michael learns that Emma's broken body has been found outside her home, the victim of an apparent accidental fall from her bedroom window, or so the coroner's inquest rules. Michael, however, begins to suspect that Emma's vicious sister-in-law, Kate Howard (Kellino), had something to do with her death. While feigning romantic interest in Kate, Michael concludes that his suspicions are justified and decides to kill her by forcing her to jump from the same window. After the lecture, he successfully implements his plan of committing a "murder conceived in perfect sanity," but disposing of the body and convincing himself of his "perfect sanity" turn out to be more problematic. *The Upturned Glass* is a dark tale of revenge and insanity, nicely acted by Mason and his real-life wife, Kellino. The unexpected downbeat ending more than compensates for the film's sluggish script.

Urge to Kill
★★ (1960)

MRS. WILLIS: I'd like to get my hands on the chap what done it. I'd teach him a thing or two.
MR. FORSYTHE: "Vengeance is mine, saith the Lord. I will repay."
MRS. WILLIS: That may be but something should be done in the meantime.

Length: 58 min. **Cast:** Patrick Barr, Ruth Dunning, Howard Pays, Terence Knapp, Wilfrid Brambell. **Production Company:** Merton Park Productions. **Directed by:** Vernon Sewell. **Photographed by:** John Wiles. **Written by:** James Eastwood.

A local girl is strangled near the waterfront while taking a shortcut home from the cinema. Police determine that her dead body had been mutilated with a piece of broken glass and think they've found their killer in Hughie (Knapp), "a half-witted lad living in a queer world of his own." The mentally retarded Hughie, who collects broken glass as part of a secretive project he calls the "Lord's work," lives at a boarding house operated by his Aunt B (Dunning). Aunt B and her lodgers, the religious Mr. Forsythe (Brambell) and ladies' man Charlie Ramskill (Pays), are convinced of Hughie's innocence, but try telling that to the angry customers at The Anchor pub, who seem ready to take matters into their own hands. *Urge to Kill* is a whodunit until approximately 25 minutes into the film when the identity of the real killer is revealed and it becomes apparent that poor Hughie is being framed. Nothing special but watchable.

Vengeance Is Mine
(NR) (1949)

Length: 59 min. **Cast:** Valentine Dyall, Anne Forth, Richard Goolden, Sam Kydd. **Production Company:** Grossman-Cullimore-Arbeid Productions. **Directed by:** Alan Cullimore. **Photographed by:** Jimmy Wilson (lighting), Bill Oxley (camera operator). **Written by:** Alan Cullimore.

Told he has only six months left to live, a man who had been wrongly convicted of murder hires a hit man to kill him and to see to it that the man who framed him gets the blame.

The Verdict
★½ (1964)

JOE: I had juries in my pocket and judges on my payroll.
LARRY: Joe, you're in England now.
JOE: Money talks anywhere.

Length: 55 min. **Cast:** Cec Linder, Zena Marshall, Nigel Davenport, Paul Stassino. **Production Company:** Merton Park Productions. **Directed by:** David Eady. **Photographed by:** James Wilson. **Written by:** Arthur la Bern.

After being deported by American authorities, gangster Joe Armstrong (Linder) returns to his native England with his lover (Marshall). Within hours of his arrival, Armstrong learns that Scotland Yard has discovered evidence of a murder he committed 24 years ago. After his arrest, Joe orders his flabbergasted British underling, loan company official Larry Mason (Davenport), to fix the trial. Mason concocts a wild scheme involving the interception of letters addressed to potential jurors and the replacement of the chosen twelve jurors with those desperate men and women whose loan applications he had once turned down. Meanwhile, rival gangster Danny Thorne, who is worried about Armstrong trying to take over his protection racket, gets wind of the plan. The plot is highly implausible and often puzzling. (Part of the "Edgar Wallace Mystery Theater" series.)

The Vicious Circle
(U.S. Title: *The Circle*)
★★ (1957)

Everything's piled up on top of me. [Dr. Howard Latimer]

Length: 84 min. **Cast:** John Mills, Derek Farr, Noëlle Middleton, Wilfrid Hyde-White, Roland Culver,

Mervyn Johns. **Production Company:** Beaconsfield Films. **Directed by:** Gerald Thomas. **Photographed by:** Otto Heller. **Written by:** Francis Durbridge.

Dr. Howard Latimer (Mills) of the Mayfair Clinic, thinking he's doing an old friend a favor, picks up a German actress at London Airport, almost missing an opera date with his girlfriend, Laura James (Middleton). Later that evening he finds the actress' dead body in his flat. Thus begins a series of bizarre incidents that turn the golf-loving doctor's neat little world upside down as he finds himself framed for not one but two murders. Latimer complicates things by doing a bunk (the British equivalent of "taking a powder") and hiding out in the flat belonging to his best friend, Ken Palmer (Farr), while he tries to find out who has set him up and why. Scotland Yard Inspector Dane (Culver) seems strangely content to allow the suspect to move around freely, and a suspicious looking but grandfatherly gent (Hyde-White) makes Latimer an offer he can't refuse. Johns plays a physician whose soon-to-be-murdered patient tells Latimer that she recently stumbled upon a dead man on Hampstead Heath and that the body mysteriously disappeared while she sought help. A bit far-fetched, the sluggish, convoluted plot revolves around a desperate citizen who finds himself ensnared in a noirish web spun by Scotland Yard, Interpol and an assortment of major criminals (murderers, blackmailers, forgers, and narcotics thieves). The talented cast (especially Mills as the increasingly paranoid patsy) and Heller's interesting nighttime shots of London may help sleepy viewers stay awake until the film's all-too-predictable ending.

Victim
★★★★ (1961)

It used to be witches. At least they don't burn you. [Frank to Jack Barrett about the treatment of homosexuals in England]

Length: 100 min. **Cast:** Dirk Bogarde, Sylvia Syms, Peter McEnery, Donald Churchill, Derren Nesbitt, Dennis Price, Anthony Nichols, Peter Copley, Nigel Stock, Charles Lloyd Pack, John Barrie, John Cairney. **Production Company:** Parkway Films. **Directed by:** Basil Dearden. **Photographed by:** Otto Heller. **Written by:** Janet Green, John McCormick.

Wages clerk Jack Barrett (McEnery) has been embezzling funds from his company to pay off the blackmailers who are threatening to expose Melville Farr (Bogarde), a prominent attorney with whom Barrett has fallen in love. With the cops hot on his trail, Barrett tries to contact Farr, an inactive homosexual since his marriage to Laura (Syms), but Farr, fearing Barrett is attempting to blackmail him, refuses to speak with him. When the police catch up with Barrett and his scrapbook of newspaper clippings about Farr's career, the embezzler hangs himself in his cell. When Farr learns of the boy's suicide, the guilt-ridden nominee for Queen's Counsel (QC) risks his marriage and career in an attempt to track down the blackmailers with help from Barrett's homosexual friend, Eddy Stone. Another extortion victim eventually puts Farr in touch with one of the blackmailers, a motorcycle-riding street thug named Sandy (Nesbitt), a particularly nasty piece of work whose own sexual preference the filmmakers leave open to question. (The identity of Sandy's blackmail partner, an equally vicious homophobe, is not disclosed until the end of the film.) With homosexual acts against English law, other blackmail victims, such as a well-known stage actor (Price), an aristocrat (Nicholls), an artist (Copley), an elderly barber (Pack) who had been imprisoned three times for his sexual preference, and a frightened Rolls-Royce salesman (Stock), are well into the closet and not too keen on joining Farr in his self-destructive scheme. Scotland Yard Det. Inspector Harris (Barrie) and the proudly puritanical Sgt. Bridie (Cairney), however, are glad for a bit of help. Meanwhile, Laura, who was aware of her husband's homosexuality when she married him, struggles with Farr's admission of having had a sexual attraction to Barrett. Much has been written about this groundbreaking film and its effect on the both the British and the American film industry. The first British film to deal openly with homosexuality, *Victim* may seem a bit outdated, but one must remember the climate of the era in which it was produced (homosexuality was a criminal offense in England until 1967). Technically, the film is flawless, with some terrific camerawork from Brit-noir veteran Heller.

A homosexual attorney (Dirk Bogarde, right) seeks out his blackmailers after the suicide of a young man who tried to protect him in *Victim* (Parkway Films, 1961).

Bogarde turns in nice low-key performance, but his character's surprising willingness to go the distance in his quest for justice is never fully explored.

Violent Playground
★★★½ (1958)

> They're like lepers, only they don't warn you with a bell. [Detective about juvenile delinquents]

Length: 108 min. **Cast**: Stanley Baker, Anne Heywood, David McCallum, Peter Cushing. **Production Company**: Rank Organisation Film Productions. **Directed by**: Basil Dearden. **Photographed by**: Reginald Wyer. **Written by**: James Kennaway.

Sgt. Jack Truman (Baker), a tough cop who is a member of the Liverpool Police Department's Criminal Investigation Department, is removed from a case involving a series of arson-related crimes and assigned to be a juvenile liaison, with the job of preventing potential delinquents from committing that second crime, the one that could seal their fate as hardened criminals. A life-long bachelor and not particularly fond of children, Jack reluctantly does as he is ordered and is relentlessly teased by colleagues who have taken to calling him "Uncle Jack." On his first day on the new job, Jack picks up the pre-pubescent Murphy twins, Patrick and Mary, for stealing from a local shop owner. Returning them to their slum apartment, he meets their beautiful sister, cop-hater Cathie (Heywood), who has been caring for the kids since their mother ran out on them. Jack learns that Cathie's other brother, Johnny (McCallum), is the leader of a teen-aged gang whose members blindly obey his often whimsical orders. From a clue he found at the previous arson-related fire, Jack suspects that Johnny may be the perpetrator. Torn between his growing attraction to Cathie and his sense of duty, Jack withholds facts from his colleagues hoping to find information to prove that he is wrong about Johnny. The film's explosive and somewhat shocking climax is the highlight of this rock n' roll noir, which has been likened to the American juvenile delinquent film, *Blackboard Jungle*. Despite the superfluous romantic subplot, the film succeeds with strong performances by Baker and Heywood and a good, if frenzied, acting job by relative newcomer McCallum. The Scotland-born McCallum later went on to become a household name in America as secret agent Illya Kuryakin in the smash TV series *The Man from U.N.C.L.E.* Future British horror icon Peter Cushing appears as an ineffective but game priest.

The Wall of Death
see *There Is Another Sun*

Wanted for Murder
★★½ (1946)

> You poor halfwits. Six murders and you haven't even a clue. There'll be another corpse tonight. [Postcard addressed to Scotland Yard.]

Length: 101 min. **Cast:** Eric Portman, Dulcie Gray, Derek Farr, Roland Culver, Barbara Everest, Stanley Holloway. **Production Company:** Excelsior Films. **Directed by:** Lawrence Huntington. **Photographed by:** Mutz Greenbaum (as Max Greene). **Written by:** Rodney Ackland, Emeric Pressburger.

Londoner Anne Fielding (Gray), a pretty clerk working at a gramophone shop, has been dating well-to-do businessman Victor Colebrooke (Portman), who, unbeknownst to Anne, is the serial strangler Scotland Yard has been trying to catch. When Colebrooke murders female victim number six on Hampstead Heath, he accidentally leaves behind a handkerchief, which Yard Inspector Conway (Culver) and Sgt. Sullivan (Holloway, the film's comedy relief) trace back to him. Without solid evidence, however, they are left only with their well-founded suspicions, and when victim number seven is found in Regents Park, Conway assigns a man to follow Colebrooke day and night. Tormented by his crimes ("Oh, God, set me free," he prays), the psychopath thinks he can find redemption by marrying a woman who is like his doting mother (Everest). The only female who seems to fit the bill is Anne, but while Colebrooke has been out murdering young women Anne has found herself another beau, bus conductor and innocent murder suspect Jack Williams (Farr). The upper-crust killer is not happy about getting dumped by a woman for a mere bus conductor, so he invites Anne for an early evening rowboat ride in Hyde Park to discuss the matter. Portman gives an interesting if over-the-top performance as the class-conscience mama's boy who seems to have inherited his bloodlust from his late father, Queen Victoria's official hangman, who has been honored with a waxed likeness in the Chamber of Horrors museum. At times, *Wanted* is a suspenseful film, but the distracting theme song, "A Voice in the Night," a catchy tune sung by a young woman Colebrooke is preparing to strangle, plays almost incessantly from the opening credits to the disappointing climax.

Waterfront
(U.S. Title: *Waterfront Women*)
★★★½ (1950)

> It's unnatural to hate your own father, but I just couldn't help it. [Nora McCabe]

Length: 80 min. **Cast:** Robert Newton, Kathleen Harrison, Avis Scott, Susan Shaw, Robin Netscher, Richard Burton. **Production Company:** Conqueror Productions. **Directed by:** Michael Anderson. **Photographed by:** Harry Waxman. **Written by:** John Brophy, Paul Soskin.

Ne'er-do-well drunkard Peter McCabe (Newton), a sailor "born under a wandering star," abandons his family and takes to the sea, unaware that his wife (Harrison) is pregnant. Soon after he leaves, Mrs. McCabe gives birth to a boy. Over the next fourteen years, during difficult economic times, the McCabes struggle to survive in their tenement slum near the

Liverpool docks. Now a teenager, Peter's son, Alexander McCabe (Netscher), wins a scholarship to a prestigious school; Peter's daughter, Nora (Scott), reluctantly falls in love with a sailor, the decent but out-of-work Ben Satterthwaite (Burton); and Nora's kid sister, Connie (Shaw), hooks up with a wealthy playboy who is determined to bed her under the guise of a serious relationship. Then, just as suddenly as he left, Peter returns from sea after losing his job over a dispute with his ship's engineer. Expecting a warm welcome from his family after never sending a letter or any financial aid, McCabe is shocked when Nora tells him that she despises him. He is, however, pleasantly surprised to learn that he has a son and seeks out the nearest pub to celebrate retroactively the birth of 14-year-old George Alexander. The celebration ends abruptly when, drunk as usual, he becomes involved in another confrontation with the man who cost him his job. Unfortunately, McCabe pocketed his old razor blade before leaving his family's flat and soon finds himself imprisoned for murder. *Waterfront*'s strength lies not in its simple but ironic storyline, but in the astute character study of each member of the poverty-stricken family—the cowardly drunkard who hopes to find his redemption in the son he never knew; his loving and forgiving wife; their bitter eldest daughter and her loose sister, each seeking love in their own fashion; and the shy teenaged boy, tormented by peers who cruelly tease him that everyone else's seagoing fathers eventually return except his. Newton and Harrison are superb, and newcomer Burton gives an impressive low-key performance as a sailor out to prove to his fiancée that not all seafaring men are untrustworthy.

Waterfront Women see Waterfront

Waterloo Road
★★★ (1945)

The more we coddle them, the more they cry. The more they cry, they more we coddle them. It's a vicious circle. Probably explains Hitler. [Dr. Montgomery to the mother of a crying baby]

Length: 77 min. **Cast:** John Mills, Stewart Granger, Alastair Sim, Joy Shelton. **Production Company:** Gainsborough Pictures. **Directed by:** Sidney Gilliat. **Photographed by:** Arthur Crabtree. **Written by:** Sidney Gilliat.

The simple plot of *Waterloo Road* tackles the unfaithfulness of some military wives during World War II. Lonely newlywed Tillie Colter (Shelton), weary of living with her in-laws and heartbroken over her husband's refusal to have children during wartime, warily dates Ted Purvis (Granger), a caddish spiv and lady's man who got out of serving his country by purchasing a phony medical certificate from "a quack down in the docks." When Tillie's husband, Jim (Mills), an Army enlisted man, gets wind of his wife's interest in Purvis, he goes AWOL after his commanding officer refuses to grant him leave. With the military police hot on his trial, the desperate soldier searches for his wife in the dives around London's Waterloo Station. *Waterloo Road* offers a fascinating peek at war-time London and the disrupted lives of its war-weary citizens. Sim is entertaining as the crusty neighborhood doctor who serves as the film's narrator, and Mills and Shelton do well as the troubled newlyweds separated by war. Granger's character, who is a despicable and cowardly homme fatale, has been described as Britain's first film spiv (a dapperly dressed small-time crook). *Waterloo*'s highlight is a nicely staged fight scene that occurs during a German bombing raid.

The Way Out see Dial 999

The Weak and the Wicked
(U.S. Title: *Young and Willing*)
★★ (1954)

All right, so he's rotten through and through. But he's mine. [Betty Brown]

Length: 88 min. **Cast:** Glynis Johns, John Gregson, Diana Dors, Sidney James. **Production Company:** Marble Arch Productions. **Directed by:** J. Lee Thompson. **Photographed by:** Gilbert Taylor. **Written by:** J. Lee Thompson, Anne Burnaby, Joan Henry.

Gambling addict Jean Raymond (Johns) passes a bad check at a casino, prompting the owner to even the score by framing her for insurance fraud, for which she is sentenced to a year in prison. At H.M. Prison Blackdown, she befriends a number of inmates, including Betty Brown (Dors), who has loyally taken a two-year rap for her boyfriend; a woman whose neglect caused the death of her infant; and Nelle Baden (Sloane), who was nabbed for shoplifting along with her husband (James) and children. After saving the life of a matron, Jean is transferred with Betty and Nellie to The Grange, a "prison without bars," part of a social experiment in which convicts are taught trades and permitted to visit the nearby town unescorted when their sentences are nearing an end. So far, no prisoner has betrayed the governor's trust, but Betty, who has been permitted to visit town to encourage her good behavior, has just received a letter telling her that her no-good boyfriend, Norman, has taken up with another girl. So much for the prison's unblemished record in this program. Another subplot involves whether or not Jean's boyfriend (Gregson), a newly licensed physician, will wait for her for a whole year. There's really more "weak" than "wicked" in this insipid clone of the American film noir *Caged* (1950), a film in which women prisoners are subjected to the hell of the good old American prison system and where brutal matrons know how to treat their unruly charges other than by constantly scolding them to "keep quiet."

We Shall Rise Again
see *Uncensored*

We Shall See
★★ (1964)

The devil is in that woman. [Ludo]

Length: 61 min. **Cast:** Maurice Kaufmann, Faith Brook, Alec Mango, Alex MacIntosh, Talitha Pol, Bridget Armstrong. **Production Company:** Merton Park Productions. **Directed by:** Quentin Lawrence. **Photographed by:** James Wilson. **Written by:** Donal Giltinan.

Airline pilot Evan Collins (Kaufmann) is being victimized by his psychopathic wife, Alva (Brook), who has been making anonymous telephone calls to his employer, accusing Evan of being a carousing alcoholic and a danger to his passengers. After a car accident, Evan is hospitalized, much to the satisfaction of his wife, whose sick objective has been to destroy his career as "an aerial bus driver" so he can pay more attention to her. Her plan backfires, however, when Evan meets pretty Nurse Rosemary (Armstrong) and they fall in love. In the meantime, Alva's brother, Greg (MacIntosh), has been having an affair with Alva's longsuffering maid, Jirina (Pol), and has been snooping around the house seeking a key to a safety deposit box that contains his share of the inheritance that his sister has been withholding from him. Adding to Alva's growing paranoia, the Collins' gardener, Ludo (Mango), has set up an apiary without realizing that one bee sting could mean death for his highly allergic mistress. Faith Brook's campy performance as the neurotic housewife on the verge of a complete breakdown is alone worth the price of admission. (Part of the "Edgar Wallace Mystery Theater" series.)

The Weapon
★★★½ (1956)

I know what's it's like to be dead and not fall down, believe me. [Capt. Mark Andrews]

Length: 81 min. **Cast:** Steve Cochran, Lizabeth Scott, Herbert Marshall, Nicole Maurey, George Cole, Jon Whiteley. **Production Company:** Periclean Productions. **Directed by:** Val Guest. **Photographed by:** Reg H. Wyer. **Written by:** Fred Freiberger.

Ten-year-old Erik Jenner (Whiteley) flees into the dark London night after accidentally shooting a playmate with a gun he found in a bombed-out building. Scotland Yard Inspector Mackenzie (Marshall) contacts U.S. Army CID officer, Captain Mark Andrews (Cochran), because the bullet removed from the wounded child matches the one that killed an American soldier ten years earlier. With his contemptuous attitude and hard-nosed tactics ("I'm a soldier not a diplomat," he is fond of saying), Mark antagonizes the boy's mother, waitress Elsa Jenner (Scott), the American widow of a British soldier. However, Elsa's concern over her missing son touches a compassionate nerve Mark never knew he had, and the search for the boy rather than the murder weapon soon becomes his priority. The killer, Joshua Henry (Cole), meanwhile has also been searching for the boy in order to retrieve the evidence that could send him to the gallows. During his search for the missing boy, Henry snuffs out the life of hardened dance hall hostess, Vivienne Pascal (Maurey), who was about to share information about the decade-old murder with Mark. Cole is terrific as the suave, gentlemanly villain, and American film noir veterans Cochran and Scott, appearing together for the first and last time, have a nice chemistry going on. Young Whiteley, who was so good opposite Dirk Bogarde in 1952's *Hunted*, does not disappoint here. Suspenseful, fast-moving and stylistically dark, *The Weapon* also contains several traditional noir characters and plot elements, such as a cynical by-the-book cop (in this case a military one), a whore with a heart of gold, an on-the-run child in jeopardy, and a desperate killer trying to cover up his tracks.

Web of Evidence
see *Beyond This Place*

West 11
★★ (1963)

I'm an emotional leper. I don't feel anything. [Joe Beckett]

Length: 93 min. **Cast:** Alfred Lynch, Kathleen Breck, Eric Portman, Diana Dors, Kathleen Harrison, Finlay Currie, Freda Jackson, Marie Ney, Harold Lang. **Production Company:** Dial Films. **Directed by:** Michael Winner. **Photographed by:** Otto Heller. **Written by:** Keith Waterhouse, Willis Hall.

Fired from his job as a salesman at a clothing store, kicked out of his flat by his landlady (Jackson) for being behind on the rent and fed up with his on-again, off-again romantic relationship with the flighty Ilsa Barnes (Breck), Joe Beckett (Lynch) roams the streets of West London seeking meaning in his life. After determining that life has no real significance, he agrees to commit a murder at the urging of former Army captain Dickie Dyce (Portman), a ne'er-do-well who wants his inheritance now rather than having to wait for his wealthy aunt to die of natural causes. Dickie has come up with a "foolproof" murder scheme but soon learns he hasn't chosen his killer very carefully. Complicating matters is the creepy character called Silent (Lang), known as a copper's nark (stool pigeon), who hangs around the local jazz joints ogling girls and playing chess. West 11 is a long merry-go-round ride going nowhere and taking a long time to get there. Portman, nearing the end of a long and successful film career, is a disappointment, and the only time Lynch's sullen character shows any life is when he is dancing The Twist at a London hot spot. And he really doesn't do that very well. The film's most interesting character is Gash (Currie), the eccentric bookworm who has no real connection to the plot. Harrison gives the film's best performance as Joe's dying mother, while Dors merely manages to look good as a lonely divorcee who allows herself to be taken advantage of by both Joe and Dickie.

Wheel of Fate
★★★½ (1953)

Come on, coppers. You won't get me alive. [Ted Burrows]

Length: 70 min. **Cast:** Patric Doonan, Sandra Dorne, Bryan Forbes, John Horsley. **Production Company:** Kenilworth Film Productions. **Directed by:** Francis Searle. **Photographed by:** Reg Wyer. **Written by:** Guy Elmes.

Stepbrothers Johnny and Ted Burrows couldn't be more different. While artist wannabe Johnny (Doonan) tends to both his invalid father and the family garage, Ted (Forbes) squanders his dough on the horses, has little patience for his father's constant need for attention and has a tendency to become involved in brawls. When a drunk tries to kiss Ted's girl, nightclub singer Lucky Price (Dorne), he whacks the fellow over the head with bottle, nearly killing him. Johnny's former Army pal, Det. Sergeant Jack Simpson (Horsley), pays a visit to the garage looking to question Ted about the incident, but Johnny reluctantly provides a brotherly alibi.

Later that night, Ted shows up at home with Lucky and, unfortunately for him, sparks fly between her and Johnny. Dejected, broke and in debt to an impatient bookmaker, whose goon has already paid him a threatening visit, Ted begins thinking about the pub he wants to open, the large sum of money his seriously ill father has stashed away and how easy it would be to withhold the old man's medicine the next time he needs it. *Wheel of Fate*, an almost unknown film, is a gratifying noir surprise. Bryan Forbes is terrific as the bad seed who seems destined to lose. His scene in the old man's bedroom, during which the viewer never sees the bed-ridden father but only his gnarly hand desperately pounding his cane on the floor, is a high-point in British film noir and one that viewers can expect to long remember. Darkly photographed by Brit noir veteran Reginald Wyer and ably directed by Francis Searle, *Wheel of Fate* proves what a talented cast and crew can accomplish on a limited budget.

While I Live
★½ (1947)

You're a domineering, self-centered old spinster.... When I came along and tried to bring a breath of fresh air into your musty little world you hated me. [Christine Sloan to Julia Trevelyan]

Length: 85 min. **Cast:** Sonia Dresdel, Carol Raye, Tom Walls, Patricia Burke, Clifford Evans, John Warwick, Audrey Fildes. **Production Company:** Edward Dryhurst Productions. **Directed by:** John Harlow. **Photographed by:** F.A. Young. **Written by:** John Harlow, Doreen Montgomery.

Tormented by her inability to please her overbearing sister, who wants her to put the final touches on an unfinished piano concerto, "The Dream of Olwen," composer Olwen Trevelyan (Fildes) sleepwalks herself right off a cliff near her Cornwall home and into the raging sea below. On the 25th anniversary of her tragic death, a beautiful girl (Raye) suffering from amnesia wanders into the Trevelyan home, sits down at the piano and plays the concerto flawlessly, prompting Julia Trevelyan (Dresdel) to jump to the conclusion that her long-dead sister has been reincarnated. Julia's live-in cousin, newlywed George Grant (Warwick), takes an interest in the girl, causing his bride, Christine (Burke), to move out of the house in a fit of jealousy. Julia thinks this is just dandy and hopes that George will hook up with the amnesiac and drop Christine, whom she considers an outsider. When Londoner Peter Sloane (Evans) shows up in Cornwall looking for his missing writer wife, Sally, smug Christine is delighted to help him locate her. Meanwhile, Julia's butler, Nehemiah (Walls), the local "layer on of hands," is convinced that he can snap Sally out of her amnesiac state through hypnosis. Most sources list this film as having a running time of 85 minutes, but the available U.S. copies all seem to run 58 minutes, which might help explain why *While I Live* is almost incomprehensible even with two explanatory flashbacks. Charles Williams' music is terrific, though.

Whirlpool
★½ (1959)

ROLF: You are afraid to accept this world as anything better than a place of garbage and filth.
LORA: That's my world.

Length: 95 min. **Cast:** Juliette Gréco, O.W. Fischer, Marius Goring, Muriel Pavlow, William Sylvester. **Production Company:** Rank Organisation Film Productions. **Directed by:** Lewis Allen. **Photographed by:** Geoffrey Unsworth. **Written by:** Lawrence P. Bachmann.

Lora (Gréco), a pretty but jaded French waitress working in a Cologne biergarten, goes on the run when her ex-boyfriend, Herman (Sylvester), stabs a man during a black market money-exchange deal that has gone wrong. She tells Herman that she will meet him in Amsterdam but wisely thumbs a ride aboard a river barge heading in the opposite direction. When Herman learns of her deception, he tries to catch up with the boat, killing a cop in the process. Meanwhile, Lora begins to fall for the barge's handsome captain, Rolph (Rischer), unaware that he has reluctantly agreed to use her as a decoy to help German police capture Herman. Despite the promising first ten minutes, the film quickly deteriorates into a Rhine River travelogue. Filmed in Eastmancolor, the scenery is pretty but some of the close-ups obviously have been superimposed upon footage of the shoreline. *Whirlpool* (not to be confused with the 1949 American film noir of the same title) is a tedious story with a paucity of noir elements and no help from the mostly average cast, which includes Goring as the staid first mate and Pavlow as his wife. Greco is stunningly beautiful, but it is American actor William Sylvester (*2001: A Space Odyssey*), who gives the best performance as the desperate cop killer.

White Fire see 3 Steps to the Gallows

Wicked as They Come
(U.S. Title: *Portrait in Smoke*)
★★ (1956)

TIM: There isn't a single thing that's ever happened to you in your whole life that you haven't planned and figured out all for yourself.
KATHY: I didn't plan to be born in a stinking slum to be raised with hoodlums as playmates.
TIM: So what makes you so special? A million other dames have been born in the dirt and haven't wound up like you, baby.

Length: 94 min. **Cast**: Arlene Dahl, Philip Carey, Herbert Marshall, Ralph Truman, Michael Goodliffe, Sidney James. **Production Company**: Film Locations. **Directed by**: Ken Hughes. **Photographed by**: Basil Emmott. **Written by**: Ken Hughes, Robert Westerby, Sigmund Miller.

Kathy Allen (Dahl) wins a beauty competition sponsored by a small New York City newspaper after both the lonely middle-aged editor and his romantically obsessed son fix the contest in the hopes of cozying up to the beautiful factory worker. First prize? A thousand dollars and a trip to Europe, which she claims immediately after dumping the two patsies. Turns out that Kathy has an aversion to men, a disgust for them really, ever since "that thing that happened to her when she was a kid." She can't even tolerate being touched by a man — until she meets the handsome and sensitive Tim O'Bannion (Carey). Confused by her newly aroused feelings for, ugh, a man, Kathy becomes even more determined to claw her way to the top of the corporate world. After charging a new wardrobe to her short-tempered current boyfriend, London photographer Larry Bickhan (Goodliffe), she disappears, leaving Bickhan to serve a six-month term in prison for assaulting the department store manager who tried to collect the debt. After graduating from secretarial school, Kathy finagles her way into a clerical position under middle-aged corporate executive Stephen Collins (Marshall) by using O'Bannion's name. She then earns a promotion by getting Collins drunk and pretending that they had intimate relations. Collins becomes her sugar daddy, setting her up in an expensive apartment, but when he reneges on a promise to divorce his wife, Kathy sets her sights on Collins' elderly father-in-law (!), John Dowling (Truman), the president of the corporation, whom she quickly seduces into marrying her. It is then that the vengeance-minded Bickhan arrives in town and starts sending anonymous and threatening letters to the new Mrs. Dowling. American actress Dahl does the best she can with her character, a poor excuse for a femme fatale who couldn't hold a candle to the likes of her more lethal cousins in American noirs. There's nothing special about this snooze producer except for fans of British character actor Sid James, who has a minor role as Kathy's stepfather.

Wide Boy
★★★ (1952)

A professional man who's married and gets himself involved with another woman is bad enough. But when his wife is dying! You can imagine the effect that will have on the people I'm hoping will vote for me. [blackmail victim Robert Mannering]

Length: 67 min. **Cast**: Sydney Tafler, Susan Shaw, Ronald Howard, Melissa Stribling, Colin Tapley. **Production Company**: Merton Park Productions. **Directed by**: Ken Hughes. **Photographed by**: Jo Ambor. **Written by**: Rex Rienits (original story).

Recently busted for selling stolen nylons, street hawker Benny (Tafler), a London "wide boy"(i.e., a small-time crook), gets big ideas after lifting a wallet from a woman's purse in a night spot. In addition to some dough, Benny finds a letter written to the woman, Caroline Blaine (Stribling), by her married lover, Robert Mannering (Tapley), an eminent surgeon with political aspirations. Benny, under pressure from his hairdresser girlfriend, Molly (Shaw), to spend a little more money on her, decides to blackmail Mannering. After collecting £200 from the doctor, Benny reneges on his end of the deal and holds on to the letter. He then doubles the demand on his next extortion attempt and purchases a gun when Mannering insists on a face-to-face meeting. Before Benny knows it, he's on the run from Scotland Yard for murdering his blackmail victim. The low-production values are hardly noticeable in this enjoyable, old-fashioned, crime-doesn't-pay story photographed in the film noir style. Tafler, in a rare starring role, is believable as the small-time criminal caught in a downward spiral that ultimately leads to tragedy.

A Window in London
(U.S. Title: *Lady in Distress*)
★★ (1939)

> I can't stand this idiotic jealousy any more. It's killing even the pity I have for you. And I warn you, when that goes I shall go, too. [Vivienne to The Great Zoltini]

Length: 77 min. **Cast:** Michael Redgrave, Sally Gray, Paul Lukas, Patricia Roc. **Production Company:** G&S Films. **Directed by:** Herbert Mason. **Photographed by:** Glen McWilliams. **Written by:** Ian Dalrymple, Brigid Cooper.

While riding the Underground on his way to work, Peter (Redgrave), a London crane operator, witnesses what he thinks is a man stabbing a woman on the balcony of an apartment building. He reports the incident to a constable and together they find the flat and confront the man who lives there. However, the "murdered" woman is very much alive. It turns out that the couple, the Great Zoltini and his wife, Vivienne, had been rehearsing their illusionist act with a collapsible knife. Peter is happily married to Pat (Roc), even though they only see each other long enough each day to say hi and bye because he works the day shift and she works nights as a hotel switchboard operator. However, he is strangely drawn to the beautiful Vivienne, whose marriage to the arrogant, middle-aged magician is floundering. The jealous Zoltini, who is beginning to wonder why it is that every time he turns around he sees Peter with Vivienne, makes the mistake of slapping his wife before their act begins at a second-rate burlesque club. In retaliation, she spitefully ruins his performance by leaving the theater instead of popping up in a locked trunk. This infuriates Zoltini, who learns that she was last seen leaving the theater in a taxi with Peter, whose idea of showing a girl a good time is to bring her to his construction site and show her his crane. When Peter and Zoltini next meet, somebody ends up in the Thames. This overly lighthearted film is even less dark than the similarly plotted American film noir, *Lady on a Train* (1945), where it is at least obvious that filmmakers had their tongues firmly in cheek. In addition to *Window*'s disappointing ending, Redgrave is miscast and awkward as the laborer with an unexpected proclivity to cheat on his sweet, hardworking wife. The beautiful Sally Gray, however, is just fine as the unintentional femme fatale.

Wings of Danger
(U.S. Title: *Dead on Course*)
★½ (1952)

> ALEXIA: My future's no dream from a bottle. I've had too much of attic rooms and runs in my stockings and 10-cent bar loungers trying to paw me to death not to know what I want out of life. And to recognize it when I've got it. All you have to do is hitch your wagon and I'm tossing you the hook.
> VAN: Thanks for the hook. And the information.
> ALEXIA: You've taken me for a ride, haven't you?

Length: 73 min. **Cast:** Zachary Scott, Robert Beatty, Kay Kendall, Naomi Chance, Arthur Lane, Colin Tapley, Harold Lang. **Production Company:** Hammer Film Productions. **Directed by:** Terence Fisher. **Photographed by:** Walter Harvey. **Written by:** John Gilling.

Richard Van Ness (Scott), a pilot carrying freight for Spencer Airlines, loses his best buddy, Nick Talbot (Beatty), when Nick's plane crashes

A pilot who suffers blackouts (Zachary Scott) discovers a ring of counterfeiters in Wings of Danger *(a.k.a.* Dead on Course*) (Hammer, 1952).*

over the Atlantic. Nick's body is never found but debris from his plane is discovered drifting in the ocean. After the accident, "Van" becomes a busy fellow, consoling Nick's pretty sister, Avril (Chance); dealing with a slimy character named Snell (Lang), who's blackmailing Avril over Nick's past criminal activities; trying to convince Inspector Maxwell (Tapley) that he's not involved in a gold smuggling ring; seeking to get the low-down on his boss, Boyd Spencer (Lane), who he believes is involved in Nick's death; and playing femme fatale Alexia LaRoche (Kendall) for a sucker while pumping her for information about her lover, Spencer. That's a lot of running around for a pilot who suffers from sporadic blackouts, but there is still a big surprise waiting for Van (but not for the savvy viewer who will see it coming a mile away). *Wings* has its share of noir elements, including voiceover narration by the main protagonist, who is a war hero struggling with a combat-related disability and the psychological distress that accompanies it; a war veteran who turns to crime; a scheming femme fatale and her "good-girl" counterpart; and a plethora of criminal activities such as blackmail, counterfeiting, smuggling, and murder. In the end, despite the noir content and the presence of noir icon Scott, this is a torturously boring movie that comes close to being unintelligible.

Witness in the Dark
★★½ (1959)

Is there anything worse than blindness? [Mr. Finch]

Length: 62 min. **Cast**: Patricia Dainton, Conrad Phillips, Madge Ryan, Nigel Green, Enid Lorimer. **Production Company**: Ethiro Productions. **Directed by**: Wolf Rilla. **Photographed by**: Brendan J. Stafford. **Written by**: Leigh Vance, John Lemont.

Blind switchboard operator Jane Pringle (Dainton), who lost her fiancée along with her sight in an automobile accident years earlier, believes one way to deal with her disability is to help others. Thus, she has volunteered to teach a recently blinded boy how to read Braille and visits the elderly widow who lives in her apartment building. The widow, Mrs. Temple (Lorimer), owns a valuable brooch worth more than £2,000. Thanks to neighborhood gossip Mrs. Finch (Ryan), word has gotten around the neighborhood that Mrs. Temple hides the brooch in a canister of lentils. The wrong person (Green) hears about the brooch and pays Mrs. Temple a deadly visit. After killing her, however, he is unable to find the jewelry because, unbeknownst to her gossipy neighbors, the wily old lady was in the habit of changing hiding places. On his way down the stairs, he bumps into Jane, who touches his Macintosh raincoat before he flees the building. While Scotland Yard Inspector Coates (Phillips) scours the neighborhood for a man wearing a ragged Macintosh raincoat, Mrs. Finch is busy spreading the news around the local pub that the old lady left the brooch to Jane in her will. Before long, the newspapers pick up the story, alerting the killer that the brooch is still up for grabs. He eventually shows up at Jane's flat pretending to be a newspaper photographer. *Witness*' familiar storyline — a blind girl terrorized by a vicious killer — doesn't fare too badly here, relying mainly on a good performance by Dainton. The claustrophobic ambiance of the film, especially the scene on the staircase where the killer and the blind girl brush up against each other, will be appreciated by noir fans, but its positive effect is negated by the otherwise unexciting cinematography and the silliness of the supposedly ominous musical score.

The Woman in Question
(U.S. Title: *Five Angles on Murder*)
★★★ (1950)

I always get what I want, when I deserve it.
[Agnes Hoosten]

Length: 88 min. **Cast:** Jean Kent, Dirk Bogarde, John McCallum, Susan Shaw, Hermione Baddeley, Charles Victor, Duncan MacRae. **Production Companies:** Javelin Films, Vic Films. **Directed by:** Anthony Asquith. **Photographed by:** Desmond Dickinson. **Written by:** John Cresswell.

Five people tell Superintendent Lodge about their relationship to Agnes Hoosten (Kent) (a.k.a. Madame Astra), an arcade fortune teller who was found strangled in her home. Each of the five, four of whom Lodge considers suspects, has a different impression of the dead woman: her housekeeper, Mrs. Finch (Baddeley), whose young son discovered the body, saw her as the perfect lady; Agnes' sister, department store clerk Catherine Taylor (Shaw), viewed her as a drunkard who callously refused to visit her war veteran husband as he lay dying in a naval hospital; out-of-work stage magician Bob Baker (Bogarde), who wanted Agnes to become a part of his mind-reading act, was convinced that her interest in him was only sexual; marriage-minded pet shop owner Albert Pollard (Victor), "an elderly, insignificant little man," built his world around Agnes, viewing her as a prime candidate for marriage after the death of his invalid wife; and Irish sailor Mike Murray (McCallum) knew her as a tough, cynical broad with a heart of gold but whose tainted past had hardened her, making faithfulness an impossible virtue. Their stories, told by way of voiceover narration and flashback, eventually lead Superintendent Lodge to the killer. The film's fascinating characters are what holds the story together, with Kent doing a sensational job in a complicated role. The film's weakness turns out to be the perplexing ending, in which Lodge implausibly links seemingly insignificant details that help him to identify and entrap the killer.

The Woman with No Name
(U.S. Title: *Her Panelled Door*)
(NR) (1950)

Length: 83 min. **Cast:** Phyllis Calvert, Edward Underdown, Helen Cherry, Richard Burton. **Production Company:** Independent Film Producers. **Directed by:** Ladislas Vajda, George More O'Ferrall. **Photographed by:** Otto Heller. **Written by:** Ladislas Vajda, Guy Morgan.

An amnesiac (Phyllis Calvert) seeks her real identity in *The Woman with No Name* (a.k.a. *Her Panelled Door*) (Independent Film Producers, 1950).

A woman loses her memory during a German bombing raid on London and falls in love with the Norwegian pilot who saved her life. After the pilot's death, the amnesia victim, who is pregnant with his child, is tracked down by her crippled husband. She begins to investigate her past and learns a dark family secret.

Women of Twilight
(U.S. Title: *Twilight Women*)
★★★½ (1953)

> You know, I don't agree with murder but when it comes to a showdown my sympathies are always with the bloke in the dock. I suppose it's because I've been inside meself. [Olga]

Length: 89 min. **Cast:** Freda Jackson, René Ray, Lois Maxwell, Laurence Harvey, Vida Hope, Joan Dowling, Dorothy Gordon, Dora Bryan, Mary Germaine, Ingeborg von Krusserow (as Ingeborg Wells). **Production Company:** Daniel Angel Films. **Directed by:** Gordon Parry. **Photographed by:** Jack Asher. **Written by:** Anatole de Grunwald.

When Vivianne Bruce's lover, London nightclub singer and "cheap little Romeo" Jerry Nolan (Harvey), is arrested for murdering a countess, Vivianne (Ray) finds herself pregnant and an unwanted victim of media attention. Her landlord, revolted by all the bad publicity, kicks her out of her flat. When she is unable to find another place because of her notoriety, she reluctantly moves into a rooming house run by Helen Alistair (Jackson), the day care provider from hell. The widow Alistair and her accomplice, the horrible Jessie Smithson (Hope), take in unwed pregnant women and new mothers, cramping them together in tiny rooms and taking their paychecks and welfare payments in return for room and board and sloppy, even criminal, baby-care services. Emotionally exhausted because of the dragged-out murder trial and the subsequent execution of her boyfriend, Vivianne readily agrees to Mrs. Alistair's offer of a nurse and a nice little cottage in the country where she can have her baby without the publicity she would encounter in a hospital. Unbeknownst to Vivianne, Mrs. Alistair operates a baby farming racket and has another equally dirty little secret that the police would be only too glad to find out about. Combination soap opera and crime melodrama, the *Women of Twilight* is nothing short of intriguing. Jackson and Hope are terrific as the exploiters of the unfortunate women (Ray, Maxwell, Dowling, Gordon, Germaine, von Kusserow, and Bryan) who come to the boarding house seeking shelter and security for themselves and their babies. Harvey, whose obviously dubbed singing voice at The 23 Club threatens the believability of his character, redeems himself in a moving prison scene on the day he is scheduled to hang. Although today it would hardly raise an eyebrow, the film received an "X" rating from the British Board of Film Censors because of its controversial subject matter.

Women Without Men
(U.S. Title: *Blonde Bait*)
★½ (1956)

> Like most women in prison, I'm here because of a man. [Angela Booth]

Length: 73 min. **Cast:** Beverly Michaels, Thora Hird, April Olrich, Paul Carpenter, Ralph Michael. **Production Company:** Hammer Film Productions. **Directed by:** Elmo Williams. **Photographed by:** Walter Harvey. **Written by:** Richard Landau, Val Guest.

Angela Booth (Michaels), an American singer in London, makes plans to meet and wed her boyfriend, Nick Randall (Carpenter), when he returns on New Year's Eve from a three-month-long deep-sea diving assignment. When she tells her abusive manager, Julian Lord (Michael), that she is planning to quit, he assaults her. She defends herself by hitting him in the face with a hand mirror. He presses charges and she is sentenced to six months in prison for assault. Unaware of Nick's location, she is unable to tell him that she can't meet him at the Ox Head Inn as planned, so she breaks out on New Year's Eve, along with prison mates Gran' Rafferty (Hird), an escape artists of sorts, and Marguerite Chavez (Olrich), a young girl who wants to avoid having to turn over to welfare officials the baby she gave birth to in prison. The escaped convicts make it to London, where Angela rushes off to her rendezvous with her fiancé, not knowing if he will even show up. The only interesting aspect of *Women Without Men* is its history. The film was later released in the U.S. as *Blonde Bait* and included new footage of Beverly Michaels and several new characters, as well as an entirely different plot. American audiences saw singer Angela Booth become the victim of her crooked fiancé, Nick Randall (played by Jim Davis), a former Nazi collaborator. His marriage proposal is merely a pretense for involving her in one of his illegal schemes. Meanwhile, a U.S. State Department official and a Scotland Yard inspector (Richard Travis and Paul Cavanagh, respectively) allow her to escape from prison so she will lead them to Randall, who is wanted for murdering an American government official. In the new script, the kindly Gran' Rafferty is a prison stool pigeon who helps Angela escape in order to earn an early release. Both versions are boring, but *Blonde Bait* contains more noirish plot elements than the original.

The Yellow Balloon
★★★ (1953)

> FRANKIE: Have you done something bad?
> LEN: Oh, of course not. I've just had an unlucky break. I'm the most law-abiding man in the world. I've been framed.

Length: 80 min. **Cast:** Andrew Ray, Kathleen Ryan, Kenneth More, Bernard Lee, William Sylvester, Sandra Dorne. **Production Company:** Marble Arch Productions. **Directed by:** J. Lee Thompson. **Photographed by:** Gilbert Taylor. **Written by:** Anne Burbnaby, J. Lee Thompson.

Young Frankie Palmer (Ray) snatches a balloon from a playmate, flees into a bombed-out building and dares his friend to catch him. The boy chases his tormenter through the ruins, climbs to the upper stories of the building and slips and falls to his death. Len, an adult who witnessed the accident, intentionally terrifies Frankie, convincing him that the police will never believe his story and will probably arrest him for murder. Pretending to befriend the boy, Len swears he would help him get away if he only had the money to do so. So Frankie steals from his parents, Emily (Ryan) and Ted (More). He gets caught, however, is spanked with a belt by his father while his mother attributes his sullenness and bad behavior to his friend's recent death. When Frankie returns to his new friend broke and discouraged, Len expresses understanding and tells him there is a way they can get their hands on enough money so the both of them can get out of town. There's this pub, Len tells him, where his girlfriend, Irish (Dorne), works, and the owner is certain to open it after business hours to a child who needs some brandy for his sick mum. Of course, Len's attempted robbery goes sour and he ends up strangling the proprietor during a scuffle, while Frankie runs away. Determined to silence the boy, Len finds him and lures him into a dark, abandoned Underground station. The little known *The Yellow Balloon* starts out as a poignant message movie (i.e., kids, tell your parents everything, the policeman is your friend and keep away from strangers) but soon heads in the apparent direction of *Hunted* and *Tiger Bay*, two films in which the killers bond with their innocent young victims. *Balloon*, however, turns into a frightening child-in-jeopardy tale reminiscent of the 1949 American film noir *The Window*. Andrew Ray does a fine job as the frightened and guilt-ridden young boy, and American actor William Sylvester is simply odious as his bogus protector. Bernard Lee, "M," of the early James Bond films, appears in a small role as a kindly constable.

Yellow Canary
★★½ (1943)

Wouldn't it be nice to do something violent? [ship passenger Mrs. Towcester moments before tripping a German officer]

Length: 98 min. **Cast**: Anna Neagle, Richard Greene, Albert Lieven, Lucie Mannheim. **Production Company**: Herbert Wilcox Productions. **Directed by**: Herbert Wilcox. **Photographed by**: Mutz Greenbaum (as Max Greene). **Written by**: Miles Malleson, De Witt Bodeen.

After being nabbed for deliberately violating the blackout during a German bombing raid on London, Sally Maitland (Neagle) is deported to Canada. Tagging along on her ship is undercover British intelligence agent Lieutenant Commander Jim Garrick (Greene), who can't make it to first base with the pretty Nazi sympathizer because she seems to have eyes only for Jan Orlock (Lieven), a charming Polish refugee who is on his way to Nova Scotia to visit his wheelchair-bound mother (Mannheim). With her reputation arriving in Halifax before she does, Sally is not surprised to find herself being shunned by almost everyone except the elderly Mrs. Orlock, who seems strangely nice to her considering she herself was a victim of a German air strike on Warsaw. Obviously, not everyone is what he or she seems. Spies, counterspies, patriots and traitors—you can't tell them apart without a scorecard in this fair-to-middling, war-time propaganda film. Beloved English character actress Margaret Rutherford, who is probably most familiar to American viewers as Agatha Christie's amateur detective Miss Marple, has a small but entertaining role as a feisty traveler with a set of loose lips.

Yield to the Night
(U.S. Title: *Blonde Sinner*)
★½ (1956)

I know every mark and blemish in this cell, every crack in the wall, scratches on the wooden chairs, the place where the paint has peeled off the ceiling, and the door at the foot of my bed, the door without a handle. I know it better than any room I ever lived in. [condemned prisoner Mary Price Hilton]

Length: 99 min. **Cast**: Diana Dors, Yvonne Mitchell, Michael Craig, Marie Ney. **Production Company**: Kenwood Films. **Directed by**: J. Lee Thompson. **Photographed by**: Gilbert Taylor. **Written by**: John Cresswell, Joan Henry.

During the sensationally photographed opening sequence, Mrs. Mary Price Hilton (Dors) empties her revolver into a romantic rival, a wealthy married woman who ruined Mary's adulterous relationship with pianist boyfriend Jim Lancaster (Craig). So much for the interesting portion of *Yield to the Night*. The remainder of the film revolves around Mary's time in prison while she awaits either execution or reprieve. The viewer learns by way of multiple flashbacks and voiceover narration about the events that led Mary to this predicament (although the first several minutes of the film seemed to have addressed that issue sufficiently). Overly pampered by the matrons assigned to watch her during her final days, especially the kindly Hilda MacFarlane (Mitchell), Mary walks around in a self-pitying, zombie-like daze while she awaits word about her fate from the prison governess (Ney). Boring and not very well acted (although loyal Dors fans see her performance here as having forever silenced the critics who stereotyped her as just another blonde bombshell), *Yield to the Night* is strictly for the cult of Diana Dors worshippers, of which there are many, and for those who agree with its undisguised anti-capital punishment message.

The Young and Willing
see *The Weak and the Wicked*

Young Scarface see *Brighton Rock*

Young, Willing and Eager
see *Rag Doll*

Appendix A. British Films Noirs Listed by Rating

★★★★★

Gaslight
Great Expectations
Seance on a Wet Afternoon
Third Man

★★★★½

They Drive by Night
Black Narcissus
Brighton Rock
Night and the City
Night of the Demon
Odd Man Out
Oliver Twist
Peeping Tom
The Rocking Horse Winner
Room at the Top
They Made Me a Fugitive

★★★★

Across the Bridge
Chase a Crooked Shadow
The Criminal
Dead of Night
Dear Murderer
The Fallen Idol
Footsteps in the Fog
Frieda
The Gentle Gunman
Give Us This Day
Green for Danger
Hatter's Castle
I See a Dark Stranger
Love on the Dole
Mine Own Executioner
Outcast of the Islands
Poison Pen
Sapphire
Seven Days to Noon
Shake Hands with the Devil
The Ship that Died of Shame
Silent Dust
So Evil My Love
The Spy in Black
Stage Fright
Tiger Bay
Victim

★★★½

Another Man's Poison
Blanche Fury
The Blue Lamp
The Damned
The Frightened City
Good-Time Girl
The Heart of the Matter
Hell Drivers
Hell Is A City
Hysteria
I Believe in You
I Met a Murderer
Jigsaw
The Key
Madeleine
Madonna of the Seven Moons
The Man in Grey
The Man in the Back Seat
Mr. Denning Drives North
Mr. Perrin and Mr. Traill
My Brother's Keeper
Never Let Go
Nightmare
1984
The October Man
Paranoiac
A Prize of Arms
The Secret Place
Serious Charge
The Shop at Sly Corner
The Small Back Room
The Small World of Sammy Lee
The Snorkel
So Long at the Fair
The Spider and the Fly
Strongroom
The Third Secret
Time Without Pity
21 Days
Violent Playground
Waterfront
The Weapon
Wheel of Fate
Women of Twilight

★★★

Act of Murder
All Night Long
Assassin for Hire
The Brothers
Cage of Gold
Cast a Dark Shadow
Cloudburst
Contraband
Counterblast
Crimes at the Dark House
Daughter of Darkness
Do You Know This Voice?
Don't Talk to Strange Men
Dual Alibi
Eight O'clock Walk
Fanny by Gaslight
The Flying Scot
For Them That Trespass
Forbidden
Golden Salamander
The Good Die Young
Great Day

Appendix A

Home at Seven
Hotel Reserve
The House Across the Lake
Hunted
The Informers
An Inspector Calls
It Always Rains on Sunday
The Long Haul
The Long Memory
The Man Between
The Night Has Eyes
Night Without Stars
No Room at the Inn
No Trace
Obsession
Offbeat
On the Night of the Fire
One Way Out
Payroll
Personal Affair
Piccadilly Third Stop
Playback
Pool of London
Rough Shoot
Secret People
The Set-Up
The Shakedown
The Share-Out
So Well Remembered
The Square Ring
Stolen Face
Take My Life
Three Weird Sisters
To Have and to Hold
Tread Softly Stranger
Turn the Key Softly
Uncle Silas
The Upturned Glass
Waterloo Road
Wide Boy
The Woman in Question
The Yellow Balloon

★★½

Appointment with Crime
Bang! You're Dead
Beyond This Place
Black Limelight
Blind Corner
Blind Date
Boys in Brown
The Brain Machine
The Breaking Point
Cairo
Calling Bulldog Drummond
Candidate for Murder
Cat Girl

Circle of Deception
The Clouded Yellow
The Clue of the New Pin
Confession
Corridor of Mirrors
Cosh Boy
Cottage to Let
Crow Hollow
Dancing with Crime
The Dark Eyes of London
Daybreak
The Depraved
Desperate Moment
Downfall
The Embezzler
The Face at the Window
Face of a Stranger
Faces in the Dark
Five to One
The Flesh Is Weak
Floods of Fear
Fortune Is a Woman
The Green Cockatoo
The House in the Woods
House of Darkness
I'll Get You for This
Information Received
The Intimate Stranger
The Intruder
Joe MacBeth
Kill Me Tomorrow
The Last Page
Locker Sixty-Nine
London Belongs to Me
The Long Dark Hall
Man Detained
The Man Who Wouldn't Talk
Marriage of Convenience
Murder Without Crime
Naked Fury
The Narrowing Circle
Night Beat
No Trees in the Street
Nowhere to Go
On the Run
Once a Sinner
Operation Diplomat
Panic
Passport to Shame
Pink String and Sealing Wax
Pit of Darkness
A Place to Go
Portrait from Life
Queen of Spades
The Quiet Woman
Ricochet
The Rivals
The Rough and the Smooth
Saraband for Dead Lovers

The Seventh Veil
The Sleeping Tiger
Stormy Crossing
The Stranger's Hand
Street of Shadows
There Is Another Sun
They Can't Hang Me
13 East Street
Tiger in the Smoke
Wanted for Murder
Witness in the Dark
Yellow Canary

★★

Alias John Preston
The Bank Raiders
Beat Girl
Bedelia
The Big Chance
Bitter Harvest
Black Orchid
Black Widow
Blackout
Calculated Risk
Carnival
Case of the Frightened Lady
Circle of Danger
Crossroads to Crime
The Dark Man
The Dark Tower
Double Confession
Escape by Night
Escape Route
Face the Music
Five Days
The Flanagan Boy
The Girl Hunters
Guilt Is My Shadow
Impact
Impulse
Incident at Midnight
The Interrupted Journey
Jassy
Johnny Nobody
Jungle Street
Kill Her Gently
Lady of Vengeance
The Large Rope
The Late Edwina Black
The Limping Man
The Little Red Monkey
The Lost Hours
The Malpas Mystery
Man on the Run
The Man Upstairs
The Man Who Was Nobody
The Man Who Watched the
    Trains Go By

British Films Noirs by Rating

Mantrap
Marilyn
The Mark of Cain
Murder at 3 A.M.
Never Mention Murder
Nicholas Nickleby
Night Boat to Dublin
Night Was Our Friend
No Orchids for Miss Blandish
No Road Back
The Noose
The Painted Smile
Psyche 59
Radio Cab Murder
Rag Doll
Recoil
The Small Voice
Snowbound
Solo for Sparrow
Spellbound
Street Corner
Thirty-Six Hours
Three Crooked Men
3 Steps to the Gallows
Tiger by the Tail
Time to Remember
Tower of Terror
Uneasy Terms
Urge to Kill
The Vicious Circle
We Shall See
The Weak and the Wicked
West 11
Wicked as They Come
A Window in London

★½

Beautiful Stranger
The Blue Parrot
The Challenge
Deadly Nightshade
Dial 999
The Door with Seven Locks
East of Piccadilly
The End of the Line
The Gambler and the Lady
Latin Quarter
Man in Black
Murder by Proxy
Port of Escape
Return to Sender
Room to Let
The Six Men
Soho Incident
The Stranger Came Home
Third Party Risk
Three Sundays to Live
The £20,000 Kiss
The Verdict
While I Live
Whirlpool
Wings of Danger
Women Without Men
Yield to the Night

★

The Hypnotist
Murder in Soho

Not Rated (NR)

Black 13
Black Memory
Blackmailed
Dark Secret
Dead Men Are Dangerous
Delayed Action
Escape
Escape to Danger
The Fatal Night
The Flamingo Affair
The Green Scarf
Gunman Has Escaped
In the Wake of a Stranger
The Man Within
Midnight Episode
Murder in Reverse
No Way Back
Now Barabbas
The Passing Stranger
Squadron Leader X
Temptation Harbour
This Was a Woman
Three Silent Men
Traitor Spy
Trunk Crime
Uncensored
Vengeance Is Mine
The Woman with No Name

Appendix B. British Films Noirs Listed by Year

1937
The Green Cockatoo
21 Days

1938
Black Limelight
They Drive by Night

1939
The Dark Eyes of London
Dead Men Are Dangerous
The Face at the Window
I Met a Murderer
Murder in Soho
On the Night of the Fire
Poison Pen
The Spy in Black
Traitor Spy
Trunk Crime
A Window in London

1940
Case of the Frightened Lady
Contraband
Crimes at the Dark House
The Door with Seven Locks
Gaslight
Three Silent Men

1941
Cottage to Let
East of Piccadilly
Hatter's Castle
Love on the Dole
Spellbound
Tower of Terror

1942
The Night Has Eyes
Squadron Leader X
Uncensored

1943
The Dark Tower
Escape to Danger
The Man in Grey
Yellow Canary

1944
Fanny by Gaslight
Hotel Reserve
Madonna of the Seven Moons

1945
Dead of Night
Great Day
Latin Quarter
Murder in Reverse
Pink String and Sealing Wax
The Seventh Veil
Waterloo Road

1946
Appointment with Crime
Bedelia
Carnival
Daybreak
Great Expectations
Green for Danger
I See a Dark Stranger
Night Boat to Dublin
Wanted for Murder

1947
Black Memory
Black Narcissus
Brighton Rock
The Brothers
Dancing with Crime
Dear Murderer
Dual Alibi
Frieda
It Always Rains on Sunday
Jassy
The Man Within
Mine Own Executioner
Nicholas Nickleby
The October Man
Odd Man Out
The Shop at Sly Corner
So Well Remembered
Take My Life
Temptation Harbour
They Made Me a Fugitive
Uncle Silas
The Upturned Glass
While I Live

1948
Blanche Fury
Corridor of Mirrors
Counterblast
Daughter of Darkness
Escape

British Films Noirs by Year

The Fallen Idol
The Fatal Night
The Flamingo Affair
Good-Time Girl
A Gunman Has Escaped
House of Darkness
London Belongs to Me
The Mark of Cain
Mr. Perrin and Mr. Traill
My Brother's Keeper
Night Beat
No Orchids for Miss Blandish
No Room at the Inn
The Noose
Oliver Twist
Portrait from Life
Saraband for Dead Lovers
The Small Voice
Snowbound
So Evil My Love
This Was a Woman
Three Weird Sisters
Uneasy Terms

1949

Boys in Brown
Dark Secret
For Them That Trespass
Forbidden
Give Us This Day
The Interrupted Journey
Man on the Run
No Way Back
Now Barabbas
Obsession
Queen of Spades
The Rocking Horse Winner
Silent Dust
The Small Back Room
The Spider and the Fly
The Third Man
Vengeance Is Mine

1950

Blackout
The Blue Lamp
Cage of Gold
The Clouded Yellow
Double Confession
Golden Salamander
Guilt Is My Shadow
Madeleine
Man in Black
Midnight Episode
Murder Without Crime

Night and the City
No Trace
Once a Sinner
Room to Let
Seven Days to Noon
So Long at the Fair
Stage Fright
Waterfront
The Woman in Question
The Woman with No Name

1951

Another Man's Poison
Assassin for Hire
Black Widow
Blackmailed
Calling Bulldog Drummond
Circle of Danger
Cloudburst
The Dark Man
The Late Edwina Black
I'll Get You for This
The Long Dark Hall
Mr. Denning Drives North
Night Was Our Friend
Night Without Stars
Outcast of the Islands
Pool of London
The Quiet Woman
The Six Men
There Is Another Sun

1952

13 East Street
Cosh Boy
Crow Hollow
Escape Route
The Gambler and the Lady
The Gentle Gunman
Home at Seven
Hunted
I Believe in You
The Last Page
The Lost Hours
The Man Who Watched the
   Trains Go By
Secret People
Stolen Face
Wide Boy
Wings of Danger

1953

Black 13
Black Orchid

The Blue Parrot
Deadly Nightshade
Desperate Moment
The Flanagan Boy
The Heart of the Matter
The Intruder
The Large Rope
The Limping Man
The Long Memory
The Man Between
Mantrap
Marilyn
Murder at 3 A.M.
Operation Diplomat
Personal Affair
Recoil
Rough Shoot
Street Corner
Street of Shadows
The Square Ring
3 Steps to the Gallows
Turn the Key Softly
Wheel of Fate
Women of Twilight
The Yellow Balloon

1954

Bang! You're Dead
Beautiful Stranger
Delayed Action
Eight O'clock Walk
The Embezzler
Escape by Night
Face the Music
Five Days
The Good Die Young
The Green Scarf
The House Across the Lake
An Inspector Calls
The Passing Stranger
Radio Cab Murder
The Sleeping Tiger
The Stranger Came Home
The Stranger's Hand
Thirty-Six Hours
The Weak and the Wicked

1955

The Brain Machine
Cast a Dark Shadow
Confession
Dial 999
Footsteps in the Fog
Impulse
Joe MacBeth

Appendix B

The Little Red Monkey
Murder by Proxy
One Way Out
The Ship that Died of Shame
They Can't Hang Me
Third Party Risk
Tiger by the Tail

1956

Alias John Preston
The Intimate Stranger
The Narrowing Circle
1984
Port of Escape
Soho Incident
Tiger in the Smoke
The Weapon
Wicked as They Come
Women Without Men
Yield to the Night

1957

Across the Bridge
The Big Chance
Cat Girl
The Depraved
The End of the Line
The Flesh Is Weak
The Flying Scot
Fortune Is a Woman
Hell Drivers
The House in the Woods
The Hypnotist
Kill Her Gently
Kill Me Tomorrow
Lady of Vengeance
The Long Haul
Night of the Demon
No Road Back
The Secret Place
Three Sundays to Live
Time Without Pity
The Vicious Circle

1958

The Bank Raiders
Chase a Crooked Shadow
Floods of Fear
The Key
The Man Upstairs
The Man Who Wouldn't Talk
Nowhere to Go
The Snorkel

Stormy Crossing
Three Crooked Men
Tread Softly Stranger
Violent Playground

1959

Beyond This Place
Blind Date
In the Wake of a Stranger
Naked Fury
No Trees in the Street
Passport to Shame
Room at the Top
The Rough and the Smooth
Sapphire
Serious Charge
Shake Hands with the Devil
Tiger Bay
Whirlpool
Witness in the Dark

1960

Beat Girl
The Challenge
Circle of Deception
Crossroads to Crime
The Criminal
Faces in the Dark
Hell Is A City
The Malpas Mystery
The Man who Was Nobody
Marriage of Convenience
Never Let Go
Peeping Tom
Piccadilly Third Stop
The Shakedown
Urge to Kill

1961

All Night Long
The Breaking Point
The Clue of the New Pin
The Frightened City
Information Received
Johnny Nobody
Jungle Street
Man Detained
The Man in the Back Seat
Offbeat
Payroll
Pit of Darkness
Rag Doll
Victim

1962

Candidate for Murder
The Damned
Don't Talk to Strange Men
Jigsaw
Locker Sixty-Nine
The Painted Smile
Playback
A Prize of Arms
The Share-Out
Solo for Sparrow
Strongroom
Time to Remember

1963

The £20,000 Kiss
Bitter Harvest
Blind Corner
Cairo
Calculated Risk
Five to One
The Girl Hunters
Impact
Incident at Midnight
The Informers
Nightmare
On the Run
Panic
Paranoiac
A Place to Go
Psyche 59
Return to Sender
Ricochet
The Rivals
The Set-Up
The Small World of Sammy Lee
To Have and to Hold
West 11

1964

Act of Murder
Do You Know This Voice?
Downfall
Face of a Stranger
Hysteria
Never Mention Murder
Seance on a Wet Afternoon
The Third Secret
The Verdict
We Shall See

Appendix C. British Films Noirs Listed by Director

Marc Allégret
Blackmailed
Blanche Fury

Lewis Allen
So Evil My Love
Whirlpool

Gerry Anderson
Crossroads to Crime

Michael Anderson
1984
Chase a Crooked Shadow
Night Was Our Friend
Shake Hands with the Devil
Waterfront

Ken Annakin
Across the Bridge
Double Confession
The Informers

Leslie Arliss
The Man in Grey
The Night Has Eyes

John Arnold
The Passing Stranger

Anthony Asquith
Cottage to Let
Fanny by Gaslight
The Woman in Question
Uncensored

Robert S. Baker
13 East Street
Blackout

Roy Ward Baker
The October Man
Tiger in the Smoke

Burt Balaban
Lady of Vengeance

John Baxter
Love on the Dole

Reginald Beck
The Long Dark Hall

Compton Bennett
Daybreak
Desperate Moment
The Flying Scot
The Seventh Veil

Thomas Bentley
Three Silent Men

Daniel Birt
No Room at the Inn
The Interrupted Journey
Third Party Risk
Three Weird Sisters

John Boulting
Brighton Rock

Roy Boulting
Seven Days to Noon
Trunk Crime

John Nelson Burton
Never Mention Murder

Muriel Box
Street Corner

Alan Bridges
Act of Murder

Anthony Bushell
The Long Dark Hall

Jack Cardiff
Beyond This Place

John Paddy Carstairs
Dancing with Crime

(Alberto) Cavalcanti
Dead of Night
For Them That Trespass
Nicholas Nickleby
They Made Me a Fugitive

Don Chaffey
The Flesh Is Weak
The Man Upstairs

Jack Clayton
Room at the Top

St. John L. Clowes
No Orchids for Miss Blandish

Lance Comfort
Bang! You're Dead
Bedelia
Blind Corner
Daughter of Darkness
Eight O'clock Walk
Escape to Danger
Great Day
Hatter's Castle
Hotel Reserve
Pit of Darkness
Rag Doll
Silent Dust

233

Appendix C

Squadron Leader X
Temptation Harbour
The Breaking Point
The Painted Smile

Arthur Crabtree
Dear Murderer
Madonna of the Seven Moons

Charles Crichton
Dead of Night
Floods of Fear
Hunted
The Third Secret

Alan Cullimore
Vengeance Is Mine

Antony Darnborough
So Long at the Fair

Jules Dassin
Night and the City

Alan Davis
The Clue of the New Pin

Basin Dean
21 Days

Basil Dearden
A Place to Go
All Night Long
Cage of Gold
Dead of Night
Frieda
I Believe in You
Pool of London
Sapphire
Saraband for Dead Lovers
The Blue Lamp
The Gentle Gunman
The Ship that Died of Shame
The Square Ring
Victim
Violent Playground

Jeffrey Dell
The Dark Man

Thorold Dickinson
Gaslight
Queen of Spades
Secret People

Paul Dickson
The Depraved

Edward Dmytryk
Give Us This Day

Obsession
So Well Remembered

Clive Donner
Marriage of Convenience
The Secret Place

David Eady
Faces in the Dark
In the Wake of a Stranger
The Verdict

Maurice Elvey
The Late Edwina Black

Cy Endfield
Hell Drivers
The Limping Man
Impulse

Terence Fisher
Face the Music
Kill Me Tomorrow
Mantrap
Murder by Proxy
Portrait from Life
So Long at the Fair
Stolen Face
The Last Page
The Stranger Came Home
Wings of Danger

Gordon Flemying
Five to One
Solo for Sparrow

Bryan Forbes
Seance on a Wet Afternoon

Freddie Francis
Hysteria
Nightmare
Paranoiac

Charles Frank
Uncle Silas

Harold French
Dead Men Are Dangerous
The Man Who Watched the Trains Go By

Seymour Friedman
Escape Route

Lewis Gilbert
Cast a Dark Shadow
Cosh Boy

Once a Sinner
The Good Die Young
There Is Another Sun

Sidney Gilliat
Fortune Is a Woman
Green for Danger
London Belongs to Me
Waterloo Road

John Gilling
3 Steps to the Gallows
Deadly Nightshade
Escape by Night
No Trace
Panic
Recoil
The Challenge
The Embezzler
The Quiet Woman
Tiger by the Tail

Gerard Glaister
The Set-Up
The Share-Out

Godfrey Grayson
Room to Let

Guy Green
The Snorkel

Mutz Greenbaum
Escape to Danger
Hotel Reserve

Edmond T. Greville
Beat Girl
The Noose

Richard Grey
A Gunman Has Escaped

Val Guest
Hell Is A City
Jigsaw
The Weapon
They Can't Hang Me

John Guillermin
Never Let Go
Operation Diplomat

Gordon Hales
Return to Sender

Robert Hamer
Dead of Night
It Always Rains on Sunday

British Films Noirs by Director

Pink String and Sealing Wax
The Long Memory
The Spider and the Fly

Guy Hamilton
An Inspector Calls
The Intruder

Victor Hanbury
Hotel Reserve

John Harlow
Appointment with Crime
Delayed Action
Spellbound
The Blue Parrot
The Dark Tower
While I Live

Norman Harrison
Calculated Risk
Incident at Midnight
Locker Sixty-Nine

Frank Harvey
Seven Days to Noon

Sidney Hayers
The Malpas Mystery
Payroll

Stanley Haynes
Carnival

Alfred Hitchcock
Stage Fright

Seth Holt
Nowhere to Go

Ken Hughes
Black 13
Confession
Joe MacBeth
The Brain Machine
The House Across the Lake
The Little Red Monkey
The Long Haul
The Small World of Sammy Lee
Wicked as They Come
Wide Boy

Lawrence Huntington
Man on the Run
Mr. Perrin and Mr. Traill
Night Boat to Dublin
The Upturned Glass
Tower of Terror
Wanted for Murder

Brian Desmond Hurst
On the Night of the Fire
The Mark of Cain

Harold Huth
East of Piccadilly
Night Beat

Pat Jackson
Don't Talk to Strange Men

Charles Jarrott
Time to Remember

Patrick Jenkins
The Gambler and the Lady

Roy Kellino
Guilt Is My Shadow
I Met a Murderer

Anthony Kimmins
Mine Own Executioner

Anthony Kimmins
Mr. Denning Drives North

George King
Case of the Frightened Lady
Crimes at the Dark House
Forbidden
The Face at the Window
The Shop at Sly Corner

Bernard Knowles
Jassy
The Man Within

Frank Launder
I See a Dark Stranger

Michael Law
The Six Men

Quentin Lawrence
Playback
We Shall See

Reginald Le Borg
The Flanagan Boy

David Lean
Great Expectations
Madeleine
Oliver Twist

Jack Lee
Circle of Deception
Turn the Key Softly

Norman Lee
Murder in Soho
The Door with Seven Locks

John Lemont
The Frightened City
The Shakedown

Joseph Losey
Blind Date
The Criminal
The Damned
The Intimate Stranger
The Sleeping Tiger
Time Without Pity

Arthur Lubin
Footsteps in the Fog

Robert Lynn
Information Received

David MacDonald
Alias John Preston
Good-Time Girl
Snowbound
The Brothers
The Lost Hours

Joseph L. Mankiewicz
Escape

Herbert Mason
A Window in London

Peter Maxwell
Impact

Michael McCarthy
Assassin for Hire
Crow Hollow

Fergus McDonell
The Small Voice

William Cameron Menzies
The Green Cockatoo

David Miller
Beautiful Stranger

Oswald Mitchell
Black Memory
House of Darkness

Ernest Morris
Three Crooked Men
Three Sundays to Live

John Moxey
Downfall

Appendix C

Face of a Stranger
Ricochet
The £20,000 Kiss

Maxwell Munden
The Bank Raiders
The House in the Woods

Ronald Neame
Golden Salamander
Take My Life

Frank Nesbitt
Do You Know This Voice?

Sam Newfield
The Gambler and the Lady

Joseph M. Newman
I'll Get You for This

George More O'Ferrall
The Green Scarf
The Heart of the Matter
The Woman with No Name

Stefan Osiecki
No Way Back

Cliff Owen
A Prize of Arms
Offbeat

Robert Parrish
Rough Shoot

Gordon Parry
Midnight Episode
Now Barabbas
Tread Softly Stranger
Women of Twilight

Nigel Patrick
Johnny Nobody

Anthony Pélissier
Night Without Stars

Anthony Pélissier
Personal Affair

Anthony Pélissier
The Rocking Horse Winner

Michael Powell
Black Narcissus
Contraband
Peeping Tom
The Small Back Room
The Spy in Black

Emeric Pressburger
Black Narcissus
The Small Back Room

Alvin Rakoff
Passport to Shame

Irving Rapper
Another Man's Poison

Carol Reed
Odd Man Out
Outcast of the Islands
The Fallen Idol
The Key
The Man Between
The Third Man

Michael Relph
I Believe in You

C. Pennington Richards
Stormy Crossing

Ralph Richardson
Home at Seven

Wolf Rilla
Cairo
Marilyn
Piccadilly Third Stop
The Large Rope
Witness in the Dark

Maclean Rogers
Dark Secret

Alfred Roome
My Brother's Keeper

Roy Rowland
The Girl Hunters

Charles Saunders
Black Orchid

Charles Saunders
Jungle Street
Kill Her Gently
Naked Fury
The End of the Line
The Narrowing Circle

Victor Saville
Calling Bulldog Drummond

Peter Graham Scott
Bitter Harvest
The Big Chance

Francis Searle
Cloudburst
Man in Black
Murder at 3 A.M.
One Way Out
Wheel of Fate

Vernon Sewell
Black Widow
Latin Quarter
Radio Cab Murder
Soho Incident
Strongroom
The Man in the Back Seat
Uneasy Terms
Urge to Kill

Alfred Shaughnessy
Cat Girl

Horace Shepherd
The Flamingo Affair

Alexander Singer
Psyche 59

Robert Siodmak
The Rough and the Smooth

Mario Soldati
The Stranger's Hand

Paul L. Stein
Counterblast
Poison Pen
Black Limelight

Walter Summers
The Dark Eyes of London
Traitor Spy

Ralph Thomas
The Clouded Yellow

Gerald Thomas
The Vicious Circle

J. Lee Thompson
Murder Without Crime
No Trees in the Street
The Weak and the Wicked
The Yellow Balloon
Tiger Bay
Yield to the Night

Jacques Tourneur
Circle of Danger
Night of the Demon

Alfred Travers
Dual Alibi

Robert Tronson
Man Detained
On the Run

Montgomery Tully
Murder in Reverse
Boys in Brown
Dial 999
Five Days
The Man Who Was Nobody
No Road Back
The Hypnotist
Thirty-Six Hours

Ladislas Vajda
The Woman with No Name

Max Varnel
The Rivals

Richard Vernon
Street of Shadows

David Villiers
Candidate for Murder

Tim Whelan
This Was a Woman

Herbert Wilcox
The Man Who Wouldn't Talk
Yellow Canary

Herbert Wise
To Have and to Hold

Elmo Williams
Women Without Men

Michael Winner
West 11

Arthur Woods
They Drive by Night

Terence Young
Corridor of Mirrors
Serious Charge

Tony Young
Port of Escape

Mario Zampi
The Fatal Night

Appendix D. British Films Noirs Listed by Cinematographer

Josef Ambor
The Brain Machine
The Little Red Monkey
Wide Boy

Jack Asher
Cast a Dark Shadow
Cosh Boy
Passport to Shame
Portrait from Life
The Good Die Young
The Snorkel
Women of Twilight

Lionel Banes
No Road Back

Paul Beeson
Nowhere to Go

Monty Berman
13 East Street
3 Steps to the Gallows
Blackout
Deadly Nightshade
Escape by Night
No Trace
Recoil
The Lost Hours
The Quiet Woman

Cyril Bristol
Boys in Brown
House of Darkness

Hal Britten
This Was a Woman

Bernard Browne
The Spy in Black

Alex Bryce
The Door with Seven Locks

Jack Cardiff
Black Narcissus

Edwin Catford
The House in the Woods

Christopher Challis
Blind Date
Floods of Fear
Footsteps in the Fog
Never Let Go
The Small Back Room

Wilkie Cooper
Beyond This Place
Green for Danger
I See a Dark Stranger
London Belongs to Me
Man on the Run
Mine Own Executioner
Silent Dust
Stage Fright
The Long Dark Hall
There Is Another Sun
Trunk Crime

Jack Cox
Alias John Preston
Cottage to Let
Madonna of the Seven Moons

Arthur Crabtree
Fanny by Gaslight
The Man in Grey
Uncensored
Waterloo Road

Eric Cross
Black Orchid
Escape Route
Hunted
In the Wake of a Stranger
The Dark Man
Tiger Bay
Tiger by the Tail

Stephen Dade
Dear Murderer
Don't Talk to Strange Men
Good-Time Girl
Snowbound
The Brothers
The Flesh Is Weak
The Late Edwina Black

Desmond Dickinson
Cairo
The Frightened City
The Man Between
The Rocking Horse Winner
The Woman in Question

Gordon Dines
Circle of Deception
Frieda
I Believe in You
Nicholas Nickleby
Pool of London
Secret People
The Blue Lamp
The Challenge
The Gentle Gunman
The Man Who Wouldn't Talk
The Ship that Died of Shame

Basil Emmott
Blind Corner
Joe MacBeth

British Films by Cinematographer

Pit of Darkness
Rag Doll
Soho Incident
Strongroom
The Breaking Point
The Long Haul
The Painted Smile
They Drive by Night
Wicked as They Come

Geoffrey Faithfull
Kill Me Tomorrow
Marilyn
Offbeat
Panic
Radio Cab Murder
Stormy Crossing
The Large Rope
Three Silent Men

Frederick Ford
The Flamingo Affair

Freddie Francis
Room at the Top
Time Without Pity

Claude Friese-Greene
Black Limelight
East of Piccadilly
Murder in Soho

Gerald Gibbs
Black 13
Delayed Action
Fortune Is a Woman
The Man Upstairs
Night Was Our Friend
No Orchids for Miss Blandish
Operation Diplomat
A Prize of Arms
The Intimate Stranger

Hone Glendining
Crimes at the Dark House
Midnight Episode
The Face at the Window
The Noose
The Shop at Sly Corner
Case of the Frightened Lady
Forbidden

Arthur Grant
Hell Is A City
Jigsaw
Paranoiac
The Damned

Cyril Gray
The Bank Raiders
The House in the Woods

Guy Green
Blanche Fury
Carnival
Great Expectations
Madeleine
Night Without Stars
Oliver Twist
Take My Life

Mutz Greenbaum
Hatter's Castle
Night and the City
So Evil My Love
Squadron Leader X
The Green Cockatoo
Wanted for Murder
Yellow Canary

Philip Grindrod
Confession
Dial 999
Street of Shadows
The Hypnotist
Port of Escape

Henry Hall
The Bank Raiders

Walter J. Harvey
Black Widow
Cloudburst
Dark Secret
Face the Music
Five Days
Jungle Street
Kill Her Gently
Murder by Proxy
Naked Fury
One Way Out
Spellbound
Stolen Face
The Big Chance
The End of the Line
The Flanagan Boy
The Gambler and the Lady
The House Across the Lake
The Last Page
The Stranger Came Home
Third Party Risk
Thirty-Six Hours
Tower of Terror
Wings of Danger
Women Without Men

Otto Heller
I'll Get You for This
Night Boat to Dublin
Now Barabbas
Peeping Tom
Queen of Spades
Temptation Harbour
The Dark Tower
The Man Who Watched the Trains Go By
The Rough and the Smooth
The Square Ring
The Vicious Circle
They Made Me a Fugitive
Victim
West 11
The Woman with No Name

Peter Hennessy
Cat Girl
The Flying Scot

Jack Hildyard
The Green Scarf
The Heart of the Matter
Home at Seven

Erwin Hillier
Chase a Crooked Shadow
Great Day
Mr. Perrin and Mr. Traill
Shake Hands with the Devil
The Interrupted Journey
The Mark of Cain
The October Man

Ken Hodges
Faces in the Dark

Jonah Jones
The Embezzler
Impulse
The Limping Man
The Narrowing Circle

Roy Kellino
I Met a Murderer

Bernard Knowles
Gaslight

Günther Krampf
Latin Quarter
The Night Has Eyes
This Was a Woman

Robert Krasker
Another Man's Poison
Odd Man Out

Appendix D

The Criminal
The Third Man
Uncle Silas

Gordon Lang
Boys in Brown
My Brother's Keeper

Bryan Langley
The Dark Eyes of London

Robert LaPresle
Assassin for Hire
Crow Hollow
Traitor Spy

Walter Lassally
Beat Girl
Psyche 59
The Passing Stranger

Arthur Lavis
Do You Know This Voice?

Bert Mason
Candidate for Murder
The Clue of the New Pin
Locker Sixty-Nine
Man Detained
Playback
The Set-Up
The Share-Out
Solo for Sparrow
Time to Remember

Gerald Massie-Collier
The Man Upstairs

William McLeod
Calculated Risk
Guilt Is My Shadow
Murder Without Crime

Glen McWilliams
A Window in London

Ted Moore
Johnny Nobody

Oswald Morris
Circle of Danger
The Key

Gerald Moss
Impact

Robert Navarro
No Way Back
The Blue Parrot

Frank North
Once a Sinner

S.D. Onions
Black Memory
Murder at 3 a.m.
The Six Men

Bill Oxley
Vengeance Is Mine

Ernest Palmer
The Door with Seven Locks
Murder in Reverse
The Three Weird Sisters
Uneasy Terms

Stanley Pavey
Daughter of Darkness
Dead of Night
Pink String and Sealing Wax
Rough Shoot
The Small Voice
They Can't Hang Me

C.M. Pennington-Richards
1984
Desperate Moment
Give Us This Day
Obsession

Georges Périnal
Serious Charge
The Fallen Idol

John Read
Crossroads to Crime

Michael Reed
The Malpas Mystery

Brian Rhodes
The Man Who Was Nobody
Marriage of Convenience

Nicolas Roeg
Information Received

Edward Scaife
All Night Long
An Inspector Calls
Beautiful Stranger
Night of the Demon
Home at Seven
The Intruder
Outcast of the Islands

Enzo Serafin
The Stranger's Hand

Douglas Slocombe
Cage of Gold
Dead of Night
It Always Rains on Sunday
Saraband for Dead Lovers
The Third Secret
Tread Softly Stranger

Brendan J. Stafford
Bang! You're Dead
Eight O'clock Walk
The Shakedown
Witness in the Dark

Jan Stallick
21 Days

Ernest Steward
Bitter Harvest
Payroll
Piccadilly Third Stop
The Secret Place

George Stretton
Blackmailed

Ian Struthers
Lady of Vengeance

Wolfgang Suschitzky
The Small World of Sammy Lee

Ken Talbot
The Girl Hunters

Philip Tannura
Poison Pen

Gilbert Taylor
No Trees in the Street
A Prize of Arms
Seven Days to Noon
The Weak and the Wicked
The Yellow Balloon
Yield to the Night

André Thomas
Corridor of Mirrors

Gerry Turpin
Seance on a Wet Afternoon

Geoffrey Unsworth
Double Confession
Hell Drivers
Jassy
The Clouded Yellow
The Man Within

The Spider and the Fly
Tiger in the Smoke
Turn the Key Softly
Whirlpool

Václav Vích
Night Beat
On the Night of the Fire

James Watson
Dual Alibi

Harry Waxman
Brighton Rock
Sapphire
The Long Memory
The Sleeping Tiger
Waterfront

John Wilcox
Hysteria
Mr. Denning Drives North
Nightmare
Outcast of the Islands

John Wiles
Urge to Kill

Cedric Williams
A Gunman Has Escaped

Cedric Williams
Man in Black
Room to Let
The Fatal Night

Derick Williams
For Them That Trespass

James Wilson
Act of Murder
Appointment with Crime
Counterblast
The Depraved
Downfall
Face of a Stranger
Five to One
Incident at Midnight
Love on the Dole
Never Mention Murder
No Room at the Inn
On the Run
Three Crooked Men
To Have and to Hold
Return to Sender
Ricochet
The Rivals
Three Sundays to Live
The £20,000 Kiss
Vengeance Is Mine

The Verdict
We Shall See

Reginald H. Wyer
A Place to Go
Across the Bridge
Dancing with Crime
Daybreak
Mantrap
Personal Affair
So Long at the Fair
Street Corner
The Informers
The Man in the Back Seat
The Seventh Veil
The Upturned Glass
The Weapon
Violent Playground
Wheel of Fate

Frederick A. Young
Bedelia
Calling Bulldog Drummond
Contraband
Escape
So Well Remembered
While I Live

Appendix E. Edgar Wallace Mystery Theatre

Between 1960 and 1965 producer Jack Greenwood and Merton Park Productions (a.k.a. Merton Park and Merton Park Studios) made forty-six* films that eventually found their way to British and American television screens as an anthology of crime films entitled, *Edgar Wallace Mystery Theatre*. Most of these short (approximately one hour in length), low-budget films, were based on the crime stories of popular British mystery writer Edgar Wallace and were shot in and around Merton Park. Of the series' forty-seven films, I have identified at least twenty-six that I consider to be films noirs or at the very least marginal noirs (see first list below). The remaining twenty-one films, in my opinion, have little of the noir style or narrative.

"Edgar Wallace Mystery Theatre" Films
Noirs and/or Marginal Noirs

Act of Murder	1964
Candidate for Murder	1962
The Clue of the New Pin	1961
Downfall	1964
Face of a Stranger	1964
Five to One	1963
Incident at Midnight	1963
Locker Sixty-Nine	1962
The Malpas Mystery	1960
Man Detained	1961
The Man Who Was Nobody	1960
Marriage of Convenience	1960
Never Mention Murder	1964
On the Run	1963
Playback	1962
Return to Sender	1963
Ricochet	1963
The Rivals	1963
The Set-Up	1963
The Share-Out	1962
Solo for Sparrow	1962
The £20,000 Kiss	1963
Time to Remember	1962
To Have and to Hold	1963
The Verdict	1964
We Shall See	1964

"Edgar Wallace Mystery Theatre"
Non-Films Noirs

Accidental Death	1963
Attempt to Kill	1961
Backfire!	1961
Change Partners	1965
The Clue of the Silver Key	1961
The Clue of the Twisted Candle	1960
Dead Man's Chest	1965
Death Trap	1962
The Double	1963
Flat Two	1962
The Fourth Square	1961
Game for Three Losers	1965
The Main Chance	1964
Man at the Carlton Tower	1961
Never Back Losers	1961
Number Six	1962
The Partner	1963
Partners in Crime	1961
Strangler's Web	1965
The Sinister Man	1961
Who Was Maddox?	1964

*There were actually forty-seven films in the series, with one (*The Malpas Mystery*) being produced by Julian Wintle and Leslie Parkyn for Independent Artists-Langton.

Bibliography

While not all of these sources concern British films noirs (some do not even mention the term), they all proved to be valuable resources to the author of this book.

Borde, Raymond, and Etienne Chaumeton. *A Panorama of American Film Noir, 1941–1953*. Translated from the French by Paul Hammond. San Francisco: City Lights Books, 2002.
Chibnall, Steve, and Robert Murphy. *British Crime Cinema*. Oxon, England: Routledge, 1999.
Cross, Robin. *The Big Book of British Films*. Devon, England: Charles Herridge: 1984.
Crowther, Bruce. *Film Noir: Reflections in a dark mirror*. New York: Continuum, 1988.
Duncan, Paul. *Film Noir: Films of Trust and Betrayal*. Harpenden, England: Pocket Essentials, 2000.
Durgnat, Raymond. "Some Lines of Inquiry into Post-war British Crimes." In *The British Cinema Book*, Robert Murphy, ed. London: British Film Institute, 2001.
Everson, William K. "British Film Noir." In *Films in Review*, May 1987, and June/July 1987.
Falk, Quentin. *The Golden Gong: Fifty Years of the Rank Organisation, Its Films and Its Stars*. London: Columbus Books, 1987.
Gifford, Denis. *The British Film Catalogue: 1895–1985*. London: Facts on File, 1986.
Hardy, Phil, ed. *The BFI Companion to Crime*. Berkeley and Los Angeles: University of California Press, 1997.
Hare, William. *Early Film Noir: Greed, Lust and Murder Hollywood Style*. Jefferson, North Carolina: McFarland, 2003.
Keaney, Michael F. *Film Noir Guide: 745 Films of the Classic Era, 1940–1959*. Jefferson, North Carolina: McFarland, 2003.
Lyons, Arthur. *Death on the Cheap: The Lost B Movies of Film Noir!* New York: Da Capo Press, 2000.
McFarlane, Brian. *The Encyclopedia of British Film*. London: Methuen, 2003.
Miller, Laurence. "Evidence for a British Film Noir Cycle." In *Re-Viewing British Cinema, 1900–1992*, Wheeler Winston Dixon, ed. Albany: State University of New York Press, 1994.
Murphy, Robert. *Realism and Tinsel: Cinema and Society in Britain 1939–49*. London: Routledge, 1989.
_____. "Dark Shadows Around Pinewood and Ealing." *Film International*, vol., 2, no. 7 2004:1.
_____. "British film noir." In *European Film Noir*, Andrew Spicer, ed. Manchester, UK: Manchester University Press, 2007.
Pettigrew, Terence. *British Film Character Actors: Great Names and Memorable Moments*. Devon, England: David & Charles, 1982.
Selby, Spencer. *Dark City: The Film Noir*. Jefferson, North Carolina: McFarland, 1984.
Silver, Alain, and Elizabeth Ward, eds. *Film Noir: An Encyclopedic Reference to the American Style*. Woodstock, N.Y.: Overlook Press, 1979; 3rd ed., 1992.
Slide, Anthony. *"Banned in the USA": British Films in the United States and Their Censorship, 1933–1960*. London: I.B. Tauris, 1998.
Spicer, Andrew. *Film Noir*. Essex, England: Pearson Education, 2002.
Williams, Tony. "British Film Noir." In *Film Noir Reader 2*, Alain Silver and James Ursini, eds. New York: Limelight Edition (Proscenium), 1999.
_____. "The British Gangster Film." In *Gangster Film Reader*, Alain Silver and James Ursini, eds. Pompton Plains, New Jersey, 2007.

Index

Numbers in ***bold italics*** indicate pages with photographs.

Abney, William 119
Academy Award ("Oscar") 18, 35, 79, 127, 140, 167, 171, 175, 198, 208
Accidental Death 242
Achilles, Peter 9
Ackland, Rodney 81, 162, 193, 209, 214
Across the Bridge 7, 227, 232, 233, 241
A.C.T. Films 23, ***118***, 118, 134
Act of Murder ***8***, 8–9, 227, 232, 233, 241, 242
Adair, Robert 57, 194–95
Adam, Noëlle 12–13
Adam, Ronald 104, 174
Adams, Jill 147
Addams, Dawn 209
Adés, Vivian 53
Adrian, Max 158
The Adventuress see *I See a Dark Stranger*
Aimée, Anouk 74–75, 120
Ainsworth, John 126
The Alamo 163
Albiin, Elsy 199–200
Alderdale Films Limited 207
Aldrich, Robert 137
Alexander, Patrick 152
Alexandra Film Studios 32
Alias John Preston 2, 9, 228, 232, 235, 238
Alison, Dorothy 118–19
"All in the Family" (TV series) 201
All Night Long 9–10, 227, 232, 234, 240
Allan, Elizabeth 24, 82
Allégret, Marc 19, 20–21
Allegro Films 139
Allen, Jack 24
Allen, Lewis 183, 218
Allen, Patrick 37, 109–10, 207
Alliance Film Studios 44, 45–46, 137, 184, ***196***, 196
Allied Film Makers 171
alter 27, 74, 92
Alva Films 173
The Amazing Mr. X 186
Ambler, Dail 12
Ambler, Eric 142, 168
Ambor, Jo see Ambor, Josef
Ambor, Josef (Jo Ambor) 24, 107, 219

Anatole de Grunwald Productions 140
Anderson, Gene 109–10, 176
Anderson, Gerry 42
Anderson, Michael 33, 134, 136, 175, 214
Anderson, Rona 19, 108, 185
Andrews, Dana 133–34
Andrews, David 156
Andrews, Harry 35, 95
Angel Street see *Gaslight*
Anglofilm 60
Anglo-Guild Productions 37, 96
Annakin, Ken 7, 53, 95
Another Man's Poison 10, 227, 231, 236, 239
A.P. Films 42
Apollo Films 38
Appointment with Crime 10–11, 228, 230, 235, 241
Aqua Film Productions ***83***, 83
Archard, Bernard 36–37, 58, 115
Archdale, Alexander 87
Archers Film Productions 17, 180
Arden, Jane 17, 81
Arden, Robert 49, 185
Argyle, J.F. *see* Argyle, John
Argyle, John (J.F. Argyle) 44, 207
Arliss, Leslie 116, 133
Armstrong, Bridget 216
Armstrong, Leslie 60
Arnold, Grace 87, ***88***
Arnold, John 151
Around the World in 80 Days 33
Artna Films 169
Asher, Jack 30, 39, 75, 152, 159, 182, 223
Ashley, Eve 196–97
Ashley, June 23, 129
Aslan, Grégoire 41, 100
Asphalt Jungle 27, 155
Asquith, Anthony 39, 60, 209, 222
Assassin for Hire 11, 227, 231, 235, 240
Associated British Picture Corporation 16, 25, 54, 67, 81, 117, 127, 133, 139, ***157***, 157, 162, 193, ***194***, 206
Associated Dragon Films 33, ***34***
Atkinson, Michael 17
Attempt to Kill 242
Attenborough, Richard 9, 23, 25–

26, 43–44, 54–55, 109, 118–19, 121, 171, ***177***, 177–78, 198–99
Audley, Maxine 84, 130, 153, 164
Ault, Marie 202
"The Avengers" (TV series) 61
Aylmer, Felix 30, 186
Ayres, Robert 19, 31–32, 39, 49, 199

B & A Productions ***80***, 81
Bachmann, Lawrence P. 218
Backfire! 242
Bad Blonde 205; see also *The Flanagan Boy*
Baddeley, Hermione 25–26, 39, 95, 137–38, 163, 166–67, 194, 222
Badel, Alan 16
BAFTA (British Academy of Film and Television Arts) 103, 162, 166–67, 170, 171, 198, 204, 206
Bailey, John 117
Baines, John 47, 56
Baird, Anthony 47
Baird, Harry 169–70
Bait 122
Baker, George ***177***, 177, 207
Baker, Jane 149
Baker, Mark 65
Baker, Pip 149
Baker, Robert S. 20, 142, 199
Baker, Roy (Ward) 205
Baker, Stanley 13, 21–22, 36, 41–42, 75, 83, 83–84, 84, 160, 213–14
Balaban, Burt 104
Balchin, Nigel 35, 123–24
Balcon, Jill 76–77, 131
Balfour, Michael 20, 155, 162, 181, 199
Banes, Lionel 137
Bang! You're Dead 11–12, 228, 231, 233, 240
The Bank Raiders 2, 12, 228, 232, 236, 239
Banks, Leslie 39, 52–53, 112, 208–9
Banned in the USA (book) 243
Bannen, Ian 160–61
Banner Films 107
Banner Pictures 56
Barnabe, Bruno 155
Barnes, Barry K. 13–14, 43–44
Barnes, Peter 144
Barnum, P.T. 54

245

Index

Barr, Patrick 19, 24, 30, 56, 104, 146, 211
Barrett, Ray 205, 206
Barrett, Sean 11
Barrie, John 212
Bartley, Penelope 15
Barton, Margaret 193
Barzman, Ben 21, 73, 205
Basehart, Richard 75, 96–97, 190
Bass, Alfie 98, 137, 188
Bassani, Giorgio 190
Bate, Anthony **8**, 8, 173–74
Bateman, Andrew 81
Baxt, George 152
Baxter, Alan 55–56
Baxter, Anne 33, **34**
Baxter, John 112
Beaconsfield Films 212
Beat Girl 12–13, 228, 232, 234, 240
Beatty, Robert 10, 29, 40, 71, 159–60, 176, 188, 220–21
Beautiful Stranger 13, 229, 231, 235, 240
Beaver Films 171
Beck, Reginald 109
Bedelia 13–14, **14**, 228, 230, 233, 241
Beeby, Bruce 93, 163
Beeson, Paul 140
Bell, Tom 152, 160
Ben Hur 167
Bendix, William 101–2, 168
Bennett, Charles 133
Bennett, Compton 46, 49, 65, 174
Bennett, Jill 41
Bennett, John 32–33
Bennett, Richard Rodney 22
Benson, Martin 56, 63–64, 92–93, 164, 185
Bentley, John 18, 37, 50–51, 111
Bentley, Thomas 201
Bergerac, Jacques 13
Bergh, Eva 111
Bergman, Ingrid 71
Berkeley, Ballard 23, 93, 147–48
Berkeley, Martin 189
Berkman, Edward O. 79
Berlin Express 134
Berman, Monty 20, 48, 56, 111, 138, 162, 164, 199, 201
Bernauer, R. 81
Berry, Eric 56
Bettison, Ralph 136
Between Midnight and Dawn 112
Beyond a Reasonable Doubt 134
Beyond This Place 14–15, **15**, 228, 232, 233, 238
The BFI Companion to Crime (book) 243
The Big Chance 15–16, 228, 232, 236, 239
The Big Frame see *The Lost Hours*
The Big Punch 3
The Bikeldore 49–50
Billy Liar 166
Binder, Sybilla 40
Bird, Richard 52
Bird, Thora 191
Birt, Daniel 96, 137–38, 198, 202
Birt, Louise 202

Bitter Harvest 16, 228, 232, 236, 240
Black, Ian Stuart 107, 185
The Black Glove see *Face the Music*
Black Limelight 16–17, 228, 230, 236, 239
Black Memory 17, 229, 230, 235, 240
Black Narcissus 17–18, 227, 230, 236, 236, 238
Black Orchid 18, 228, 231, 236, 238
Black 13 19, 229, 231, 235, 239
Black Tide see *Stormy Crossing*
Black Widow 2, 19, 228, 231, 236, 239
Blackboard Jungle 214
Blackmailed 19, 229, 231, 233, 240
Blackman, Honor 45–46, 184
Blackout (1940) see *Contraband*
Blackout (1950) 19–20, 228, 231, 233, 238
Blackout (1955) see *Murder by Proxy*
Blair, Betsy 9
Blake, Grey 99
Blake, Katharine 11, 206
Blakeley's Films **149**, 149, 163
Blakely, Colin 95
Blanche Fury 2, 20–21, 227, 230, 233, 239
Blanshard, Joby 84
Blind Corner 2, 21, 228, 232, 233, 238
Blind Date 21–22, 228, 232, 235, 238
Blonde Bait see *Women Without Men*
Blonde for Danger see *The Flamingo Affair*
Blonde Sinner see *Yield to the Night*
Blood on the Moon 36
Bloom, Claire **115**, 115
The Blue Gardenia 33
The Blue Lamp 22–23, 227, 231, 234, 238
The Blue Parrot 23, 229, 231, 235, 240
Bluebeard 107
Blues in the Night 11
Boddey, Martin 58
Bodeen, De Witt 225
Body and Soul 3
Boehm, Carl 153
Bogarde, Dirk 19, 22–23, 30–31, **31**, 44, 49–50, **50**, 71–72, 88–89, 180, 184, 212–13, **213**, 217, 222
Bogart, Humphrey 196
Boland, Bridget 71
Bombsight Stolen see *Cottage to Let*
Bond, Derek 131, 162, 189, 209
Boomerang 134
Boone, Richard 163
Booth, Anthony 155–56
Borde, Raymond 243
Born to Dance 152
Borneman, Ernest 11, 58
Borsody, Hans 29
Both Sides of the Law see *Street Corner*
Bouchier, Chili 127
Boulter, Rosalyn 67
Boulting, John 25, 174

Boulting, Roy 174, 207
Box, Muriel 26, 46, 48, 121, 159, 174, 191
Box, Sydney 26, 46, 48, 121, 159, 174, 191
Boyd, Stephen 198–99
Boyer, Charles 71
Boys, Arthur 162
Boys in Brown 23–24, 228, 231, 237, 238, 240
Brackett, Leigh 190
Brady, Scott 201–2
The Brain Machine 24, 228, 231, 235, 238
Brambell, Wilfrid 181, 211
Bramble, A.V. 148
Brand, Christianna 122
Brando, Marlon 207
Brauns, Marianne 103
Bray, Robert 73
The Breaking Point 24–25, 228, 232, 234, 239
Breck, Kathleen 217
Brennan, Michael 20, 138, 199
Brent, George 105
Brent, Romney 145
Bride of Frankenstein 196
Bridges, Alan 8
Bridges, Lloyd 107, 198
Brierly, David 27
Brighton Rock 25–26, 227, 230, 233, 241
Bristow, Cyril 23, 87
British Aviation Pictures 54
British Board of Film Censors 5, 112, 152, 166, 224
British Cinema Book (book) 243
British Crime Cinema (book) 243
British Film Catalogue: 1895–1985 (book) 5, 243
British Film Characters: Great Names and Memorable Moments (book) 243
The British Film Institute 5
British Film Makers 49, **50**, 88
"British Film Noir" (essay) 2, 3, 243
British Lon Production Assets 85, 114, **115**, 125, 132
British National Films 10, 37, 40, 53, 71, 106, 112, 127, 137–38, 144, 148, 174, 180, 202, 210
Britten, Hal 201
Britton, Tony 168
Brook, Faith 33–34, 96, 210, 216
Brook, Lesley 87
Brook, Lyndon 147
Brook-Jones, Elwyn 146, 202
Brooke, Hillary 86–87
Brooke, Michael 172–73
Brooks, Victor 144
Brophy, John 214
The Brothers 26, 227, 230, 235, 238
The Brothers Rico 162
Brousse, Liliane 173
Brown, George H. 49
Brown, Pamela 154
Brown, Phil **141**, 141
Brown, Robert 104–5

Index

Brown, Walter 94, 108
Browne, Bernard 187
Browne, Coral 16–17
Browne, Irene 173
Brubeck, Dave 9
Bruce, Brenda 133, 135
Brute Force 41
Bruton Film Productions 42
Bryan, Dora 35, 138, 162, 191, 223–24
Bryce, Alex 52
Buchholz, Horst *203*, 203–4
Buchman, Harold (Derek Frye) 180
Bull, Peter 37–38, 170, 179
A Bullet for Johnny 57
Burbnaby, Anne 224
Burke, Alfred 209
Burke, Patricia 68, 218
Burnaby, Anne 215
Burrell, Richard 8
Burrell, Sheila 18, 35–36, 116, 150
Burton, John Nelson 130
Burton, Peter 185
Burton, Richard 136, 140, 214–15, 222
Bushell, Anthony 109
Bushey Studios 17
Busman's Honeymoon 4
Butcher's Film Service 24, 93, 155, 201
Butler, Gerald 60
Buxton, Sheila 176
Byrd, John 201
Byrne, Eddie 108, 147
Byrne, Paula 50–51, 58, 129
Byrne, Peter 104–5
Byron, Kathleen 17–18, 70, 180

Cabaret 208
Cabot, Bruce 207
Cadell, Jean 106
Cage of Gold 2, 26–27, 227, 231, 234, 240
Caged 77, 216
Cagney, James 175–76
Caine, Michael 152, 185
Cairney, John 123, 212
Cairo 27, *28*, 228, 232, 236, 238
Calculated Risk 27–29, 228, 232, 235, 240
Callahan, George 92
Callard, Kay 31, *32*, 65
Calleia, Joseph 139–40
Calling Bulldog Drummond 2, 29, 228, 231, 236, 241
Calvert, Phyllis 60, 112, 116, 125, 209, 222, **223**
Cameron, Earl 158, 169
Campbell, Beatrice 179
Campbell, Judy 54, 79–80
Campbell, Keith 182
Candidate for Murder 29, 228, 232, 237, 240, 242
Canning, Victor 74
Cannon, Esma 42, 98–99
Canon City 202
Cardiff, Jack 14, 17
Carey, Macdonald 43
Carey, Philip 219

Carillon Films 36
Carlson, Richard 184
Carmichael, Hoagy 75
Carney, George 112
Carney, James 93
Carnival 3, 29–30, 228, 230, 235, 239
Carol, John 98, 155, 186
Carpenter, Paul 58, 61, 89, 129, 137, 190, 210, 224
Carreras, Michael 190
Carroll, Leo G. 183
Carroll, Paul Vincent 123
Carroll, Ronnie 21
Carry On (film series) 128, 168
Carson, John 8, 173–74
Carstairs, John Paddy 44
Cartier, Rudolph 38
Cartland, Robert 81
Casablanca 1, 121
Case of the Frightened Lady 30, 228, 230, 235, 239
The Case of the Little Red Monkey see *The Little Red Monkey*
Caspary, Vera 13–14
Cast a Dark Shadow 30–31, **31**, 227, 231, 234, 238
Castle, Mary 201–2
Cat Girl 31–32, *32*, 228, 232, 236, 239
Cat People 32, 134
Catford, Edwin 87
Catto, Max 46
Cause for Alarm 1
Cavalcanti, (Alberto) 47, 67–68, 131, 196–97
Cavanagh, Paul 224
Cellier, Frank 112
Chaffey, Don 63, 118
The Challenge 32–33, 229, 232, 234, 238
Challis, Christopher 21, 64, 66, 130, 180
Chamber of Horrors see *The Door with Seven Locks*
Chamberlain, Cyril 55, **157**, 204
Champion 3
Chance, Naomi 70, 220–21
Chance Meeting see *Blind Date*
Chandos, John 102, 111, 147, **177**, 199–200
Change Partners 242
Chaplin, Charles 37
Chaplin, Sydney 37
Chapman, Edward 98, 117–18, 142, 157–58
Chapman, Marguerite 105–6
Charles, Moie 45
Charter Film Productions 207
Chase a Crooked Shadow 33–34, **34**, 227, 232, 233, 239
Chaumeton, Etienne 243
Cherrell, Gwen 51
Cherry, Helen 222
Chesney, Arthur 62
Chester, Hal E. 133
Chevreau, Cecile 61
Cheyney, Peter 210
Chibnall, Steve 243

Chiltern Film Productions 208
Christ in Concrete see *Give Us This Day*
Christie, Agatha 225
Christie, Campbell 98
Christie, Dorothy 98
Christmas Holiday 43
Chrystall, Belle 157–58
Churchill, Donald 212
Churchill, Sarah 173
Ciannelli, Eduardo 190
Cilento, Diane 151, 198–99
Cineguild Productions 20, 78, 112, 144, 193
Cinemascope 85
The Circle see *The Vicious Circle*
Circle of Danger 34–35, 228, 231, 236, 240
Circle of Deception 35, 228, 232, 235, 238
Citizen Kane 1
City for Conquest 3
Clancey, Vernon 47
Clare, Mary 133, 145, 202–3
Clarion Film Productions 182
Clark, Dane 61, **61**, 70, 126
Clark, Jameson 14
Clarke, Michael 29
Clarke, T.E.B. 22
Clarkson, Stephen 53
Clash by Night 1
Clay Pigeon 150
Clayton, Jack 166–67
Clemens, Brian 49, 201, 202
Cloudburst 3, 35–36, 227, 231, 236, 239
The Clouded Yellow 36, 228, 231, 236, 240
Clowes, St. John L. 137
The Clue of the New Pin 36–37, 228, 232, 234, 240
The Clue of the Silver Key 242
The Clue of the Twisted Candle 242
Cobby, Brian 24–25
Cochran, Steve 216–17
Code of Scotland Yard see *The Shop at Sly Corner*
Coen, Guido 129
Coenda Films 129
Coffee, Lenore 66
Cole, George 39–40, 97, 128, 216–17
Coleridge, Sylvia 91–92
Coles, Michael 115, 130, 185
Colin, Ian 15–16
Colleano, Bonar 56, 73–74, 76–77, 100–1, **101**, 158
Collins, Joan 39, 75, 91, 188, 208
Collins, Michael 175
Collins, Wilkie 41
The Come-On 33
Comfort, Lance 11, 13, 21, 24, 54, 57, 77, 81, 86, 149, 155, 163, 179, 187, 193
Compton, Fay 19, 109
Concanen Recordings 139
The Concrete Jungle see *The Criminal*
Condor Film Productions 81
Confession 37, 228, 231, 235, 239

Index

Connell, Maureen 103, 118–19, 189
Conner, Rearden 175
Connery, Sean 70, 84, 137
Conqueror Productions 214
Conrad, Jess 163
Conrad, Joseph 148
Constantine, Eddie 152
Constellation Films 181
Conte, Richard 107, **108**
Contraband 37–38, 227, 230, 236, 241
Cook, Whitfield 188
Cooper, Brigid 220
Cooper, George A. 135, 172
Cooper, Terence 27–28
Cooper, Wilkie 14, 79, 92, 109, 117, 123, 179, 188, 194, 207
Cope, Kenneth 102, 129
Copley, Peter 212
Coppel, Alec 125, 141
Le Corbeau 158
Corbett, Harry H. 64, 123, 176, 205
Cordell, Cathleen 71
Cordet, Héléne 107
Cornelius, Henry 98
Cornered 74, 141
Coronado Productions 34
Coronet Films 44
Corri, Adrienne 15–16
Corridor of Mirrors 38–39, 228, 230, 237, 240
Cortese, Valentina 172
Corvin, Maria 173
Cosh Boy 39, 228, 231, 234, 238
Cottage to Let 39–40, 228, 230, 233, 238
Cotten, Joseph 71, 198
Coulouris, George 104, 148
Counterblast 40, 227, 230, 235, 239
Court, Hazel 29, 48, 68, 119, 129, 176
Court, Joanne 27
Cowan, Maurine 208
Cowley, John 95
Cox, Jack 9, 39, 112
Crabtree, Arthur 48, 60, 112, 116, 209, 215
Craig, Ivan 179
Craig, Michael 152–53, 169–70, 225–26
Crawford, Andrew 26, 109, 132, 191
Crawford, Anne 13–14, 45, 45–46
Crawford, John 64, **84**, 85, 119, 154
Cresswell, John 30, 222, 225
Crest 94
Crichton, Charles 47, 64, 88–89, 198
Crimes at the Dark House 40–41, 227, 230, 235, 239
The Criminal 41–42, 227, 232, 235, 240
Crisham, Walter 137
Cronon, A.J. 82
The Crooked Circle 3
Cross, Eric 18, 45, 56, 88, 94, 203, 204
Cross, Hugh 174
Cross, Robin 243
Cross-Up see *Tiger by the Tail*

Crossfire 74, 141
Crossroads to Crime 42, 228, 232, 233, 240
Crow Hollow 42–43, 228, 231, 235, 240
Crowdy, Francis 122
Crowley, Dave **194**
Crowther, Bruce 243
Crutchley, Rosalie 193
Cry Vengeance 112
Cry Wolf 43
Cullimore, Alan 211
Culver, Roland 47, 89, 106, 177–78, 211–12, 214
Cummings, Constance 96
Cummins, Peggy 56, 83–84, 133–34, 191
Cunningham, Anne 16
Currie, Finlay 26, **66**, 66–67, 78, 198, 217
Curse of the Demon see *Night of the Demon*
Curtis, James 195
Cusack, Cyril 64, 142, 175
Cushing, Peter 136, 205–6, 213–14
Cusick International Films 109
Cuthbertson, Allan 95, 114, 166, 185

Dade, Stephen 26, 48, 51–52, 63, 106, 182
Dahl, Arlene 68–69, 219
Daily Mail 189
Dainton, Patricia 137, 147–48, 221–22
Daisy Kenyon 134
Dalby, Amy 118–19
Dalrymple, Ian 82, 220
Dalton, Audrey 37
The Damned 43, 227, 232, 235, 239
Dancing with Crime 43–44, 228, 230, 233, 241
Daneman, Paul 36–37, 108, 205–6
A Dangerous Profession 57
Daniel, Jennifer 123, 164
Daniel Angel Films 10, 223
Danielli, Wendy 158–59
Daniely, Lisa 119, 147, 204
Dankworth, John 10
Danziger Photoplays 9, 201, 202
Danziger Productions 49
Dark City: The Film Noir (book) 1, 3, 243
The Dark Corner 112
The Dark Eyes of London 44, 228, 230, 236, 240
The Dark Man 44–45, 228, 231, 234, 238
Dark Secret 45, 229, 231, 236, 239
"Dark Shadows Around Pinewood and Ealing" (article) 243
The Dark Tower 45, 228, 230, 235, 239
Darnborough, Antony 184
Dassin, Jules 131–32
Daughter of Darkness 3, 45–46, 227, 230, 233, 240
Davenport, John 77, 86
Davenport, Nigel 164, 211
Davey, Stan (Stan Pavey) 181

David Henley Productions 126
Davidson, Lewis 8
Davies, Betty Ann 39, 98, 116, 126, 144, 148
Davies, David 70
Davies, John Howard 165–66
Davion, Alexander 21, 150
Davis, Allan 36
Davis, Bette 10
Davis, Desmond 95
Davis, Jim 224
Davis, Winifred 186
Dawson, Anthony 109, 144, 203–4
Daybreak 2, 46, 228, 230, 233, 241
Dead Man's Chest 242
Dead Men Are Dangerous 46–47, 229, 230, 234
Dead of Night 47, 227, 230, 233, 234, 240
Dead on Course see *Wings of Danger*
The Deadliest Sin see *Confession*
"Deadlock" (play) 10
The Deadly Game see *Third Party Risk*
Deadly Nightshade 47–48, 229, 231, 234, 238
Dean, Basil 208
Dear Murderer 2, 48, 227, 230, 234, 238
Dearden, Basil 9, 22, 26, 47, 69, 71, 91, 156, 158, 169, 170, 171, 177, 188, 212, 213
Death of an Angel 5
Death on the Cheap: The Lost B Movies of Film Noir! (book) 4, 243
Death Trap 242
Death Wish 2 84
de Banzie, Brenda 152
Deception 121
The Defiant Ones 128
de Grunwald, Anatole 39, 85, 223
Delamar, Mickey 173
De Latour, Charles see Endfield, Cy
Delayed Action 49, 229, 231, 235, 239
Dell, Edith 49
Dell, Jeffrey 45
Delta Films 104
de Marney, Derrick 106–7, 139, 201, 209–10
de Marney, Terence 53–54
Denham, Maurice 53, 54–55, 89, 91, 133, 173
Denham Productions 208
De Niro, Robert 132
Denison, Michael 58–59
The Depraved 2, 49, 228, 232, 234, 241
Derek, John **63**, 63–64
De Rouen, Reed 129, 179
Derrick Williams Productions 51
Design for Murder see *Trunk Crime*
Desni, Tamara 207
Desny, Ivan 112
Desperate Moment 49–50, **50**, 228, 231, 233, 240
Deutsch, Ernst 198

Index

The Devil Inside see *Offbeat*
The Devil's Plot see *Counterblast*
Devlin, William 91–92
Dial Films 217
Dial 999 50–51, 229, 231, 237, 239
Dickens, Charles 78, 131, 145
Dickinson, Desmond 27, 70, 114–15, 165, 222
Dickinson, Thorold 71, 162, 172
Dickson, Paul 49
Dietrich, Marlene 188
Diffring, Anton 94, 104, 147
Dighton, John 131, 170
Dignam, Basil 49, 202
Dillman, Bradford 35
Dines, Gordon 22, 32, 35, 69, 71, 91, 120, 131, 158, 172, 177
Dinnie, William 106
Disney, Walt 204
Dixey, Phyllis 53–54
Dixon, Wheeler Winston 2
"Dixon of Dock Green" (TV series) 23
Dmytryk, Edward 73–74, 141, 184–85
Do You Know This Voice? 51, 227, 232, 236, 240
Dr. No 4, 39
Dr. Strangelove or: How I Learned to Stop Worrying and Love the Bomb 4
"Dr. Who" (TV series) 45
Doctor Zhivago 38
Domergue, Faith 185
Donald, James 26–27, 181
Donlan, Yolande 100, 195
Donner, Clive 123, 172
Donner, Judith 171
Don't Talk to Strange Men 51–52, 227, 232, 235, 238
Doonan, Patric 20, 22, 217
The Door with Seven Locks 52–53, 229, 230, 235, 238, 240
Doré, Alexander 102
Dorne, Sandra 12, 114, 121–22, **122**, 199, 202, 217, 224–25
Dorning, Robert 119
Dors, Diana 44, 76–77, **105**, 105, 109–10, **110**, 145, **151**, 152, 207, 215–16, 217, 225–26
The Double 242
Double Confession 53, 228, 231, 233, 240
Double Indemnity 156, 206
Double Jeopardy 49
Douglas, Paul 100–1
Dowling, Joan 127–28, 223–24
Downfall 53, 228, 232, 235, 241, 242
Dracula 207
Drake, Michael 207–8
Drayton, Alfred 131
The Dream of Olwen 218
Dresdel, Sonia 36, 59, **200**, 200, 218
Drive a Crooked Road 162
Dryhurst, Edward 30, 40
Dual Alibi 2, 53–54, 227, 230, 237, 241
Dudley-Ward, Penelope 30
Dulcimer Street see *London Belongs to Me*

Dunbar, Robert 198
Duncan, Paul 243
Dunham, Joanna 24
Dunne, Philip 56
Dunning, Ruth 211
Duprez, June 187
Durbridge, Francis 212
Durgnat, Raymond 243
Duryea, Dan 51, 199–200
Dvorak, Ann 57, 187
Dwyer, Leslie 121, 123, 133, 189, 194
Dyall, Valentine 116, 167–68, 211
Dyneley, Peter 198

Eady, David 58, 94, 211
Ealing Studios 22, 26, 47, 69, 71, **72**, 91, 98, 131, 140, 155, 158, 170–71, 172, **177**, 188
Earl, Clifford 115
Early Film Noir: Greed, Lust and Murder Hollywood Style (book) 243
East of Piccadilly 54, 229, 230, 235, 239
East Side Kids 24
Eastham, Richard 179
Eastman Color 219
Eastwood, James 107, 119, 211
Eaton, Shirley 73, 94
Eaves, Hilary 40–41
Eddington, Paul 119
Eden, Mark 21, 171
"Edgar Wallace Mystery Theatre" (TV series) 9, 29, 37, 53, 58, 62, 94, 109, 114, 116, 123, 130, 146, 157, 164, 165, 165, 174, 176, 185, 205, 206, 209, 211, 216, 242; see also Wallace, Edgar
Edge, Francis 18
Edge of Doom 134
Edward Dryhurst Productions 218
Edwards, Henry 54
Edwards, Meredith 123, 194–95
Edwards, Olga (Olga Edwardes) 18, 179
Egan, Beresford 106
Eggar, Samantha 160–61, **161**
Eight O'clock Walk 54–55, 227, 231, 233, 240
Eisinger, Jo 131
Eldridge, John 158
Elgin Films 181
Elliot, Biff 73
Elliott, Denholm 82
Ellison, Tim 12
Elmes, Guy 7, 11, 62, 173, 190, 217
Elton, Eileen 104
Elvey, Gartside 106
Elvey, Maurice 106
Emary, Barbara K. 112
The Embezzler 55, 228, 231, 234, 239
Emerton, Roy 30
Emmott, Basil 21, 24, 100, 109, 149, 155, 163, 185, 192, 195, 219
The Encyclopedia of British Film (book) 243
The End of the Line 2, 55, 229, 232, 236, 239

Endfield, C. Raker see Endfield, Cy
Endfield, Cy (Charles De Latour, C. Raker Endfield) 83, 93, 107
The Entertainer 4
Epitaph for a Spy see *Hotel Reserve*
Erickson, Paul 55, 103, 201
Erskine-Lindop, Audrey 168
Escape 56, 229, 230, 235, 241
Escape by Night 56, 228, 231, 234, 238
Escape Route 56–57, 228, 231, 234, 238
Escape to Danger 57, 229, 230, 233, 234
Esmond, Jill 13, 56
Ethiro Productions 154, 176, 221
Europa British 111
Europa Films 135
European Film Noir (book) 2, 3, 4, 243
Evans, Clifford 56–57, 112, 218
Evans, David 106, 123, 146, 182
Evans, Edith 161–62
Evans, Michael 20, 179
Evans, Peggy 22–23, 29, 126
Everest, Barbara 69, 207–8, 214
Everest Pictures Limited 120
Everrett, Wallace 57
Everson, William K. 3, 4, 243
"Evidence for a British Film Noir Cycle" (essay) 2, 3, 4
Excalibur Films 156
Excelsior Films **200**, 201, 214
Experiment Perilous 134
Eytle, Tommy 129

Fabian, Robert 152
"Fabian of Scotland Yard" (TV series) 152
The Face at the Window 57, 228, 230, 235, 239
Face of a Stranger 2, 3, 57, 228, 232, 236, 241, 242
Face the Music 58, 228, 231, 234, 239
Faces in the Dark 58–59, 228, 232, 234, 239
Fairchild, William 148
Fairlie, Gerard 29
Faith, Adam 13, 129–30
Faithfull, Geoffrey 104, 121, 144, 150, 163, 189, 201
Falcon Pictures 24
Falconer, Alun 42, 95, 118, 130
Falconer, Robert 104
Falk, Quentin 243
Fallen Angel 134, 186
The Fallen Idol 59–60, 148, 227, 231, 236, 240
Fanny by Gaslight 116, 227, 230, 233, 238
Farr, Derek 11, 53, 54–55, 117–18, 127–28, 139–40, 178, 179, 186, 211–12, 214
Farrar, David 12, 17–18, 26–27, 45, 69, 106, 125–26, 135, 180
The Fatal Night 60–61, 229, 231, 237, 241
Faulkner, Keith 117, **192**, 192

Index

Fay, W.G. 142–43, *143*, 186
Faye, Janina 51–52
Fayre, Ronald 57
Fellane Productions 73
Fellows, Robert 73
Ferguson, Lester 60
Fernald, John 133
Fidley, M. Roy 13
Field, Alexander 44, 129
Field, Shirley Anne 43, 63–64
Figaro Films 100
Fildes, Audrey 218
Film locations *66*, 66, 100, *101*, 185, 219
Film Noir (book) 3, 4, 243
Film Noir: An Encyclopedic Reference to the American Style" (book) 1
Film Noir: Films of Trust and Betrayal (book) 243
Film Noir Guide: 745 Films of the Classic Era, 1940–1959 (book) 3, 4, 5, 243
Film Noir Reader 2 (book) 2, 243
Film Noir: Reflections in a Dark Mirror (book) 243
Film Workshop 12, 87
Films in Review (magazine) 3, 4, 243
Finch, Peter 82–83
Finger of Guilt see *The Intimate Stranger*
Finlay, Frank 95
Fischer, O.W. 218
Fisher, Steve 111, 200
Fisher, Terence 58, 104, 105, 121, 126, 159, 184, 189, 190, 220
Fitzgerald, Geraldine 106, 183–84
Fitzgerald, John 81
Fitzgerald, Walter 20, 77–78, 154, 187, 200
Five Angles on Murder see *The Woman in Question*
Five Days 61–62, *62*, 228, 231, 237, 239
Five Ocean 109
Five to One 62, 228, 232, 234, 241, 242
The Flamingo Affair 62, 229, 231, 236, 239
The Flanagan Boy 2, 3, 62–63, 205, 228, 231, 235, 239
Flat Two 242
Fleming, Brandon 12
Fleming, Ian 45
Flemyng, Gordon 62, 185
Flemyng, Robert 21–22, 30
The Flesh Is Weak 2, 63–64, *63*, 228, 232, 233, 238
Floods of Fear 64, *64*, 228, 232, 234, 238
The Flying Scot 65, 227, 232, 233, 239
Footsteps in the Fog 65–67, *66*, 227, 231, 235, 238
Footsteps in the Sand see *Black Limelight*
For Them That Trespass 67–68, 227, 231, 233, 241
Forbes, Bryan 95, 171, 217–18

Forbidden 2, 68, 227, 231, 235, 239
Ford, Frederick 62
Foreman, Carl (Derek Frye) 102, 180
Forth, Anne 2111
Fortress Productions 55, 103, 129
Fortune Is a Woman 68–69, 228, 232, 234, 239
Forwood, Anthony 19, 61, 121
Foster, Barry 156
Foster, Dianne 111, 162
Foster, Dudley 130, 164
Foster, Julia 181
Four Dark Hours see *The Green Cockatoo*
Fourth Square 242
Fowler, Harry 91
Fox, Bernard 185
Foxwell, Ivan 81, 138
Francis, Freddie 89, 150, 166, 205
Francis, Frederick see Francis, Freddie
Frank, Charles 106, 209
Frankau, Ronald 53–54
Frankel, Benjamin 67
Franklin, Pamela 198–99
Franklyn, William 63–64, 155
Fraser, Liz *149*, 149
Freeman, Denis 7
Freeman, Mona 50–51
Freiberger, Fred 216
French, Harold 47, 120
Frenzy see *Latin Quarter*
Freshman, William 157
Frieda 69–70, 227, 230, 234, 238
Friedman, Seymour 56
Friend, Philip 49–50, 77–78
Friese-Greene, Claude 16, 54, 127
The Frightened City 2, 70, 227, 232, 235, 238
The Frightened Lady see *The Case of the Frightened Lady*
Frobisher Productions 30, *31*
From Russia with Love 39
Frye, Derek see Buchman, Harold; Foreman, Carl
Frye, Dwight 207
"The Fugitive" (TV series) 139
The Fugitive see *On the Night of the Fire*
Furse, Judith 17

G&S Films 145, 220
Gabin, Jean 111
Gabor, Zsa Zsa 120–21
Gabriel, John 176
Gainsborough Pictures 23, 39, 48, 60, 98, *99*, 112, 116, 128, 159, 171, 182, 184, 209, 215
Gamble, Rollo 112
The Gambler and the Lady 70, 229, 231, 235, 236, 239
Game for Three Losers 242
Game of Danger see *Bang! You're Dead*
Gamma Films 91–92
Gangelin, Paul 195
Gangster Film Reader (book) 243
Gardner, Hy 73

Garner, Rex 126
Garnett, Tony 94, 165
Gaslight (1940, British) 60, 71, 227, 230, 234, 239
Gaslight (1944, U.S.) 71
Gauge, Alexander 96, 158–59
Gawthorne, Peter 47
Genn, Leo 37–38, 79–80, 154
The Gentle Gunman 71–72, *72*, 227, 231, 234, 238
"The Gentle Gunman" (play) 72
George Minter Productions 168
Georgefield Productions 14, *15*
Germaine, Mary 223–24
Germi, Pietro 19
Ghost Story 186
Gibbs, Gerald 19, 49, 68, 96, 118, 134, 137, 147, 160
Gibbs, Susanne 20
Gibraltar Film Productions 137
Gifford, Alan 65
Gifford, Denis 5, 243
Gilbert, Lewis 30, 39, 75, 146, 194
Gilbert Betterson, Ralph 207
Gilliat, Sidney 68, 79–80, 92, 109, 215
Gilling, John 17, 20, 32, 47, 55, 56, 81, 87, 111, 116, 138, 150, 162, 164, 167, 199, 201, 204, 220
Giltinan, Donal 216
Gingold, Hermione 39
The Girl Hunters 2, 72–73, 228, 232, 236, 240
The Girl in the Painting see *Portrait from Life*
Give Us This Day 73–74, 227, 231, 234, 240
Glaister, Gerard 173, 176
Glendining, Hone (Hone Glendinning) 5, 30, 40, 57, 68, 123, 139, 178
Glenville, Peter 76–77, 112
Gloria Films *196*
Glory Alley 3
Glyn-Jones, John 108
Goddard, Patricia 210
Goddard, Paulette 190
Godsell, Vanda 84, 104–5
Goff, Ivan 175
Goldbeck, Willis 204
The Golden Gong: Fifty Years of the Rank Organisation, Its Films and Its Stars (book) 243
Golden Salamander 74–75, 227, 231, 236
Goldfinger 46, 73
Goldner, Charles 73–74, 92–93, 172
Goldoni, Lelia 89–90
Gomez, Arthur 55
The Good Die Young 3, 75–76, 227, 231, 234, 238
Good-Time Girl *76*, 76–77, 227, 231, 235, 238
Goodliffe, Michael 50–51, 100, 209, 219
Goolden, Richard 211
Gordon, Colin 107, 192–93
Gordon, Dorothy 223–24
Goring, Marius 30, 34–35, 120, 125–26, 168, 193, 218–19

Gorman, Shay 27, 103
Gotell, Walter 43
Gotfurt, Frederic 193
Gough, Michael 19, 20, 29, 87, 134, 170, 180
Graham, David 42
Graham, Genine 205
Graham, Winston 135, 193
Grahame, Gloria 75
Granger, Stewart 20–21, 60, 65–67, 112–13, 116, 170–71, 215
Grant, Arthur 43, 84, 100, 150–51
Grant, Rita 40–41
Gray, Barry 42
Gray, Coleen 92–93
Gray, Cyril 12, 87
Gray, Dulcie 123–24, 214
Gray, Janine 150
Gray, Nadia 135, 186
Gray, Sally 29–30, 56–57, 79–80, 122–23, *141*, 141, 179, *196*, 196–97, 220
Grayson, Godfrey 167
The Great Armored Car Swindle see *The Breaking Point*
Great Day 77–78, 227, 230, 233, 239
Great Expectations 2, 78–79, 227, 230, 235, 239
Gréco, Juliette 218–19
Green, Danny 94
Green, F.L. 142
Green, Guy 20–21, 29, 57, 78–79, 112, 135, 144–45, 182, 193
Green, Janet 30, 36, 169, 212
Green, Nigel 156, 221–22
Green, Phillip 10, 155, 170, 176
The Green Cockatoo 2, 4, 79, 228, 230, 235, 239
Green for Danger 79–80, 227, 230, 234, 238
The Green Scarf *80*, 80–81, 229, 231, 236, 239
Greenbaum, Mutz (Max Greene) 5, 57, 79, 81, 86, 131–32, 183, 187, 214, 225
Greene, David 181
Greene, Graham 7, 25, 59, 191, 198, 208
Greene, Howard 165
Greene, Max see Greenbaum, Mutz
Greene, Richard 140, 225
Greenwood, Jack 114, 242
Greenwood, Joan 106, 121, 142, 170
Greenwood, Walter 112
Greeves, Vernon 104
Gregg, Christina 51, 163
Gregg, Olive 151
Gregory, Thea 61
Gregson, John 58, 70, 215–16
Gregson, Michael 55
Greville, Edmond T. 12, 139
Grey, Lita 37
Grey, Richard 81
Griffith, Hugh 180
Griffith, Kenneth 70, 118–19, 149, 152, 163, 178, 199–200
Griffiths, Jane 202
Griffiths, Kenneth 68
Grindrod, Philip 37, 50, 89, 159
The Grissom Gang 137

Gross, Arthur 129
Grossman-Cullimore–Arbeid Productions 211
Gudrun, Ann 199–200
Guest, Val 10, 84, 100, 195, 216, 224
Guest in the House 33–34
Guillermin, John 130, 147
Guilt Is My Shadow 81, 228, 231, 235, 240
Guinness, Alec 144–45
Gun Crazy 84, 134, 191
A Gunman Has Escaped 81, 229, 231, 234, 241
Gunn, Gilbert 52
The Guns of Navarone 33
Gurney, Claud 79
Gwillim, Jack 165
Gwynn, Michael 172–73

Haas, Hugo 122
Hafner, Ingrid 62
Hagen, Jean 27
Haines, Brian 130
Hale, Elvi 115
Hales, Gordon 164
Halevy, Julian 160
Hall, Henry 12
Hall, Robert 133
Hall, Willis 217
Hamama, Faten 27
Hambling, Arthur 201
Hamer, Robert 47, 98, 111, 155, 186
Hamilton, Guy 95, 97
Hamilton, Patrick 16
Hammer Film Productions (Hammer) 19, 21, 47, 35, 43, 58, 61, *61*, 62, 70, 84, *85*, 86, 89–90, *90*, *105*, 105, 116, 121, 126, 150, 167, 182, 189, 190, 198, 199, 220, *221*, 224
Hammerscope 85
Hammond, Peter 37
Hanbury, Victor 86
Handl, Irene 45
Hanley, Jimmy 21, 23, 98, 127, 163, 167–68
Hanslip, Ann 58
The Harder They Fall 3
Hardwicke, Cedric 131, 140
Hardy, Phil 243
Hare, Doris 156
Hare, William 243
Harefield Productions 123, *124*, 187
Harlequin Productions 151, 205
Harlow, John 10, 23, 45, 49, 186, 218
Harper, Barbara S. 159
Harris, Paul 9
Harris, Richard (actor) 176
Harris, Richard (screenwriter) 108, 115, 146, 192
Harris, Vernon 39, 75
Harrison, Kathleen 30, 140, 208, 214–15, 217
Harrison, Norman 27, 94, 108
Harrison, Rex 56, 109
Harry Reynolds Productions 53
Hartnell, William 10–11, 25–26, 45, 53, 56, *66*, 66–67, 83, 89, 127, 140, 154–55, 193, *194*, 206

Harvey, Frank (Frank Harvey, Jr.) 111, 128, 159, 174
Harvey, John 81, 111
Harvey, Laurence (Lawrence Harvey) 75, 87, *88*, 91, 117, 163, 166–67, *167*, 194–95, 223–24
Harvey, Walter J. (Walter Harvey, James Harvey, Jimmy Harvey, Jimmy W. Harvey) 15, 19, 35, 45, 55, 58, 61, 62, 70, 86, 102, 103, 105, 126, 129, 147, 186, 189, 190, 198, 200, 206, 220, 224
Hatter's Castle 81–82, 227, 230, 233, 239
The Haunting 4
Hauser, Philo 159
Havelock-Allan, Anthony 78
Hawkesworth, John 203
Hawkins, Frank 81
Hawkins, Jack 59–60, 68–69, 85, 97–98, 198–99
Hawtrey, Charles 167–68
Haye, Helen 30
Hayers, Sidney 114, 152
Hayes, George 30, 54
Hayes, Melvyn 139
Hayne, Murray 165
Haynes, Stanley 29, 112, 144
Hayter, James 127
Hayward, Frederick 40
Hayworth, Rita 202
He Walked by Night 202
Heal, Joan 204
The Heart of the Matter 82–83, 227, 231, 236, 239
Heat Wave see *The House Across the Lake*
Heath, Gordon 169–70
Hell Drivers *83*, 83–84, 227, 232, 234, 240
Hell Is a City 84–85, *85*, 227, 232, 234, 239
Heller, Lukas 29
Heller, Otto 45, 92, 120, 133, 140, 153–54, 162, 168, 188, 193, 196–97, 212, 217, 222
Hemmings, David 149–50
Heneghan, Patricia 42
Hennessy, Peter 31, 65
Henreid, Paul 121, 189
Henrey, Bobby 59
Henry, Joan 215, 225
Henson, Gladys 69
Hepburn, Audrey 172
Her Panelled Door see *The Woman with No Name*
Herbert Wilcox Productions 225
Here's the Knife, Dear: Now Use It see *Nightmare*
Heston, Charlton 167
Hewer, John 11
Heywood, Anne 49, 64, *65*, 213–14
H.H. Films 19
Hibbert, Geoffrey 55, 112
Hicks, Seymour 179
Hickson, Joan 158–59, 174
The Hidden Room see *Obsession*
The Hideout see *The Small Voice*
Highway 301 90

Index

Hildyard, Jack 81, 82, 85
Hill, Jacqueline 23
Hill, Rose 12
Hiller, Wendy 148
Hillier, Erwin 33, 77, 96, 122, 125, 142, 175
Hills, Gillian 12–13
Hilton, James 185
Hird, Thora 146–47, 204, 224
Hitchcock, Alfred 37, 96, 150, 186, 188
Hitchcock, Patricia 188
Hobson, Valerie 20–21, 37–38, 78, 96, 165–66, 181, 187
Hodges, Ken 58
Hogan, Brenda 60
Holden, William 102–3
Holiday Camp 4
Holiday Film Productions 136
Hollow Triumph 121
Holloway, Stanley 123, 131, 139–40, 182–83, 214
Holm, Sonia 163, 199
Holt, Patrick 81, 122–23, 190, 199
Holt, Seth 140
Home at Seven 85–86, 228, 231, 236, 239, 240
Homeier, Skip 137
Homolka, Oskar 102–3, 178
Hope, Vida 121–22, 223–24
Hopkins, Joan 53, 117–18
Horne, David 36–37, 40–41, 52
Horner, Penelope 108
Horsley, John 47–48, 162, 164, 189, 217
Hotel Reserve 86, 228, 230, 233, 234, 235
Hour of Glory see *The Small Back Room*
The House Across the Lake 2, 86–87, 228, 231, 235, 239
The House in the Woods 87, 228, 232, 236, 238, 239
House of Darkness 87–88, **88**, 228, 231, 235, 238
House Un-American Activities Committee 180
Houston, Charles 84, 118–19, 150
Houston, Donald 42, 104–5, 118–19, *167*
Houston, Glyn 150, 185, 208
Howard, Arthur 97
Howard, Eldon 201
Howard, Joyce 10, 133
Howard, Peter see Koch, Howard
Howard, Ronald 11, 18, 87, 114, 132, 134, 139, 140, 161–62, 191, 219
Howard, Trevor 36, 74–75, 79–80, 82, 92, 102–3, 148, 167, 184, 190, 196–97, 198
Howes, Sally Ann 47, 131
Hubris Productions 198
Hud 161
Hudd, Walter 16–17
Hudis, Norman 65
Hughes, Harry 47
Hughes, Ken 19, 24, 37, 86, 100, 107, 109, 181, 219
Hulke, Malcolm 117

Hulme, Anthony 202–3
The Human Monster see *The Dark Eyes of London*
Hunt, Martita 54, 78
Hunted 88–89, 204, 216, 225, 227, 232, 234, 241
Hunter, Ian 13, *14*, 54–55
Hunter, John 97
Huntington, Lawrence 117, 125, 133, 206, 210, 214
Huntley, Raymond 92, 109, 125–26, 183
Hurst, Brian Desmond 122, 145
Hurst, David 168–69
Hurst, Veronica 11
Hurt, John 136
Huth, Harold 54, 132
Hyde-White, Wilfrid 74–75, 23, 211–12
Hylton, Jane 128, 162
The Hypnotist 89, 229, 232, 237, 239
Hysteria 2, 89–91, **90**, 135, 227, 232, 234, 241

I Became a Fugitive see *They Made Me a Fugitive*
I Believe in You 91, 227, 231, 234, 236, 238
I Confess 34, 37
I Met a Murderer 2, 91–92, 227, 230, 235, 239
I Promised to Pay see *Payroll*
I See a Dark Stranger 92, 227, 230, 235, 238
I, the Jury 73
I Wake Up Screaming 140
I Walked with a Zombie 134
I'll Get You see *Escape Route*
I'll Get You for This 92–93, 228, 231, 236, 239
Illing, Peter 92, 148
Imbarco a mezzanotte 88
Immoral Charge see *Serious Charge*
Impact 93, 228, 232, 235, 240
Impulse 93–94, 228, 231, 234, 239
In the Wake of a Stranger 94, 229, 232, 234, 238
Incident at Midnight 94, 228, 232, 235, 241, 242
Independent Artists 16, 21, 45, 88, 117, 130, 152, *203*, 203
Independent Artists–Langton Productions 114
Independent Film Producers 190, 222, **223**
Independent Producers 17, 20, 92, 144
Independent Sovereign Films *141*, 141, 179
Individual Pictures 79, 92, 109
Information Received 2, 94, 228, 232, 235, 240
The Informers 95, 228, 232, 233, 241
Ingram 150
The Inheritance see *Uncle Silas*
The Innocents 4, 199
Insignia Films 31, *32*, 65, 104, 163, 180

An Inspector Calls 95–96, 228, 231, 235, 240
Inspiration Pictures 62
International Motion Pictures 87, **88**
The Interrupted Journey 2, 96, 228, 231, 233, 239
Inter-State Films 160
The Intimate Stranger 96–97, 228, 232, 235, 239
The Intruder **97**, 97–98, 228, 231, 235, 240
IRA see Irish Republican Army
Ireland, Jill 102
Ireland, John 58–59, 75, 189
Irish Republican Army (IRA) **72**, 72, 92, 143, 175–76
Iron Curtain 134
Iron Man 3
It Always Rains on Sunday 98, 228, 230, 234, 240
It Takes a Thief see *The Challenge*
It's Cold in the Channel (book) 190
Ivan Foxwell Productions **97**, 97

Jack the Ripper 168
Jackson, Freda 63–64, 78, 137–38, 217, 223–24
Jackson, Gordon 155, 201
Jackson, Pat 51–52
Jackson, Ray 69
James, Sid (Sidney James) 17, 56, 62–63, 73–74, **83**, 86–87, 100–1, **101**, 116, 132, 188, 215–16, 219
Jarrott, Charles 205
Jassy 98–100, **99**, 228, 230, 235, 340
Javelin Films 222
Jayne, Jennifer 19, 55, 89
Jeans, Desmond 179
Jenkins, Megs 79–80, 154
Jenkins, Patrick 70
Jerrold, Mary 125–26
Jessel, Patricia 63–64, 118–19
Jigsaw 100, 227, 232, 234, 239
Joe MacBeth 100–1, **101**, 228, 231, 235, 238
John, Rosamund 79–80, 191, 210
John Argyle Productions 44, 146
John Corfield Productions 13, *14*
John Harvel Productions 68
Johnny Angel 57
Johnny Guitar 202
Johnny Nobody 101–2, 228, 232, 236, 240
Johns, Glynis 69, 154, 175, 215
Johns, Mervyn 40, 47, 96–97, 129–30, 155, 212
Johnson, Celia 91
Johnson, Fred 58
Johnson, Nunnally 109
Johnson, Richard 27
Johnson, Van 14–15, *15*
Jolly Bad Fellow 4
Jones, Barry 36, 43–44, 174, 187, 210
Jones, Emrys 45, 47–48, ***200***
Jones, Evan 43
Jones, Griffith 76–77, 103, 196–97, 209
Jones, Jacqueline 94

Jones, Jonah 55, 107, 129
Jones, Ken 144
Joseph, Robert L. 198
Judd, Edward 32–33
Jungle Street 102, 228, 232, 236, 239
Jungle Street Girls see *Jungle Street*
Jurassic Park 44
Jürgens, Curt 160–61, **161**
Justin, John 29

Karam, Mia 209
Karas, Anton 198
Karlin, Miriam 42, 181
Kash, Murray 73
Kath, Katherine 120–21
Kaufmann, Maurice 216
Kay, Charles 154
Kaydor Productions 92
Keaney, Michael F. 243
Keegan, Barry 152
Keel, Howard (Harold Keel) 64, **65**, 181
Keen, Geoffrey 58, 88, 114, 140, 164, 172
Kelley, James 21
Kellino, Pamela 91–92, 210–11
Kellino, Roy 81, 91–92
Kelly, Judy 47
Kelly, Michael 49
Kelsall, Moultrie 14
Kemp, Jeremy 58
Kendall, Kay 121, 191, 220–21
Kendall, Victor 47
Kenilworth Film Productions 18, 45, 47, 49, 55, 217
Kennaway, James 213
Kennedy, Arthur 93–94
Kennedy, Margaret 116, 193
Kenney, James 39, 71
Kent, Jean 14–15, 29–30, 60, **76**, 76–77, 111, 112, 121, 222
Kenwood Films 225
Kerima 148
Kerr, Bill 158–59
Kerr, Deborah 17–18, 81, 92, 112
Kerr, Geoffrey 98
Kersh, Gerald 132
Kershaw, Phoebe 37–38
The Key 102–3, 167, 227, 232, 236, 240
Keyes, Evelyn 168–69
Kill Her Gently 103–4, 228, 232, 236, 239
Kill Me Tomorrow 104, 228, 232, 234, 239
Killer's Kiss 147
The Killing 42, 153, 155
Kimmins, Anthony 123, 125
Kind Hearts and Coronets 4
King, Diana 186
King, George 30, 40, 57, 68, 178
King, Nel 9
King and Country 4
Kingston, Claude 104
Kinnear, Roy 95
Kirkwood, Pat 146
Kirwan, Patrick 44, 49, 101, 145
Kiss Me Deadly 73
Klee, Richard 93

Knapp, Terence 211
Knight, David 7, 135
Knight, Esmond 37–38
Knott, Frederick 105
Knowles, Bernard 71, 98, 121
Knox, Alexander 9, 33, 43, 176, 180
Koch, Howard (Peter Howard) 96
Kogan, Ephraim 58
Konstam, Anna 195
Kossoff, David 136
Krampf, Günther 106, 133, 201
Krasker, Robert 10, 41–42, 142, 198, 209
Krüger, Hardy 21–22
Kruse, John 83
Kurnitz, Harry 114
Kydd, Sam 211

Labarr, Marta 207
la Bern, Arthur 94, 205, 211
Lacey, Catherine 29, 157
The Lady Gambles 36
Lady in Distress see *A Window in London*
The Lady Killer 4
Lady of Vengeance 104, 228, 232, 233, 240
Lady on a Train 220
Laird, Jenny 17
Lambert, Peter 24
Lamble, Lloyd 12, 121
Lamont, Duncan 97, 150, 151
Lampell, Millard 21
Landau, Richard (Richard H. Landau) 62, 126, 189, 224
Landis, Carole 139–40
Landone, Avice 81
Landry, Gérard 135
Lane, Arthur 58, 220–21
Lang, Gordon 23, 128
Lang, Harold 35, 63, 111, 126, 186, 199–200, 217, 220–21
Langley, Bryan 44
Langley, Noel 196
Langova, Sylva 94, 107
LaPresle, Robert 11, 42, 207
The Large Rope 104–5, 228, 231, 236, 239
La Rue, Jack 127, 137
Lassally, Walter 12–13, 151, 160
The Last Page 2, **105**, 105–6, 228, 231, 234, 239
The Late Edwina Black 106, 228, 231, 234, 238
Latham, Stuart 37–38, 146
Latin Quarter 106–7, 229, 230, 236, 239
Launder, Frank 68, 80, 92
Laura 134, 159
Laurence, Michael 67
Laurie, John 60, 138
Lavis, Arthur 51
Law, Michael 179
Lawrence, D.H. 166
Lawrence, Delphi 12, 146
Lawrence, Marc 103–4
Lawrence, Quentin 156, 216
Lawrence, Sheldon 189
Lawrence of Arabia 38

Lawson, Sarah 146, 201
Lawson, Wilfrid 60, 133, 206–7
Leach, Rosemary 58
The League of Gentlemen 4
Leake, Barbara 47
Lean, David 78, 112, 144–45
Leave Her to Heaven 1
LeBeau, Madeleine 26–27
Le Borg, Reginald 62–63
Lee, Belinda **66**, 66–67, 126, 172–73
Lee, Bernard 7, 14, 29, 102–3, 118–19, 127, 140, 156, 176, 177–78, 198, 224–25
Lee, Christopher 9, 12–13, 39
Lee, Jack 35, 208
Lee, Norman 52, 127
Leech, Richard 164
Leeds, Charles 137
Lehman, Carla 39–40
Lehmann, Beatrix 160–61
Leigh, Vivien 208
Leighton, Margaret 29, 75, 85
Leister, Frederick 184, 186
Le Mesurier, John 23
Lemont, John 70, 176, 221
Lennard, Maria 165
The Leopard Man 134
Lesley, Carole 139
Leslie, Dudley 16, 168, 201
Lestocq, Humphrey 155–56
Levell, Raymond 202
Levis, Carroll 49
Lewis, Duncan 8
Lewis, Ronald 100, 172, 188
Lieven, Albert 49, 69, 174–75, 225
The Life and Adventures of Nicholas Nickleby see *Nicholas Nickleby*
The Limping Man 107, 228, 231, 234, 239
Lind, Gillian 51–52
Linden, Jennie 135
Linder, Cec 211
Lindfors, Viveca 43
Lindo, Olga 95, 169
Lindop, Audrey 20
Lindsay, Vera 186
Lindsell, Stuart 60
Linehan, Barry 165
Lines, David 98
Lister, Francis 127
Lister, Moira 107, 158, 210
The Little Red Monkey 107–8, **108**, 228, 232, 235, 238
Livesey, Roger 96
Llewellyn, Richard 139, 158
Loan Shark 57
Locke, Harry 117
Locke, Philip 58, 94, 146
Locker Sixty-Nine 2, 108–9, 228, 232, 235, 240, 242
Lockwood, Margaret 13, **14**, 30–31, 98–100, **99**, 116
Lodge, David 129–30, 205
The Lodger 3, 168
Lom, Herbert 10–11, 13, 26–27, 33–34, **34**, 45, 53–54, 70, 74–75, 76–77, 83–84, 86, 120, 125, 131–32, 133, 139, 152, 159, 168–69, 174

Index 254

London Belongs to Me 109, 182–83, 228, 231, 234, 238
London Film Productions 59, 82, 85, 114, 115, 123, *124*, 125, 148, 174, 180, 187, *197*, 198, 208
London Independent Producers 79, 191
The Loneliness of the Long Distance Runner 166, 228, 231, 233, 238
Long, Reginald 107
The Long Dark Hall 109
The Long Haul 109–11, *110*, 228, 232, 235, 239
The Long Memory 2, 3, 111, 228, 231, 235, 241
The Long Rope see *The Large Rope*
Longden, John 19
Look Back in Anger 4, 5, 166, 170
Lord, Justine *8*, 8, 94
Loren, Sophia 102–3
Lorimer, Enid 221–22
Lorre, Peter 53
Losey, Joseph (Victor Hanbury, Joseph Walton) 41–42, 43, 88, 96, 180, 205–6
The Lost Hours 111–12, 228, 231, 235, 238
The Lost Illusion see *The Fallen Idol*
Love, Bessie 140
Love on the Dole 112, 227, 230, 233, 241
Lovegrove, Arthur 129
Lovell, Dyson 150
Lovell, Raymond 10, 37–38, 86, 133, 209
Lubin, Arthur 66
Lucas, Victor 23
Lucas, William 27, 152–53
Lucky Nick Cain see *I'll Get You for This*
Lugosi, Bela 44
Lukas, Paul 220
Lunge, Romilly 52, 207
Lupino, Ida 27, 111
Lustgarten, Edgar 120
Lynch, Alfred 217
Lynn, Ann 192–93
Lynn, Robert 94
Lynne, Ann 129
Lynne, Betty 46–47
Lynx Films 152
Lyon, Ben 45
Lyons, Arthur 4, 243

Maben, Alvys 190
MacDonald, David 9, 26, 111, 182
MacDonald, Philip 34
MacDougall, Roger 71–72
MacGinnis, Niall 54, 133
MacIntosh, Alex 216
MacKendrick, Alexander 170
MacKenzie, Compton 30
Mackenzie, Mary 189
Mackie, Philip 36, 176, 209
MacKinnon, Allan 19, 23
Macnee, Patrick 60–61
The Macomber Affair 36
MacPhail, Angus 47, 69, 98
MacRae, Duncan 26, 222

Madame Tussaud's Wax Museum 169
Madden, Peter 51
Maddern, Victor 191–92
Madeleine 112–13, 227, 231, 235, 239
Madison, Leigh 129, 173
Madonna of the Seven Moons 60, 113–14, 227, 230, 234, 238
Magee, Patrick 41–42, 160, 164
Mailbag Robbery see *The Flying Scot*
The Main Chance 242
Major Productions 15, 147
Malin, Edward 179
Mallalieu, Aubrey 57
Malleson, Miles 74, 186, 187, 225
Malo, Gina 52–53
The Malpas Mystery 114, 228, 232, 235, 240, 242
Maltby, H.F. 40
The Maltese Falcon 1, 210
A Man About a Dog (book) 141
A Man and a Woman 120
The Man at the Carlton Tower 242
Man Bait see *The Last Page*
The Man Between 114–15, *115*, 228, 231, 236, 238
Man Detained 115–16, 228, 232, 240, 242
The Man from U.N.C.L.E. 84, 102, 214
Man in Black 116, 229, 231, 236, 241
The Man in Grey 60, 116, 227, 230, 233, 238
Man in Hiding see *Mantrap*
Man in the Attic 168
The Man in the Back Seat 117, 227, 232, 236, 241
Man in the Dark see *Blind Corner*
Man of Evil see *Gaslight*
Man on the Run 117–18, 228, 231, 235, 238
The Man Upstairs *118*, 118–19, 228, 232, 233, 239, 240
The Man Who Never Was 5
The Man Who Seeks His Murderer 62
The Man Who Was Nobody 2, 119, 228, 232, 237, 240, 242
The Man Who Watched the Trains Go By 2, 120, 228, 231, 234, 239
The Man Who Wouldn't Talk 120–21, 228, 232, 237, 238
The Man Within 121, 229, 230, 235, 240
Manahan, Sheila 174
Mancunian Film Corporation 21
Mango, Alec 216
Mankiewicz, Joseph L. 56
Der Mann, der seinen Mörder sucht 62
Mannheim, Lucie 86, 225
Mansfield, Jayne 32–33
Mantrap 121, 229, 231, 234, 241
Marble Arch Productions 215, 224
Marilyn 2, 121–22, *122*, 229, 231, 235, 239
Marion, Joan 16–17
The Mark of Cain 122–23, 229, 231, 235, 239

Marks, Alfred 70
Marks, Leo 35, 153
Marksman Films 13, 109, *110*
Marlé, Arnold 107, 159
Marlowe, Kit 67–68
Marlowe, Linda 93
Marquis, Max 192
Marriage of Convenience 3, 123, 228, 232, 234, 240, 242
Marriott, Sylvia 40–41
Marsh, Carol 25
Marsh, Garry 43–44, 68, 111–12, 155, 178
Marsh, Jean 58
Marshall, Herbert 216–17, 219
Marshall, Roger 62, 164, 173, 185
Marshall, Zena 47–48, 55, 211
Maskell, Virginia 118–19
Mason, Bert 29, 36, 108, 115, 156, 173, 176, 185, 205
Mason, Elliott 16–17
Mason, Herbert 220
Mason, James 60, 81–82, 86, 91–92, 114–15, *115*, 116, 133, 142–43, 174–75, 210–11
Massey, Anna 153
Massey, Raymond 16–17
Massie, Paul 169–70
Massie-Collier, Gerald 118
Matthews, Eddie 62
Mature, Victor 109–10, *110*
Maude, Joan 38
Maugham, Robin 97
Maurey, Nicole 216–17
Maxwell, Lois 104, 121, 223–24
Maxwell, Peter 93
May, Hans 203
May, Jack 31
Mayflower Pictures 186
Mayne, Ferdy 15–16, 23, 42, 120, 121–22, 129, 198, 201
Mazhar, Ahmed 27
Mazurki, Mike 131
McCallum, David 102, 111, 172–73, 213–14
McCallum, John 98, 158–59, 222
McCallum, Neil 51
McCarthy, Michael 11, 42
McCormick, F.J. 142–43
McCormick, John 212
McCowen, Alec 205
McCrea, Joel 168, *169*
McDermott, Brian 62
McDermott, Hugh 76–77, 137, 174–75
McDonell, Fergus 181
McDonnell, Burgess (Fergus McDonell) 181
McEnery, Peter 212
McFarland, Olive 70
McFarlane, Brian 243
McGivern, Cecil 20, 78
McGoohan, Patrick 9–10, *83*, 83–84
McGrath, Pat 163
McGuire, Tucker 133
McIntosh, Ellen 53
McKenna, Siobhan 45–46
McKenna, T.P. 53
McKenna, Virginia 177

Index

McKern, Leo 205–6
McLaughlin, Gibb 24
McLeod, Bill 127
McLeod, William 27, 81
McLeod Productions 27
McNaughton, Jack 196–97
McWilliams, Glen 220
Meadows, Stanley 150
The Mechanic 84
Medima, Patricia 86
Medwin, Michael 11, 17, 80, *97*, 97–98, 191
Meeker, Ralph 73
Meillon, John 27, 144
Melachrino, George 87
Melford, Jack 142
Mellinger, Michael 201
Melville, Colette 62
Menzies, William Cameron 79
Meredith, Burgess 123–24, *124*
Merrall, Mary 47, 112, 131, 202–3
Merrill, Gary 10
Merritt, George 30
Merton Park Productions 6, *8*, 11, 24, 29, 36, 42, 50, 53, 58, 62, 89, 94, 96, 107, 108, *108*, 115, 119, 123, 130, 146, 156, 164, 165, 173, 176, 185, 191, 205, 206, 209, 211, 211, 216, 219, 242
Merzbach, Paul 81
MGM 27, *28*
MGM British 29
Michael, Ralph 47, 224
Michael Powell Theatre 153
Michaels, Beverly 224
Michell, Keith 9
Mid-Century Film Productions 18, 55
Middleton, Guy 133
Middleton, Noëlle 211–12
Midnight Episode 123, 229, 231, 236, 239
Mikell, George 103
Miles, Bernard 29, 78, 131, 169–70
Miles, Vera 14–15, *15*
Milland, Ray 34–35, 183
Millar, Ronald 69, 183
Miller, David 13
Miller, Francis 207
Miller, Joan 139
Miller, Laurence 2, 3, 4, 243
Miller, Mandy 182
Miller, Martin 94, 133
Miller, Peter 21
Miller, Sigmund 219
Mills, Freddie 104
Mills, Hayley 142, 203–4
Mills, Hugh 19, 184
Mills, John 39–40, 71–72, *72*, 78, 79, 111, 125, 142, 165, 184–85, 203–4, 211–12, 215
Mills, Juliet 142
Milroy, Vivian 42
Milton, Ernest 31
Mine Own Executioner 123–24, *124*, 227, 230, 235, 238
Mingus, Charlie 10
Minter, George 207
Miranda, Isa 51

Mr. Arkadin 49
Mr. Denning Drives North 124–25, 227, 231, 235, 241
Mr. Perrin and Mr. Traill 125–26, 227, 231, 235, 239
Mitchell, Julien 13, 86
Mitchell, Oswald 17, 87, 137
Mitchell, Warren 181, 201
Mitchell, Yvonne 101–2, 161–62, 169–70, *203*, 203, 208, 225–26
Möhner, Carl 32–33
Moisiewitsch, Maurice 62
Molloy, John 41
Molnar, Lily 137
Monaghan, Jno (John) P. 210
The Monkey's Paw 5
Monlaur, Yvonne 205
Montague, Lee 62
Montgomery, Doreen 60, 129, 157, 218
Montgomery, Douglass 68
The Monthly Film Bulletin 137
Moontide 111
Moore, Eileen 95, 125
Moore, Kieron *80*, 80, 102–3, 121, 123–24, 164, 202
Moore, Ted 101
More, Kenneth 36, 117, 224–25
Morell, André 36, 112–13, 174, 189, 195
Morgan, Charles 84
Morgan, Diana 155
Morgan, Guy 54, 132, 194, 222
Morgan, Michèle 59
Morgan, Terence 154, 176, 191, 195, 207, 208
Morley, Robert 76, 148, 180
Morris, Ernest 201, 202
Morris, Lana 19, 81, 163
Morris, Oswald 34, 74, 102
Morrison, T.J. 125, 132
Morse, Barry 45–46, 138
Morton, Clive 36–37
Moss, Gerald 93
Movita 206–7
Moxey, John 53, 58, 164, 209
Mullard, Arthur 12
Mullen, Barbara 38, 71
Munden, Maxwell 12, 87
Munro, Janet 16
Murcell, George 42, *83*
Murder at 3 A.M. 126, 229, 231, 236, 240
Murder by Proxy 126–27, 229, 232, 234, 239
Murder Can Be Deadly see *The Painted Smile*
Murder in Reverse 127, 229, 230, 237, 240
Murder in Soho 127, 229, 230, 235, 239
Murder in the Night see *Murder in Soho*
Murder Is My Beat 147
Murder, My Sweet 74, 141
Murder on Monday see *Home at Seven*
Murder Without Crime 127–28, 228, 231, 236, 240

Murphy, Mary 96–97
Murphy, Robert 3, 4, 243
Murray, Barbara 10, 23, 191
Murray, Don 175
Murray, Stephen 67, 109, 140, 179, 190
Murum, William 106
Musel, Robert 35
My Brother's Keeper 128, 227, 231, 236, 240
My Gun Is Quick 73
My Learned Friend 5
Myers, Peter 182
Myra Breckenridge 156
Mystery at Tiger Bay see *Tiger Bay*

Nader, George 140
Nagy, Bill 7
Naismith, Laurence 205
Naked City 100
Naked Fury 128–29, 228, 232, 236, 239
"Nanny and the Professor" (TV series) 142
Napier, Russell 107, 129, 190
The Narrowing Circle 129, 228, 232, 236, 239
Navarro, Robert (Bob Navarro) 23, 139
Neagle, Anna 120–21, 225
Neal, Patricia 160–61, 199
Neame, Derek 181
Neame, Ronald 74, 78, 193
Neff, Hidegarde 114
Nelson, Gene 50–51
Nesbitt, Cathleen 117, 184
Nesbitt, Derren 95, *192*, 192, 212
Nesbitt, Frank 51
Netscher, Robin 137–38, 214–15
Nettlefold Productions 45, 121, *122*, 147, 194
Never Back Losers 242
Never Let Go 129–30, 227, 232, 234, 238
Never Mention Murder 2, 130, 229, 232, 233, 241, 242
"The New Avengers" (TV series) 61
New World Pictures 79
Newfield, Sam 70
Newlands, Anthony 89, 185, 209
Newley, Anthony 144–45, 181–82
Newman, Joseph M. 92
Newman, Nanette 58–59, 149, 155–56, 171
Newton, Robert 46, 71, 79, 81–82, 133, *141*, 141, 142–43, 144–45, 150, 157–58, 182–83, 193, 214–15
The Next of Kin 5
Ney, Marie 217, 225–26
Nicholas Nickleby 131, 229, 230, 233, 238
Nichols, Anthony 212
Nichols, Dandy 8
Nicholson, Nora 42
Nicol, Alex 58, 86–87
Night and the City 131–32, 182, 193, 227, 231, 234, 239
Night Beat 2, 3, 132, 228, 231, 235, 241

Index

Night Boat to Dublin 132–33, 229, 230, 235, 239
Night Comes Too Soon 5
Night Editor 147
The Night Has Eyes 133, 228, 230, 233, 239
Night of the Demon 133–34, 227, 232, 236, 240
Night of the Eagle 5
Night Was Our Friend 134, 229, 231, 233, 239
Night Without Stars 134–35, 228, 231, 236, 239
Nightfall 134
Nightmare 90, 135–36, 227, 232, 234, 241
1984 136, 227, 232, 233, 240
Nineteen Eighty Four 136
No Man of Her Own 27
No Orchids for Miss Blandish 136–37, 229, 231, 233, 239
No Road Back 137, 229, 232, 237, 238
No Room at the Inn 137–38, 228, 231, 233, 241
No Trace 138–39, 228, 231, 234, 238
No Trees in the Street 139, 228, 232, 236, 240
No Way Back 3, 139
Nobody Lives Forever 106
Nocturne 57
Nolan, Lloyd 73
The Noose 139–40, 229, 231, 234, 239
Norden, Christine 19, 96, 123–24, **124**, 132
North, Frank 146
Northwest Frontier 170
Now Barabbas 140, 229, 231, 236, 239
Now Barabbas Was a Robber see Now Barabbas
Nowhere to Go 140, 228, 232, 235, 238
Number Six 242
Nystrom, Carl 13

O'Brien, Edmond 136
O'Brien, Pat 104
O'Brine, Manning 104
Obsessed see The Late Edwina Black
Obsession 140–41, **141**, 228, 231, 234, 240
O'Casey, Ronan 56, 204
O'Connell, Arthur 127
O'Connell, Myra 17
The October Man 141–42, 227, 230, 233, 239
Odd Man Out 60, 142–44, **143**, 148, 175, 186, 227, 230, 236, 239
O'Dea, Denis 59
O'Dell, Denis 207
O'Donnell, Cathy 54–55
O'Farrell, Bernadette 188
O'Ferrall, George More 81, 82, 222
Offbeat 3, 144
O'Keefe, Dennis 104
Oliver, Anthony 42, 195
Oliver, Charles 79

Oliver Twist 144–45, 166, 227, 231, 235, 239
Olivier, Laurence 208–9
Olrich, April 224
On the Night of the Fire 2, 4, 145, 228, 230, 235, 241
On the Run 146, 228, 232, 237, 241, 242
Once a Sinner 146–47, 228, 231, 234, 240
One Way Out 147, 228, 232, 236, 239
Onions, S.D. 17, 126, 179
Open Road Films 102
Operation Diplomat 147–48, 228, 231, 234, 239
Orde, Julian 181
Orme, Geoffrey 49
Oroe, Julian (Julian Orde) 181
Orton, J.O.C. 39
Ortus Films 174
Orwell, George 136
Osborn, Andrew 126
Osborn, David 33
Oscar, Henry 16–17, 145
Osiecki, Stefan 139
Osmond, Lesley 87
O'Sullivan, Richard 190
Oury, Gérard 82
Out of the Past 1, 134
Outcast of the Islands 148, 227, 231, 236, 240, 241
Owen, Alun 41
Owen, Bill 46, 176, 177, 188
Owen, Cliff 144, 160
Owen, Yvonne 128
Owens, Pat 42
Ox-Bow Incident 134
Oxley, Bill 211

Pack, Charles Lloyd 212
Padovani, Lea 73–74
Page, Christopher 179
Paice, Eric 117
Paid to Kill see Five Days
The Painted Smile 148–50, **149**, 229, 232, 234, 239
Palmer, Ernest 52, 127, 202, 210
Palmer, Lilli 52–53, 109
Palmer, Toni 181
Panic 2, 3, 150, 228, 232, 234, 239
A Panorama of American Film Noir, 1941–1953 (book) 243
Paramount British Productions 81, 183
Paranoiac 90, 150–51, 227, 232, 234, 239
Parély, Mila 182
The Paris Express see The Man Who Watched the Trains Go By
Parke, Macdonald 137
Parker, Cecil 91
Parker, Suzy 35
Parks, Larry 204
Parkway Films 212, **213**
Parrish, Robert 168
Parroch-McCallum Productions 51
Parry, Gordon 123, 140, 207, 223
Parry, Natasha 42, 45, 168

The Partner 242
Partners in Crime 242
Passing Clouds 186
The Passing Stranger 151, 229, 231, 233, 240
Passport to Shame **151**, 151–52, 228, 232, 236, 238
Pastell, George 93
Patch, Wally 39–40
Paterson, Neil 166–67
Patrick, Nigel 95, 101–2, 139–40, 169, 179
Patterson, Lee 65, 151, 185
Pavey, Stan (Richard S. Pavey, Stanley Pavey) 47, 155, 168, 181, 195
Pavlow, Muriel 133, 178, 205, 218
Paxinou, Katina 209–10
Paxton, John 184
Payroll 2, 152–53, 228, 232, 235, 240
Pays, Howard 102, 211
Payton, Barbara 62–63, 205
Peach, Mary **167**
Peacock, William 152
Pearson, Donna 165
Peck, Brian 173
Peeping Tom 153–54, 227, 232, 236, 239
Pélissier, Anthony 135, 154, 165–66, 205
Penington-Eady Productions 58
Pennant Picture Productions 30, 40, 57, 68, 178
Pennebaker Inc. 175
Pennington-Richards, C.M. (C. Pennington-Richards) 49, 73, 136, 141, 189
Penwarden, Hazel 116
Percy, Esme 208
Periclean Productions 216
Périnal, Georges 59–60, 173
Perry, Linette 172
Personal Affair 154, 228, 231, 236, 241
Pertwee, Michael 96, 134, 179
Pertwee, Roland 113
Peters, Scott 73
Petrie, Hay 40–41, 139, 186, 207–8, 208–9
Pettigrew, Terence 243
Pettingell, Frank 71
Phantom Lady 109, 193
Phelan, Brian 41–42
Phillips, Conrad 93, 221–22
Phillips, Leslie 107
Phipps, Nicholas 56, 112
Piccadilly Third Stop 154–55, 228, 232, 236, 240
Pickup 122
Pidgeon, Walter 29
Pilbeam, Nova 40, 202
Pinewood Films 74, 112, 186
Pink String and Sealing Wax 155, 228, 230, 235, 240
Pious, Minerva 100
Piper, Frederick 142
Pit of Darkness 155–56, 228, 232, 233, 239
Pithey, Wensley 104

Index

A Place of One's Own 5
A Place to Go 156, 228, 232, 234, 241
Plantaganet Films 73
Platt, Victor 115
Playback 2, 3, 156–57, 228, 232, 235, 240, 242
Pleasence, Donald 84, 136, 176
The Pleasure Lovers see *Naked Fury*
Plunkett, Patricia 63–64, 67, 98, 127
Pohlmann, Eric 20, 27, 70, 109, 199–200, 201
Poison Pen **157**, 157–58, 227, 230, 236, 240
Pol, Talitha 216
Pollock, Ellen 89
Poncin, Marcel 184
Ponto, Erich 198
Pool of London 158, 228, 231, 234, 238
Port of Escape 158–59, 229, 232, 237, 239
Port of New York 202
Portman, Eric 38, 46, 48, 57, 77–78, 122–23, 186–87, **187**, 209, 214, 217
Portrait from Life 159–60, 228, 231, 234, 238
Portrait in Smoke see *Wicked as They Come*
Portrait of a Sinner see *The Rough and the Smooth*
Portrait of Jennie 159
Possessed 174
The Postman Always Rings Twice 63, 121
Powell, Michael 17, 37, 153, 180, 187
Pravda, George 156
Present Day Productions 73
Presle, Micheline 21–22
Pressburger, Emeric 17, 180, 187, 214
Preston, Robert 35–36
The Pretender 62
Prévost, Françoise 152–53
Price, Dennis 48, 68–69, 76–77, 97–98, 98–99, 126, 127–28, 182, 212
Price, Nancy 202–3
Price, Vincent 82, 150, 209
Priestly, J.B. 95
Private Hell 36 147
A Prize of Arms 160, 227, 232, 236, 239, 240
Production Film Service 121
The Prowler 147
Pryse, Hugh 45
Psyche 59 160–61, **161**, 229, 232, 236, 240
Psycho 1, 150
PT Raiders see *The Ship That Died of Shame*
Pughe, George 54
Puppet Master 187
Pushkin, Alexander 162
Pushover 147
Pyramid Amalgamated Productions 186

Quayle, Anthony 32–33, 120–21, 171, 173
Quéant, Gilles 135

Queen of Spades 161–62, 228, 231, 234, 239
Query see *Murder in Reverse*
The Quiet Woman 162, 228, 231, 234, 238
Quinn, Derry 163

Race Gang see *The Green Cockatoo*
Race Street 57
Radio Cab Murder 163, 229, 231, 236, 239
Raft, George 56–57, 92–93, 196
Rag Doll 163, 229, 232, 233, 239
Raglan, Robert 94
Raine, Jack 139
Rains, Claude 120
Rakoff, Alvin 152
The Rank (Rank Film Productions, Rank Organisation Film Productions, Rank Organisation) 7, 9, 64, **65**, 83, **83**, 95, 172, 205, 213, 218
Rapper, Irving 10
Rattigan, Terence 25, 209
Rawlings, Margaret 13, 137
Rawlinson, A.R. 45, 57, 71, 147
Ray, Aldo 101
Ray, Andrew 56, 173, 224–25
Ray, Philip 150
Ray, Rene (René Ray) 75, 79, **196**, 196–97, 223–24
Ray, Ted 56
Raye, Carol 218
Raymond, Cyril 51–52, 200
Raymond Stross Productions 63, **63**, 120, 168, **169**
Read, John 42
Realism and Tinsel: Cinema and Society in Britain 1939–49 (book) 243
Rebecca 43
Recoil 163–64, 229, 231, 234, 238
Red Light 57
Redgrave, Michael 47, 80, 121, 136, 175, 205–6, 220
Redmond, Liam 45–46, 92
Redmond, Moira 100, 123, 135–36, 155, 176
Reed, Carol 59, 102, 114–15, 142–43, 148, 198
Reed, Maxwell 20, 24, 26, 36, 45–46, 46, 48, 121–22, **122**, 132, 188, 194
Reed, Michael 114
Reed, Oliver 13, 43, 150
Rees, John 93
Reggiani, Serge 172
Regin, Nadja 53, 185
Reid, Dorothy 66
Reid, Trevor 129
Reinhardt, John 206
Relph, George 91
Relph, Michael 91, 156, 177
Remberg, Erika 29
Remus Films 75, 166, **167**
Rennie, Michael 206–7, 210
Return to Sender 164, 229, 232, 234, 241, 242
Re-Viewing British Cinema 1900–1992 (book) 2, 243

Reynolds, Peter 12, 19, 24–25, 32–33, 81, **105**, 105–6, 149
Rhodes, Brian 119, 123
Rhodes, Christopher 205
Rialto Productions 52, 207
Rich and Rich 104
Richard, Cliff 173
Richardson, Ralph 59, 85–86, 145, 148
Richfield, Edwin 23, 24, 27, 108
Richmond, Anthony 11
Richmond, Irene 135
Richmond, Susan 42
Ricochet 164, 228, 232, 236, 241, 242
Rienits, Rex 11, 219
Rietty, Robert 205
Rilla, Wolf 27, 104, 121, 154, 221
The Rivals 165, 228, 232, 237, 241, 242
Riverside Studio 39
RKO Radio Pictures 57, 77, 86, 187
Road House 27
Roadhouse Girl see *Marilyn*
Roberts, Ben 175
Roberts, Ewan 62
Robertson, Dale 52
Robinson, Edward G. 11
Robinson, Joe 63–64
Robson, Flora 17, 69, 76, 77–78, **157**, 157–58, 170–71
Roc, Patricia 26, 34–35, 87, 89, 98–100, **99**, 112, 184, 201, 220
Roche, Jonathan 147
Rockett, Sam 190
The Rocking Horse Winner 165–66, 227, 231, 236, 238
Roddick, John 164, 165
Rodney, Jack 176
Roeg, Nicolas 94
Rogers, Erica 165
Rogers, Ginger 13
Rogers, Howard Emmett 29
Rogers, Maclean 45
Rogers, Peter 48
Rogue Cop 57, 147
Rolfe, Charles 206
Rolfe, Guy 147–48, 159, 186–87
Romain, Yvonne 70, 164
Roman, Ruth 100–1
Romero, Cesar 191–92
Romney, Edana 38, 54
Romulus Films 92
Room at the Top 166–67, **167**, 227, 232, 233, 239
Room 43 see *Passport to Shame*
Room to Let 167–68, 229, 231, 234, 241
Roome, Alfred 128
Roosevelt, Eleanor 77–78
Rope of Sand 121
Rosay, Françoise 170
Rose, George 188
Rose, William 92
Ross, Hector 132
The Rough and the Smooth 2, 168, 228, 232, 236, 239
Rough Shoot 168–69, **169**, 228, 231, 236, 240
Rowbatham, Bill 44

Index

Rowland, Roy 73
Royal Academy of Dramatic Art (RADA) 188
Ruddock, John 133
Rusoff, Lou 31
Russell, William 15–16, 164, 176
Rutherford, Margaret 225
Rutland, John 27
Ryan, Edmon 44, 127
Ryan, Kathleen 73–74, 142–43, **143**, 224–25
Ryan, Madge 221–22
Ryan, Robert 76
Ryan's Daughter 38
Ryder, Paul 94, 160

Saad, Margit 41–42, 156
Sabre Film 133
Sabu 17–18
Sachs, Leonard 120, 155
St. John, Betta 9, 182
Salew, John 58, 139
Salt to the Devil see *Give Us This Day*
Sanders, George 27, **28**, 190
Sands, Leslie 10
Sangster, Jimmy (John Sansom) 58, 89, 150–51, 182, 206
Sansom, John *see* Sangster, Jimmy
Sapphire 169–70, 227, 232, 234, 241
Saraband see *Saraband for Dead Lovers*
Saraband for Dead Lovers 170–71, 228, 231, 234, 240
Sarne, Mike 156
Saturday Night and Sunday Morning 166
Saunders, Charles 18, 55, 102, 103, 129, 129
Saville, Philip 11, 126, 201
Saville, Victor 29
Scaife, Ted (Edward Scaife) 9, 85, 95, 97, 133–34, 148
The Scar 121
Schmid, Helmut 160
Schroeder, Ernst 114
Scorcese, Martin 153
Scotland Yard Dragnet see *The Hypnotist*
Scott, Alex 164
Scott, Avis 61, 214–15
Scott, Elizabeth 30
Scott, Janette 150
Scott, Lizabeth 189, 216–17
Scott, Margaretta 60
Scott, Martha 184
Scott, Peter Graham 15, 16
Scott, Zachary 220–21, **221**
Seance on a Wet Afternoon 171–72, 227, 232, 234, 240
Searle, Francis 35, 116, 126, 147, 217
Sears, Ann 104, 115–16
Sears, Heather 166
Secret Beyond the Door 43
Secret People 172, 228, 231, 234, 240
The Secret Place 2, 172–73
Selby, Spencer 1, 3, 243
Sellars, Elizabeth 35–36, 71–72, **72**, 81, 88–89, 111, 113, 129–30, 134, 164

Sellers, Peter 129–30
Selway, George 172
Serafin, Enzo 190
Serious Charge 173, 227, 232, 237, 240
Sernas, Jacques 74
The Servant 5
Sessleman, Sabina 94–95
The Set-Up (1949, U.S.) 3, 166, 188
The Set-Up (1963, British) 2, 173–74, 228, 232, 234, 240, 242
Seton, Bruce 79
Seton, Joan 106–7
Seven Days to Noon 174, 227, 231, 233, 235, 240
The Seventh Veil 174–75, 228, 230, 233, 241
Sewell, Vernon 19, 106, 117, 163, 185, 192, 210, 211
Sexy Beast 3
Seyler, Athene 133–34
Shadow Man see *Street of Shadows*
Shadow of a Woman 43
Shake Hands with the Devil 175–76, 227, 232, 233, 239
The Shakedown 176, 228, 232, 235, 240
Shakespeare, William 100–1
The Share-Out 2, 176, 228, 232, 234, 240, 242
Sharif, Omar 27
Shaughnessy, Alfred 31
Shaw, Denis 49
Shaw, Sebastian 54, 98, 109, 187, 201, 222
Shaw, Susan 104–5, 158, 194–95, 214–15, 219–20
She Played with Fire see *Fortune Is a Woman*
Shearer, Moira 153
Shearing, Joseph 183
Shell, Maria 82
Shelley, Barbara 21, 31–32, 55–56
Shelton, Joy 93, 137–38, 146, 210, 215
Shepherd, Elizabeth 21
Shepherd, Horace 62
Shepley, Michael 123–24
Sheppard, Morgan 192–93
Sheridan, Dinah 20, 45, 138
Sherriff, R.C. 142
Shield for Murder 147
The Ship That Died of Shame **177**, 177–78, 227, 232, 234, 238
Shoot First see *Rough Shoot*
The Shop at Sly Corner 178, 227, 230, 235, 239
Short, Jean 60
Signoret, Simone 166
Silent Dust 179, 227, 231, 233, 238
The Silk Noose see *The Noose*
Silva, Simone 56, 191, 198
Silver, Alain 1, 2, 243
Silver, Christine 167
Sim, Alastair 39–40, 79–80, 95–96, 109, 188, 215
Sim, Sheila 43–44, 77–78
Simmonds, Annette 20
Simmons, Anthony 151

Simmons, Jean 17–18, 26–27, 36, 65–67, 78, 184, 209–10
Simon, Simone 193
Sims, Sylvia 139
Sinatra, Frank 52
Sinclair, Charles 33
Sinclair, Hugh 34–35, 121, 138, 165
Sinden, Donald 205
Singer, Alexander 160
Singer, Campbell 85–86
The Sinister Man 242
Siodmak, Robert 62, 168
The Six Men 179, 229, 231, 235, 240
Skutezky, Victor 193
The Slasher see *Cosh Boy*
Slater, John 62–63, 98, 111, 127, 156
Slaughter, Tod 40–41, 57
Slavin, Martin 156
"Sleep Long My Lovely" (play) 100
The Sleeping Tiger 180, 228, 231, 235, 241
Slide, Anthony 243
Sloane, Olive 174
Slocombe, Douglas 26, 47, 98, 170–71, 198, 207
The Small Back Room 180, 227, 231, 236, 238
The Small Voice 64, 181, 229, 231, 235, 240
The Small World of Sammy Lee 181–82, 227, 232, 235, 240
Smith, Alexis 180
Smith, Brian 165
Smith, Constance 93, 167, 204
Smith, Cyril 111–12
Smith, Madeleine 112–13
Smith, Maggie 140
Smith, Shelley 203
The Smugglers see *The Man Within*
The Snake Pit 112
The Sniper 74, 141
The Snorkel 182, 227, 232, 234, 238
Snowbound 182–83, 229, 231, 235, 238
So Evil My Love 2, 106, 183–84, 227, 231, 233, 239
So Long at the Fair 184, 227, 231, 234, 241
So Well Remembered 184–85, 204, 228, 230, 241
Soho Incident 2, 3, 185, 229, 232, 236, 239
Soldati, Mario 190
Solo for Sparrow 185, 229, 232, 234, 240, 242
"Some Lines of Inquiry into Post-war British Crimes" (essay) 243
Somewhere in the Night 150
Soskin, Paul 214
The Spell of Amy Nugent see *Spellbound*
Spellbound 185–86, 229, 230, 235, 239
Spicer, Andrew 2, 3, 4, 243
The Spider 2
The Spider and the Fly 186–87, 227, 231, 235, 241
Spigelgass, Leonard 183
Spillane, Mickey 73

Spin a Dark Web see *Soho Incident*
The Spy in Black 187, 227, 230, 236, 238
The Spy Who Came In from the Cold 3
Squadron Leader X 187, 229, 230, 234, 239
The Square Ring 3, 187–88, 228, 231, 234, 239
Squire, Anthony 97
Squire, Ronald 165
Stafford, Brendan J. 11, 54, 176, 221
Stage Fright 2, 188–89, 227, 231, 235, 238
Staiola, Enzo 92
Stallick, Jan 208
Stamp-Taylor, Enid 81
Stanley, Kim 171
Stassino, Paul 115, 211
Steel, Anthony 10
The Steel Trap 16
Steiger, Rod 7
Stein, Paul L. 16, 40, 157
Stella see *The Key*
Stepanek, Karel 57
Stephens, Ann 137–38, 210
Stephens, Robert 35, 181
Stephenson, Henry 144
Sterling, Jan 136
Sterndale, Martin 102
Stevens, Mark 111–12
Stevens, Marti 9
Steward, Ernest 16, 152, 154, 172–73
Stewart, Jack 192–93
Stewart, Robert 53, 123, 156
Stewart, Robert Banks 130
Stock, Nigel 25, 206, 212
Stolen Face 121, 189, 228, 231, 234, 239
Stolz, Clarissa 108
Stone, John 202
Stoney, Kevin 119, 146
Storm, Lesley (Leslie Storm) 54, 74, 77, 154
Storme, Sandra 127
Stormy Crossing 189–90, 228, 232, 236, 239
The Strange Affair of Uncle Harry 106
The Strange Mr. Gregory 116
Stranger at Home (book) 190
The Stranger Came Home 190, 229, 231, 234, 239
The Stranger in Between see *Hunted*
Stranger on the Prowl 88
Stranger on the Third Floor 1, 11
The Stranger's Hand 190–81, 228, 231, 236, 240
The Strangler see *East of Piccadilly*
The Strangler's Web 242
Stratton, John 32–33
Street Corner 2, 191, 229, 231, 233, 241
The Street Has a Thousand Skies (book) 16
Street of Shadows 191–92, 228, 231, 237, 239
The Street with No Name 112, 199
Stretton, George 19

Stribling, Melissa 219
Stride, John 16
Strong, L.A.G. 125
Strongroom **192**, 192–93, 227, 232, 236, 239
Strueby, Katherine 54, 68, 178
Struthers, Ian 104
Stuart, John 112
Sullivan, Francis L. 78, 121, 131–32, 144, 193
Summerfield, Eleanor 58, 109, 126, 139, 191
Summers, Walter 16, 44, 207
Suschitzky, Wolfgang 181
Sutton, Willie 144
Swallow Productions 43
Swanson, Maureen 114, 198
Swinburn, Nora 60
Sydney, Basil 98–99
Sylvester, William 21, 73–74, 94, 144, 190, 218–19, 224–25
Syms, Sylvia 212

Tabori, Paul 9, 61, 114, 121
Tafler, Sydney 11, 12, 50–51, 98, 137–38, 146, 147, 219–20
Take My Life 2, 193
Talbot, Ken 73
"Tales of Wells Fargo" (TV series) 52
Tani, Yoko 154
Tannura, Philip 157
Tapley, Colin 35, 219, 220–21
Taste of Fear 5
Tate, Reginald 56, 123, 157–58, 172
Taylor, Gilbert 139, 160, 174, 215, 224, 225
Taylor, Ken 14
Taylor, Marjorie 57
Taylor, Valerie 193
Technicolor 1, 18, 21, 67, 100, 120
Teed, John 87
Tempean Films 20, 56, 93, 111, 138, 162, 164, 189, 199, 201, 204
Temple-Smith, John 18
Templeton, William (William P. Templeton) 53, 123, 136
Temptation Harbor see *Temptation Harbour*
Temptation Harbour 193–94, **194**, 229, 230, 234, 239
Terror at Midnight 202
Terror House see *The Night Has Eyes*
Terror Street see *Thirty-Six Hours*
Tess 208
Teynac, Maurice 135
Thatcher, Torin 30, 78
Thaw, John 62
Theatrecraft 102, 174, **192**, 192
There Is Another Sun 3, 194–95, 228, 231, 234, 238
These Are the Damned see *The Damned*
Thesiger, Ernest 195–96
They Can't Hang Me 195, 228, 232, 234, 240
They Drive by Night (1938, British) 2, 4, 195–96, 227

They Drive by Night (1940, American) 57
They Made Me a Fugitive **196**, 196–97, 227, 230, 233, 239
They Met in the Dark 5
The Thin Man 193
The Third Man 59, 148, 162, **197**, 197–98, 227, 231, 236, 240
Third Party Risk 198, 229, 232, 233, 239
The Third Secret 3, 198–99, 227, 232, 234, 240
13 East Street 199, 228, 231, 233, 238
The 13th Letter 158
Thirty-Six Hours 199–200, 229, 231, 237, 239
This Gun for Hire 36
This Man Is News 5
This Was a Woman **200**, 200–1, 229, 231, 237, 238, 239
Thomas, André 38–39
Thomas, Dylan 138, 202
Thomas, Gerald 212
Thomas, Ralph 36
Thompson, J. Lee 54, 67, 127–28, 139, 203, 215, 224, 225
Thorburn, June 49
Thorndyke, Sybil 175
Thorne, Anthony 184
Thorp, Richard 209
Thorpe, George 45
Three Cases of Murder 5
Three Crooked Men 3, 201, 229, 232, 235, 241
Three Guys Named Mike 64
Three Silent Men 201, 229, 230, 233, 239
3 Steps to the Gallows 201–2, 229, 231, 234, 238
Three Stooges 92, 160
Three Strangers 106
Three Sundays to Live 202, 229, 232, 235, 241
Three Weird Sisters 202–3, 228, 231, 233, 240
Thunder Rock 5
Thunderball 39
Tierney, Gene 131–32, 154
Tierney, Lawrence 202
Tiger Bay 170, **203**, 203–4, 225, 227, 232, 236, 238
Tiger by the Tail 204, 229, 232, 234, 238
Tiger in the Smoke 204–5, 228, 232, 233, 241
"Till Death Do Us Part" (TV series) 201
Tiller, Nadja 168
Time to Remember 205, 229, 232, 235, 240, 242
Time Without Pity 205–6, 227, 232, 235, 239
Timetable 112
To Have and to Hold 3, 206, 228, 232, 237, 241, 242
"To Tell the Truth" (TV series) 73
Todd, Ann 46, **80**, 80, 112–13, 157, 157–58, 174–75, 183–84, 205–6

Index

Todd, Richard 33–34, 67, 96, 129–30, 188
Tomlinson, David 29, 128, 184
Toone, Geoffrey 114, 157–58
Torén, Märta 120
Torso Murder Mystery see *Traitor Spy*
Tottenham, Merle 167–68
Tourneur, Jacques 34, 133–34
Towb, Harry 162
Tower of Terror 207–7, 229, 230, 235, 239
Traitor Spy 207, 229, 230, 236, 240
Travers, Alfred 53
Travers, Ben 209
Travers, Bill 66–67, 66, 121, 188
Travers, Linden 137
Travis, Richard 224
Tread Softly Stranger 2, 207, 228, 232, 236, 240
Triangle Films 123
Triton Films 26, 46, **76**, 210
Tronson, Robert 115, 146
Troy Films 175
Troy-Schenck Productions 160, **161**
Truman, Ralph 14, 144–45, 219
Trunk Crime 207–8, 229, 230, 233, 238
Tudor Films 137
Tully, John 58, 94
Tully, Montgomery 23, 50, 61, 89, 119, 127, 137, 199–200
Tunick, Irve 104
Turn the Key Softly 2, 208, 228, 231, 235, 241
Turpin, Gerry 171
Tushingham, Rita 156
Twentieth Century–Fox Film Corporation 35
20th Century-Fox Productions 131
Twentieth Century Productions 56
21 Days 208–9, 227, 230, 234, 240
21 Days Together see *21 Days*
The £20,000 Kiss 2, 209, 229, 232, 236, 241, 242
Twilight Women see *Women of Twilight*
"Twilight Zone" (TV series) 103
Twist, Derek 195
Twist of Fate see *Beautiful Stranger*
Two Cities Films 29, 122, 125, 142, 142, **143**, 154, 165, 209
Two O'clock Courage 150
2001: A Space Odyssey 219
Tynan, Kenneth 140

U-Boat 29 see *The Spy in Black*
Uncensored 209, 229, 230, 233, 238
Uncle Silas 209–10, 228, 230, 234, 240
Under Capricorn 5
Undercurrent 43
Underdown, Edward 45, 94, 108, 117, 164, 191–92, 222
Undertow 202
Underworld Informers see *The Informers*
Uneasy Terms 2, 210, 229, 231, 236, 240

The Unholy Four see *The Stranger Came Home*
United Co-Productions 94, **151**, 152
Unpublished Story 5
Unsworth, Geoffrey 21, 36, 53, 83, 98, 121, 186, 205, 208, 218
The Upturned Glass 210–11, 228, 230, 235, 241
Urge to Kill 211, 229, 232, 236, 241
Ursini, James 2
Ustinov, Peter 30

Vadim, Roger 19
Vajda, Ladislas 222
The Valachi Papers 84
Valentine, Val 195, 201
Valiant Films 96
Valk, Frederick 47, 62–63, 106, 170
Valli, Alida 190, 198
Vance, Leigh 63, 70, 154, 176, 221
Vandyke Picture Corporation 19, 179, 195
van Eyck, Peter 182
Van Eyssen, John 123
Van Lusil, Jan 207
Varley, Beatrice 81, 128, 138
Varnel, Max 165
Vedey, Julien 79
Veidt, Conrad 37–38, 187
Vengeance Is Mine 211, 229, 231, 234, 240, 241
The Verdict 211, 229, 232, 234, 241, 242
Vernon, Richard 176
Versois, Odile **151**, 152
Vertigo 38
Vic Films 222
Viceroy Films 101
Vích, Vacklav (Václav) 132, 145
The Vicious Circle 211–12, 229, 232, 236, 239
Victim 212–13, **213**, 227, 232, 234, 239
Victor, Charles 29, 50–51, 55, 191, 222
Victor, Herbert 13
Villiers, David 29
Villiers, James 36–37, 43
Violent Playground 213–14, 227, 232, 234, 241
Vitale, Milly 63, **63**
von Krusserow, Ingeborg (Ingeborg Wells) 223–24

Wade, Michael 109–10
Waescher, Aribert 114
Wager, Anthony 78
Wagstaff, Elsie 40–41
Walbrook, Anton 71, 161–62
Walker, Martin 127
The Wall of Death see *There Is Another Sun*
Wallace, Edgar 6, 53, 117, 119; see also "Edgar Wallace Mystery Theatre"
Walls, Tom 96, 218
Walsh, Dermot 23, 24–25, 98–99, 122–23
Walsh, Kay 30, 78, 142, 144–45, 188

Walsh, Raoul 196
Walter, Wilfred 44
Wanamaker, Sam 41, 73–74, 125
Wanted for Murder 214, 228, 230, 235, 239
Ward, Elizabeth 1, 2, 243
Ward, Michael 199
Ward, Ronald 57
Wardwell, Geoffrey 40–41
Warner, Jack 11, 22–23, 23, 48, 98, 100, 128, 188
Warner, Richard 176
Warner Brothers First National Productions 45, 188, 195–96
Warren, Barry 51
Warren, Kenneth 41–42
Warrender, Harold 179
Warwick, John 30, 44, 47, 57, 218
Washbourne, Mona 30, **31**
Waterford, Gwen 51, 227, 231, 233, 241
Waterfront 214–15
Waterfront Women see *Waterfront*
Watergate Productions 95
Waterhouse, Keith 217
Waterloo Road 2, 3, 215, 228, 230, 234, 238
Waters, Russell 123, 198
Watling, Jack 146
Watson, Jack 153
Watson, James 53
Watson, Wylie 25, 109
Waugh, Hilary 100
Waxman, Harry 111, 169, 180, 214
The Way Out see *Dial 999*
Wayne, John 163
Wayne, Naunton 34–35, 53, 141
Wayne, Patricia 109
We Shall Rise Again see *Uncensored*
We Shall See 216, 229, 232, 235, 241, 242
The Weak and the Wicked 215–16, 229, 231, 236, 240
The Weapon 216–17, 227, 232, 234, 241
Web of Evidence see *Beyond This Place*
Webb, Denis 62
Webber, Robert 89–90, **90**
Webster, Joy 189
Welchman, Harry 54–55
Welles, Orson 49, **197**, 198
Wellesley, Gordon 81, 114
Wellington Films 11, 158
Wells, Ingeborg see von Krusserow, Ingeborg
Welsh, John 37
Welwyn Studios 47
Wenham, Jane 95
Went the Day Well? 5
Weske, Brian 102, 150
Weske, Victor 10
West, Anita 93
West 11 217, 229, 232, 237, 239
Westbrook, John 166
Westerby, Robert 13, 132, 186, 188, 219
Westwood, Russell 204
What Ever Happened to Baby Jane? 33

Wheatley, Alan 10–11, 25, 49, 86, 107
Wheel of Fate 217–18, 227, 231, 236, 241
Whelan, Tim 201
Where the Sidewalk Ends 134
While I Live 218, 229, 230, 235, 241
While the City Sleeps 134
Whiley, Manning 178, 207–8, 209
Whiplash 3
Whirlpool 218–19, 229, 232, 233, 241
Whistle Stop 57
The Whistler 62, 116
White, Barbara 123–24, 200
White, Carol 117, 129–30
White Fire see *3 Steps to the Gallows*
White Heat 176
Whitelaw, Billie 152
Whiteley, Jon 88–89, 216–17
Whiting, John 177
Whiting, Margaret 95
Whittaker, Ian 39
Whittingham, Jack 26, 40, 57, 88, 91, 158
Who Was Maddox? 242
Wicked as They Come 2, 219, 229, 232, 235, 239
The Wicked Lady 5
Wicked Woman 146
Wickert, Tony **149**, 149
Wide Boy 219–20, 229, 230, 235, 240
Widmark, Richard 131–32, 163
Wilcox, Herbert 120, 225
Wilcox, John 89, 125, 148
The Wild One 97
Wilding, Michael 29, 39–40, 188
Wiles, John 211
Wilhelm, Wolfgang 57, 77, 172, 187
William Nassour Productions 191
Williams, Brock 37, 45, 163, 189

Williams, Cedric 60, 81, 116, 167
Williams, Derick 67
Williams, Elmo 224
Williams, Emlyn 10, 14, 81–82, 195
Williams, Esther 188
Williams, Harcourt 106, 137–38
Williams, Hugh 44, 97, 193
Williams, J.B. 109
Williams, Tony 2, 4, 243
Willis, F. McGrew 127
Willis, Ted 16, 104, 139
Willman, Noel 7, 129–30
Willoughby Film Productions 12
Wilson, James (Jimmie Wilson, Jimmy Wilson) 8, 10–11, 40, 49, 53, 58, 62, 94, 112, 130, 138, 146, 164, 164–65, 165, 201, 202, 206, 209, 211, 211, 216
Wimperis, Arthur 29
Winchell, Walter 128
The Window 173, 225
A Window in London 220
Windsor, Marie 153
Wings of Danger 2, 220–21, **221**, 229, 231, 234, 239
Winner, Michael 217
Wise, Herbert 206
Withers, Googie 47, 98, 127, 131–32, 155, 158–59
Witness in the Dark 221–22, 228, 232, 236, 240
Wolfit, Donald 166–67
The Woman in Question 222, 228, 231, 233, 238
The Woman in White (book) 41
The Woman with No Name 222–23, **223**, 228, 231, 233, 238
A Woman's Devotion 121
Women of Twilight 223–24, 227, 231, 236, 238
Women Without Men 224
Wood, Mary Laura 18
Woodbridge, George 198

Woods, Arthur 195
Woods, Aubrey 131
Woodthorpe, Peter 89–90
Woodville, Catherine 95
Wooland, Norman 56, 112, 137
Worth, Brian 95
Worth, Irene 172
Wright, Tony 58–59, 62–63, 94, 168, 205
Wyer, Reginald (Reg H. Wyer, Reginald H. Wyer, Reg Wyer) 7, 44, 46, 95, 117, 121, 154, 156, 174–75, 184, 191, 210, 213, 216, 217–18
Wyler, William 167
Wyman, Jane 188
Wynter, Dana 175
Wynyard, Diana 71, 145

Yates, Pauline 130
The Yellow Balloon 224–25, 228, 231, 236, 240
Yellow Canary 225, 228, 230, 237, 239
Yesterday's Enemy 170
Yield to the Night 225–26, 229, 232, 236, 240
Yordan, Philip 100
Young, Arthur 61–62, 95
Young, Frederick A. (F.A. Young, Freddie Young) 13, 29, 37–38, 56, 184, 218
Young, Terence 38–39, 145, 173
Young, Tony 158–59
Young and Willing see *The Weak and the Wicked*
Young Scarface see *Brighton Rock*
Young, Willing and Eager 163

Zampi, Mario 60
Zbyszko, Stanislaus 131
Zetterling, Mai 19, 49, **50**, 58–59, 69, 144, 154, 159–60
Zodiac Productions 70